VANIER

Soldier, Diplomat and Governor General

VANIER

Soldier, Diplomat and Governor General

A BIOGRAPHY

ROBERT SPEAIGHT

Jamais aucun homme ne posséda à un plus haut degré cette paix intérieure qui nait du sentiment du Devoir sacré, et la modeste insouciance d'un soldat à qui il importe peu que son nom soit célèbre, pourvu que la chose publique prospère.

Alfred de Vigny on Admiral Lord Collingwood

COLLINS

TORONTO, 1970

© Robert Speaight 1970

ISBN 0 00 262252 1

PRINTED IN GREAT BRITAIN

Published by Wm Collins Sons & Co. Canada Ltd
100 Lesmill Road, Don Mills, Ontario

TO PAULINE VANIER

My dear Pauline,

The train of circumstance is strange indeed. If I had not happened to be suffering from a severe cold and a half strangled voice in the middle of a lecture tour in the United States, I might never have been given the honourable burden of writing this book. You will remember how I sent you a *cri de coeur* shortly before Easter 1966, and craved the hospitality of Government House; and I am not forgetting how I first came to Canada twenty years ago, armed with letters of introduction which you had so kindly given me. And that brings back memories of simple Sunday evening suppers in the rue Dosne, when we knew each other much less well than we do now. But it was those two visits to Government House – the second only a few weeks before Georges' death – that gave you the thought which these pages have tried to put into effect.

So this book belongs to you, because you and Georges belonged to one another. It belongs, in a lesser degree, to all the members of your family, and very particularly to Michel who not only classified Georges' papers – and how voluminous they were! – but stood at my side while I was at work on them. Your own prodigious memory has stood me in wonderful stead, and I look back with pleasure and gratitude to those happy week-ends in Redpath Place. Jock McEwen, a former Under-Secretary of State for Scotland, used to say that Georges was the only saint he had ever known in public life, and Diana Cooper wrote to me in very much the same terms. Well, public life is not a sphere where sanctity has much competition, and in any case canonization has no place in objective biography. But you know how deep were my affection and admiration for Georges, and it is for that reason that the burden of this book has lain lightly on my heart though heavily enough on my conscience.

Yours affectionately,
ROBERT

Acknowledgments

THE principal source for this biography was General Vanier's personal papers to which I was given unrestricted access. Through the generosity of the University of Ottawa, these were sorted and classified by Mr George Cowley, M. Michel Vanier and Madame Châteauvert. To all three I owe a warm debt of gratitude. Without their preliminary work and constant help, my task would have been much longer and much more laborious. Madame Châteauvert acted as my secretary while I was at work in the Public Archives and I cannot adequately express my thanks for her assistance. I also enjoyed every courtesy and consideration from Dr Kaye Lamb and his staff.

I have already expressed my thanks to Madame Vanier and the members of her family. Others who have aided me include the Right Hon. Lester B. Pearson; the Right Hon. Sir Michael Adeane; the Hon. Lieut-Colonel Keiller-Mackay; Major-General J. P. Bernatchez; Général de Brigade L. P. Archambault; General Sir James Marshall-Cornwall; The Earl of Bessborough; M. Jules Léger; Mr Saul Rae; Mr Charles Ritchie; Dr Francis Leddy; Mr Murray Ballantyne; Professor C. E. Carrington; Lord Hylton; M. Maurice Schumann; the late Norman Robertson; Mr Arnold Heaney; Mr Michael Pitfield; Mr James Goodall; Nurse Attrill; Lieut-Commander Price; Sergeant Chevrier; Mr Paul Hutchison Q.C.; M. René Pléven; M. Pierre-Henri Teitgen; M. Louis Closon; M. Claudius Petit; M. Edmond Michelet; Madame Gilbert Gadoffre; Miss Gladys Arnold; and Mademoiselle Elisabeth de Miribel. To these, and to the Right Hon. John F. Diefenbaker and to others who have allowed me to quote from their letters, I am much indebted.

A special word of thanks must go to Mr and Mrs Esmond Butler. As General Vanier's Secretary, Mr Butler was always at hand with correction or advice; and during my second visit to Ottawa he and his wife most kindly offered me the hospitality of Rideau Cottage.

I am much indebted to Mr Eugene Forsey for the loan of his writings on the constitutional position of the Governor General; and to my secretary Mrs Pat Brayne for her speed and efficiency in typing a MS which had to make a quite unusual number of Atlantic crossings.

The letters from Sir Michael Adeane to General Vanier are reproduced by gracious permission of Her Majesty the Queen.

For an intimate study of General Vanier's spiritual life by a member of his family, the reader is referred to Dr Jean Vanier's *In Weakness, Strength*, Griffin House, Toronto.

Contents

Illustrations

The author wishes to thank the National Film Board of Canada for permission to reproduce the illustrations numbers 1, 15-19, 22-24; the Department of National Defence, Canada for numbers 7, 13, 14; The Globe and Mail, Toronto for number 20; The Gazette, Montreal for number 21. Photographs 6, 9, 11, 12 were taken by Topicat, J. Belin, Presse Libération, Jean Fargeas.

PART ONE

THE SOLDIER

GROWING UP

I

I T was said of Guillaume Vanier, a citizen of Honfleur, the second and last of his family who emigrated to Canada towards the end of the seventeenth century, that he arrived there with the following possessions – his wife, his three children, and his gun. Very quickly he acquired a cow. But if we extend the notion of possessions to include a man's posterity, he had a very large number of descendants, so that Vanier became a fairly common name in the Province of Quebec. Guillaume lived in Quebec city and was among the archers of the Maréchaussée until, after returning from doing battle with the Iroquois, he accidentally discharged the gun against his own person. He left six children to continue his line. Other members of the family would travel northward and hunt beaver, returning with the skins which they sold profitably for fur. By 1767 they had settled at Côte de St Michel on the outskirts of Montreal, and it was here that Jean-Baptiste, the grandfather of Georges Vanier, was born in 1810. The family had property around what is now the intersection of the Trans-Canada Highway and the Montée St Léonard, only a short distance from the north shore of the St Lawrence and the tunnel which today links Boucherville with Ville d'Anjou. It was still woodland when Georges Vanier was a boy and used to go there to gather the nuts in May as well as to visit his relations.

Philias Vanier, from whom Georges took his second name, was the eighth and youngest son of Jean-Baptiste. He was born in 1862 and married Margaret Maloney – known to all her friends as 'Maggie' – the eldest child of John Maloney from Co. Cork. Now, for the first time, blood other than French entered the family. John Maloney, with his square dark beard, was a very silent and austere character. He would rarely speak of his childhood, only recalling how he used to do his homework in a corner and how his parents had never corrected him. His wife had died leaving him with seven children, and they lived between Drummond and Mountain on the frontier between English and French-speaking Montreal.

Philias had made quite a lot of money out of real estate, but he and his Irish wife lived modestly over an *épicerie taverne* on the corner of the rue St Jacques and the rue de la Seigneurie. It was here that Georges, the eldest of their five children, was born on the 23rd of April 1888. He was baptized in the Church of St Joseph. Afterwards the family moved to the rue St Antoine, and then to 810 Dorchester Boulevard between the rue St Mathieu and the rue St Marc. These addresses were providential, and indeed prophetic. It was difficult for a family so situated to be indifferent to the message of the Gospel; or to be unaware that 'never the twain shall meet' was not an adage that could, or should, be applied to the French and English-speaking communities of Canada, whatever appearance or prejudice might suggest to the contrary.

Philias Vanier had a strong sense of humour and an acute flair for business, combined with a certain inferiority complex. This may have been the result of a very primary education. He liked to make others talk, but spoke little himself. 'You'll have to account for every idle word' was one of his favourite maxims. Margaret, his wife, was a beautiful and warm-hearted woman, with coils of luxuriant golden hair. She was sensitive and understanding, and very ambitious for her children, inculcating the virtues of decision and perseverance. 'Don't go back on things' she would say, and Georges Vanier was never tempted to go back on his deep devotion to her. Great men are supposed to owe a large debt to their mothers, and in this case it was generously repaid.

There were two sisters and two brothers. Eva, closest to Georges in age, shared her mother's distaste for gossip and dispute, but his favourite was always Frances, the youngest of the family. He was interested in his other relations, particularly his first cousin Arthur, who wished to become a priest but died before he could enter the seminary; and he was much attached to his aunt, Katie Maloney, writing to her when he was only nine years old: 'As soon as I got the letter, I suddenly ran into the house and cried out aloud I got a letter from Aunt Katie.' The holidays were spent either at Cacouna, on the south bank of the St Lawrence, where the Vaniers took a house for the summer, or on Lake Memphremagog in the Eastern Townships where they had bought a farm. Here there was boating – in their own yacht, and bathing – when the water was not too cold, and rides on the hay carts, and walking in the woods. Georges had no mechanical sense, but as time went on he would organize games for the family and

friends. They were happy times and many years later Philias
Vanier was to recall them:

There was one day that I remember very well. It was a Saturday and
we had spent the day on the Ile du Camiel and towards six o'clock
in the evening a storm suddenly got up. We left hurriedly, for the
angry tide was quickly coming in. That time I was really in a blue
funk! I carried you on my back, and had to make a long *détour* to
get away. What frightened me was the darkness which was beginning
to close in upon us. Those were *the best days of my life*, when you
were all little.[1]

At home English was habitually spoken, presumably because
Margaret was more at ease in it and Philias found it commercially
useful. Georges, and his brothers, received an English education
at Loyola College, run by the Jesuits and then situated in the
former Convent of the Sacred Heart on the south-east corner of
St Catherine and Bleury Streets. The students remembered the old
violinist who played at the corner every night as they went to
bed, and the fire that broke out in January 1898. As a result of
this the College moved to 68 Drummond Street, where it remained until 1916. Georges was nine years old when he went
there in 1897, a serious, studious, considerate boy, but not in
the least aloof. At times, however, his Irish blood came out, and he
remembered smashing his fist through a pane of glass in a fit of
temper – a painful gesture which was painfully rewarded. An
early photograph shows him in an Eton suit and a frilly shirt,
looking alarmingly like Little Lord Fauntleroy to whom in other
respects he bore no resemblance whatever. It was something of
a walk from home to school and, thus attired, he had to run the
gauntlet of rotten eggs and ripe tomatoes thrown at him by the
other boys of the neighbourhood. At Loyola, where he remained
until 1906, his tastes and aptitudes were mainly literary. A strain
of romantic melancholy, not unusual in adolescence, was quick
to make itself apparent, whether in verse or prose. Such thoughts
were naturally inspired by the sun setting over Westmount:

Nature is viewed at her best, arrayed in all her sublimity and
grandeur, decked in all her finest garments, and glowing with the
radiance of beauty, bestowed upon it by its creator, when the sun
has all but reached his long required sleep, and when the dark
shadows begin to deepen along the foot of the high and thickly
wooded forest. Then it is we have the glorious, though common,
opportunity of viewing the work of God's hand in one of its

1. 8th October 1929.

highest forms: we see the sun nearing the hill-tops: we see its far reaching beams, fading more and more into oblivion, reflected in the gently swaying lake, that idly rolls now that way at the mercy of the light refreshing breeze, that fans the cheek with a sweet caressing touch. The heavens lie peaceful and tranquil in their bluish depths: the balmy air is fragrant with the sweet, exhilarating perfume of autumn's harvest, whilst casting over all a mantle of fiery red, the sun now half beyond the sight of human eye, sinks lower and lower down the horizon, enveloping more and more, as it travels its inevitable course, this earth in a gradually thickening darkness. And this scene though perhaps conveying no sublime thoughts to the uneducated, still conveys to the refined and cultivated mind a volume of thoughts that art can never give!

These exercises, in the long, broad and rather sloping script which always characterized Georges Vanier's handwriting, were evidence, if not of high literary talent, at least of delicate sensibility and literary appreciation. The essays he wrote at school, punctiliously corrected by his teachers, are an early indication both of mentality and style. The style was at times a little precious; at others a little diffuse. The tone is didactic, although the thought is beginning to run deep. He writes at length on friendship, with apt quotations from Cicero, Socrates, and La Rochefoucauld. He entreats the Catholics of Canada to unite, as Leo XIII had entreated the Catholics of France to a similar *ralliement*. Indeed *ralliement* was to be the watchword of Georges Vanier's career. He discusses La Bruyère's maxim that the nature of the French disposes them to satire and robs their thinking of a corresponding depth. Georges disagreed:

If depth consists . . . in obscuring what is clear rather than in clarifying what is obscure, I will freely admit that the French are not profound. But if the greatest artist is the one who knows how to conceal his art, then the Frenchman who knows how to bring the most complex questions under the light of day is the master artist of profundity. Whatever the Germans may say, depth is not in proportion to obscurity.

La Bruyère himself was an example of this, since he had so clearly analysed the evils of French society and foreshadowed, indirectly, the Revolution of which they were the cause.

Georges wrote, in high, romantic strain, about the 'pleasures of the imagination', and supported the paradox of Sainte-Beuve that 'there is nothing living in the present but the past'. Like many another adolescent, he had his heroes. Here George Washington held pride of place, not because he had helped to found the United States but because he was a hero to those who followed him and also, no doubt, because he was reputed never to have told a lie. With his literary leanings, Georges was ambitious to appear in print, and sent up a number of compositions to the local press – a poem, a short story, and a one-act play. The first of these was designed for the 'young people's corner', and the tone of all three was naïvely edifying. If the Georges Vanier that Canada knew was all things to all men, in the Pauline sense of the word, the young Georges Vanier was resolved to be all things to all readers. Writing under the pseudonym of George Raymond, he knew the popular press well enough not to quote Sainte-Beuve.

It does not appear that the reading at home was of a very high order. A magazine to which the family subscribed contained a serial by E. F. Benson entitled ' A Woman's Ambition', and indeed the paper seemed interested in little else. There were articles on how women could make money, on the art of etiquette and courtship, on health and strength for girls with the following recipe: 'secure an ordinary broom and let one girl hold it as high as she can over her head. The other girl should attempt to grasp it and pull it down. This is rather a vigorous exercise but it makes rather an interesting contest, and is very fine for chest and general bodily development.' Whether this advice was followed by Eva and Frances we are not told, but Georges' mind was on more virile matters. He frequented, indefatigably, the second-hand bookshops and came back armed with Scott, Thackeray, Macaulay, Pitt, Disraeli, and Trollope – in a word, the English classics. His favourite novelist was Thackeray, and remained so to the end of his life.

It is a curious fact, indicative of a nature in some sense always withdrawn, that Georges Vanier, who was the most companionable of men, never had a really intimate friend among his own contemporaries. He gave himself more freely only to those older or younger than himself. Naturally the staff at Loyola College were English-speaking, but there was one exception – a French Jesuit, Père Gaume, with whom Georges' relations were very close and confiding. Gaume was writing to him, a little nervously, during the summer holidays and regretting that he had not met 'any young people of your own age, well brought up and well behaved, who would have made your stay in the country more agreeable. But on the other hand I am glad to see that you have enough character and judgment not to associate with people from whom you would have nothing to gain. You have a boat at your disposal – so much the better; quite apart from the fun of it, you will be able to strengthen your muscles; rowing is capital exercise.'[2] So was the recital of the Rosary, which the good Father urged him not to neglect.

It was another Jesuit with a French name, if not a French nationality – Father Gagnieur – who taught him to love Shakespeare, and this was a love affair that lasted all his life. Georges was President of the Literary and Debating Society where Socialism, National Moderation, Champlain, and Canada's attitude towards Britain were subjects under discussion. We find him arguing that Canada had no need of a navy, on the grounds that a navy was the property of an independent nation, 'not a colony'; that there was no necessity for it, since Canada was under British protection; that the expense incurred would be enormous; that the result, even if the experiment were tried, would be a small and incapable fleet; and that Canada could best contribute to the strength of the empire by developing its own resources before thinking of defence. These were sensible views at the time, but they were a long way from the Statute of Westminster; and the admission of colonial status was a hostage to any speaker on the other side for whom the Heights of Abraham were more than a place on the map.

For Georges Vanier himself they were already rather more than that. The Victorian novelists, for all his delight in them, represented a world in which he had no ancestral stakes – a world almost as remote from Munster as it was from Montreal. He was in search of an identity which the home on Dorchester did not effectively provide. He did not doubt that he was a Canadian, but what kind of Canadian should he be? He talked English and was taught in English, but he could not forget that for generations his family had been French. If he were to be a useful Canadian, he must take his stand upon one side or other of the frontier upon which he had been born. He had not yet been to France and his mother, when she left the country, sent him postcards of Grant's tomb from New York, a bird's eye view of Baltimore, and William Penn's house in Philadelphia. Yet France – the *terra incognita* – seemed to call him like a vocation. Partly, no doubt, it came to him through his friendship with Père Gaume; and it may well have been the influence of this exemplary priest that decided him to settle down seriously to the study of the French language. Georges Vanier, with the determination that marked his

2. 5th August 1904.

character, resolved, for better or worse, to turn himself into a French-Canadian.

Here again he was fortunate, as he was always to be fortunate in the people who had a decisive effect on his career. Camille Martin was a retired professor, tutoring in Montreal, in whom the love of his native France was intensified by exile. He lived with his Italian wife and an adult, unmarried daughter in the upper flat of a house on lower Mackay Street, near Dorchester Boulevard. A tall, patriarchal figure with a full grey beard, he was a Parisian with an intense love of his native city and a corresponding hatred of the Germans, which he passed on to his pupils. He would turn the lessons into imaginary walks through the French capital, strolling down the streets and explaining the historic sites and monuments. Martin was not his real name and he was not, in fact, a teacher by profession. The story went that he had been a prominent banker, subsequently ruined by the Germans, and that he had known many of the outstanding literary and political personalities of his day – not only members of the Imperial family, but Victor Hugo and Edmond Rostand. In his study – which adjoined the living-room where he gave his lessons, and to which only privileged pupils were admitted – there were three signed photographs over the desk; the Emperor Napoleon III, the Empress Eugénie, and the Prince Imperial as a young man.

The Professor's interests were divided between literature and history. He introduced his pupils to Corneille, Racine and Molière, and told them anecdotes about the siege of Paris, the Commune, and the Franco-Prussian war, for these had left a profound imprint on his memory. But his chief business with the English-speaking pupils was conversational French. He left the grammar and genders to look after themselves until a certain fluency had been achieved, stressing a correct pronunciation and building up a vocabulary. It used to be said that Georges Vanier spoke like a well-educated Frenchman rather than a French-Canadian, although he spoke the language more slowly and more carefully than one who had never been at such pains to acquire it. A younger pupil[3] remembered him as upstanding, good-looking and tall, with a gentle and even courtly manner. The Professor thought him unusually gifted and prophesied for him a brilliant future. The Protestant boys would refer to their teacher as 'Père Martin', not because he was clerical but because he was venerable. A good

3. Mr Paul Hutchison, Q.C., to whom I am indebted for much of the above.

Catholic, he nevertheless refused to be dictated to by the local clergy. When a certain Canon, and afterwards a Bishop, demanded that the Professor play down any criticism of the Church's interference in politics, Martin replied curtly: 'When I teach history, I teach history.' Did he also teach the fastidious use of the *passé simple* which Georges Vanier clung to, like a moral principle, all through life? He certainly taught him what France could mean to a Frenchman, and very soon both the professor and his wife and daughter were welcomed into the family circle, sharing the same pew with them in church.

Georges Vanier's interests, however, went beyond literature and history; they touched upon science and religion, and the difficult relationship – more difficult than now – between the two. An essay on Darwinism, read aloud in class, reflected much credit both on himself and his Jesuit teachers:

There must be life already existing before Natural Selection has anything to select . . . In the Darwinian system, the initiating force has no more to do with the subsequent career of its productions than has the base which lifts a balloon in the direction in which it travels . . . The success of Darwinism has been throughout *popular* rather than *scientific* and as time went on, it has lost ground among the class of men best qualified to judge. Evolutionists there are plenty – but very few genuine Darwinians and among these not a few profess doctrines which cannot be reconciled with those of Darwin himself . . .

The soul, we know from psychology, is the great and immortal principle that animates the body – that stirs in every limb, that throbs in the over-burdened heart, that strives in the seething brain. The soul is that immaterial substance that looks out of its prison house of clay and gazing beyond this puny earth, interprets the signs in the heavens, measures the distance and magnitude of the stars, traces their paths through sidereal space, or turning to earth, reads its history in the very rocks, robs the seas and the mountains of their hidden treasures and compels the powers of nature to serve its purpose and to do its will. What then is the origin of the soul?

In the margin of this Georges had pencilled the following note: 'Do you remember our little discussion on the nature of the soul? Please excuse this poetic description?' With whom had he been talking? With Père Gaume, perhaps, or another whose company he sought out of school hours.

His notebooks were filled with scientific and metallurgical jottings, and at Christmas 1906 he did particularly well in the oral examination in chemistry, getting fifty marks out of a possible fifty-five. He also excelled in mathematics, logic, and ontology, and in the paper on Revelation and the Church. Among those who sat on the same benches with him was 'Chubby' Power,[4] better at history but not so good at Latin. The impression is of an exceptionally diligent and competent 'all rounder', with a taste for boxing that anyone who saw him browsing in the second-hand bookshops might not have suspected, and a love of hockey which long survived his inability to play it. The hours of recreation were spent on a large field on St Catherine Street, between Scott's Confectionary and Dionne's Grocery. One of George's more painful memories of Loyola was of a three-round bout under the railroad bridge on Guy Street with a fellow-student of his own weight, but more expert than himself; and one of his proudest was of kicking a decisive goal a minute before time was up.

In 1906 he was Prefect of the Loyola Sodality and delivered the Valedictory Address for the graduating class of seven before going on to Laval University where he had decided to study Law. It would have been more natural for a Loyola boy to go to McGill, but Laval was the obvious place for a young man who had no doubts that he was a French-Canadian. The University had certain of its Faculties in Montreal, where the teaching was of course in French. The decision to study Law was not a quick, or perhaps a very enthusiastic, choice, and it would not in the future generate much enthusiasm. Like many boys at Catholic schools, Georges Vanier had anxiously pondered the question of a religious vocation. He had made two Retreats at Sault au Récollet and, at the second of these, in May 1908, he had followed the Exercises of St Ignatius. A letter, presumably from Père Gaume, and written from Quebec, makes it clear that he had been careful and conscientious in making up his mind:

I thought that perhaps you had a religious vocation, and I should have been happy if God had called you, but He prefers to have you in the world, and that is perfect. Remember what I told you two years ago on one of our walks. Whatever decision you arrived at would have my approval, if I knew that you had taken it seriously, weighing the arguments for and against before God. Now that your decision has been made, I wholeheartedly approve your choice. You have acted honourably and reasonably; have no regrets. You will be walking resolutely forward along the path, clearly marked out,

4. The Hon. Senator C. B. Power, Q.C., 1888-1968.

along which God has impelled you through the mediation of your spiritual director.

You are going ahead with your Law, and you will profit by these years of study, developing at the same time your knowledge of French. I am glad that you have followed my advice, because a thorough knowledge of two languages will be of incalculable benefit to you in the profession you have chosen.[5]

For all his confidence in Père Gaume, Georges did not speak his mind easily, at least on paper, and the good priest reproached him for his reserve. Georges replied that 'intimate feelings – joys, sorrows and aspirations – are not things to write about. They can be spoken, and even so they are generally better understood by gestures, looks, and the tone of voice.' Gaume was also nervous about Georges' visits to the bookshops:

I approve of the books you have bought, but not without certain reservations. Molière, for example, is not to be read in his entirety. Some of his plays are abominable, and I rely on your good taste and delicacy to leave them to the oblivion they deserve. But perhaps you have bought an expurgated edition? In that case all is well.

Here we catch a clear hint of the Jansenism which was to infect religious life in the Province of Quebec for many years to come, and from which Georges Vanier took a long time to free himself. Not all of his teachers, however, were so nervous of Molière. One of the more interesting exercises he was set was a funeral oration that might have been delivered in honour of Molière by a member of the Académie Française. Here he caught, with rare imitative skill, the intonations that have so often reverberated *sous la Coupole*. He quotes Boileau, and he might have been reading Bossuet. Molière had 'transformed the literary manners of France', holding up the *précieux* of his time to a merited ridicule and making his genius for rhyme serve the purpose of comedy. But more than rhyme was required for dramatic poetry:

Molière had a profound love for humanity and studied it in depth. He reads the hearts of men like an open book. He observed their absurdities and depicted them as he saw them. He is the painter of nature, as Corneille is the painter of the ideal.

Georges had sent Père Gaume a pen and a pair of gloves, for which the priest was duly grateful; but what he craved were letters. Georges had been unwell and had said that he would be writing 'shortly'. 'For goodness sake' replied Gaume 'don't say "shortly";

5. 5th June 1908.

the "shortly" of your last letter but one lasted for six weeks.'
Gaume returned to France soon after this; and rather easier, maybe because moralism had no part in them, were the long literary
and philosophical discussions with Camille Martin. Meanwhile
Georges had become indented as student and apprentice to Charles
Casgrain, Advocate, in June 1908, and although his health was
none too good at this time, he was feeling stronger in body and
more settled in mind when he resumed his studies at Laval in
September 1909. The professor had read some of his youthful
outpourings on the beauties of nature and found in them 'an admirable eulogy of nature, which is the instrument of reconciliation between the two great schools of realism and idealism . . .
the inspiration of literary masterpieces and – to go further – the
fruitful basis for an agreement between reason and faith.' To
read what Georges had written, he said, was like 'drinking milk',
and he went on to quote Anatole France – hardly an author to
win the approval of Père Gaume – 'Madness is wiser than wisdom,
for it is the madness of the martyr without which nothing great or
useful has been constructed by mankind.'

Among his own contemporaries Georges' closest friend was the
poet Paul Morin, who wrote to him from Paris with exciting news
of meetings with Maurice Barrés and Henri de Régnier. Georges
was evidently suffering from pre-examination nervous depression,
for in May 1911 Morin asks him:

Was it too much civil code, Georges old boy? or too many 'gentes
demoiselles haultaines mais propices à l'amour'? Heart troubles or
supertension of the grey matter? I hope that you will go up for the
June exams – in fact, I know you will, and a nice, fat, juicy L.L.L.
will reward you.

Morin addressed Georges as 'Alma soave e cara'[6] – a description
that no one who knew him would ever have contested. He took
his Bar exam in June (1911), and a telegram to his mother – who
was at Memphremagog – on the 6th of July announced that he
had passed it. Père Gaume sent a postcard from Paray-le-Monial,
happy that his prayers had been answered; an uncle and aunt
wanted to know whether he would like a signet ring or a scarf
pin; and Camille Martin – less interested in law than in literature,
and here Georges would have been at one with him – recommended a book of essays by Emile Faguet and others which resumed 'all that a cultivated French mind should possess after his
classical studies.'[7]

6. Sweet and dear soul.   7. 18th July 1911.

2

Some men are born leaders; some achieve leadership; and some have leadership thrust upon them. Each of these was true of Georges Vanier, but perhaps the third is truer than the others. His ambition was the ambition to serve, and so we find him at Laval replying, with an almost precocious felicity, to the toast in honour of the students. The speaker's words were a surprise because, after all, there were students and students. There were students who studied – if the pleonasm might be allowed – and there were students who did not study. Everyone knew – or at least had heard – of students who danced with a rather particular freedom; who made a noise in the theatre and created disorder in the street; but Georges proceeded to paint his own portrait of the student who was a student in nothing but name:

He gets up rather late, and you will find him at the Bar, leading a merry life for as long as the paternal allowance lasts, and very ingeniously obtaining his funds under the most unlikely pretexts. He wants to buy legal text-books which have never existed, and to pay tailors' bills for suits that have never been made. But here I stop . . . my portrait is wholly imaginary, because you know, Messieurs les Professeurs, that this kind of student is unknown at Laval. The unenviable reputation of the students, outside the University, is exaggerated. If a sign-post is broken, or a policeman jostled in a scuffle, a student is always held responsible by the mob. One would say that the beret seems to sit well on every rascally scalp.

The speaker – a certain M. Fauteux – had complimented the students on their good behaviour during a recent visit to Ottawa. Georges agreed that in order to demonstrate their intellectual superiority it was not 'absolutely necessary to knock the police on the head, or to keep the peaceful inhabitants of the capital from their sleep.' But he claimed, eloquently, the rights of the *joie de vivre*; and this could only be nourished by the enthusiasm for a great ideal:

> *Il faut avoir l'amour, il faut avoir la foi*
> *Tant qu'on n'a pas laissé l'azur derrière soi.*

All that was lacking to make of Laval the El Dorado of their dreams was a closer union between the students of the different faculties. Professors and students worked together in the Maison des Etudiants, but the pupil tended to be embarrassed by the presence of his teacher. 'The humble reed does not dare to

look up to the heights of the great oak.' So Georges asked for a
general council of students, composed of delegates from all the
faculties, to organize the banquets, concerts, demonstrations,
inter-collegiate debates, and Olympic games. Such a council would
be a power for unity:

> C'est la force d'en haut qui fait joindre nos mains
> Par dessus les grands murs des préjugés humains.

Georges went on to speak of the French-Canadian student's rôle
in Canada:

It seems to me that our mission here is clear, great and generous.
We must spread the spirit of the Latin countries, we must develop
the Latin civilization, and the culture of our forbears, by the
mediation and the use of the most beautiful language which has ever
existed for the translation of human thought. . . . To our neighbours who forget it and would make us forget it, I will answer – we
are the descendants of a Latin race, we shall always preserve the
cult of the Latin genius. Listen to the eulogy recently pronounced by
the most delicate stylist of contemporary France:
  'It was by this that in Rome the fate of the universe was deliber-
ated, and the form conceived in which the peoples of the world are
still contained.'
  May the same mould serve for the conception of the Canadian
intellect; of the Canada which will give its name to the twentieth
century.

Evidently the Professors took the hint, for presently Georges
is pleading his record as student representative on the sports
committee and asking, modestly enough, for larger responsibilities. He had obtained a reduction in price for the orchestra
stalls and the gallery at the Tuesday evening performances of the
Comédie Française – then visiting Montreal – for any student who
wished to attend, and he hoped to secure a similar reduction for
the other seats in the house. It was unfortunate that Laval had no
skating-rink:

What would you say, he went on, if I promised you an open
skating rink, of the regular size, illuminated at night and always at
your disposal? A rink adjoining a warmed room which would serve
as a changing room, and as a place for rest and conversation? Does
the idea of this installation smile on you? Well, I can't promise it
to you, for the good reason that I have already obtained it. Besides
aren't promises such fragile things that one can very well apply to
them the words of Sully Prud'homme: 'Don't have anything to

do with them'? The Maison des Etudiants has undertaken to give us a rink, to light it, and to keep it in repair – a rink which will be at your disposal at any time and which will cost you nothing. And there is a further detail. Those who like playing hockey but don't belong to either of our regular teams will have the privilege of playing on the rink at certain times, and have absolute freedom to practise there.

Georges had other projects up his sleeve; the students' banquet which would justify Boileau's couplet:

> *On est savant qui boit bien*
> *Qui ne sait boire ne sait rien,*

the concert to which the friends of the University were to be invited, and the tour up into the Province of Quebec. And then there was the problem of oral examinations:

You know as well as I do that under the present system we jostle one another before the door of the examination hall for two or three days, we get tired out, and then it sometimes happens that after waiting all the afternoon they tell us that the exams have been put off till the next day. I should like to see a list published in advance, giving the names of the candidates and the times at which they will be examined . . . and I undertake to make all the necessary representations to get the system modified.

In asking for a confirmation and extension of his mandate Georges stressed the obvious necessity of the student representative being perfectly bilingual, since all discussion with McGill was in English, and he wished to see Laval taking part in the inter-University debates. It was an absurd anomaly that Laval, the oldest University in Canada, should be excluded from them. In these speeches, which for cogency of argument, elegance of phrase, and aptness of quotation heralded many that he was to make in the years ahead, Georges Vanier not only spoke the language of his French-speaking compatriots but upheld their academic and linguistic rights.

3

It was now decided that he should spend some time in travel before he started life as a barrister. Except for a short visit to Washington in January 1911, he had not been out of Canada. In September, therefore, he set out for the United States and western Ontario. Already he was feeling the compulsive need to jot down his impressions. He thought – surprisingly enough for a French-Canadian – that Montreal had a great deal to learn from Toronto.

The residential district was superior to Westmount or Outremont; the streets were cleaner and better paved; the lighting was efficient; and the public buildings impressive. In fact, the only thing wrong with Toronto was that he met 'scarcely half a dozen attractive women'. He thought London pretentious, and he was disconcerted – to say the least – when he crossed to the American side of the Niagara Falls.

The officials are discourteous, the travellers vulgar and children ill-bred. . . . After viewing the Falls a Guide will say: 'Register in here.' You go in and are set upon by a couple of irrepressive sales-ladies. You are disgusted. The American Falls are simply a shadow of the Canadian Falls. Very amusing to see tourists trying to see more than there is to be seen.

Buffalo reminded him of Montreal, and it lacked 'the atmosphere of refinement and home life so marked in Toronto'. Detroit pleased him better; but in Minneapolis he was unable to find a decent restaurant, and in Chicago he noted that the men did not remove their hats when ladies were in the elevators.

We must suppose that on his return he began to feel his way about Casgrain's office, but on the 4th of February 1912 he boarded the S.S. *Franconia* at Halifax and started out on the first stage of the Grand Tour. A certain Madame Rodier was also on the ship, and Georges was her guest at dinner, enjoying the bouillabaisse. In Paris he stayed at the Regina in the rue de Rivoli, meeting Paul Morin and relishing what he afterwards described as 'the sacred thrill of contact with the intellectual life of Paris.' Morin, whose poems had been published by Francis Jammes in *Les Tablettes*, was at work on *Le Paon d'Email*, and one of these jewels he dedicated to Georges Vanier. He also introduced him to Albany cigarettes, which you bought in metal boxes of ten, and sent him a copy of Shelley's *The Sensitive Plant*. Now, and for some time to come, Shelley, more than any other poet, met the mood of Georges' romanticism.

The excitement of travel did not tempt him to forget his friends in Canada, and they in turn kept in touch with him. Camille Martin sent him a copy of Anatole France's *Les Dieux ont Soif*, and he received more than one kindly letter from the Minister of Justice in Ottawa. In March he was in Brussels, and towards the end of June his father and his sister Eva joined him. Together they went to Dresden and other German cities, and on to Italy. Milan reminded Georges of Lyon and he did not appreciate the Lombardy plain 'because it is too cheerful – it has not suffered.

It is perfectly unassuming but too self-sufficient.' *Weltschmerz* was the *mot d'ordre*, and in Venice, where they arrived at sunset, there was enough of it and to spare. The city appeared to him as an 'enchantress, cruel and subtle. I will be rocked by you not into sleep but into a fever of excitement. You are the city that intoxicates, that renders feverish and as such I am one of your devotees. . .'

They took a gondola from the station to the Hotel Napoleon I, under the light of a crescent moon, and after dinner, as they were rowed out to the Lido, the gondolas around the San Marco landing stage were lyrical with singers and musicians. The next afternoon the Lagoon was 'laughing' and at night it would be 'full of infinite sadness'. The reader may smile at Georges Vanier's romantic *Angst*, but how many young men, seeing Venice for the first time, have seen it so! Georges did not imagine himself another Robert Browning, but as they glided in the dark by the *palazzo* where Browning had lived, he could not resist the impulse to put pen to paper:

Venice is only the shadow of her former self but I like her as she is and as she must be – it is the destiny of all men and all cities to crumble. What more beautiful death for Venice than to sink slowly – very slowly – into the waters of the Adriatic. A Swan Song you are singing now and I like the Swan Song better than the gay and rich melodies of yore. The narrow *calles* with one solitary gas-jet at the end, with deserted houses on both sides, the shadows playing across the bob of the gondola, and only the regular swish of the oar to break the silence – this is Venice, but the gay barks of orchestras are a resurrection of the past, and what more awful than trying to revive something that never can be. No, Venice, sleep on, die on, you are greater in your misery than in your happiness and gaiety. You are the personification of all that is decayed and decadent. An attempt to rehabilitate you would be a sacrilege. . . . Silently we pass over the Ponte della Guerra, on all sides abandoned gondolas, ghosts fretting to and fro, five-storey houses. . . . Picture of the Madonna over the staircase in Santa Barbara: You are in the presence of a smiling, almost roguish looking child, you hardly look at the Madonna, but you stand electrified before the Child and you smile – tears almost come into your eyes. Such grace, the left hand clutching in a convulsive grasp the robe of the Madonna. The right hand in which rests His head is gently laid on the Virgin. It is more natural than nature. It is the first picture in Venice that moved me, that enthralled me . . . the Child is fair with laughing eyes.

They spent the last four days in Venice gliding up and down the canals in a gondola, for the *sirocco* had come to depress them 'so that the whole dead past seemed to rise out of the Lagoon to stifle and smother us'; and they were glad to move on to Rome, where a photograph shows Georges in a wide, floppy hat standing by Keats' grave in the Protestant cemetery. 'The violets no longer spring as they did in March, but the green is more luxuriant, only the sun touched the top of the trees and with bowed heads we left.' A postcard of St Peter's Square told Frances that 'this is where I saw His Holiness Pope Pius X'; but since Pius X never set foot in St Peter's Square the indication is that they were received in audience. They returned to France by way of Turin and the Mont Cenis. Georges found the French that he met casually 'forward, overbearing and soi-disant omniscient', but he did not doubt that the 'better classes' were 'refined, cultivated and considerate'. On the 10th of August they were at Rouen; on the 23rd at Windsor; on the 29th in Dublin; and at the end of the month they sailed from Liverpool for Montreal. A letter from his favourite sister no doubt quickened the pulse of Georges' homecoming:

The dog just fell ill today. I think she has the measles. I hope not. From your 'lovely' little sister, Frances.

Three months later Paul Morin was writing gaily of a dinner in Paris with bunches of asparagus, langoustes, and pigeon *sauté*; and if this revived hopes of a return to France, they were soon to be realized under circumstances of which neither Georges Vanier nor his friend had the slightest premonition.

CHAPTER 2

THE 'VAN DOOS'

I

A T some point during the next six months Georges Vanier went to work with Messieurs Dessaules and Garneau, another firm of advocates in Montreal. This may have been a temporary arrangement since he kept in touch with Casgrain, who wanted him to accept a lieutenancy in the 6th Brigade, Canadian Field Artillery. Georges did not feel inclined to fall in with this plan, but Casgrain was persistent:

I hope you will not let the question drop permanently but that you will see your way clear in the near future to accept a commission. Any time that you may consider the matter more favourably, just let me know, and if there is a vacancy I shall be glad to welcome you to fill the same.[1]

The truth is that Georges had no particular interest in military matters. The security of Canada was not threatened, and attached as he was to France, he was not thirsting for the return of the lost provinces. True, there was always Camille Martin at his elbow, but the professor was no chauvinist. A letter to Georges, recommending a book by Funck Brentano, makes it clear that he had no royalist sympathies – popular as these might have been in the Province of Quebec where the fleur-de-lys commanded a good deal more respect than the tricolour.

It is a real lesson in history – and at the same time the public condemnation of those self-styled ultramontane historians who monarchize the history of France in her own despite, by truncating or mutilating the texts.

Here the reference is obviously to Jacques Bainville, Charles Maurras and the dogmatists of the *Action Français* – writers with whom Georges probably had no acquaintance.

The outbreak of war in August 1914 took Canada, with the rest of the world, by surprise. Contingents for service overseas were immediately mobilized, and on the 24th of September

1. 7th May 1913.

the press published an open letter to the Prime Minister, Sir Robert Borden,[2] by Colonel Mignault, medical officer with the 65th Carabiniers Mont-Royal. This asked for authority to recruit a regiment composed exclusively of Canadians of French descent. The request was warmly received by press and public alike, and volunteers quickly came forward. A group of French-Canadians, officers of the militia and a number of civilians without any military experience, met together in the Mess of the Fusiliers de Mont-Royal. Georges Vanier was among them. This was the beginning of what afterwards became the Royal 22nd Regiment. The choice of commanding officer fell, by general assent, upon Colonel F. M. Gaudet, a regular soldier who for many years had been superintendent of the arsenal at Quebec. The son of an engineer, he was himself a member of the Canadian Society of Civil Engineers. A short, dark man, with a bristling black moustache and large bright eyes, he proved eminently fitted to organize and lead the regiment.

On the 15th of October there was a big rally in the Parc Sohmer. Twenty thousand people crowded the hall, with Mignault in the chair, and Sir Wilfrid Laurier, Sir Lomer Gouin, Senator Dandurand, and M. Casgrain on the platform. Laurier had to withstand an ovation of twenty minutes before he was able to speak, and it seemed as if the *union sacrée* had been achieved in Quebec before it was achieved in France. A week later the *Gazette du Canada* gave the new regiment its birth certificate as the 'Royal French-Canadian' – a mistake which was subsequently rectified, since the title of 'Royal' is not normally given to a regiment until it has been under fire. Throughout the war the 'Van Doos' were known as the 22nd French-Canadian Battalion, and it was not until 1920 that it became the 'Royal 22nd'.

Georges Vanier was undoubtedly in the hall on that memorable night. From the beginning of October he had been training with the McGill O.T.C. Equitation Class at the Riding Academy in Montreal, either in riding breeches or in uniform; and on the 10th of November, after a most perfunctory medical examination, he formally enlisted, with the rank of lieutenant, at St Jean d'Yberville, quite close to Montreal, He had already, it seems, been active in recruiting, since a room in the offices of *La Presse* had been placed at his disposal for this purpose. Out of 2,000 volunteers 900 were rejected for one reason or another. The first draft of about twenty men had reached St Jean on the 22nd of October,

2. Lord Borden, 1854-1937.

and from then onwards they arrived daily, a few hundred at a time, with an officer in charge. On the 29th of October a guard was mounted at the main gate.

What, we may ask, were Georges Vanier's motives in responding so promptly to a call which others of his own age and milieu left unanswered? A letter to Frances gives a clue:

During the last months of 1914 I could not read the accounts of Belgian sufferings without feeling a deep compassion and an active desire to right, as far as it was in my power, the heinous wrong done.[3]

Like so many others of that doomed generation, he acted upon some instinctive sense of honour, for delicacy and determination were twin facets of his character. With his English-speaking home and his English education he might, however, just as well have joined up in an English-speaking regiment where he would have found several boys from Loyola alongside of him. But it was not for nothing that he had come to regard himself as a French-Canadian. Moreover many of those first officers in the 'Van Doos' were men with an ancestry rich in military tradition and bearing names of the old French Seigneuralty, illustrious in the history of Quebec. Gaudet's uncle had fought with the British in the Crimea. He was himself a direct descendant of the Grosbois, allied to the de Beaujeu and the de Bellefeuilles, and his father had been an intimate friend of Charles de Salaberry the hero of Châteauguay, and Lieutenant La Roque de Roquebrune was de Salaberry's great-grandson and had an uncle serving with the first Canadian contingent in France. Major de Lanaudière was directly descended from Mademoiselle de Lanaudière whose salon in Old Quebec had been frequented by the élite of the French and English aristocracy in the days of Governor Murray. These names brought echoes of the time when men fought for their King before they fought for their country, and although Georges Vanier did not boast their lineage he was proud to serve with them. To be frank, if we may judge from the photographs, they were a tough and not particularly prepossessing lot. The young Lieutenant Vanier was taller than any of them, and more distinguished than most. He gives the impression of a poet strayed into uniform beside a bunch of hardened campaigners.

They were, in fact, anything but hardened. Enthusiasm does not make an army; the men had no uniforms; and eighty-five per cent of them, we are told, had never learnt to march in step. They

3. 1st February 1919.

Georges Vanier, 4 years old.

Philias and Margaret Vanier
on the occasion of their
golden wedding, 1937.

On active service 1915–18. From a portrait drawing by Alfred Bastien.

The 'Van Doos' in training at St Jean d'Yberville, January 1915, Georges Vanier in the centre.

did not salute because they saw no need to; their quarters were bad; and they slept pretty well anywhere. Of the officers only Gaudet and Captain Henri Archambault, the second-in-command, came from the regular army. Archambault was inspector of the cadet corps in the military district of Montreal, but he left, soon after the arrival at St Jean, to command the 41st Battalion, another French-Canadian unit. His namesake, 'Lipi' Archambault[4], has recorded that Georges Vanier was the first officer he met and that Georges immediately offered him his bed. The historian of the regiment has compared the recruits of the 'Van Doos' to Napoleon's conscripts after the *levée en masse*, and they were inspired by the same zeal. Georges Vanier was quick to exercise such authority as he had, and he did so with justice tempered with mercy. On the route marches, which were an essential part of their training, the men were forbidden to talk when they were passing through a village. This was not easy, because their passage drew all eyes to the windows – and many petticoats into the street. On one occasion a soldier in Vanier's platoon replied with some jocular gallantry, and Georges, turning round, sentenced the man to three days' confinement to barracks. Another soldier, Private Rancourt, spoke up and admitted that it was he who had broken the rule of silence – whereupon the sentence was transferred. Later, it was remitted because Rancourt had had the candour to 'own up'. Rancourt was to be in many a tight corner with Georges Vanier, and he described him as the justest officer under whom he had ever served. The day would come, a little later on, when Georges protected him from Court Martial.

I taught the men what I had learnt the night before. Since I was a little – oh a very little – better educated than they were, I assumed an air of authority and self-confidence which intimidated the recruits. . . . The training at St Jean went along quite well until Christmas and the New Year when we had a bitter experience. Most of our men gave themselves leave until the Feast of the Epiphany – oh, with the best will in the world and perhaps without knowing what one had to do to get permission to go on leave. The climax came on New Year's Day when the family spirit was so strong that practically everyone went home. The poor Colonel was in despair, wondering if his men would come back. Well, they did come back, explaining that they loved their families so much – which was very edifying but not very convincing, and the Commanding Officer was so hard-hearted as not to believe them. I needn't tell you that they didn't absent themselves a second time. It's

4. Général de Brigade L. P. V. Archambault.

only fair to say that as an additional reason for their absence without
leave they declared that they had joined up in order to fight.[5]

On the 17th December the regiment was inspected by the
Duke of Connaught, Governor General of Canada, and on the 2nd
of March 1915, it was ready to leave. Two flags presented to it
were committed to the safe keeping of the Order of St Sulpice
until it should return. Now numbering four companies, eight
platoons, thirty-six officers, and 1,093 non-commissioned officers
and men, it moved off from the Richelieu parade ground at St
Jean and left in trains at one hour intervals for Amherst, Nova
Scotia. The journey was enlivened by a grand reception at
Chaudière Junction where friends had come to meet them by
special train. Nova Scotia was not quite *terra incognita* for
the French, since the Cumberland district had once been the
home of the French military with its headquarters at Fort Beausé-
jour. The local press announced that the 'Van Doos' had carried
Amherst by 'bloodless storm'; nevertheless their arrival ushered in
a period of arduous training. The men looked eagerly forward to
the morning hour of physical drill, sometimes in a foot or more
of snow. The officers were quartered at various hotels, and the
men on the premises of the Canada Car Foundry Company. A
twenty mile route march in biting cold, wind and snow was the
order of the day; and on the 29th of April they marched to Sackville and back in weather conditions that were still atrocious. In
many places the water and mud were knee-deep. Georges Vanier
was in 'D' Company, under the command of Major Dubuc,[6] and
on this occasion he was in charge of the vanguard. Dinner was
served on the College campus at Sackville, and by the end of
the day the 'Van Doos' had marched twenty-two miles between
9.30 a.m. and 5.30 p.m. with a two-hour break for their midday
meal – and only five stragglers.

After four and a half months of training, the regiment prepared to leave for Europe. On their last evening the officers gave
a military ball in the hall which had been the scene of so much
tedious, though necessary, drilling. Colonel and Madame Gaudet
received the three hundred guests under balconies draped with
the Allied flags and the letters '22nd F.C.R.' picked out with the
sheaths of bayonets. There were no individual programmes and
the dances – waltzes and one steps and a single set of the lancers –

5. Speech at the Annual Meeting of the 'Amicale' of the Royal 22nd Regiment,
Montreal, 1955.
6. Lieut-Colonel A. E. Dubuc.

were announced on posters hanging from the walls and by a blast from the buglers. The last Military Ball in Amherst had been held in honour of the Duke of Kent in 1800. On the following morning, the 20th of May, the regiment paraded in full equipment, except for rifles and side arms. Soldiers of the 6th Mounted Rifles lined the streets, and 5,000 people had assembled behind them from Amherst and the neighbouring towns. The Amherst Military Band turned out in their khaki greatcoats and played 'O Canada', 'Tipperary' and 'The Soldiers of the King', with the children from the West Highlands school adding their trebles to the brass. The Lieutenant Governor and Prime Minister of Nova Scotia were also there as the two trains, each composed of ten carriages, took the 'Van Doos' to Halifax. The mood of that day, and the morale of the regiment, is given in a letter of Georges Vanier to his mother:

Our departure from Amherst was very enthusiastic, the whole town turned out to say farewell. The streets were lined with people carrying flags and bunting . . . Our train ran onto the wharf at Halifax where the *Saxonia* was waiting for us, with the 25th Battalion on board . . . the embarkation taking about one hour. No disorder, no noise on the part of the men, discipline perfect. The sight was impressive as we drew away to the sounds of 'O Canada' played by our band. Quietly we left the wharf, the people waving flags, handkerchiefs and hats. It was the most 'living' moment of our existence so far. It is a privilege (Lloyd George said so first) to be of this age, when instead of leading mediocre, colourless lives we can forget the dollars and the earth and think of principles and the stars. We have been looking at the ground so long that we have forgotten that the stars still shine.[7]

The standing orders for the troops on board included a daily inspection, physical training, sports, occasional parades with lifebelts, and at least one in marching kit. A very successful concert was also given in aid of the Liverpool Sailors' Orphanage Asylum. Georges took his turn as Officer of the Guard, but the duties were minimal and he killed a good many hours playing shuffle-board and quoits. The sea was calm and the weather sunny; and at night they sat up on deck under a full moon, thinking about their friends in Canada, and wondering if they would be torpedoed – for the ship was sailing without escort. On the Sunday 'it was wonderful to hear Mass in the open air with the sky and the sea and the clouds as witnesses. The most impressive moment

7. 21st May 1915.

was when the priest raised his hands to the sky preparatory to giving us his blessing.'[8] A few days later they could have dispensed with the light of the moon, for they were now in the danger zone, sleeping in their clothes and with lifebelts at their side. On the 28th of May they sighted two destroyers, the first war vessels to be seen since they had left Halifax; and on the 29th they reached Devonport – and what Georges noted in his diary as the 'laughing' English countryside.

The regiment now went into training at East Sandling camp, on high dry ground two miles from Shorncliffe and Hythe, and four from Folkestone. Here they lived in water-proof huts, but on the 3rd of June Georges was in London, staying at the Savoy, and stealing a visit to the Alhambra, in order to buy a motor-car for the regiment and a portable bath, periscope, water bottle and other necessities for himself. He was even playing with the idea of acquiring a motor-cycle, and eventually took a half share in one. In camp he would rise with the others at 5.30 a.m.; learn how to read a map, handle a machine-gun, and point a bayonet. Later, there was firing with dummy cartridges, and rehearsals for trench warfare. Religious services were held in the open air, and Georges described how more than a thousand voices chanted the 'Magnificat'; and then, at the end of Mass, 'Nous vous invoquons tous' to the tune of 'God Save the King', so that the men of the 24th Battalion, also training at Shorncliffe, thought that they were singing the National Anthem. The regiment was reviewed by Sir Robert Borden; Sam Hughes,[9] the Canadian Minister of Defence; and Bonar Law,[10] himself a Canadian by birth:

As the platoons marched by Mr Bonar Law removed his black bowler, had his head drenched and probably his back also, as the water was trickling down our spines.

    . . . to complete the day, Mr Bonar Law spoke to us at the drill hall, Folkestone, in the evening. His speech was retrospective and prospective: a synopsis of what England had done and what she was likely to do. He spoke with deep conviction. He is a quiet unassuming speaker, with little gesture and no theatrical tricks. He speaks in a conversational tone (very pleasant timbre) and unless you listen intently (especially at the back of the hall) you miss snatches here and there. He has a delightful sense of humour, a

8. Letter to Mrs Vanier, 23rd May 1915.
9. Lieut-General the Hon. Sir Sam Hughes, 1858-1923.
10. Andrew Bonar Law, 1858-1921, Leader of the Conservative Opposition in the British House of Commons, and afterwards Prime Minister.

remarkable command of idiomatic English and a supple turn of mind. I felt as if I could have listened to him for three or four hours without tiring.

The meeting was for Officers only. It was a touching and inspiring scene, this gathering of Canadian Officers come from every part of the Dominion and belonging to every walk of life, united in the mother country and proclaiming the solidarity of the English peoples.[11]

At the same time Georges was receiving *Le Temps* regularly from Paris, and had no doubts of 'France's determination to continue the war until German autocracy is destroyed.'[12]

For recreation there were dinners at the Grand Hotel and at *Chez Maestroni* in Folkestone; or a visit to Saltwood Castle where the assassins of Thomas à Becket had spent the night before setting out on their fatal mission; or a twelve mile ride on horseback with Tommy Tremblay[13] up into the Kentish weald, and supper at a country inn. At the week-end he often went to London, staying at the Savoy or the Cecil, close by in the Strand. Georges Vanier was an insatiable play-goer, and it was a time of very light entertainment. *Betty* at Daly's; *Gamblers All* at Wyndhams; Yvette Guilbert, Vesta Tilley and Charles Hawtrey at the Coliseum – the theatre was an opiate rather than an inspiration. Georges would visit the poorer quarters of the city; walk in Hyde Park; have tea at the Regent Palace; and he went up in an aeroplane for the first time with Tremblay, Captain Boyer, and Major Dubuc. 'Not the least nervous tension' he noted 'one has gone up and one is completely satisfied. The whole nervous system relaxes deliciously. It's like being in a rocking-chair; as you ascend, coast along, and come down again, without any shock or fear. It's like a beautiful and strange dream.'[14] On Sunday he would hear Mass at the Jesuit church in Farm Street, listening to Father Bernard Vaughan. 'No longer the same man' he noted 'he has lost his fire, but kept his sense of the theatre. The sermon was full of images and poetry, very French. The Latin formation of Father Vaughan comes through.'[15]

On his return, two parcels of boots, made to measure, arrived from Dangerfield's in Montreal. He was now appointed machine-gun officer for the 22nd – 'the responsibility is greater and so is

11. Letter to Mrs Vanier, 5th August 1915.
12. Ibid.
13. Major-General Thomas-Louis Tremblay, 1886-1951.
14. Diary.
15. Diary, 6th June 1915.

the interest'[16] – as the day of embarkation drew near. He had arranged to send home the following coded messages: 'How is Arthur?' would mean that they were leaving for France; 'Expect you shortly' that they were leaving for the Dardanelles. On the 2nd of September the battalion was inspected by King George V, who radiated hope and confidence; and Cardinal Bourne[17] came down to preside and preach at the Mass in Beachborough Park. He spoke in French and English, and Georges noted the good accent which was among the legacies of St Sulpice. On the 13th of September the first detail of the battalion entrained for Southampton. This comprised the transport and machine-gun section, composed of twenty-four privates, two sergeants, a corporal, a batman, six drivers, four guns, four limbered waggons, thirteen horses – twelve for draught and one for riding. Georges slept on the wharf, with a horse blanket for a mattress. Even at the Savoy, he wrote, he had seldom slept so well; and the cable 'How is Arthur?' was duly sent off in the morning.

Disembarking at Le Havre, they found the inhabitants surprised that they were talking French, and a French Captain with whom they were in conversation seemed to know nothing of French-speaking Canada. The officers were comfortably settled in a second-class railway carriage, the men much less so in a goods waggon – thirty-six or forty in each – without seats or lights. They were not depressed, however, and left the station at Le Havre singing 'O Canada' and the 'Marseillaise'. Meanwhile the rest of the battalion had embarked at Folkestone, and Georges Vanier with his machine-gun and transport section met them at Pont-de-Brigues, near Boulogne. It was at Boulogne, as they marched through the streets, that the 'Van Doos' received the nickname of 'petits cochons' – not because they had misbehaved themselves, but because they wore a beaver on their caps. At St Omer they were joined – to the general astonishment – by an interpreter from French military headquarters. Gaudet received him politely, explaining that while they were grateful for his services as Adjutant they could dispense with his interpretations – a fact of which he very quickly became aware. From St Omer it was a long and fatiguing march to Wallon-Capelle, nine miles further on. The infantry had new boots and many of them had not slept for three nights. Georges was luckier since he rode on horseback, carrying all his effects in saddlebags, except for his revolver, ammunition, haversack and water-bottle.

16. Diary, 4th September 1915.   17. Archbishop of Westminster.

At Wallon-Capelle, where they arrived at 11 p.m., the officers were billeted at the Mairie, sleeping on the hard floor with a mackintosh for a mattress. It was 2 a.m. before they were able to turn in after seeing to the feeding and quartering of the men, and in the morning they were on the road to Rouge-Croix. The regimental headquarters were at Meterem, four miles further on, and Georges wrote that he was 'billeted in a farmhouse with a few other officers and my men are in a neighbouring barn; I have never been so well in my life; the food is excellent. There are farmers quite near to the front who can supply you with delicious eggs, butter, coffee, milk, in fact any nutritious food.'[18] This country had been Flemish before the Napoleonic wars, and many of the inhabitants still spoke Flemish. But for Georges Vanier it was France. 'Never in my wildest flights of imagination could I have foretold that one day I would march through the country I love so much in order to fight in its defence; perhaps I should not say in *its* defence because it is really in defence of human rights, not of French rights solely.' In feeling thus he was both exceptional and fortunate. Only a very small fraction of the British and Canadian Forces can have had a similar feeling about a country they did not know at all, and which many of them, if the truth be told, did not particularly like.

Two days later the battalion arrived at Scherpenberg, only three and a half miles from the front. On the 20th of September seven platoons went up into the trenches, and the rest followed on the 22nd relieving the King's Own Yorkshire Light Infantry. The normal routine was to spend six days in the trenches and six in rest billets behind the lines. Even in the trenches everything was done to keep the men as contented and occupied as possible. At 5 p.m. the section commanders examined each man's fire position, and at 5.30 reported to the company commander that these were correct. At 6 p.m. the company commander met the officers and N.C.Os of the company to discuss what offensive action could be taken against the enemy, how the line could be strengthened, and how the trenches could be made more comfortable. Half the company worked from 11 p.m. to 2.30 a.m., when the other half took over till 6 a.m. The whole company stood to arms until breakfast, after which everyone, except for sniping and observation posts, turned in to sleep in the dug-outs.

Each platoon had its own mess, with fresh meat well cooked instead of tinned food, and hot soup at night when on duty. Any

18. Diary, 17th September 1915.

man heard grousing was liable to one to four days fatigue, which entailed working in the afternoon; but there seems to have been very little grousing, although these were early days. Even when they were standing to arms, the men were discouraged from merely stamping their feet and complaining how cold it was. Work was arranged for them close to their fire positions where they could have their rifles at their sides. All hand grenades were removed from the front line when the company went into reserve and placed in a depot, where they were cleaned and overhauled. When the men returned to the trenches they took in aprons, boxes or haversacks whatever bombs were thought necessary to hold the line. Special precautions were taken against 'Trench Feet'. No leave was granted to company officers in units where this was prevalent. The men were stripped, and anti-frost grease rubbed in from waist to feet. Every man had to have with him at least one extra pair of dry socks, and both boots and socks were removed once in every twenty-four hours. They were also made to take whatever exercise was possible while they were in the trenches.

Such were the routine and orders for everyone in the 2nd Canadian Division, and Georges Vanier was not in the least depressed by them. He was quick to send his first impressions to his father, writing, as he always did to Philias Vanier, in French:

At night the effect is fairy-like – fireworks illuminating the German lines, the shells exploding in a burst of light which is fantastic and picturesque, the men singing and working and happy to be where they are – all this is deeply impressive. The game is well worth the candle; the intense reality of the life we are leading gives you a human outlook which you'll never lose. Don't imagine that the first sensations are unpleasant; they're not. A little astonishment and surprise at first, after which you're almost indifferent. (I say 'almost' because you still have a little respect for these weapons of destruction). You see, one gets so quickly accustomed to the most abnormal sort of life.[19]

At the same time he was writing to his mother:

During the six days in we seldom sleep at night; the Boche trenches are only seventy-five to two hundred yards distant. The trenches are relatively safe and if a chap keeps his head well down he is not likely to be hit. This applies of course to rifle and machine-gun fire: shell fire is harder to avoid and whether you are hit or not

9. 18th September 1915.

is largely a matter of chance. This morning I witnessed a most striking scene: some time before dawn artillery duels were opened all around us and the sky was red with the thousand flashes from the cannon. Slowly dawn crept up, the flashes became more intermittent and less distinct and the morning broke on a plain zigzagged by trenches of all kinds. It is the sort of sunrise one does not forget. The game is worth the candle: I would not exchange the marvellous experiences I have gone through for five years of life.

Just at present we are marking time and watching one another like field mice. We nibble at one another occasionally, as General Joffre would say. So far the weather has been very favourable and the trenches have been very dry, but as soon as the wet weather sets in we shall probably be ankle-deep in mud. Really it is very good sport.[20]

When the company was in reserve there was a chance to explore the country a little and talk to the inhabitants. The war might appear to have settled into a tedious immobility, but Georges caught many echoes of his own optimism:

Today I left camp at 10 a.m. and returned at 7 p.m. The country about is very beautiful and picturesque: there are all sorts of interesting spots, small chapels, windmills, etc. . . . It is hard to believe that there are people in Canada who dare criticize the French; if we had more like them in Canada we would be a nobler, a better race. What France has gone through in this way no one will ever know, what her women have suffered without murmur can never be adequately told. The French will start the offensive any moment and we will follow it up: after twelve months of hardship and of privation, the old time dash of the most gallant of nations will carry us through – and we are *going* through.[21]

On the 4th of October Georges went out on his first patrol, describing the experience in his diary which, in contrast to most of his letters home, was written in French:

Out in front of the trenches from 9 till 11 p.m. As we were coming back one of our sentries fired on us at short range. It might have been a fatal mistake. Beyond the parapet you drag yourself along on your stomach, your face in the mud. Bullets whistle and cross overhead. You are under an incessant fire. Actually the danger is not so great as you might think. In creeping along you are pretty sure to avoid the fire of machine-guns and artillery. The German rifles are pointed at the top of our parapet and the bullets pass three or four feet above our heads. The only immediate danger is from stray

20. Letter to Mrs Vanier, 23rd September 1915.
21. Ibid, 30th September 1915.

bullets, and from the bombs and hand grenades that the Boches throw between the lines, precisely in order to catch the patrols. The sensation of being underneath this sort of fire – bullets, machine-guns, etc. – is stirring; the imagination is seized, the nerves remain very firm, and you keep your head.

A fortnight later he was over the parapet again under cover of the early morning mist, and found several German corpses in an advanced state of decomposition. They must have been lying in the open for several months, each man lying close to a hole two feet deep. They had evidently been trying to dig a trench when the Canadian machine-gun fire had caught them. Georges took away from them a few buttons and a Missal; and they were buried on the following days – once again under cover of the mist.

Every day Georges would make his report and send his requests to Battalion H.Q. Where was Private X? What punishment should he receive for being drunk on parade? Had he been warned? Georges held that he could not have time to get drunk between the parade and the order to parade, and that the charge as formulated could not be proved. Two of the guns were defective; might they be speedily replaced? A man of the 26th Battalion had been left sick in one of the huts. How should he be got away? The machine-gun emplacement in Trench K-I showed signs of caving in. Might the men rest till noon before moving off into reserve, since they would have had so little sleep? Complaints that rations were short. Would Captain Boyer, O.C. 'B' company please ask Lieutenant de Martigny to keep his eye on Lieutenant Vanier's things in his old dug-out? 'The horse I had yesterday belongs to my M.G. transport and is under my direct orders. I have chosen him as my riding horse and wish him to remain with the other riding horses. I am returning the other horse you sent me and will thank you to let me have my horse as soon as possible.' Georges' sense of justice was impartial; he was as careful about his own rights as he was about other people's.

The officers had two dug-outs, both underground, with an opening between them; one was used as a dining-room, the other as a bedroom. Their batman had found an old stove, in perfect working order, in a house which had been shelled to pieces not a hundred yards from the front line, and it was soon blazing away in their bedroom. Even in the worst weather they had dry socks, dry boots, hot coffee, bovril or cocoa – not to mention galantine of pheasant, veal and rice, vegetable soup and mutton cutlets. They were, in fact, very well fed and there was usually enough left

over for the 'thousands of rats and mice which invade our dug-
outs.'[22] The régime of 'D' Company was now slightly changed.
They rose and breakfasted at 11 a.m., lunched at 4 p.m., and dined
at 11 p.m. Dinner, Georges noted, was their best meal:

We take it at 11 o'clock to keep ourselves awake and to help pass
the long hours of the night. It's a gay meal, as a rule. The five members of the mess, Major Dubuc, Captains Plante and Beaubien,
Lieutenant de Martigny and myself get along splendidly, and during
the meal we are very open and gay. This gaiety makes life possible
in the trenches.[23]

So the weeks went by with their alternations of vigilance and
repose. The amenities of 'D' Company mess were improved by a
mess basket sent from London, easily portable, and complete with
plates, cutlery and other utensils. On the 27th of October a dinner
was held to celebrate the birthday of the regiment in the Hospice
St Antoine at Locre. This was an old Flemish convent, half broken
down, but the walls were still standing in spite of the shelling.
Colonel Gaudet was in the chair, with Generals Watson and
Turner at his side. Gaudet spoke feelingly of Major Roy,[24] and the
patriotic songs of France, England and Canada raised whatever
remained of the roof. The fine weather continued through October,
and at night there was sometimes a perfect silence under the
stars and the new moon, broken by a sudden fusillade. 'If it were
not tragic and horrible, it would be beautiful.'[25] Towards the end
of the month Georges launched a number of hand-grenades for the
first time:

New sensation: rather nervous to begin with: then one gets used
to it, one calculates the time, and one throws steadily. The grenades
are the most effective way of capturing new trenches. Shells and
bullets have a too level trajectory. A man lying flat in a trench is
sheltered from them, but grenades can do a lot of damage when the
trench is deep and very narrow.[26]

With November the rain began to fall in a fine drizzle and the
mud thickened intolerably. Georges Vanier's reflections now
strike a sombre note:

A dismal morning; low clouds; everything is heavy. You feel

22. Letter to Master Georges Pelletier, 6th December 1915.
23. Diary, 6th October 1915.
24. The first officer of the 22nd to be killed in action.
25. Diary, 18th October 1915.
26. Diary, 26th October 1915.

oppressed and stifled; you paddle in a foot of mud and water. These are appropriate conditions for the month of the Dead. The earth sweats, and the departed return to us in a gust which is disconcerting and revealing also. We are ourselves the essential link between what is past and what is to come.[27]

When they were relieved on the 14th of November after the most painful spell yet experienced in the trenches, Georges had seen all his personal effects 'floating around merrily' in five inches of water, and he was himself caked with mud. Nevertheless he had cured himself of a cold; and a ride on horseback, a bath at a neighbouring convent, and a delicious cake provided by the Sisters, did much to restore his morale. The routine was now slightly altered, the company spending four days in the trenches and four behind the lines. At the least fall of rain or drop in the temperature the men's feet began to swell, and there was the risk of pneumonia. Georges found it impossible to inspect the gun positions without walking on the top of the parapet; this he did at night or before dawn. It was a strange transformation in two months. At first, the idea would never have entered his head to walk outside the trenches; now, it had become a habit and he did not trouble about the stray bullets. Once again, he came upon a dead soldier 'pale in the clear moonlight, his hands clasped on his breast, and his face serene.'[28] As the rain fell interminably, making all work impossible, Georges Vanier sat in the dug-out, reading his pocket edition of Shelley or the copy of the *Imitation of Christ* which Père Gaume had sent him, writing his diary or his letters home, and watching the other officers playing bridge. It was extraordinary, he told his mother, how one could find 'a sentence and a thought appropriate to any prevalent mood' simply by opening the *Imitation* at hazard.

News came to him regularly from Montreal. Frances wrote of the new two-decker buses, and of her rabbit that was so tame and yet so cunning. While Philias Vanier and his friends were shooting the wild duck at Memphremagog, Antoine wrote as well, missing the long Sunday walks that he and Georges had been used to take together, and missing Georges in the big bedroom they had shared. The 'Van Doos' were already acquiring a reputation in Montreal. Major Roy was spoken of as if he were Lord Nelson himself, and Antoine had heard from 'two persons of good

27. Diary, 1st November 1915.
28. Ibid, 20th November 1915.

authority' that Georges and Major Dubuc were 'among the finest officers in the battalion'. Georges thrilled to read of Casgrain's appeal for unity between the two founding races of Canada, but there was a strong undercurrent of dissent in the Province of Quebec. Henri Bourrassa's propaganda had affected the lower clergy, and this was reinforced by the Canadian Government's dealings with the Church, and by the treatment of the Church in Russia. Mgr Bruchésie, the Archbishop of Montreal, had issued a public letter condemning political corruption and unfairness to minorities, and emphasizing the constitutional rights of those who had 'first brought Christian civilization to Canada'. In reply to this Olivier Asselin, himself an ardent nationalist, had offered to raise a regiment. He renounced none of his opinions, but he believed the cause of humanity to be at stake.

Early in December, with the announcement of his sister Eva's engagement to Joseph Trudeau, Georges received a Christmas parcel of underwear, socks, cigarettes and chocolates. The socks were too thin; he wanted the thick ones, worn by the *habitants* and procurable at the Maison Beausecours. Another, less welcome gift, was a first taste of poison gas. Although the company were two and a half miles from the point under attack, they found themselves red-eyed and weeping like children. They came out of the line on Christmas Eve, very muddy and wet but indomitably cheerful, as they marched singing through the moonlit night to their billets four miles in the rear. There was just time to wash and clean up before parading for Midnight Mass in the parish church of Locre:

I have attended Midnight Masses when the singing was better, when the lighting was more brilliant, when the crowd was gayer and the clothes brighter but never have I attended a more stirring or a more impressive Mass than last night's. The church is small and could not hold our Battalion seated. The men stood filling the church to the doors and the officers occupied the Sanctuary. We sang the old Christmas hymns in front of the Child Jesus lying with outstretched arms in his cradle of straw and the deep rough voices of the men stirred me to the soul and the sound was like the noise of the heavy sea breaking against the shore. Often I would take a surreptitious look back at the upturned faces of the soldiers; they were strong faces, with the straightforward look of the born fighter, of the man who will follow you anywhere. After Mass we had a 'réveillon' at the Convent of which I have already spoken . . . and we sang Canadian songs and ate Canadian dishes (pigs' feet, etc.). We turned in at four o'clock. Today I distributed Christmas presents to my section. These consisted of cigarettes, stockings, magazines and chocolates which had been forwarded from all parts of Canada.[29]

Hospitality was in the air and a message had been sent in German to the German lines inviting the enemy to surrender in small parties, with assurances that the Canadians would take good care of them. But the invitation was not accepted.

Georges Vanier had now spent three months in the trenches, and he declared himself 'stronger, happier, and more resolute than at the beginning'.[30]

29. Letter to Mrs Vanier, Christmas Day 1915.
30. Ibid, 16th December 1915.

CHAPTER 3

BAPTISM OF FIRE

I

On the 29th of December 1915 Georges Vanier received the following message in pencil from his friend Major Tremblay, now in command of the battalion:

The General tells me that the special task you are on might have to be carried out tomorrow night; depending of course on the condition of the weather, so would advise you to hasten your preparations tonight in order to be ready tomorrow night.

The 'special task' was defined in a secret standing order of the 30th of December:

A patrol under Lt. Vanier, consisting of one Officer and five men, supported by a bombing party of one N.C.O. and ten men, will undertake the capture of a certain shack in front of the German lines opposite trench L-4 with the idea of seizing anything that the shack may contain and afterwards blow it up. (Part of larger operation).

Georges replied immediately to Tremblay's message asking for the two engineers and the four pairs of handcuffs he had been promised. On the following night two patrols went out to reconnoitre, one of them under Georges' command. He reported that there was no one in the hut and no flares or firing from it, and no one in the sap leading to the main German trenches. The hut was riddled with bullets and was probably thought too unhealthy for permanent occupation. Its construction was primitive, and it might well have been used as a listening post or flare point. Georges did not think that it was a regular emplacement for machine-guns, although these could have been moved up to it for occasional shooting. There was a small hole in one side, presumably for purposes of observation, and from two sides it would be possible to cover No-Man's-Land with rifle or machine-gun fire.

On New Year's Eve there was a 'petit réveillon' in Major

Dubuc's dug-out with the usual toasts to a glorious peace and happy homecoming. The New Year had come in like a lamb – would it go out like a lion? Georges was warned that his operation might have to be carried out the following night, but later he received word that it was fixed for the night of the 2nd of January. The story can best be taken up from his own diary:

Sunday: Jan 2nd.
My men are eager to attack the little hut opposite our trenches; I fervently hope that the weather will be favourable this evening – too long a delay gets on the nerves of the men. I have spent part of the day observing from L-4 trench.
8 p.m. Wind, rain, thick darkness – an ideal night for our little operation.
10 p.m. Receive word that it is to go forward.
1.35 a.m. Order received to leave our trenches; two minutes later the patrol jumps over the parapet. The following men accompany me: Sergeant Maurice Levin, Lance-Corporal L. Rancourt, Private John Watt, of the 22nd, and Corporal Leclerc. Levin acts as a guide, Rancourt carries the 15-lbs. of gun-cotton, and Leclerc the wire which he unrolls behind him. We easily get across our three lines of barbed wire. Sometimes on our stomachs, and sometimes on our hands and knees, we make our way straight towards the German line with the intention of getting behind the right hand side of the hut. Levin and I are ahead of the others, who are slowed down by the weight of the gun-cotton and the unwinding of the electric wire. We reach the German barbed wire, four feet in depth, very thick and new, and three and a half feet high. We had to cut it in thirty places in order to get through. The Boche flares continually showed up the hut against the dark background, and could incidentally have shown us up as well. The bullets whistled in a normal way above our heads and on either side of us. We were thirty feet from the hut – was it occupied? In a few seconds we had crossed the barbed wire and were inside the hut. No one was there. A foot and a half of water in the hut and in the trench connecting it with the main trenches. Originally it was probably a machine-gun post. After placing the gun-cotton on the roof and joining the electric wire to the box containing the explosive, we left with a steel plate which served as a loophole.
2.25 a.m. The patrol returned without mishap. It was only at 5.30 a.m. that we were given permission to blow up the hut. A minute later the spark had done its work – a dull explosion, a very bright flash, a cloud of black smoke. The daylight showed us a hole where the hut had been; the gun-cotton had left nothing standing. Must write a report, send the loophole to H.Q., and a piece of the Boche barbed wire, and a piece of tarred paper that was covering the roof.

To bed at 10 a.m. Very happy.

In his report to Battalion H.Q., sent at 8.30 that morning, Georges noted the superiority of the German barbed wire, and the virtual absence of noise or talking in the enemy trenches. He particularly commended 'the work done by Sergeant Levin who showed qualities of daring and of coolness, and who was in great measure responsible for the success of the little excursion through the excellent information procured in a preliminary patrol. In spite of the darkness of the night Sergeant Levin's guidance was perfect.' Georges Vanier had little sense of material possessions, except for his war souvenirs. He was not going to let Battalion H.Q. hold on to the steel plate and the barbed wire, and he asked Lieutenant de Martigny to keep an eye on them. The plate is now among other trophies in the Citadel Museum, Quebec.

Four days later General Watson[1] sent the following letter to the 'Van Doos':

With reference to the minor operation carried out by your Battalion on the night of the 2nd to the 3rd instant, I wish to take this opportunity of conveying to you my sincere thanks and appreciation at the manner in which the task was carried out on that occasion. This reflects great credit on your Battalion and I would particularly mention in this connection Lt. Vanier and his party for the expeditious and efficient manner in which the work was performed. The distance to be traversed toward the enemy line, cutting the wire, the placing of the charge and although a long time elapsed awaiting the progress of the unit working on your right, the charge was successfully fired with such good results. I mention the specific case but it is typical of the manner in which your Battalion has acted in all its undertakings since arriving in this country. This has been noted and mentioned in my report which has been rendered to higher authorities.

As we shall presently see, the 'higher authorities' lost little time in taking the action expected of them. Meanwhile, on the 15th of January, Georges was woken up with the news that the London Gazette of the 12th of January had recorded his promotion to Captain with effect from the 15th of October 1915. He had known for some time that this was in the air and he received the information philosophically: 'I am a little sorry to give up the two stars which I have been wearing almost since the war began. Anyway, my men will never get used to calling me Cap-

1. Major-General Sir David Watson, 1871-1922, Brigadier commanding the 5th Infantry Brigade.

tain.'[2] Such pleasure as he took in the promotion was clouded, the same afternoon, when Major Dubuc was wounded for the second time in the head, although the injury proved to be only slight. Shortly afterwards Georges left his machine-guns to become second-in-command of 'C' Company under Major Hudon, who had been his superior officer during the early days of the 'Van Doos'. Gaudet was promoted to Major-General and assigned to the command of certain munition factories in England, and Tremblay took over the battalion with Dubuc as his second-in-command. Captain Chassé[3] replaced him at the head of 'D' Company. Amid all these changes Georges continued to be struck by the contrasts of war – the contradiction of charity and hate.

Jan. 9: Sunday. Mass at 10 o'clock. At the beginning of Mass the silence was complete; at the Gospel one heard the familiar sound of our heavy artillery, the whistle of shells above our heads and their dull and distant explosion in the German lines. This accompaniment continued until the end of Mass. It was more impressive than the purest music. All one's soul was caught up in it and the heart ached. There, in front of us, was the symbol of charity – was charity itself – and above us the symbol of destruction and hate.[4]

The contrast was equally striking, as he came back from patrol under a full moon on a night 'made for lovers rather than for warriors'. It was difficult to believe that only two hundred yards away were men 'whose only desire is to kill us – and vice versa.' Yet nature was 'so peaceful'. And the contrast was driven home when a particularly good friend was shot through the lung:

Poor chap, do you know I met him as recently as Jan. 17th not a mile from the firing line? Out of the darkness he came up to me saying 'Hello George, happy New Year – I am back from hospital' . . . Barrack room life had not changed Adrian: he was an angel. Without exaggeration, he had the cleanest mind and the best heart of any youth I have ever met. He was unspoiled. He received Communion on the mornings of Jan. 16th and of Jan. 17th. He was buried on Jan. 20th, in a little cemetery within sound of the rifle shots. A white cross marks his grave, next to that of Lieut. Buchanan, 24th Battalion, who was killed the day before. . . . Adrian's death gave me the worst shock I have had since I reached Flanders.[5]

On the 24th of January Georges went on a week's leave to Paris,

2. Diary.
3. Lieut-Colonel Henri Chassé.
4. Diary.   5. Letter to Mrs Vanier, 21st January 1916.

staying at the Hotel Regina. The theatres were beginning to re-open, with their audiences of women and soldiers on leave – many of them wearing the ribbon of the *Croix de Guerre* or the *Médaille Militaire*. The plays were more serious than the plays that Georges had seen in London. The shadier cafés and theatres were shut; and Montmartre was dead. The boulevards were quite dark, and no restaurant stayed open after 9 p.m. The number of women in mourning was already impressive at a time when the defence of Verdun had not yet raised its hecatombs of dead. But the muted gaiety of Paris only made it dearer to Georges Vanier; never had he felt so close to the protracted French ordeal. 'Bonjour affectueux de Paris, centre de la civilization' he writes on a postcard of the Musée de Cluny; and 'Ah, the sheer joy of it' he notes in his diary 'to visit Paris on leave from the trenches where we are all trying to do our bit for the triumph of civiliza-tion, and to avenge 1870.' He served Mass for Père Gaume at Notre Dame des Victoires; had his photograph taken at Gaume's request; and spent an interesting half hour at the Invalides, exam-ining the trench mortars and machine-guns captured by the French during their short-lived offensive in Champagne.

During the second week of February a German attack was expected, and Tremblay issued his order :

I am confident that the French-Canadians will defend all their trenches with a desperate vigour and will hold firm at whatever cost, even to the death. Let us not forget that we represent an entire race, and that a great deal – even the honour of French Canada – depends on the way we conduct ourselves. Our forbears have left us a brave and glorious past which we must respect and emulate. Let us con-tinue in the ancient and fine traditions.

The 2nd Canadian Division had followed the example of the Australians in throwing a blanket over a hand grenade when it fell in a trench, and they were now covering their steel helmets with a sandbag, drawing in the edges with a string and cutting the superfluous material away. On the 21st of March Georges Vanier was transferred from second-in-command of 'C' Company to Temporary O.C. 'A' Company, replacing Captain Papineau who had been wounded in the eye. Parcels were now arriving regularly from Montreal with candy, sardines, chicken, ham, tongue, choco-late, cigarettes, Quesnel tobacco, a slice of Eva's wedding cake, and rather a surfeit of 'habitant' socks. Georges already had twenty pairs and there was really no need for more. He asked

for maple syrup instead. He evidently believed that an army
marked time, as well as marched, on its stomach, for among his
messages and signals were requests for a chicken '2 wings, 2 legs
(oh! oh!), the whole breast (ah! ah!), and no stuffing' . . .
bottled fruit – strawberries, pears or peaches – sardines, ketchup,
Camembert cheese, haricot beans, *petits pois*, tinned lobster, and
port wine. Some of the men were in the habit of shooting local
game, chiefly rabbits, but this was strictly forbidden under threat
of Penal Servitude.

Not all the news from Quebec was such as to fortify morale.
Paul Morin, writing from Smith College, Massachusetts, was
anxious to enlist himself after enlisting other people; academic
life was a 'swamp'; his 'exquisite Germaine' had become engaged;
and he asked Georges to send him a line 'between two hand-grenades'.[6] Morin's parents had been vigorously opposed to his joining up, but he signed on as a lieutenant and returned to Montreal
hoping to enlist in Asselin's battalion. But although a hundred
boys from Loyola were now with the colours, Antoine wrote of
narrow-minded priests at the school who discouraged those eager
to fight for 'a party who were slowly crushing them out'. On the
other side it was being said of the French-Canadians that they
were instructed to stay at home by their parish priests; that the
few who did enlist got a few weeks' pay and immediately deserted; that the 69th Battalion was filled up with Scotsmen,
Russian and Poles; and that the 32nd French-Canadian Battalion
had to be moved from St Jean d'Yberville on account of the
wholesale desertions. A reply to these accusations came from
spectacular recruiting in the streets of Montreal, particularly
for the 148th Battalion which paraded with an open street-car
on the side of which was written: 'Hop on and join the 148th',
and promised to certain of its men a dollar and forty-eight hours
leave for every recruit they took in; and also by M. Martin, the
Mayor of Montreal, who recalled that the first recruiting speech
since the outbreak of war had been made by Sir Wilfrid Laurier,
and pointed to the three French-Canadian Hospitals which had
been organized in France through the generosity of their French
speaking compatriots. Colonel Pelletier, the Agent General for
Quebec in London, argued that all French-Canadians were Canadian born, whereas most of the British settlers had ties with
Britain. The French-Canadians were mostly farmers and it was
less easy to leave a farm than for a business man to leave an

6. 3rd March 1916.

office. Nationalist agitators had certainly had some influence, but the Provincial Government and the majority of better educated people were behind the French-Canadian war effort. Still it was one thing – argued the man from Toronto – to give your money; it was another to give your life. Georges Vanier was happily more remote from these provincial squabblings than he was to find himself thirty years later. Nevertheless it was a fellow officer, Captain Talbot-Papineau, D.S.O., who addressed a long public letter to his cousin Henri Bourrassa in defence of French-Canadian participation.

I have just seen this morning the 22nd French-Canadian Battalion in the trenches. The men are gay and confident. Many of them will die on the field of battle, but I think that they are better Canadians and better nationalists than the pseudo-patriot Bourrassa, who is sitting so comfortably and so pleased with himself in Montreal . . .

It would be untrue to say that Georges Vanier viewed the war objectively – very few people in the circumstances of the time did that, and warriors are not called upon to be objective. But he did see it in its human and cosmic dimensions, with compassion and courage. He had given ample proof of both, and now he found it comforting 'to hear the birds singing again, to see the grass turn green, and to see the flowers beginning to bud and what is more wonderful and surprising still, to see the mud slowly but surely drying.'[7] Things were livening up in the sector held by the 'Van Doos', and on Good Friday, when Papineau returned to the battalion, Georges noted:

At the first streak of dawn in the east I heard a cock crow, once, twice, and then a third time. I remembered that it was Good Friday. Who is now denying the Lord? Alas, we all are. Really you would never believe that it was Good Friday. . . no religious service.

A week later the birds had come back and one heard their gentle singing at 'stand to'. It was restful and made you think you were on holiday, sitting out on the broad verandah at Memphremagog. The weather was superb. And then, on the 30th of April the Germans attacked with poison gas, followed by several days of bombardment. Two friends of Georges – Gordon Ross and Johnny Howe, an old Loyola boy – were killed, and the strain was proving too much for Papineau whose eye was troubling him a good deal. The Germans were throwing over kerosene tins, containing three hand grenades and a good sized trench mortar.

7. Letter to Mrs Vanier, 21st March 1916.

Georges' dug-out was only two and a half feet high, and since the floor was too muddy to sit on, he was forced to write perched on a small ammunition box so that his head was continually banging against the corrugated iron roof. When the bombs had demolished the parapet in front of the dug-out, he thought it wise to move to a fire-step with his blanket and shaving articles:

These instruments of torture (not shaving articles) are not so bad when studied a bit: one usually has time to see what the general direction of the bomb will be and to run . . . in the opposite direction. I have never done fifty yards in quicker time, the end being a dive on to the trench mat and a painful wait for the hellish explosion. Enfin c'est la guerre.

'Curiously enough', Georges laconically observes, 'the dug-out was hit the next day by a 77 shell.'

2

He had already been mentioned in despatches (3rd of March 1916) and on the 4th of June he was called to the telephone by Tremblay, informing him that he had been awarded the Military Cross. All the others taking part in the action of the 2nd of January received the Military Medal. Two days later his friend Captain Beaubien was killed: 'an excellent fellow and a good company commander. I was very fond of him. His death is a blow to me.'[8] And on the 9th of June a shell exploding a few feet away from where Georges was standing stunned, deafened, and knocked him out completely. 'If the ground had not been soft, I should have been killed.'[9] He was obliged to leave for the Cistercian Monastery of Mont des Cats which had been turned into a hospital for officers and other ranks, and from here he sent daily letters home:

I am receiving the best of treatment and I am getting what I need more than anything else – complete rest. The surroundings are very beautiful. This morning I heard Mass in the old chapel which the monks still use.

(11th of June)

Fortunately we are out of sound of the artillery which I could not stand just now. One reaches a point sometimes where one feels that one cannot stand very much more. And I am beginning to get over that feeling.

(13th of June)

8. Diary, 6th June 1916.   9. Ibid, 9th June 1916.

I am still enjoying the quiet life of the very high spot chosen as a rest hospital by people who understood the importance of beautiful surroundings and of soothing solitude. In the valley – or rather on the plains – far below, villages here and there dot the ground and the bricks of the buildings look like red spots against the green of the fields and the hedges of the woods. From the centre of each spot of red a spire protrudes and one is reminded of the village churches of Quebec. There are beautiful walks and gardens about the Monastery . . . and through these I stroll in spite of the wind and cold, because I do not wish to lose my taste for the open air life. . . . The war is not by any means over and a great deal of fighting remains to be done yet. . . . I am very happy here, why shouldn't I be? I am going through one of the periods not unusual in a soldier's career, and I am very fortunate that I have not been crippled for life, or something like that, instead of having received only a severe shaking up.

(15th of June)

Among the patients was Canon George Frederick Scott, a popular writer of war poems. Georges described him as a 'delightful talker and a very fine type of Canadian'. He knew his son William, who was a member of the Junior Bar in Montreal.

A few days afterwards Georges was moved to a Casualty Clearing Station a little further from the front. News reached him here that his friend Jacques Brosseau had been killed in action:

When I look back over the two years we have lived together and played together and fought together, it is almost as if I had lost a brother. I knew *no one* so devoted to and thoughtful of his mother. He wrote to her each day and numbered his letters, which had reached, I believe, the five hundred mark.[10]

Towards the end of the month Georges was sent back to England. He stayed at the Savoy; fitted in four theatres, including *Mr Manhattan* at the Prince of Wales, *The Happy Days* at Daly's, and *Please Keep Smiling* at the Playhouse; and spent a night at the Moorlands Hotel, Hindhead, visiting the 4th Canadian Division at Bramshott Camp. Since he was not yet completely recovered, a bed was found for him at the Perkins Bull Hospital for Convalescent Canadian Officers on Putney Heath. Perkins Bull, an advocate from Toronto, had founded the Hospital in what had once been the home of Sir Ernest Shackleton. He himself lived with his family a few doors away. All the V.A.Ds were Canadian girls from the 'best families'; they cooked and served the meals, made the

10. Letter to Mrs Vanier, 23rd June 1916.

beds, and attended to the wants of the patients in every possible way. There was a tennis court – 'tennis and tea are my principal pastimes' – and Georges was able to go in to London for matinées. Among his fellow-convalescents was Chassé – 'very gay on crutches'; he had caught a bullet through the foot on the same day that Georges had been shell-shocked. For once Georges allowed himself a caustic comment on the clergy when he was forced to listen to a sermon forty minutes in length and wholly abstract in content. The heat was overpowering, so that finally even the preacher could not stand the sound of his own voice any longer and the congregation were of the same mind.

On the 4th of July Georges had appeared before a Medical Board which gave him six weeks' sick leave, and Tremblay had been encouraging him to rest for as long as possible. The 'Van Doos' had fourteen supernumary officers – 'quelle avalanche!' Meanwhile his parents and Pierre Casgrain had been using what influence they possessed to get him returned to Canada; and in fact he had permission to spend his leave there if he travelled at his own expense. It was thought, reasonably enough, that with his decoration and his experience, he would be a valuable recruiting agent in the Province of Quebec. But he told his father that he did not think he would be likely to succeed where Sir Wilfrid Laurier and Sir Rodolphe Lemieux had failed. On the 24th of July he was notified that he could return to Canada if he wanted to, but he wrote on the same day to his mother:

I appreciate very much what all my friends in Canada have done for me, but somehow I can't go back. I must be at the front so long as I am fit. I should be unhappy anywhere else. Of course if I am offered an appointment where the work is less trying than in an infantry company, it is possible that I may accept it: however I shall be very sorry to leave the 22nd where so many of my friends are.

He next received two letters from the Canadian H.Q. at Shorncliffe, offering to send him home, and if the offer had come at the beginning of his sick leave he might have agreed to return to Canada – in order to recuperate, but not to remain there. Now, his sick leave would be up in a fortnight, and it was too late.

If by that time I have not secured a combatant position with the 4th Canadian Division, a little less trying than infantry work, I shall return to the 22nd Battalion which has kept up its very good work. I can't go back to Canada now, with the boys fighting in France. I should be as unhappy as I was in the early months of the war before I enlisted. Please do not think that I am ungrateful for all you and the dear Governor . . and Pierre Casgrain have been doing for me. (1st of August)

His leave was extended until the 14th of September, and General Watson now suggested that he accept the post of Pay-master-Captain in a battalion of the 4th Division; but Georges' mind was made up, and he wrote again to Montreal:

You are not angry that I refused. It isn't that I am not anxious to see you all, dear, but I feel that it is my duty to see this sacred war through and with God's help I shall. The further I get from the firing line, the more unhappy I am. I don't mean that I revel in the noise of bursting steel, because I don't, but there's the tremendous consolation of being in the thick of it, of the biggest fight that has ever taken place for the triumph of liberty. At some time or other we have all wished that we had lived in Napoleonic days: but the present days are fuller of romance, of high deeds and of noble sacrifices. (16th of August)

The realities of war had tempered, but they had not soured Georges Vanier's romanticism. Yet these letters do not give us the whole of his mind. He would say afterwards that the reason why he had not returned to Canada was because he feared he would not have the courage to go back to France.

All through his life one can trace a pattern where each stage in his journey seemed to be a preparation for the next. If his leave had not been extended, almost at the last moment, he would certainly have played his part in the battle of Courcelette. It would be a 'life-long sorrow', he wrote, that he had not been able to do so – for Courcelette was the greatest feat of arms in the annals of the 'Van Doos'. He read of it in Philip Gibbs' despatch on the 21st of September – 'with tears in his eyes'.[11] But if he had been there on the 15th of September, he might never have come back. Out of the twenty-three officers taking part in the action, which lasted for three days and ended victoriously in the capture of the village, seven were killed and eleven more or less seriously wounded. Courcelette was described by Sir Douglas Haig as 'the most effective blow yet delivered against the enemy by the British army'. The details of the battle lie outside our present story, and they illustrate in retrospect not only the valour of the troops but the atrocious carnage to which the strategy of the western

11. Diary.

front had committed them. For the larger campaign which Georges Vanier had left and to which he would presently return was still the Battle of the Somme.

On the 29th of August he received a telegram from the Lord Chamberlain inviting him to luncheon at Windsor on the occasion of his investiture with the Military Cross. He travelled down by train in service dress on Friday, the 1st of September. About twenty-five officers were there to receive their decorations, and the King spoke for a few minutes with each of them. He appeared surprised to learn that Georges was a French-Canadian. After the investiture luncheon was served in the dining-room overlooking the gardens of the Castle; Georges can little have guessed when he passed through Windsor on his first visit to Europe that he would shortly have a more intimate and significant glimpse of it. The menu certainly did not suggest the privations of war time, with Homard à l'Américaine, Tournedos Parisienne, Grouse à la Broche, red currants and Framboises Alsaciennes. Among those at table was Mademoiselle Dussan, French governess to Princess Mary. Glad to find someone who spoke her own language in what was anything but a bilingual household, she made friends with Georges Vanier and afterwards sent him a book of French war poems, thanking him for his 'hauts faits d'armes' of which she had read in the newspapers.

3

Georges was still playing tennis at Roehampton on the 25th of September, and received his orders to leave on the 29th. He sent his Military Cross home to Montreal in the care of a friend. Reaching the lines on the 9th of October, he found Major Dubuc, 'Lipi' Archambault, and Captain de Martigny stationed in a small village near to a particularly violent sector of the front. Dubuc was in temporary command of the battalion. Most of Georges Vanier's other friends had been either killed or wounded at Courcelette. Further details of the engagement had been given him by Gaudet, who had learnt of them at first hand from the Adjutant, Major Gingras, himself wounded and sent back to London. The battalion had changed, almost unrecognizably, and Georges missed the 'cheery faces' of those who had been with it from the start. There was no longer the old gaiety; and it was not easy to be gay. Nevertheless, he wrote, it was 'necessary not to be downhearted, so we try to think of the present and the living, and not of the past and of the dead.'[12] Later he wrote that the battalion was 'shaping splendidly' after the arrival of much fresh material; that the new draft of officers – twelve of them for 'A' Company of which he was now in command – was of excellent quality; and that the spirit of the 'Van Doos' was what it had always been. For a short time he was acting as Temporary Adjutant, with a good deal of office work; and he was promoted to the temporary rank of Major when he took over the company command. Tremblay – who had so magnificently led the battalion at Courcelette with his cry 'We must get there in time, at whatever cost' – was sent on sick leave, and Dubuc – his short, square figure in sharp contrast to Tremblay's leanness and height – was appointed Acting Lieut-Colonel on the 24th of November.

At the beginning of January 1917 Georges Vanier was painfully occupied with Courts Martial, and later in the month was on leave with Dubuc in London. On the 15th of February he was officially appointed Adjutant with larger responsibilities, longer hours, and generally comfortable quarters. A fellow officer described Georges as the 'model of an Adjutant-Major – one of the few officers who knew how to keep his friends in spite of his rather delicate duties – and who represented politeness and courtesy in uniform' and still remained 'a very brave soldier, and a strict and efficient officer.'[13] Ever since the arrival of the regiment in Europe Battalion H.Q. had been plagued with requests that they should acknowledge the receipt of some fur caps which had not in fact been asked for and on which no one had set eyes. Denial, however, was useless and the same request came in with exasperating regularity until the dossier in question had assumed formidable proportions. One day Georges Vanier and Tremblay found themselves regarding it with something like desperation. They looked at each other; they looked at the fire in their billet; and then they put the dossier on the fire. After a decent interval it was easy to compose a reply to Ottawa: 'destroyed by enemy action'.

On another occasion the Adjutant and his Commanding Officer were not quite of the same mind. It was New Year's Day; the battalion was in reserve billets; and the General of the Division expressed his intention of inspecting it on the 2nd or 3rd of January.

Our men were excellent fellows, but they were not angels. Never-

12. Letter to Philias Vanier, 15th October 1916.
13. Colonel X, *Souvenirs of the 22nd.*

theless, having received the order, we had no choice – we had to
march. As the Adjutant responsible to the Commanding Officer, I
was responsible for the training and turn-out of the men, and I
nearly went sick when I realized that an inspection so soon after
New Year's Day would leave much to be desired. At last the tragic
morning broke, the battalion was lined up, the General arrived, and
I noticed with dismay that some of our men gave the impression of
having celebrated the New Year with too much enthusiasm. My
presentiment was confirmed when I saw that the General and
Colonel Tremblay were both displeased, so I decided to move away
from the Colonel beside whom the Adjutant normally stands during
an inspection. Under one pretext or another, I was pretty invisible
and thus avoided the General's and the Colonel's wrath. When the
General had gone, Colonel Tremblay said to me in that voice that
some of you know so well: 'Vanier, I order you, at any future
inspection, to stay beside me the whole time.'[14]

Tremblay had returned to the battalion at the end of February,
and it received a visit from Olivier Asselin in March. Already a
Major in the 163rd Battalion from Montreal, he got himself
seconded as a Lieutenant in a platoon of the 22nd in order to
have the pleasure of cutting a path through the barbed wire.
'You wouldn't want me' he said 'to let another have this fine
opportunity of doing something' – for the attack on Vimy Ridge
was in preparation. The position of honour and glory was
assigned to the 5th Brigade, with the 'Van Doos' in support to
the 24th, 25th and 26th Battalions. At 5.30 in the morning, on
Easter Monday, the 9th of April 1917, the attack began with a
barrage of fire from 2,000 guns. The infantry leapt out of the
shell holes and trenches or emerged from the tunnels – right up
against the enemy lines – in a hail of bullets and a bitter north-
west wind. But the barbed wire in front of the Canadian trenches
was not sufficiently cut to permit a rapid assault, and a fatigue
party had to be sent out into No-Man's-Land. When Georges
heard that it was Olivier Asselin's turn to take charge of it, he
observed that it was 'too bad' and then added, charmingly: 'My
dear Major, I would willingly offer you a cup of tea, but that
would delay the execution of your plans.' The leading battalions
gained their objectives quickly and the 'Van Doos' followed
through capturing several machine-guns, trench mortars and
hundreds of prisoners. On the 14th of April Georges was writing:

14. Speech at the annual meeting of the 'Amicale' of the Royal 22nd Regiment,
Montreal, 1955.

Things are going with a tremendous swing and we are pursuing the Boches. The morale of our troop is magnificent, we cannot lose – what is more we are winning quickly and the war will be over within six months. It is a wonderful consolation to be driving the Boches out of France.

The battalion was relieved two days later, and marched to billets at Aux-Rietz. On re-entering the line it spent a couple of gruelling months in front of the Ridge, and in July took part in the capture of Hill 70. Then it was moved north to the Ypres sector. Here its objectives were gained with relatively light losses, although it suffered heavily for six days resisting no less than seventeen counter-attacks by the enemy. It was relieved on the 21st of August, and sent to the rear for a month's rest. On the 15th of September the anniversary of the arrival of the regiment in France, and also of the battle of Courcelette, was celebrated at Cambligneul.

On the 2nd of August Georges Vanier was decorated with the Cross of the Legion of Honour by Paul Painlevé, the French Minister for War. The news of this was music to the ears of Camille Martin, who wrote that 'just as we say that the man who has the job best fitted to him is the "right man in the right place", so would I gladly say that this is "the best Cross in the right place".' There was no one in history whom Georges less resembled than François Ier, but this did not deter the ardent professor from suggesting the comparison. A photograph of Georges now had a place of honour in his study, with the Imperial family, other of his former pupils, and a rather cheap lithograph of 'Papa' Joffre. It told him all he wanted to know, and had guessed already. The distinctions Georges had won were due to 'a determination not to act upon impressions and prejudice, but upon reason and deliberation', and this had 'left upon his features the imprint of strength and serenity'.[15] They were long to remain there.

The pace of the campaign gave him little time for writing home; but news of him from other sources was hardly less welcome:

He is quite the tallest and largest of the Officers and is quite stout. You would have to look twice to be sure it was he. He has filled out and says that he enjoys his life here. Certainly he looks as if he did. His Military Cross colours look quite as if they ought to be there and he seems to be a general favourite with the other Officers,

15. 5th June 1917.

notwithstanding the fact of his being Adjutant, which appointment requires endless tact and diplomacy to fill properly.[16]

At the end of September Georges went to London on twelve days' leave, staying at the Savoy; dining at Simpson's, next door, and feeling 'very much alone'; seeing *Arlette* at the Shaftesbury and *Zig-Zag* at the Hippodrome; playing tennis at Wimbledon; revisiting his friends at Putney; and sending home some more souvenirs by Perkins Bull, with whom he lunched at the Union Club. There were Zeppelin raids almost every night. The middle of October saw a further move to Belgium, and in November the battalion acted as a reserve guard for the attack and taking of Passchendaele by the 5th Brigade. Passchendaele became a synonym for the waste of life on the western front, and when the 'Van Doos' relieved one of the forward units it lost ninety officers and men, either killed or wounded. Captain Chassé, as he then was, would afterwards describe something of their ordeal:

We had been ordered to rest our right flank close to the church at Passchendaele, but when we arrived there after a night of marching through the mud the village no longer even existed. That march, I can assure you, was the most painful of all our adventures. To begin with we had to follow a little pavement of trenches, three feet wide, for more than six miles in order to reach the reserve line. This pavement was a landmark for the German batteries. We were forced to follow it as best we could, although in certain places it was partially demolished, for you risked death by submersion in the mud if you put your foot to one side. Unfortunately a number of our comrades met their end in this horrible way.

The officers, who led the march, had never known such difficulties. At last we came to what had once been the village of Passchendaele. The enemy, supposing that there was still a wall left standing, continued his bombardment. We spent twenty-four hours in this hell before we were relieved and sent in support to the Heights of Abraham near Ypres. As the result of a misunderstanding, one of our platoons was not relieved, and I had to spent an extra twelve hours in the front line. We returned to the rear, marching in the mud up to our waists under the fire of an unrelenting bombardment. Really, Napoleon's veterans of 100 years ago couldn't have been more miserable than we were.[17]

Chassé was also to recall the part played by the 'Van Doos' in the assault on Hill 70:

16. Letter to Mrs Vanier, 15th October 1917, from Bernard Brady.
17. *Souvenirs de Guerre*, talk given at the Académie Commerciale, Montreal, under the auspices of the Société des Arts, Sciences, et Lettres, 5th February 1920.

The aim of this attack was to force the enemy to evacuate the town of Lens by capturing Hill 70 and the surrounding trenches. The 25th from Halifax was to attack on our right, and we had the 5th Battalion on our left. . . . 'A' Company, which I was commanding, and 'B' Company, commanded by Major John H. Roy, were in the first wave of the assault. 'D' Company, with Captain Paul Emile Coté, killed in action, in command, was in support and 'C' Company, commanded by Captain W. Morgan was in reserve. Lieut. Col. Tremblay commanded the battalion, with Major Georges P. Vanier as Adjutant.

The 22nd had as their objective a German trench – 'Catapult' – stretching in a north-easterly to south-westerly direction, and crossing the miners' houses in St Emile, which is a kind of suburb of Lens. It was difficult work, because the Boches had nests of machine-guns hidden in many of the houses, and these only stopped firing when the men of the 22nd could get to grips with them hand to hand.

The 22nd had completed its preparations for this attack at the farm of Marqueffles. We had left the farm – about six miles from the line of fire – in the evening of the day before, and in a driving rain which lasted until 3 a.m. We passed through Bully-Grenay where the population, hearing that we were about to attack the enemy, gave us a magnificent ovation. Our men were in great spirits and sang as they went along. Our own songs mingled with the acclamations of the French in Bully-Grenay. 'Vivent les Canadiens' cried the good peasants; 'Vive la Canadienne et ses jolis yeux doux' intoned one of our foot-sloggers, and his comrades took up the refrain 'et ses jo-o-lis yeux doux'. Sometimes women and children would interrupt one of our best singers with a kiss. It was a magnificent and charming sight to see the old France applauding the young France which was on its way to die for her.[18]

Georges had his own more intimate memory of the same occasion. It was the scene of general absolution at Marqueffles farm before the battalion went in to the attack.

It was raining. The Chaplain gave absolution to the men as they stood in line under the weeping sky and the battalion set off on the march to Bully-Grenay. One after another the platoons disappeared over the crest of the hill. In spite of the rain the men were singing. Would they have sung in the same way without the great peace that the blessing of the priest had given them?[19]

On the 11th of November – just a year before the signing of the Armistice – the regiment returned to the line near Méharicourt and remained there until the middle of February 1918. It had

18. See note 17.   19. Speech in Montreal, undated.

been a year of desperate engagements, appalling casualties, and
epic heroism – but the end of the war was not in sight. The
submarine campaign had nearly brought Britain to her knees,
although it had also brought the promise of American help which,
in the event, was to prove decisive. When Georges Vanier wrote
home on Christmas Eve, he little guessed that the 'Van Doos'
would once again have their backs to the wall before they had
their faces to the St Lawrence:

It is my intention to go through the line tonight with a sandbag containing cake, sucre à la crème, and cigars, all gifts from Canada,
and to act as Santa Claus to the Company officers. As I go down the
deep dug-outs, I shall feel like St Nicholas in his chimney.

CHAPTER 4

HORS DE COMBAT[*]

I

GEORGES Vanier was beginning to interest himself in politics. His family had always voted liberal – which was as much to say, although not much more, that Catholics in Quebec did not generally vote like Protestants in Toronto. Liberalism can mean many different things, according to the time and place. Georges' sympathies were generally to be found where we should expect to find them – very much in the centre. He was too humane to be a reactionary and too disciplined to be a rebel. He now subscribed not only to *Le Temps*, but also to Clemenceau's paper, *L'Homme Libre*. The 'Tiger's' virulent anti-clericalism did not rob him of widespread support; people who would never have tolerated him in peace followed him ardently in war. By contrast, the Socialists were losing their hold on the industrial masses and they had never made much appeal to the peasantry. 'The more I see of the peasant class' Georges wrote 'and it is the class I see most often, the greater is my admiration for the French nation and the greater is my faith in the triumph of Latin civilization.'[1]

With these preoccupations he was glad to leave the trenches at Souchez, and go on leave to Paris. Here he stayed at the Meurice and visited the Ecole Polytechnique, the Palais de Justice and Père Gaume's Orphelinat St Charles, distributing candies to the orphans, and listening to a blind musician play Chopin. This was more amusing than *Ohé Cupidon!* at the Théâtre des Variétés. Georges Vanier was a fervent but not – at least at this time – a very discriminating theatre-goer; yet for once he complained of a 'big disappointment'. The title of the play, like those of the others he had seen in London, should not have aroused excessive expectations. More amusing, too, was the case he watched at the *cour de cassation* in the Palais de Justice:

A very pretty woman was accused of selling faked furniture to an antique dealer. She was seated in front of her counsel, a fat barrister

1. Letter to Mrs Vanier, 14th January 1918.
* Map of battlefields on p. 76.

with a pasty complexion. She continually rose to interrupt the man who was accusing her, the witnesses and the magistrate, and each time her own counsel seized her by the shoulders and made her sit down. This was as good as the Palais Royal.[2] She was acquitted, since the evidence showed that her accuser was an expert who had had plenty of time to examine the furniture.[3]

Georges was greatly moved by his visit to the Orphanage:

For me, who am so fond of children and have seen so few of them for more than two and a half years, this was a great joy. Many of them are crippled and walk with crutches. They were all grateful and gay. One case was particularly sad – a child whose mother is dead and whose father is a prisoner in Germany. He was the youngest – three years old – and he called me 'Papa'.[4]

He was fascinated to watch the X-ray apparatus at work:

The flesh seems to melt away, leaving the skeleton. You see the heart very clearly, expanding and contracting with each pulsation. As if the rays were passing across a purse, eliminating the paper and the leather and leaving only the solid coins. You think that you're in the presence of a miracle; anyone not initiated into the mysteries of science would say that the rays should be called by any other name than 'X', and thus perpetuate the fame of whoever helped to discover them.[5]

Attached to the Canadian Commission in Paris was an old acquaintance of Georges Vanier, Jean Désy. Both, in their time, were to be Ambassadors to France, but if the idea had entered either of their heads in 1918 it was more likely to have occurred to Désy than to Vanier. Each seems to have carried away a similar impression of the other. Georges noted that 'Désy has matured. He is robust'; and Désy wrote to Mrs Vanier:

We were both delighted at the chance which brought us together again. Georges has changed physically. He is far more robust and vigorous than when he was practising law. The handling of arms has made of him a strapping fellow and he bears himself splendidly. . . . From the moral point of view he has kept intact the sincere enthusiasm of the early campaigning days, still the same smile and warmth, the same unshakable confidence.[6]

A performance of *Thais* at the Opera with Marthe Chenal –

2. The home of French farce.
3. Diary, 19th February 1918.
4. Ibid, 21st February.
5. Ibid.
6. 22nd March 1918

'always radiant and royal' – did something to compensate for *Ohé Cupidon*!; and then Georges went down to Nice, staying at the Westminster on the Promenade des Anglais. He took long walks by the sea and explored the coast as far as the Italian frontier; bought some perfume at Grasse for his mother and Frances; but was kept from the tables at Monte Carlo, since gambling was forbidden to officers in uniform. At Nice there was also a Théâtre des Variétés, where *Mignon* was in the bill:

The roles of Mignon and of Philine were very well sung and that of Meister very badly. Meister was amusing, played by a man at least six foot six and weighing 300 pounds, with enormous hands which were always in the way. He strutted about the stage saying 'Ah vraiment?' (or words to that effect because he mouthed his words continually and we did not know whether he was talking, singing or simply gesticulating). To complete the tragedy he wore really fine clothes and considered himself a 'lion'. If I were wealthy I would settle him down in the butcher business. He should be able to fell an ox, *perhaps* with an axe, *certainly* with his voice.[7]

The return journey to Paris was crowded and exhilarating. A French Commandant with the Légion d'Honneur and six palms to his Croix de Guerre, two other French officers, a Belgian Colonel, a Russian woman and Georges Vanier were all in the same first-class compartment, drinking and playing cards. On his way through Paris Georges consulted two doctors about the inadequate nasal respiration which had been troubling him. The diagnosis reported a deviation of the nasal septum, but no adenoidal enlargement.

On the 9th of March he was back with his battalion, having visited Amiens Cathedral en route, and just in time for Ludendorff's last offensive. Only a week before this decisive challenge we find the most sombre entry in his diary:

A— D— sentenced to death. His attitude is calm and we leave him alone with the Chaplain. I have been put in charge of the troops that will assist at the execution tomorrow morning. A sad task – a sad command.[8]

By the 26th of March, when the British Divisions had been falling back between the Scarpe and the Oise, the military situation was grave; and on the following day Lieut-General Sir Arthur

7. Letter to Mrs Vanier, 27th February 1918.
8. 14th March 1918.

Currie,[9] commanding the Canadian Corps, sent out his inspiring order:

I place my trust in the Canadian Corps knowing that where Canadians are engaged there can be no giving way. Under the orders of your devoted officers in the coming battle, you will advance or fall where you stand facing the enemy. To those who will fall I say 'You will not die but step into immortality. Your mothers will not lament your fate but will be proud to have borne such sons. Your names will be revered for ever and ever by your grateful country and God will take you all to Himself.' Canadians, in this fateful hour, I command you and I trust you to fight as you have ever fought with all your strength, with all your determination, with all your tranquil courage. On many a hard fought field of battle you have overcome the enemy. With God's help you shall achieve victory once more.

The 22nd Battalion was at Ecoivres and the day of the 27th of March was passed in the expectation of an immediate move. At 6 p.m. Georges was summoned to Brigade H.Q. and informed that the battalion would leave at about 11 p.m. The whole of the 2nd Division was being shifted southward through Maroeuil, Dainville, Bailleulval and Bienvillers-au-Bois. Georges dined at the officers' club at Ecoivres; passed the orders to the company commanders; and by 11.30 they had started out on their nocturnal march. The gravity of the situation, the darkness of the hour, and the secrecy of their movement all gave food for reflection:

11.30 p.m. We leave Ecoivres – noise of enemy aircraft – in the distance a bomb explodes. The moon is up; at the turning of the road leading to Maroeuil an enormous crucifix throws a shadow which we cross silently – shadow and reality – without any sense of blasphemy, each one of us seems to make a comparison. The great Apostle of civilization and of love inspires the humble disciples. O God of battles, one would like to think that this is your cause as well as ours, and one thinks that it is.

The men march a little heavily, weighed down with all their equipment. The night is cold and it warms them to be kept on the move. When we halt, some of them fall asleep. No one falters – that would be a moral and physical failure, and the soldier's honour lifts him above his own strength and gives him fresh resources.

Obliged to halt for an hour on the Doullens-Arras road between Dainville and Beaumetz. Lorries, ambulances, motor vehicles of every sort follow one after another. An incident – we met a cart

9. General Sir Arthur Currie, 1875-1934.

driven by a little girl, accompanied by her brother – even younger. We asked her where she was going. 'I don't know, sir. My father was killed this morning and I was left in charge of the cart with hay for the horse. I have brought all the bread and meat we had left, and my little brother and I are getting away.' They went off into the night – it was sad to watch them, and significant too. I could have wished that certain young girls I know could have seen them . . . but would they have understood? At last I feel that I know something useful – the war that I have experienced up to now has been so impersonal, an affair of metal and gas and barbed wire . . . so that I sometimes forgot that I was not a cog in a huge machine. Contact with these poor folk in flight from the barbarian is far from depressing. It's exalting – and you feel it a great privilege to contribute, even in the slightest degree, to the defeat and rejection of the savages.[10]

The battalion had a few hours of sleep in spite of a flood of messages, orders and reports. Rumour and counter-rumour contradicted one another. At 11.30 next morning each company was alerted to expect an attack, but it was announced later that the enemy's assault had been contained. The villages of Hébuterne and Bucquoy were still in Allied hands. Georges Vanier's diary tells the story of the dour defensive. Having tasted the rewards of attack, the 'Van Doos' were restive – though implacably resistant – under the new rôle assigned to them. The men were short of ammunition and hot food. No movement was possible during the day, and the only communication was by telephone. 'A' Company was heavily attacked, but the enemy retreated at the point of the bayonet. Out of 'C' Company there were forty casualties, killed or wounded. One of the chaplains to the regiment, Father Crochetière of Nicolet, was killed on the 2nd of April:

We buried him in a little village not many miles from the front, after the funeral service in the parish church at which Father Fortier of Ottawa officiated. The priest's death had a marked effect on the men whose friend he was. Many of the men could not keep back their tears.[11]

On the 15th of April the battalion left Bailleulmont for Brétencourt, headquarters of the 2nd British Division. Georges was billeted with Dubuc, and they found the hospitality a little less warm than elsewhere, for the aged proprietress had had enough of military squatters, not all of whom were as considerate as these,

10. Diary, 27th March 1918.
11. Diary.

and very few of whom can have conversed in her own langu-age. On the 18th the 'Van Doos' retired to a line in front of Ytres, where the German advance on territory which it knew so well was hitting them all the harder. On the 30th they were in trenches opposite Neuville-Vitasse.

I run along the fresh earth for the umpteenth time, but the earth has never done us any harm. It receives us like her own sons. When we are tired she comforts us. When we are ill she cures us. When we are on edge she calms us. She is a mother to us all, and then one day we shall go back to her. This premature return must please her and take her by surprise.[12]

One of the best and most intelligent officers of the battalion, Captain Guay, was killed on the 1st of May, and on the 9th of May Corporal Keable won his Victoria Cross; but from that date onwards the 'Van Doos' took part in no large-scale action, con-solidating their position in the line and putting all their faith in American reinforcement and the strategy of Marshal Foch. On the 1st of July they went into rest billets at Lignereuil and St Quentin, having lost four hundred men, killed and wounded, in three months, and Major Chassé had been taken prisoner. Gradu-ally the German offensive spent itself, and on the 22nd of July the enemy was in retreat to the south of the Marne. The hour of reckoning, so long awaited and so long delayed, had come.

At 9.05 a.m. on the 9th of August the 22nd battalion was ordered to attack in the direction of Méharicourt, passing across the 2nd Brigade of the 1st Division occupying the line of defence for Amiens. Tremblay sent Georges Vanier forward to reconnoitre, giving him a rendezvous in the last house of Caix on the road to Harbonnières. Georges left on horseback with a couple of cyclists by way of Guillaucourt, leaving the rest of the mounted troops in the valley. At 10.00 a.m. he dismounted a kilometre beyond Caix and met Tremblay, as arranged, at 11.40. The battalion fol-lowed on their right flank through Caix and Vrély against strong opposition and with heavy losses, going forward in short sallies, dislodging the remaining snipers and machine-guns, and waiting for those in the rear to catch up with them. At 3.30 p.m. a mes-senger arrived, summoning Tremblay to Brigade H.Q., and Georges Vanier was put in command. The battalion was reformed and continued its advance towards Méharicourt, capturing fifteen machine-guns and two hundred prisoners. Beyond Méharicourt

12. Diary.

there was a consultation with officers of the 24th, 25th and 26th Battalions, and the decision was taken to push on to the further side of Chilly, where they awaited orders from Brigade H.Q. Tremblay, now in temporary command of the Brigade, came back at 7.15 p.m. and approved the decision to remain in ambush. The Brigade had reached all its objectives, and the flow of prisoners continued down the road, The 22nd now occupied positions six hundred yards beyond Méharicourt, between the roads to Maucourt and Hallu, with its headquarters to the east of Chemin Chilous.

At 7.30 p.m. Georges returned to Brigade H.Q. The action had been an extraordinary success. Monchy-le-Preux was taken, and Wancourt had offered very little resistance. As Georges wrote afterwards to Frances:

The advance of course was unprecedented – 22,000 yards in a little over two days. The Huns were no match for our men who charged M.G.s with perfect coolness as if they were on the parade ground. Their indifference before death was little short of sublime.[13]

The Brigade, with all its four battalions, was in position to the south of the Arras-Cambrai road, and it was decided not to attack on the following day. Georges had two hours of well-earned rest in the afternoon, and then visited all the officers of the 'Van Doos'. The projected assault on the Somme canal was put off owing to the partial failure of the 4th Division beyond Chilly. A reinforcement of tanks was awaited, and on the 12th of August Georges went ahead with Archambault to reconnoitre the place of assembly. The attack was fixed for the morning of the 15th of August, with a limited objective. It was not intended to reach the canal in a single leap. By the 17th the battalion was in trenches to the north of Chilly, and remained there until it was relieved the same day by the 87th Canadian Battalion. The final assault on the Somme was expected for the 22nd, but nothing was known for certain. Orders were constantly changing to put enemy agents off the scent, and the troops could only move by night.

The exhausted men of the 'Van Doos' were now glad to find themselves in the Bois de Blangy, ten kilometres to the east of Amiens – territory which had been recaptured between the 8th and the 10th of August. Georges lay stretched on the grass among the brushwood, and sleeping till 1 p.m. It had been a testing week, but his luck still held. 'I have seen some of my comrades fall

13. 17th August 1918.

beside me and I have had so many narrow escapes myself that I am beginning to think that one should not worry much about possible eventualities.' Among those fallen was a particular friend, Basil Kingston. 'The day before his death I had quite a long talk with him in the front line trench. He was always the same courteous, quiet, gracious gentleman' – a description just as applicable to Georges Vanier himself. His heart's desire was still 'to be given another chance at the retreating line. Providence has continued its special protection and in spite of some narrow escapes, I have come through without a scratch.'[14] He was very quickly to be given his chance, although Providence had its surprises in store.

Georges had hardly woken from his sleep on the good earth than he received word that the battalion was to leave on the evening of the following day. So there would be one more night of sleep under the stars. The transport left the same evening for Frévent. Tremblay came to dinner, as the sun was setting in a splendour of crimson and gold, with the towers of Amiens silhouetted in the distance. Georges described this as 'one of the beautiful moments of my life . . . what an honour to have contributed, even slightly, to the deliverance of Amiens and its pure cathedral!' As the sun went down in the west, the full moon got up.

In the morning there was a thick mist, just as there had been on the morning of the attack on the 8th of August. You could only see two hundred yards ahead, and then, little by little, the sun came through. The Bois de Blangy stood revealed and, once again, the towers of Amiens. The heat was overpowering and it was not until 7.30 p.m. that the battalion moved off in buses to the north, travelling all through the night, and scarcely pausing until midday of the 22nd August. The heat reminded Georges of Canadian summers, and he was glad to lie out on the grass. On the 23rd they left, just after noon, for Pithouvin, and from there by train to Aubigny. Several men fell out under the pitiless sun. At 9 p.m. they were billeted – very uncomfortably – at Wanquetin, and on the evening of the 24th Georges was sleeping on bales of straw in a hut at Berneville. The moon was still riding high and clear, and he slept well.

The 25th of August was a Sunday and they attended Mass in the church at Parvins. At 10.30 a.m. the battalion commanders of the 5th Brigade met for consultation; the attack was provisionally fixed for the next morning. At 5.30 in the afternoon Dubuc sent

14. Letters to Mrs Vanier, 11th and 15th August 1918.

Georges ahead to reconnoitre a convenient assembly area to the north of Beaurains. A sudden storm got up with torrential rain and flashes of lightning; but it soon passed and the night was again moonlit and clear. In the early hours of the 26th of August Georges left with Dubuc for Brigade H.Q. Tremblay appointed him liaison officer with the 3rd Division and the 7th Brigade, and sent him off to their headquarters at Beaubourg St Sauveur. Zero hour was 3 a.m.; the artillery opened up a deafening barrage and by 7 a.m. the first prisoners were coming in – evidently second-class troops of inferior physique. By 7.15 a.m. the 8th Brigade had reached all its objectives, and at 7.30 a.m. Georges returned to headquarters of the 5th Brigade where Tremblay informed him that the 5th would not attack that day. The four battalions were still in position to the south of the Arras-Cambrai road. Georges had left that morning with no idea that he would be appointed liaison officer, and had therefore neither washed, shaved, nor eaten. 'Fortunately two tins of "Bully Beef" that I discovered in a trench saved my life.' He was grateful for two hours rest in the afternoon, and to renew contact with the officers of the 'Van Doos'. At 10 p.m. the battalion commanders were again summoned to Brigade H.Q., and informed that it would attack on the 27th of August, with Cagnicourt as objective.

There are two main roads branching out from Arras in an easterly or south-easterly direction, the first leading to Cambrai and the second to Bapaume. It was between these two roads that the battle of Chérisy was fought. Chérisy itself is a small village on the light railway from Boisleux to Cambrai. The country is open and slightly undulating, and the little stream of the Sensée runs through the valley. Chérisy stands on its north-western slope. The village had been captured by the 18th Division on the 3rd of May 1917, but it was retaken the same night. Its importance lay in its position commanding the side road leading to Haucourt which was on the main Arras-Cambrai highway. This whole region comprised what was known as the Hindenburg line. It consisted of five successive zones of defence – the former network of German trenches to the east of Monchy-le-Preux, now consolidated and reinforced; the line between Fresnes and Rouvroy; the redoubtable double line running between Haucourt and Quéant; and the bed of the Canal du Nord, which was heavily defended. Once the Allied armies had broken through the Hindenburg line the war would become a war of movement with Cambrai as its immediate objective.

Movements of the 22nd Battalion

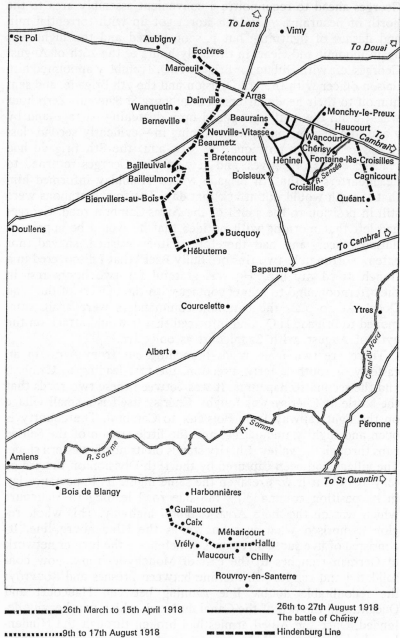

St Pol

To Lens

Vimy

Aubigny

To Douai

Ecoivres

Maroeuil

Arras

Dainville

Wanquetin

Berneville

Beaurains

Monchy-le-Preux

Haucourt

To Cambrai

Neuville-Vitasse

Wancourt

Beaumetz

Chérisy

Brétencourt

Héninel

Fontaine-lès-Croisilles

Bailleulval

Boisleux

R. Sensée

Cagnicourt

Bailleulmont

Croisilles

Bienvillers-au-Bois

Quéant

Doullens

Bucquoy

To Cambrai

Hébuterne

Bapaume

Courcelette

Ytres

Albert

Canal du Nord

R. Somme

Péronne

R. Somme

Amiens

To St Quentin

Bois de Blangy

Harbonnières

Guillaucourt

Caix

Méharicourt

Vrély

Hallu

Maucourt

Chilly

Rouvroy-en-Santerre

▬■▬■▬■▬ 26th March to 15th April 1918

▬▬▬▬▬ 26th to 27th August 1918
The battle of Chérisy

▪▪▪▪▪▪▪▪▪▪▪ 9th to 17th August 1918

▬ ▬ ▬ ▬ ▬ Hindenburg Line

The 82nd Division held the sector on the right between Neuville-Vitasse and the Arras-Cambrai road. On the morning of the 26th of August, at 3 a.m., the 3rd Division opened the attack and captured a network of German trenches. More than five hundred German corpses were afterwards discovered on the terrain. Meanwhile the 'Van Doos' had left Beaurains an hour later, advancing over the plain through the night over unfamiliar ground. Throughout the following day they remained in reserve, with the 4th Brigade on their left, and under the shelter of the recently captured German trenches. On the morning of the 27th of August they assembled at 4.30 for the attack. At 10 a.m. the artillery thundered its overture, and three minutes later they were over the parapet with Dubuc in command, Georges Vanier acting in liaison with the 4th Brigade, and Tremblay, now promoted Brigadier-General, in overall charge of the operation. For a couple of hours the advance was slow, as the men spurted from one shell hole to another, but by noon a good number of prisoners were filing to the rear. Dubuc went forward to reconnoitre while the men were in position behind a hut above the Sensée ravine. Their job was to cross it and capture the ridge beyond. It was raining hard when they continued the attack, having lost during the morning half of their effectives. Privates found themselves commanding platoons. Dubuc, who was here, there, and everywhere, had a bullet through his head which cost him his eye, and might well have cost him his life. He was taken from the field and the command passed to Archambault. It was now 5 o'clock in the afternoon. The 'Van Doos' had already gained a foothold on the opposite slope when Archambault was wounded in his turn and Major Morgan took over what remained of the battalion. Operations were suspended at 5.45, and it was at this point that Tremblay put Georges Vanier in command.

Georges rejoined the unit at dusk. The men were at the end of their tether, in occupation of no definite line, crouched in shell holes or the debris of trenches. He established a single H.Q. with Lieut-Colonel Clark-Kennedy, who commanded the 24th Battalion, and at about 9 a.m. the following morning they received orders to renew the attack shortly after noon. They looked at each other in a silence more eloquent than words. At last Clark-Kennedy simply remarked: 'It'll be all right', and Georges Vanier indicated his agreement. He then got together a few officers in a shell-hole and told them that the attack would be renewed at 12.30 p.m. Since he had no staff he would himself advance at the centre of the battalion where everyone could see him. The attack went forward as planned, under cover of a light artillery barrage. This time the 'Van Doos' did not get very far; the battalion was still further decimated by machine-gun fire. What happened to Georges Vanier can best be told in his own words:

Very shortly after zero hour, I was shot (MG or rifle bullet) through the right side splitting a couple of ribs. The wound however was a very clean one (most bullet wounds are) and I should have been very fortunate indeed to come off with it only. But this was to be one of my bad days: as I was being dressed by the bearer a shell exploded at my side causing rather unpleasant shrapnel wounds to my right and left legs. I was taken to a Casualty Clearing Station near Ligny St Flochel where I was examined. The right knee was shattered and the M.O. then said even if the leg were saved I would never be able to use the knee. I asked him if he might wait until the following day for a reply. He agreed and the leg was amputated next day. A short time after my return to bed following the operation, I suffered a severe haemorrhage and was hurried back to where the operation took place. There the transfusion was done in direct contact with the donor. The immediate effect was a feeling of active physical resuscitation. I have no doubt whatever that the transfusion saved my life. When it was over, somebody suggested – perhaps I did – that a glass of port might do me good. Everybody agreed, and another voice was heard (it was the man next to me) saying: 'I'd like one too.' Later I was transferred to No. 8 British Red Cross Hospital, Boulogne.[15]

The stretcher-bearer was killed instantly, and on his way to the dressing-station Georges met the Chaplain to the regiment, who asked if there was anything he could do for him. 'Yes' replied Georges 'you can give me three things – absolution for my sins, a drop of rum, and a cigarette.' It was the first cigarette he had smoked since enlisting with the 'Van Doos', but the Chaplain decided that rum would not be good for him.

2

A clue to the character of Georges Vanier is to be found in the contrast between the letters he now wrote home and the entries in his own diary. He could not conceal from his parents the nature of his injuries, but he was silent about his suffering. In

15. Letters to Mrs Vanier, 6th September 1918; and to Dr Norman M. Guiou, 3rd March 1966. Remarks recorded for the C.B.C., 14th January 1965.

his diary he put down everything he felt. It was not only that he wished to spare anxiety to those concerned for him; it was also that there were certain things he told only to himself. But where the same protective armour of reserve would have petrified the sympathies of another man, with him it seemed only to make them warmer. They radiated from a centre of increasing self-knowledge and self-control.

At 6 p.m. on a sunny September evening he left the Casualty Station with an aching heart and a last look at the old farmsteads and immemorial roads of France which he had come to know so well. It was good-bye to the humours and the precarious intimacies of war. Even now, his first thought was for others besides himself. A young officer, wounded in the battle of Haucourt-Quéant, was brought to the Casualty Clearing Station, and coming out of the anaesthetic found himself in a marquee ward. Georges was in the adjoining bed.

Never shall I forget the sympathetic kindness of that officer who, despite his own suffering and much more severe wounds, concerned himself with cheering and rallying a very young subaltern (I was twenty years old at that time).

I still remember a devoted young batman who appeared to have remained with his officer from the time the latter was wounded, and I heard the Major ask a hospital authority to try and keep the lad a day or two before returning him to the Battalion as he had had a very hard time.

Later, in convalescent hospital in England, other officers from the 22nd told me that that Major was one of the most illustrious and well-beloved officers in the Battalion.[16]

Now, with his wounds superficially dressed, Georges was driven to the hospital train, waiting at Ligny, and into this he was carried with thirty other officers. The heat was intolerable and the blinds drawn. The train left at 9 p.m. and travelled slowly and smoothly to Boulogne where it arrived at 7.30 a.m. on the morning of the 4th of September. He was given a light meal of soup and tongue, and his wounds were dressed again – that on his right leg under a gas anaesthetic. He was suffering a great deal in spite of medical encouragement. The pain was partially relieved by constant injections of morphia, but this did not prevent insomnia:

God! how the nights are long! Every half hour I hear the distant echo

16. Major Eric A. Henderson, letter to the author, 4th April 1968.

of the sea, and the sea winds; the weather is cool; still no letters; agonizing pains in the right leg. 6 p.m.: sudden attack of weakness; I have been reading too much – certain pages of *Nemesis* by Bourget. Lieut.Col DesRosiers[17] gave it to me.[18]

DesRosiers from the 10th Reserve Battalion was taking over command of the 'Van Doos' in the absence of Chassé who was still a prisoner. He had spent two hours with Georges, and told him that not a single officer in the battalion had escaped alive or unwounded at Chérisy. Georges was greatly cheered by Des-Rosiers' visit and thought he would make an excellent commander. It was also an encouragement to learn that the whole Allied line from Ypres to Rheims was now moving forward. Three other officers from the regiment were in the same hospital: and Georges was visited by Mgr Gauthier, the new Archbishop of Montreal. Fortunately the wound in his side was not serious, although the bullet had passed within one and a half inches from the spine, but he was suffering intensely from the damage to his right leg. At times the pain was almost unbearable, and outside the windows of his room the sky was grey and sullen, and the autumn winds moaned across the Channel. On the 24th of September he was moved to the Third London General Hospital at Wandsworth, and writing home that he expected to be getting about in three weeks 'with difficulty, of course, but still getting about'. It was an optimistic prediction, quite in keeping with his character; and the following letter, sent two days later, was not less so:

Fortunately, no bones were broken in the left leg and I expect to have the complete use of it very soon. But the right one was badly shattered, more especially about the knee and it was found necessary to amputate just above the knee. Do not think that I have suffered because with the modern surgical methods, pain and discomfort are reduced to a minimum. By this time, of course, the stump is almost healed and I shall probably be about without a bandage in a few weeks.

There is absolutely no cause for the slightest worry on your part. The loss of the leg does not affect one in the least.[19]

The operation was completely successful, and on the 8th of October Georges expressed the hope that his mother was sleeping as well as he was: 'I have never been so "tranquil" in my life.' He had reason for sound sleep, for on the same day Trem-

17. Lieut-Colonel H. DesRosiers.
18. Diary, 9th September 1918.
19. Letter to Mrs Vanier, 26th September 1918.

blay had written to tell him that a Bar had been added to his
M.C., and again on the 9th of October that he had been awarded
the D.S.O. The citation read as follows: 'He led his Battalion to
the capture of a village and his exemplary courage so stimulated
his men that this important position was carried by assault.'
Georges was now finding it easier to read, and Stephen Leacock's
Literary Lapses amused him not a little. There was also plenty
of time for pure contemplation:

Today . . . I have indulged in another pastime – watching spiders
spin webs. They have put me in a sort of summer-house outside
the regular ward and when I woke this morning I found four spiders
industriously spinning beautiful regular webs outside one of my
four windows – trying to seal me in, as they did the King in
English History whose name I forget.[20]

On the 4th of November he was transferred to the Canadian
Hospital, 1 Hyde Park Place, where it was decided that a second
operation on what remained of his right leg would be necessary.
This was performed on the 11th of November, and Georges awoke
from the anaesthetic to the sound of cannon announcing the
Armistice. A week later the frenzied celebrations had not yet
subsided, but Georges Vanier's thoughts were with the 'Van
Doos':

The Canadian troops in France will be marching towards the Rhine
in a few days – one of the greatest disappointments of my life will be
my inability to take part in this march. What a tremendous reward
and consolation to see the goal of all our ambitions – to actually
tread on German soil, to feel that the efforts and the sacrifices of
years have not been in vain.[21]

Georges was determined – obstinately, as we shall see – to have
his artificial leg fitted in London, since he did not wish to arrive
on crutches in Montreal. By the 7th of December he was getting
up and down stairs on crutches, but not as yet about the streets.
His left leg had recovered much better than he expected; neither
the nerves nor the muscles seemed to be in any way affected.
Lieut-Colonel G. de Martigny of the 10th Canadian Reserve
Battalion reported to Madame Vanier that he had found Georges
'gay, looking well, and surrounded by friends' and that his 'famous appetite' was undiminished. In the middle of the month he
was being measured for a peg leg – a kind of preliminary limb

20. Letter to Mrs Vanier, 26th September 1918.
21. Diary.

which had to be worn for a month or two before any work could be done on the permanent replacement. This enabled the stump to harden and prepared it for the more laborious work it would have to do later on. At the same time Georges received an offer that pointed in the direction which his career was eventually to take. Philippe Roy, Canadian Commissioner in Paris, asked him to accept a secretaryship at the Commission at a salary of $4000 a year. This would put him in touch with the leading politicians and men of affairs in Canada, and might be the first step towards some other position of importance. Sir Robert Borden had approved the offer, but Georges was in no hurry to make up his mind. Meanwhile he spent the first Christmas of a world at peace at the Perkins Bull Hospital, and what Christmas was like at the Perkins Bull may be gathered from the Hospital's own bulletin:

A bevy of beauteous femininity, plus flocks and flocks of gallant young striplings, clad in the customary khaki, somewhat toned down – the young element, not the khaki – by the presence of glowing middle age. Add the cheeriness and glow of Christmas spirits. Mix well and season the whole with plenty of Canadian pep, and one may draw a fairly complete idea of Christmastide at the Perkins Bull Hospital.

CHAPTER 5

RETURN TO CANADA

I

A s soon as he was disabled for further action in the field Georges reverted to the substantive rank of Captain – an injustice against which he was quick to protest. He maintained that his substantive Majority should have been put through when he had the best right to it. The question of his pension and his permanent disability made the matter urgent, and Tremblay replied sympathetically to his complaint. Meanwhile he retained the honorary rank of Major, but without the appropriate pay.

These considerations may have been in his mind when he wrote to Philippe Roy accepting the Paris offer on three conditions; that he should remain in uniform until he knew whether the wounds in his side and his left leg would give further trouble; that the period of his secretaryship should be limited; and that he should receive a salary of $5,000 a year. His parents had agreed to his taking the job, but in his heart of hearts Georges did not really want it; and he was rather relieved when Roy replied that he could not accept a temporary secretary or agree to any advance on the salary he had proposed. This was already double what had previously been paid.

Georges had written off his second operation as a matter of 'minor importance' since its purpose was only to remove the scar tissue and a piece of bone. The stump had healed in less than three weeks, leaving a clean scar no more than one eighth of an inch wide. As for the wound in his side, the result was only a bruised patch just above the appendix. A second bullet had merely smashed his revolver; it might otherwise have lodged in his abdomen. 'The surgeons' he wrote on the 18th of January 1919 'have given me a complete re-examination and look upon me as a curiosity without any claim to existence'. With this relatively clean bill of health he was sent to the Granville Special Hospital at Buxton – which in peace time had been the Palace Hotel. Every morning his stump, left leg, and scar in the side were massaged in order to loosen the scars, strengthen the muscles and stimulate the nerves. At 11 a.m. there was a walking class for officers with pegs; and in the afternoon rowing exercise and punching the ball in the gymnasium. The patients were made to walk on a narrow strip of wood, backwards, forwards and sideways; and then upstairs and downstairs. Georges soon found that he could walk on his peg without crutches or sticks, though for a short distance only – 'perhaps' he noted 'I could make a career as an *equilibrist*' – and the peg was giving him a good deal of trouble.

What he chiefly suffered from was the cold, for the hospital had no central heating. 'I sometimes long' he wrote 'for the winter weather of Canada when I experience the hybrid variety of Derbyshire. This is the first complete winter I have spent in England and I pray Heaven it may be the last one.'[1] The only heating was coal fires – as long as the coal lasted; and thereby hung a tale. Georges shared a room with Captain J. P. Cathcart, and their orderly was instructed, under threat of dire penalties, to see that the coal box was always full and the fire at all times blazing:

The result has been miraculous. The rest of the hospital patients are allowed to freeze (more or less) but room 23 sometimes presents the aspect of a Turkish bath; so far so good – but the horror of the thing does not end here. Our room communicates with a second room in which are two other officers whose eyes bulge when they see the coal being brought into 23 and whose hearts grow black with rage. We fear some awful tragedy of revenge: whenever I stoke the fire, Cathcart – to drown the noise – either attempts to sing or throws the furniture about and the sound of the shovelled coal does not reach the ears of the infuriated patients in 22. The other night we heard a strange song from 22 and Cathcart swore it was the Scottish death-song. (The patients in 22 are Scots). We waited in fear and trembling for the onslaught: finally I ventured forth and attempted to placate them with offerings of candied ginger and of 'Cresca' figs. But the suspense is terrible! Cathcart and myself spend – alternately – sleepless nights watching the fire and the precious box of coal. Needless to say we keep a vigilant eye on the frenzied inhabitants of 22.[2]

Once again, the resilience of Georges Vanier's letters does not give us the whole of his mind. In another adjoining room was J. Keiller Mackay,[3] and it was to him that Georges uttered the despairing cry: 'I'd better have been killed'. But these moments were rare. The monotony of convalescence was relieved by much hospitality from the neighbours, and expeditions into the country

1. 12th March 1919.
2. 8th February 1919.
3. The Hon. Colonel J. Keiller Mackay, Lieut-Governor of Ontario 1957-1963.

foraging for food. The Matron of the Remedial Department had
been family masseuse to the Duke of Connaught, and the Duke
visited the Hospital. One of the Canadian Nursing Sisters died of
heart failure after an attack of influenza, and was given a complete military funeral, with the patients following behind in their
blue suits with white facings, red ties and slippers. Influenza was
very rife, and to prevent infection the officers were given drops of
oil of cinnamon on a tea-spoonful of sugar several times a day.
The civilian working women in the adjoining annexe threatened
to go on strike, but Nurse Attrill – who was looking after Georges
Vanier – managed to dissuade them. On Sports Day competitions
were held between teams of American and Canadian Service men
from the Discharge depots, although some of the contestants were
anything but sporting. Off the battlefield, as well as on it, they
fought to win. Georges himself made various attempts to play
golf, 'but the result was always a disaster to the lawn, and language that would make me weep under less strained circumstances.'[4]

He continued to read widely – from Shakespeare to Napoleon's
campaigns. He also followed current affairs with interest and
anxiety. In England he noted the signs of civil disaffection, and
he was strongly affected by Charles Rivet's *Le Dernier des
Romanoffs*. Rivet had been correspondent for *Le Temps* in Petro-
grad, and the reading of his book, with its picture of the Russian
aristocracy, filled Georges with a repulsion of which he was unable to rid himself. In Canada he already saw separatist tendencies
at work between the eastern and western provinces, and thought
that the time had come for the formation of an independent
party. Sir Wilfrid Laurier had died in March, and Georges wondered whether the country would ever again have a French-
Canadian as Prime Minister. Laurier had opposed conscription,
although he had encouraged recruitment, and his obituaries in
the English press were in consequence a little reserved. The
chauvinism of Quebec, in its more extreme manifestations, was
directed against the British as well as the British-Canadians.
Georges Vanier caught an echo of it from his sister Frances, replying to her with some heat:

This young friend of yours who considered all Englishmen barbarians
must be a very curious person; I wish she could visit some of the
hospitals in England and see the hundreds of thousands of maimed
'barbarians' – it might open her eyes.[5]

4. Letter to Mrs Vanier, 24th April 1919.
5. 8th November 1918.

Georges did not believe that the war had been engineered by British commercial interests, and he remembered the young French girl in her hay-cart fleeing from the advancing enemy:

That was one of the moments when I did not care whether the English were barbarians or not, but when I did care whether we could save the poor people of France from the horror of every imaginable crime. You may tell your little friend that the 'English barbarians' for four long years have been sacrificing their finest manhood in the service of humanity in order to make the world habitable for her and her children and her children's children. Strange barbarians these![6]

In March 1919 another death touched Georges more nearly. He had come to love Camille Martin 'as a member of my own family. . . . He was above all a large-hearted man. His love for France was almost a religion and it is to him I owe to a large extent my own love and pride in this most wonderful of nations.'[7] He had sent his old professor a bottle of whisky on his 80th birthday, and Mgr Gauthier had told Camille Martin that Georges Vanier was 'the master product of his professional teaching in Montreal'.

The doctors were determined that Georges should have his artificial leg fitted in Toronto, and Georges was equally determined that it should be fitted in England. It was not that he had any particular dislike for Toronto, but he did not wish to wait there in a queue for two or three months, and he was even prepared to be demobilized in England to avoid doing so. For a time the authorities were adamant, but Georges wrote that he expected 'to outwit them'. In the event he was successful. General Watson not only saw that his substantive Majority was restored, but took him to see Sir Edward Kemp,[8] Overseas Minister of Militia, who gave orders that the leg be fitted in England. Georges left Buxton on the 22nd of April and moved into the Perkins Bull Hospital at Putney. He had enjoyed himself at Buxton, but felt that it was time for him to get out. The local hospitality was at once tedious, overwhelming and difficult to refuse. And the excuse of a previous engagement was unlikely to work, since everyone knew what everyone else was doing at every moment of the day.

The 'Van Doos' came to London in May and paraded, with other

6. 1st February 1919.
7. Letter to Mrs Vanier, 28th March 1919.
8. The Hon. Sir Edward Kemp, 1858-1929.

Canadian troops, through the streets. Georges noted that the public was cold and that very few people saluted the colours, not through disloyalty but ignorance. It was sad not to be marching with them, but there were happy reunions with Tremblay and 'Lipi' Archambault. The day would come, many years hence, when Georges Vanier would describe Tremblay as 'the soul of the Royal 22nd', and 'the greatest French-Canadian soldier since Salaberry'. He knew – none better – the man he was speaking of:

Tremblay is a prince, he has been wonderful to me at all times. Very often he has been anxious to spare me fatigue and danger and on two or three occasions wanted to leave me out of shows in which he was taking part. I felt that as long as I followed him no harm would come to me. I have been in tighter corners than the one in which I was hit but always I felt certain that his star wd bring us through.[9]

The 'Van Doos' sailed for Canada on the 19th of May, with Tremblay, O.C. 5th Canadian Brigade, DesRosiers in command of the regiment, and of the original officers only Dubuc, Archambault, and Routhier. Georges regretted not to be returning with them – the excitement and exertion would have been too much for him – but he sent all his souvenirs ahead in a trunk under the care of Archambault, with his blood-stained tunic and the muddied boots from Dangerfield's. 'Please do not clean the boots' he instructed 'I wish to keep the soil of France which clings to them and to sprinkle some of it over the grave of M. Martin.' He also warned his parents that he was not in good condition. 'I am organically as well as I ever was, *but* I do not look well.' He had lost 50-lbs. since March 1918 – such was the toll of the last six months campaigning and of the weakness from his wound. Nevertheless, he added, 'I am happy that I had the courage to return to my boys in 1916, and that God gave me the strength of body and mind to do my duty under fire.'[10]

On the 27th of May he reported that his new leg was quite satisfactory after certain minor repairs, and on the 11th of June he received a telegram from the Lord Chamberlain requesting his attendance at Buckingham Palace on the 14th to be invested with his D.S.O. and the Bar to his Military Cross.

The King was very considerate to me, wishing me not to stand when speaking to him and questioning me at length upon the condition of my

9. Letter to Mrs Vanier, 5th June 1919.
10. Ibid, 13th May 1919.

stump and the comfort of my artificial leg. He looked extremely well and I should say that, with age, his appearance improves. He has a quiet direct manner which pleases by its manliness. He reminds one of the soldier or sailor rather than the courtier.[11]

On the 18th of July Georges Vanier sailed home in the S.S. *Minerva* for Quebec.

2

The future was now uncertain. After a long rest at Memphre-magog, where the only exercise he could take was sawing logs, Georges played with the idea of returning to the Bar, but his heart was with the regiment and in September 1919 we find him at the first Annual Banquet of the officers, at the Windsor Hotel in Montreal, proposing the health of the 'nurses and the god-mothers'. (Each officer had been in correspondence with a French 'godmother', generally unknown to them, while they were in France). It was apparently a most felicitous speech, with a pretty turn of phrase, evoking the devotion of the women who had 'consoled the living in the name of their wives and mothers, and closed the eyelids of the dead. They were examples of strength and comfort to the wounded, and there was sweetness in the wound which was healed by a woman's hand. Where the nurses cured our wounds, the godmothers cured our depression.' He raised his glass to the 'roses of the war'.

The 22nd was now constituted as a permanent unit with Chassé in command. It was to be quartered at the Citadel in Quebec; to comprise twelve officers, twenty-five N.C.Os, and two hundred men; and to consist of two companies, each commanded by a Major. Georges Vanier consulted Sir Arthur Currie about his future, and when Currie questioned the utility of an officer with only one leg, Georges replied: 'I suppose you want officers with brains?' So the matter was settled and he went to the Citadel in command of 'A' Company, and second-in-command of the battalion.

One day, shortly after Georges Vanier's return to Canada, a very tall and beautiful young woman was sitting in the Ritz Hotel in Montreal, having tea with Tommy Tremblay. She was perhaps rather more interested in Tremblay than he was interested in her. 'That's the man for you' he remarked, pointing to Georges Vanier who happened to be in the hotel at the same time – and

11. Letter to Mrs Vanier, 14th June 1919.

Tremblay was nothing if not a judge of men. Pauline Archer was the only child of Judge Charles Archer of the Quebec Superior Court and his wife Thérèse. Charles Archer's mother was a French-Canadian and his father, an emigrant from Brixham in Devonshire, had been converted to Catholicism. His wife, Thérèse, was a direct descendant of Charles de Salaberry – and the Salaberrys had been the *seigneurs* of Chambly de Rouville in early colonial times. Although her own branch of the family had been settled in Canada for many years, she had numerous relations in France. She was a woman of tiny physique and very considerable intelligence.

Pauline had spent a sheltered and privileged childhood in the big sandstone house on Sherbrooke Street. After four years' schooling with the Madams of the Sacred Heart, she had been taught by a governess at home where she had an entire floor of the house to herself – bedroom, sitting-room, class-room, and accommodation for a nanny and governess. She was to remember with nostalgia the pink and white bedroom, and the rosebuds on the curtains, and the ivory lacquered desk where she worked at her lessons, and the dolls' house with its miniature furniture. Until she was seventeen she was never allowed to leave the house unaccompanied. On Saturday mornings, she would walk with her father to his office in the Place d'Armes and there, in the high-ceilinged room, she was allowed to play with his typewriter. At Christmas all the Archers would gather at her grandfather's house in Quebec City, where the eleven cousins regaled themselves on charlotte russe, ginger ale and jelly; and in Montreal there was a Christmas tree for the needy children of the parish. Already, when she was still a girl, Pauline Archer dreamt of giving herself to great causes; she would be a missionary, or a nun, or perhaps an artist.

She was twenty-two years old when Tremblay introduced her to Georges Vanier. Georges, never quicker off the mark than now, invited her to luncheon the following day. Since she was just leaving for a six months' holiday in France, he lent her his staff maps so that she could visit the battlefields with a detailed knowledge of the terrain. Naturally she expected a message, or something more than a message, when she got to the boat. Nothing came, however, and she concluded that appearances were deceptive. During her stay in France she became engaged to another officer who had lost an arm. The last thing she asked of her suitors was that they should be sound in wind and limb. Tremblay was not alone in thinking that Georges was the man for Pauline Archer. Madame Philippe Roy, wife of the Canadian Commissioner in Paris, gave a dinner for Pauline and her fiancé. 'All the same,' she observed, as she proposed their health, 'I have always thought that Pauline should really be marrying Georges Vanier.' Pauline thought so, too, but when her engagement was announced Georges sent her a telegram of congratulation. Once again she concluded that appearances had been deceptive.

The engagement, however, did not go well and it was soon broken off. In the summer of 1920 Pauline was on holiday in the Gaspé, where she happened to meet a friend of Georges Vanier. Learning that she also knew him, he suggested that they send him a postcard, and rather reluctantly she agreed. Later in the year she was staying at her father's old home in Quebec, where her grandfather, at the age of ninety-six, had sat with a tartan rug over his knees and solemnly blessed the family. Georges was at the Citadel, and when Pauline met him again she soon discovered that he had indeed sent a message to the boat – but to the wrong boat! They dined together very often, and Georges talked to her of Bergson and Ernest Psichari, who had reached an acceptance of the Faith through the discipline of arms; talked to her of everything, in fact, except the one subject upon which she wished to hear his views. At last, on the 13th of January 1921, she told him that she was going back to Montreal the next day, and then he spoke up. In the morning he phoned her for clear confirmation that he had proposed to her the night before.

We do not know exactly at what point Georges was telling his Buxton room-mate, Captain Cathcart, that Pauline was 'the only girl in the world', but when their engagement was announced in April 1921, Cathcart wrote: 'I knew that nothing short of that would ever stir you out of that hermit's life you were leading', and went on to recall 'our little conversations while sitting about the grate fire in our room at the Palace Hotel – waiting for the tomato soup to boil and even longer for it to cool. Of course my love affairs were a constant suggestion to you to do something yourself.'[12] Camille Martin's daughter, Thérèse, wrote that Georges had found 'une âme d'élite, comme la vôtre'; and another friend, Marie Chauvin, reminded him of an occasion, twelve months before, when he had expressed his envy of those who 'give themselves for ever under the stars'. Georges may not have known very much about women, but he was no stranger to

12. 26th April 1921.

the chivalries of hearth and home. He knew that when a man proposes to give himself in marriage, it is customary to give also some token of his commitment. A ring was *de rigueur*, and he then bethought him of the muddied boot from Dangerfield's which had once encased the leg that he had lost, and which 'Lipi' Archambault had obediently brought home to Montreal. There was still a little mud that had not been sprinkled on Camille Martin's grave, and this he put in a tiny box and presented to Pauline. Throughout the summer months of their engagement when they were often separated – he at Quebec and she in Montreal or at Murray Bay – he sent her roses every Saturday, and for good measure sent them to Mrs Archer also. 'You know so well' she wrote 'and with such infinite charm, the way in to the heart.' She, on her side, knew the quality of the young woman Georges was proposing to marry: 'the intense ardour of her nature. . . . My God, what exuberance of life, heart and soul; how impressionable – almost too much so for her nervous organism.'[13]

In June Georges sat for an examination by the Civil Service Commissioners and qualified, second among the candidates, as a First Class Interpreter. During the same month Marshal Foch, who had accepted the invitation to become Colonel of the Royal 22nd, presented a flag to the regiment. This was brought over by Marshal Fayolle, and Georges was appointed his A.D.C. in Quebec. Huge crowds watched the presentation on the parade ground of the Citadel. The flag was a replica of the one offered to the battalion by its Chaplain, Père Doyon, before it left St Jean d'Yberville in 1915. Fayolle compared it to Jeanne d'Arc's immortal banner, and Chassé, in receiving it, described it as 'the mother's affectionate caress for her Canadian child, for we have two countries – our own and France.' Fayolle was staying at the Château Frontenac. Fifty men composed the guard of honour as he came out, and as the troops marched past to the strains of 'Sambre-et-Meuse', the flag was seen waving in the wind and the sun darted its rays on to the gilt badges and regimental motto of the 'Van Doos'. The battalion was formed up for inspection at the western extremity of the Parc des Champs de Bataille, with all the officers who had commanded it – Gaudet, Tremblay, Dubuc, DesRosiers and Chassé.

A striking coincidence of good fortune gave Georges his future wife and the best friend of his maturity almost at the same moment. In 1921 the Duke of Devonshire's term as Governor

13. 18th July 1921.

General had expired and General Lord Byng of Vimy[14] had been nominated in his place. It was a popular and appropriate appointment. The seventh son of the 2nd Earl of Strafford, he had been born in 1862 and served with the 10th Royal Hussars of which he was appointed Colonel in 1900. As Commander of the Third Army on the Western Front, of which the Canadian Corps was a part, he had organized the victory from which he took his title; and earlier, at the Battle of Cambrai, he was the first to demonstrate how tanks could be used with decisive effect. A soldier of patrician birth, distinguished bearing, simple piety, acute intelligence, and high sense of public duty, he dedicated himself to the service of Canada, and left behind him not only a respected name but the memory of a controversy which broke his heart.

This we shall examine in due course. In the meanwhile he thought it high time that he should have a French-Canadian A.D.C. on his staff at Ottawa, and on the 27th of August 1921 the post was offered to Georges Vanier. It would carry his present pay and allowances, with an extra $200.00 a year, and the appointment was to end in December 1923. Byng was not personally acquainted with Georges, but he had heard enough about him to know that he was the man he was looking for, and he was already interested in his future career. He proposed that he should go to Ottawa for the last two weeks in September and then to Quebec, and that afterwards he should follow a course at the Royal Military College, Kingston. If he passed the necessary examinations in July, he could proceed later overseas to the Staff College at Camberley. Even when he was on duty in Ottawa he would be given opportunities for study. With these qualifications the path to higher promotion would be open to him.

Georges accepted the offer and on the 7th of September he met Byng in Ottawa to discuss his future duties. Byng agreed to the postponement of these until after Georges' wedding, which had been fixed for the 29th of September in the Basilica at Montreal. He and Pauline were married by Mgr Gauthier in front of the High Altar and its gilded baldachino. Pauline was given away by her father, with Tremblay as the best man; and when the ceremony was over the bridal pair passed to their waiting car under the swords of the bridegroom's brother officers, wearing service dress and medals. Lord and Lady Byng were the only significant – and very reluctant – absentees from a brilliant social occasion. The honeymoon was spent among the White Mountains at Dix-

14. Field-Marshal Viscount Byng of Vimy, 1862-1935.

ville Notch in New Hampshire. Georges' brother, Antoine, came with them as chauffeur; but three is never the best company, and never less so than on a honeymoon. There were occasions when Georges slipped his brother a five dollar bill to keep out of the way.

Although it had been arranged that the Vaniers should live at Rideau Cottage – the charming and spacious mid-nineteenth century house which stands in the grounds of Rideau Hall – they were not able to occupy it immediately. Most of the next two months were spent in lodgings at Kingston – 252 King Street – while Georges was studying at the Royal Military College. It was an unromantic residence – with a bed threatening to collapse – in a rather romantic setting, for the College on its peninsula, surrounded by maples and poplars, with lawns from the Officers' Mess running down to the water, and flanked by the Martello towers, looked out on to Lake Ontario and Simcoe and Wolfe islands not far from the shore. Here there were courses on topography, sketching, the use of outposts and advanced guards, and dispositions for attack and defence. By December the Vaniers were back at Rideau Cottage, and equally at home at Government House where the friendship with Lord Byng was very quickly cemented. On their first entrance into his study he had laid his hands on their shoulders and observed: 'Now you're members of the family.' Edward Greene, M.C. was Comptroller, and Captain Willis O'Connor,[15] Captain the Hon. F. W. Erskine, and Captain W. G. N. Jolliffe[16] were the other A.D.Cs. Georges had enough experience of the British army to find his feet easily in this entourage; and all the grace of manner to see that guests were properly looked after and that the right person was not put next to the wrong one. Willis O'Connor – whose presence at Government House was as permanent as anything can be in this changing world – had assured him that 'it's the only life; nothing like it'. Georges Vanier, who had knowledge of life elsewhere, might not have been so categorical; but he was well content.

His usefulness to Byng lay partly in the fact that he was able to improve the Governor General's very imperfect French. Even a British Governor General – and in 1921 no other kind was dreamt of – was expected to speak French on occasion. He was constantly being called upon to thank somebody for their 'bon accueil'. 'Accueil' was Byng's Waterloo – indeed the only Waterloo he had

15. Colonel Henry Willis O'Connor, 1886-1957.
16. Lieut-Colonel Lord Hylton, 1898-1967.

ever met – and eighteen months later we find him writing to Georges:

Your letter of 4th March had the warmest 'accool', 'acurl' – damn! I'll look it out – *accueil*, that's the one. I am getting better at it. I find a slight suspicion of a yodel, just where the vowels are thickest – u, e, and i – adds wonderfully to the effect. I tried it on a French M.P. who said it reminded him of the noise he made to entice a kitten.[17]

The Governor General's evident approval gave to the Vaniers an easy entry into Ottawa society, which was normally inclined to regard all French-Canadians as second class citizens. Hostesses ambitious for their débutante daughters came whispering round with 'Can't you get us into the ball?'

Relief from the duties of protocol came in December when Marshal Foch himself was a guest at Government House. Georges was quick to note his first impressions: 'strength and movement – an active, quick, almost hurrying man with well-knit body set on legs that have retained the form of the horse: the Commander-in-Chief of the Allied Armies and the Commander of the Third Army meet again; one has for the other a deep admiration.'[18] On the 12th of December Georges rejoined his regiment for the visit of its Colonel-in-Chief. 'I should have liked to arrive here as Colonel of the 22nd' the Marshal observed as Chassé greeted him 'but I could find nobody in the United States to make me a khaki uniform. Still, I have my little stick and I am proud to carry it.' A powdery snow was falling on the Parc des Champs de Bataille, whitening the moustaches and uniforms of the military, and clinging to the overcoats of the spectators. Archambault, now second-in-command, was acting as the Marshal's A.D.C., and Georges Vanier, standing with his brother officers, was free to record the details of a triumphant day:

A day of glory: the honorary colonel comes to review his regiment. Marshal of France and of Great Britain he is a symbol of the Entente Cordiale in the same way as is the French-speaking regiment serving under an oath of allegiance to the King.

At noon Marshal Foch arrives at the Citadel; he is carrying the regimental swagger-stick which, on his appointment, was sent to him by the Colonel; the guns of the R.S.G.A. thunder in his honour. The 'Royal 22e Régiment', under the command of Colonel Chassé,

17. 24th March 1923.
18. Personal Notes.

salutes: Marshal Foch inspects . . . shakes hands with each officer
. . . the Band plays 'La Madelon' . . . the regiment marches past to
the strains of 'Sambre et Meuse'. The Regimental Colour, a gift from
Marshal Foch, unfolds its wings. The Marshal congratulates Colonel
Chassé and the regiment. History writes and turns its pages quickly
– 1759 Montcalm – 1921 Foch.

Luncheon in the Officers' Mess: Colonel Chassé proposes the
Marshal's health who responds: 'It is with joy that I accepted the
appointment of Honorary Colonel of this Regiment. The "22e
Bataillon" took part and distinguished itself in most of the important
engagements between 1915 and 1918 . . . it is an honour for me to
belong to it . . .'[19]

Georges returned to Kingston in January 1922 while Pauline
stayed with her mother, and early in July he passed his examination at the Royal Military College with adequate marks, if not
with flying colours. Evidently his experience as Adjutant stood
him in good stead, for he did best in the papers on Business and
Imperial Organization. On the strength of these results, and with
high recommendation from Byng, he was accepted for the Staff
College at Camberley, and it was arranged for him to go there
in January 1923. Byng was naturally sorry to lose him, but agreed
that he would 'get more for his money' in Camberley than in
Canada. As the day drew near for them to leave, Pauline was
subject to a good deal of teasing as the other A.D.Cs began to
initiate her into the idiom and the necessities of English life. If
she wanted petrol she must not ask for gas; and if she wanted
ironmongery she must not ask for hardware; and she must not
pronounce 'schedule' as if she were pronouncing 'school'. She
was not a particularly logical person, but she must be more
illogical than she was already. Byng's affection for them both
grew as the months went by. Very often, in the early morning,
they would hear the pattering of pebbles on their bedroom window, and a voice below: 'Get up, you little Vaniers'. It was the
Governor General on his morning ride. On the night before they
left, Pauline shed such tears of emotion that he complained that
she had 'taken all the starch out of my front' – for in those days
shirts were really, not figuratively, boiled. Before the year was
out he was writing to her:

We miss you two dreadfully. We miss you inside and outside the
house. We miss you the sunny side and the blizzard side. We miss you
greatly.[20]

19. Personal Notes.   20. 29th December 1922.

To Georges he wrote – as always, in long hand – with thanks for

... help unstintingly given, unsparingly thorough and helpful, of a value which it is not possible to express tho' quite possible to appreciate. Your work here has been admirable, always for good and always of a nature to merit my deepest approval and affection.

I suppose an Englishman should keep his pipe of affection very carefully soldered, but somehow with you and Pauline I have allowed a leakage, I could not help it, and I feel I should like you to know how sincere my affection is for you both.[21]

This was only the beginning of a great creative friendship which counted equally for the younger man and for his chief. When the Vaniers left Government House they little imagined under what circumstances they would return to it; but they had been set an example of constitutional authority which they were not likely to forget.

21. 18th September 1922.

CHAPTER 6

TOWARDS COMMAND

I

ON arrival in England on the 3rd of December the Vaniers went straight to the Stafford Hotel, in the heart of London's West End. Flowers and a letter from Lord Byng's sister, Lady Margaret Boscawen, were waiting for them, and when Georges met her at luncheon the next day he found her very much like her brother – with a charm less physical than moral, the reflection of an innate goodness. Only a few doors from the Stafford in St James's Street was Sifton Praed's Map House where Georges made the acquaintance of Mr Praed himself and bought a Bartholomew's Guide to London. Other military books and maps he would acquire there in due course. Mr Praed spoke of the great officers he had known and served – Horne[1] and Haig and Lord Byng himself, whose hand he claimed to have shaken before the General left for Canada.

The Vaniers then went on to spend a fortnight with Lord Byng's nephew, the Earl of Strafford, at Wrotham Park in Hertfordshire. The establishment, with its footmen standing with candles at the bottom of the stairs, was not such a far cry from Government House. The contrast to Rideau Hall, and even to Rideau Cottage, came when they settled down at Camberley in a house called 'Balgonie', named after a place in Fife with a ruined castle and a coal pit but bearing no resemblance to either. Byng had sent Georges a few words of fatherly advice:

I think you will really like the good young Englishmen you will meet at Camberley. Unlike the Frenchman, whose nimble brain and vivacity make him such a lively and fascinating acquaintance, you may find my countrymen ponderous in thought, but remember it is national, and our very ponderosity, tho' irritating, has led to some sound judgments and careful decisions. So don't altogether despise it, tho' it may probably give you many a moment of amusement.

One little word more of advice. Don't be too keen to write your opinions for others to read. They frequently take the form of

1. General Lord Horne of Stirkoke, 1861-1929.

'spasms', and everybody has a spasm occasionally, but people invariably like their own spasms best and only read the other fellow's out of civility. Read all you can of other people's opinions before giving your own to the world. I think it is best, and I think you will find it so.

Georges had a natural propensity for putting down his thoughts on paper, but how or where he had been circulating them is not clear. He was most unlikely to have done so at Camberley where the Vaniers had little to do in their spare time but contemplate the rhododendrons when they happened to be in bloom. An overheard 'There go the little colonials!' gives the measure of their exclusion from the social establishment. All this, however, was presently to be changed; and in the meantime encouragement came from the C.I.G.S. himself, Lord Cavan,[2] a nephew of Lord Byng by marriage, who had procured them a cook – an acquisition not altogether due, as Byng wrote, 'to Pauline's way with the male':

'So if at any time', he continued, 'you are desirous of undeserved promotion or unauthorized indulgence, a line enclosing a cheque to me will probably produce anything from a F.M.'s baton for yourself to another reinforced pyramidical knitting-needle for yr wife. . . .'

Pauline could certainly do with knitting-needles for she was expecting her first baby. Thérèse Marie Chérisy Vanier was born at Camberley on the 27th of February 1923 and baptized on the 4th of March. 'She's the Major all over' was an early comment, to be justified abundantly as the years went by. Byng wrote that he liked the accents over her first name: 'like Jiggs' eyebrows'. Jiggs was his favourite cat.

Camberley lies thirty-five miles to the south-west of London, and the Staff College is situated in beautiful grounds, adjoining the Royal Military Academy of Sandhurst. Originally it occupied the west wing of the R.M.A. The present building of honey-coloured stone and brick was designed in the contemporary Italian style by James Pennythorne, and founded in 1859 by the Duke of Cambridge, whose bewhiskered portrait has a place of honour inside. A third storey, with slate facing to the roof, was added in 1912; and there have been several subsequent enlargements. But the general appearance of the building, at once solid and elegant, with an observatory – now of purely decorative interest – on the north end of the roof, has remained unchanged.

2. Field-Marshal the Earl of Cavan, 1860-1946.

The interior is built round a central hall, on the model of a Roman bath, embellished by lances from the Crimea, pistols from the Tower of London, and swords and cuirasses from the battle-field of Edgehill. The War Memorial of blue and brown Hornton stone, also quarried from Edgehill, and commemorating the 203 officers who had passed through the College since 1873, now stood in place of a door in the north wall. It was some time, however, before baths were provided for the inmates. The library, with its alcoves and barrel roof – all lit from above by stained-glass windows – oak panelling and fluted pilasters, was particularly congenial for study. The croquet lawn and tennis-courts, sur-rounded by beeches, pines and rhododendrons, led down from the west front through well-kept borders to an ornamental water. On the other side were the stables – for every officer was entitled to a horse and batman and expected to ride in the local 'Drag'. Lord Byng had been secretary of this in 1893-4.

The College was organized in two Divisions with sixty students in each, none of them below the rank of Captain. These were sub-divided into Syndicates of ten, and the relations between the students and the Directing Staff were of the greatest ease and friendliness. Among Georges Vanier's contemporaries were a number of men who later won distinction in the Second World War; Major and Brevet Lieut-Colonel H. G. D. Crerar D.S.O.,[3] from the Royal Canadian Artillery; A. R. Goodwin-Austen, the explorer and author of *The Staff and the Staff College*; Major C. W. M. Willoughby Norrie,[4] one of the mechanised cavaliers of the West-ern Desert; Captain A. E. Nye;[5] and Brigadier J. G. Smyth.[6] Major Alan Brooke (later Field-Marshal Lord Alanbrooke) was a mem-ber of the Directing Staff. Harry Crerar was the only other Canadian student, and Georges was to remember how he 'made certain representations on my behalf when I got fed up with study and teachers.'[7]

The Commandant was Major-General Sir Edmund – 'Tiny' – Ironside.[8] In his introductory lecture he stressed that British Staff work in the 1914-18 war had not been good, and in many

3. General H. G. D. Crerar, 1888-1965.
4. Lord Willoughby Norrie of Wellington, New Zealand and Upton, Gloucestershire.
5. Lieut-General Sir Archibald Nye, British High Commissioner in Ottawa 1952-6.
6. Brigadier the Right Hon. Sir J. G. Smyth.
7. Letter to H. D. G. Crerar, 28th April 1962.
8. Field-Marshal Lord Ironside of Archangel and Ironside, 1880-1959.

instances inferior to the French and German. The College was not a dead academy for the teaching of dead subjects. It was a live institution and the business of the instructors was to find out what was alive in those who came to study there. 'I do not care' he said, 'about the bald facts of military history – what a certain general did on a certain day at such an hour. Apply what you read to your own experience and to the future.' He would not ask the students for lectures in the ordinary way, except on such foreign countries as they happened to visit. But he would arrange lectures for them on psychology and logic, for in future wars – and here he showed considerable prescience – it would be 'easy enough to be a soldier, but a civilian's life won't be worth living'. He stressed the value of improvisation, and went on to speak of the little room where the portraits of many Field-Marshals were hanging:

Go there and have a look at their faces – some are very refined faces. I like that room very much, so don't make a bear-garden of the place, have your fights elsewhere – or I shall come down on you like a ton of bricks.

The course of study lasted for two years, and Georges Vanier – for all the active service he had seen – was in the position of a 'new boy'. Here again Byng was ready with encouragement and advice:

The senior term will probably patronize you a bit, but let them; you will get yr own back next year and it is great fun being told about things you probably already know. . . . Your professors will be summing you up but not so much as you will be summing them up. They will ask you seemingly innocent questions such as 'Can one use a mashie in the middle of a Canadian winter?' This will really be meant to know if you consider that 'surprise is the hand-maid of victory' – but you will find it all out for yrself, and I have told you all I know.

Among the many other things that Georges learnt at the Staff College was that a newspaper is an essential part of an officer's equipment in the Officers' Mess, and that to clap a British officer on the back during breakfast is a very unsafe proceeding, however amiable the intention.

Ironside, with his imposing height and command of several languages, had all the authority he required; and he was ably

9. 3rd January 1923.

seconded by Colonel J. E. C. – 'Boney' – Fuller[10] who was Chief
Instructor. 'Prevision' he told them in his initial lecture, 'is the
highest form of judgment', and as a foremost proponent of
mobile tank warfare he had given signal proof of it. This, he
emphasized, had been the secret of Napoleon's success. War must
be studied first as a science, and then as an art. Nothing should
be taken at its face value: 'if you don't ask yourself "why?" you
are mentally standing at ease.' Knowledge, judgment and method
must all be cultivated, but method should mean something more
than manuals. Manuals were for average men, and armies were
composed of average men. An army with a bad method was better
than an army with no method at all. But manuals did not exon-
erate a soldier from using his own brains. 'We give you the food
to swallow – you do the digesting afterwards – and the digesting is
the more important. We will assist you to work, but we will not
drive you.'

In discussing the science of war Fuller borrowed Huxley's
definition of 'co-ordinated common-sense', and he defined common-sense as 'thought or action adapted to circumstances'. War
itself was a means to an end and should be prosecuted with as
little force as possible. The Battle of Ligny was an example of this
economy. For reading he recommended Bloch's *The War of the
Future*, Dodge's *Great Captains* and, at the suggestion of the
C.I.G.S., Manders' *Campaign in Mesopotamia*. But he advised the
young officers not only to study great captains, but fools and
charlatans as well; to distinguish between Napoleon or Gustavus
Adolphus, and others who had merely copied their methods and
used brute force in doing so. All the students had some experience
of soldiering, but personal experience – Fuller emphasized – was
both useful and dangerous. He encouraged them to study the
peace time conditions of other countries – the workings of their
politics and finance. Finally he stressed the value of sport, since
'the rules of war are very like the rules of sport'. Here Georges
Vanier was at an obvious disadvantage. His favourite game was
tennis and inspired by Suzanne Lenglen, whom he watched at
Wimbledon in July, he even took lessons from a professional.

If the drawing-rooms of Camberley were closed to the Vaniers,
Windsor Castle was open to them. Here Lord Stamfordham,[11]
Private Secretary to King George V, and a nephew of Lord Byng
by marriage, entertained them to luncheon in the Winchester

10. Major-General J. F. C. Fuller, 1878-1966.
11. Lord Stamfordham, 1849-1931.

Tower; and on the 22nd of May they were invited to dine with
the King and Queen at Aldershot for Byng's pen had not been idle.
The King had a brief word with Georges before dinner, and Lady
Ampthill, Lady-in-Waiting to Queen Mary, had a brief word with
Pauline about her hair-do. She then presented her to the Queen,
who made polite enquiries about Georges' leg, and observed that
although she quite understood the French wanting their repara-
tions she did not think they were going about it in the right way.
In this she was in accord with the consensus of British opinion.
She had been well briefed and also enquired about Thérèse.

During dinner the King talked most of the time with Ironside;
afterwards he came up to Georges and spoke with him for about
five minutes. The conversation went as follows:

K :   How did you get on as A.D.C. with your leg?
G.V. Quite well, your Majesty.
K :   Do you ride?
G.V. Not very well, Sir.
K :   That's right, don't try to ride. It's dangerous – you can't get
      your balance. Is Lord Byng popular?
G.V. Nobody can be more popular. He was appointed at the psy-
      chological moment –
K :   Yes, yes. Is Lady Byng popular?
G.V. Yes, Sir. One of her great assests is her knowledge of French.
K :   Does she speak well?
G.V. Like a Parisienne.
K :   Ah yes, I remember. Have you much unemployment?
G.V. No, your Majesty.
K :   Ah yes, unfortunately we have that great trouble – one million
      unemployed – very sad. There is no work for them. In spite of
      the War there are 150,000 more people in England than in 1914.
      No wonder we have unemployment. We must send English-
      men to Canada. But you have too many Americans, you mustn't
      let them in. Some people tell me Canadians talk of separation
      from the Empire – I don't believe it. I know the Canadians too
      well.

The conversation also turned on Baldwin's appointment as
Prime Minister. The King then told Georges to sit down and a
chair was brought, while the Queen was asking Pauline whether
she pronounced her name Vanier or Vanié and observing – with
a somersault of royal diplomacy – that she 'loved the Canadian
climate'. Then the King came up and found Georges disregarding
the chair which had been brought for him.

K :   I've told your husband to sit down, but he won't even listen to

the King. . . . Have you been to Toronto? Aha! French-Canadian,
you have never been to Toronto. You don't like Toronto. Aha!
the rivalry between the two cities.

G.V. I hope you don't think we're so narrow-minded.

K : No, I was only teasing you. I hope you know Ottawa?

G.V. Yes, we were there sometime with Lord Byng.

K : Of course you had to go there, but you didn't like it?

G.V. Oh yes, we loved it.

K : I'm only ragging you. The first time I went to Canada you
weren't born – that was in 1883. But you never can tell (with
a sly glance at Pauline) women know how to hide their age. But
you're not forty.[12]

He then asked where and when Georges had lost his leg, and
hearing that it was in August 1918 observed what a 'terrible show'
that had been. Princess Mary was also in the party, but the
Vaniers found her less easy to talk to.

The result of these conversations was that Camberley society
changed its tune overnight. Where the Vaniers had hitherto contented themselves with Harry Crerar – who was also studying
at the College and as an English Canadian was considered slightly
less 'colonial' – they were now flooded with invitations. Georges
lectured to the College on the organization of the Military Forces
in Canada during the late war, and Crerar on their organization
prior to 1914. An essay of Georges on Sir John Moore won high
praise from Fuller; there were phrases here which might stand
as an epitaph on Georges Vanier himself:

As nature was kind to Moore, so Moore was kind to nature. Every
talent he received was returned twofold when the time of accounting
came. His was a good stewardship. . . . The fight was always uphill
with – at the end of the fight – a wound and another hill.

The future of tank warfare was discussed in detail during the
winter term of 1924. Tanks would become the decisive arm on all
ground over which they could move freely; and infantry should
therefore be trained for operation in mountains, forests or
swamps. The function of cavalry would be no longer to fight, but
to observe and report; and artillery must be motorized. As the
use of tanks was developed, the work of the Field Engineer would
consist in delaying or facilitating their movement. The main
exercise of the term – proposed by the War Office – was particularly interesting in view of subsequent events. This envisaged the

12. Personal Notes.

despatch by Japan of an Expeditionary Force for the capture of
Singapore. The Naval, Army and Air Force Staff Colleges combined to work this out with an eye to the time when Singapore
had been reasonably fortified and its garrison increased. By an
ironic chance the man responsible for the defence of Singapore
was one of Georges Vanier's fellow-students, and one would like
to know how far the scheme anticipated tactics against which
neither garrison nor fortifications were of any avail whatever.

2

On the 16th of April 1924 Georges set out with Harry Crerar
and three other officers on a tour of Czechoslovakia and Hungary.
Their object was to study the political conditions and military
dispositions of these countries. Passing through Germany they
were struck by the many new factories along the line and the
general appearance of prosperity. During a four hour wait at
Dresden Georges visited the Art Gallery. On arrival in Prague
they were installed at the Palais Passage Hotel, and afterwards
shown the 'Aero' factory where five hundred workmen were employed in turning out five or six military aircraft a week. Later
they visited the Aviation Centre at Kbelj, six miles north-east
of Prague, and on the following day were much impressed by the
size of the Skoda works at Pilsen and the variety of its manufactures. The Ecole de Guerre in Prague was modelled on its French
counterpart; both the Commandant and many of the staff were
French. Among the officers training there no marked difference
was observed between those who had served in France, Italy and
Siberia, but the difference was clear between those who had fought
with the Czech Legion and those who had served throughout the
war with the Austrian army. The officers were not well turned
out – one was seen to have neither his belt nor his buttons polished
– and they did not appear to represent the best type of young
man, nor to occupy a very high position in the social life of
the country. Their attitude towards the French Military Mission
was anything but cordial. The men were largely of peasant stock
and sturdy physique, but not very amenable to discipline. The
visiting officers from Camberley concluded that the German elements in the army would be the most efficient, in the event of war,
and they suspected that the sympathies of many Slovaks would
lie with Hungary rather than with their own country. Consolidation of its various races was essential if Czechoslovakia were to
hold its own; and in any case the shape of the country and its

internal communications made it difficult to defend. Fear of a
German-Austrian combination, with Hungary ready to take advantage of it, was very strong; and Georges Vanier concluded that,
if the crunch came, the Czechs probably would not fight. In this
prediction he was correct.

On Easter Sunday he walked round the city; visited the Church
of St Vitus on the Hradzy heights; and attended a performance of
The Bartered Bride at the National Opera in the evening. The following day the Camberley 'Syndicate' were shown the grottoes of
Macocha, where the stalactites and stalagmites grew at a rate of
one square inch in thirty-two years. They were then taken to the
battlefield of Austerlitz. A Czech officer explained the battle from
the Pratzen Heights, and Georges noted that 'the God of Battles
was certainly with Napoleon, so that from his point of view in
the morning he could see the Russians withdrawing from the
Pratzen Heights, whilst his own dispositions in the valley were
hidden by fog.'[13] The landscape was practically unaltered since
1804, but certain features of tactical importance showed up in
contrast to pre-conceived ideas. One noticed in particular the
open and rolling character of the terrain; the low elevation and
gradual slopes of the Pratzen Heights; the strength of the main
French position despite its lower elevation; the insignificance of
the Goldbach river which could not have constituted a serious
obstacle, except to artillery; the virtual lack of cover which gave
extensive visibility, except from relatively low elevations; and
the facilities afforded by numerous slight valleys for the conceal-
ment of troops not actually in movement. One detail, however,
their guide omitted to explain to them. In 1804 the ground to the
right of the French position had been broken by a number of
small lakes. These had since been filled in, but they would have
naturally modified Napoleon's freedom of manoeuvre. The
attempt to elucidate his reasoning by a study of the battlefield
justified his own maxim that 'the whole art of war consists in a
well-reasoned and extremely circumspect defensive followed by
a rapid and audacious attack'.

A visit to Bratislava followed. Here they watched a small combined exercise, in the presence of the French General, Spiré, who
was in command of the army in Slovakia. Spiré observed that the
Bratislava bridgehead between Czechoslovakia, Austria and
Hungary was quite inadequate. A broad belt of barbed wire en-
tanglement, in a bad state of repair, was the only sign of defence,

13. Diary.

and this had been erected in 1920 during the Béla Kun régime in Hungary.

The party next proceeded to Budapest where a certain Mr Braun, who had lost a leg on the Russian front and spoke fairly good English, acted as their cicerone. Georges described him as 'a very fine-looking man, with a charming personality, and a gentleman to his finger-tips. We thought he must represent the best type of Hungarian aristocrat'.[14] Conversation with Braun and the officers – equally aristocratic – to whom he introduced them revealed the bitter intensity of Hungarian nationalism. Deprived of two thirds of her territory and the natural resources to assure a prosperous future, reduced from a population of twenty millions to a bare eight and a half and encircled by hostile neighbours, Hungary was little more than a living skeleton. Rumania had gained territory at her expense because she had backed the winning side; Czechoslovakia had recovered its nationhood because it had revolted against the losing side. She had been rewarded for her revolt where Hungary had paid the price of her loyalty. It was small wonder the Treaty of Trianon was derided as iniquitous. The Syndicate met a Hungarian with a Czech wife whose father had died in Czechoslovakia. The Czech government refused him leave to attend the funeral. His own mother lived in Transylvania and it was only after the intervention of the Hungarian Minister in Bucharest that he was allowed to visit her. Finally, his household effects were all in Vienna where he had lived before the war. 'Thank God,' he exclaimed, 'I have nothing in Yugoslavia.'

Moving as they did in an aristocratic milieu – for the Hungarian nobility had close personal ties with England – the Syndicate observed that the upper classes were remote from the mass of the people – not through lack of sympathy but through ignorance of the revolution which was transforming societies elsewhere. Their own experience of Béla Kun was hardly calculated to foster radical opinions. Taking the support of the peasantry for granted without realizing the need for democratic progress, they had addressed an appeal to the English Bishops – whose political influence they rather naïvely overrated – and were disappointed when this met with no response. Where others talked of 'before the war' the Hungarians spoke of 'in the peace'; the war was too disastrous to be mentionable. The extreme nationalists were also violently anti-Semitic. M. Gombos, a young man of thirty-six, a member of Parliament, and previously a Staff Captain in the regular Hungar-

14. Diary.

ian army, was the leader of a party called 'Protectors of the Race'. It was even imagined that Lord Northcliffe was a Jew; and the Syndicate remarked that the Jews were an essential factor in the business life of the country, many of the Hungarians standing aside and not wishing to soil their hands with trade. Any afternoon in the tea room of the Ritz Hotel in Budapest was like a Jewish festival. To the Socialist who wanted the world to be 'a forest with trees of equal height' the nationalists replied that they wanted nothing of the kind. They wanted 'the tree of Hungary to be the tallest and the best'. Regarding Rumania and Yugoslavia as former enemies and therefore entitled to some share of booty, they reserved their special hate for the Czechs. If one warned them about the output of the Skoda works, they answered that the man behind the Skoda gun was more important than the gun itself, and they were confident that they could go through the Czech army 'like a knife through butter'.

The Rumanians were despised rather than feared, because they were such bad judges of horse-flesh; the Prussians were admired, but without affection; the Poles were given a very short lease of life; the English were grouped with the Germans under the 'Saxon' label, and should have known better than to enter the war on the wrong side; the French and Russians were equally hated; but the old antagonism to Austria seemed to have disappeared. The ancient Crown of Hungary was waiting for a claimant, and if an English Prince of the Blood could not be persuaded to accept it – for this would be the most popular choice – they would favour a Bavarian Prince. There were moments when the Syndicate must have fancied themselves in Ruritania, but there was no mistaking the national mood of fanatical revisionism as they heard the school-children chanting the new Hungarian Credo:

> I believe in One God;
> I believe in a single Fatherland;
> I believe in the eternal truth of God;
> And I believe in the resurrection of Hungary.

Before they left, the British and Canadian officers visited the Royal Palace with its superb ballroom and terraced gardens – now sadly neglected. In the afternoon they were received by the Regent, Admiral Horthy, dressed in naval uniform with six rows of medals and speaking fluent English. On either side of the door leading to his apartment was a flag. One had been presented by the Veuds, a people living in a part of old Hungary which now belonged to Yugoslavia. It bore the inscription: 'National Flag of the Hungarian Veuds mourning for Hungary. We will mourn until we are reunited with Hungary once more.' The other had been presented by the Hungarian women of Transylvania, and expressed similar sentiments. The Admiral invited his guests to sit down at a small table and offered them cigarettes. They remained with him for more than an hour. He gave them an impression of honesty and straightforwardness; of a man more accustomed to action than the diplomacy with which he was now concerned; without personal ambition, but prepared to accept heavy responsibilities from a sense of patriotism and public duty. He looked into the future with a tempered optimism, believing a restoration of Hungary's historic frontiers to be inevitable and just, but not expecting to see them restored tomorrow, or even the day after. Georges Vanier noticed an iron safe built into the wall of the study. It was here that the Hungarian Crown was kept – the 'last remaining symbol of the Kingdom of Hungary saved from the Bolsheviks by the efforts of the English General Gorton and the American Admiral.'[15]

On the following day the Syndicate was part of a large crowd watching the mounting of the Palace Guard. Georges observed that the thirty-two men of the rank and file handled their arms well and goose-stepped smartly, but their marching did not otherwise impress him. As the Governor of the Palace drove up in his closed car, the band broke into the very sad strains of the Hungarian National Anthem. It was an appropriate *envoi* to the Syndicate of Officers from the Staff College, who had come to see what was happening in a country with which they had recently been at war.

3

In the middle of June Georges Vanier received a letter which is of exceptional interest because it foreshadowed the non-political influence that he was afterwards to exercise in Canadian affairs. A friend in Montreal, Robertson Fleet, was worried – with many others – about the signs of national disunity. Groups to counteract this were being formed at the University Club and elsewhere, with the blessing of the Governor General, and became known as the Canada League. Fleet's letter showed how people were already looking to Georges as an instrument of reconciliation:

15. Diary.

We here in Montreal are living in a hot-bed of prejudice, where everyone damns the Westerner and calls him selfish and says he cares nothing for the country as a whole, whereas the Westerner doubtless is
living in a somewhat similar atmosphere on the other side of the
fence. The manufacturer in the East is yelling for more production
and the farmer in the West is complaining bitterly of the fact that
he can't be protected and the cost of living is exorbitant. The
Westerner thinks salvation lies in the Hudson Bay Rly – the
Montrealer will not hear of such a wild scheme.

And where is all this leading us to? One trembles to think of it.
If this country is split, everyone will suffer, and shdn't each man
realize that his future – his prosperity – is bound up with that of his
neighbour even tho' the two be separated by the Lake Superior District or the long line of the Intercolonial Railway. Up at Ottawa we
have our representatives – some doing their best – others grafting or
voting on party lines and some too stupid to know what they are
doing or care.

I won't enlarge on these things – you know all about them, no
doubt, better than I do but we want your ideas. We want them on
the main big subject of what can be done and at the same time on a
very important phase of the question – namely what can be done with
the French Canadians. They come into this, and very vitally, not
only because they form a large proportion of the inhabitants of the
country but also because . . . their prosperity is wrapped up with
Canada and they constitute one of the sanest, if not the sanest element.
Wd it be possible to get them interested, and how? Whenever this
so-called 'French-English' question . . . comes up, I always think of you
as a solver of difficulties. So in distress I turn to you now.[16]

The Byngs were over in England during the summer and the
Vaniers saw them at their home at Thorpe-le-Soken in Essex. The
Governor General had had four teeth out in the spring and 'managed "acurl" without foaming at the mouth'. Georges had sent him
a bottle of brandy to which he replied with 'mes chaleureuses (sic)
remerciements pour votre bonté et au nom du roi je vous donne
congé – as I tell the Mayor when I have made certain he is an
Englishman'. He brought news of Willis O'Connor going down a
gold mine wearing a miner's hat which made him 'look like a
dyspeptic charwoman' and 'warbling "Don't go down the mine,
Daddy" at intervals.' The Governor General thought it was meant
for himself. He told Georges of Archambault who had
succeeded him as A.D.C., and was greatly liked, but did not
always have a forthcoming manner with guests. 'With six French
M.Ps for dinner, his only remark was "Pass the salt, please" in

16. 22nd June 1924.

broken English.' And there was an account of a dinner in Montreal at which the Governor General was to meet eight men 'who had not had the privilege of meeting me', six of whom he had seen the same day or the evening before.

During the summer term exercises were held to illustrate the organization of an overseas base in an allied country already at war. Falmouth was chosen as the available port, with Britain presumed to be at a distance of eight days steaming from it. It was shown that effective military assistance to an ally, under these circumstances, was essentially an administrative problem, provided that command of the sea were assured. In June a week of mountain warfare exercises near Harlech, in North Wales, was found to duplicate very closely conditions on the North-West Frontier of India. Other exercises included the hasty reconnaissance of a position behind which a hard pressed army could re-form, in a situation parallel to that which confronted the Fifth Army in March 1918; the employment of a highly mobile mechanical force to strike a decisive blow at the enemy flank and rear – here Colonel Fuller envisaged a rather bolder action on the part of the force engaged, for the problem was to minimize the interval between the tank attack and the infantry consolidation; and a raid on the enemy's main railway communications, with the destruction of a vital bridge in anticipation of a subsequent decisive attack.

In the autumn Fuller lectured on training. Self-control, self-confidence, voluntary action and originality were the four qualities which would permit an officer to distribute his forces to the fullest effect. As usual, he emphasized the rôle of tanks – which was not the protection of slow-moving infantry. They should be used in strength, and when their work was completed should rally in the rear. They should be given elbow-room to facilitate manoeuvre, and be trained to debouch properly from their position of assembly. Very soon another military theorist would be propounding similar ideas, but Colonel de Gaulle's *armée de métier* was condemned to remain largely theoretical while Rommel and Guderian were putting the theory into effect.

Some of the indoor exercises were confidential, in order not to give offence to friendly nations. It was assumed, for example, that the Government had decided on military action against Afghanistan which was in a state of unrest and had been guilty of hostile activities on the borders. Here it was concluded that the Chaman-Kandahar route should be followed, although the distance to

Kabul was two hundred miles further than by way of Jamrud and Jellalabad. A war was also presumed between England and Scotland, in which England had a powerful air force and a weak army and navy, and Scotland the reverse. Or how would Military Intelligence deal with the despatch of an expeditionary force to Turkey? There were also visits to the school of artillery at Larkhill, and to the Naval Dockyard at Portsmouth, with trips in submarines and coastal motor boats. In December Georges Vanier, now with the rank of Lieut-Colonel, went on a course for Commanding Officers; and Byng was writing from Ottawa:

There is a lot which will cause you to sniff, to smile, to hausser les epaules (French), to frotter les mains (more French) and to se moquer (still more French) about it all, but being ultracareful not to take a hand in the Military arrangements here, I contented myself with silence not unmixed with wonder.

He added that Willis O'Connor – 'l'enfant prodigue d'Ottawa' – was in grand form, but, having so many babies in the house, got mixed with the diets and ended by eating them all himself, and then complained that he was tired. There had also been the usual Household Dance, where 'I capered with the new cook – her temperature seemed about 80° above, so it was like dancing with a baked apple.'[17]

In spite of his disclaimer Byng was naturally hoping that Georges would get the command of the Royal 22nd; and his appointment was gazetted on the 29th of July 1925, dated from the 24th of April. The autumn term ended with the usual theatricals, dances and other revelries; and when these were over the Vaniers went off to St Cergues in Switzerland for winter sports. In a circular letter sent to his friends at the New Year Georges wrote:

The snow forgot to fall with the result that most of our time was spent in praying. As a matter of fact I do not know what I was praying for, because it was much more pleasant to bask in the sunshine than to pretend that I was taking part in the sports. Whilst others were skiing when there was snow I hired a funny little truncated bob-sleigh and played with myself or with any little playmate, male or female, that happened along.

After spending enough time in Switzerland to feel like a lion we returned to England and I proceeded to the S.O.S.[18] Sheerness. Whether it was too much Staff College and too much Switzerland my whole being revolted at the idea of lectures and schemes and I lay down and was ill.

17. 28th December 1924.   18. Special Officers School.

When Pauline went to his rescue, he met her in a green Citroën with all his luggage packed – and the agreement of Ironside that he had much better return to Canada. 'I hear you speak seven languages' Pauline had observed to the towering Commandant. Not many men were tall enough to look down on Pauline Vanier, but 'Tiny' Ironside was one of them. 'Twelve' he replied benignly.

CHAPTER 7

THE CITADEL

I

THE Vaniers had not long been installed at the Citadel when the Royal 22nd was drawn into an ugly industrial dispute. In the spring of 1924 the British Empire Steel Company, which owned several mines on Cape Breton island, was losing its Montreal market and being undersold by American coal. It was therefore decided to reduce the cost of coal production in Nova Scotia. A number of inspectors, superintendents and other officials were dismissed, and salaries were cut from 10 to 25 per cent. This resulted in an annual saving of about a million dollars. The United Mine Workers were informed that their existing contract, due to expire on the 15th of January 1925, would be cancelled, and the U.M.W. convention replied by asking for an increase in wages. This demand was subsequently dropped, and the miners agreed to continue at their existing rates of pay if the business of the coal company were submitted to investigation. The Vice-President of BESCO, McLurg, did not make things easier by stating that a man with a family could live on $17.50 a week, and the workers refused to recognize either the Conciliation Board or the Royal Commission that was set up. On the 5th of March 1925 the crisis was exasperated by a shortage of food. The store credit was stopped at three of the mines, and when McLurg refused to restore them a strike was called. By a majority of over a thousand the men favoured the Government's proposal for a settlement.

The physical conditions in the Cape Breton coal-mines were very inferior to those in the United States; the children went about in sackcloth and lived on four cent meals. The serious trouble began at Glace Bay where incendiaries took possession of the mining town of Reserve. A powder magazine was set on fire, and the relatives of a coal company stableman were seized by masked men in the crowd. It was at this point that the Royal 22nd was called in to assist the police. Barbed wire was stretched all along Union Street, and sentries put on guard. The Lake Power Plant at Waterford was occupied, and a second company, with

Lewis guns and full war-time equipment, stationed at Glace Bay. It was uncongenial employment, although the police – and above all the British Empire Steel Company – had to bear the brunt of popular indignation. The following verses give the measure of local sympathies:

The Waterford Raid.
T'was on a Thursday morning, and all was going well,
Until those Besco Policemen marched in and raised up Hell,
All mounted on Pit horses, with Billies by their side,
Into the town of Waterford those Besco Bums did ride.

And straight toward the Power Plant where wires were all
    pulled down.
And lights and water were shut off and left a gloomy town.
When the miners heard of this, to vengeance they gave vent,
And straight toward the Power Plant, twelve hundred men sent.

But ere that day was over it was a sad affair,
For one of our poor fellow-men was shot while standing there.
Some injured here, some injured there, a broken leg or arm
Those Besco Bums were carried home after doing so much harm.
I guess it will be a long time before those Cops shall dare,
To ride the streets of Waterford and look at the miners and sneer.

One of the local magistrates was himself a striker. He normally drove a Donkey engine and was paid twelve dollars for an eight hour day spent entirely in the mine. Another maintenance man, whom Georges met in the shower room, was sixty years of age and still spent twelve hours stoking in the hottest weather. In general, the 'Van Doos' held a watching brief in the dispute, and the most unfortunate incident was when Georges was awakened at 2.40 a.m. with the news that one of his Sergeants had had a leg broken in the Guard Room during a scuffle with a drunken miner, who had been brought in to sleep off his liquor.

On the 30th of November 1925 Pauline gave birth to a son at the Citadel. He was christened Georges, but since Lord and Lady Byng had agreed to be godparents he became known as Byngsie. The Governor General wrote with characteristic generosity and good sense:

The suggestions I have in mind are the usual mug, cup, pot, horn or tankard suitable for liquid refreshment during infancy, adolescence, youthful manhood, riper years and possibly the period (at which I have arrived) described as senility. The other alternative, which I think a better one, is to insure Vanier Jr's education – i.e. invest a sum of money now to which he becomes entitled at the age of 13 when he might possibly be considering a course of tuition.[1]

Georges wrote to a friend that he meant to make of Byngsie 'the champion amateur boxer of Canada'. As we shall see, he became something very different. Georges himself was laid up for a fortnight with a feverish cold and intestinal infection, but what concerned him more than this was the danger of fire in and around the Citadel. There had already been a spectacular fire at the Château Frontenac, which had been partially destroyed, and his own garage had been burnt to the ground, with three cars belonging to officers of the regiment. In these circumstances he thought it wise to remove the explosives from the powder magazines, which were bedded deeply in the rock, since the stronger the container the greater would be the explosion. He recommended that the wooden snow porch be removed; that the roof be recovered if and when it was found necessary; and that a barrier be constructed to keep unauthorized persons at a distance. This could not be done without the sanction of the Quartermaster-General, and by the end of April the explosives had not yet been removed, as Georges Vanier had advised, to Levis on the southern shore of the St Lawrence. Georges protested respectfully but vigorously – the more so since three fires had broken out in the grass between the Citadel and Cove Field Barracks. The existing conditions, he wrote, 'would not be tolerated for a moment in any well conducted civilian establishment'. The magazines were unsafe for even the smallest quantity of explosives; barriers were essential. 'Any man can jump over the low wall around A Magazine and set fire, if he has incendiary tendencies, to the roof which is of wood, or the platform leading to and touching the main entrance to the Magazine.' He went on to quote an Order-in-Council of the 21st of April 1926:

No permanent Magazine shall be located at a distance less than 400 ft. from any other building, railway, highway, or working place; except where the Magazine is surrounded by an embankment of stoneless earth, of sufficient thickness, and exceeding by at least three feet in height the coping of the building.

He renewed his protests before leaving for camp on the 21st of May, but it was not until the end of June that the explosives were removed.

1. 4th January 1926.

Georges Vanier was never afraid to speak his mind to superior authority; it was not by docility that he had won his way to this important command. A high-ranking officer had been entertained in the Mess, and in writing his thanks had expressed the hope that 'in future the officers will take things more seriously'. Vanier was not going to take this lying down and at once asked for an explanation. 'The best years of my life are bound up with the 22nd . . . and anything that touches my officers affects me vitally.' The staff officer replied that the officers of the Royal 22nd should work harder in order to pass their promotion exams. He was also annoyed by political interference on their behalf. Vanier was still not appeased and the officer in question expressed his surprise at the stand he was taking on what was intended to be a private letter of thanks for hospitality.

On the 7th of June Georges was invited to give the Commencement Address at Loyola. The College had moved its premises and grown apace since he had been there. In 1900 there were only seven graduates; now there were twenty-two, and among them students from the United States, Mexico, and British Honduras. Having been an ardent pugilist himself, and cherishing similar ambitions for Byngsie, he quoted Milton's advice to the young: 'They must be also practised in all the locks and grips of wrestling, as need may often be in fight, to tag, to grapple, and to close'. He also quoted Julian Grenfell:

> For life is colour and warmth and light
> And a striving evermore for these
> And he is dead, who will not fight
> And who dies fighting has increase.

The main theme of his address was character. He recalled a Loyola boy killed in action and hardly out of his teens, in command of a platoon of men who knew more about war than he could ever have learnt; and an officer ordered to attack after a costly engagement:

I watched the officer's face, it gave no indication of feeling. He looked up and said 'I think the attack ought to go very well'. He knew it wouldn't go well, he knew it couldn't go well. No I shan't try to define character.

Nevertheless he did define it very clearly. He told the story of a platoon commander ordered to take his men to a village four miles away. After an hour's walking they came to a signpost saying 'Four miles to St Servin'. The optimist gaily remarked: 'Well, thank God we're holding our own.' It was a fine but difficult thing to be a graceful winner, and it was not a bad training to begin by being a graceful loser. Georges Vanier had a strong, and very personal, sense of humour; and humour, unlike wit, could be cultivated. 'Perhaps its most valuable trait' he suggested 'is to prevent people taking themselves too seriously.' Georges took everything seriously, except himself.

Lord Byng now approaching the end of his term of office, had been devoting his energies to the Canada League in pursuit of Canadian unity. When he asked Georges' advice about sending a team of 'absolute John Bulls' to Quebec, Georges replied: 'The Buller the better'. The moment came when Byng could write 'There is no more French or English in the Canadian League – thank God!'[2] He had been a remarkably successful Governor General, although Georges heard down the grapevine that the King – a stern sartorial martinet – had expressed strong views about his clothes! In March he was raised to a Viscountcy, but his departure was over-clouded by the most painful constitutional crisis in which any Governor General of Canada had been involved. Mackenzie King, who had succeeded Sir Wilfrid Laurier as leader of the Liberal Party, was now Prime Minister at the head of a minority Government, held in office by permission of the Progressives since 1925. It had been three times defeated in the House, and on the 26th of June 1926, fearing a further rebuff on a matter which had been thoroughly debated before a mixed Commission, appointed by a Liberal M.P., King asked Byng for a dissolution. Byng refused since the Conservative Party, led by Arthur Meighen, had the means to form a Government, if the Progressives supported him. Very surprisingly, King – who was a stickler for Canadian autonomy – suggested that Byng should consult the Secretary of State for the Dominions as to the constitutional propriety of this refusal. But the Governor General was too wise to put his head into that particular noose, and felt obliged to take the responsibility on his own shoulders.

Constitutional lawyers and historians[3] are generally, though not quite unanimously, agreed that Byng was right in acting as he did. But Mackenzie King was furious. He resigned on the 28th of June, and Arthur Meighen became Prime Minister without a seat

2. 17th November 1925.
3. For an excellent account of the crises see William Lyon MacKenzie King, Vol. II by H. Blair Neatby, pp. 130-175.

at the head of a Cabinet without portfolios.[4] He was defeated three days later and in the election that followed King – confident, as ever, that 'the God of our fathers has chosen me' – was returned with a clear, though not very decisive, majority. The new Government was sworn in on the 26th of September.

Georges Vanier was an anxious spectator of the crisis not only as an honorary A.D.C. to Byng, but as his intimate friend. The Governor General was spending his summer leave at Pointe-au-Pic in the Maison Bleue on Murray Bay. This was next door to Judge Archer's house, Rayon d'Or, where the Vaniers were staying. Georges was able to get down there for three or four days in the week, and there were few mornings when he did not step across to the Maison Bleue at 11 a.m. The weather was generally fine. He and the Governor General would walk down to the shore, or along the Boulevard, or in the direction of the plateau which stood above it, talking all the time. The conversation turned on many subjects, but it always came back to the crisis for which Byng felt himself to be, however rightly, responsible. He put his case as follows:

It seems to me that when Mr Mackenzie King came to ask for dissolution, there were only two courses open to him – to resign or to fight it out in the House. The courageous course was to fight it out and to stand or fall by the verdict of Parliament. The proper jury, it seems to me, to decide on a question is the one which has heard the evidence; and Parliament in this case had the right, I believe, to pronounce its verdict. That is my idea of Government of the people, by the people and for the people. If dissolution can be obtained each time a P.M. fears an adverse vote in the House, it is the negation of Parliament's authority; Parliament represents the people – Parliament should judge. Mr King had always said in the past 'Let Parliament decide' and now when Parliament was to be given an opportunity to decide, he asked for a dissolution, thus seeking to deprive Parliament of its prerogatives and casting the issue into the confusion of a general election.

But some may say – even granting that Parliament should normally be allowed to pronounce on a matter that has been thrashed out before it – should not the Governor General accept the advice of the Prime Minister the mouthpiece of the people? What did Mr King represent? A discredited minority – a minority which three times had been defeated in the House – a minority over whose head a vote

4. A new Prime Minister, taking office during the lifetime of the same Parliament, had to stand for re-election. The same held good for Cabinet ministers. Meighen evaded the difficulty by making them 'acting' heads of their departments.

of censure was hanging. How can Mr King say that he represented
the people when he had been beaten three times, and if he repre-
presented the people, why should he fear the verdict of Parliament
which is the voice of the people? If Mr King, who represented a
minority, a discredited minority, had been given a chance to govern,
why should not the man who represented the numerically greatest
party be given a chance to govern before throwing the country
anew unto the throes of a general election.

I have often asked myself – is there anything I should have thought
of that I did not think of? And frankly I don't think there is. It is
the hardest thing I have done for Canada.
And the best, added George Vanier.
I don't know.[5]

Sometimes Byng would go for a walk with Pauline, but then
he would say nothing, only heaving at regular intervals a deep
sigh. Before leaving Ottawa he had asked for Mackenzie King to
come to the station and shake hands with him, since he wished to
dispel some of the clouds which hung over his departure. When
he sailed from Quebec on the 30th of September he had tears in
his eyes, and there were barely a dozen people to see him off.
Needless to say, Georges Vanier was one of them; and an hour or
two later the following cablegram was sent to the *Empress of
France* by the late Governor General's A.D.Cs. 'Our thoughts are
with you; although in a few hours Canadian shores will fade from
view, there are hearts in that land which will always remember.'

Byng was succeeded by Lord Willingdon,[6] who visited the
Citadel on arrival in Quebec the following month and asked for
the Viceregal quarters to be put in order. The Devonshires had
often stayed there, and the Byngs for a fortnight in 1921; but nobody since then. Willingdon also asked for Georges to stay on as an
Hon. A.D.C., and in December the Vaniers were in Ottawa for
the opening of Parliament, bearing a plum-pudding that Archambault had sent from the S.O.S. at Sheerness. There followed in the
New Year a prolonged correspondence with Archambault, which
reflects the leisurely preoccupations of peace time soldiering.
Georges Vanier had set his mind on obtaining a bearskin cap for
the Royal 22nd, similar to that worn by the Royal Welch Fusiliers
with whom the regiment was 'in alliance'. The original *bonnet à
poil* dated from 1760 with a badge bearing the fleur-de-lys; this
was more in accord with French-Canadian tradition than the

5. Personal Notes.
6. The Marquess of Willingdon, 1866-1941.

Napoleonic model. Archambault was in touch with the military antiquarians in Paris, but unfortunately a sheet of paper on which Georges had expressed his caustic opinion of the French authorities was mistakenly included in the correspondence. This resulted in ruffled sensibilities and further delays. When the bonnet at last arrived at the Citadel it was approved with certain modifications, and permission was asked from Ottawa to wear it with full dress uniform. Georges insisted that it must sit on the head without discomfort; that it should be too big rather than too small; and slightly rounded in front. With some expectation of obstruction from the Quartermaster-General, he told Archambault that he 'wanted to be ready to parry any ultimatum'. Ottawa agreed to the fleur-de-lys; the bearskin was duly approved; and the first consignment of them arrived, although Georges was by then no longer at the Citadel to admire them, in time for the unveiling of a tablet by the Royal Welch Fusiliers. They were cleared through the Customs on a Friday; fitted on the Saturday; and embellished the Guard of Honour on the Sunday afternoon. General Panet,[7] the Adjutant-General wrote to Georges in warm approval:

It was very hot, about 80°. I think the men suffered a great deal, but no one fell out. All the officers seemed very pleased with the splendid showing the regiment made. Much credit – in fact, all the credit is due to you, hence my congratulations.[8]

In January 1927, the Willingdons paid their first official visit to Montreal and Quebec. The Governor General had written that he wanted 'to have plenty of police about'. Georges wrote his speech in reply to the Mayor's address of welcome in Montreal. Already a reference to the 'sister nations' was becoming the diplomatic recognition of an indubitable fact. Lord Willingdon had secured that the ancient armorial shield of Quebec should be returned from Hastings to the city where it properly belonged. When people in Hastings talked about the 'Conquest' they meant one thing; when people in Quebec talked about it, they meant another. Willingdon referred to Montreal as 'the metropolis of Canada'; Georges was not called upon to suggest what he should say when he went to Toronto. Arrangements were made for him to visit the Villa Maria Convent – traditionally the Governor General called on this before the others – the Nazareth Institution, and the Compagnie

7. Major-General Henri Alexandre Panet.
8. 9th July 1928.

de St Sulpice – which was the official title of the clergy at Notre
Dame Cathedral. In Quebec a dinner for military and civilians was
organized at the Garrison Club. The Willingdons had asked for
'not too many speeches'; in Toronto they had been saturated with
oratory. At the Garrison Club only an informal reply would be
required, since 'by then plenty of wines would have been drunk'.
Willingdon renewed his request that the Viceregal quarters at the
Citadel be made habitable, and Georges had a long conversation
on the subject with the Prime Minister of Quebec, M. Taschereau.
There were certain difficulties. Parliament would have to be summoned to obtain a grant, and there might be opposition since the
Citadel had previously been cared for by the Federal Government.
The Prime Minister did not wish the Viceregal home to become a
bone of contention; even 'Spencerwood', the residence of the
Lieutenant-Governor, had been the subject of regrettable comment. Eventually the matter was peacefully settled with a vote of
$100,000 from the Federal Government.

On the 4th of April a second son, Bernard, was born to Pauline,
and the family then rented a house at Pointe-au-Pic from an
American, Dr Jones; but their stay was dramatically cut short by
a disastrous fire which broke out during the last week of June.
Georges sent details of this to the owner:

At about 6.45 a.m. Sunday my wife woke me saying that she smelt
smoke. I got up at once, rushed to the open window, and looking
down saw smoke issuing from the direction of the living-room
window. I hurried to the upper landing of the stair leading to the
ground floor from where I saw smoke. Hoping to be able to extinguish
the fire I ran down the stairs but on reaching the ground floor I was
caught in a sudden burst of flame and I had just time to reach
the front door and thus make my escape. Meanwhile I had shouted
to my wife not to come down the main stairway: my wife, the two
nurses and three children were able to escape by the back stairs. A
guest of ours, Major Scaife, who was in the room with the bow-
window facing the sea, had to jump from the window because of the
rapidity with which the flames spread.

The whole thing happened so quickly that nothing could be saved,
neither jewellery, nor papers, nor belongings of any kind. Almost as
soon as we had made our escape the whole house was a mass of
flames and it would have been impossible without grave danger to
remove anything from the house.

Nothing stands except the shed (or garage) and the ice-house: the
latter has been very badly damaged by fire, but parts are standing.
The flower garden in front of the house is completely destroyed.

However, some parts of the garden in the rear may be put in condition.

We had no insurance on our things except on my wife's jewels. . . .

Immediately after the fire I had a guard put on the ruins pend-
ing any action which the insurance company in which my wife's
jewellery was insured, wished to take. This guard is still on the ruins.
However, there is really nothing that can be of any value in the
ruins except things like precious stones that probably would not
melt. . . .

One word about the origin of the fire; we really have no definite
idea of how it started. This only is certain. The fire originated in the
living-room or in the small den off it. The night before there had
been a fire in the stone fire-place and also in the small stove in the
hall. Saturday night was quite cold. I should think that the fire had
been smouldering for sometime judging by the suddenness with which
the whole house burst into flames.[9]

The Vaniers hastily returned to Quebec and replenished their
wardrobe in time for Georges to entertain Lord Willingdon at a
men's dinner aboard the *Empress of Austria* on the 4th of July,
and the Prince of Wales and Prince George at a luncheon given
by the Provincial Government at the end of the month.

2

Frustrated of their summer holiday, the Vaniers decided to take
an autumn one, and sailed for England in October. For Georges
Vanier the wedding of Lord Byng's niece, Mary, at St James's,
Piccadilly, was a more than nuptial occasion:

I knew that I should see the man whom I was so longing to see
again. He looked well, with a better colour, and more rested than
when I said Good-bye to him in Canada. It was a great joy to shake
him by the hand. There was the same warm welcome, the same
gentle and penetrating regard.[10]

During their stay in London the Vaniers met the publisher
John Murray. He showed them the MS of Canto III from *Childe
Harold*, the MS of Scott's *The Abbot*, a Shakespeare First Folio,
and a fifteenth century Book of Hours. They took tea in the
room where Scott and Byron had met, and where John Murray's
grandfather had burnt Byron's *Memoirs*. Later they spent a few
days with the Byngs at Thorpe-le-Soken. It was a large white
house, of no great antiquity, standing in beautiful grounds. But

9. 28th June 1927.
10. Diary.

size and splendour did not matter; it was 'the home of the old and beloved chief. He received us with open arms. After dinner I talked to him alone about friends in Canada and Canadian affairs.' The next morning they went out for a walk in spite of the intermittent rain.

'This is a very old part of England' Byng remarked 'these fields were cultivated a thousand years ago. Boadicea drove over this ground in her chariot. You know the Germans were to come through here . . .' They walked again in the afternoon, taking a look at the Working Men's Club. 'If these young men weren't here this afternoon' said Byng 'where would they be and what would they be doing?' The conversation continued on a more personal note:

'George, I have been putting down lately what I think of myself, what I know about myself. I find it very interesting and right to put on paper my views on what I am, why I act, and what I shall become.'

'Now's the time to do it, sir.'

'Yes, before I die.'

'I didn't mean that, I meant now that you have the leisure. Later you will be busy doing something for the good of man and of your country. I for one hope that you will be engaged on some other and great work.'

'What work?'

'I don't know: but there are many things you could do better than most men.'

'I don't know – there has been some talk of offering me South Africa, but I don't think I would take it. I have had the best, Canada. If you like, after tea I shall show you what I have written about myself. I have never as yet shown it to a living person.'

'I am very grateful to you, sir.'

Their talk then reverted to the constitutional crisis:

'History, I feel sure, will vindicate the stand you took when Mackenzie King asked for a dissolution.'

'George, I am only sorry the Prime Minister of Canada should have put the Governor General in the position in which he did. After the mutual understanding which existed between us, he must have known that I would refuse his request. It was understood between us that if he did not succeed, Meighen was to have been given a chance. The *wiser* course for him would have been to give Meighen a chance.'

'Wiser does not seem to me to be the correct word. More honest is better.'

After tea Byng handed Georges a MS of several pages with the title: *Know Thyself*. It set forth the author's personal beliefs, and what he had learnt about life and men. Among the subjects treated was the anxious question of immortality:

A great number of people have tried to prove immortality to me. They have not succeeded and I am rather pleased they have not succeeded. I believe in it as implicitly as anyone, but I like the faith in it better than the proof. . . . I want to keep my faith in it and not have it proved.

Georges Vanier spent the hours till dinner time reading the MS and laid it down with the impression of 'a gentle and consoling philosophy, very human and at the same time divine, resting upon a very simple faith.'

Byng had instructed the Vaniers to call him by any name they liked, except 'Lord Byng'; and when they had gone he wrote to Pauline:

You know what we both wish you and George. It is impossible to put it on paper, because paper cannot convey how deep our sentiments really are. I believe Lao Tze, the Chinese philosopher, said 'those who feel cannot speak, and those who speak cannot feel'. That is the case with us, but you do know what we feel.[11]

The visit had done a great deal to strengthen still further the friendship between two men who occupied, each in his own time, the highest position in Canada, and had each earned it by the discipline of arms.

Georges had spent part of his leave in Paris, and one of the objects of his visit was to call at Marshal Foch's Headquarters, 8 Boulevard des Invalides, and present to the Honorary Colonel of the Royal 22nd the respects and good wishes of all ranks.

Under the shadow of the Dome which rises above Napoleon, the Marshal works; in truth it is a soldier's setting – history, glory, space and light (there are shadows like Napoleon's which are luminous) combine to make of this corner of Paris, the predestined last 'poste de commandement' . . .

Through iron swing gates one passes into a cobbled court-yard – to the right a patch of grass no longer green, to the left a tall slender tree, with turning leaves – leading to the narrow buildings in one of which, on the first floor, the Marshal and his staff are housed: simplicity, bare almost shabby simplicity, is the key-note.

Captain Lhopital, who accompanied Marshal Foch to Canada is

11. 22nd December 1927.

cordial and helpful: he does not think it will be necessary to come back later but hopes the Marshal, who has just returned from Brittany after his summer holidays, will be able to receive me now.

After a few minutes' wait, I am brought to Marshal Foch: he has aged a little since December 1921, or perhaps his dark civilian clothes contrast meanly with the colour and line of tunic, breeches and high boots . . . the face is sun-tanned, the eyes bright behind mobile eyelids that wink in a 'knowing' fashion: the eyelids are so expressive, so changing in form and place that one would say they were of rubber if any substance could rival the living elasticity of flesh.

The room is bright, large, scantily furnished, unpictured, unornamented . . . on the walls a few maps . . . the room, like the man, is clear, vast, simple . . . only essentials. A generous table – upon which are piled books, papers, unopened letters – is placed in such a way as to receive the maximum of light from the two windows.

The Marshal is standing – and remains so for the greater part of the half hour and more which he grants me – if one may apply the word 'standing' to the various, ever-changing attitudes of walking to and fro and of gesticulating with hands and head and body: he insists on my being seated.

Having given to the Marshal the Regiment's message of admiration and of gratitude, I look at the pile of unopened letters and apologise for coming at such an inopportune moment – 'No, no, I am very glad to see you' – but he looks himself at the work before him and adds 'one of these days I hope I may be able to rest . . .'

He speaks with enthusiasm, of his visit to the Regiment in December 1921 and of his Canadian friends. 'I remember,' he says, 'the view over the snow at the Citadel' . . . the beauty of Quebec has impressed him.

I tell the Marshal of our joy, at the battle of Amiens, when for the first time, we moved forward in miles instead of yards. His eyes brighten, he walks over to the door, brings back a pipe which he has taken from his overcoat and speaks, in rapid unfinished sentences – interspersed with 'ahs' and 'ohs' which read badly because Marshal Foch uses a medium all his own – a language depending more on motion than on word. Why say 'strike' if you can act it?

'On the 8th August we felt that we were going forward to victory. You M. le Maréchal had known it for some time . . .'

'Ah, not since very long . . .' (One feels that the battle of Amiens is a pleasant recollection.)

'Yes, the attack of the 8th August, prepared with Sir Douglas Haig and carried out in silence, so that the Germans would have no knowledge of it . . . and later Byng towards Bapaume . . . Haig said to me "I have few men". I replied "It does not matter go ahead anyway". Hearing that I have been on Lord Byng's staff he adds 'Yes, General Byng is 'un homme de valeur.'

Speaking of German strategy and of the psychology of war in general, Marshal Foch states 'Often the Germans struck terrible blows but they did not continue – do not let go, but strike, strike . . . after a time the 'break up' (décollement) begins: one must not let go but strike here and there . . . victory is like an inclined plane . . . an army which advances has the wind in its sails.

He recalls a conversation – dramatic in its simplicity – which took place on the night of the 26th of March 1918, after he had assumed command of the Allied armies.

'When I returned to Paris after having been appointed Commander-in-Chief my wife said to me: 'So they have passed you the whole "paquet"?'

'Yes.'

'What are you going to do with it?'

'Pray God that it may not be too late.'

When I tell the Marshal that the history of the 'Royal 22e Régiment' had not been written yet, he exclaims:

'Write the history of your regiment, you will draw lessons from it.'

The time of parting is at hand: the Marshal asks me to carry back to the regiment and to his friends of Quebec his Greetings and his thanks for the way in which he was received in 1921.

I take the liberty, as I leave, to congratulate Marshal Foch on his birthday (he was 76 on the 2nd October) and on his youthful appearance in spite of his age; the Marshal replies 'You have before you a young man of 76. '

The last words are uttered smilingly: Marshal Foch bows, with arms slightly raised and extended, a warm and lasting hand-shake . . . Yes indeed a young man still, in mind, in gesture and in voice.[12]

3

The reputation of the Royal 22nd in peace time was not quite what it had been in war. The men may not have been brutal, but they were more than occasionally licentious, and their behaviour had caused some complaint in the city of Quebec. Blasphemy in the field or on the parade ground does not, of course, mean what it says; Georges Vanier, however, liked it none the better for that. So it was with the good name of the regiment in mind that he invited Cardinal Rouleau, O.P., Archbishop of Quebec, to dinner in the Officers' Mess. The arrangements for the evening and his own speech of welcome preoccupied him to an extraordinary degree. He instructed Rancourt, now Sergeant-Major, that he was on no account to be disturbed. 'But supposing the Brigadier rings up?'

12. Personal Papers, 6th October 1927.

Rancourt enquired. 'Tell him I can't speak to him.' 'Or Madame Vanier?' Rancourt persisted. 'Tell her I can't speak to her' Georges replied with redoubled and thunderous emphasis.

With its elegant silver centrepiece, its table made of a single oak beam taken from one of the adjacent buildings, its lamps fixed into the butts of old rifles, and its chairs made by the Government cabinet maker in Montreal, the Mess provided a good setting for ceremonial dinners. At one of these, Jean Brunhé introduced the officers to the pleasures of French tobacco. Music was played in the vestibule and the Royal toast was drunk in champagne, followed by 'O Canada' and the 'Marseillaise'. Then a soldier passed round the snuff which the officers and guests took from the huge horn of a buffalo. 'Tobacco is here the ritualistic symbol' declared Georges Vanier 'of a comradeship worthy in every respect of the French army.' Brunhé was the initiator of a new science called 'human geography'. Georges regretted that he had not learnt geography according to this method. 'Perhaps I should have been a good pupil, knowing a little more than the capitals of the world.'

For three months in summer the battalion went into training at Valcartier, seventeen miles from Quebec, where the Jacques Cartier river winds its way through the flat country. In fact Georges had more to worry about than blasphemy and 'trouble with the girls'. The authorities were alarmed by the number of desertions from the army, and Georges sent a memorandum to Ottawa setting out what he believed to be the immediate and fundamental causes of this. Desertion was encouraged by the slowness to apprehend the deserter and by the leniency of the punishment if he were caught. But the real causes went deeper. Recruits presenting themselves at the Citadel were often men who had failed in civilian life, for whom it was impossible to obtain references, and who only wanted to tide over a period of temporary unemployment. Moreover recruits were so few that one could not be too nice about accepting them; in winter there were hardly enough men to mount the guard and shovel away the snow. The military establishments were so small that city parades were liable to excite the ridicule of the onlookers, who would ask derisively: 'Is this your regiment?' The ordinary existence of the soldier in peace time was very drab, with no appeal to what Georges Vanier went on to define as the 'soldier type':

He is a curious mixture: there is in him something of the sentimentalist, of the bohemian and of the adventurer. He likes to swing down the street to the strains of the band or of the drums: he likes to walk out, with his lady-love, in an attractive uniform; the unexpected in life appeals to him; he certainly does not care to be continuously employed on fatigues. He will enlist at $1.20 a day as readily as at $3.00 or $4.00 a day. At present the man who will stay in the army for a smaller remuneration than he can find in civilian life does not enlist.

Georges thought that the money spent in making quicker arrests would be saved on fitting out fresh recruits with uniform and equipment:

To put the matter bluntly, at present when a soldier is discontented with military life he deserts, with the quasi-certainty that he will not be punished at all, and with the complete certainty that if apprehended he will be dealt with leniently.[13]

Little as he may have realized it at the time, this was something of a military testament, for except for a short period during the Second World War, Georges Vanier was never to exercise military command again. On his return from England in December 1927 he was offered the post of military representative on the Canadian delegation to the League of Nations in Geneva. Byng approved his acceptance of it, although he had been trying to get him to the War Office in London. Byng was no cynic about the League of Nations, but he believed that friendship – through the intercourse of art, science, hygiene, education and religion – must precede disarmament. 'Love your enemies' was a better slogan than 'Reduce your cruisers'. Byng had no children of his own, and his feeling for Georges Vanier was that of a father for his son:

The thought of our friendship is stark reality, existing on the transcendental plane where the spirit alone can reach and indulge itself. If there is going to be a bigger life hereafter it seems to have its beginnings here and now when thoughts of one's deep friendships lift one up to what can only be called the realm of reality. There you are, dear old George, I felt I wanted to say this to you and I know you will not mind.[14]

Nevertheless it was a sad farewell to the Citadel. On arrival there he had written that he 'would not exchange the work for any other, not even on the Staff', and he had turned down an offer to join the Judge Advocate's office in Ottawa. He would

13. 7th January 1928.
14. 15th February 1928.

probably not have exchanged it now if the term of his command were not coming to an end. A dinner was given for him at the Garrison Club, with Tremblay in the chair. Edward Pope[15] wrote afterwards:

I was sitting in the midst of a group of 'Canayans' who were busy counting the large no. of French chaps present and speculating (the tone was bitter) as to whether Tremblay or you would speak in French. It was not thought that he would – about you it was uncertain. I hope you will forgive me for not having remembered that doing the right thing at all times is your *forte*.[16]

Since the Chief Justice of Quebec congratulated Georges on a speech 'imprinted with delicacy and tact, remarkable and re-marked upon'[17] we may assume that he spoke in French. Perhaps he spoke in English as well; it would have been the right overture to diplomacy. In the train bearing the family to Montreal he put down in his diary the melancholy details of that last day; for, as he was many years later to remind the Governor General's Foot Guards, 'a regiment is not merely a group of men; it is a way of life'.

What a day of emotions! Up at 6.20. To the office at 8.00 to arrange my papers. Very tired. 9.00 Farewell parade. Shook hands with everybody. Said a word and then there was the march past in the wind and snow. 11.45 visit to the P.M., M. Taschereau. 'Don't stay too long out there. Come back to us'. 2.30 called on S.E. Cardinal Rouleau who gave me his blessing for the family. I thanked him for dining in the Mess. 5.30 we left. The Tremblays, Colonel Benôit, the Archambaults, the officers of the regiment. At last the terrible ordeal is over – it was time – we were at the end of our tether.

15. Henry Edward Pope.
16. 18th February 1928.
17. 18th February 1928.

PART TWO

THE DIPLOMAT

CHAPTER 8

GENEVA

I

THE Vaniers had booked their passage on the *Paris*, sailing from New York on the 23rd of February, with three children and two nurses. A telegram from the Adjutant-General brought the comforting news that the Department of External Affairs would pay for one of the latter. Georges noted this as an 'unexpected success', since it was contrary to all the regulations; and inside cabins would alleviate the cost of the voyage. Before sailing he went up to Ottawa and had a long conversation with Willingdon whom he found irritable and depressed. The Conservative opposition was speaking as if the country were on the verge of bankruptcy, whereas the financiers prophesied an imminent wave of prosperity. Willingdon had learnt that the City Council of Montreal were proposing to give twelve acres for the American Legation, and had promptly quashed the idea. If ground could be given for the Americans, why not for the French and the Japanese? Why not for the British?

The question of Canadian representation abroad came up in conversation with Senator Dandurand,[1] head of the Canadian Delegation at Geneva, who was also travelling on the *Paris*. The Conservatives, opposed to Japanese immigration, did not wish for a Legation in Tokyo, whereas the Liberals, who wanted to restrict immigration in both countries on an equal basis, were more favourable. But it was thought inadvisable to establish a Legation in Tokyo before establishing one in Paris. Briand, the French Minister for Foreign Affairs, had concurred, and the Japanese eventually agreed. With regard to Canadian representation at Geneva, Dandurand recalled the observation of Austen Chamberlain[2] that it was he, Chamberlain, who represented Canada on the League of Nations. 'Not Canada' Dandurand had replied, and Smuts had added 'Not South Africa'. Only Desmond Fitzgerald,[3]

1. The Hon. Raoul Dandurand, 1861-1942.
2. The Right Hon. Sir Austen Chamberlain, 1863-1937.
3. Irish Minister for Defence 1927-1932.

speaking for the Irish Free State, had not demurred. This was the more surprising since Fitzgerald had been active in the Easter Rising, and had spent some time in gaol chained to Mr de Valera. His subsequent hostility to de Valera may have been due to this unnaturally close alliance; but like his friend, Kevin O'Higgins,[4] Fitzgerald had come to see the point of the Commonwealth.

The Imperial Council of 1926 had laid down that the Dominions, unrepresented on the Council of the League, were not bound by British decisions, but a year later Chamberlain declared that the British Delegate represented the Empire. In reply to Ottawa, he explained that he had been misunderstood; he spoke for the Empire, excluding the Dominions. When Canada was elected to the Council she received twenty-six votes – ten certain and thirteen doubtful. Great Britain headed the doubtfuls. Chamberlain and Stresemann[5] were the scrutineers, and as the result of the voting became apparent Chamberlain's expression was severe. 'He certainly voted for Canada' Dandurand explained 'but he hoped perhaps she would not be elected.'

In the train from the Gare de Lyon Vanier read Mussolini's reply to Mgr Seipel[6] on the rights of minorities. 'If the League of Nations penetrates the labyrinth of so-called minorities, she will never get out again.' 'Decidedly' Georges noted 'I am arriving in Geneva at the right moment.' The heat in the compartment was unbearable; one could either quarrel with one's fellow-passengers or merely simmer to oneself. Georges opted for the second alternative, spending the greater part of the journey in a state of coma. At one point Briand[7] passed down the corridor. 'I saw him from behind, without his hat. Fugitive impression of an *immense* hunchback, with a bush of hair round his neck.'[8] Georges was met at Geneva by Dr W. A. Riddell[9] who took him round to the Hotel de la Paix. His room looked on to the lake and a full moon, eclipsing every star but one.

The next day, after meeting Dandurand at the station, he sat behind him at the meeting of the Council, at the left end of the horse-shoe table, between Holland and Finland. The other members of the Council were Great Britain, France, Germany, Japan, Italy, Poland, Chile, Rumania, Cuba and China. Austen Chamber-

4. 1892-1927.
5. Gustav Stresemann, 1878-1929.
6. Ignaz Seipel, 1876-1932, the Austrian Chancellor.
7. Aristide Briand, 1862-1932.
8. Diary, 4th March 1928.
9. Walter Alexander Riddell, 1881-1957.

lain was head of the British Delegation, with Colonel H. A. C.
Temperley[10] and Rear-Admiral Aubrey C. H. Smith[11] as his
military and naval advisers. Georges Vanier's work lay with the
Permanent Advisory Commission for Military, Naval and Air questions. Each country represented on the Council of the League had
the right to appoint three delegates to this, but Vanier represented
all three services, with Dr Riddell to speak for the Government.
The Commission met whenever the Council or any of its Delegations or sub-commissions, required. The recommendations of
the Commission were expected to be unanimous, although
majority reports with minority objections were also admitted.
The main business on the agenda was to prepare suggestions for
the Disarmament Conference to be held at a later date. A letter
to Lieut-Colonel H. H. Mathews[12] in Ottawa gives an account of
the discussions and the difficulties:

The Draft Convention submitted by the Soviet delegation and based
upon complete and immediate disarmament has been definitely killed.
The suggestion made by Count Bernstorff[13] (Germany) for inser-
tion in the Armament Yearbook of certain information and tables
might be considered by you and I would be grateful if the General
Staff would give me instructions with regard to this document.

Asking for instructions with regard to the new Draft Convention
for the *Reduction of Armaments* submitted by the Soviet delegation, Georges continued:

The two main bones of contention are tonnage and conscription.
Great Britain would like tonnage to be divided into various categories
whereas France would like global tonnage. In the matter of conscription, France appears to be adamant judging from conversations I have
had with their representatives here. An interesting situation arose when
General de Marinis (Italy) stated, in a very tactful way (but one understood) that he was unaware of any conversations being carried on. His
tone was polite, but one felt that it might be wise to bring Italy into
the conversations mentioned. This of course is purely a personal
impression, but I think it correct. . . . It would seem almost certain
that at the next session of the Disarmament Commission there will
have to be a 'show down'; if the political ground is not prepared
before the technical people get together, I am afraid that the German
and Soviet protests will be such as to awake a certain amount of
public interest. . . . Just now the technical aspect of the case is over-

10. Major-General H. A. C. Temperley, 1877-1940.
11. Rear Admiral Sir Aubrey C. H. Smith, 1877-1940.
12. Lieut-Colonel H. H. Mathews.
13. Count Johann Heinrich Bernstorff, 1862-1939.

shadowed by the political. It is for the General Staff to decide whether it is advisable to give an opinion until it is asked for by External Affairs. However, I consider it my duty to bring to your attention, at least unofficially, all matters having a military, naval or air aspect, upon which I might later be called upon to deliberate. I should be quite happy to carry on without definite instructions until some point of controversy arose, when the matter would be referred to you through External affairs. The last thing I should wish would be to render the work of External Affairs more complicated because of my presence here.[14]

Georges added that he and Dr Riddell got on very well together, and understood the situation perfectly.

On the 29th of June Georges was asked to represent the Royal 22nd at the unveiling of the statue to Marshal Foch at Cassel. It was the first time he had revisited the battlefields he knew so well; they stirred poignant and splendid memories:

En route for Cassel to attend the unveiling of the equestrian statue of Marshal Foch; La Compagnie du Chemin de Fer du Nord has organized a special train upon which travel the Marshal and his family, the State – and more particularly Army – officials and invited guests including the Military Representatives and Attachés of the Allied Forces. Field-Marshal Lord Allenby has come from London, the Honourable Philippe Roy, Minister to France, represents Canada.

Paris-Cassel. . . . . The journey, towards the end of it, recalls memories. Here is Farbus: on the heights of Vimy skeleton trees stand against the sky – trees that have not regreened or rebudded – with outstretched and twisted arms they remain dead things . . . perhaps, one wonders. . . . Lens, with its prosperous railway station, with its rows and rows of small, new houses, standing phoenix-like where only yesterday – one has but to raise the eye of memory – ashes lay.

Along the railway line, masses of flowers, all yellow – what a revealing colour yellow can be. . . .

Cassel . . . in a motor car to the 'Place' – there is the Mairie where the Marshal in October 1914 – then General and Commander of the group of Armies of the North – established his Headquarters. Many fateful months he spent in Cassel: in the beginning of November of that year, the Kaiser had come to Flanders for the offensive that was to lead to the sea.

On foot, through winding streets alive with people and colour, from the 'Place' to the highest spot above Cassel – cries of 'Vive l'Angleterre, Vive le Canada'. Colonel (now General) Réquin, French Military Representative at the League of Nations begins, with me in

14. 4th April 1928.

tow, a patient, steady, effective advance, through the dense crowd to the statue: thanks to his courteous but impressive insistence we reach the monument.

What a view there is over the green smiling plains of Flanders – one has known them otherwise . . . there are the old familiar windmills . . .

M. Hanotaux,[15] of the French Academy, is speaking: towering above him and his voice is the monument. Seated firmly in the saddle, with reins held loosely, the bronze marshal looks intently into space – does he see the fields or beyond the fields? The horse knowing his master, stands quiet but, with head up ready to move – – who knows, with such a rider?

Around the monument, hundreds of flags make a silken noise in the fresh breeze.

Where is the man – the centre to which point colours, men and things . . . ? There he is seated in a curious, reclining, sideways fashion, arms crossed, legs crossed, his képi pulled down over his eyes which are turned to earth. He is almost scowling – this is the greatest ordeal . . . to hear his eulogy: perhaps also the greatest test . . . how many men could attend the unveiling of their own monument?

The Marshal has aged more much more since November 1927 than during the six preceding years.

After M. Hanotaux, M. Poincaré,[16] Premier of France, rosy-cheeked as a child, speaks in his characteristically rasping tones, but with a note of conviction which softens the unpleasantness. Following M. Poincaré's speech, which is the last, the Marshal's face clears – he breathes again, he jumps up, he chats with General Gouraud[17] to whom he points out spots in the plains which he knows so well . . . the band strikes up a march, somehow the crowd around the statue untangles itself, irregular ranks are formed . . . flags and men march past the Marshal who, képi still over his eyes, salutes.

Later a reception is held at the Mairie: there, no longer under the weight of the monument, the Marshal expresses thanks in response to a toast to his health. He authorizes the dispatch of a cablegram of good wishes to his regiment in Quebec.[18]

At the third session of the Committee on arbitrage and security the suggestions by the German Delegation were unanimously adopted, with some amendments, by the Preparatory Commission; and it was agreed that a model treaty sponsored by Germany should be proposed to the General Assembly in September. The

15. Gabriel Hanotaux, 1853-1944.
16. Raymond Poincaré, 1860-1934.
17. General Henri Eugène Gouraud, 1867-1946.
18 Personal Papers, 7th July 1928.

Canadian representatives held firmly to the principle of unanimity, since their own Constitution depended on it; and their views were generally approved. The German proposals were as follows:

1. If a dispute were submitted to the Council, the States involved might undertake in advance to execute provisional recommendations of the Council to prevent any aggravation of the dispute.
2. In case of threat of war, the States might undertake in advance to accept and to execute the recommendations of the Council to the effect of maintaining or re-establishing the military status quo normally existing in time of peace.
3. In case of hostilities and if, in the Council's opinion, all possibilities of peaceful settlement had been exhausted, the States might undertake in advance to accept an armistice on land, sea and air and to withdraw any forces which had penetrated into foreign territory.
4. To be considered whether the above obligations should be undertaken only in case of a unanimous vote of the Council or whether the majority, simple or qualified, might suffice.
5. These obligations might constitute the subject of an agreement or protocol open for signature by all States Members and non-Members of the League of Nations.

It was impossible to discuss disarmament without considering the weapons – or, worse, the potential weapons – that were to be disarmed. In a long letter[19] to Mathews Vanier took a realistic look into the future. The whole problem had been completely changed by the new phenomena in time and space, and by the frightening possibilities of chemical warfare. It was no secret that the methods of poison gas used by the Germans in 1918 were now obsolete. Whatever regulations were introduced, large quantities of gas could be manufactured at the last moment and diffused from the air. At a moment when the Kellogg Peace proposals were on the point of signature the British Government were still not prepared to ratify the Geneva Protocol of 1925 prohibiting the use of poison gas in warfare, unless the other signatories to the Protocol did the same. There was also the danger that whereas guns, shells and warships could not be made or built in secret, commercial aircraft could rapidly and secretly be converted into offensive or defensive weapons. The signing of the Kellogg Pact would be a superfluous ceremony unless the nations acted as if peace were a possibility as well as an ideal.

After the fifth session of the Preparatory Disarmament Com-

19. 27th August 1928.

mission in March 1928 progress was held up by the inability of
the French and British to agree on naval limitation and trained
reserves. The Anglo-French Agreement, the terms of which leaked
out in August before the Ninth General Assembly, suggested no
limitation whatever on surface vessels of, or under, 10,000 tons,
armed with six-inch guns, and none on submarines of six hundred
tons or under. The U.S. Government's contention that any limitation of naval armament should apply to all classes of combatant
vessels met with general approval; but Georges Vanier appreciated the British dilemma. Of what use would her six-inch guns
be against the eight-inch guns of the large American cruisers?
France, previously in support of the American position, had now
turned to Great Britain – firstly because some agreement was imperative, and secondly because in exchange for permission to build
an unrestricted number of six hundred ton submarines, Britain
would be tolerant in the matter of her trained reserves. France
would not accept the abolition of these, unless she were forced to
do so by world opinion. Britain, on her side, though she realized
– and with good reason – the menace of six hundred ton submarines, was prepared to accept them if she could build an unrestricted number of cruisers with six-inch guns. The proposed
Agreement, when it became known, stirred the waters it was
intended to calm, and Georges told Mathews that there was 'only
one course to follow now – scrap it.' He did not believe the impasse could be bridged constructively at the next meeting of the
Disarmament Commission. The only hope was in an agreement
sufficiently vague to allow the nations to build whatever vessels
suited their particular requirements.[20]

The Vaniers were now living in a flat at 6 rue Bellot, and it was
here that Jean Vanier – generally known as Jock – was born on
the 10th of September. Lord Byng wondered if Pauline was 'thinking of starting a little League of Nations of her own.' In the
following month he was appointed head of Scotland Yard:

I am the head of a fearful and wonderful machine. It moves along
creaking and groaning at every point, getting tied up in its own
cobwebs, and occasionally covering itself up under quilts of official
goose-down, but it moves along. It has a venerable past, a muddy,
present, and an incomprehensible future.[21]

Among the more frequent visitors to the flat was Colonel

20. Letter to Lieut-Colonel H. H. Mathews, 8th October 1928.
21. 9th November 1928.

Réquin,[22] French representative on the Disarmament Commission. Small in stature and quick in mind, he was an accomplished artist who found many subjects for his pen among the *dramatis personae* of the League of Nations. One would have liked to see him illustrate Georges Vanier's pen picture of a diplomat of the old school:

What is he best fitted for – to create, or to complicate, irritate, and destroy? What a master *saboteur* he is, with his mobile and ravaged features, his eyes with their cobwebs of wrinkles, his thick and facile laugh, contrasting with his sinister smile – the effect, I believe, of the wrinkles which furrow his face in every direction.[23]

These sardonic comments were inspired by a four hour meeting of the General Assembly:

A ship without a rudder – suggestions and resolutions rained down one after another – and all of them, hopelessly mixed up, clashed without anyone attempting to find a solution or coming to a decision. A pitiful sight.

As for the Preparatory Commission, Hugh Gibson, the U.S. representative had a word for it:

> The firefly is brilliant
> But he hasn't any mind
> He wanders through existence
> With his headlight on behind.

Commander Dillon R.N.[24] of the British Delegation, had told Georges that matters discussed behind the scenes were far more important than those discussed before the curtain. The days of secret diplomacy were far from over, and opportunities were plentiful of meeting the diplomats – when they were off duty. There was Senator Dandurand, of course, who certainly looked the part – a Voltairean from Montreal, of whom a friend wrote to Georges that although 'not as pious as I would like him to be, would not object to putting three medals of the Madonna in his pocket, along with some gramophone records of some rather naughty French songs'.[25] There was Baron Moncheur,[26] formerly Belgian Ambassador in London, wavering and resigned; and Sir

22. General Edouard Réquin, 1879-1953.
23. Personal Notes, 17th March 1929.
24. Captain George Crozier Dillon, R.N.
25. Letter from Harry Baldwin, 25th January 1929.
26. Baron Ludovic-Alfred-Ghislain Moncheur, 1857-1946.

Rennell Rodd,[27] in Geneva for the Rockefeller Library Committee
– 'charming and sympathetic and a great admirer of Lord Byng'[28]
– with whom Georges discussed tobacco – a subject on which he
was at no time an expert. Rodd described to him how Lord Cromer,
faced with a difficult decision, would light his pipe, smoke it for
a little, empty it, fill it again, and so on until at the end of the
day he was faced, no longer perhaps with the difficult decision, but
with a heap of unsmoked tobacco. The conversation took place at
the house of Sir Eric Drummond,[29] Secretary-General of the
League, and as Georges was leaving he perceived a stoutly built
man with an impressive moustache and an umbrella. 'He's a
detective' Drummond explained. 'The Macedonians have stated
that they will commit a crime in Geneva in order to draw attention to their claims. Hence – rather far-fetched I consider – the
police protection.'

Then there was M. Titilesco,[30] the Rumanian representative,
who did not share Sir Eric Drummond's *sang-froid*, although he
had nothing in particular to fear from Macedonia. Leo Kennedy,[31]
Assistant Foreign Editor of *The Times* and a good friend of Georges
Vanier, had been to see him at Titilesco's request. The interview
was singular in the extreme:

The Secretary seemed scared to death, rapped on the door, sounds
from inside. I was shown in. Titilesco in bed was dressed in red
dressing gown under which was a sort of heavy blue waist-coat
and under that I saw more than one pyjama or shirt. Bed clothes
piled over him. Titilesco very excited. Looking for all the world
like a Chinese woman. At times spoke in a rambling fashion. He
said: 'The English have two things, prestige and bookkeeping.
Scratch an Englishman once: he does not appear to notice it. Scratch
him twice, perhaps three times, he does not appear to notice it. But
after many scratches he suddenly wakes up and then he remembers
the other scratches that went before.' Whilst saying all this he jumped
out of bed and locked the door. He wore a sort of brown trousers
under his dressing gown.[32]

The principal actors might have been surprised if they had
known how closely the Canadian Military representative was
observing them as they sat in the oblong room at the oblong

27. Lord Rennell of Rodd.
28. Personal Notes, 13th March 1929.
29. The Right Hon. Earl of Perth, 1876-1951.
30. Nicholas Titilesco, 1883-1941.
31. A. L. Kennedy, 1885-1965.
32. Personal Notes, 14th March 1929.

table under the oblong paintings and the blue skylights, under the
gaze of four marble statues. There was Briand, the incomparable
orator: 'his head falls lower, it touches his sleeve, he lifts his
head like a surprised child, it is all right – the translator is
Dronnigan. When Briand yawns, his face opens. He is in a bad
mood, and looks greyer than usual.' There was Dandurand, looking for all the world like a politician of the Third Republic, 'nerves
on edge and speaking too hurriedly'. There was the Turkish
representative; 'tortoise shell glasses with one side broken. Only
goes beyond his left temple. A small, dark moustache which fails
to hide a trembling, sensitive mouth, a sparse beard which he
swathers sometimes. He gesticulates quietly with his glasses in
his right hand . . . a study in brown'. There was Stresemann: 'a
barrel with the cork come out – the collar is the bung. Cork
coloured face, but not a bouncing cork but a dead, ill-fitting one.
To quit the figurative, looks like someone who has been doing
without all the good things of life he loves so well.'[33]

The ratification of the Anglo-French Naval agreement was still
bedevilled by the British objection to conscription, and the French
objection to the cruiser tonnage which the British thought essential to their needs. Vanier admitted that he could not as yet make
up his mind which attitude was the more reasonable; but he
recognized that the needs of the two countries were diametrically
opposed. The rôle of the British Fleet was active, if not aggressive;
that of the French was passive and defensive. Submarines were
essential for defence, cruisers to protect imperial communications.
Lord Cushendun,[34] for the United Kingdom, manoeuvred skilfully;
but everyone else was manoeuvring as well.

When the fifth session of the Preparatory Commission opened
on the 15th of March, it was decided not to tackle the two most
important questions – the Soviet proposals for complete disarmament and the Convention on the reduction of armaments – before
the arrival of the Turkish Delegation. The discussion turned instead on the work of the committee on arbitration and security.
This was criticized by M. Litvinoff[35] as tending to exasperate the
causes of war, and to turn 'a local conflict into a general butchery'.
Comte Clauzel for France and Count Bernstorff for Germany
intervened. 'The former protested without energy – in any case,
his physique puts energy out of the question; he would be ridi-

33. Personal Notes.
34. 1861-1934.
35. Maxime Maximovitch Litvinoff, 1876-1951.

culous; even in his calmer moments his body trembles like a jelly – and the second *congratulated everybody*, even the committee on arbitration and security, but ended up by saying that, in spite of all the work accomplished, "the first step towards disarmament has not yet been taken: I hope it soon will be".[36]

In occupying his front seat in the stalls Georges may have been prepared for a comedy; he was not expecting a farce. Later, when the Russian proposals were discussed, the farce turned to melodrama with the Muse of Tragedy hovering in the wings:

One breathes at last. Everyone was revolving round the Soviet balloon (why not say bladder?), everyone knew (particularly the Germans and the Turks) that the air inside was poisoned, but they were afraid to touch it for fear of bursting it. Some (the Germans and the Turks) wanted it intact to annoy the countries who are making a serious effort towards disarmament, the others were literally terrified to give it the least enquiring knock . . . in case it should fly away. Really, in this atmosphere of fear and almost of panic, I was ashamed – it was a sight to make the League of Nations blush.

Italy and France spoke, without saying anything. Is it conceivable? These countries found nothing to say to the Bolshevists who spread anarchy and civil war throughout the world, and who have the impudence, the effrontery, to come here and say in effect: (a) 'the work done by you (the Disarmament Commission) is futile and will only result later on, in transforming a local conflict into a general war (following the treaties and conventions which will bind the nations of the world. (b) We bring another remedy for war – complete and immediate disarmament – we are not concerned with security – our remedy is based on principles diametrically opposed to the [Kellogg] Pact – that doesn't matter – abolish the Pact.'

One breathes at last. Lord Cushendun spoke – firmly, frankly and logically. He brought out the contradictions, the anomalies, the futility – to take the words out of M. Litvinoff's mouth – of the Soviet plan for a convention. He burst the Soviet balloon and everyone (except the Turks, the Germans and the USSR, applauded. It is the first time that I have heard applause at the League of Nations. Lord Cushendun deeply impressed his listeners. The prestige of Great Britain at the League of Nations has grown. He dissipated the atmosphere of worry, timidity, uneasiness, and even of fear – and how? Simply by saying what everyone was thinking. What an admission, all the same![37]

Meanwhile Briand and Austen Chamberlain were putting their heads together to settle the problem of cruisers and conscription.

36. Personal Notes, 15th March 1929.
37. Personal Notes, 20th March 1929.

As Cushendun had observed to the French Ambassador in London: 'We don't want to find ourselves lined up with Russia and Germany against France.' Not for the first time, or the last, the Entente Cordiale was creaking. The session of the 22nd of March was a 'battle of flowers: bouquets of doubtful perfume were thrown by Litvinoff to Cushendun, by Clauzel to Litvinoff and Bernstorff, and from Bernstorff to Clauzel. They need a little golf to calm them down.'[38]

2

When a natural optimist like Georges Vanier could write as he did about the international horse-coping at Geneva, one is not surprised that he should have turned with relief to the military virtues. On the 22nd of March Foch died in Paris, and Georges was there:

Marshal Foch is dead – the morning paper lies before me – One knew he was ill, very ill but somehow it is hard to think of him . . . dead.

I go to his home 138 rue de Grenelle to sign the register in the name of the regiment: already, so few hours after the Marshal's death, people are gathering, cinema operators and photographers are waiting for the great of the earth who will come to see the dead: in the cobbled courtyard, leading to the house, lists which lie upon long narrow tables are being signed, by men, women and children: some of the children cannot write, their small hands are guided by hands that have held a rifle . . . the one-legged porter, with tears in his eyes, looks on. A few people cross the courtyard to the house . . . I follow . . . Marshal Pétain, in horizon-blue uniform, escorted by General Weygand, in mufti, is leaving . . . Commandant Bugnet who, for eight years, has been 'officier d'ordonnance' to Marshal Foch, recognises and receives me, leads me through corridors and up a flight of stairs to the room in which, the night before, the Marshal died.

Marshal Foch, in his dark grey-blue uniform, lies upon the bed. . . . The face – nothing else in the room matters – seems strange, unknown – wondering, I gaze at it: has death alone wrought such a change . . . ? then I understand . . . the moustache bushy, mobile, characteristic has been cut (by a whim of destiny it had been removed at the Marshal's request the day before he died). Without the moustache, the features stand out with the sharpness of a death-mask, the nose has thinned, the mouth is set, the profile recalls – does it really or is it only a trick of imagination? – that of Napoleon. But the face is different, entirely different, in death: curious phenomenon, the dead face gives an impression of greater strength than in life.

38. Personal Notes, 22nd March 1929.

A bronze crucifix is in his skeleton hands, joined in prayer: thrown over the knees and hiding the feet is the grey-blue coat – lighter and shorter than our greatcoats – which the Commander-in-Chief wore when he reviewed the French troops entering Metz. In the light of the candles the many rows of ribbons and the star of the Legion of Honour colour the tunic; on a side table to the left and at the head of the bed are the Médaille Militaire and the Croix de Guerre – no other decorations or insignia, no marshal's baton.

Covering the wall, at the head of the bed, is a large quilt-like tapestry, made of the flags of the Allies; the flag of Canada is in the upper left hand corner under that of Belgium.

La Maréchale and a few members of the family are there and two praying nuns in black. . . . I kneel to add my prayers to theirs.

Sunday, 24th March.
Morning 8.30

Near the Arc de Triumphe we stand: the body of Marshal Foch is to be brought from 138 rue de Grenelle. Radiant sunshine . . . thousands, scattered over the broad spaces, stand expectantly, silently, reverently. The unknown soldier awaits the coming of the soldier known to all. A fitting tribute to both that they should lie together and be worthy to lie together.

The clatter and movement of horses, the play of sun on helmet and sword – Marshal Foch is under the Arch of Glory: the people of Paris file before the coffin draped in the tricolour, lying on a gun-carriage: the great and small, the old and young, the poor the rich, all classes, all manner of men and women and children have come to say their thanks and their sorrow. We join the queue – ten or twelve abreast – on l'Avenue Kléber, and we advance, in one hour, a little less than one hundred yards.

Night 10.45.

A cool clear night under a bright moon, so bright that only two or three stars appear in a slate-coloured sky. Looking up the Champs Elysées one sees two double rows of lights narrowing to a point at the Arc de Triomphe, the top of which holds tricolour lights which cut eerily across the sky: four enormous torches around the gun-carriage radiate a greenish light.

Night 11.00.

A gun booms . . . in the distance myriads of flashes rise; like lights on boats moving down a quick running stream, nearer, nearer, they come – they are the torch-bearing cavalry preceding the Marshal on his way to Notre Dame Cathedral. The moon throws over the lighted riders and their horses strange opalescent colours . . . the lights at the top of the Arc de Triomphe disappear – the unknown soldier is alone once more.

26th March.

Eight years ago today, at Doullens, Marshal Foch was appointed Commander-in-Chief of the greatest army in history . . . today he is to be buried.

Notre Dame Cathedral
Morning 09.00.

Cardinals, Princes, statesmen, diplomats and soldiers are gathered before the altar: the scarlet and gold, the purple and silver of robe and uniform rise to meet the red, white and blue of the catafalque and then the black of the mourning streamers, falling from the roof. The Prince of Wales, tanned and fit – has come disregarding etiquette to mourn and honour: Mr Merrick,[39] the US Ambassador, with his mask of tragic beauty is to die a few days later, perhaps the long march behind his friend's body will contribute to his death. . . . Great Britain has sent her Ambassador, an Admiral, several Field-Marshals and an Air Chief-Marshal. Canada is represented by the Honorable Philippe Roy, National Defence by General Sir H. E. Burstall;[40] the Honorable Peter Larkin[41] attends also.

After the service the Cathedral mourners form up on the Place du Parvis de Notre Dame: behind the troops, already in position far ahead, come the Papal Nuncio, the Cardinals, the Marshal's charger draped in black, the 75' gun-carriage upon which lies the Marshal. Nine nations, in addition to France, are represented among the pall-bearers: Field-Marshal Lord Plumer[42] is given the place of honour. Directly behind the coffin, three officers – British, French, Polish – carry on cushions the Marshal's batons: then follow, twelve artillery N.C.Os holding decorations and insignia, the nurses attending during the last illness, the family, the officers who, at various times, served on Marshal Foch's staff. . . . The President of the French Republic standing alone, the Prince of Monaco, the Prince of Wales and Prince Charles of Belgium, Ambassadors, Ministers. . . . Then a group composed of naval, military and air representatives and attachés, at the head of which is the British Delegation – Admiral Wemyss, Field-Marshals Methuen, Allenby, Jacob, Milne and Air-Marshal Trenchard: Field-Marshal Methuen, in spite of his 84 years, will complete the arduous march from Notre Dame to Les Invalides (a few days later *The Times* will publish a letter from him to say that he attended Wellington's funeral and that he has not been in Paris since the Germans marched in and out during the Franco-Prussian War). I am with the latter group: Commandant Cuny, a French Cavalry officer and a friend of Staff College days, provides a strong helpful arm of which I will take full advantage.

39. Myron Timothy Merrick, 1854-1929.
40. General Sir H. E. Burstall, 1875-1945.
41. 1856-1930.
42. Field-Marshal Viscount Plumer, 1857-1932.

The sky is darkening now. The historic march begins, through the section of Paris where Kings and Emperors have been made and discarded.

Pont d'Arcole, a grey Seine: Hotel de Ville, fifty and more stone figures of France's past look down, among them Richelieu, Molière, Tourville. Rue de Rivoli, the corridor of faces – an unending strip of faces unrolls as the cortège advances – faces from the street to the roof, from the roof to the street, faces pale, tense, thrust forward – faces . . . they are merging, there is only one face now, the face of Paris anxious and wondering. Place du Louvre, one breathes here – the obsession of faces is ended – The Musée du Louvre, Ney, Kléber, other soldiers in niches, overlook the street; there are empty niches, one day Marshal Foch will have his. . . . Place des Pyramides, Jeanne d'Arc – one of the Marshal's last acts was to write of the Maiden-warrior.

The sky is quite dark now, by a curious and impressive phenomenon of nature, Paris is shrouded in an ashen mist, through which the draped street-lamps stand out like enormous funeral candles.

Jardin des Tuileries, behind the iron gratings the 'mutilés' and their families look through the bars. . . .

La Concorde – faces again . . . but with spaces to counteract the oppression . . . a grey-black mass covered by a flesh-coloured open-work quilt. . . . The Strasbourg monument . . . the dead liberator passes. Champs Elysées – one looks in vain for the Arc de Triomphe, it is hidden in the eclipse-like atmosphere – the unknown soldier does not see, from afar, the passing Chief . .

Pont Alexandre III – slowly, out of the haze rises, from where one knows Les Invalides to be, the Cross in which Marshal Foch believed above the sword . . .

The darkness is lifting.

The people of the Procession take their places in two large stands facing Les Invalides . . . the tricoloured gun-carriage lies between. . . .

Monsieur Poincaré proclaims – in an oration worthy of Bossuet – the admiration and the thanks of France. General Gouraud, one-armed and limping, takes his stand before the iron gates of Les Invalides of which he is Governor: he draws his sword to salute. . . .

The march past begins . . . the sun gilds the Dome.

No funeral airs now – there are no dead – only the triumphant blast of trumpets, the stirring strains of march music. The French army is passing in battle array – men, horses, guns and tanks, they are all there. Flags dip, swords flash, turrets turn. . . . The tricolour over the gun-carriage has felt the hot breath of the passing tumult. . . . It too is moving now. . . .

More troops are coming, not French – but British, Guardsmen, Highlanders, Air Force; men wearing the uniform of the U.S.A.:

Belgians, in service greatcoats, steel helmeted: Italian Chasseurs Alpins. . . .

It is 1918 . . . the Commander-in-Chief is reviewing his troops . . .

From Les Invalides Napoleon has seen and wondered at the armies of the world passing by. . . . Why should mankind have waited so long before paying this armed tribute to his genius . . . still it is pleasant even now – better late than never – Yes, even the British Guard. . . . A happy moment that . . . worth waiting for . . . What! Not for him, not for Napoleon! . . . Then what manner of man is here? He must not be kept waiting . . .

Napoleon beckons. . .

The gates of Les Invalides are opened – Napoleon and Foch are together.[43]

43. Personal Notes.

CHAPTER 9

BETWEEN FRIENDS

I

THE corner stone of the League of Nations Building was laid on
the 7th of September 1929. The ceremony was to take place at
3 p.m. and Georges was commissioned to deposit in the stone –
whose hollowness was ironically prophetic – a number of Canadian coins and some papers which had been received from Canada.
Through some mistake or minor fatality he reached the stone
just before it was sealed. For a long time afterwards he was to ask
himself the agonizing question – what would he have done if he
had got there too late? Would he have admitted the tragic omission, which might only have been discovered five hundred years
afterwards when the building had crumbled into dust – if indeed
it was ever discovered at all?

This was not his only *mauvais quart d'heure*. He described the
26th of April 1929, as Black Friday because on that day the USA
and Great Britain declared themselves no longer interested in the
matter of trained reserves. He considered general conscription incompatible with peace; the two could no more live together than
cat and dog. Britain and America had thus forfeited the moral
authority which might just have persuaded the other nations to
abandon the principle of conscription.

Georges' appointment in Geneva was to end in 1930, and he was
wondering what he would be doing next. Sir Eric Miéville, Private
Secretary to Lord Willingdon, sent him pertinent advice:

You say that you do not know what will happen to you after 1930.
I know what *ought* to happen to you and that is that you should join
the Diplomatic Service. . . . It is a matter on which I am very keen,
because, to be perfectly frank, I do not consider that Canada is
getting the best men to assist her representatives abroad. And it is
really frightfully important.[1]

A friend from Brussels had also written: 'Dieu vous a marqué pour
quelque grande chose'. These prophetic intuitions were timely,

1. 11th May 1929.

for the suggestion was now put forward that he should join Vincent Massey's[2] staff at the Canadian Legation in Washington with the rank of First Secretary. The post would carry a salary of $3,840 a year with $3,000 allowances, and the probability of disarmament work on the spot. Dandurand had warmly recommended him, but Georges twice declined the offer. Dr Skelton,[3] the Canadian Under-Secretary for External Affairs agreed about his high qualifications, but told Dandurand that it was impossible to give him the rank of Counsellor immediately. This might be possible in a year or two when some alternative post fell vacant. Meanwhile Georges was writing to Harry Baldwin, Private Secretary to Mackenzie King:

I have not yet made up my mind whether I shall stay on in the army indefinitely. . . . I shall have to take a decision in this matter within the next two years, but meanwhile it would be a mistake, I believe, to accept a position the duties of which would be entirely foreign to army work Such a course would close definitely all access to any other military appointments.[4]

And he gave a further reason in a subsequent letter to Mathews:

I am beginning to understand something about the history and problems of disarmament and I feel that if I can be of any use to National Defence in Geneva it is from now onwards. Disarmament is entering a most interesting phase which may lead in a relatively short time to the General Conference on Disarmament.[5]

He wrote in the same sense to Massey, adding that he had been strongly tempted to accept; and Willingdon regretted that he had not done so: 'You and Pauline would have been ideal'.

In a further long letter to Mathews Georges described the sense of shame and uneasiness which prevailed among the members of the Disarmament Commission:

The President of the Commission, Monsieur Loudun, stated that he had received thousands of letters, which had been packed in large boxes placed in view of the delegates as a constant reminder. These letters came from organizations of many kinds representing several million people and a section of public opinion in 17 countries: it may interest you to know there were no letters from Canada.

France, Japan and Chile were opposed to the Soviet proposals,

2. The Right Hon. Vincent Massey, 1887-1967.
3. Oscar Douglas Skelton, 1878-1941.
4. 13th May 1929.
5. 20th September 1929.

whereupon the Soviet representatives threatened to withdraw if they were not accepted. The matter was then referred to the Bureau of the League, which ruled that the Soviet memorandum be annexed to the proceedings of the Commission when its report was completed. No specific reference was to be made to gas warfare in the draft convention to be submitted to the Disarmament Conference – this having been covered by the Protocol of 1925 – and on the question of bombing Georges recorded a long conversation with Group-Captain W. F. MacNeice-Foster,[6] the British Air Expert on the Commission, who maintained that:

a) The State which in good faith did not build *bombing* machines might find itself defenceless against a State whose *civil* aviation had reached a high degree of development, particularly in the way of large, long range machines.
b) To ensure that the amendment would be operative *for all* States, it would be necessary to limit the size and power of civil aircraft (which of course States would never consent to do), otherwise States carrying out the provisions of the prohibition would be at a disadvantage vis-à-vis less scrupulous States possessing a strong civil air fleet which might be used for bombing.[7]

To sum up the discussions – or, more precisely, the divergences – it was beginning to look as if:

a) Military powers will dispose of land armaments and naval powers will dispose of naval armaments.
b) As a natural corollary of 'A', powers without important naval or military interests will have little influence in the councils of disarmaments.
This looks like the substitution of a purely subjective standard by which to measure the limitation and reduction of armaments.

The first part of the 6th Session of the Preparatory Commission had covered twenty-one meetings:

Why it should have been called the *first part* I cannot imagine. Here is one of those subtleties in which international commissions sometimes seem to take delight. But whether we give to the 21 meetings held the name of session or first part of a session, the fact remains that we have just gone through a phase of 'concessions' which bring the Disarmament Conference nearer but which may be harmful later on in the ultimate and definite settlement of disarmament problems.[8]

6. Air-Commodore W. F. MacNeice-Foster.
7. 28th April 1929.
8. 18th May 1929.

The Council of the League of Nations was meeting that year in Madrid, and the Vaniers, accompanied by Frances, went there with Dandurand, Riddell and Jean Désy, Counsellor to the Canadian Legation in Paris. Some amusing drawings describing 'the arrival of the Vanier family greeted by *banderillos* of honour' were sent by Réquin to welcome them at the Ritz Hotel. They were entertained by the Duke of Alba[9] at the Palacio Liria. The Duke, with his never-failing ancestral piety, showed them several letters of Mary Stuart, set out under a glass case above the letters of Queen Elizabeth. 'You see', he remarked, 'as a Stuart, I have made Queen Elizabeth take second place.' Briand, examining the letters, observed that the two Queens were probably continuing their polemic under the glass. On the same evening the Canadian party were presented to King Alfonso XIII and Queen Ena; the King promised that when he came to America he would come by the way of the St Lawrence out of regard for the 'Latin' population of Quebec. A dinner and reception followed at the British Embassy, where Sir George Grahame had invited Primo de Rivera[10] and members of Madrid society. The dictator's son, Miguel, had recently spent some time in America, and Frances Vanier recalled dancing with him in Washington. Miguel and his brother José – the founder of the Spanish Falange and executed soon after the outbreak of the Civil War – put themselves at the disposal of Frances and Pauline. Dandurand remembered them on the night of the reception at the Royal Palace:

the young officers in full-dress uniform entering the *salons* with these ladies and Colonel Vanier. Everyone around was whispering 'They're the Canadians'. It was delightful to see our pretty compatriots, so tall, and elegant, and with such a rare distinction of mind and carriage.[11]

Another brilliant evening was spent at the house of Pablo and Margaret de Doriga. Señora de Doriga was a Canadian by birth and her husband was a man of wide culture and fastidious taste. After dinner an Andalusian ensemble of dancer, guitarist, and singers entertained the company, their songs laden at times with a reminiscence of Arab incantations. There were visits to the Escorial and Toledo, where Maurice Barrés had gone to discover the secret of El Greco; and it was in El Greco's house, with the elongated and ecstatic apostles hovering over the tea table, that

9. The Duke of Berwick and Alba, 1878-1958.
10. General Miguel Primo de Rivera, 1870-1930.
11. Speech in Quebec, 8th March 1929.

Eugenio d'Ors' description of El Greco's art as 'ascetic deforma-
tion' was vividly brought to mind. For Georges Vanier, whose
interest in painting was growing day by day, the Prado was a
supreme experience. The great series of Velasquez impressed him
beyond everything else.

Throughout July Georges Vanier, with Dr Riddell, was engaged
with the Diplomatic Conference convened in Geneva to revise
the Red Cross Convention of 1906 and to prepare a Convention
for the treatment of prisoners of war. Forty-seven states sent
delegates, in addition to the League of Nations, the International
Committee of the Red Cross, and the Sovereign Order of the
Knights of Malta – although the last three bodies were not able
to vote. To expedite the work of the Conference two committees
were formed to deal, respectively, with the subjects under discussion. Vanier concerned himself with the revision of the Red
Cross Convention, and it will only be necessary here to single out
the points on which he exerted – or tried to exercise – his
influence.

To the article prescribing that the 'wounded and sick shall be
respected' it was proposed to add the words 'and protected in all
circumstances'; and to the phrase 'shall be taken care of' it was
proposed to add 'shall be treated with all humanity'. Vanier considered these modifications redundant; and he joined with the
majority in opposing a Hungarian proposal that only the
wounded, the sick or the medical services should be allowed to
approach within fifty metres of a medical establishment. In the
chapter dealing with medical units and establishments he supported the French proposal to substitute the word 'munitions' for
'cartridges'. Article Nine of the 1906 Convention had granted complete immunity to the guards of medical establishments, but this
exemption – hitherto supported by the Canadian Delegation – was
suppressed on the ground that serious abuses might result if the
guards themselves were not to be considered as prisoners of war
in the event of capture. Georges Vanier rallied to the majority
opinion, and did not press the point of view expressed in a
previous Despatch to External Affairs. He also supported a minor
French amendment replacing the words 'à son ennemi' by the
more generic 'à l'ennemi' covering the hypothesis of more than
one adversary. A recommendation from the tenth and eleventh
International Red Cross Conferences that, under circumstances of
special urgency, aid societies of neutral countries might go to the
help of the sick and wounded belligerents in close proximity to

these states was turned down by the Canadian Delegation, with the French, Belgian, Spanish and Polish Delegations in support. It was felt that this attempt to legislate for an exceptional occasion might be open to abuse. In the matter of medical transport three suggestions – mainly verbal – introduced by France, Germany and the United States were supported by Georges Vanier on behalf of the Canadian Delegation.

The Vaniers spent their summer leave at St Lunaire in Brittany, where they were joined by Judge and Mrs Archer.

The children were . . . literally . . . wild with joy : they raced about the broad stretch of hard fine sand, carrying and waving all the beach paraphernalia . . . shrimping nets, pails, shovels : in Geneva they knew little real freedom of movement (an apartment restricts youth's need of space and particularly of *displacement*). The beach of St Lunaire is the finest I have ever seen.[12]

Colonel Réquin also came for a few days. It was not only a common interest in painting and a mutual disillusion with disarmament which drew him and Georges together. 'You who love history and its realities'[13] Réquin was writing to him about this time.

The holiday was interrupted, however, when Georges was called upon to represent the Canadian Minister to France at the opening of the chapel at the cemetery of Notre Dame de Lorette, only a few miles from Vimy Ridge. With its 30,000 graves this was the only large French Memorial in the British sector of the Western Front. Six windows, designed by Henry A. Payne and placed at the end of the transepts, with St George and St Joan of Arc as their central figures, were the gifts of the British War Office on whose behalf, and on that of the Imperial War Graves Commission, the Secretary of State for War offered them to the Bishop of Arras. Georges Vanier spoke eloquently in French for his former comrades-in-arms :

The high places of France are well guarded : your dead keep watch on these uplands where the country's soul seems to escape and mount towards heaven. If Notre Dame de Lorette is yours, and altogether yours, Vimy belongs in part to Canada since the dawn of 9th April, 1917, when the Canadian Corps, under the command of our beloved chief, General Byng, who later took the title of Viscount Byng of Vimy, went forward to victory and sacrifice. Our brothers

12. Letter to Mrs Vanier, 10th August 1929.
13. 28th July 1929.

lie there under your generous soil where we are proud to leave them, and where they have found another fatherland, in communion with your own dead who are lying here, in a glory that is always fresh and in the luminous peace of immortality. Notre Dame de Lorette and Vimy are neighbours, and it is my wish to unite them in a common thought, as I salute this sacred corner of France.

Lord Byng had been gravely ill, shortly after writing to Georges that he was 'studying the claims of a rascally Italian to conduct a house of ill fame'. The Vaniers had seen him in London, still barely convalescent:

He looked very ill, although at the time the trip to South Africa had been set definitely for the end of December – it will be a long, a very long time before he is well again, because of the state of exhaustion in which he is. However there is no reason, according to the doctors, why he should not recover completely.[14]

Georges was recalled to Geneva for three days at the end of August for the Fourth Session of the Special Commission to prepare a Draft Convention on the supervision of the private manufacture of arms, ammunition, and implements of war, and of the publicity pertaining thereto. He again accompanied Riddell, who put the Canadian point of view on the problems under discussion. In the autumn he was appointed to represent Canada at the Naval Conference due to open in London early in the New Year. The General Assembly of the League was in session, and Georges got the impression that the British experts were not consulted in any way by their Government, the Prime Minister – Ramsay Mac-Donald – holding that disarmament was a political rather than a technical problem. Georges admitted that he might be right, but this did not make things easier for the experts. Looking ahead to the Naval Conference, he doubted whether France and Italy would accept definite figures for ships and tonnage, since they regarded the reduction of naval, air and land armament as interdependent, and held that specific figures under specific heads could only be agreed to as part of a total settlement – in other words, at a general disarmament conference. One was back at square one: 'They might accept a lower tonnage and fewer ships if Great Britain and the United States agreed, in what is called here a spirit of conciliation, to forget about trained reserves.'[15] The position of Great Britain and the United States was quite

14. Letter to Mrs Vanier, 29th August 1929.
15. Letter to H. G. D. Crerar, 21st October 1929.

different, since neither was the least interested in land armaments, and could arrive at a naval agreement without waiting for a general conference. Where their views were diametrically opposed was on the freedom of the seas.

'The Conference' Georges wrote to his mother 'will be tremendously interesting – not so much from the *technical* standpoint as from the *political*: the details of disarmament are unimportant compared with the aims, the aspirations, the interests and *fears* of the nations.' He went on to describe the family Christmas at Geneva:

Pauline and I had quite as much fun as the children . . . the tree was brought to the apartment at 8 o'clock after the young ones had gone to bed. I had read them the poem you taught me years ago 'T'was the night before Christmas and all through the house, not a creature was stirring, not even a mouse'. They had never heard it before so it had a great success. We had sixteen electric bulbs of various colours which were bright with tinsel and toys of all kinds. When the children came into the room they went first to the manger where they said a prayer and afterwards they were given Santa's many wonderful gifts. The children behaved well, much better than I used to, and managed to get through the Christmas period *without indigestion*. We were all very sorry when the 25th came to an end. . . . Thérèse is becoming quite expert with her electric questionnaire . . . a very ingenious game.[16]

2

The London Naval Conference opened at St James's Palace on the 21st of January 1930. It was attended by the representatives of five powers – the British Commonwealth, France, Italy, the United States and Japan. The Canadian Delegation, acting independently but in concert with the British, consisted of Commodore Walter Hose, Chief of the Naval Staff, Colonel J. L. Ralston,[17] Minister of National Defence, and Georges Vanier. Mr L. B. Pearson was also there, staying with the other Canadian Delegates at the Mayfair Hotel. On the 20th of January they were all entertained by the Prime Minister, J. Ramsay MacDonald, at 10 Downing Street. The food was so inedible that the Vaniers and Réquin escaped as soon as they could to find another luncheon elsewhere. Moreover the Prime Minister was far declined along the slope of senility. He was quite unaware of what country they came from, and could

16. December 1929.
17. Colonel the Hon. James Layton Ralston, 1887-1948.

speak of little more important than the beauty of Nancy Astor's legs! This was light relief, in its way, and more innocent amusement was provided by Réquin who was staying with the French Delegation at the Ritz. Every morning a neat and amusing coloured sketch would be sent across to the Mayfair – Pauline Vanier putting on the Golf Course, with Georges and Frances trailing behind, and Réquin bringing up the rear – 'Comment je me suis engagé dans le Corps des Caddies'; the Vaniers trapesing along the corridor of their hotel, Georges carrying his hair-brush, because they were constantly having to change their rooms; sketches of fish, lions and tigers; and *pointilliste* or impressionist views of the Thames.

By the 1st of April, when Ralston returned to Canada to be replaced by Philippe Roy, the Conference had been dragging along very slowly. It was essentially a political conference, in which the experts had little to do. A cynical view of its proceedings was provided by Henri de Jouvenel who compiled a lexicon for the enlightenment of those who wished to follow them. The British Admiralty was defined as 'our enterprise of international philanthropy'; equality as 'an obsolete word replaced by "parity" to which not everyone was entitled'; the United States as 'a great nation which could not forgive Europe for having discovered it'; fair play as 'an Anglo-Saxon system for doing and getting others to do whatever England wanted'; freedom of the seas as 'freedom for the United States to dispose of the elements'; and security as 'the kind of feeling M. Tardieu did not experience when he was in the presence of Mr MacDonald.'

Georges regretted Ralston's departure; he thought him 'head and shoulders above any other of the Delegates from the Dominions.'[18] A five power agreement looked unlikely – and ultimately proved to be so – because Italy was demanding a parity which France refused. Parity having been accepted by both sides at the Washington Conference, it was a matter of amour-propre for Italy to stick to it. The French, on the other hand, insisted that as they had a longer coast-line and much longer sea communications to protect, they needed more ships. There was also the more basic reason of mutual mistrust. As for Canada, Ralston authorized the Delegation to state that her naval requirements would not be such as to cause the naval services of Great Britain, the different Dominions and India to exceed the total strength allocated to the British Commonwealth of Nations

18. Letter to H. G. D. Crerar, 1st April 1930.

in the proposed Agreement. On the 12th of April Vanier was writing to Crerar:

There is an atmosphere of hurry and haste at St James's Palace, which, in some respects, is not quite in keeping with the dignity of the place, and the importance of the work to be done. There is no use hurrying in the last stages of an important Treaty like the present one. There was an element of comedy in the fact that in adjoining rooms two Committees were meeting, one an Experts Committee and the other a Drafting Committee, and members of both Committees went from one room to the other to consult one another; I suggested to Massigli[19] that the doors be left open, and that an attempt be made by the various members of both Committees to listen to what was being said in both rooms at the same time.

The dominating personality of the Conference was Dwight Morrow,[20] who led the American Delegation. Like most Americans, he was content with a light luncheon:

At 12.45, Mr Dwight Morrow, who is a terrible driver, suggested that instead of adjourning for lunch, sandwiches and coffee be served to the Delegates. There was consternation on the part of the Latin representatives, who are used to no breakfast and a very copious and satisfying lunch; however, no one dared to object for fear of being considered responsible for delay in the drafting. At 1.30 the members of the Committee went downstairs to a buffet lunch that had been prepared, and which was excellent. Mr Dwight Morrow, who is very restless, and apparently never still, walked from table to table, talking to the various members of the Committee, meanwhile leaving his plate of ham and tongue untouched. Occasionally he murmured: 'What about a cup of coffee?' or, 'Where is that cup of coffee?' but nobody seemed to take any notice of his quest for a cup of coffee.[21]

The Conference ended in April with the Four Power Agreement which was generally foreseen. Georges Vanier attended all the meetings of the Drafting Committee, on which jurists sat as well as draftsmen. They sat all day – including Sunday – for a week and sometimes on into the night. Georges wrote to the husband of his private secretary: 'I suppose life will lose its thrill when the day, or rather the night, comes that there are not in her room to be guarded like the Ark of the Covenant numerous ugly boxes and files containing 'The Secret Records of St James's Palace – or why is the Navy Blue? by Sir Maurice

19. René Massigli, a member of the French Delegation.
20. Dwight Whitney Morrow, 1873-1931.
21. Personal Notes, 17th April 1930.

Hankey.' The work was so hectic that at times Pauline was called in as a deputy.

Back in Geneva, Georges found the Chairman of the Preparatory Commission, M. Loudun from the Netherlands, recovered from his influenza but not from his neurosis. He was huddled in a corner of the room, listening to the woes of the Delegates as if he were hearing their confessions. When Georges saw that he had 'no further penitents',[22] he went over and talked to him. They agreed that it would be a mistake to call another meeting of the Commission before the General Assembly in September. Georges then returned to London, where Pauline was on the eve of a serious operation. The entries in his diary at this time betray his deep concern:

21st May: Lady Carnarvon allows me to see Pauline as she is starting to regain consciousness. Her colour is good and clear. She says 'Is it all over . . . is it really finished?' I assure her that it is. 'Poor Georges – will you put some water on my tongue . . . have they cut me up? Give me some air, Georges.' A nurse gives her an injection of morphine, and little by little, as I hold her hand, she goes to sleep, repeating the same words, and I leave her. The nurse moistens her lips with cotton wool; Pauline's hands are white and bloodless, like wax, but gentle and no warmer than usual.

4.30 p.m. I saw Pauline for a few moments before they gave her another injection of morphia. I told her again that everything had been all right. . . . When I asked her how she felt, she made a face but said nothing. Pauline looks well, her pulse is good, and she is breathing normally. She doesn't appear to be in such pain as she was this morning.

Pauline's illness and slow convalescence forced the Vaniers to remain in London. Georges was now seeing a great deal of Lord Byng who had resumed his work at Scotland Yard. The two friends, with Lady Byng, would often dine together at 4 Bryanston Square. The conversation ran on the crisis in the Conservative Party. They agreed that Baldwin was a man of character, but doubted his capacity for leadership. Byng's opinion of Beaverbrook was higher than Georges', who questioned – unjustly – his patriotism but suspected, no doubt, his appetite for power. Unemployment was the agonising problem of the day, and when Georges asked whether any party could settle it, Byng replied: 'No, *a man*.' The man was wanting; but it is significant that both Byng and Vanier were impressed by Oswald Mosley's latest speech.

22. Letter to H. G. D. Crerar, 7th May 1930.

The country was prepared for drastic remedies, although the nature of Mosley's remedy had not yet been made clear. Byng thought that politicians thought too much of peace and too little of prosperity. 'They disband a few regiments and they scrap ships . . . and they throw more men on the dole'. There is a touching account of the meeting between Byng and Byngsie:

2nd July: 7 p.m. Went with Byngsie to see H.E. at Bryanston Square. H.E. was seated and smoking his pipe. When he saw us, he half got up, a little awkwardly; since he is not (alas!) used to children, he was not quite certain what to do. Byngsie went straight over to him, put his arms round his neck, and kissed him affectionately. H.E. was moved, and not far from tears. H.E. took Byngsie's hands in his own and held him close.

'How you have grown, Byngsie! How old are you?'

'Four and a half, sir.'

'And where are you going to soon?'

'To St Lunaire.'

H.E. takes a little note-book out of his pocket – a sort of diary with a tiny pencil fixed in the back of the cover – and said to me:

'Do you think he would like a little present?'

'I am sure he would, Sir.'

Then he opened the note-book and took out a 10/- note which he must have hidden there for the purpose. Byngsie accepted it with joy and thanked him. H.E. went on talking to Byngsie, who was pale but not intimidated. I said to Byngsie:

'Lord Byng is one of the finest men in the world, my boy.'

'And so is he,' said H.E., blushing.

He was nervous and unsure of himself – I confess that I don't know whether H.E. was talking to Byngsie about me. . . . There was a short and embarrassed silence.

I asked H.E. to add his signature to the photo of himself in Police Commissioner's uniform, and the words 'To Byngsie', which he did with a good grace. Byngsie, at my suggestion, wished H.E. 'Good health'. I thanked H.E., and Byngsie kissed him tenderly, and H.E. accompanied us into the hall where Nurse had been waiting. He shook hands with her and asked her how she was. Byngsie put on his straw hat, saluted H.E., and then we were on our way, leaving H.E. with a sad and tender smile on his lips.

H.E. is not well. God knows how long he'll last. Nurse, who had not seen him since 1926, found him bent and aged.

On the 5th of July Georges was at Thorpe-le-Soken, with Lord and Lady Titchfield, for the week-end. There was much talk of politics. Georges agreed with Titchfield that there should be some kind of permanent Imperial Council, having a purely consultative character, and he thought that after a few years, when Canada had achieved an important position among the nations of the world, she would lose her 'adolescent susceptibility'. Byng observed that if a Dominion wished to have a distinct foreign policy, it must be able to enforce that policy; and Georges added that the politicians could not go on declaring that Canada had no need of a navy. A country with a big merchant fleet must have an armed fleet as well. He had put the point to Dandurand, but Dandurand had disagreed with him. They talked of Vincent Massey, who was being spoken of as the next Canadian High Commissioner in London. Byng wondered if he were not 'too Balliol' for the job, and Georges agreed that he was the least typical of Canadians. Georges and Titchfield also talked of the war – but on this, as usual, Byng would say nothing.

A fortnight later Georges was again at Thorpe-le-Soken. Pauline's illness had involved him in considerable expense, and Byng broached the possibility of helping him. Nothing illustrates more clearly the character of the two men, and the delicate *rapport* between them, than George's record of their conversation:

23rd July. At breakfast. H.E.: 'There is something I want to speak to you about. I know you have had a hard time lately. Can I help you? I would like to do something for you . . . and Pauline.'

He seemed a little embarrassed as he said this, and his tone was very affectionate. I wasn't expecting this offer, and wishing to understand what H.E. was really thinking, I answered: 'May I think about it, Sir, and may I say how much I appreciate the thought?'

Reflections of G.P.V. during the day. Perhaps H.E. thinks that I am momentarily embarrassed and would like to advance me the money to pay Richardson or Cassidy, or both. . . . I can manage, and even manage very well, since the grandfathers are generous . . . the truth is that I can pay everything, and pay it now, but . . . H.E. wants to help me, I know it would please him . . . have I the right to refuse? I decide – no; I shall accept the offer and repay him in a few months' time. I shall speak to him about it tomorrow.

24th July: At breakfast. 'I have thought of what you said yesterday . . . really I can manage very well . . . on the other hand I suppose one should pay these bills as soon as possible . . . Richardson's account is paid.'

'How much was it?'

'The operation itself cost about £120 – that is paid – but Cassidy's bill – he was very reasonable in his charges – is not paid yet and it amounts to one hundred guineas.'

Reply: 'Why don't you let me pay that?'

G.P.V.: 'Well, Sir, it would be a great help and I could pay you back in a few months . . .' (I see that I have struck the wrong note . . . I look at H.E. . . . it's a *gift* that he wants to make me . . . I wait). H.E. hesitates: then: 'Oh George, it's a little douceur I would like to offer you. I have some pennies and I would like to give you some of them.'

I try not to show my surprise . . . what should I reply?

'It is very nice of you, but' (I proceed tentatively, he *wants* to help us . . . what should I do or say?)

'Not nice at all – it gives me pleasure. . . . I have thought a great deal about this. . . . I have wondered whether we are great enough friends – we are great friends aren't we? – to do this – only very great friends could do this without any *arrière pensée*. I would like to pay Cassidy's bill, George . . .'

'Before you go on, I think it only fair to explain the situation to you, Sir. *I can afford* to pay the account. It would be a temporary relief to me . . . but there must not be any false pretences on my part, it will not be a hardship for me to pay. . . .'

'False pretences – my dear George! . . . I *want* to help you and perhaps I am putting you in a position of embarrassment . . . of obligation to me? . . . I hope not . . .'

'There is no one else in the world' (apart from our parents, I meant, and he understood) 'from whom I would accept such a gift. . . .'

'I know that George, I had hoped that . . . George . . .' (But a hundred guineas, no, really that has no sense, I must protest. . . .)

'Perhaps you might pay half of Cassidy's bill . . . it would be a great help. . . .'

'No George – the whole of it . . . let me. . . .'

After breakfast I am in my study (Eva's[23] room), and H.E. brings me a cheque for £105. 'Let's hear no more about it, George.'

No man has ever given me such proof of trust and affection – I accept this money with joy – it is the finest and most touching compliment that H.E. could have paid me, and I believe that *in accepting it* I am paying him the finest compliment that one man can pay another – to accept his money, for the medical care given to my wife, *a miracle of friendship*.

Georges Vanier's fears for the health of his former chief were only too well founded. On the 26th of July, after some talk about the Canadian General Election, and betting on a Conservative victory, Byng handed Georges a heavy stick and thistle cutter, and they went out into the field. The conversation turned on hawks

23. Eva Sandford, a friend and formerly lady-in-waiting to Lady Byng.

– not yet a political synonym – and the gamekeeper observed that he had shot one the previous afternoon. Georges' diary takes up the story :

H.E. 'There is a hawk on the tree (tree about 200 yards away) do you see it?'

I say 'Yes'. H.E. goes quickly in the direction taken by the keeper, walks 75 yards when the bird flies away. 'He's gone' (I don't think however it was a hawk but a rook.) I go towards him to centre of field – we then walk towards fringe of cart road about 15 yards from the road. He says :

'We might start here – don't start too near anyone when cutting the thistles. . . .' Cutting thistles we move slowly away from one another. I go on cutting. Occasionally I look up and see H.E. who seems to be taking things easy. A little after 11 (I should say) I look up and see Eva near him – cutting thistles also – I am about 75 yards from them. . . . About 10 minutes later I look up again and see H.E. in a sitting posture . . . then I see him quietly and slowly fall over on his side. Eva sees incident at same moment. I run towards H.E. – Eva already there – we raise him to sitting posture – undo collar, tie, shirt . . . eyes closed, he is quite unconscious, breathing heavily and with difficulty at rather lengthy intervals – I mean about once each second – his colour to me does not seem too bad – he is rather brick coloured, there is a trickle of saliva from his mouth. He is quite helpless. Eva runs for brandy and for doctor. About four minutes later Orchin[24] arrives with brandy – all the while H.E.'s breathing is the same, heavy and difficult . . . give him a little brandy . . . breathing becomes easier, he seems relieved . . . after about five minutes of easier breathing and two or three small doses of brandy, breathing becomes heavier and harsher again. The first words H.E. says (about 15 to 20 minutes after falling over) are : 'I'm absolutely all right.' 'Yes, Sir, you're all right.' Eyes begin to open. 'I'm quite all right.' Car arrives in field about 20 minutes after the accident. We (Orchin and others) lift H.E. in and seat him on floor of car. En route to house H.E. opens eyes and says : 'What's happened George?' 11.40 a.m. by my wrist-watch. This is the first time he realizes (I believe) that something has happened. 'Oh you were just a little ill. . . .' 'I'm very sorry, George, about this . . . I'm very sorry I've given you all this trouble.' (His first thought is for us. H.E. has beads of perspiration on his head). He is lifted into the house and placed in his chair in his study, feet on a footstool. Dr W. arrives a few moments later. H.E. looking a little better . . . While Dr is sterilizing his needle, H.E.: 'What's happened George? What an idiotic thing to do when one is perfectly well . . . What a d . . . fool I am . . . What a devil of a fuss I have made . . .' To Eva and

24. The butler.

to me: 'I am very grateful dear people . . . but I'm very sorry I gave you all this trouble . . .'

The recovery was very slow, if indeed it was recovery at all. For nearly three weeks Georges Vanier never left the large white rectangular house with the heavy creepers, and whenever Byng was able to talk Georges talked with him. The Doctor had told Byng that he had had a 'close call' and seemed surprised when the information did not 'frighten him into a jelly'. 'Perhaps it was a close thing and that I was near death – perhaps one was dead for just a moment – but each one of us is near death each day. Sometimes several times in a day. . . . some of these doctors have no knowledge of human nature.' They spoke of Heaven and Hell, and the difficulty of believing that Heaven was a place of happiness if the people one loved were in Hell; and as they talked Georges noted the 'sad, wistful look' in Byng's eyes which were very close to tears. They discussed mind and matter, Byng expressing his admiration for Bergson and quoting the American philosopher who had described him as 'a David out to slay the Goliath of materialism'. Tolerance was essential to philosophy. 'Plato and Socrates were tolerant, George; Aristotle was not. What is it someone said of Plato, that he had a ferocious love of humanity?'

They discussed the nature of good. Would you do something for a person you disliked as readily as for one you liked? If so, would it make you love that person any better? Byng thought not. In that case, weren't you disproving the idea that good was founded on love? Would Georges distribute tickets for an interesting meeting at Geneva impartially to people he liked and disliked? Georges said no. Very well, then, would it be wrong not to do so—These two supremely good men did not get very far in their definition of goodness; altruism and utilitarianism were always getting in the way.

The result of the elections brought the Conservatives, under R. B. Bennett,[25] to power. Byng did not conceal his satisfaction, and he asked Georges why there were no French-Canadian Conservatives. Georges explained that the French-Canadians were naturally conservative, but that Laurier had changed their orientation, and that since 1917 the Provincial elections in Quebec had been decided by the issue of conscription.

I deplore the dishonest attitude of the Liberal leaders who exploited the conscription issue in 1930 – Lapointe, Dandurand, Lemieux –

25. The Right Hon. Viscount Bennett, 1870-1947.

whom one would have thought above such manoeuvres. I say that I 'deplore', because I am still theoretically a Liberal. I have no official politics while I am on the active list of the army. If I were a Conservative, I would use a different word.

Byng observed that Georges was 'a funny kind of Liberal', and Georges replied simply: 'Before being a Liberal I am some other things' – and they went on to talk of Mackenzie King:

'I have tried not to be vindictive, George.'
'It's a thing you've never been, Sir.'
'I mean with King . . . it would have been awful to be vindictive . . . What is good for Canada, George, is good for me.'

Byng suggested that Bennett might bring Georges Vanier into his Government, but Georges – not wishing to contradict him – said nothing. 'I am not a Conservative' he noted 'I am a Liberal, pro H. E., anti-King, that is my political faith.' It was a profession that would not have got him very far inside politics, but did not prevent him going a very long way outside them. He was to owe his two most important appointments respectively to a Liberal and Conservative Prime Minister, and it was a source of sadness to him as the years went by that, for all his gratitude to Mackenzie King, he could never forget what King had done to the man he revered above any other man in the world. Indeed the contrast was striking between Byng in 1926, 'shattered by the dishonesty of a man who did not keep his word', but still strong in body, and Byng in 1930 'physically ill but spiritually serene.'

The rain fell on the August Bank Holiday, but did not depress the relative merriment of the breakfast table. No English breakfast table is really merry. Then Byng told a story about his mother, and Georges remarked that she must have been a very charming woman, and Byng – 'a delicate film over his eyes and a very beautiful – in a way childlike – smile on his face' – agreed that she was. The depth of Georges Vanier's feelings about his own mother rarely came out in his letters to her, but in recording the conversation he notes in a moving parenthesis:

Mother, how we come to you always near the end . . Oh the wonder and the beauty of the Mother-Child and particularly the mother-son relationship – there is something in it of the divine . . . Although smiling – H.E. will always smile – he is very tired.

But although Byng was tired, scarcely lifting his feet from the ground as he walked, he could still discuss *la bonne cuisine* and ask why the good things like oysters, asparagus, mushrooms and mackerel lasted such a short time? Someone might have answered that mushrooms and mackerel were comparatively long-lived. When a rabbit was spotted on the lawn, everyone agreed that it was very sporting of this endearing and destructive animal to appear in full view of the dining-room during the luncheon hour. In the afternoon there was a little pruning in the garden, and in the evening Byng would play Patience – wondering, with that alert curiosity of his, what exactly was the meaning of the Ace of Spades? A natural philosopher, Byng believed there was a meaning in everything – 'if only philosophy could find it out'. Nothing escaped his vigilant eye, for now he had nothing to do but look and think and listen. They noticed that the rooks were coming home to roost earlier than usual, and when a bird swooped on to the grass just outside the window, Byng observed: 'What wonderful breakfasts go on there . . . I saw that bird pull out something – a worm I suppose – it came out just like macaroni – probably just as good.' And he wondered if the King would send them grouse from Balmoral.

With his favourite stimulant of a Fine Champagne, the General talked more freely at dinner, asking Georges about the Staff College:

We had a very fine lot of fellows, George . . . most of them are gone now . . . several killed in the South African war . . . others in the last war. . . . If I had any fault to find with them it would be this – about one third of them had only one ambition – to be on a Staff . . . Had you the same experience at the Staff College?

Georges replied that, like himself, nearly all his contemporaries at Camberley had seen active service during the war. About the war itself again they spoke very little – Georges was worried because the reports to Third Army H.Q. had not given Byng a proper appreciation of Tremblay – and only rarely of religion. 'Do you consider yourself a good Catholic, George?' Georges replied that it was not altogether a question of being 'good', and Byng went on:

I agree that good is not the word I should have used . . . I have been reading about Luther and Erasmus . . . The Reformation was caused by bad priests . . . I think the Reformation – although deploring the bloodshed – did good . . . *people are better now* . . . If I thought I should be better as a Catholic than as a Protestant, I might become a Catholic, but I don't think I should be any different to

what I am . . . I was born a Protestant and I shall die a Protestant
. . . I am an ad.'

'And what is that, Sir?'

'One who does not believe in religious controversy.'

One morning he wished to revisit the field where he had collapsed with his heart attack. The thistles were lying on the
ground and Byng remarked that they had done good work in
cutting them down, and apologized for spoiling the morning's
sport. 'It's very nice' he said, looking over the valley and then,
surveying the hedge, thought it a mistake on nature's part that
blackberries did not come from blackthorns. He was delighted to
receive one day a letter addressed to 'Lord Byng, Vimy Ridge,
Thorpe-le-Soken'; the incongruity appealed to him, and Georges
observed :

'It's a nice title – Byng of Vimy.'

'None finer, George.'

'And splendid for Canadians to be associated with it.'

'I wouldn't have had it if it hadn't been for the Canadians.'

'Oh, they just happened to be there, Sir.'

It was said of Georges Vanier by one who knew him well that
his attitude towards Almighty God was that of a Major-General to
a Field-Marshal. There was more – and in a sense less – to it than
that. Georges was not yet a Major-General and Byng was not yet
a Field-Marshal, but whenever Georges looked for an authority
whom he could love without presumption and admire without a
trace of fear, it was to Julian Byng that his mind instinctively
turned. Byng would receive his baton in due course, and the
Field-Marshal would have played a vital part in Georges Vanier's
progress along the path where Byng had preceded him.

CHAPTER 10

CANADA HOUSE

I

WHILE Georges was in attendance on one General, Pauline was convalescing with another in the room adjoining her own. General Gordon, who was indirectly descended from Gordon of Khartoum, gallantly sent her books of poetry, with the favourite passages marked for her perusal. Later she took the family to St Lunaire where Georges joined them as soon as Byng was well enough to release him. In September they returned to Geneva in time for the General Assembly of the League. Sir Robert Borden[1] had succeeded Dandurand as head of the Canadian Delegation, and was often with the Vaniers in the rue Bellot. When the conversation turned on the suppression of titles for Canadian citizens, Borden surprised them by saying that he hoped Bennett would reverse this prohibition. He had been in power himself when the request had been made to the King – to whom it was not at all congenial – but it had gone forward without his knowledge. Georges saw the point of Sir Thomas Wilford's[2] argument that a title was the only honour in which a wife could share – and Georges Vanier knew the importance of wives. He found Borden 'a most delightful man to work with and under; he has a very keen sense of humour and, I believe, made a good impression on the Assembly . . . In spite of his seventy-six years, he was energetic and active and his mind is as clear as that of a young man.' It was never clearer than when General Herzog, the Wilfords, Leo Kennedy, Judge Archer, Dr and Mrs Riddell, Princess Radziwill, and others met at the Vaniers for dinner. Borden and Wilford 'told stories after the port and entertained the rest of the men for over half an hour'. It was only a pity they could not have entertained the ladies.

Meanwhile the deadlock between France and Italy was slightly relieved when both countries agreed to suspend naval construction until the end of the year. At the meeting of the Preparatory

1. The Right Hon. Viscount Borden, 1854-1937.
2. Sir Thomas Wilford, 1870-1939, the New Zealand High Commissioner in London.

Commission in November a draft convention was at last agreed upon as a basis for the general Disarmament Conference expected for 1932 – in Georges Vanier's opinion, ten years too late. There was now little hope that the contracting parties would agree to minimum figures for arms and personnel lower than the ones existing already. When the Draft Convention was submitted to the Council of the League in January, it was generally approved, except by the German representative, Dr Curtius.[3] Having been forcibly disarmed herself, Germany was naturally anxious that those who had disarmed her should do something more effective to disarm themselves. The beginning of February 1932 was fixed on as the date for the Disarmament Conference, and Geneva chosen as the place. There was no agreement as to who should be Chairman, in spite of considerable support for Dr Beneš.[4] With these further deliberations Georges Vanier had nothing to do, but he accurately foresaw their fruitlessness:

The present situation and the present Convention lead to a complete *impasse*. You can be quite sure that, barring a revolution or a cataclysm of some sort, Germany will not agree to sign a convention which requires that the Versailles military obligations imposed upon her be respected, and that France, will not agree to the same military clauses being put aside. So there you are! – and what will the result be? I can see only one: the great majority of States will be in favour of the Versailles clauses being respected and a few will be against; the Convention will be signed by those in favour but certainly not by Germany. It is possible that as a result of the above situation Germany might withdraw from the League, and that undoubtedly would be a most serious matter.[5]

Germany did withdraw, and the result was serious indeed. The only error in Georges Vanier's prediction was that the cataclysm came after the withdrawal rather than before.

Pauline had returned to England, but was back in Geneva for Christmas, still needing 'rest, recreation, outdoor exercise and air and proper diet, and very exhausted nervously'.[6] Frances was with them, and in February Georges returned to Canada. The idea had already been mooted that he should replace Lucien Pacaud as Secretary to the Canadian High Commission in London, but neither he nor Pauline were anxious for another posting in

3. Julius Curtius, 1877-1948.
4. Dr Edvard Benes, 1884-1948.
5. Letter to H. G. D. Crerar, 6th February 1931.
6. Letter to Mrs Vanier, 1st January 1931.

Europe. A letter from Lord Byng, recuperating in the South of France, was influential in deciding him to accept:

The whole point of my argument is that I would like to see you in a job where your abilities, knowledge of men and matters, manner and Manners etc. would have some scope – in fact where you would have some ideal of life to chew upon. Geneva does not give it, the Royal 22nd does not give it, and beginning again in the Law, which is probably overcrowded, offers at best the academic future that one sees everywhere in that profession. You and Pauline should make a huge success of London, and a huger success of French and English Canadianism in London.[7]

Georges left for Europe in the *Berengaria* on the 31st of March, preoccupied as usual, not with himself but with other people. Pacaud had not been considered in all respects satisfactory, and there was some doubt as to whether he would receive a pension. Before sailing, therefore, Georges wrote a letter to the Prime Minister, R. B. Bennett, which was as bold a *démarche* as any subordinate ever made to his chief:

Dear Mr Bennett,
    Since I saw you I have thought a great deal about poor Lucien Pacaud's message. I was so surprised at the tone of the cable that my immediate reaction was not clear and definite enough to give expression to at once. But I must say now – at the risk even of being thought importunate – what is in my mind.
    What manner of man wrote it? A beaten man, and I should think a penniless – perhaps an indebted – man to whom one year's salary seems now to be a fortune.
    During the last nine years Pacaud has carried out to the best of his ability – the duties of a very responsible appointment (or so I consider it); for personal reasons over which he may have no control he is to leave the London office. Perhaps for the same personal reasons he cannot see his way clear to go to Tokio; possibly he may wish to ability the duties of a very responsible appointment (or so I consider it); for personal reasons over which he may have no control he remain with his daughter. He is 51 – before him – nothing. His message to you shows that he cannot fight for himself. He asks for a year's salary when, if he had a proper appreciation of life values, he would ask for a pension, if there is nothing to offer him except far-away Tokio. Putting myself in his stead, I take the liberty of imploring you to give him a pension – He has been a member of the House of Commons; he has been Canada's Acting High Commissioner for a very long period, he has been a good servant of the country – he is broken now – You have the wonderful opportunity, Sir, of being

7. 1st March 1931.

magnanimous and helpful to one who was not of your party – it will be a great satisfaction to you and a relief to those who still believe that an ideal is not incompatible with party politics. You will have the whole-hearted support of the opposition, which may or may not be indifferent to you. Every Canadian would hate later on to see, in regrettable straits, one who for nearly a year was Canada's representative and spokesman in London.

I shall not write further, knowing that you dislike unnecessary words. But if I had the great honour of being Prime Minister I would give Pacaud a pension, if this were at all possible, and if, Sir – pushing the fantasy further – you were George Vanier I would not be angry with you for writing this letter.

I shall write to you from the *Berengaria* to express adequately my deep feeling of gratitude and of appreciation not only for the confidence which you have shown in me but for the kind and understanding manner with which you have treated me and for the frankness with which you have allowed me to speak to you.

> Believe me, dear Mr Bennett,
> Your Obedient Servant and Debtor,
> (signed) George P. Vanier.[8]

Georges' appointment was announced by the Prime Minister in the House of Commons on the 8th of May in reply to a question by Mackenzie King. His duties were very much those of an understudy to Howard Ferguson,[9] the High Commissioner. Should the Prince of Wales or the Duke of York open the Regina Grain Exhibition in 1932? If the Duchess went, a great deal of extra expense would be involved in difficult times. What could be done for Mrs G. J. Howard pleading for some recognition for her daughter who had been running Nova Scotia House since her father's death? Mr Howard had been promised a Knighthood by the Nova Scotia Prime Minister who had then forgotten all about it and Mr Howard had given thirty-seven years of his life, and much of his fortune, to Nova Scotia. The Wheat Conference at Canada House in May, with forty delegates from eleven wheat-exporting countries; the unveiling of a commemorative plaque to Douglas Haig at the Château de Beaurepaire at Montreuil-sur-Mer, which had been the General's H.Q. during the Great War; a speech at the Canadian cemetery at Shorncliffe; the presentation of a walking stick to the Captain of the *Farnworth* at the Royal Victoria Docks in recognition of the first shipment of grain from Western Canada to the United Kingdom by the Hudson Bay route – all

8. 30th March, 1931.
9. The Hon. George Howard Ferguson, 1870-1946.

these required Georges Vanier's presence, participation, and – when occasion demanded – felicity of phrase.

If anyone wanted employment at Canada House, it was Georges Vanier's business to receive them and generally to send them empty away. This produced some ludicrous incidents, one of which threatened to be macabre.

A man who had been to Canada and thought that fact alone entitled him to an appointment, became abusive when told that there were no vacancies and said I would hear from him again. I did, indeed . . . He wrote later to say he would be coming on a certain day to Canada House, when to punish me for my iniquity he would commit suicide. This was rather depressing but I thought it better than murder. I had never before received a man the object of whose visit was so unpleasant. But as hospitality is a great virtue and Canada had tried to uphold a reputation for hospitality, I decided to receive him with the honours due to his rank or rather suitable to his mission. So with the aid of the County Council an ambulance was produced and with the aid of Scotland Yard a few policemen. The stage was beautifully set and we awaited the hero's coming with bated breath. But he never turned up. We had the stage but no actor. Perhaps the sight of the ambulance put him off or perhaps it was the police.

In the second case it was again a question of employment, and again the man was told there was no hope of giving him work.

He then turned to me and asked: 'Are you a Canadian anyway?' And I answered very slowly and deliberately: 'I have been a Canadian for 300 years.' He looked at me, rose at once and made for the door. I could see what was going through his head. He may have been crazy but he thought I was crazier.[10]

Georges had a very clear view of the English character from his windows overlooking Trafalgar Square. He watched the hunger march when the desperate participants assembled for their protest, each group led by a friendly policeman and flanked by other policemen with whom they engaged in amiable conversation. They were shown politely to their places in the square, and the policemen appeared to enjoy the many hard things that were being said. At about 4.30 there was a slight drizzle; the crowd became a little restless – not with hunger but with thirst. It was tea-time; and tea was the great imperative of English life. Georges Vanier was not deceived by the modest appearances of English understatement. He saw it as 'a sure sign that the speaker does not suffer from an inferiority complex. It is only someone pretty sure of

10. Address to the University Club, Montreal, undated.

himself who can afford to indulge in understatement. The English without understatement would not be the English. They would give me some concern.'[11]

On the 21st of July 1931 Georges dined with the Prince of Wales at St James's Palace, where the Duke of Alba was among the guests; but the Vaniers' own standard of living and hospitality was now affected by the world economic crisis. Philias Vanier's company in Montreal had paid no dividends at the end of 1930, and Georges' private income was correspondingly reduced. They had to maintain a staff of five servants at Cornwall Terrace, and for eighteen months both the cook and governess were unpaid – although their arrears of salary were made up afterwards. Looking back, Georges was able to view these difficulties in humorous perspective:

I believe I enjoyed the unique distinction of having an overdraft in all the Canadian banks, and I fondly imagined that each one of the Managers did not know of my interest – distressing interest – in the other banks. Naïveté is a great asset – the only one I had at the time. One of the bankers, who shall be nameless, because he acted with utter disregard for sacrosanct banking principles, granted me a substantial loan without security, but he used to send me a reminder at the end of each month. I don't say this practice offended me, but it didn't exactly cheer me up. Cracks began to appear in the ceiling of my morale but fortunately, before the roof blew off, I had a brilliant idea. I decided to have a heart to heart talk with the banker and in substance this is what I said to him: 'I assume that we both hold the same view that it would be advantageous if, in due course, I repaid my loan. I am afraid the technique you have adopted is the wrong one. This monthly reminder of my indebtedness is beginning to tell on me. I am a relatively young Civil servant with perhaps fairly good prospects if I do not break down under the strain. With time, promotion may come my way. I suggest, therefore, that it is in the bank's interest to maintain my morale at as high as level as possible. Instead of sending me these "billets doux" – I should say, "billets due" – why don't you ask me out to dinner, say once a month, and entertain me perhaps with a little champagne? In this way I shall face an awkward situation in a much more cheerful manner, conducive to the bank's solvency and to mine'.[12]

On arrival in London the family stayed at the Leinster Court Hotel, and in June they were still house-hunting. Since Georges

11. Address to the Ottawa Canadian Club, 10th December 1959.
12. Address of welcome to the Ambassadors of Ireland, the Netherlands and Belgium.

had used his annual leave, they spent August at Bexhill-on-Sea, where there were three golf courses and where he could go down for week-ends. A suitable home – though elegant beyond their means – was eventually found at 19 Cornwall Terrace, overlooking Regents Park. Georges and Pauline moved in at the end of August, and the family at the end of September. The children were delighted to be near the Zoo, and to feed the swans, ducks and gulls in the lake which they passed on their daily walk. There was no house allowance attached to Georges' new appointment, since Pacaud had occupied the top floor at Canada House. The rent of 19 Cornwall Terrace was £600 per annum, unfurnished, plus a proportion of rates and taxes. Georges wrote to Dr Skelton, asking for the same allowances, including a house allowance, that were given to the First Secretaries in Washington and Tokyo: i.e. $4000 a year. At the depreciated rate of exchange his expenses for rental alone would be $2500.

Although not a single Canadian bank had failed, the economic crisis was continually reflected in the speeches that Georges was called upon to make. At an exhibition of Canadian goods and produce at Southend-on-Sea he told his audience that 'the world is now at a very low ebb and it is in danger of seeing the waters ebb so far back that it may be left lying in a desert. We must do something soon to bring back to earth its freshness and its fragrance, or we shall all suffocate.' This was what the Ottawa Economic Conference was designed to accomplish, and Georges asked whether the Commonwealth were not 'the greatest political organization in history capable of infusing a new economic life into the world?' In a lighter mood he described Labour Day to the Institute of Mechanical Engineers, assembled for their annual dinner, as 'so called because it is a day upon which nobody does any work of any kind'. Whether or not the gaiety of nations was about to be eclipsed in financial ruin, he could at least promise them an eclipse of the sun at Memphremagog on the 21st of August. Sitting next to him was Mr Asa Binns, Chief Engineer of the Port of London Authority, who insisted on reciting to him *in toto*, and without a mistake, Kipling's *The River's Tale*.

Georges knew Kipling quite well. They both sat on the Imperial War Graves Commission, and when the meetings grew tedious Kipling would be seen doodling on his writing pad shapes curiously reminiscent of the Citadel at Quebec. Georges remarked to him one day: 'I have a son who says you know how to make jungle noises'; whereupon Kipling wrote his autograph for Byngsie: 'To the boy who says I know how to make jungle noises.' Georges liked Kipling as a man and admired him as a writer. When James McGregor Stewart, one of the youngest Canadian K.C.s, and a courageous victim of polio, came to England, he said that the one thing he wanted was to see Kipling. So Georges took him down to luncheon at Burwash, arriving flustered and contrite one and a half hours late. Kipling greeted them imperturbably: 'Quite all right, Vanier; have a glass of sherry.' When Kipling died Georges paid him a warm tribute at a meeting of the War Graves Commission:

What struck one more particularly was his simplicity which in a way is not surprising, because one always felt that his heart had remained young. Few writers have been able to write for children and for men. Kipling was able to do this. I think another way to put it is that anyone who has known him or read his books is the better for it, and it is a very great tribute that a great writer could have been at the same time a man of infinite virtue, and in these days when art and letters are sometimes made the instrument of weakness, not to say vice, Kipling stands out as a true apostle of art, realizing that real art should be based on eternal truth.

Georges' own literary judgment was called upon when the question arose of the French inscription on the Somme Memorial Cross at Thiepval. In such matters he was a perfectionist to the point of pedantry, preferring in this case 'rappelant au monde' to 'pour rappeler au monde'; 'frères d'armes pour l'Eternité' to 'compagnons pour l'Eternité'; 'reposent' to 'dorment'; and 'soldats de l'Empire Britannique et de la France' to 'soldats Français et Britanniques'. He was present at the unveiling by the Prince of Wales on the 1st of August, 1934.

Another ceremony on the site of the old battlefields was nearer to his heart. In the village of Neuville-St-Vaast, between Arras and the Vimy Ridge, and close to the great French cemetery where Georges had already spoken, fifteen houses had been built for men who had been permanently injured in the war but were still capable of looking after the graves. Each of these had been named after a famous French soldier – Joffre, Pétain, Fayolle, de Castelnau, Gouraud – and one of them had been named after Byng. This was the first house in the village on the road from Arras to Béthune. In an open square beside the Cité des Mutilés, as it was called, a gigantic stone hand held aloft the torch of civilization, eight metres in height. Georges was there to bring back the gold key of the Villa Byng to the man after whom it had been named, and a bronze replica of the torch. The inaugural ceremony was performed on the 2nd of August by M. Ducos, Under-Secretary of State, on behalf of the French Prime Minister. There was a procession beside the row of Canadian maple trees, planted in memory of the fifty-three Neuvillois who had lost their lives in the war; and the symbolic lighting of the torch was entrusted to the deputy Scapini who had been blinded at Neuville, guided by General de Ponydraguin, a former Governor of Strasbourg, whose two sons had been killed in the village.

In February 1934 Georges represented all the Canadian troops who had fought on Belgian soil at King Albert's funeral in Brussels. The cathedral of St Gudule was so crowded that he was compelled to stand for one and a half hours. On the homeward journey from Ostend he shared a cabin with the Prince of Wales, who was surprised to learn that Canada possessed a Navy.

2

The news from Montreal was now disquieting. Frances wrote that Mrs Vanier was suffering from astronomic blood pressure and could come downstairs only once a day. For a time she was under observation in hospital, and then underwent two operations in the autumn of 1933. Judge Archer had also been gravely ill, and Pauline was able to get home before he died in June 1934. Since Mgr Gauthier, a particularly cherished family friend, was in hospital and not thought likely to recover, Pauline wrote that she was losing her 'spiritual father and her temporal father' at the same time. She herself was still feeling the after effects of her illness, but Frances wrote to Georges reassuringly that she was 'one of the most magnificent soldiers in life that I have ever known' – a verdict that many people would have reason to endorse. Frances was married to William Shepherd at the end of June, and Pauline stayed on for the wedding. She had seen few people in Montreal outside French-Canadians, feeling that this would have been Georges' wish; but an interview with Dr Skelton threw out a hint of things to come. 'I think,' he told her, 'that Georges ought to have Paris, and I am doing all I can to say so, and to further the idea.' Pauline confessed that she felt *dépaysée* in Canada and she was anxious to get back to London, where the family – and urgent material problems – were awaiting her. Already there was talk of leaving Cornwall Terrace and moving to a small hotel.

The crunch came with the stair carpet. Pauline said they must have a new one; and Georges said, of course they must have a new one; but the new one never came. When Georges, having long put off the evil day in the manner of husbands who do not want to disappoint their wives, explained that they could not possibly afford it, Pauline – with her characteristic and impulsive generosity – sold all her jewels and replaced them with fake stones from the Burma shop. She never, as we have seen, had much luck with her jewellery. At Christmas 1934 the children's presents were on an unusually modest scale: Henty's *With Wolfe in Canada* and – to give fair play to the British – *Under Wellington's Command*, H.B. pencils and sharpener, a fretsaw and wood for carving. For entertainment there was the Circus, *Sinbad the Sailor*, *Treasure Island*, and *Hamlet*. Wisely, Georges believed that the children should be taken to see Shakespeare performed before they were made to study him, although they were indoctrinated with Wolsey's 'Farewell, a long farewell to all my greatness' from an early age. Then there were the dolls' houses, and the bus ride to Canada House on Sunday mornings, and the family lunch, and the children's plays in the afternoon. These were written and produced by Thérèse, and they were liable to go on for a very long time with the angels and the Wise Men muffled in scarves and draperies. There was much throwing about of cushions, and readings aloud at bedtime with the children gathered round attentively in their red dressing-gowns. It was a remarkably happy family with few psychological problems and no physical punishments. A temporary abstinence from sweets or a brusque despatch to the bedroom were sufficient to ensure obedience.

In January 1935 the Vaniers were moving into a new house at 15 Oxford Square:

Our new house is a great success, smaller, easier to run and representing an appreciable economy, all of which is very welcome just now. Really the house has some advantages over the other, it is quieter at night because it is not on a main thoroughfare like Cornwall Terrace, along which nearly all the cars passed en route from Portland Place to Hampstead. Then there is a nice garden in front which gives one an open and green outlook, especially in the summer – with a few flowers in the dining-room window-box one can fool oneself into believing that there is a real garden in front, which is a help on a grey morning, more particularly if the breakfast isn't quite up to par (a thing that never happens, of course, at 15 Oxford Square).[13]

13. Letter to Frances Shepherd, 21st June 1935.

Byngsie was at Egerton House school and Thérèse at the Convent of the Holy Child in Cavendish Square. In quickly joining the Boxing Class Byngsie was apparently setting out on the career that Georges had designed for him, and in winning a prize of 2/6 for drawing Bernard was already set on the career which he would design for himself. Byngsie's school report, which Georges had enclosed, was acknowledged in the last letter Georges was to receive from Julian Byng: the familiar handwriting was much weakened and changed:

It is strange, but if one analyses the causes of the Wars in the last 200 years one nearly always finds that the politicians talked us into them and then accused the soldiers for not winning them in five minutes. You and I, at their instigation, fought for four years to make the world safe for hypocrisy (wasn't it!) and even now they don't seem happy about it. I wish I had Byngsie's brains; if so, I might write a sensible letter. What a beautiful report he got! If he were to see mine, he might have a heart attack.[14]

The words were prophetic. Byng had listened to a broadcast talk by Georges soon after the Vaniers came to London, and had written: 'Some well-known writer once said that a real live Canadian voice was the loveliest in the world with the music of grinding ice in it and the softness of all nature'.[15] But the Vaniers now saw less of him than formerly, since his nearly fatal collapse at Thorpe-le-Soken. He had made a trip to America, but returned in so frail a condition that it was thought inadvisable for them to meet him at the station, since the emotion of seeing such old friends might be bad for him. Those who did see him were shocked at his appearance, and he died shortly afterwards, following a minor operation. Georges wrote to a fellow-officer, who had also been on the Field-Marshal's staff at Ottawa: 'Well, Sandy, we have lost a very dear friend, and the world for us will never be quite the same again.'[16]

In September 1935 the Abyssinian crisis was boiling to a head, and Georges Vanier was in no doubt that if nothing were done to resolve it at Geneva, the result would be a severe, and perhaps a mortal, blow to the League of Nations. Howard Ferguson was in Geneva for the General Assembly, but he was unlikely to remain at Canada House much longer. If Mackenzie King won an overall majority at the forthcoming elections, Ferguson would resign.

14. 20th April 1935.
15. 14th November 1933.
16. To Lieut-Colonel H. M. Urquhart, 1st August 1935.

In the event, the Liberals, under King, were returned to power and Vincent Massey was appointed High Commissioner in London. Georges Vanier's relations with Massey were cordial, but never close. Massey stood in a long succession of distinguished Canadians who had been to Balliol at a time when Balliol was something that Balliol men never forgot. Indeed, it is doubtful whether any other institution on earth commands quite the same attachment – and for reasons which those who have not been to Balliol find a little hard to understand. This was as far beyond Georges Vanier's comprehension as Georges Vanier's attachment to the Royal 22nd was beyond Vincent Massey's. There was here a certain incompatibility between two *mystiques*. Each man represented the best in his respective tradition, with the difference that Massey had not yet been brought into contact with the personality and the problems of French Canada, whereas Vanier's military and diplomatic experience made him equally at home on either side of the racial boundary, and on either side of the Atlantic. The Masseys had no daughter of their own, and Pauline found herself cast for the rôle of a lady-in-waiting rather more often than she would have liked, and of a hostess more often than she could afford.

Georges continued to be in demand for such speeches as the High Commissioner was unable or disinclined to make himself. Replying for the British Empire at the City of London Tradesmen's dinner, he quoted Burke on the Colonies which his oratory had failed to save:

The fierce spirit of liberty is stronger in the English Colonies, probably, than in any other people of the earth. . . . The colonists emigrated from you when this part of your character was most predominant, and they took this bias and direction the moment they parted from your hands. They are therefore not only devoted to liberty, but to liberty according to English ideas and on English principles.

Taking the chair for Sir Ernest Shackleton, Georges recalled the thrill of seeing Shackleton and Humphreys off at St Catherine's Dock:

I recollect that it was quite a hot day, and thinking of the cool-white snows to which they were going I felt sorely tempted to rid myself of the shackles of office work and civilization; the thought of my wife and children only just restrained me from jumping aboard. The age of romance is not over yet.[17]

17. 12th March 1936.

For Georges Vanier it never was.

Receiving a gift of cutlery from the Sheffield Company of
Master Cutlers on behalf of the Empire Marketing Board, he
asked:

What would the housewife do without your scissors, and nearly
all the men of the world, and some of the women, use your razors.
Without you no meal would be complete, your knives and forks
gleam upon the table and are an incentive to man's appetite: the
sportsman uses your skates, and the naughty boy your penknives
with which to carve the school desks. May I pass on to you a
wonderful secret, which, however, unlike other secrets, you must
not keep to yourselves. Canadian food tastes wonderfully good
when eaten with Sheffield cutlery.

And in order not to leave the Empire quite out of the picture, he
added a quotation from Isaac Watts:

> Birds in their little nests agree,
> And 'tis a shameful sight
> When children of one family
> Fall out and chide and fight.

Mackenzie King headed the Canadian Delegation at Geneva in
September 1936, passing through London on his way home.
Pauline saw that flowers were waiting for him at the Ritz – the
first of many such bouquets – and both the Vaniers were at the
station to see him off. 'I am glad to carry away from England'
he wrote from the *Empress of Britain* 'as one of the last and
sweetest of remembrances, the glimpse I had of you both as I
said Good-bye.'[18] It was the first of many such acknowledgements.

After the trauma of the Abdication Georges spent Christmas
in Montreal where his mother's precarious health made his
presence imperative. Bernard sent a drawing of three cats sitting
at a table surrounded by a horse-shoe; and Jock wrote that he
was a witch in the school play 'with a black cloak, red dress,
black hat and wand'; and Thérèse had bought *Seven Little
Australians* and *What Katy Did Next* with her Christmas money.
They cannot have done her any harm since she was described
as a 'splendid influence in the school'. Georges was the only
absentee from his parents' golden wedding in May, with the
organist playing 'Here Comes the Bride', so that strangers in the
Church thought it was a real wedding, and seven baskets of

18. 1st November 1936.

flowers with fifty roses in each, and a wedding cake four storeys high.

Arrangements were now in hand for the Coronation of King George VI, and shortly after his return Georges was requested by the Secretary of State for the Dominions to attend a meeting at the Dominions Office. The High Commissioners for South Africa and the Irish Free State, with Major Keith Officer[19] from Australia, were also there. It was proposed to set up a Coronation Committee, but all those representing the Dominions expressed their concern that their Governments had not been approached with regard to the advisability of Dominion representation on it. Apart altogether from the constitutional aspect of the matter, Georges wondered what the reaction would be on public opinion in the Dominions if there were no Dominion representation on a committee which was to deal with the Coronation of the King who was King of Canada as well as King of the United Kingdom. He added that if the names of the Coronation Committee were published tomorrow, in accordance with tradition, it would then be too late to add Dominion representatives, because it would be obvious that this was an afterthought. He did not know whether his Government would want representation on the Committee or not, but he felt that it was a matter of importance to which consideration should be given.

At 8 p.m. the same evening Malcolm Macdonald[20] phoned him that the next day's agenda had been changed, and that no action would be taken in connection with the setting up of the Committee. Georges' timely intervention had forestalled a situation which would have caused embarrassment on every side. At a further meeting of the Committee, when it had been duly formed, he suggested that owing to the special difficulties in selecting representative Canadian troops, and taking into consideration the short distance involved, the Canadian contingent should consist of 250 troops (instead of 150) with a band of thirty-five. No objection was raised by the other Dominions. Georges and Pauline attended the Coronation in the Abbey and they took Thérèse to see the Naval Review at Spithead – the last ceremonial display of British naval power. At the end of July the whole family went to Montreal for the summer holidays, returning in the middle of September.

The arrival of Lester Pearson as political secretary at Canada

19. Sir Keith Officer, 1889-1969.
20. Secretary of State for the Dominions.

House, and an important Memorandum which he addressed to External Affairs, brought to light the ambiguity of Georges Vanier's duties as the Official Secretary. At present he was a kind of Deputy High Commissioner without either the title or the authority to act as such. Pearson saw the job of the Secretary to co-ordinate the administrative, commercial, publicity, political and economic activities of the High Commission. He complained that the High Commission was often kept in ignorance of Canadian affairs. It was 'humiliating to be asked by Whitehall officials to comment on certain actions that the Canadian Government has taken when no official knowledge of that action is available here. It is even more humiliating to be told by Whitehall officials what the Canadian Government has done. It is equally deplorable to have the Dominions Office forward a weekly list of dispatches which have passed between the two Governments.' External Affairs were not anxious for the Political Secretary to visit the Foreign Office too frequently, and Dr Skelton had written that he should be permitted access to papers in the same way as his opposite number at the British High Commission in Ottawa. 'That virtually means' Pearson replied 'that I should see very little of anything.'

The Memorandum was an extremely able document, and much of it has since been adopted. Pearson pointed out that Georges Vanier had been carrying on both as political and administrative Secretary; he suggested therefore the establishment of a political section under the High Commissioner, with Georges Vanier, Mr Maclean[21] and himself, each to be given specific duties, and each acting, in the High Commissioner's absence, as the spokesman in all discussions, and as the draughtsman of all communications, on the matters which he had made his speciality. Since the Official Secretary and the Private Secretary had other duties, the third member would have to undertake more of the political work than his colleagues. Pearson suggested that Georges Vanier should continue with his present political activities, but that he, Pearson, should relieve him of representation on committees. As far as Georges himself was concerned these proposals, however sensible, were soon to become academic, for throughout the following year (1938) he was to be racked by private anxiety, and preoccupied by future diplomatic prospects.

21. Private Secretary to Vincent Massey.

3

In the middle of April his brother Antoine – aged thirty-seven and a lawyer in Montreal – underwent an exploratory operation for a large tumour in the abdominal cavity. This was found to be malignant, although his parents were not immediately advised of its nature. Georges, however, was kept informed by Frances and the doctor. It was not possible to remove the tumour and the only hope of prolonging Antoine's life by a few months lay in concentrated treatment by X-ray. He had been suffering for some time from what was thought to be a strain on the ligaments of the spine, but even if the real cause of the trouble had been discovered earlier X-rays would have been the only remedy, and Antoine would have had so many more months of mental anxiety. He returned home at the end of April; was able to walk about a little; and there remained an outside chance that if the tumour were sufficiently reduced by the X-rays, it might be possible to operate again. Frances wrote: 'His expression is so tragic, though his words are brave; his mouth determined';[22] and again, as the feelings of those looking after him fluctuated between hope and resignation: 'Frankly, Georges, I think you would be happier if you came out for two weeks this summer. . . . If you saw him as we see him, you too – I think – would feel as we do, and that's why I say – if you want to see him, you should come this summer.'[23]

There seemed, however, no immediate urgency, and it was not easy for Georges to get away. The Vaniers took the children to Varangeville, near Dieppe, for the holidays; and Georges, with Pauline, went to Lisieux to pray for Antoine's recovery. Then, on the 7th of September, the blow fell – although it was not the blow they expected. Three telegrams in quick succession came from Frances:

> Mother ill after two gall bladder attacks.
> Mother very low. Slim chance.
> Mother died quietly 6.40 this morning.

She was seventy-five years old. Further details came from Eva Trudeau:

She had the death she always desired; she gave me the impression of just leaving us for heaven. You know, she always said 'I don't mind

22. 30th April 1938.
23. 20th June 1938.

dying, but I hope God will take me quickly'. I think she was spared the pain of seeing Anthony go. Poor child, it was pitiful to see him. Since last week, he can't walk, his right leg pains him terribly . . . Father walked all the way to the Cathedral. . . .[24]

and again from Frances:

All Tuesday she kept saying 'tired – tired'. Asked for Father Langlois, the Franciscan Father who lately has been her confessor and Tony's during his illness. Her speech, of course, was faint and I understand her with the greatest difficulty. Her eyes questioned and followed me – they seemed to want to tell me so many things. I felt there were so many messages she wanted to give me. And when I said in her ear 'You're all right old soldier' she smiled that lovely smile of hers. . . . When John came to see her, she said 'Have you had your supper John' – always thinking of others, never of herself . . . A day never went by without her visit to me or mine to her – and so she was with all her children.[25]

Only two weeks before her death Mrs Vanier had written in her last letter to her son: 'I have always had a great admiration for the Carmelites and the life of St Teresa. When I was sixteen I thought seriously of joining the Order';[26] and Georges had written in his last letter to his mother:

If you did not become a Carmelite, it is because God had work for you to do elsewhere and you have done it like a Saint. Who knows, He may have special designs on one of those – perhaps a grandchild or a great grandchild – who would not have existed if you had become a nun.

This letter did not reach Montreal until after Mrs Vanier's death, and in the meanwhile he asked Frances to send him a rosary which had touched his mother's lips. The 'special designs' of which he had spoken were to be made clear in the fullness of time.

On the 17th of September Georges received a telegram inform- ing him that Antoine's condition had suddenly become worse; that he might die at any moment; and that it was advisable for Georges to come out immediately. The international crisis was at its height and he replied that he could not leave Pauline and the children until the peak of danger was past. He hoped to get away in a few days. There was, however, yet another unexpected

24. 10th September 1938.
25. 12th September 1938.
26. 26th August 1938.

blow in store; Philias Vanier died just two weeks after his wife. Eva Trudeau again gave the details of his passing:

The first days after mother's death, he was depressed and did not sleep very well; of course we had not left him a minute alone since mother's passing. I had him examined by the doctor, who found him no worse than a year ago, when he told him of the heart lesion and his rather weakened kidneys. . . . Wednesday, Frances and I were out with him, we went to see Anthony. I left him at five. Frances and Father had tea together at 6. Father had a light meal. Frances was addressing some envelopes about 7.30 when he told her he had a pain in his chest from the left shoulder down. Frances had barely time to go with him in the living-room (he had been in the bath-room) when he collapsed. The priest and doctor arrived just as he had breathed his last, perhaps ten minutes later. He died in Frances' arms.

Anthony is gradually weakening; he has slept very little since mother's death on the seventh of September. I have a vague idea he might possibly live a few weeks longer, but even the Doctor does not say.[27]

The 1st of October – five days after the signing of the Munich Agreement – Georges was able to sail on the *Empress of Britain*, and spent four weeks with his dying brother. He saw him every day, sometimes for hours on end, but Antoine never complained of his suffering or of the fact that he was dying so young. Indeed he did not, even now, appear to believe that he was dying. 'I believe the miracle has happened' he said. 'I am not worrying about the main thing, but about minor things.' Georges could only reply: 'Go on *believing* it has happened – that is all important – to have faith. Remember the woman in the Gospel to whom Christ said: "Thy faith has made thee whole".' The doctor was still saying that Antoine might live for months, and Georges could not stay on indefinitely, although he was hoping to return early in the New Year. Antoine's condition weakened a few days after he had left. Frances wrote that it seemed 'as if his courage had kept him while you were here – but once that you had gone, and there was no more immediate business he grew weaker.'[28] And Eva wrote that the long hours Georges had spent with him had been 'a source of great spiritual comfort'.[29] On the 5th of December Dr Reford brought him some books – the life of Ollier, founder of the Sulpicians, among them; and the next day he told

27. 27th September 1938.
28. 8th December 1938.
29. 9th December 1938.

the Doctor: 'You know, Lewis, I am awfully weak, but I know
that I am going to get well.' The Doctor congratulated him on
the comfort he was getting out of his religion. The end came
peacefully on the evening of the 8th of December, with his wife
Jeanne, the curé, and all the family around him. He was talking
to them quietly until a few minutes before he died. The morning
of the funeral was grey and wet, with the snow turning into rain,
difficult for the men walking to the Requiem at Notre Dame de
Grace, and cold at the cemetery. Jeanne Vanier was too overcome
to stand at her husband's grave, and Georges was with her in a
community of absence and grief.

4

In the early summer of 1938 the question arose of establishing
a Canadian Legation in Brussels, and Georges Vanier's name was
mooted for the post. Colonel Ralston wrote to him in anticipation
of this: 'Your advancement is due to nobody, but the aptitude
and qualification of personality and prescience possessed by your
wonderful wife and yourself.'[30] On the 23rd of June, M. Spaak,
the Belgian Minister for Foreign Affairs, was informed by the
British Ambassador in Brussels that the Canadian Minister would
also be accredited to the Netherlands; and on the 4th of July the
Ambassador informed him that the Canadian Government
definitely wished to establish the proposed Legation. Spaak welcomed the proposal. Early in December the *Montreal Star*
announced Georges Vanier's appointment to Brussels and the
Hague, and this was almost the last news that Antoine got before
he died. When Dr Reford was discussing it with his brother,
Robert Reford observed: 'Yes – but why not Paris?' In recount-
ing the conversation to Georges, the Doctor added: 'Paris will
come.'

It came very quickly. The *Star* had its facts wrong, for on the
5th of December the Canadian Government expressed its wish to
nominate Georges Vanier to Paris and asked for the King's
approval. This was given on the 12th of December, and at once
communicated to Georges. In a subsequent letter to Dr Skelton,
he wrote:

I do not like to introduce a note of disappointment in this letter but
the information that the salary would be on a sliding (a word which,
to me, has always had an ominous sound of going down instead of
up) scale in future and the implications that the allowances might

30. 21st May 1938.

be lower were just sufficient to nip in the bud the sin of pride which the devil might have taken the opportunity to cultivate – so perhaps you have done me a service after all![31]

He presumed that the Canadian Government would indemnify him for the remaining lease of 15 Oxford Square, and asked permission to go to Paris immediately. The Brussels and Hague appointment went to his old acquaintance, Jean Désy.

Georges said 'Good-bye' to London in one of the happiest speeches he ever made. The Canada Club entertained him to dinner at the Savoy, with Sir Edward Peacock in the chair; Lord Willingdon – only lately returned from India – proposed the health of the new Canadian Minister to France. The indefatigable pro-consul recalled his arrival in Quebec and how Georges had helped him 'to explore the heights as well as the depths' of the Citadel. A previous and also a more recent Governor General of Canada – the Duke of Devonshire and Lord Bessborough – were there as well; but none could have guessed that the man they were honouring would afterwards follow in their footsteps. In reply Georges paid a tribute to Pauline; he had owed 'much to her inspiration, much to her advice and criticism with which, for my good, she is not always sparing' – and to R. B. Bennett who was among the guests:

I am very glad to see Mr Bennett here. As you know, it was he who brought me to London in 1931. He has a great deal to answer for. Mr Bennett's presence gives me an excuse for saying publicly that he sent me a message of congratulations on my appointment . . . I mean the one to Paris, not the one he made in 1931. I don't suppose he would ever deny having done so – but it is as well to have on record this rash admission of the ex-Conservative Prime Minister. The document is being put in a safety deposit vault for future reference.

He went on to speak of the view from his room in Canada House:

For eight years I have looked out on to Trafalgar Square. . . . From my window I saw many things – the home of our Sister Dominion, South Africa, St Martin's-in-the-Fields, the National Gallery, Nelson's Column. . . . I have seen meetings of protest and of denunciation of all kinds, some of them beautifully organized by the police, sometimes with bands. I have heard vociferous speakers at 3 o'clock in the afternoon but I have seen them leave their audience at the tea

31. 30th December 1938.

hour. Oh the power of tea in England! . . . I cannot imagine a revolution taking place here, but if one ever did start, it would most certainly be interfered with by the tea hour – and I am sure that any explosive used would be T.N.T.! And I have seen the pigeons. In my spare time at Canada House I felt tempted to write poems on the pigeons . . . On hot days I have seen and envied little boys who bathed in the fountains and then were chased by policemen who didn't try to catch them. But the things I have seen most, because they happened to be in a direct line with my desk, are the lions. Their attitude is a peaceful one, but they look as if they could spring. I'd hate to be looking at one if I thought he might spring. My admiration for those British lions has grown and grown, and if they ever decide to move I would rather be behind them than in front.

Don't think me impertinent, men of these Northern Isles, if I pay tribute to your character and virtues. My praise, in any event, cannot be suspect because I haven't a drop of English blood in my veins. Don't blush if I tell you that, during the eight years that I have been your guest in England, you have won my heart in kindness and my head by your quiet humour and wisdom based on human understanding.

And so, I go from you full of gratitude, but not only of gratitude, full of confidence as well in the genius and destiny of a very great people. I count it a high privilege to have lived with you during these years. Almost a century ago, Emerson, in a speech delivered at Manchester, referring to 'this aged England' as he described her 'with the possessions, honours and trophies, and also the infirmities of a thousand years gathering around her', added 'I see her not dispirited, not weak, but well remembering that she has seen dark days before; indeed with a kind of instinct that she sees a little better in a cloudy day, and that in storm of battle and calamity she has a secret vigour and a pulse like a cannon. I see her in her old age, not decrepit but young, and still daring to believe in her power of endurance and expansion'. And now, 92 years after Emerson spoke, *that* is the way *I* feel about England.

Yes, England has given me a great deal which will remain ingrained. She has given me things material and spiritual, some of them so well described by Rupert Brooke in an immortal poem – She has given me

'Her sights and sounds; dreams happy as her day;
And laughter learnt of friends; and gentleness;
In hearts at peace, under an English heaven'

And for these and many other things I shall be forever grateful.

Then, turning to the French Ambassador, M. Corbin, he spoke for a few moments in French:

And now I go from this great country to another great country –

to your country, Excellency, to France, with behind her a magnificent history of over 1,000 years, and I pray God as glorious a one ahead . . . It is one of the great joys of my life to go to the land of my fore-fathers as His Canadian Majesty's representative, proud of that allegiance, brooking no other, although attached to France by blood and cultural ties which nothing can eradicate and with which I would allow no one to interfere.

There is no contradiction here – this is only one small example of how our wonderful community of independent nations carries on in complete freedom of thought and action under one Crown, whose light shines equally to and for each of these nations scattered through-out the world.

Edward Peacock wrote to Pauline that Georges had 'held three hundred highly sophisticated men in the hollow of his hand'; and Lord Willingdon was overheard to remark, as he was leaving, 'I never heard a better speech in my life' – and he had heard a good many. Nothing that Georges Vanier had done in London became him better than the way he left it.

Much had happened to him, and in the world of politics and diplomacy, during those eight years. Leo Amery was a particular friend, and it was at his house in Eaton Square, where the Vaniers often lunched or dined, that they met Sir John Simon,[32] Sir Samuel Hoare,[33] and the young Anthony Eden.[34] These names alone reflect a sufficient diversity of attitude, without straying beyond the fairly wide limits of the National Government. Margot Asquith, with her mingled astringency and idealism, grew very attached to Georges; so attached indeed that she invited him to dine without Pauline. Georges replied that he did not go out to dinner without his wife, for whom an invitation came by the next post. It was a large party, and Pauline was thankful to be lost in the crowd where those eagle eyes could only reach her distantly. Among Georges' compatriots resident in London, Sir Edward Peacock[35] held a special and abiding place in his affections.

But he had not spoken – because he could not have spoken – of the most important event of all. The date cannot be precisely fixed – and the date does not matter; the day, however, mattered a great deal, for it was a Good Friday. Pauline had been deeply impressed by the sermons and retreats given by Father R. H. J. Steuart, one of the Jesuit Fathers on the staff of Farm Street

32. Viscount Simon.
33. Viscount Templewood.
34. The Earl of Avon.
35. Sir Edward Robert Peacock, 1871-1962.

Church. Steuart was a remarkable spiritual director, with a profound and accurate knowledge of mysticism. Pauline had long been trying to persuade Georges to hear him, and her importunity had met with some resistance. Georges Vanier was of course a convinced and devout Catholic, but he still had a good deal of inherited Jansenism in his blood, and he was reluctant to frequent the Sacraments with a regularity which he would afterwards have considered normal and even necessary. However, on this particular Good Friday, he remarked – a little impatiently – to Pauline: 'All right, then, I'll go and hear your Father Steuart.' Steuart was preaching the Three Hours Meditation in a London church, and after hearing him Georges went to Mass every day until the end of his life, unless he were unavoidably prevented from doing so.

In the C.B.C. memorial programme which followed Georges Vanier's death the speaker said of the Vaniers – 'we always think of them together'. This was a tribute to public appearances, and the appearances were not deceptive. They were rooted in a private harmony which was not, however, easily achieved. Georges was the soul of chivalry. He wrote to Pauline every day whenever he was away from her, and sent her flowers on every anniversary. But where she was extrovert and communicative, he was naturally reserved. She had his heart, but she would have liked to have more of his mind – as much as she was eager to give him of her own. Suddenly, however, under the influence of Father Steuart's Meditation, the barrier was removed. Henceforward she was able to speak and he to listen. In his more reflective, less impulsive, way he spoke as well. He had always been a rock upon which she could rely, and now the hidden springs within it were released to their mutual enrichment.

CHAPTER 11

PARIS 1939-1940

I

T H E Vaniers were met at the Gare du Nord by General Réquin, their old friend from Geneva days, and cheered by a letter from Norman Robertson.[1]

I feel I'm entitled to put in a prophetic postscript – reminding you that it is nearly eight years since Sir Robert (Borden) very strongly recommended you for the succession to the Paris Legation. Had he lived he would have been much prompter and more felicitous than I can ever be in his congratulations.[2]

Robertson was a Balliol Rhodes scholar, but this did not prevent him from understanding the other side of the Canadian mentality, and no one in Ottawa had a more just appreciation of Georges Vanier's gifts, or was a better friend to him in the critical years to come. He spoke French easily and was familiar with contemporary thought in France. Only recently, writing from a Presbyterian standpoint, he had been pointing out to Pauline the inadequacies of Maurice Blondel's metaphysics. This was ground on which neither Georges nor Pauline would have felt very competent to challenge him.

The offices of the Canadian Legation in Paris were situated on the ground floor of 1 rue François 1er, and the Minister occupied an apartment at 55 Avenue Foch. The staff consisted of twelve persons including secretaries. M. Pierre Dupuy, with the rank of First Secretary, would act as Chargé d'Affaires in the absence of the Minister. Georges took up his duties on the 25th of January and presented his credentials to President Lebrun[3] on the 21st of February. Oswald Balfour had lent him all the necessary clothes – Sulka ties and shirts – for this ceremonial occasion. Only the top hat was too small, and he was obliged to carry it. A *pourboire* of five hundred francs for the *personnel* of the Elysée was duly

1. 1904-1968.
2. 22nd January 1939.
3. Albert Lebrun, 1871-1950.

appreciated. On the 22nd he was received by Edouard Herriot,[4] President of the Chambre des Députés, at the Palais Bourbon.

How did he conceive his duties as a diplomat? A speech delivered later in the year on a short visit to Canada gives the answer. He must see the Foreign Minister of the country to which he was accredited as often as possible, without becoming a nuisance – a *via media* not always easy to follow. 'Daily and deadly' dinners loosened the tongue as well as surfeiting the appetite, and much interesting information might be gleaned at them. Vanier would have liked to suppress the word 'diplomat'; he was not sure that the best representative was always 'a gentleman with a diploma'. Vanier was romantic about many things, but he was not romantic about diplomacy. There was no need for so much 'mystery and mummery'; the chief quality required was judgment or common sense. He quoted in approval or refutation Paul Cambon's 'Solid good sense is as much the essential quality of a diplomat as it is of a grocer'; and Frederick the Great's 'Ambassadors are the least honourable of spies'; and Sir Henry Wooton's 'An Ambassador is an honest man sent abroad to lie for the good of his country'. Vanier, on the contrary, held that it was his duty to tell the truth in all circumstances, both to the Ministers of the country to which he was accredited and to his own colleagues. 'Perhaps not more truth than is good for them or might harm his own Government – nevertheless, nothing but the truth.'[5] He must also have the courage to displease.

He began by making the customary round of diplomatic calls. One of these envoys had an electric button on the arm of his chair; Georges wondered if the reason for this was fear of violence or fear of boredom. The visits enabled him, nevertheless, to take the pulse of international opinion.

On the 11th of November he was placing a wreath on the tomb of the Unknown Soldier, and standing behind him was General Gouraud with his Father Christmas beard. It was very soon apparent that the new Minister was the right man in the right place, as a French-Canadian newspaper had foreseen:

Lieutenant-Colonel Vanier has to his credit the prestige of a hero in the 1914 war, and a wide knowledge of international circles acquired in the course of several missions. To these advantages he adds a simple manner and a friendliness about which there is nothing either conventional or constrained. All the elements making up this fine per-

4. 1872-1957.
5. Speech at a dinner given by the Comité France-Amérique.

sonality contribute to an openness which commands admiration and trust – qualities more useful in diplomacy than in all the other professions. In addition, Colonel Vanier adapts himself easily to the ways of a country, without falling into snobbery – and this favours the success of everything he undertakes abroad. There can be no doubt that the highly polished society of Paris will accord the best of welcomes to our new representative and to Madame Vanier who is the perfect wife of a perfect diplomat.[6]

On the 28th of March Vanier presided over a Canadian programme at the Collège Stanislas – *A la Gloire du Canada* – at which speeches and songs were given by the school. These were followed by a play – *Le Secret de Champlain* by Marc Villeneuve. Earlier in the month he had visited Réquin, now in command of the Fourth Army at Nancy; and in April he was received by Marshal Pétain on the eve of the Marshal's departure for Madrid.

He received me with the greatest cordiality. I expressed my gratitude and my admiration, and I bowed before this great man who, at the age of 83, has written, 'A Frenchman's task is never finished so long as he thinks he can be of service'.[7]

The words summed exactly the guiding principle of Georges Vanier's own life, and it is among the sadder ironies of that life that he should have found himself, during the second World War, in opposition to the soldier beside whom he had fought in the first. Both men had turned from arms to diplomacy, and where the soldiers had agreed the diplomats were constrained to differ.

Gradually the Vaniers were getting the Legation into the shape and style they wanted. It was rumoured in Montreal[8] that Georges never had a fire in his room, even on the coldest day, and that his desk was completely bare. The second of these idiosyncrasies sounds highly improbable; it would have been astonishing if there had not been a Larousse dictionary and a Fowler's English Usage within easy reach. Pauline observed that a lot of trouble would be saved if electric bells were put in French houses as well as on the armchairs of foreign diplomats.[9] In the middle of April Arctic landscapes by Canadian painters were still stacked against the walls, and if Georges really did

6. *Le Jour*.
7. Speech at a dinner given by the Comité France-Amérique.
8. *The Daily Telegram*, 5th January 1939.
9. Interview with Gladys Arnold, *Windsor Daily Star*, 13th April 1939.

refuse a fire in his room this must have made the house that much colder. There was little entertaining as yet, and when it started first consideration was given to Canadian students, of whom there were a good number in Paris.

While the international situation simmered ominously through the summer months, a more personal anxiety recalled the Vaniers to England. Byngsie was taken dangerously ill at Beaumont with peritonitis. After the operation he hung for several days between life and death. Georges stayed at the college and Pauline at a hotel in Windsor. She was as close to despair as her courageous nature could ever come, and there was a dramatic moment when the Rector of Beaumont, Father Lillie, threw his rosary across to her where she was sitting in the chair opposite and told her that she must accept the outcome either way. She repeated the words: 'I accept it either way,' and the abscess which was threatening Byngsie's life broke just in time.

On the 25th of August Georges Vanier was advising all Canadian nationals to leave Paris, and on the following day he learnt that Daladier was extremely pessimistic about the possibility of preserving peace. He had reason to be, for the Molotov-Ribbentrop pact had just been signed. Nevertheless Georges Vanier saw further into the future:

The Moscow Agreement has confirmed the impression which has never left me that Hitler, sooner or later, would crumble. One cannot construct anything durable on force alone without any respect for truth and justice. Up to now, Hitler could be said to be fighting for an idea or an ideal directed against the Communist Doctrine but now that he has put his hand in the red hand of Stalin, he has lost his soul.[10]

2

The Vaniers were staying at Varengeville, near Dieppe, when war broke out. A. P. Herbert and his family were also in the hotel, and Jacques Emile Blanche was a close neighbour. If Blanche spoke his mind in person as freely as he did on paper, he cannot have left the Canadian Minister with many illusions about the French *haute bourgeoisie*. Although Georges Vanier was to find himself entangled in so many of the complexities which the second World War brought in its train, his attitude to the war itself was essentially simple. He regarded it as just, inevitable, and also – in a sense – sacred. True, he took note of Jacques Maritain's distinction

10. Personal Notes.

between a just war and a holy war, but Vanier was a soldier, not much given to philosophical refinements. He considered himself, and those for whom he spoke, as engaged in a crusade. General Gouraud had given him the word in a letter to *The Times*, and Vanier wrote to thank him for it. What he saw immediately was the French war effort, and here it must be admitted that, perceptive as his view of the French situation subsequently became, he at no time between September 1939 and May 1940 suspected the weakness of the French army, the deep fissures in French society, or the intrigues that were already undermining the Government. He did not frequent the salons where the Comtesse de Portes and Madame de Crussol were pushing the claims of their respective candidates.[11] His chief friend in political circles was Champetier de Ribes, Under-Secretary for Foreign Affairs, and a *mutilé* of the first war, who shared Georges Vanier's own views on the second. Among the military high command he relied upon Réquin, who wrote that he had 'taken the offensive on the 9th of September, and everything went well, without any setback. It's a great advantage to know the country and to have the best troops under one's command.'[12] Georges had spent a few days in Normandy during September, and noted the mood of mobilisation:

The order and discipline, and also the dignity and calm, were admirable. No shouts or exaltation; the general behaviour was beyond praise. Even the women held back their tears, in order not to soften or trouble the men. In everything you do, you have such a sense of proportion.

He had also attended the Fête du Triomphe at the Military Academy at St Cyr:

I wonder whether any other country in the world would be capable of achieving this perfection. There is something not only serious but sacred about this traditional ceremony. And at the same time your young people know how to mix with it all a humour and a sort of boyish imagination which can make one laugh without in any way diminishing one's emotion. This is a masterpiece of proportion![13]

In October he visited Réquin at Nancy, where the impression of ardour, discipline and efficiency was amply confirmed. Nor were these appearances altogether deceptive; the French army

11. Paul Reynaud and Edouard Daladier.
12. 14th September 1939.
13. Interview in *Le Petit Journal*, 12th September 1939.

was excellently trained for a war which it would not be called upon to fight. Meanwhile in Quebec there were the first rumblings of dissension, but Vanier took comfort in Maurice Duplessis' heavy defeat in the Provincial elections.

Three days after war had broken out Georges was receiving Holy Communion at St Honoré d'Eylau carrying a gas-mask. With the general expectation of gas attacks on the civil population, and with his own knowledge of the new possibilities of bacteriological warfare, he was naturally anxious to bring the family together and put them out of reach of danger. So the children were brought over from their English schools and installed, with Pauline and Mrs Archer, at the Château de Baillou, near Le Mans, in the Sarthe. This belonged to the Marquis de Courtavel, to whom Pauline had been introduced by a distant connection, Odette de Roussy de Sales. The Marquis was concerned to prevent his house being taken over by the military, and he assigned a wing of the unattractive and sombre building to the Vaniers. Separated from his wife who was a pianist, he did not have very much in common with them, and since they took their meals together, conversation cannot have been easy. Not being on good terms with the curé, he had a sharp dispute with Mrs Archer, who was looking after the more difficult cases in the village. The Vanier boys went to the local school, and Pauline, Thérèse, and Odette de Roussy de Sales took turns in teaching the catechism, since the curé was too far declined in years to do so. Georges would come down by car for the week-end and restore order in a family which was becoming rather turbulent. When the boys pushed a heifer into a pig-trough, Pecquard – the gardener – thought it was time he came down with a ton of bricks.

The deceptive tranquillity of those winter months was emphasised by a matinée poétique devoted to Canada, and introduced by Jacques de Lacretelle, at the Comédie Française;[14] and in April Georges and Pauline paid an official visit to the Maginot Line. At each point in the line they were surprised and flattered to be greeted by a Canadian flag, and asked how this had been arranged. An officer explained that it was taken down immediately they had passed, rushed forward by motor-cycle, and rehoisted at the next point. The French authorities had tried to obtain a copy of 'O Canada', but the only copy in Paris was with the Canadian Legation, and could not be parted with. The problem was solved by the making of photostat prints, which were hurried to the

14. 2nd March 1940.

front and arrived at the same time as the Vaniers themselves. An impromptu concert was organized at one of the forward posts, where a *poilu*, who had been a tenor at the Opéra Comique, sang all five verses of the anthem in French. Pauline was even photographed with a group of girls in native costume. Lorraine has always been a nerve centre of French patriotism, and when the youngest of them, presenting her with a bouquet, addressed her in the following words – 'Je suis une petite fille de Lorraine très heureuse de présenter à Votre Excellence le signe de bien-venue dans notre pays' – Pauline was reminded of another 'jeune fille de Lorraine', not quite so 'petite', whose name would be desperately invoked before many days went by.

Réquin, no longer on the very limited offensive, led them to a place where they could see the German lines only a thousand yards away. They were in full view of the enemy and were certainly observed; but no shot was fired. Georges remarked to Pauline that she had done what he had never succeeded in doing throughout the last war – to stand in full view of the enemy without drawing his fire. Réquin assured them that there was very little firing; if one side sent over half-a-dozen shells – 'for banging purposes perhaps' – the other replied with a similar dose. Pauline was struck by the intricacy and efficiency of the Maginot Line, and also by its comfort. Was it, she wondered, a shade too comfortable? Nevertheless, Georges wrote afterwards to Gamelin, C.-in-C. of all the Allied Armies on the western front:

Our visit filled us with enthusiasm. A simple letter would not suffice to convey our deep impressions. Whether it was your officers or your men that we saw at rest or at work, we felt that their minds and hearts were given unreservedly to the task assigned to them. Their calm and natural behaviour – even their modesty – struck us very much indeed.

Among the men whom Georges had met and so much admired was Joseph Darnand, head of the Corps Franc, who was later to distinguish himself in the brief and calamitous campaign. Out of loyalty to Marshal Pétain he became chief of the Vichy *milice* and was executed shortly after the Liberation. He met his death at the hands of a firing squad with the same courage that he had risked his life in the field.

Another officer in Réquin's Army, where he commanded the 14th Infantry Division, was General de Lattre de Tassigny, whose personality both fascinated and disquieted Georges Vanier from the moment of their first meeting. The scion of an old Royalist family, de Lattre had been Chef de Cabinet to Weygand, when Weygand was Chief-of-Staff to the 5th Army. He was not only a soldier of originality and daring – qualities he was very shortly to display – but also something of an artist. Since there was no fighting immediately to be done, the Generals vied with each other in setting up the most comfortable 'Centres d'Accueil' (Soldiers' Hostels), and here de Lattre outshone his rivals, as he was later to outshine most of them in personal *réclame*, if not in military exploits. From one of these Centres Vanier brought away a beautifully carved stick, which he was proud to include in his private museum of souvenirs. His first impression of de Lattre was of a dynamic, intelligent, well-mannered, good-looking and debonair commander – impeccably turned out. He fitted exactly the description of a 'dashing cavalry officer' – which in fact he was, although he was commanding an Infantry Division. Georges described him as 'a little too *séduisant* – a word for which 'seductive' is too strong and 'charming' too weak.

General Gamelin[15] had visited and addressed the Canadian troops stationed in England, and Georges had heard from the Chaplain to the Royal 22nd how moved they had been by his encouragement. It was a matter of pride to Georges Vanier that the Royal 22nd had mounted guard outside Buckingham Palace. Tremblay wrote of the tremendous welcome that had greeted them: 'I am rather amused to compare the atmosphere of the present moment with the atmosphere in 1915 when we were at East Sandling.'[16]

Shortly afterwards (29th of April) Georges had a long interview with Gamelin at the General's H.Q. Mr Norman Rogers,[17] the Canadian Minister of National Defence, was also present. Gamelin thought it reasonable to suppose that the Germans would invade Holland or Belgium – more particularly Holland – and half encircle the United Kingdom by the occupation of Holland, Denmark and Norway. He did not believe there would be any substantial change on the French front, since it was well guarded and it was not the German method to attack places strongly held. He thought the attack on Norway would ultimately favour the Allies because it involved an expenditure of men and material. It did not seem to occur to him that the Allies were expending much needed men and material in the same campaign. He thought Canadian troops well suited to fight in Norway, but

15. Maurice Gustave Gamelin, 1872-1958.
16. 15th May 1940.   17. 1894-1940.

Rogers replied that they had sentimental reasons for preferring to fight where their brothers and fathers had fought. Gamelin was already assuming that the German attack on Norway was partially unsuccessful, and that the destruction of a large part of Hitler's navy would deter Mussolini from entering the war. In common with many other people, the Allied Commander-in-Chief was not without his illusions.

On the same day Georges Vanier and Rogers were received by Daladier at the Ministry of War. Madame de Portes had prevailed over Madame de Crussol, and Paul Reynaud had replaced Daladier as Prime Minister. The horns of the 'bull of Vaucluse' were shown to be remarkably blunted. Rogers explained that 23,000 Canadian troops were now in England, and 100,000 under arms. They were arriving overseas with their personal equipment, small arms and some light guns. The rest of the necessary *matériel* would have to be found in Britain. Canada had been told to prepare for a three years' war, and Daladier agreed that it might continue for as long as that. He thought that it would be more brutal and ruthless than the last one.

The arrival of Canadian forces in France, expected shortly, raised certain political problems. Since they would be the forces of a sovereign state, should not the First Division be met by representatives of the French civil and military authorities, and should not its Commander come to France and establish relations with these authorities before the troops arrived? The Canadian Government would naturally wish them to be under General Gamelin's over-all command, to whom their Commander should have direct access. But how far would this privilege of approach, and consequently of independent action, be extended in practice to operations and administration? Vanier did not advocate Canadian representation on the Imperial General Staff, but if it were so represented the situation would be altered in the sense that the I.G.S. would then no longer take its orders from the United Kingdom Government alone. Mr Price Montague, however, the Canadian Judge Advocate General, had laid down in a Memorandum to General Andrew McNaughton,[18] commanding the Canadian Forces overseas, that these would only be under General Gamelin's command in the sense that they would be a part of the British Expeditionary Force, and that Gamelin's command could only be exercised through Lord Gort,[19] Commander-in-Chief of

18. General the Hon. Andrew McNaughton, 1887-1966.
19. Field-Marshal Viscount Gort, 1886-1946.

the B.E.F. There would be no direct relationship between Gamelin and the Canadian Divisions.

Georges Vanier wrote to McNaughton (22nd of April 1940) that he thought the position as defined by Montague would be found by the French difficult to reconcile with the prerogatives of a sovereign state. He had no wish to impair the unity of command. 'I realize as an ex-soldier how essential unity of command is to success' – but he wished to establish a principle which appeared to him more in keeping with the Statute of Westminster. He had already personally emphasized these views to Mc-Naughton at a meeting at the Canadian Legation on the 10th of January; and when Canadian troops were sent to Norway three months later their relevance became clear. 'We are told what has happened; very seldom what will happen or may happen. . . . Yesterday it was Norway, tomorrow it may be Holland or Belgium – or the Mediterranean.'

The fault lay in defective contact between the War Cabinet and the Services – and for this Canada herself was largely responsible. She was not represented on the Committee of Imperial Defence; looked with suspicion on all Imperial Committees; and even demurred – as Lester Pearson had pointed out – at regular meetings between the High Commissioner and the United Kingdom Secretaries of State for the Dominions and Foreign Affairs. She insisted on loose informal consultations in London, and direct consultation between the two Governments when necessary. Ottawa had never encouraged its representatives in London to consider it their duty to discover the purposes of British policy in time of peace, with the result that as far as policy and planning in the present war was concerned, the status of the senior Dominion was little better than that of a colony. It was unrepresented on the War Cabinet, or the Cabinet Secretariats, or the Planning and Operations Boards. The Allied War Council met with Norwegian and Polish representatives, but not Canadian. There had been an important meeting of the Council: 'We have not yet received any information of what took place at that meeting; neither has North Borneo. . . . Are the Air Ministry – without consultation with Canadian representatives – to send Canadian squadrons at will all over Europe? Personally, I dislike this rôle of unpaid Hessians.'

To remedy these anomalies Vanier proposed that Canada should be informed of all decisions of the War Cabinet; should have the right to send a representative to its meetings when questions of Canadian participation were under discussion, and to meetings of the Allied War Council in London and in Paris; and that Canadian Staff officers should be attached to the Secretariat of the Chief of Staffs Committee and to the Military Secretariat of the War Cabinet. These suggestions were not without effect.

Meanwhile life continued placidly at Baillou, where the only casualties were Bernard and Jock who went down with the measles. F. C. Turner, S. J. who had been teaching Byngsie at Beaumont, came over during his Easter holidays to supplement the rudimentary instruction at the village school. He noted that the optimism of the family was secure, and undisturbed by the Norwegian campaign. Confidence in the French army was absolute, and even the sight of Madame Weygand walking in the Paris streets was enough to reinforce it.

3

On the evening of the 9th of May Pauline was in Paris for a dinner at the American Embassy. It was an important occasion with Daladier, Champetier de Ribes, Campinchi[20] – Minister of Marine – and Air-Vice-Marshal Barratt among the guests. The prevailing mood was heavy, and as the evening wore on the men were seen gathering in groups and leaving early. The Vaniers were among the last to go, and at 3 a.m. they were woken by the sirens screaming over Paris. The German attack in the west had broken at midnight, and some inkling of this had reached the American Embassy, where the guests had dispersed to their war stations, like the officers at the Duchess of Richmond's ball on the eve of Waterloo. Later that morning Pauline left for the country, while Georges remained at the Legation. For the next three anxious weeks he watched the incredible collapse of French resistance. On the 17th of May a message from the British Embassy advised him to burn all secret documents, while others were burning in the courtyard of the Quai d'Orsay, and he prepared to move the archives at a moment's notice. For the first time the *gendarme* outside the Legation was carrying a rifle. Gamelin's Order of the Day recalled Joffre's message on the eve of the Marne; and on the afternoon of the 19th of May, Vanier was kneeling in Notre Dame with Marshal Pétain – now a member of the Government – and other politicians to whom prayer was not an habitual occupation. It had occurred to them that it might be

20. César Campinchi, 1852-1941.

a useful, if desperate, measure of defence. Only a week before Champetier de Ribes was telling Georges Vanier how Herriot, in 1926, had asked him to join his ministry 'not in spite of your ideas, but because of them'. Herriot was, in every sense of the word, a bigger man than Daladier; but even Daladier, in making a similar offer in 1938, had ventured to suggest: 'il faut réchristianiser la France'. Now, supplanted by Reynaud at the Présidence du Conseil, the 'bull of Vaucluse' thought he might end up as a believer.

For Georges Vanier the service of intercession in Notre Dame was a deeply moving experience. General de Castelnau[21] – a revered name from the first World War – and General Gouraud were there, as the Auxiliary Bishop of Paris invoked the Saints whose names reverberate through the history and geography of France – St Michel, St Rémy, St Louis, St Denis, St Geneviève – the patroness of Paris – and St Jeanne d'Arc whose standard and relics were carried down the nave of the cathedral. The vast assembly repeated the invocations and then chanted the 'De Profundis' and sang the 'Marseillaise'. It was the last manifestation of hope – if hope it could be called – in a situation which all but a few were coming to recognize as hopeless.

Georges was now spending his nights at Villennes, a small village outside Paris. As he made his way in to the Legation he would pass the convoys of refugees – women, children and old men, sometimes with a cart-load of rabbits. At Mass that morning the *curé* had spoken of courage, recalling the definition of a colonel in the last war. Courage, he had said, had nothing to do with insensibility or excitement; it was an act of the will; it was to continue the struggle in full awareness of its dangers; it was to be brave when one was brave no longer.

On the 21st Vanier had tea at the British Embassy, watching the melancholy bonfire of documents in the garden of what had once been Pauline Borghese's house, and where in normal times the *beau monde* – now paralysed with fear – would soon have been parading in honour of the King's birthday. Sir Ronald Campbell[22] already foresaw the possibility that Germany would offer France a separate, and superficially attractive, peace. Few people as yet foresaw that France would sue for it. On the 22nd the wives and families of men engaged on Government service in France, Belgium, Holland and Switzerland were advised by

21. General Edouard de Corières Castelnau, 1851-1944.
22. The British Ambassador Sir Ronald Campbell, 1883-1955.

External Affairs to return to Canada immediately. And on the 24th Vanier drove down to Pernay, eighteen kilometres north-west of Tours, to inspect the Château de l'Herissodière which had been allocated to the Legation in case it were forced to move. Pauline joined him at Blois, and after dining at Vouvray they returned for the night to Chitenay in the Loir-et-Cher, where Pauline and the family were now staying with her cousin, the Marquis de Pothuau. Thérèse had a message from the Canadian Military Attaché, Major-General LaFlèche,[23] that the military situation was still precarious.

Marshal Pétain had never been the austere figure of later legend, and two days later when Georges Vanier was dining at the Restaurant Chaulant he was informed that the Marshal had been there for luncheon. Asked whether the Marshal was a big eater, the proprietor replied: 'Well, this morning the Marshal said that he wasn't hungry. In spite of that, however, he ate a melon, a mutton cutlet, *petits pois*, cheese and fruit. His companion asked him what he would have eaten if he *had* been hungry, and the Marshal replied: "I should have ordered some fish as well".' The same afternoon Georges had attended the public prayers at St Etienne-du-Mont where thirty thousand people filled the square and the relics of St Geneviève were carried in procession. He remembered that in the sombre days of 1914 the reliquary had been exposed in the porch of the church. The French had been thinking of Paris then; they were thinking of Paris now; they were not thinking of very much else.

On the 28th of May King Leopold of the Belgians capitulated with his army, and was bitterly denounced by Reynaud. Pierlot[24] and Spaak, respectively Prime Minister and Foreign Minister of Belgium were in Paris, laying wreaths on King Albert's monument. Georges had been dining with Paul Claudel, the eminent poet and recently retired ambassador. Claudel remarked that small nations unable to defend their neutrality constituted a serious danger to nations that conformed to international law, and that after the war the conception of neutrality for smaller nations would change – and Vanier agreed with him. Two days later he received a visit from a man with whom he was to be closely associated in the years to come. Before the war René Pléven had lived in London, where he was in business. He had also collaborated with Charles Flory on the review *Politique*, and it was through Flory

23. Major-General Leo R. LaFlèche.
24. Comte Hubert Pierlot, 1883-1963.

that Vanier had met him. He had only just returned from the United States, and was perhaps less concerned about French morale than he might have been if he had been longer on the spot at a time when it was declining so quickly. Nevertheless he recognized that inspiration and initiative were lacking from the top – something that Clémenceau had given in the last war and Churchill was giving now. He asked Georges Vanier what he thought of organizing a resounding inter-allied demonstration, without defining exactly what form this should take. Georges replied that he was sympathetic to the idea but that he could not take the matter up with his own Government unless he were asked to do so by the French. In any event the time for demonstrations was quickly passing although on the following Sunday another fervent ceremony took place at the Sacré Coeur. It was all very well for Cardinal Suhard[25] to consecrate Paris to the Sacred Heart and for General de Castelnau to make a public vow to organize a day of Masses. What was needed was for other Generals to close the widening gap between the northern and the southern armies; and for those in power who had so ardently addressed their prayers to St Geneviève to heed the words of a very humble subordinate when he observed to Georges Vanier: 'It would be a cowardly thing to let Paris be taken after praying to St Geneviève; it would show a want of faith.'

After a brief visit to Chitenay, Vanier returned to find the Avenue Foch blocked by disused buses and lorries, placed there to prevent a landing by hostile aircraft. If they were removed after a few hours it was not because the aircraft were less hostile. Through all these alarms and excursions Georges kept a cool head, and on the 5th of June he was still in the mood to order a copy of Thackeray's *Henry Esmond* and Churchill's *The Aftermath* from the American Library. General Gamelin, whom Weygand had just replaced as Commander-in-Chief, occupied two floors above the Vaniers at 55 Avenue Foch; and as Georges was leaving the house for Mass at 6.50 a.m. on the 9th of June, he met him outside saying good-bye to his wife who was driving off into the country. The General complained bitterly of his dismissal, more especially as other high-ranking commanders had been retained. He also criticized the dispersal of man-power for the Norwegian expedition, and implied that the Government bore him a grudge for his opposition to it. He contradicted the rumour that he had lost his head after the German break-through; on the con-

25. Emmanuel Cardinal Suhard, 1874-1949.

trary, he had signed an order for attack on the morning of the day – the 19th of May – when he had been relieved of his command. His voice, as he justified his conduct to Georges Vanier, betrayed his emotion. He seemed a broken man, and Vanier was disposed to accept the information he had previously been given that at the critical moment, when Corap's army had cracked, Gamelin had been quite useless. A nominee of Daladier, he evidently regarded himself as a casualty of the Comtesse de Portes' victory over Madame de Crussol, although he was too polite to say so.

Major-General LaFlèche, had been received the previous night by Weygand at General Headquarters. Weygand had stressed the numerical superiority of the enemy and the French lack of reserves both in men and material. LaFlèche had also been told by the Armament Bureau of the Ministry of War that there were only six tanks and twelve field-guns available for replacement – information that he must have found incredible. Weygand declared to the U.S. Military Attaché, who was also present, that prolonged resistance was impossible unless America declared war at once. When Vanier heard this, he realized that the defeat of France could only be a matter of time – and probably a very short time – not because America was unlikely to declare war, but because no army could hope to win under the command of a man who did not believe in victory.

Malise Graham,[26] the British Military Attaché, had learnt from Weygand that neither General Georges,[27] commanding the Allied Armies in the field, nor his Chief of Staff were at all confident that they could hold the Germans on the Somme. Vanier replied that if Georges felt that way he had no right to be in command, and he told Malise Graham that it was his duty to urge the British Government to press the French Government for his removal. Churchill, however, and his military liaison with Reynaud, General Spears,[28] both had a high regard for Georges and knew him well, even though they wondered what he was doing at the moment. If Malise Graham had made any such representations, they were unlikely to have had much effect.

After sending Pierre Dupuy to the Quai d'Orsay – where he learnt that a decision whether to move the Government to Tours would be taken in a few hours – Georges Vanier called during the

26. Brigadier Lord Douglas Malise Graham.
27. General Joseph Georges, 1875-1951.
28. Major-General Sir Edward Spears, Bart.

afternoon on M. Charles Roux, Secretary-General for Foreign Affairs. He was informed that arrangements had been made for the immediate departure of certain Ministries, but that the Government hoped to remain in Paris indefinitely. This information, confirmed later the same evening, was falsely reassuring, since Paris was now regarded as part of the battle zone, and German mechanized units were already pushing towards the city. At the Legation preparations went ahead for a move to Pernay. The occupation of Paris had not been remotely contemplated, but as the situation worsened a part of the office records, filing cabinets and other equipment had been transferred to Pernay during the first week of June. In Paris the mood was grave, but not as yet alarmist, and restaurants and cinemas were still open. Quietly, however, by road and rail, the exodus had begun.

The guarded optimism of the Quai d'Orsay was quickly belied. On the 10th of June LaFlèche was informed that the Ministry of Air and the Ministry of War were leaving, and it was obvious that the Government would follow shortly. The United States Ambassador – W. C. Bullitt[29] – agreed to take over the Canadian Legation, if it were forced to leave, and to assume protection of Canadian interests. A letter from the Quai d'Orsay gave authority for the evacuation of all diplomatic missions to the area assigned to them, and Dupuy obtained confirmation that this was to be regarded as notice to quit – not merely permission to do so. Seals were then affixed to the Legation, and the staff, with their wives and families, left in five cars at intervals of a few hours, each filled to its maximum capacity. After picking up some personal effects, Georges was the last to go. There were eight people in the Buick when it took the road to Tours – and beyond – at 11.30 p.m. Already there was an air of battle about the city. The Germans had crossed the Seine to the north-west, and the wind was blowing their smoke-screens over the Champs Elyseés and the Bois de Boulogne like a pall of doom, carrying with it the smell of cordite – the same smell, again, after twenty-eight years. As the Buick swung out into the Bois its huddled occupants caught sight, here and there under a shaded street lamp, of detachments of police or bus-loads of soldiers standing by for orders. Here were all the appearances of a last stand; but they were no more than the décor for a play upon which the curtain never went up.

A motorist would normally reckon three hours to travel from

29. William Christian Bullitt, 1891-1967.

Paris to Tours by way of Orléans and Blois; on this night of exodus, with vehicles of every description crawling bumper to bumper along the road, it took seventeen. They reached Pernay at 4 p.m. the following afternoon. Sometimes they were brought to a complete halt and one of the Canadian cars decided to wait by the roadside till the morning. Moving a hundred and fifty yards from the main road, the party got out and were about to go to sleep on some hay under a tarpaulin beside a stone wall, when they were roused by some soldiers who thought they were parachutists. It was a plausible suspicion, since the spot chosen was next door to one of the largest gunpowder factories in France.

There was just room in the château for the senior members of the staff, with LaFlèche and two others. The rest were billeted in the village. The Ministry for Foreign Affairs was established at Langeais, only eighteen kilometres to the south, but LaFlèche had to motor 150 kilometres by less frequented side roads to find the Ministry for War at Faverolles. On the 13th of June Vanier drove to Langeais where he found Charles-Roux in a state of deep depression. The Germans still had twenty fresh divisions to throw into the battle, and the French had none. Ministers and officials could talk of nothing but a chimerical declaration of war by the United States. Vanier heard the same story of disaster from the British Military Attaché at Clère – ten kilometres from Pernay – where the British Embassy was temporarily installed. The first Canadian contingent had just disembarked, and would be thrown piecemeal into the *mêlée*. Vanier would have liked to welcome them, but with the probability of a move further south this was impossible. On the same day, at a meeting of the Supreme War Council, Paul Reynaud asked that the French Government be relieved of its undertaking not to conclude a separate peace, and the United Kingdom decided to await the result of an appeal to President Roosevelt before giving a reply.

In the very early morning of the 14th of June Vanier received a personal letter from Sir Ronald Campbell. It had been written at 12.30 a.m., despatched at 5.30 a.m., and marked 'Immediate – to be wakened up'. Although the beds at L'Herissonière were comfortable, it may be conjectured that in all the circumstances Georges was already awake. The note passed on the information received from Mandel, Minister of the Interior, that the British Ambassador must be away and on the road to Bordeaux by 10 a.m. German tanks had forced a passage at Evreux and might enter Tours before the day was out. At 9 a.m. a telephone message from the Ministry of Foreign Affairs requested the Canadian and South African Ministers to leave the neighbourhood of Tours, proceed to Bordeaux, and apply to the Prèfet for accommodation. This might only be available for the Ministers and one Secretary apiece.

It was a fine day, with a light mist giving cover from aerial bombardment, when the Canadian party left Pernay at 10 a.m., leaving behind some office furniture and equipment, stationery and personal effects. Vanier instructed the personnel of the Legation to make for Margaux, twenty-eight kilometres north of Bordeaux, where General Brutinel, who had commanded the Canadian Machine-Gun Corps in 1918, had a château and would be prepared to welcome them. Progress from Pernay to Bordeaux was easier than from Paris to Pernay, and the Buick arrived there at 6.40 p.m. An Admiral, allocating billets at the Préfecture, informed the Canadians that the Château de Suau at Barsac, thirty-seven kilometres to the south-east, had been allotted to them; but when Georges arrived at the château, he was informed by the châtelaine that she had received no instructions, and in any case could only let them have one room. This seemed inadequate for twelve people, even in time of war; so the party set off for Margaux, sixty-five kilometres away. Here they were greeted by General Brutinel, with his one leg and his crutches, shortly before midnight, and – even more importantly – by Pauline and the children who had driven down from Chitenay the day before. Chitenay was crowded with refugees who went round in circles of bewilderment and alarm while Thérèse picked flowers and strawberries in the garden. Jean Désy – a diplomat in flight like themselves – had arranged billets for them, and for the others, in the village of Cantenac near by. At the same time the news came through that the Germans had entered Paris. Reunited with his family, his Chancery established at the Mairie, and so traumatic a day behind him, Vanier could hardly have done other than sleep well. Nevertheless, as Byngsie was to write later in his reminiscences of those days, 'billeted in an old farmhouse . . . with a candle in an empty bottle for comfort, our dreams were a little uneasy.'[30]

On the 15th of June Georges motored into Bordeaux, met his South African colleague, Mr Bain-Marais,[31] and together they called on Charles-Roux at the Law Faculty Building of the Uni-

30. B.M.A. *Blitz*, March 1945.
31. Colin Bain-Marais, 1893-1942.

versity. The Secretary-General could only tell them what they knew already – that the military situation was hopeless. Vanier decided to remain at Cantenac, where the Mayor and inhabitants were doing all they could to make him comfortable; he also realized that the village was on the main road to the port of Le Verdon, whence he might eventually be able to make his escape. On the following day Reynaud resigned, having failed to persuade his colleagues to accept Churchill's offer of a union between France and Britain; and shortly after midnight on the 17th of June Marshal Pétain formed a Government from which the three ministers most firmly in favour of continuing the struggle – Mandel,[32] Campinchi and Louis Marin[33] – were significantly excluded.

At 11 a.m. the same day Vanier received a message from the British Embassy that one of His Majesty's destroyers would be leaving Bordeaux for Le Verdon at 1.30 p.m., and that ships were at anchor at Le Verdon to take on refugees for the United Kingdom. Pauline was warned by telephone to leave with the family and members of the Legation staff – twenty-nine in all – as soon as possible. After a fast drive to Bordeaux – where the Stars and Stripes were hoisted on every British-owned building, Barclays Bank among them – they boarded H.M.S. *Berkeley*, and were transferred at Le Verdon to the cargo ship *Nariva* of the Royal Mail Steam Packet Company, which normally carried meat from the Argentine. It remained at anchor for a further twenty-four hours. There were three hundred people aboard – including the President of Poland and the British Ambassador in Warsaw, Madame Geneviève Tabouis,[34] Alexis Léger,[35] and a group of English nuns – huddled under tarpaulins in the holds, in the cabins, or on the decks, and wondering who would get the sixty life-belts if they were torpedoed. When three bombs dropped on the wharf during the afternoon the destroyer, still moored alongside, opened up with all her guns before casting off. Those who had life-belts tightened them; those who hadn't tightened their lips. A bell was found for the Vanier boys, who took much delight in announcing the successive distributions of tinned salmon sandwiches – for the menu was invariable. 'First Service – Premier Service.' The nuns were resourceful and suggested sponge bags in

32. Georges Mandel, 1885-1944.
33. 1871-1960.
34. The eminent French journalist.
35. Formerly head of the French Ministry of Foreign Affairs, and better known as the poet St Jean-Perse.

the event of seasickness. More bombs fell during the night of the 18th of June and at dawn the refugees were informed that planes were dropping magnetic mines in the harbour. There were fifty ships around them in the estuary under the rather distant protection of a cruiser lying off-shore. A Heinkel bomber, flying low with its engine on fire, was the only encouraging prospect until the *Nariva* put out to sea at 4 p.m. Two days later it anchored at Milford Haven where a ship from Montreal, flying the Canadian flag, reminded them that there was a new world waiting to come to the rescue of the old. The disembarkation was not easy, and one of the nuns explained how she had been 'passed from one man's arms to another'. When a passenger expressed his relief at being back in England, wrath fell on him from a local townswoman: 'Look you, it is not England at all, it is Wales.' Vincent Massey cabled Georges the news of the safe arrival.

Having said Good-bye to the family on the quay, Georges returned with Bain-Marais to the Ministry of Foreign Affairs. Charles-Roux informed them that Marshal Pétain had asked General Franco to appeal to the German government for an immediate cessation of hostilities and to enquire about its terms for an armistice. He added that France would not agree to surrender the Air Force or the Fleet, and that she had no intention of turning against Britain. Considering that France and Britain were allies, the remark struck Vanier as surprising. The British Government had only agreed to the French *démarche* – a similar approach had also been made to Italy – if the French fleet sailed for British harbours. On the 18th of June Sir Ronald Campbell, supported by the First Lord of the Admiralty[36] and the First Sea Lord,[37] were desperately trying to ensure that it should not fall into German hands. Meanwhile German troops were approaching Lyons, and no reply had been received from the German government. In the course of a brief conversation the Papal Nuncio, Mgr Valerio Valeri, observed: 'Il faut s'en remettre à Dieu.' It was the only thing that a Papal Nuncio could be expected to say, and it was advice that Georges Vanier was never reluctant to follow.

The 19th of June brought notice from Sir Ronald Campbell that he was sending most of his staff to England that night on H.M.S. *Arethusa*, and he asked Vanier and Bain-Marais if they wished to go with them. The two Ministers decided to remain for the time being, but instructed their own staff to embark on H.M.S. *Berkeley* and transfer to the *Arethusa* at Le Verdon. News then

36. Mr A. V. Alexander.   37. Admiral of the Fleet Sir Dudley Pound.

came from the French Ministry for Foreign Affairs that the Germans had agreed to meet a French delegation, and the Ministers were asked to make known to their Governments that the French would welcome some more positive action from the United States. This would encourage public opinion in France and might deter the enemy from pressing unacceptable demands. Charles-Roux repeated his assurances with regard to the Fleet and Air Force: nothing was said about a possible move of the French Government to North Africa, but Vanier learnt from Sir Ronald Campbell that, in the event of the enemy approaching Bordeaux, the President of the Republic, the Presidents of the Senate and the Chamber of Deputies, with three or four ministers, would go there – probably to Algiers. Charles-Roux added that the messages from Mr Roosevelt and the British Government, warning the French that the goodwill of their two countries would be forfeited if the French Fleet were allowed to fall into the hands of the enemy, were very displeasing to the distinguished Marshal to whom they were addressed.

On that same day, the 19th of June, LaFlèche had breakfasted with General Colson, the new Minister of War and a close associate of Weygand and Pétain; and he had also heard from U.S. officials that the French cabinet, then in session, were thinking of selling the Navy to the United States. It was a strange idea, if it ever existed, and it did not get very far – perhaps because these paralysed politicians realized that history would laugh at it. Admiral Darlan, who was not insensitive to *amour-propre*, cannot have relished the thought of his officers and crews wandering about ashore while the Americans – as it was still fondly hoped – fought in their ships. The Head of the Ier Bureau had told LaFlèche of a new projectile being developed in France which was thought to be very effective against tanks. The plans for this had been placed with French industry too late for use – too little and too late accurately summed up the situation – but an officer had taken them to Lisbon whence they were being despatched to Washington. They would also be given to LaFlèche for Canada, and the British had been informed.

Meanwhile Vanier, with his South African colleague, had joined Sir Ronald Campbell at the Hotel Montré in Bordeaux, handing over the Buick to his chauffeur to dispose of as he liked, informing the Préfet that he had done so, and leaving the three other Legation cars with Brutinel. In less than a week the population of the

38. François Darlan, 1887-1942.

city had expanded from 260,000 to nearly a million, a good number of fifth columnists among them. People were sleeping in the parks or in their motor cars. Many young men were heard proclaiming that they wished to join the British Forces, but the British Consulate, hitherto besieged, had been moved to Bayonne. The Germans were not only dropping their magnetic mines in the estuary of the Gironde, but during the night of the 19th-20th of June there was a heavy raid on Bordeaux. The electric power gave out, and the diplomats took refuge in a cellar. By the light of a torch they could only discern a vista of vintage clarets, General Gouraud in uniform, and Lord Lloyd[39] in a silk dressing-gown. The raid lasted for a little under two hours. In the morning the two Ministers were received by Paul Baudouin, the new French Minister for Foreign Affairs. He stated that no reply had as yet come from the Germans to the French request for a safety zone around Bordeaux, and that the Government were moving the same afternoon to Perpignan. Later, they would probably go to North Africa. Vanier was struck by Baudouin's youthful appearance, decisive manner, and nervous speech : he had the feverish glare of the fanatic, with obviously no sense of detachment or of humour. It was an accurate impression.

The Ministers were preparing to leave for Perpignan when they learnt that the French Government had changed its mind, since the Germans had promised to restore the telephone line between Bordeaux and Tours. The Government would thus be able to communicate with its Armistice Delegation. In the evening some French pilots gave an exhibition of low flying and diving close to the Hotel Montré; Vanier could not help thinking that their acrobatics might more usefully have been directed against the enemy. It was no time for sowing aeronautic wild oats. He and Bain-Marais dined that evening at the 'Chapon Fin'. The great restaurant remained, as always, above suspicion, but it was filled with people who deeply suspected one another – Sir Ronald Campbell and Pierre Laval, Mr Drexel Biddle[40] and the Spanish Ambassador. Campbell came over to the table where Georges and Bain-Marais were seated, expressed his distrust of Baudouin, and invited them to accompany him in quest of further information. They obtained the address of Marshal Pétain at the Ministry of Foreign Affairs and drove – a longish distance – to his quarters. It was then 11 p.m. Hearing that the Marshal was resting, and

39. Lord Lloyd of Dolobran, 1879-1941 Secretary of State for the Colonies.
40. A. J. Drexel Biddle, 1874-1948. U.S. Minister in Paris.

that the Armistice Delegation was on its way to Tours, Campbell asked to be informed as soon as the terms for an armistice had been received, and the three diplomats returned to their hotel.

The next morning (the 22nd of June) Vanier and Bain-Marais called on Charles-Roux with their Governments' reply to Baudouin's request of the previous day. Both Governments had pressed the matter on the United States, and would make further representations. Meanwhile the Armistice Delegates had been delayed by the destruction of the bridges over the Loire, and had then been summoned to Compiègne where Hitler had planned a ceremonial consummation of his revenge. Vanier later received word that the French cruiser *Emile Bertin* had arrived at Halifax, N.S., with a large consignment of gold from the Bank of France to be placed in the safe keeping of the Bank of Canada. The Captain had orders to deliver the gold to the Island of Martinique, which the Canadian Government considered vulnerable and lacking the required facilities. Vanier was instructed to take the matter up with the French authorities, but a subsequent cable informed him that it had now been settled.

At 2 a.m. that night the Ministers, sleeping in adjoining rooms, were woken by Mr Harold Mack,[41] Counsellor at the British Embassy, with a message from Sir Ronald Campbell inviting them to join him at the offices of the French Prime Minister, where the Cabinet was then in session. On arrival they were shown into a large entrance hall, with a high ceiling supported by marble columns. A dozen men, most of them in uniform, were sitting there in silence with their heads bowed. The hall was in semi-darkness, feebly lighted by a few electric bulbs. The atmosphere was deathly. The Ambassador was seated at the foot of the staircase leading to the first floor, and Vanier took the vacant place beside him. Campbell whispered the information he had just been given regarding the proposals for the disposition of the French Fleet. The Ambassador had already poured scorn on the German undertaking not to make use of the Fleet for its own ends. They had never respected any undertaking they had given; why should they respect this one?

At 3.20 a.m. the large doors leading to the adjoining room were thrown open, and the members of the French Cabinet came in. Baudouin assured Sir Ronald Campbell that the French Government would propose the disarmament of the French Fleet and its internment in North African waters or ports. If the Italians tried

41. Sir Harold Mack.

to seize it, the crews would scuttle their ships. The conversation was not particularly cordial, and in face of Baudouin's refusal to give more precise information, Sir Ronald protested formally against the procedure he had adopted. President Lebrun[42] then came into the room; shook hands with the diplomats; and confirmed Baudouin's statement that there was as yet no draft of the reply to the German terms. Baudouin complained of Sir Ronald Campbell's suggestion that he was wanting in frankness, but shook hands with the Ambassador and the two Ministers before they left. Dawn was breaking as they walked the short distance to their hotel through the deserted streets.

It was by now a little before 4 a.m. Campbell had extracted from Baudouin a copy of the Armistice terms and he invited the two others to study them in his room. Owing to the lack of cypher personnel it was not possible to cable a complete text to Ottawa, which would in any case have received the details from London, where adequate facilities existed. A meeting of the French Cabinet had been called for 8.30 a.m., before which Sir Ronald Campbell obtained an interview with Marshal Pétain. He again protested against the proposal to recall the Fleet to French ports. Vanier and Bain-Marais remained in the hall adjoining the Council Chamber until the members of the Cabinet began to arrive. Weygand, whom Vanier knew very well, passed him without recognition. The reply to the German terms was approved a little later; and in the matter of the Fleet, which was of primary concern to the Allied diplomats, it did nothing to meet their objections.

In a subsequent meeting with Charles-Roux the Dominion Ministers discussed the probability of their leaving France very soon. They did not relish the prospect of being taken prisoner as belligerents. The Secretary-General suggested that they might continue their mission in unoccupied territory, but could give no guarantee that they would be able to communicate with their respective Governments. M. Charles-Roux was depressed, but philosophic; France had fallen before and she would rise again. By 7.30 that evening the decision to leave had been taken, and half an hour later the Ministers accepted the offer of Sir Ronald Campbell to accompany him in the British cruiser, H.M.S. *Galatea*, which was at anchor off Arcachon, sixty kilometres to the south-west of Bordeaux. There was a last, melancholy dinner at the 'Chapon Fin', and then they set out on a final round of

42. Albert Lebrun, 1871-1950.

courtesy calls. Protocol, informed with compassion, was keeping its stiff upper lip to the end. President Lebrun had gone to bed, but they left appropriate messages with the head of his civilian household. Marshal Pétain was not at his provisional quarters, but they were received in a very kindly manner by General Weygand. The General confirmed the signature of the Armistice, and agreed that the danger of capture was very real, since there was nothing to stop the Germans entering Bordeaux. When Georges Vanier observed that the conduct of the Italian Government had been ignoble, Weygand described it as 'infamous'. They expressed their admiration and sympathy for a man who had taken over command of the Allied Armies under almost impossible conditions. With a sad thought for his own army, now reduced to defeated fragments, Weygand remarked: 'Notre armée est belle – oui' – and laid the greater responsibility for its defeat on the politicians.

Vanier reaffirmed his conviction that France would rise from her present humiliation, and the General agreed, but added that he was too old to witness a resurrection which at that moment seemed so remote. Vanier knew that Weygand, like his master Foch, was a man of deep religious beliefs, and he tried to comfort him by saying that if he did not see the restoration of his country in his own lifetime he would see it in the life to come. The General was moved and bowed his head. After signing Bain-Marais' card of diplomatic identity and writing in the date, he remarked bitterly: 'cruel date'. While he was giving a similar autograph to Vanier, and hearing that he possessed a signed photograph of Foch, he said that if Foch had been alive things might have turned out differently. He accompanied the diplomats to the head of the stairs and said Good-bye to them with some emotion. They noticed that although tired and grave, he betrayed no agitation either in speech or movement. His signature on their cards was firm and clear.

Baudouin received them in a bright blue dressing-gown and slippers. Apart from the usual courtesies, he expressed his regret that the British Ambassador had so little faith in the assurances of the French Government with regard to the disposition of the Fleet. The two diplomats were not inclined to pursue the conversation. With General Weygand they had been speaking to a defeated general; with Paul Baudouin they were speaking to a political opportunist. In the former case they had taken their leave with sympathy; in the latter with suspicion.

After returning to the hotel they left for Arcachon by car at 11.30 p.m., through a fine drizzle of rain. Lodging had been arranged for the night within sound of the sea breaking on those sandy shores. Shortly after 7 a.m., in company with Sir Ronald Campbell and Mr Oliver Harvey,[43] they boarded a small sardine fishing vessel called Le Cygne, but bearing no resemblance to its name. It put out to sea, pitching and tossing violently in the drenching rain, until a Canadian destroyer – H.M.C.S. Fraser – picked up the retching and discomfited passengers. The Captain[44] of H.M.S. Galatea, warned of enemy submarines, had sailed south to St-Jean-de-Luz and ordered the Fraser to follow as soon as the diplomats were aboard. Vanier was pleased and proud that a Canadian vessel should have helped to bring him to safety. They spent four hours on board her – a grateful memory only clouded two days later by the knowledge that the Fraser had been sunk in those same, unfriendly waters.

The Galatea sailed from St-Jean-de-Luz shortly after midnight on the 24th of June. The sea was calm and she was making something better than twenty-five knots. Vanier went up on deck at 3 a.m. The moon was full, shedding a silver light over the furrowed waves, and the sky was clear, except in the east, where the great clouds weaving a shroud over France were an appropriate décor for tragedy. They reached Plymouth at 8.30 p.m. the following evening. The Admiral C-in-C.[45] sent his barge to take them off, and entertained them at Admiralty House until the night train left for London. They arrived at Paddington at 9.30 a.m. on the morning of the 25th of June. Vanier was met by Lester Pearson, members of his own Legation, Pauline and all the family. When Pauline discovered, after the first embraces, that Georges had been fed on chicken during the voyage, she decided, with memories of less delicate fare on the 'sardinier', that in future they had better escape from difficult situations in company. The Ministers sent a cheque to be distributed among those who had looked after them on the Galatea, and another to the telegraphist from the Calcutta who had dived overboard to rescue the crew of the Fraser. Georges had left his rosary behind in the cabin which Captain Schofield had kindly given up to him, but he had kept his faith intact. In the weeks and months to come he would have need of it.

43. Lord Harvey of Tasburgh, 1893-1968, then Minister at the British Embassy.
44. Captain Schofield, R.N.
45. Sir Martin Dunbar-Nasmith, R.N.

CHAPTER 12

DISSENSION AND DEFIANCE

1

WHATEVER Georges Vanier may have known of the corruption, incompetence and intrigue which had helped to bring about the fall of France – and he must have known a good deal – he did not dwell on it in his correspondence or his conversation, or even brood upon it in his own mind. Beneath the mire and the *malaise* there was an essential France which he knew because he belonged to it. He believed, beyond all reasonable belief, that it would rise again. Where Vincent Massey had seen betrayal, Pauline – who was listening to the news of capitulation at his elbow at the Dorchester – had seen only misfortune, and reacted accordingly. Where many people in England were proud to be 'going it alone', the Vaniers never ceased to feel the pulse of a hidden, as yet hardly articulate, France which others would come to feel as time went by. Within a few days of his return Georges was broadcasting his invincible confidence to Canada.[1]

The forces of regeneration were already gathering in their twos and threes. A young woman, Elisabeth de Miribel, only twenty-four years old, conscious of a personal mission and like a firebrand in pursuit of it, was in London. A great-grand-daughter of Marshal Macmahon – whose sword hung on the walls of the family house in the rue Bellechasse – she was attached as translator to Paul Morand's mission, and immediately after the French collapse got herself engaged as secretary to General de Gaulle. It was she who typed out his message of the 18th of July. By the natural contagion of kindred spirits she quickly became a close friend of the Vaniers, and for the next eight years she was never far from their side. Pléven was in London too, and arranged a dinner at his flat for the Vaniers to meet the General. He and Georges liked and trusted each other immediately. Hearing that

1. 27th June 1940.

Pauline was visiting the French soldiers evacuated from Dunkirk, de Gaulle reminded her that it was her duty to make them rally to his standard. When she explained that she was the wife of a diplomat and could not say everything she thought, he failed, imperiously, to see the force of the argument. It was, in fact, a rather mixed bag of adherents that he was then collecting around him at Carlton Gardens; not all of them were the kind of people with whom British officials were accustomed to deal, and few were known to them. At the French Embassy Corbin was urbane and hesitant, and Roland de Margerie – who knew England so well and on whom much reliance had been placed – returned with his chief. Corbin went into retirement and de Margerie to Shanghai. One by one the pillars of diplomacy were falling or holding up the house, according to the way one looked at it.

Vanier noticed that intelligent Englishmen differentiated sharply between the French Government and the French people. They blamed the Government and sympathized with the people. The Free French knew that the restoration of France depended on the victory of the British Commonwealth; felt that the destruction of the French Fleet at Oran was a justified tragedy, however terrible; and looked upon Canada as a land of spiritual and material promise, to which all Frenchmen, without distinction, were drawn by ties of blood and sentiment. Every Frenchman Vanier had met in London, outside the diplomatic enclave, had expressed the wish to go to Canada or enlist in the Canadian Forces. It would be a noble work for Canada to maintain, if possible, friendly relations with France while the United Kingdom and the present French Government were at odds, and to hasten the day when the French people would repudiate it.

There were two tendencies at work among the men of Vichy. Pétain, with Maurras[2] and the *Action Français* behind him, spoke for the advocates of the Latin *bloc* – a natural and soi-disant Catholic alliance with Spain and Italy, and an eye cast on Quebec; but there were others, more powerful, ruthless and realistic, who saw the future of France with Germany and were soon to be working for it. Pierre Laval, still lurking in the shadows, would be their principal agent, with Bergery and de Brinon[3] among his henchmen. In the tug of war between the collaborators and the *attentistes*, the collaborators had the whip hand because the hand behind them held the whip.

The most important recruit to the standard of the Free French

2. Charles Maurras, 1868-1952.   3. Fernand de Brinon, 1885-1947.

was Colonel Philippe de Hauteclocque, to be known afterwards – and to immortality – as General Leclerc. A cousin of Pauline Vanier, he had been taken prisoner at Lille and escaped; found his brother in the battle of Champagne; been taken prisoner again and escaped from a hospital at Avallon, escaped a third time from his sister's château, with the help of a Sudeten-German; and found his wife at a small château belonging to her near Bordeaux. 'You're leaving for England?' she said – and fortified by this encouragement he reached Paris and changed into civilian clothes; bicycled through occupied France; heard de Gaulle's appeal from the house of a peasant near Bordeaux; crossed the Spanish border with a forged passport; and made his way to England. He gave Georges an account of prevailing conditions in France and Georges, reporting this, suppressed his name since he was known to have joined de Gaulle and his future movements might be compromised. But although there was no doubt where Georges Vanier's own sympathies lay, he was obliged to remain in close touch with External Affairs and with what remained of the French Embassy. He was tied to policies which he could influence, but not dictate. On the 9th of July the Marquis de Castellane, Chargé d'Affaires, expressed the hope that Canada might find it possible to maintain some form of representation in France, since Canada – in his opinion – was best placed to act as an intermediary between the United Kingdom and the new French Government, and on the 18th the idea was formally proposed by the French Minister in Ottawa. No immediate decision was taken by the Canadian Government; it would depend on whether the seat of Government was in occupied or unoccupied territory. On the 23rd Georges Vanier wrote to Colonel Ralston offering his services in some military capacity if he were not sent back to France. He was still on the active list of the permanent forces and one of the few Canadian officers who had been to the Staff College at Camberley. He did not wish for an office appointment because 'a bit of movement and outdoor work would be good for me just now'; but he believed that 'my future, for what it is worth, lies in the diplomatic service', and that he could do something 'to better Franco-British relations, especially after Oran'.

On the 1st of August he was informed by Massey that Lord Halifax[4] – the British Foreign Secretary – would approve the resumption of diplomatic relations with France by Canada and South Africa, and that the British Government had under con-

4. The Earl of Halifax, 1881-1959.

sideration the appointment of an Agent without diplomatic status. Halifax did not think that Commonwealth solidarity need be affected by this discrepancy, but Georges Vanier, as we shall see, would beg to differ. The Marquis de Castellane had in mind that Paul Morand, who had returned to France with the rest of the Embassy staff on the 17th of July, should come back a fortnight later in some representative capacity. He could hardly – in the light of Morand's subsequent attitudes – have proposed a more un-welcome envoy. Morand had written a book on London, based on his experience of the drawing-rooms and literary circles he fre-quented, and this may have been the reason why he was con-sidered *persona grata*. He had described the city as a 'masterpiece'; it was shortly to become a masterpiece in a sense that he had not suspected.

By the 22nd of August the Canadian Government were prepared to consider sending Georges back to France if there were no likeli-hood of a further break in relations between Britain and France – badly strained already by the attack on the French Fleet – and if his presence there were likely to be useful in interpreting the French situation. But it would be difficult to maintain a Legation if the Government were moved to Paris, which was then rumoured as possible. Financial assistance was being organized for distressed Canadians in occupied France, where they would be regarded as enemy aliens and liable to internment. Four males of military age were already in prison at Fresnes. Canadian citizens in unoccupied territory would be treated like other foreigners, except that no exit visas would be issued to men between the ages of seventeen and twenty-eight. Their accounts were not blocked and money could be sent to them from Canada. M. Duchastel, a member of the Legation staff, returned to Paris to protect Canadian interests in so far as it was possible to do so, and it was suggested in the meanwhile that Georges Vanier should return home. The idea that he should resume his military duties was already in the air.

Georges was in no hurry to leave. General Leclerc had passed through London, and on the morning of his departure to raise the Cameroons for de Gaulle the Vaniers had accompanied him to Mass at Farm Street. It was a memorable parting, and the meeting had been memorable also. On the 29th of August Leclerc cabled: 'Amitiés les plus vives de Duala redevenu libre'. For Georges it was the first step on the road to Algiers, and on the 3rd of September it looked as though developments in French West Africa were of such importance that they might conceivably result in the setting up of a French Government there – in which case Canadian representation would presumably follow. Might it not, therefore, be wiser to delay his departure? The Canadian Government, however, did not foresee the likelihood of a régime sufficiently durable to warrant the transfer of an envoy to its headquarters; and since it would be inopportune to send Vanier either to Vichy or to Paris, they renewed their request that he should return as soon as possible.

On the afternoon of the 26th of August he had been summoned to the Foreign Office. Since the sirens had just sounded he was taken down to the air raid shelter from the reception room where he had been asked to wait. He insisted that Lord Halifax be informed of his arrival, and was shown up to the Foreign Secretary's room on the first floor, with the large french windows overlooking the Horse Guards Parade thrown open to prevent the shattering of glass, if bombs should fall in the vicinity. Massey was there with Halifax. Vanier presented his arguments against Canadian representation at Vichy if the United Kingdom were not represented also, quoting Paul Baudouin's 'Great Britain wants to starve us. France regards this dictatorship of famine as inhuman, unworthy of a Christian country, inept and ineffective. The blows of battle can be forgotten, but the memory of the children and women who suffer is graven in the hearts of a generation.' It would be lamentable, Georges argued, if any excuse were given for supposing that the Canadian Government shared these views, and Massey supported him. Halifax then admitted, very frankly: 'You have shaken me.' He added that his previous view, which he was now prepared to modify, had not been that of his permanent officials. They would, he was sure, be pleased to hear of the change in his attitude. Churchill, however, was anxious to keep a channel of communication open with Vichy, and Vanier did not demur at the suggestion that Pierre Dupuy should remain in London as Chargé d'Affaires, able to make such *sorties* into unoccupied France as were deemed advisable. But it was not a solution to his liking, and as time went on he liked it less and less.

Many people were critical of the Free French movement and organization. They pointed out the failure of de Gaulle to enlist the services of Generals returning from the Norwegian campaign, and they attributed the fiasco of the attempted landing at Dakar to clumsy diplomacy and to the lack of a fifth column ashore. They also criticized dictatorial methods of recruitment. No support had been given, or asked, from the French Military Mission in Britain at the time of the French collapse, and outstanding adherents to de Gaulle's movement were few. Georges Vanier would have recognized many of these arguments, but he had a faith in the forces of French resistance which went beyond appearances. His own position was anomalous and he would soon find it intolerable. He was still the titular Minister to France, but he ceased to have any connexion whatever with the Government to which he was accredited, and of whose policies he profoundly disapproved.

Working once again from Canada House, he was concerned that his staff should be indemnified for their loss of clothing and other necessaries – indeed he was very short of clothes himself – and that employment should be found for as many of them as possible. Some were taken on, for the time being, at Canada House. Mrs Archer and the children had sailed for Canada early in July, and the Vaniers had found a flat at 48 Grosvenor Square. It was from here that they saw the Battle of Britain and the beginnings of the Blitz – the arc of flame over London and St Paul's silhouetted against the sky. They came to have an admiration for the British people 'as deep as the waters over which they rule'.[5] There was Mrs Knipe who cleaned the church at Farm Street: 'I am going to have to speak to that Mr Hitler' she told Pauline 'every time I get it all clean, he comes and makes a mess of it. Never mind, I'll have the last word each time. I must go and polish the saints now, so that they'll be all smart when they come out of retreat.' A bomb had fallen a hundred yards or so from Egerton House School, and when the Headmaster hurried to the dormitory on the ground floor where the boys were sleeping, one of the smaller ones merely exclaimed, 'That *was* a ripping one.' Georges Vanier, who had always liked to go to the best tailors, had arranged a fitting for a new suit at Hawkes. When he got there, the fitter remarked: 'I don't think I ought to fit you today because there is a delayed action bomb near by which may explode at any moment and all my fitting rooms have glass doors and windows.' Four hours later the bomb exploded. On a similar errand to his bootmaker in the Burlington Arcade, Georges discovered that a large part of the Arcade had collapsed. Even Austin Reed – sartorially speaking, one or two drawers, as well as one or two streets, below Hawkes – where he was hoping to buy an overcoat, was inaccessible for the same reason. Georges was as

5. Speech to the Rotary and Associated Clubs, 27th May 1941.

unlucky with his clothes as Pauline had been with her jewellery. One morning, as they were leaving the house for an early Mass at Farm Street, they met the night policeman with a handful of jagged fragments of shell. 'Would you like some?' he said, 'I always have a supply for my customers.' They were the kind of souvenirs that Georges had once sent back from Flanders with 'Lipi' Archambault; only now Pauline was at his side. 'We work as one' he emphasized, and indeed she was working, as hard as he, for the Red Cross and visiting the wounded French soldiers evacuated from Dunkirk. 'I know you are not English' one of them said to her 'because you talk a great deal – just as we do.' It was a compliment that no one who knew Pauline Vanier would ever have contested.

One can say, with only a slight change of metaphor, that Britain was still playing bowls while Hitler was mustering his Armada. It would be an abuse of language to describe the Vaniers as devotees of cricket; nevertheless on the 27th of July they were both at Lords, where the Beaumont *versus* the Oratory match was being played as usual. Gracie Fields would soon be singing 'The Convoys *must* go through'; so must the cricket balls through the stumps. Georges wrote to Thérèse:

The sister (I think in some cases they were not sisters) of the Beaumont boys were very smart in their summery frocks (with heavy clouds above dripping from time to time) and hats perched at a dangerous angle. Two young ladies who discovered they had the same hat were in a state of desperation, but a solution was found by putting them in different stands and tea-rooms.

He added that it was essential the boys should brush their teeth, and instructed Thérèse to see to it. They were all staying with Frances at a summer camp in the Laurentians.

Georges and Pauline were preparing to leave for Canada on the 14th of September, although Georges was writing to Malise Graham that 'North Africa remains, I suppose, a possibility'. With his intuitive premonition of future events, his eyes were always fixed on those distant shores. He had been reading an article by Malise Graham which recalled 'many memories, most of which, unfortunately, are unpleasant, but I would not have been out of it for worlds.'[6] The Vaniers were due to leave for Glasgow. After spending the night in the basement shelter at 48 Grosvenor Street, they emerged for Mass at 6.50 a.m. and Georges then

6. 13th September 1940.

called to say Good-bye to the Masseys at Canada House. At 9.40,
as the sirens screamed their warning, he slipped round to the Sun
Life Insurance Building next door. Incendiary bombs were falling
in Cockspur Street and Northumberland Avenue, burning harm-
lessly before a stationary bus while a fireman on the top of a
ladder directed a stream of water on to a roof aflame. By the time
Georges arrived at Euston, the train for Glasgow had left and
Pauline, who was to join him at the station, had returned to
Grosvenor Street. One of the Legation staff, who had gone to see
them off, called later with the news that two bombs had fallen
twenty yards from where he was standing in the station, and
that there had been some casualties. After saying a Good-bye –
which was only to be an Au Revoir – to the Dutch Foreign Minister
and his wife, M. and Mme Van Kleffens, who had been sleeping
in the Vaniers' dining-room, Georges and Pauline travelled north
from King's Cross. Many people were dying in London on that
day, as on all the other days; but the noise of a real battle was
better than the silence of a false peace. That was the difference
between the capital Georges Vanier had left in June and the one
he was leaving in September.

2

On their return to Canada the Vaniers spent two weeks with the
Athlones[7] at Government House. Lady Byng was also staying
there for the week-end and one night Mackenzie King came to
dinner. Lady Byng had never forgiven the Prime Minister for his
part in the constitutional crisis which had overshadowed her
husband's last weeks in office, and she was not at all pleased to
see him. While the men were talking over their port, she sat in
the drawing-room grimly knitting and hoping they would continue their conversation for as long as possible. Just as they
returned, she dropped her ball of wool which rolled inconveniently under the piano. Mackenzie King, never wanting in
courtesy, was down on his knees in a flash, trying to retrieve it;
and Lady Byng was down beside him. Their heads, if not their
hearts, were together; and the other guests had a unique view of
those parts of their anatomy which they were not usually
anxious to display. After the wool had been recovered Lord
Athlone persuaded Lady Byng to dance a Highland fling, remarking : 'Evelyn, the best thing you ever did was to drop that wool.'

7. The Earl of Athlone and H. R. H. Princess Alice.

The only sad note in the hilarious scene was that Byng himself was not there to enjoy it.

An enemy in command of the whole coast-line of Europe from Norway to the Spanish frontier, and expected to invade Britain from one day to another, could no longer be regarded as remote from North American shores. A Joint Defence Board between Canada and the United States was therefore set up, and Vanier was appointed to sit on it – but not before he had answered an urgent appeal for blood donors. The first meeting in Montreal was held on the 20th of January, 1941, in the Windsor Hotel under the joint chairmanship of Colonel Oliver Mowat Biggar and Fiorella LaGuardia, Mayor of New York. Canada had an obvious interest in the defence of Alaska, and both Canada and the United States in that of Newfoundland. Until the development of air power Canada had relied for its defence against direct attack on the British Navy. Subject to certain qualifications, that was also true of the United States. It would be a good many months before the United States could regard its sea forces as adequate for the complete protection of its own coasts independently of the British Navy. If an enemy succeeded in establishing air bases on any part of the North American continent, no defending force could count on preventing his aircraft carrying death and destruction over a wide area. There had to be an understanding about the way the forces of each country were to be reinforced by those of the other. Troop movements must be co-ordinated; transport facilities taken into account; communication between the forces of each country arranged; and problems of supply worked out in detail. The setting up of the Board imposed no obligation on either country. Its function was to study the problems and report to the two Governments the steps that it thought should be taken.

A more active participation in military affairs was thought to be incompatible with Georges' diplomatic status. He still kept in touch, as far as possible, with what was happening in France. General Réquin wrote describing the battle on the Aisne to which the Fourth Army had been summoned from the south, and the 1,600 tanks before which he had retreated into Auvergne. The letter revealed what a patriotic and intelligent man thought of those Frenchmen who were trying to restore their country from overseas:

I have remained in contact with the United States, and particularly with my friend Bullitt, whom I saw again before he left . . . but I realize from the information that has reached me from over there what a hateful propaganda is being made by the Jews, the Freemasons, and the guilty politicians who have fled from the justice of their country. I know that you are inaccessible to these shameful goings on. You know France and the French too well to have any doubts of the true significance of Marshal Pétain's Government and his work of national recovery in the three fields of *morality* (public and private), *patriotism*, and *authority*. . . . You are not the person to believe that, after the crushing of her army, France could still stand on her feet? Where, and *with what*, in face of a decisive combination – armoured divisions and aerial bombardment – against which we had *nothing* to bring? For anyone who saw the condition of France and her armed forces in June the question does not even arise.

What follies have been committed since then! Otherwise the whole of France would be pro-English today, its feelings *undivided* – whereas now . . . you can imagine the drama.

Nevertheless we shall emerge from this ordeal, and we shall emerge *all the better* for it, on condition that we all remain united behind the Marshal. The army is setting an example in the work of national recovery which is taking place around it, and thanks to it – and it is prepared for any eventuality.[8]

These were the accents of Vichy and they came to Georges Vanier through the voice of a trusted friend. The same secure confidence in Pétain echoed in a letter from Père Gaume, now seriously ill in the south of France. 'The Marshal's energy is magnificent in the midst of terrible difficulties,' although he added: 'if Germany is victorious, France will simply cease to exist. It would mean death by asphyxiation.'[9] Henry de Kérillis, the only French deputy of the Right who had voted against the Munich Agreement, was in Montreal and Georges met him at a luncheon at the Mount Royal Club. De Kérillis had known Weygand for a long time and recounted a conversation with him at Tours. Weygand had prophesied that the British would be beaten within eight days. 'In that case' de Kérillis replied, 'why not give ourselves the luxury of perishing with them; but supposing they are not beaten?' Weygand smiled as he answered: 'People like you ought to be shot.' When de Kérillis maintained that the French should carry on with the war, Weygand snapped back: 'You are mad . . . with what?' – and de Kérillis had his answer ready: 'With the Fleet which is intact, with the Air Force, and with 400,000 men in North Africa.'

Nevertheless he was to write later to Georges Vanier, 'Even in

8. 7th October 1941.
9. 15th January 1941.

Canada my task was impossible. I shall never forget that you were among the very few, if not the only one, to listen to me with sympathy and comprehension.'[10] Réquin's arguments were plausible. The Vaniers heard them in Montreal and Quebec where friendly doors were closed to them when they pleaded the case for continued resistance. The divisions of which de Kérillis had spoken were only too manifest in the province of Quebec. A certain encouragement came from M. Francosky, the former Polish Ambassador in Paris. He exposed the illusion of 'unoccupied' France; in fact, the Germans were everywhere. Nobody was pro-German or pro-Nazi, and the BBC was widely listened to. Cordial relations with the enemy existed only to protect class or private interests – a rather large qualification. It would be several months before France could take any part in the war, but even now preparations were going forward.

A more direct source of information was Pierre Dupuy, Canadian Chargé d'Affaires, not only to the French but also to the Dutch and Belgian Governments. Dupuy still had the rank of First Secretary, but Georges was doing his best to have him appointed Counsellor since he was 'watching by the bedside of three countries seriously ill.' On the 12th of December the Press was informed that Dupuy had recently proceeded to Vichy for 'the primary purpose of looking into the situation of Canadians in France'. This information had not been given to Vanier and it moved him to energetic protest. He was not questioning the propriety of Dupuy's mission; he was deeply anxious for news of Canadians stranded in France, and made it his business to transmit news of them to their relatives at home. He was merely asserting his right to be informed.

On the 24th of October, 1940, Marshal Pétain met Hitler at Montoire and announced a policy of friendly collaboration with Germany. This was more than Georges Vanier could stomach; here was a contingency which, in the last analysis, he viewed in terms of the absolute. On the 17th of May, 1941, he addressed the following letter to Mackenzie King:

There can be no doubt now of Marshal Pétain's intention to collaborate with Hitler. I have felt always that the Marshal's hand would be forced whenever it suited our enemy's convenience. This time has arrived, it could not be long delayed because the Vichy Government, in addition to being powerless, was conceived in the sin of betrayal;

10. 23rd November 1941.

its every act, therefore, must needs be marked with the original stigma.

So long as H.M.'s Governments in Canada and the U.K. believed that some useful purpose could be served by maintaining relations with the Vichy Government, so long as that Government's collaboration with Germany was not too overt or shameless, I felt it my duty to retain the title of Canadian Minister to France. You will appreciate, I know, that to do so now would not be consistent with a sense of honour, of decency, or of patriotism.

I take this opportunity of expressing my opinion that the French people, for whom my affection and admiration remains intact, were misled in 1940 and are still misled by a weak and deluded Government, some members of which moreover are dishonourable. I have never believed that the French nation could approve of collaboration with Hitler, the anti-Christ.

In the above circumstances I trust that you will find it possible to relieve me of my title of Canadian Minister to France.

May I be permitted here to express, or rather to repeat, my deep gratitude for the confidence you showed me when you appointed me to the Legation in Paris. I pray that before long Free Frenchmen throughout the world will set up a Government which will conform to the glorious traditions of freedom which are part of France's natural heritage, and that you may then consider me not unworthy of being accredited to it: this is my fondest hope.

To this letter he appended an explanatory note:

I feel that I should send you an explanatory note to the enclosed letter in which I ask to be relieved of the title of Canadian Minister to France. I need hardly say that there is no desire on my part either to force your hand or to embarrass you in any way. I know that you are in constant touch with Mr Churchill and Mr Roosevelt and that such an important matter as the complete breaking off of diplomatic relations with the Government of Maréchal Pétain will call for joint consideration and possibly joint action. I quite realize therefore that it may not be possible for you to give immediate effect to my request. At the same time I know that you will appreciate my position and understand that, in conscience, I can delay no longer the expression of the wish to be relieved of my present title as soon as circumstances permit.

The sequel to this important *démarche* was curious indeed. Two years later Georges noted in a personal memorandum:

There has never been any written reply or reference excepting the Order in Council appointing me Minister to the Allied Governments in the U.K. in which it is stated that my resignation has been accepted without specifying the date of the resignation. Only one verbal comment was made on my resignation; this was by Mr Norman Robertson[11] who stated that my resignation at that particular time would be much less embarrassing to the Government than if it had been made some time before. I replied that I had no wish whatever to embarrass the Government, and drew attention to my explanatory note.

When Mr Church, the Conservative member for Toronto Broadview, asked the following questions in the Canadian House of Commons two weeks[12] after Georges had sent in his attempted resignation – Had Canada an envoy or Minister or Ambassador to the Vichy Government? If so, who was he, where was he, what functions did he perform, and would he be recalled? – the brief and bland reply was given that the Minister was Lieut-Colonel Vanier; that he was a member of the Joint Board of Defence; that the Canadian Legation was established in London, with Pierre Dupuy in charge of it; and that Colonel Vanier's recall was a matter of Government policy, depending on circumstances. Doubtless many eyebrows were raised, and Georges Vanier's were certainly among them.

Early in 1941 Jacques Maritain came up from New York to Montreal. He had just published his views on the French disaster in a short essay, A Travers le Désastre, which had given encouragement to the Free French, although, writing as a philosopher, he had been careful to safeguard his independent judgment. The Gaullist headquarters were anxious to make use of this for propaganda purposes, but Maritain – whom Georges had met in New York – was concerned not to compromise his chances of influencing those who were still under the spell of Vichy. He therefore wrote to Georges that he considered more harm than good might be done by quoting from the book at the present time:

If this book has any force, it is because it has been written with the sole intention of getting at the truth. It seems to me very important to avoid anything that might alter its meaning in the eyes of French opinion, and to make people regard it as an incitement to polemic even before they have read it. That is why I hope that the B.B.C. will not speak about it in their broadcasts to France, at least for the moment, for many people might classify it as 'British propaganda' – which would create the most unfortunate misunderstandings. On the other hand, if it arrives in France through the spontaneous initia-

11. He succeeded Dr Skelton as Under-Secretary for External Affairs early in 1941.
12. 2nd June 1941.

tive of some reader, it may have a chance of enlightening men of good faith and of very diverse opinions. So I should be particularly grateful if you would convey to the authorities of the B.B.C. the wish that I am expressing here.[13]

Georges cabled to Lester Pearson in London and wrote later:

He has been extremely fair in his judgment of men and events; it would not be just to him to broadcast, for instance, that Pétain's decision morally was a wrong one (which in effect he says) without adding his comments on the Marshal's action and character. You will appreciate, therefore, that extracts from the book, unless chosen with very great care, would not give a correct picture. As I sympathize with Maritain's view, I took the liberty of cabling to you.

Maritain had referred to 'a friendship that God sometimes brings to birth at a single stroke' and Georges, in giving him the assurances he asked for, added that 'for me too . . . our meeting was a joy. Indeed I felt the sudden birth of a friendship that I was not prepared for. The sympathy of a man like yourself means a great deal to me.[14]

Eventually, however, miniature editions of *A Travers le Désastre* were dropped into France by Allied aircraft.

3

On the 25th of July 1941 Norman Robertson telegraphed that Mackenzie King would like to see Georges in Ottawa. The result of this interview was his appointment to command the military district of Quebec and his promotion to the rank of Brigadier-General. Both were to date from the 15th of August. The Vaniers had taken a cottage at Cartierville for the summer. Pauline was expecting another baby, and her fourth son was christened Michel Paul in St James' Basilica on the 13th of August. Thérèse – now taking a secretarial course – and Byngsie were the godparents. The other two boys had been continuing their education at Loyola. In the last week of August Georges was invited by Mackenzie King to fly with him to London. Norman Robertson – who had never flown before – and Jack Pickersgill,[15] Private Secretary to the Prime Minister, were also of the party. Georges Vanier's presence was attributed in some quarters to the seizure of St Pierre and Miquelon by the Free French and to the possibility of breaking off relations with the Vichy Government.

13. 18th February 1941.   14. 8th April 1941.
15. The Hon. John W. Pickersgill.

Melodramatic precautions attended their departure. They moved to the take-off point in small groups so as not to excite curiosity, the Prime Minister going aboard his private railway car at a secluded spot in the shunting yard at Ottawa several hours before it was attached to the train. At the airport it was parked on a siding, and he remained aboard until a few minutes before the plane was due to leave. All the passengers had been fitted with flying suits, and Mr King was observed to put cottonwool in his ears. Georges had brought with him a leather case containing what might have been a rather large musical instrument, but he explained that it was his 'spare leg'. Since he was unable to curl up in the bomb-rests of the aeroplane, he travelled in relative comfort with the Prime Minister. They talked during the flight, King drawing consolation from the fact that they 'had ideas in common about things celestial'. Mr King was very keen on things celestial, and claimed to have a more direct acquaintance with them than Georges Vanier. He was not an intellectual, he said, and did not consider Georges an intellectual either. But he thought the intellect should be the servant of the spirit, like the eyes and the ears and the other senses. Georges would not have disagreed with him.

Pipers greeted their arrival in Glasgow, and in London King had an interview with Churchill who told him that Dupuy was the only British contact with Vichy, and that the information he brought back was extremely useful, even if it erred on the side of optimism. Georges accompanied King to Aldershot, where he was to address the Canadian troops, As he rose to speak there was some booing, apparently organized, from somewhere to the right of the Royal Box where the Canadian party were seated. There was cheering also, but the booing and catcalls were unmistakeable. King referred to the applause as confirmation of what he was saying, and Georges hoped that he had not noticed the hostile manifestation; but on the way back King remarked that 'there were a lot of Tories there'. It was significant, however, that the Prime Minister was wildly applauded when he sympathized with the troops' desire to get into action: Captain Margesson, the Minister for War, asked him about conscription in Canada, indicating that he thought this might be desirable; but Churchill did not think it would be necessary. Neither did General Macnaughton. Like everyone else, Churchill was impatient for the United States to declare war on Germany, and at a meeting of the War Cabinet which King attended there was uncertainty about winning the war unless they did so. Georges, who accompanied his Prime Minister to Downing Street, described as rather 'pitiful' the discussion about ways and means of bringing them in,[16] although he had not, of course, been present at the meeting. Churchill – in the way of British Prime Ministers when they want to be polite – had come out on to the steps to greet the Canadian visitors: 'The first impression I received was most favourable. Mr Churchill has almost a school-boy colour, fresh . . . it might even be described as rosy. His step was light and he appeared to have a reserve of vitality'. The Press Secretary gave Georges – as always avid for souvenirs – two pieces of shrapnel which had fallen on Number Ten, one for himself and one for Michel. Having left Mackenzie King at Downing Steet, he immediately drove to Lock's in St James's Street and bought himself a black Trilby. It was an oversight to have come to London with two artificial legs, but no hat in which he could decently present himself at Buckingham Palace. He had been forced to borrow one from Major Simson, a valued member of his staff at the Paris Legation.

On the 15th of September the Royal 22nd celebrated the 25th anniversary of Courcelette in the stadium at Montreal, with a military and theatrical display, an open-air Mass, and a parade and march past. A symbolic play, *La Guerre des Croix*, was staged in a theatre specially constructed at one end of the auditorium. Other French-Canadian regiments – many of which had sent reinforcements to the 'Van Doos' – were represented. The Régiment de Joliette, the Régiment de Châteauguay, the Régiment de Trois Rivières, the Régiment de Maisonneuve – the very names were a call to arms; and a photograph shows Georges Vanier – strangely enough the only officer in mufti – standing with his former comrades – DesRosiers, Gaudet and the others – behind Tremblay who was taking the salute, as the 4,000 troops went by. No more spectacular answer could have been devised to those who believed that the crushing of Nazi Germany and the succouring of France was no business of those who claimed the fleur-de-lys for an emblem.

The Vaniers moved to Quebec in September, occupying the District Commander's official residence in the rue St Louis. Thérèse and the boys remained behind in Montreal with Mrs Archer. Georges was elected President of the Garrison Club and of the 'Amicale' of the Royal 22nd. Memories of active service crowded round him. Of those whom he had led to the German hut across No-Man's-Land Sergeant Leclerc was now a Brigadier

16. Diary.

like himself, and Corporal Rancourt was now a Sergeant-Major. The other two members of the party, Watts and Levine, had lost their lives later in the campaign. Now, once again, there were the ceremonial calls on the Cardinal and the Prime Minister; and now there was the walk to daily Mass in the chapel of the Missionnaires du Sacré Coeur, thickly hung with its votive tablets, in the rue Sainte Ursule. It was here that he met the Flemish philosopher and theologian Charles de Koninck, then teaching at Laval University, who dedicated his *Scandale de la Médiation* to Georges Vanier.

Already, however, the Quebec appointment was having a more provisional look than it subsequently acquired. Nothing could have been less provisional than Willis O'Connor at Government House, and he reported the Governor General as saying: 'I don't think Georges Vanier will be very long in Quebec.' There was, in fact, talk of bringing him into the Cabinet to replace Ernest Lapointe,[17] who seemed 'to be losing a bit of ground in the Province of Quebec.'[18] He had been tepidly received by the Canadian Clubs, and he was in poor health. It was hinted that a seat might be found for Georges in the St Mary's Riding at Montreal, and that he might succeed Pierre Cardin,[19] who was also too unwell to take an active part in the work of his Department. The Government were short of French-Canadian Ministers, and the Prime Minister – who held Georges in high esteem and had a warm personal affection for him – was unwilling to move Godbout from the Premiership of Quebec, even if Godbout had agreed to go. Harry Crerar, on taking over command of the 2nd Canadian Division, was writing:

I have something more than suspicion that you, also, will be required for another form of national service before very long. From the point of view of the Army and Quebec, I sincerely hope my suspicions are unfounded, but in respect to the nation as a whole you may be more needed for responsibilities in a wider sphere.[20]

In the event, better – or at any rate second – thoughts prevailed, and the 'wider sphere' of Georges Vanier's responsibilities would lie elsewhere.

The immediate problem was recruiting. Out of 229,700 men

17. The Right Hon. Ernest Lapointe, Minister of Justice and Attorney-General. He died in office 26th November 1941.
18. 16th October 1941.
19. The Hon. Pierre (Joseph Arthur) Cardin, Minister of Public Works 1935-1942.
20. 23rd November 1941.

serving with the Canadian Forces at the beginning of 1941, 50,000 came from the Province of Quebec, and this was considered an inadequate proportion. The question of recruitment was linked with the other political and military problems with which Vanier had already been dealing, both as a member of the Joint Board, and as titular Minister to France. If Canadians did not believe that the war should be prosecuted with the utmost vigour, they would not enlist. Vanier maintained that the re-education of the people must precede any effective attempt to recruit them in the numbers now thought to be necessary. A national crusade must be launched – especially in the Province of Quebec – and here the Federal and Provincial Governments, with the leaders of the Church, industry and education must all co-operate. Industry, in particular, must encourage, not merely accept. An intensive publicity, to which both Georges and Pauline contributed by their speeches, must accompany these efforts. People must understand what the war was really about before they could fight it with enthusiasm. They had not seen the Battle of Britain or the fall of France; the Vaniers had seen both.

What were the reasons for apathy? Many speakers had said: 'We don't need men', and Winston Churchill – though he was not talking to Canadians – had said 'Give us the tools and we will finish the job'. An appeal had gone out for 100,000 men to work in the War Industries, accompanied by such slogans as 'Do your duty', 'Buy Bonds', and 'Get into the front line'. The wages were high – $5 to $7 a day – and for many men this was the first remunerative employment for several years. Why should they sacrifice it for $1.50 to $3 a day when they had wives and families dependent on them? Those who had left their peace-time jobs in the last war had suffered for it, as many veterans of the Canadian Legion could bear witness. The nature of the war, as it was then being fought, did not encourage quick promotion; decorations were few; stimulus was lacking. The young, indoctrinated with pacifism over many years, were inclined to say: 'Why me and not him? I'll go if he goes.' Sacrifice, they claimed, should be equal. The result of high wages was materialism; there were a number of Fifth Columnists at work; the ground for a recruiting campaign had been inadequately prepared; and some were afraid to precipitate a political crisis. In Quebec little account had been taken of the French mentality. And there was much confusion over the situation in France, fostered by the lower clergy. Marshal Pétain's 'Travail' and 'Famille' were slogans calculated to appeal to a population which had never lacked respect for either – and when the French-Canadians spoke of 'patrie' they attached their own meaning to the word. Their ancestral *pietas* did not extend to the France of the Revolution or the Third Republic. They had not even, at this time, begun to talk about the Republic of Quebec.

Moreover the belief was growing that compulsory military service was on the way; so why leave a well-paid job before one had to? Georges Vanier shared this belief, and he thought that the people would accept it. But he also feared its consequences in Quebec. In a long interview with Godbout, both men were agreed that conscription enforced against the will of the local population would be harmful to relations between French Canada and the rest of the country – and also with the United States – both during the war and after it. Godbout was equally opposed to a referendum, because the result of this in French-speaking Canada would only underline the difference in sentiment between Quebec and the other Provinces. Post-war relations with the United States, and within the Commonwealth itself, would inevitably be closer, and Canada must be able to play its part in this ensemble of government. Godbout shared Georges Vanier's opinion that the fight over conscription was a fight over a word, and that many English-speaking Canadians would like nothing better than an adverse vote in Quebec because that would place them in a superior position vis-à-vis the province which they held to be theirs, in any case, by right of conquest. Whenever Georges Vanier walked into Canada House, he saw a statue of Wolfe in the entrance hall; it was not until after the second World War that a statue of Montcalm stood facing it. In the meanwhile, however, he congratulated Godbout on his declaration of the 30th of December 1941. This was 'the first time that a French-Canadian politician had had the courage to say that he was prepared to accept conscription if it was necessary. I permitted myself the observation that he was the man we needed as Prime Minister, and that he ought to stay.'[21]

The situation would be helped by larger French-speaking representation in the Canadian Forces, and Georges submitted the following proposals to the Ministry of National Defence. Training manuals and memoranda should be published in both languages. A bilingual school for N.C.Os should be established at Megantic, and bilingual instruction be given at Advanced Armoured

21. Personal Notes.

Corps Training centres. The Voltigeurs de Québec and the Régiment de Hull should be mobilised. A French-speaking field
artillery regiment should be formed, and a proportion of coastal
defence artillery personnel should be gradually replaced by men
of French extraction. Bilingual French-Canadian officers should
be appointed to English-speaking units where there was thirty to
fifty per cent of French-Canadian man power; the officers commanding such units should be encouraged to make the French-
Canadians under their orders feel at home; and Roman Catholic
chaplains be allotted to them. Men from rural areas wishing to
enlist should be provided with subsistence and pay from the time
they applied, and be given their travelling expenses to and from
the recruiting centres. French-Canadians should be represented,
proportionately, in the Army Trades Schools, and the number of
French Canadian candidates at Brockville Officers Training Centre
be gradually increased to thirty per cent. An equitable proportion
of qualified French-Canadian officers should be appointed to the
H.Q. of Military Districts 4 and 5, and elsewhere, as appropriate.
Similar action should be taken in respect of the Canadian Corps
in England. District Selection Boards at Military Districts 4, 5
and 7 should prepare lists of French-Canadian officers suitable for
staff or command appointments; and a French-Canadian journalist
should be attached to the French section of the Directorate of
Public Relations in order to prepare material specially suited to
the French language press.

These proposals showed Georges Vanier properly concerned
for the rights of his French-speaking compatriots; no one, in fact,
was more conscious of the traditions to which they consistently
appealed. He had not yet come across Chesterton's definition of
tradition as 'the democracy of the dead', but it was from the dead
that he sought his inspiration when he pleaded with the living to
sacrifice everything they had to succour the democracy of today.
He never spoke with a more passionate eloquence than at the
Dollard des Ormeaux ceremony in Montreal on the 24th of May,
1941. Recalling how Dollard and his sixteen companions had been
martyred by the Iroquois at Long Sault in 1660, he saw in their
death a special favour of Providence – for death and honour
were twins. Dollard stood at the head of a 'line of heroes that
marks out our history from the coming of the first colonists to the
present day.' He was in a direct descent from the military and
mystical tradition of mediaeval France – a tradition which Georges
Vanier had seen illustrated in his own time. He recalled Jean

Brillant, mortally wounded in the front line of the attack :

For two days he fought like a lion, and then – when he had been wounded three times – he fell. I can still see my friend on his improvised stretcher, the colour of his cheeks already livid, but he was smiling and the expression in his eyes was serene.

He recalled Corporal Keable, the other V.C. of the 'Van Doos' :

During an intensive bombardment Corporal Keable stayed at the parapet of the trench, the Lewis gun at his shoulder, awaiting the enemy. As soon as the barrage lifted from our front line, 50 Germans advanced towards his post. Corporal Keable jumped on to the parapet and with the Lewis gun at his hip fired on the advancing enemy. Wounded several times by fragments of shell and hand grenades, he still went on firing and stopped the enemy. At last, mortally wounded, he fell back into the trench. There, lying on his back, he fired his last cartridge on the enemy in retreat. Before losing consciousness he called out to the wounded lying all around him : 'Stand firm, boys; stop them – don't let them pass.'

He recalled Private Deblois;

rough in appearance but sensitive as a child. Wherever he saw a wounded comrade, his heart went out to him, and he rushed to his assistance. When I congratulated him one day, he replied simply : 'Major, one can't let them die alone.' . . . As I think of those we left behind on the soil of France, the words of Lacordaire come into my mind : 'Lord, will you not look with a special favour on the brave who come to you with the colours for a shroud?'

He recalled Olivier Asselin who had marched to battle for the sake of British institutions because he believed they were worth fighting for; he recalled the victims of Nazi tyranny, whose sufferings cried to Heaven for vengeance: and applied to them the words of the rough soldier whom he had just quoted: 'one can't let them die alone.'

Vanier was speaking to a similar tune all through the province of Quebec, from Rimouski in the east to Chicoutimi in the north; and it was an appeal for total war. He was unwilling to suppose his listeners below the level of his own altruism. Yet he would sometimes point them to a map, indicate the neighbouring land mass of Greenland, and bid them remember the Bismarck. 'Let us have an end of this talk of defending Great Britain *only*. You will be defending *your* land, *your* homes, *your* women and children.' He reminded them of what American Intelligence had discovered

of Hitler's intentions towards all religions except his own pre-
posterous Nordic cults. 'Who can doubt that a German victory,
if such a thing were conceivable, would result in the most ghastly
and bloody persecution of Christ's Church?' He read between the
lines of Papal pronouncements, and quoted the Cardinal Archbishop of Quebec, until a whispering campaign began talking about
'General Villeneuve' and 'Cardinal Vanier'. He would quote
Browning on prayer, and Macaulay on courage:

> To every man upon this earth
> Death cometh soon or late.
> And how can man die better
> Than facing fearful odds
> For the ashes of his fathers
> And the temples of his Gods.

The odds were still fearful on land and sea; and they were not
negligible in the Province of Quebec.

Pauline was speaking just as indefatigably for the War Savings
Campaign, with a motorised column travelling across the Province
under its auspices; and Elisabeth de Miribel – her closest sister-in-
arms – had arrived in Canada, flaunting the banner of Jeanne d'Arc.
As the representative of de Gaulle she was very kindly received by
Norman Robertson in Ottawa, with Gladys Arnold to plead the
Gaullist cause in English, and in Montreal she had her ear very
close to the ground – although here, and elsewhere in the Province
of Quebec, many people resented her presence and refuted her
arguments. It was all very well for Georges Vanier to preach a
crusade, but the Pope had not preached it. If Pius XII had condemned the Nazis as formally as he had condemned the Communists, French-Canadian opinion would have rallied to the war.
After all, Zouaves had been recruited in Quebec to defend another
Pius in 1870, and their names could be read on tablets in St
James's Basilica. As it was, the St Jean Baptiste Society had sent
to the Prime Minister of Quebec, and published in the Press, a
resolution demanding a slowing down of the war effort. Financial
control in the Province of Quebec was overwhelmingly in the
hands of the English-speaking Canadians, and there was a corresponding reaction against the Banks and Big Business. An anti-
quated educational system had not prepared the French-Canadians
for the technical posts to which their numbers and native intelligence entitled them. The university curricula were quite different
on either side of the language boundary, with an almost total

absence of academic contacts. The French-Canadians resented the slowness of promotion in the army, and they had no organization in the Auxiliary Services – such as the Y.M.C.A., the Salvation Army, the Canadian Legion, or the Knights of St Columbus – that they could properly call their own. All this did not, of course, excuse the scurrilous campaign against conscription with its slogans borrowed from Father Coughlin, and its anti-Semitic jibes. 'The accursed Jews of the Free French would have done better to fight in France during the spring of 1940 than escape to London and New York even before the battle was joined' – was a fair specimen of the latter. The influence of Charles Maurras, the mystique of the Latin *bloc*, the Papal Encyclicals in favour of the Corporate State, economic autarchy, and racial intolerance were all militating against the Christian democracy, which was Georges Vanier's political creed and which he had learnt – as Elisabeth de Miribel had learnt it – from Jacques Maritain. Georges had lately been reading Maritain's *Christianisme et Démocratie*. He always marked his books, and in this case the following passage was underlined:

The real essence of democracy is to preserve a faith in the advancement of mankind.

To believe in the dignity of the human person and of humanity in general.

To sustain and vivify the sense of equality without falling into a levelling egalitarianism.

To respect authority, with the knowledge that the men who wield it are only human like those they govern.

To believe in the sanctity of law.

Democracy is a paradox and a challenge to nature; to a wounded and ungrateful human nature, whose original aspiration and reserves of greatness it calls forth at the same time.

There was nothing revolutionary in all this, but it was too revolutionary for the *grands* or the *petits séminaires*.

Georges Vanier was hampered as well as helped by his prestige, his experience, his superior education, and his official status. He belonged to an older type of French-Canadian in whom there was no conflict of loyalties. He was too diplomatic to quote Mademoiselle de Lanaudière – 'our hearts belong to France, but our arms belong to England' but he might well have quoted Sir Etienne Paschal Taché, who had fought in the war of 1812:

Our habits, our laws, our religion have made us monarchists and conservatives. 'You are rebels' say the ultras 'we alone possess loyalty to the highest degree'. A thousand pardons, gentlemen, treat us as children of the same mother and not as illegitimate, treat us with more justice in your deeds as well as in your words, and I give you my word that if ever this country ceases to be British, the last cannon-shot to maintain British power on American soil will have been fired by a French-Canadian.

Georges regretted the necessity for a plebiscite to ascertain the views of the country on conscription, and he was not entirely dissatisfied with the campaign for voluntary enlistment. But since a plebiscite had been decided upon, both he and Pauline argued vehemently that an affirmative answer from Quebec was essential for the national – and international – good name of the Province. In the event Quebec voted 993,663 to 376,188 against, and the rest of the country 2,318,208 to 588,453 in favour. The discrepancy was alarming and justified Georges Vanier's worst fears.

It is interesting – and a little ironical – to note that only when he launched his campaign against blasphemy did Vanier have the undivided support of nationalist Quebec. He invited those who were inclined to use the name of their Saviour or the Blessed Virgin to express their anger or irritation to substitute the names of their father or their mother. They would not find it easy to do so. After four years on the western front he knew what he was talking about:

I shall always remember a certain evening during the battle. Painfully we were advancing in Indian file towards the front line. It was dark and the shells were exploding. Suddenly in the night, I heard a voice blaspheming. These blasphemies, at a moment when we were so near to death, frightened me because blasphemy calls down the wrath of God. I managed to reach the man who was blaspheming and I asked him: 'What has Christ done to you, my friend, that you should insult him like this?' He trembled like a child and very nearly burst into tears. He had blasphemed without thinking, almost without knowing, what he was doing. Without thinking? Without knowing? In fact, most of those who blaspheme try to excuse themselves by saying that they weren't thinking. As if one could forget![22]

This was bold advice to the soldiery, but it was meat and drink to a *bienpensant* publishing house in Montreal. Addressing the Brigadier as 'Cher *Monsieur* Vanier', they asked leave to reproduce his address as a tract for the times alongside of Pius XII on

22. Address at Valcartier Camp, 3rd March 1942.

feminine fashions, and other less eminent authors on Social Credit, the Corporate State, and the Conversion of Russia – anything except Christian Democracy. M. Lucien Dubois, a deputy from Quebec, felt 'the irresistible need to weep with joy at the thought that Quebec, like France, has her Fochs and her de Castelnaus.'[23] More encouraging, perhaps, to the Brigadier was the collective letter of the Canadian episcopate which supported his efforts against 'the irresponsible fanatics in the Province who speak with contempt of the British and British achievements.' They were 'rendering a dreadful disservice to their compatriots'; and there was 'no surer way of drawing down upon the head of Quebec the hatred and violence of the other eight Provinces. Such men will bear a terrible responsibility if they succeed in loosing this flood which might engulf us in Quebec.'[24]

He was further encouraged by a tour of inspection in the Gaspé peninsula (12th-18th November, 1942) where there were 'stout and patriotic hearts', and where several families had three, four, and even five sons serving with the colours. He complained to Ottawa that there was no need to censor their letters, and he pleaded urgently for better defence communications. On the north bank of the St Lawrence the road between Portneuf and Baie Comeau was not completed; and between Baie Comeau and Labrador there was no road at all. Why must coastal defence be limited to Halifax and Newfoundland? Why was there no naval base at Rimouski? Moreover the condition of the roads in winter, where communications between one village and another was often impossible, threatened both the convenience and the health of the population. Telegrams were often held up by bad weather, and the villages of Grande Vallée had had no mail for a week. A doctor had said to Georges: 'Brigadier, if you were suddenly taken ill with acute appendicitis in winter, you could only die.' The Brigadier lost no time in bringing these facts to the notice of the Prime Minister of Quebec.

The Canadian losses in the raid on Dieppe, earlier in the year, were a terrible foretaste of what might happen if a second front were opened in Europe before the time was ripe. If the purpose of the raid was to learn from experience, the lesson had been a costly one in human lives and it might have unfortunate political results. To the Adjutant-General in Ottawa who had asked Vanier

23. 17th March 1942.
24. May 1942.

to submit a list of appropriate awards from the Military District of Quebec, he replied as follows:

On the assumption that every officer, N.C.O., and soldier who fought at Dieppe will not receive an individual honour or award, I wonder what their feelings will be, as well as those of their comrades on active service in the U.K. or elsewhere, if army personnel who have never been out of Canada receive honours and awards.

Dieppe had been a superb demonstration of courage, and it was courage – among other qualities – that the Vaniers recognized in a young French-Canadian airman, Jacques Chevrier. He had taken part in the Battle of Britain, and his brief story can best be told in the words of those who befriended him. Georges recalled their first meeting in Ottawa, where Chevrier was serving as A.D.C. to Lord Athlone:

I was immediately attracted by this young man with the clear, deep eyes reflecting the vision of one who had seen death at close quarters. There was something grave and pure in his expression which revealed a strong, interior life.

Jacques showed a lively interest in what was going on among his compatriots in our province, and was anxious about them. So I invited him to spend a few days with us in Quebec. When he arrived at the end of March he said that he would like to get to know the students at the University. I arranged an invitation for some of them, and they spent the evening together, talking till one o'clock in the morning. Jacques summed up his impressions in a letter, inspired by deep religious feeling, which he wrote on April 11th from Dartmouth, New England.

Chevrier reported that the students were dissatisfied by the contradiction between the established facts and what the politicians were saying. At one moment they were urged to 'defend our shores'; at the next they were told that another Canadian contingent had landed in Britain. Why did not Ottawa say clearly: 'We are defending our shores and we are sending our children overseas to prevent the enemy from reaching them'? Georges Vanier went on to complete the portrait:

My wife and I grew to be so fond of him, and to trust him so implicitly, that we asked him to stay with us whenever he liked. Very soon we learnt to love Jacques almost as if he were our own son.

In the service of his country and his God he was the perfect example of a Christian hero, modest, upright, and brave.

In July 1942 Pauline was on a tour of the Gaspé and happened to be passing the R.C.A.F. station at Mont Joli. She asked to see Jacques Chevrier, but was told that he was away; and it was only towards seven o'clock in the evening that he was able to spend an hour with her at the hotel:

I found him very depressed and sad, and asked him why. He told me that he wanted to get back to England at any cost and join once again in the battle. It was only there that he saw an opportunity for greatness. We parted with an arrangement to meet the next morning at 8.30, after Mass. In saying good-night, he added: 'I wish that you could come to our Mass at the Station; its simplicity is very beautiful.' The next morning I waited for him at the hour we had fixed, and was anxious when he did not come. I had to be on my way to Matane at 10 o'clock and I had a presentiment that something had happened to our young friend. I learned on arrival at the hotel in Matane that an aeroplane had fallen into the sea a few miles from Cap Chat. I was sure that Jacques was in that aeroplane. Some minutes later a young pilot came into the hotel dining-room. I noticed how tired and sad he looked. They told me that he was young Cannon; Jacques had been talking about him the night before and telling me that he was second-in-command of the squadron. I went up to him and asked him point-blank: 'What has happened to Jacques Chevrier?' 'Madame' he replied 'he is dead.'

Georges Vanier composed his epitaph in words that have the beauty of a Greek *stele* and might have been written about some hero of antiquity lost in the waters of the Aegean:

He was proud to wear over his heart the wings that he had carried in the Battle of Britain – the wings that one summer night were folded over the waters of the St Lawrence.

They were broken then, but God stooped down to pick them up.[25]

25. Personal Notes.

CHAPTER 13

ALLIES IN EXILE

I

DURING the spring of 1942 the following poem, written from Montpelier in the occupied zone, had found its way into one of those drawers where Georges Vanier kept everything likely to interest him:

> Et dans l'aube qui danse
> Au val des quatre vents
> La rose d'espérance
> Effeuille le printemps.[1]

and even before the spring had come with its faint promise of liberation Leclerc was writing to Pauline:

I have under me a galaxy of young Frenchmen, first class material, and good examples of the Free French. Tomorrow I am undertaking a new expedition similar to those I have made already. Humanly speaking, it is almost madness, but my trust in Providence is so unshakable that I have no doubt of success. And so it's forward now over the kilometres of sand and rock until we meet the enemy.

Leclerc had taken Libreville from the Vichy commander in November 1941, and just a year later the Americans landed in North Africa to meet the same enemy. When the news came through, Georges was asked to broadcast a message to the French. It had to be composed in the early hours of a bitterly cold morning, and the only warm place in the house was the bathroom where Pauline sat typing on the lavatory seat. At the same time Montgomery had defeated Rommel at Alamein, and Churchill had said of Alamein 'This is not the end or even the beginning of the end; it is perhaps the end of the beginning.'

Georges Vanier hoped that for him, too, it would be the end of the beginning; and although he had once told Robertson Fleet that he had never 'sought for any job – that each in turn just came along', he was very anxious to recover the job that the Germans

1. And in the dawn which dances in the valley of the four winds, the rose of hope tears off the petals from the spring.

had taken from him, except in a purely titular sense. So long as it was purely titular, it had no interest for him; but now titles and what they signified were much in question. Scarcely had the Americans disembarked in Morocco than he was writing to Norman Robertson: 'I hope it is not necessary to remind you that the former Minister to France hopes and prays that he will be allowed to continue the work begun in 1939.'[2] The Canadian Government were in two minds whether formally to break off diplomatic relations with Vichy or merely to withdraw recognition from it. The second course was decided upon, since German pressure was now so great that Vichy was held to have no independent existence. On the 5th of November an Order in Council announced the acceptance of Vanier's resignation as Minister to France – at which he must again have raised his eyebrows – and he was almost immediately afterwards appointed Minister to the Allied Governments in London, with powers 'to consult with the French National Committee on all matters of mutual interest relating to the conduct of the war.' The second part of his mission was what really mattered to him, although it was not immediately made public. The Prime Minister announced it on the 30th of November.

The specific briefing was as follows. Georges Vanier would have no official status vis-à-vis the British Government: here he was to work through Massey, using the facilities available at Canada House, and reporting direct to External Affairs, and having direct access to the Foreign Ministers of the Governments to which he was accredited. He was a little concerned about his salary and allowances, since his Quebec appointment had involved a drop of $1500 a year, and with two boys at school in Montreal, and an infant in arms, he would be obliged to maintain a separate establishment in Canada. On the 3rd of December a reply to a telegram from de Gaulle indicated the thought uppermost in his mind:

From the moment I left France in June 1940 your voice has always represented for me the voice of the French people. Combatant of the first hour and the last, you incarnate the spirit of resistance sprung from the moral forces of France which have been built up over a thousand years, and are its finest heritage.

As always, Georges had his eyes fixed far beyond the accommodation of diplomacy, patiently as he would have to wrestle with

2. 11th November 1942.

them; and those who knew him best would have echoed the congratulations of Robertson Fleet:

Will you forgive an old admirer if he says that it is something quite other in you which he loves the most – the Poet? And maybe too it is that which has really counted the most all the way through.[3]

He had asked leave to postpone his departure until he had completed a tour of inspection in the district of Quebec, and it was further delayed by illness. At the beginning of February he was promoted to the rank of Major-General; and before he left Mackenzie King gave a dinner for him and Pauline, at which he spoke with characteristic eloquence to the Allied envoys accredited to Ottawa. He was to fly from New York at the end of March, and this gave him the opportunity of a rather disquieting conversation with Jacques Maritain, who was worried about the chauvinistic tendencies now manifesting themselves in General de Gaulle and in certain members of his entourage. Maritain thought that these might have dangerous consequences for a nation humiliated as France had been; and that de Gaulle had taken too much to heart the criticism of Vichy that he was under British influence. It was a mistake, in Maritain's opinion, to wish to establish a provisional French Government and to seek recognition for it. De Gaulle should confine himself to military action. Maritain expressed some sympathy with the point of view of Sumner Welles, which was also that of Roosevelt, that the United States should protect the interests of the French people until they were liberated and could decide their future for themselves. Maritain had declined the offer of de Gaulle to join the French National Committee and he found the General's attitude of 'are you for me, or against me?' too dictatorial. Maritain's views, did not alter Georges Vanier's belief, strengthened with every passing day, that de Gaulle represented the best hope of moral and political recovery in France. He listened to Maritain with the attention that so wise a counsellor and so good a friend deserved, but he had also listened to Elisabeth de Miribel. And if one doubted the reincarnation of Jeanne d'Arc in the intransigent leader of the Fighting French, to question it in the case of Elisabeth de Miribel was pushing scepticism a little too far in opposition to one's natural and reasoned sympathies.

Georges left by clipper on the 4th of April, and on arrival in London took an apartment in Arlington House, just off St James's

3. 24th November 1942.

Street. Premises for his Legation were found on the third floor of a steel and concrete building at 14 Berkeley Street, only a few minutes' walk away. These could be occupied for as long or short a time as was thought desirable. There was a large room which could be divided into two offices, and with £700 spent on improvements and A.R.P. equipment the place would be adequate for diplomatic needs. A staff of only two, however, was quite insufficient. A Counsellor or senior First Secretary, a Second or Third Secretary, and a Military Attaché were all required. Good material for Attachés was available among Reserve units in the United Kingdom. The Russians had twelve on their staff, and the Americans ten. When Georges had to be out, which was often the case, there would be no one in the office, and he was relieved when Christopher Eberts arrived as First Secretary. He advised against the acquisition of a house, with or without residential accommodation. Problems of hospitality could be solved later, when Pauline was free to join him. She left from Baltimore by the B.O.A.C. northern route, on the 21st of June.

Georges Vanier's mission was essentially informative. He was instructed to find out how far the Allied Governments were representative, or would prove to be so after the war, notably in the case of Yugoslavia, Czechoslovakia, Greece, and Poland. The gathering forces of resistance did not, generally speaking, represent the previous régimes. It was thought improbable that King George's Government could re-establish itself in Greece without domestic disorder, and possibly civil war. German ruthlessness in Poland and Czechoslovakia might create difficulties between those who had endured it and those who had not. The prestige of General Sikorski stood very high in Allied circles, but would it survive the liberation of his country and the drastic adjustment of its boundaries? What was the influence of Communism, reported to be very strong among the French Resistance? How was Europe to escape the domination of Russia in the immediate, and of Germany in the remoter, future? These were the right questions, and Georges Vanier set about to answer them.

Dr Beneš was, naturally enough, obsessed by Munich. When he referred to the humiliation of 1938, Georges observed that other countries had their share of humiliation. Beneš had been informed by Chamberlain that he was a refugee and must take no part in politics; he had consequently preferred to be a refugee in America, where he had reiterated his gloomy (and accurate) prophecies to Roosevelt. He had evidence in February 1941 that Germany was preparing to attack Russia, but no one in Britain or the Soviet Union would believe him. Two months later he warned Churchill who took the matter seriously, but thought that the Soviet Army would be defeated in a few weeks. The Imperial General Staff was of the same opinion.

Beneš emphasized that Czechoslovakia was an eastern as well as a western nation. Its future would depend on collaboration between Russia, Great Britain and France, and on a Tripartite Pact between Russia, Czechoslovakia and Poland. Georges Vanier learned, however, from Philip Nichols,[4] the British Ambassador to the Czechoslovak Government, that Beneš wished to conclude a bilateral treaty with Russia and that the United Kingdom Government was opposed to this. Beneš admired the courage and romanticism of the Poles, but thought them politically immature: they would have to accept the Curzon Line, whether they liked it or not . The Ukraine could not become an independent state, since it was the road to the Black Sea and the Mediterranean, and therefore essential to Russia. Moreover the bulk of its population was Russian in character; only the governing classes and landowners were Poles. East Prussia should be given to Poland, its Junker oligarchy fortunately dispossessed, and the rest of its population, like the Sudeten Deutsch, transferred to Germany. Dr Beneš believed that Hitler and the army leaders would stand or fall together – in which prediction he was not quite correct. Nevertheless, although he was so anxious to prove how right he had been and everyone else so wrong, his apologia was not unjustified.

About the same time Vanier called on Jan Masaryk, the Czechoslovak Minister for Foreign Affairs and Deputy Prime Minister. He was struck, like many others, by Masaryk's open and friendly manner also by his knowledge of the world and gentle cynicism. Masaryk did not like the Soviet Union, but he appreciated its power. Personally he favoured a Central European Federation of Austria, Hungary, Czechoslovakia and Poland – but this would depend on Soviet approval. There was no hope for Poland to regain its eastern frontier, and he thought that Churchill and Roosevelt should have said so – although it was impossible for Sikorski to accept a rectification of frontiers at the present time. In reply to Soviet insistence that Czechoslovakia should sign a bilateral treaty, even against British opposition, Masaryk had objected that he 'would

4. Sir Philip Nichols, 1894-1962.

be no great nation's 'stooge' – After all, as he generously reminded Vanier, 'the United Kingdom was fighting our battles long before Stalin came into the war.'

Georges Vanier's natural sympathies were with the Poles in the conflict between what he had himself described as the 'red hand of Stalin' and what Beneš was not alone in describing as Polish 'romanticism'. The situation had been aggravated by the Polish accusation against the Soviet Union, following the discovery of the mass graves at Katyn, and by the subsequent breaking off of relations between the Polish and the Soviet Governments. It was now complicated by the death of Sikorski in an air crash off Gibraltar. This accident was a mystery which has since been turned into a melodrama.[5] Madame Raskiewicz, the wife of the Polish President, remarked to Georges Vanier: 'We have the impression that the British Government knows what happened, but won't tell us.' Mikolajczyk[6] succeeded Sikorski as Prime Minister, and Sosnkowski[7] became Commander-in-Chief. Sosnkowski – with his combination of ruggedness and charm – had been Inspector-General of the Polish Army, and was extremely popular in military circles. Georges had watched an armoured division on combined manoeuvres with Canadian troops, and been much impressed by their efficiency and morale. Sosnkowski was in no doubt who had murdered the Polish officers at Katyn, but he was evasive about the eastern frontier. He was anxious, however, and with reason, that Russian troops should not reach Berlin before the Allies; and he posed the question as to where Britain should place her political frontier – on the French coast, the Rhine, or the eastern boundaries of Poland? He then made a purely personal suggestion, so startling that Georges Vanier could hardly believe his ears – that Poland should join the Commonwealth with the same status as Canada. A similar suggestion had been put forward, in all seriousness, by several members of the Belgian Government in exile. It was, however, no more startling and much more feasible than Churchill's suggestion of a union between Britain and France.

The Yugoslav situation was bedevilled not only by the rivalry between Mihailovitch and Tito, about which the British Government was still making up its mind, but by acute internal dissensions among the members of the exiled Government. Here Georges

5. Hochhuth's play, *The Soldiers*.
6. Stanislas Mikolajczyk, 1901-1966.
7. Kasimierz Sosnkowski, 1885-1969.

Vanier relied upon the balanced judgment of his friend Sir George Rendel, British Ambassador to the Yugoslavs and formerly Ambassador in Sofia, as well as upon his own contacts. The Prime Minister, Slobodan Yovanovitch, was an old-fashioned politician with static views. An admirer of Gladstone, he had listened to a primitive recording of Gladstone's voice and been struck by the way he pronounced the word 'justice'. He deplored the decline in Parliamentary manners and the informality of modern dress. The Foreign Minister, Milanovitch, assured Vanier that the whole country was behind Mihailovitch, and that the Communists, though heavily backed by Russia, represented no more than five per cent of the population. Later in the summer Yovanovitch was forced to resign owing to his opposition to larger Croat representation in the Cabinet; and Grol replaced Milanovitch in charge of foreign affairs. The new Government was rather more broadly based and slightly more progressive.

Churchill was urging King Peter to take his Government to Cairo, but the Government were unwilling to leave. Only General Zikkovitch, dynamic, adventurous and eager to become the power behind the throne, was prepared to accompany his sovereign. The King had lunched with Churchill at Chequers, and as a consequence the Yugoslav Prime Minister was informed in no uncertain terms that the British Government wished him and his colleagues to follow the King. The British Government were still playing with the idea of a landing in the Balkans, and thought it would be useful to have a Yugoslav Government ready to take over in this event. King Peter's engagement to Princess Alexandra of Greece – to which the Serbs were violently opposed – was announced on the 4th of August, although the marriage would not take place till later. In the light of this wrangling and ineptitude, Georges Vanier concluded that the monarchy was the only hope of holding the country together; that a federal system of government was essential; that loyalty to the throne was the strongest in Serbia, with Mihailovitch as its ostentatious champion; that the Slovene clericals were more mildly monarchist; and that Tito's Partisans were republican. The *emigrés* were strongly monarchist, with the exception of certain journalists with the Left-wing bias of their trade. In the United States a majority of Croats and a proportion of Slovenes were republican, while the Serbs were both monarchist and anti-Croat. The anti-monarchists contemplated a federation of republics to reflect the ethnic diversity of the nation. Sir George Rendel shared these views, which he and Vanier often discussed together. They were both proved wrong in many respects. Tito was able to hold the country together far more successfully than a predominantly Serbian monarchy could have hoped to do, assisted as he was by a military prestige for which he had the Italian surrender as well as the Allied support to thank.

On the 11th of August the reigning Prime Minister, Trufino-vitch, resigned and the King, with significant haste, appointed a non-political Cabinet under Puritch. The new Prime Minister had been Yugoslav Minister to France from 1935 to 1940. His wife was extremely wealthy, and they were living in what was then re-garded as improper luxury. He was a fairly typical career diplomat, forthcoming, well-mannered, good-natured, slightly cynical and took things rather easily. In reply to Vanier's remark that it would be a great day for him when he set foot on his native land once more, Puritch observed with a notable lack of enthusiasm: 'Yes, but the difficulties will be very great.' On the following day the King lunched privately with Vanier, who had never seen him in better spirits – obviously relieved by the demise of his wrangling politicians. He believed, quite rightly, that the future held nothing for these discredited professionals, and that new leaders would arise from the resistance groups – although when they did arise they did not keep King Peter on his throne. Vanier expressed surprise, nevertheless, at the appointment of Puritch, and he did not see the makings of a political leader in Mihailovitch. If the unity of the country were not preserved, Serbia would be drawn into the Russian orbit, with the Croats and Slovenes moving towards Austria. Soviet domination could only be prevented by the Allies, who in fact did everything they could to further it – although the domination was not to prove so absolute as Soviet Russia would have liked. On the 13th of September Vanier had a second interview with Puritch, who was advising the King to land in Yugoslavia with liberating armies, and was even expecting to land there himself. King Peter left for Cairo the next day with his new Government, and no member of the previous one to see him off. It only remained for Georges Vanier to pay a consoling visit to Yovanovitch at his flat in Grosvenor Square, suffering from rheumatism but serene – and presumably still talking about Mr Gladstone. It had all been a fascinating insight into Ruritanian politics, except that Colonel Sapt was not on hand to retrieve the fortunes of the Rassendyls.

Georges found a number of old friends among the Diplomatic

Corps and the Allied political representatives. There was M. Aghnides, Greek Ambassador to the Court of St James, whom he had known at Geneva as an agreeably straightforward member of the Secretariat and who told him of trouble between Royalists and Venezilist Republicans in the Greek Army. There was also Van Kleffens, the Dutch Foreign Minister. In the absence of Van Kleffens, Georges saw his deputy Michiels van Verduynen, who spoke his mind freely, wanting more care exercised in the bombing of military objectives in Holland. The Belgian Minister to Poland – easy-speaking, easy-going, and with an unconcealed dislike of the French – vigorously supported King Leopold against Paul Reynaud's accusations and Churchill's reluctant endorsement of them. He had little use for de Gaulle, believing General Giraud to be an inspired strategist who would lead the French army of invasion. Georges Vanier's response to these opinions cannot have been very warm; they touched nevertheless on the questions now uppermost in his mind.

2

It was a year of confusion and intrigue in Algiers. When Vanier reached England in April de Gaulle was still in London, and considerably mellowed since their previous encounter.[8] The Americans, however, now imagined they had found in Giraud a more acceptable candidate to lead the forces of French resistance. History does not record a more disastrous miscalculation. Vanier had met Giraud in London and summed him up as 'the type of man one would be always happy to meet and expect to meet in a cavalry Officers' Mess – a charming gentleman for a house party but impulsive and addicted to writing letters.'[9] Warnings from the French National Committee confirmed that, while in France after his escape from Germany, Giraud had written to Pétain approving his work of national reconstruction; that he had been willing to work even with Laval; and that he had in fact worked for a short time under Darlan. But then President Roosevelt had declared his readiness to work with Laval, if that would help.[10] It was already clear that he would work with anyone except General de Gaulle.

In the circumstances Vanier wrote a personal letter to Norman Robertson with reference to his possible appointment as Canadian representative in North Africa. 'There is no work with which I

8. Letter to Pauline Vanier, 19th April 1943.
9. Personal Notes.
10. In conversation with André Philip.

would prefer to be associated than the rehabilitation of France after the war.'[11] Three days later he had an interview with Admiral Stark, United States Representative with the French National Committee, whom he found extremely friendly. Stark had been working with de Gaulle for eighteen months, and regarded him as a patriot with high ideals but something of a *prima donna*. He thought it important that Giraud and de Gaulle should get together – a view that was shared by neither. Stark was relatively immune from the prejudice of the State Department. Some French ships, taken over by the United States, had returned to England where their crews had been recruited by the Fighting French, and Stark had refused to ask for their return, although the ships were left unmanned.

Soldiers in North Africa were shifting their allegiance from Giraud to de Gaulle because the pay was better. There was obstinacy on both sides, but de Gaulle was the more ruthless and ambitious. On the 24th of May the French National Committee accepted Giraud's proposals for a new Central Executive and on the 30th de Gaulle arrived in Algiers. At the first meeting between the two Generals there was violent disagreement about the rôle and authority of the Fighting French, and on the basic principles to be followed by any new and unified French Administration. The Gaullist programme assumed that Giraud had no real following, having lost the conservative and Vichyist support he had once enjoyed without having won over the republican elements to his side. It presumed that the elimination of a few higher officials would ensure that effective power remained with the Fighting French, and that the United Kingdom would approve such a transfer of authority, as it had already done in the case of Syria, Madagascar and French Somaliland. Giraud and the Allied authorities, on the other hand, rejected de Gaulle's claim to control the reorganization of the French Armed Forces, and were hankering after a war committee of higher officers, the majority of whom would be designated by Giraud rather than de Gaulle. Where the French National Committee saw the consolidation of their power as the framework of government in post-war France, Giraud envisaged a military resistance led by former officers of the French army. The Allied Military Staff in Algiers held that resistance activities in France should be controlled by military agencies under directives from the combined Chiefs of Staff. The dispute was between two Generals, both of whom knew something

11. 29th May 1943.

about war, and one of whom knew a great deal about politics.

Giraud admitted his political ignorance when he visited Canada in July. Many old sores were reopened in Montreal, for he never once in public or in private, mentioned de Gaulle or the Committee of National Resistance. At a Press conference in Ottawa he reviewed his own career; eulogized German culture, as he had known it; admired the National Socialist organization of society; and thought it wonderful to have sent all those winter clothes to the troops on the eastern front. He told the French community in Ottawa that they did not get up early enough in the morning; that their families were too small; and that their stenographers should not use lipsticks. This confirmed Vanier's impression that 'there was nothing of the heavy-weight about him . . . The way some Frenchmen have summed him up is that he is *léger*; that he cannot really concentrate and think out problems, but that he flits from one thing to another without real sequence.'[12]

Agreement was eventually reached on the constitution of a new Committee with de Gaulle and Giraud as co-chairmen. René Massigli, an old friend of Georges from Geneva, and André Philip[13] whom he had met in Canada, were among those appointed to sit on it. The Committee was known as the French Committee of National Liberation. Troubles, however, soon arose, de Gaulle absenting himself from all meetings unless he were appointed Commissioner of Defence with full powers over mobilization, training equipment, and organization of the new French forces, and command of all those not in active theatres of operations. The younger officers were Gaullist, with an estimated three-quarters of the 400,000 French living in North Africa, and a large majority of the 200,000 refugees from metropolitan France. Many of the Gaullists, however, were opposed to the conversion of the movement into a totalitarian party. Most of de Gaulle's measures were considered intelligent and constructive, but he insisted that he alone could be trusted to administer them. Could enough competent and independent leaders be associated with Giraud to make the new Committee genuinely representative, and permit the necessary reforms to be effected by democratic rather than dictatorial methods? That was the problem.

De Gaulle had the support of the Soviet Union, and its representative with the Allied Governments in London, M. Bogomolov, was immediately appointed to Algiers. With his sallow com-

12. Personal Notes.
13. Commissioner for the Interior on the F. C. N. L.

plexion and behind his horn-rimmed glasses, the Soviet Minister realized that the future lay with de Gaulle because he was in touch with the French people. This was no news to Vanier; he only regretted that the Soviet Union should steal an unnecessary march on the other Allies. The advantage could be offset by the appointment of a Canadian representative in Algiers. The United Kingdom was urging recognition of the French Committee on the United States, but the myth of Pétiniste *attentisme* persisted in Washington, and Eisenhower's retention of Giraud as Commander-in-Chief, with General Georges now at his side, had stirred up deep anti-American feeling in France. All the information Vanier was now receiving from Massigli and André Philip showed that if recognition were delayed, France would be handed over to the Communists. These arguments were supported by the responsible organs of the British Press, and Vanier was convinced that any delay in appointing a representative would expose the Canadian Government to serious criticism. His task in London was 'one largely of representation, whereas in North Africa the first chapter of the Fourth Republic is being written.' He was embarrassed to be pleading for his own advancement 'but I have forced myself to the unpleasant task because I feel deeply that my place is in North Africa and later in France where, with Pauline, I may be able to help in a humble way in its rehabilitation.'[14]

The Canadian Government saw the force of these arguments; and the principle of representation being now decided upon, only the details of its implementation remained to be settled. Both the spirit and the letter of Canadian recognition, when it came, were entirely to Vanier's satisfaction, and he believed that the French would be equally pleased with it. The frigid tone of the American formula was in disagreeable contrast. Paris Radio was alert to quote it as evidence that the United States regarded Vichy as the legitimate Government. No mention of diplomatic representation had been made in the Canadian statement, but Georges received his appointment on the 1st of October. He was to continue to act as Minister to the Greek and Yugoslav Governments now established in Cairo, and technically to the five Allied Governments still in London, where Dupuy was to remain as Chargé d'Affaires. This was announced by Mackenzie King in the House of Commons on the 25th of October when the French had signified their *agrément*.

14. Letter to Norman Robertson, 3rd August 1943.

3

Where the Vaniers had a will they generally had a way; both
Thérèse and Jock had found their way back to England before
either of their parents. Jock had passed into the Royal Naval College, Dartmouth, now removed to Eaton Hall in Cheshire. A
report described him as having 'no great gifts in the way of
brains or athletic ability, but he is a very likeable character and
should do well in the long run.' In view of his subsequent achievements this was an understatement wholly in keeping with the
traditions of the Royal Navy. Thérèse, who was only nineteen,
had arrived in June 1942 and was training with the Motor Transport Corps in London. Later she was sent to the Free French
Cadet Training School at Ribbesford, near Bewdley, where she was
secretary and driver to the Commanding Officer, Commandant
Beaudoin. She subsequently joined the Canadian Women's Army
Corps as a Private and was stationed at Farnborough. She had no
difficulty in passing the Intelligence test. Georges had advised her:
'When in doubt say: let us sit down and think this out'; and he
told Pauline that she was 'becoming quite unarmed-combat-
minded' and seemed to know all the secrets by which even
strong men might be permanently disabled. She passed first out
of her class at a ceremony held at Wellington Barracks before a
number of high-ranking officers; was given a good but not very
exciting job with the legal section of the Army; and apart from
keeping house for Georges at Arlington Street during her week-end
leaves, while Pauline was still in Canada, she brought them both
into contact with what the young people of her generation were
thinking:

We live from one day to another – without thinking or reading very
much – doing our little job as well as we can. I have the impression
that our generation will live for quite a long time like that, but
perhaps as we grow older we shall learn to see things in perspective
by thinking less about ourselves and more about other people.

The young Frenchmen she met were gay and carefree –

fortunately they can laugh when they want to, even when their hearts
are heavy and sometimes sad. They tell me I am someone with whom
they can enjoy themselves in a healthy sort of way, and in whom they
can confide their hopes and very often their discouragement.

Another winter of enemy occupation loomed ahead in France,

and in the autumn of 1943 she was again writing to her grand-mother:

The sun is setting already in a flaming sky, covered with little pink and golden clouds . . . the leaves were falling, and jumping a little as they fell in the calm air. For weeks now they have been shaken by the north wind and the torrential rain. But this evening everything is quiet and a little sad – one feels that another winter is approaching and one can't help thinking of what that will mean for the whole of Europe. I met a young Frenchman who arrived here a few weeks ago; we were talking of the coming winter and he said: 'You know there are limits to the physical and mental suffering that people can endure.'[15]

Pauline was struck by the war-scarred face of London, as Thérèse was struck by the shabby cosmopolitan charm which had replaced its peace-time *chic*.

It took my breath away . . . it is so much worse than I had somehow expected it. It gives one the impression of a dead city, like Pompei, it is quite weird and eerie, and St Paul's proudly standing up in the middle of this desolation, intact, even to its statues on the very top of the roof, but charred and scarred here and there. We walked through all this tragedy and went on looking for the little corners that we knew and loved, amongst others the Inner and Middle Temple. The lovely church of the Templars is nothing but a carcass, roofless, and the lovely hall is the same, I could have wept. That had always been my favourite haunt.[16]

But Farm Street church, though damaged, was still open and once again only a few minutes' walk away. Father Steuart was still there, telling Pauline that it was her duty to be as *mondaine* as war-time diplomacy required. The flat at Arlington House had a big sitting-room where friends and acquaintances could be invited for cocktails, and among the more unusual visitors were a couple of Carmelite sisters *en route* to the oculist. Pauline did not forget Father Steuart's advice that the best spiritual director was an 'enlightened Carmelite'. The Vaniers lunched in the Corvette restaurant downstairs and cooked dinner for themselves, when they were not lunching or dining elsewhere. Official hospitality was returned at the Royal Thames Yacht Club in Knightsbridge, where they gave a number of luncheon parties before Georges left for Algiers. Pauline was greatly impressed by the King of Norway and much teased afterwards for the chivalrous

15. Letters to Mrs Archer, 10th July, 18th September, 23rd October 1943.
16. Letter to Byngsie, 11th July 1943.

attentions he had paid her. Queen Wilhemina of the Netherlands combined strength of character and intelligence with an absence of charm, and simplicity of manner with a strict observance of protocol. Sir Charles Peake,[17] British representative with the French National Committee – a man of rare quality and deep religious feeling – became an intimate friend and Georges was always glad of his advice.

On the 3rd of November M. Viénot, the representative of the French National Committee in the United Kingdom, invited Vanier to dine with General de Lattre de Tassigny who had arrived in England a few days before. Many adventures had befallen de Lattre since their last meeting at Réquin's H.Q. From the 15th of May to the 11th of June 1940 his Division had three times thrown back the German columns attempting to cross the Aisne. Although he had orders to retire, and although his Division was greatly outnumbered, he obtained permission to delay his withdrawal. It then fought a gallant rear-guard action and defended the crossing of the Loire before French resistance collapsed. In September 1941 he was appointed G.O.C. in Tunisia, and in January 1942 returned to France in command of the 16th Motorized Division at Montpelier. When the Germans occupied the whole of France, de Lattre led out his garrison against them. The *coup* failed – partly, it was said, because he had failed to establish contact with local Resistance groups. He was arrested and condemned to ten years imprisonment by the Vichy authorities. In September 1943, however, his escape was engineered by the Franc-Tireurs section of the Resistance, and towards the end of October he had made his way to England with the help of the R.A.F. Also at the dinner arranged by Viénot was Claudius Petit, a delegate of the Franc-Tireur Resistance movement, with whom de Lattre had escaped. Claudius, as he was generally known, had been for fifteen years a furniture maker in Angers and Paris, and was now a teacher of design at a Lycée in Lyon. The Vaniers were to see a great deal of him in Algiers, and afterwards in Paris. De Lattre made an excellent impression on Georges Vanier. His manner was restrained; his views were reasonable; and he was obviously expecting to assume a military command.

Shortly afterwards he fell ill and spent some time in the Middlesex Hospital. Meanwhile Viénot had died, very suddenly, and been replaced by M. Dejean. On the 14th of December Dejean invited the Vaniers to dinner with de Lattre at the Ecu de France,

17. Sir Charles Peake, 1897-1958.

then, as now, one of the best restaurants in the West End, and much frequented by French official circles. Claudius Petit and Colonel Sutton from the War Office were among those present. De Lattre, barely recovered from his illness, arrived late, flushed, and in a state of extreme agitation. Vanier wondered if this were the result of drugs or aspirin, since de Lattre was not a heavy drinker. His extraordinary manner – shouting to the embarrassment of his host and hostess – was apparently due to his cavalier reception by the War Office, where Sir Alan Brooke,[18] Chief of the Imperial General Staff – had declined to see him. From his behaviour Georges concluded that he was ripe for a mental home, although he seems to have relaxed with Pauline. 'Certainly courageous,' she noted 'but his vanity makes one afraid. Very much of a lady's man, perhaps a little too much so.'

De Lattre went on to boast of his seven wounds and his fifteen citations, exclaiming: 'I have a right to speak.' It was only too clear that he felt he also had a right to lead a French army into north-western France, and that unless he did so there would be a bloody revolution and civil war. Georges Vanier had heard, only that morning, from General Morgan[19] that the French would have a merely token force in the northern landings; but de Lattre was not interested in 'carrying the tricolour through the back door' – in other words from the south. When his long outburst was over, Colonel Sutton suggested that he might come back to England, but de Lattre would have none of this. 'I am leaving tomorrow, and I have no intention of commuting. I am going to command an army, and if I come back to England it will be at the head of an army.' He did not explain what his army would be doing in England. Georges Vanier kept his own counsel for the time being but, as we shall presently see, he was no more anxious than de Lattre for the tricolour to return to France through the back door. In the event it came in from the front, and another General was waving it.

Vanier's mission did not bring him into very close contact with Canadian problems, but on the 16th of December he had a disquieting conversation with Andrew McNaughton at the General's H.Q. at Leatherhead. McNaughton was in poor health, and expected shortly to be giving up the command of the Canadian army in Europe. He had been in bitter disagreement with Colonel Ralston (Minister of National Defence) and General Stuart, Chief

18. Field-Marshal Viscount Alanbrooke, 1883-1963.
19. Lieut-General Sir Frederick Morgan, 1894-1967.

of the General Staff, over the way the army should be employed. McNaughton's aim was to keep the army together in order to preserve Canada's autonomous status among the Allies. He had, however, agreed to the despatch of the First Division to assist in the Sicilian landings on the understanding that it would return to Europe to take part in the invasion of northern Europe. Ralston and Stuart, however, had urged that other troops be sent to the Mediterranean, and the Canadian Government had backed them. It was decided, therefore, without consulting Eisenhower, that the Fifth Armoured Division should be sent to Italy, and equipped from North Africa. Ralston and Stuart believed that the army could more easily be reinforced if it were not concentrated in northern France, where casualties might be higher; and that battlefields should be found for troops which were tired of playing a purely defensive rôle. Against this McNaughton argued that Canada would virtually lose control of its army.

Vanier was wholly in agreement with McNaughton's point of view. He advised him to lay the problem before Mackenzie King, stressing that the policy adopted by the Canadian Government was a reversal of the policy for which the Prime Minister himself had always stood. McNaughton was resolved to have the matter out with Mackenzie King, and if the Prime Minister did not support him he indicated that he might feel obliged to make a public statement. Vanier very strongly advised him against doing so for the time being, although he was entirely on McNaughton's side. This was a case where political reasons had been given priority, and the politics did not make sense.

When Jock was home from the Royal Naval College there were walks along the Embankment with the views that Monet and Whistler had painted. Byngsie, now in his last year at Loyola, already seemed more likely to become a priest than a pugilist, but any decision would have to wait until after the war was over – since he was anxious to get into whatever front line he could reach. Letters of thirty-two pages to Arlington House were an indication of literary gifts as well as filial piety, while Bernard – though equally devoted – was readier with the paint brush than the pen, when he was not guarding Dorval airport in the Long Vacation – and Michel was 'sitting up like a Saxon Prince behind his birthday cake with its two candles.'[20]

20. Letter from Pauline Vanier, 3rd August 1943.

CHAPTER 14

ALGIERS

I

AIR-MARSHAL Bowhill[1] had provided Vanier with a private
Hudson aircraft in which he left for Algiers on the morning of the
30th of December. Saul Rae was the only other passenger. They
were obliged to come down, however, near an R.A.F. base in
Cornwall for some necessary repairs which, in the event, took a
couple of days. Georges Vanier, impatient to be off, was constantly in and out of the Operations room, and shared the joke
with Rae when they saw the following notation after the serial
number of their plane: 'Number of passengers 2; V.I.Ps 1'.
Finally, they took off in a Warwick aircraft at dawn on the 2nd
of January, landing at Gibraltar in time for a late breakfast at
Government House with General Mason Macfarlane,[2] and then
proceeding to Algiers where they were met by Maurice Forget,[3]
the Military Attaché. Georges invited the crew of five to dinner,
and then drove out to the Villa Simian, at Chéragas, not far from
Sidi Farouch, where the original Allied Naval landing had taken
place. The Villa stood among its orange trees laden with fruit.
The lemons were still green, contrasting with the silver grey of
the olives and the darker leaves of the eucalyptus and the pines.
Roses and wild flowers grew in rich profusion. It seemed a vast
property, with its distant view of the sea; Georges had neither
expected nor desired such luxury.

René Massigli had found it for him, and the Canadian Government had taken it on a short lease from a rich *colon*. With four
living rooms, a terrace for dining out of doors, seven bedrooms, a
studio, and servants' quarters, it would comfortably serve as a
residence for the Minister, his First Secretary – Saul Rae – the
Military and Air Attachés, and later the Commercial Counsellor.[4]
Georges wrote to Lester Pearson that even at breakfast they never

1. Air-Chief-Marshal Sir Frederick Bowhill, 1880-1960.
2. Lieut-General Sir Frank Mason Macfarlane, 1889-1953.
3. Lieut-Colonel Maurice Forget.
4. Yves Lamontagne.

quarrelled. The small household and office staff, when it arrived, was composed entirely of Canadian military personnel. All the furnishings were at the disposal of the Minister, but a good deal of kitchen equipment had to be brought out, with desk diaries, fountain pens and electric fans. Only desk lamps, waste paper baskets, ash-trays and desk pads were provided. Massigli had written that French wines were unobtainable, but that Algerian wine and brandy were good. London palates, long deprived of such normal pleasures, had been tasting them ever since the American landings – tangible proof that North Africa was really 'the end of the beginning'.

Georges Vanier's duties were comprised under the following headings:

(i)   to maintain close contact with General de Gaulle, and the leading members of the Provisional Government and the Consultative Assembly;

(ii)   to maintain an equally close relationship with the representatives of the Allied governments engaged in the prosecution of the war effort;

(iii) to keep in touch with developments within France to the extent that resources available to the Mission permitted;

(iv)   to ensure that Canadian policy and views, both current and prospective, in the context of Allied relations with France, were thoroughly understood;

(v)   to maintain contact with members of the Canadian Forces and other Canadians in transit through Algiers, or working in various phases of the war effort;

(vi)   to provide full reports to the Canadian Government, as an important partner in the war effort, on all developments seen, first from Algiers, and subsequently from liberated Paris.

But Vanier insisted that the exchange of information must be reciprocal. A number of departments in Ottawa had prepared a pamphlet entitled: 'Voici vos Alliés', intended to be dropped from planes and parachutes before the Allied landings in the summer of 1944. These were to remind Frenchmen that they were not alone, and to show them something of the Canadian war effort in text and in pictures. By some oversight Vanier had not been consulted prior to the preparation of the first issue. When he heard of this he was properly furious, and expressed himself to Saul Rae with the greatest vigour for five minutes. When it became clear that, as a very junior officer, Rae was not perhaps the right target for his criticisms, and when Rae sought patiently to explain how the pamphlet had come into being, and why, his anger disappeared as quickly as it had arisen. The General had a hot temper, but it was quick to cool. He was, however, always vigorous and forthright in the give-and-take between headquarters and posts in the field.

A close view of the Consultative Assembly was less agreeable than a distant view of the sea. This had been established by de Gaulle to keep the politicians quiet or, if one preferred, to keep them talking. When Vanier asked what they had been discussing, Massigli raised his eyebrows and queried: 'Do you think people are really interested in the discussions of the Assembly?' They certainly talked to little effect. In a semi-circular hall, uncomfortably reminiscent of the Chambre des Députés, with a raised platform for the President, the behaviour of certain speakers recalled the worst days of the Third Republic. More encouraging for Georges Vanier, and infinitely more important, were conversations with Edwin Wilson, United States Representative to the F.C.N.L., and Duff Cooper[5] who had just been appointed British Ambassador to the Committee. Wilson concurred with Georges Vanier that it would not be practicable to say to the French people immediately after the Allied landings: 'Vote and give yourselves the Government you desire.' A Provisional Government with wide powers and international recognition should be set up as soon as possible. Wilson asked for the Canadian Government, if they agreed with these views, to make them known in Washington.

It would be hard to imagine two men more different in temperament, mentality, background and physique than Georges Vanier and Duff Cooper. Inclined to indolence, irascible, *bon vivant*, highly intelligent, and indomitably brave, Duff Cooper alone among Nevile Chamberlain's Cabinet had resigned in protest against the Munich Agreement. This would have been quite enough to win Vanier's admiration. Moreover both men had a passionate love of France; both in their time had seen active service in the field, fighting in the same war against the same enemy; both had won the Military Cross; both were excellent speakers; both had a sensitive and informed apprecia-

5. Viscount Norwich, 1890-1954.

tion of literature and Duff Cooper himself was a writer of distinction; both were diplomats with a clear sense of where the limits of compromise should be drawn; and both were prepared, if necessary, to stand up to the authority which had commissioned them.

Duff Cooper worked in a small office with large glass doors, a kind of hot-house particularly conducive to sleep after luncheon; and if one called on him in the afternoon he often gave one the impression of having just woken from a satisfying doze. He and Georges Vanier were generally of one mind. Duff Cooper had the harder task with superior authority. Where President Roosevelt saw red at the mention of General de Gaulle, Mr Churchill saw pink. De Gaulle had been rude to him; and although people might disagree with Mr Churchill, they were not normally rude to him. Duff Cooper admitted that de Gaulle was difficult, but he was a fact of life and had to be recognized as such. When Vanier suggested that at least one French Division should land in northern France, Duff Cooper said that he would bear the suggestion in mind. As we shall see, it had fallen on fruitful soil.

Dr Beneš was also in Algiers; he had a genius for being everywhere. Recently returned from Moscow, he was happily convinced that Stalin, with whom he had had five interviews, was quite uninterested in the spread of world Communism, and the Poles had nothing to fear from him. M. Morawski, Polish Representative to the F.C.N.L., had different views. Since Vanier had known him in London he had been given the personal rank of Ambassador; and on the 11th of January Georges received a telegram from Ottawa informing him that his own rank had been similarly raised. Hume Wrong[6] wrote that he had 'never known such a question to be settled in the Department with such speed.'[7] Georges Vanier was now the fifth Canadian envoy to hold ambassadorial rank. M. Bogomolov and M. Vishinsky, the Soviet Under-Secretary for Foreign Affairs, were living in a luxurious villa which had belonged to a pro-German newspaper proprietor, now in a concentration camp. Georges Vanier admitted that perhaps too much territory had been ceded to the Poles in 1918, but he ventured the remark that the Russians also had a strain of romanticism. M. Bogomolov, a former professor of psychology, replied that they were no longer idealists in the abstract sense; they were

6. Humphrey Hume Wrong, 1894-1954. He had succeeded Norman Robertson as Under-Secretary for External Affairs.
7. 29th January 1944.

A visit to the Fourth French Army in Lorraine, March 1940. General Vanier shaking hands with Joseph Darnand, General Réquin in centre.

Addressing the Royal 22nd in St Peter's Square, Rome, after they had been received in audience by Pope Pius XII, July 1944.

The Villa Simian, Chéragas.

General de Gaulle and General Leclerc, 1944.

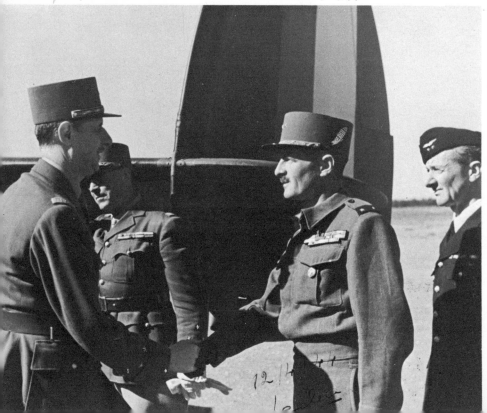

General Vanier and Général de Lattre de Tassigny saluting the Tricolour hoisted for the first time on German soil, 1945.

At the Canadian Memorial, Dieppe.

With Thérèse at Vézelay.

only interested in ideals which could be realized. He preferred not
to speak of them as Russians – which was natural enough for the
representative of a power that contemplated gathering the
Lithuanians, the Estonians, the Letts and the Ukrainians, not to
mention other ethnic minorities, into the benevolent Soviet
embrace.

The question of psychology – the war-time synonym for propaganda – arose with Mr C. D. Jackson, an Assistant Director of the
Psychological Warfare Bureau. It was essential to integrate the
activities of the Bureau with the requirements of military
strategy; otherwise the power of the Communists in France, already the strongest and best organized element in the Resistance,
would increase – with the alternatives of national chaos, or a
quasi-dictatorial régime based on the French Army and backed by
the liberating forces of the Allies. Meanwhile General Giraud had
retired from the co-chairmanship of the French Committee. As
Jackson observed, he had 'not only played his cards badly, but
dropped them altogether.' Where de Gaulle would always read the
papers he was asked to sign or initial, Giraud never did so – an
omission which led him to sign away his own authority. De
Gaulle was living at the Villa des Oliviers, El Biar. Georges paid
a visit to Madame de Gaulle – a woman of great distinction and
simplicity. In answer to his compliment that she must be very
proud of her husband, she replied: 'Yes, I am proud to have for
my husband a man who was not defeated, and for my son a man
who was not defeated either.' Philippe de Gaulle was serving with
the Naval Forces of the Fighting French.

On the 22nd of January Vanier paid his official call on the
General at the Villa des Glycines, accompanied by Maurice Forget and Saul Rae, First Secretary at the Legation. He was received
by Captain Burin des Roziers,[8] and reviewed the Spahis which
formed the Guard of Honour, looking each man deliberately in the
face. Every interview with de Gaulle had left a slightly different
impression on Georges Vanier. In 1940 he had been ardent,
dynamic and physically aggressive. In September 1941, embittered by the events in Syria, he seemed restless in mind and even
distraught in manner. In 1943 he was balanced, energetic and
serene. But now he spoke in a subdued monotone, and was
obviously tired, preoccupied and depressed. The light fell harshly
on his face, showing up the lines of anxiety; and indeed he scarcely
looked a leader at all. The contrast was marked and disconcerting

8. Later French Ambassador in Rome.

between this lassitude and his domination of the Consultative Assembly, where Vanier had twice been to hear him speak. He told Georges Vanier of the rising tide of resistance in France, where a hundred patriots were being shot every day, and he expressed impatience for the opening of a second front. Georges concluded that like so many men of genius, he was subject to the vagaries of depression; if he were an ordinary mortal, one would say that he had his ups and downs. Sir Alexander Cadogan[9] had described de Gaulle as a man 'with a head like a pineapple and the hips of a woman'; and it was not in these respects alone that he was unlike an ordinary mortal. 'De Gaulle's greatness' Georges wrote to Harold Nicolson[10] 'rests on the fact that at a time when most Frenchmen believed their country irretrievably lost, he still wanted to fight. They thought he was crazy then, but they know *now* he was right. Nothing can stop him.'[11]

The Communists already formed a cohesive *bloc* in the Assembly. François de Menthon, the Commissioner for Justice and himself a Christian democrat, was a particular friend of the Vaniers. He had a son fighting in Italy, another in the *maquis*, and the Gestapo on his heels. He thought it inadvisable to isolate the Communists, since this might have awkward consequences in France where they were collaborating loyally with the other groups in the Resistance. Some of those who had found their way to Algiers had a fine record behind them, although it was true that, here more scrupulously than in France, they accepted the discipline of their party. Georges Vanier was disquieted to learn this, but de Menthon was convinced that if the Communists were to be opposed – as they would probably have to be – the opposition had better come from within France rather than from outside. Georges was interested to learn that the detested Darnand with whom he had shaken hands at Réquin's H.Q. had offered his services to the French Committee if they would have accepted them. Georges had a photograph of that handshake; it was not the proudest of his souvenirs.

The French in Algiers were soon turning instinctively to Vanier when they were in trouble. At the beginning of the year they disposed of twelve Divisions, including Leclerc's; now four of these were being turned over to transport, lines of communica-

9 The Right Hon. Sir Alexander Cadogan, 1884-1968. Permanent Under-Secretary for Foreign Affairs from 1938-1946.
10. Sir Harold Nicolson, 1888-1968.
11. 19th June 1944.

tions, and other auxiliary services. This infuriated de Lattre and M. le Troquer, who was responsible for the re-equipment of the Army and Air Force. Le Troquer was frank, impulsive, patriotic and indiscreet, and no respecter of persons – even when they happened to be Generals. He was not particularly respectful to de Lattre, who accompanied him on a visit of protest to the Canadian Ambassador. De Lattre exclaimed: 'Instead of commanding an army, I go around inviting the Divisions to their own funeral.' Where the American and British diplomats in North Africa were doing their best to knock some sense into the heads of their political masters, the American high command – whom de Lattre and le Troquer held responsible – were displaying a crass ignorance of French psychology. The French troops were itching to get into action – why turn them over to the guarding of level crossings? But since they depended on the Allies for their equipment, the Allies had the last word, however tactless, on how they should be employed. Vanier could do no more than communicate his sympathy for these views to Sir Humphrey Gale[12] and his successor General Mark Clark, when he dined with them at the Allied Forces Headquarters Mess. He did not find them very responsive.

At the end of January a bitter and stormy session of the Assembly debated the setting up of a Provisional Government in France. De Menthon, speaking for the Committee, envisaged the continuance of its present authority, reinforced by representatives from the Committee of Liberation in each of the liberated Departments, until the country was completely free. Then the Committee would assume the title of Provisional Government, working with the Conseil Supérieur de la Résistance. Municipal elections, on a basis of universal suffrage, would be held immediately, and the Municipal Councils would then elect, within a month of their nomination, their delegates to the National Assembly – the number of these to be reckoned as roughly one for every ten thousand inhabitants. The Assembly would elect a Political Supreme Court, a Permanent Consultative Commission, and a Commission for Constitutional Reform. The General Election should take place not less than one year after the constitution of the Provisional Government.

The Socialists, with Vincent Auriol[13] as their spokesman, planned for the election of a Permanent Assembly six months

12. Lieut-General Sir Humphrey Gale.
13. 1884-1966.

after the Liberation, with legislative power vested for the time being in a Provisional Assembly, half of which would be nominated by the Councils of metropolitan and extra-metropolitan resistance, and half composed of former Deputies and Senators chosen from those who had voted against Vichy in June 1940 and from those who were not present to vote one way or the other. The main difference between the two plans was that the Socialists wished to maintain continuity with the previous legislature and to defer elections until the prisoners and deportees had returned. They also feared, and with reason, that elections held in the turmoil of liberation would not be truly representative of the popular will. The Communists proposed the immediate transformation of the Committee into a Provisional Government, and a stringent programme for the prosecution of the war. This would depend on how one interpreted its phraseology. It demanded an 'anti-Hitler army'; but what else was the Division Leclerc? It demanded that all political and administrative personnel should be called upon to furnish an autobiography; but autobiographies are scarcely impartial evidence. It demanded that the press, radio, and cinema should be reorganized in order to give the public fuller information; but the Communists wanted the portfolio of information for themselves. The only agreement at which the Assembly could arrive was to charge the Committee with the preparation of a new plan in the light of these inconclusive and intemperate discussions. General de Gaulle watched the palaver with a detachment not unmixed with irony; and he had reservations about some of his Commissioners whose *liaisons* were notorious and might even be *dangereuses*. One day, when everyone in Algiers was sheltering from an apocalyptic downpour of rain, he stood at the window of his villa and observed, 'It's the Flood. All we have to do is to summon the Commissioners to the Ark, and those who do duty for their wives.'

The rivalry between Giraud and de Gaulle had now given way to the rivalry between Giraud and de Lattre. Giraud was still nominally C-in-C. of the French Army, and he had the ear of Eisenhower. De Lattre's favour with the Left came from his advocacy of a close alliance with Soviet Russia in 1938 and 1939, and from the confidence he had won from the miners of the northern Departments, militant Communists almost to a man, whom he had under his command at Montpelier. His ideas on military strategy and the use of armour were similar to those of de Gaulle, who had first propounded them; and he despised Giraud

as the prototype of a commander whose outmoded theories of
warfare had been catastrophically disproved.

Now in command of the French Expeditionary Force, he was
drawing his officers from both Gaullist and Giraudist groups; and
he had shown tact and discretion in his relations with the two
rivals. When de Gaulle and le Troquer both suggested that he
should take over Giraud's command, de Lattre replied that his
'honour was at stake' – to which de Gaulle retorted that he didn't
care a damn about de Lattre's honour.[14] All he cared about was
France. Nevertheless de Lattre was completely overshadowing
Giraud, and many of Giraud's more capable officers were joining
him – partly because they were eager to take part in the continental campaign. De Lattre's permanent feud was with General
Juin,[15] who was Giraud's man and Eisenhower's. They had hated
each other ever since they had left St Cyr on the same day, and
Juin feared that if de Lattre replaced Giraud – which appeared
likely – he would come under de Lattre's orders. This mutual
hostility did not help de Lattre's relations with the Americans, and
at a dinner on the 8th of January he confided to Georges Vanier
his irritation and anxiety.

He had seen Eisenhower for only ten minutes, having been kept
waiting for twenty-five; and the C-in-C. had emphasized the casual
brevity of the interview by neither standing up nor sitting down,
but had half reclined on the edge of the table. General Barker[16]
had assured de Lattre that it would be an easy matter to transport
three Divisions to the northern front, and probably three more.
But Giraud favoured a landing in the south. Against this de Lattre
argued that he would have only twelve Divisions, six in the forward line and six in reserve, and that the Germans would have no
difficulty in holding them with one Division of their own against
three of the attackers. The Allied superiority in the air would be
fifty to one in the north and only ten to one in the south. If the
northern attack were successful, there would be no opposition in
the south – but still a thousand kilometres to Paris. It would be a
month before the French army got there, with no chance of dis-
tinguishing itself on the way. If the northern attack failed, the
fiasco in the south would be complete and the army would be
thrown back into the sea. De Lattre believed that the reasons for
advocating an attack from the south were less military than

14. 'On s'en fout de votre honneur. Il s'agit de la France.'
15. Maréchal Juin, 1888-1967.
16. U.S. officer in charge of transport and war material.

political; the Americans would be embarrassed by a French army marching to the rescue of its own capital.

Pauline Vanier arrived, buoyant as usual, on the 8th of February, and on the 27th the sound of a car driving up to the villa at 9.30 a.m. announced the unexpected arrival of Philippe Leclerc from Morocco. For some minutes the three friends were so moved that they were unable to speak, and it was not until the afternoon, when Pauline took him for a long walk, that Leclerc would speak of his campaigns. With his keen face, now bronzed by the equatorial sun, he conformed in every particular to the ideal of the Christian warrior. The Vaniers were not alone in putting a halo round his *casquette*. Pléven would say that he had never known anyone to keep himself so intact in the face of every possible temptation, living as he did with men who were very far from being saints, and neither smoking nor drinking in order to be at all times master of himself. More than any other leader of the Fighting French, he seemed to step out of a *chanson de gestes*. His own legendary exploits were part of a continuing story, and it was the same story that other Frenchmen were writing with their blood in the *maquis* of the Massif Central or in the perilous clandestinity of the cities and the countryside.

This was a Sunday like other Sundays at the Villa Simian. Geoffroy de Courcel,[17] Aide-de-Camp to General de Gaulle, came up to luncheon, and in the afternoon other officers were invited for tennis and tea. For all his disability, Vanier himself would never hesitate to make up a double on the court. Later he and Leclerc got down to business. It was a sombre conversation. Leclerc had come to Algiers, hoping for an authorization to proceed to England in order to discuss the incorporation of his Division in the forces of the Allied invasion. The answer had come that in England there was no material available to re-equip them. He had received the news philosophically. Georges assured him that he had raised the matter with the Canadian Government and with the Allied representatives in Algiers, and that he would continue to do everything in his power to ensure that at least a single French Division was included in the invading army. The absence of such a force, he emphasized to Ottawa, would be felt as a crowning humiliation by the French. It would be neither understood nor forgotten, whatever might be pleaded in its excuse.

Leclerc had no fears of civil war in France provided that

17. Later French Ambassador in London.

adequate authority were given to de Gaulle; otherwise the Communists would certainly take over. The French must be allowed to wash their dirty linen without interference. He foresaw the complete overturning of the social and political order with new men at the helm. Pétain had understood the need for a national revolution, but in falsifying the ideals of 'family' and 'work' he had made de Gaulle's task doubly difficult. In the evening the Vaniers accompanied him to dinner with de Gaulle. Maurice Forget and Saul Rae, with Massigli and others, were also there. The General was calm and very weary. When Pauline invited him to come to Canada after the war, he replied: 'Ah, madame, after the war I shall be so tired that I shall want to sleep and sleep and sleep.' His fatigue betrayed itself in conversation. Pauline mentioned that there were orange trees and lemon trees in the garden of the Villa Simian, and de Gaulle was astonished. 'So you have lemons growing from orange trees' he exclaimed, and blushed when Pauline assured him that he had said something that she would not forget. The General expressed his concern about French participation in the northern invasion, and Georges reiterated his fears that a serious mistake had been made and his prayers that it might not be irreparable. Duff Cooper had reinforced these arguments in an interview with General Sir Henry Maitland-Wilson,[18] the new Commander-in-Chief in North Africa, and also in a letter to Churchill, who sent an encouraging reply. Vanier feared that, exhausted by three years of personal struggle, de Gaulle would not have the nervous and physical strength for the task awaiting him when the Allied Forces had landed. But then de Gaulle was a disconcerting person; one very often had strange feelings in his presence. If one were told that he was 'better', it meant that he was at once more difficult and more dynamic. Those who were working close to him described him as a 'medium', in the sense that he always sensed, at a distance, the real feelings of the French; and if he sometimes appeared sapped of strength himself, he also sapped the strength of others. Leclerc, too, had had his struggles, but they had not been political. After three years, he said, he could still take a knock or two; and on the morning of his return to Morocco he was serving Mass in the little church at Chéragas, with the Vaniers at his side. History was repeating itself, and their memories all went back to Farm Street in 1940 on the morning of his flight to the Cameroons.

18. Field-Marshal Lord Wilson of Libya and Stowlangtoft, 1881-1964.

2

The Villa Simian quickly became known as the 'Maison de la Résistance'. Elisabeth de Miribel has left an account of one of many visits she paid there with three young Frenchmen who had come out of France. It describes the atmosphere, physical and psychological, in which the Vaniers were then living:

The road leading from Algiers to Chéragas is long and beautiful. After a final twist above the bay of Algiers, stretched out in the sunshine, it turns towards El Biar and soon plunges into a green and rich countryside.

To right and left are the stems of the vines, protected at the foot by wild flowers, purple, yellow and white; then the meadows, very green, alternating with the red earth, freshly ploughed up. In the far distance are snowy mountains, in the nearer foreground very blue hills, and ahead of us the plain and the palm trees and the orange trees laden with gleaming fruit, and the almond trees with their softly coloured blossom.

The road is long and the peace took possession of us. Nevertheless the news from France was bad. In a few words Claudius[19] evoked the terror which the Boche, who felt himself threatened, was spreading among our people. Just a few facts and figures, emphasized by the remarks of his two comrades: 'Things are going badly.' In France they were dying of hunger and suffering. In France they were waiting each week for the landings, with anguish in their hearts. In France all nerves were on edge – and for how long! – in hopes for the battle of liberation. In France they were dying.

The road turned and led through an avenue of eucalyptus to the Canadian Embassy. These fields starry with flowers, these vineyards, this red earth stretching to the sea, were much too beautiful. And the infinite calm was oppressive when one thought of France in agony.

Sitting close to each other, we didn't talk very much. What right had we to be young and free, moved by the beauty of this laughing earth, while our kith and kin were suffering? It only needed a few words from those who left France in October and November of last year – strong words emphasized by hard gestures – to bring before our eyes a whole world to which we felt as strangers, and to shatter a peace which was alien to the drama being played out there.

Gandelin said: 'These are the colours of France. Yes, they are the colours of France in springtime.'

Claudius said: 'Today, at noon, I shall not be at home for the second birthday of my boy, Dominique. There will be a cake on the table with two candles. I shall not be there to take the traditional

19. Claudius Petit.

photo. Shall I be there in May for the sixth birthday of my daughter? I am afraid I shall be too optimistic if I say Yes.'

Prigent said nothing. No doubt he was remembering the house in Paris and his wife and the eldest of his daughters, who so frightened him last year when all her teeth fell out and they had to send her away into the country because one of her lungs was affected.

The car swerved and then stopped in front of the big villa which served both as residence and office for the representative of Canada. The car was camouflaged. 'It reminds me' said Claudius as he got out 'of the great Beast of the Apocalypse, that St John talks of.'

As soon as we were inside, a friendly atmosphere surrounded us. A large, light room served the purposes of a dining-room and salon. Huge bay windows opened on to the gardens of palms and orange trees, and on to the flowering fields which reached down to the sea.

Eucalyptus, with their rustling leaves, cradled their branches under the windows. The salon was on the right; almond blossom in a blue jug and branches of mimosa in a tall copper vase, a piano, cigarettes and comfortable chairs. The office was at the end on the left, with a large map of Russia where the Russian advance was marked out each day, Canadian newspapers in both languages, French and Canadian books. A homely atmosphere.

We sat down to luncheon and the welcome was so warm and so familiar that these three Frenchmen from three different parts of France spoke without restraint. They spoke of their fears, of their disappointment at the slow campaign in Italy, of their impatience for the opening of a second front.

General Vanier asked them to say exactly what they were thinking; how did they see the future? What suggestions had they to make?

Claudius exclaimed frankly: 'What do I want? More daring; a French general on the Allied Staff, more speedy operations, and a quick landing.'

'I am no strategist' said Prigent 'but I know that in the north they have been waiting for the landings with such high hopes that when I missed the October moon to come to London, I nearly didn't leave in November for fear of not getting back in time.'

'If the Allies delay' Gandelin gently added 'they will find a cemetery.'

'You must realize' Claudius interrupted 'that for months, for two years, our people have been preparing for the landings. This can't go on. They have taken their risks. It has been a hard winter in the *maquis*. Nevertheless they refused to work for the Germans. They went into hiding, they were cold and hungry, but they waited. Now you can't hold them back any longer. Our young people are provoking the police and the Germans. They have lost their prudence. They get themselves killed for nothing. And the repressions are more severe than ever.'

Prigent underlined these arguments. 'You see' he said, 'you can make the French understand that an Allied landing is impossible before the end of the spring, that the thaw in Russia will risk delaying the opening of the second front, you can keep the French patient until May or June, but you mustn't disappoint them any further.'

There was a silence, heavy with thought, and then General Vanier observed gently:

'I am touched and moved by all that you have said. Like you, I am haunted by the thought of the French who are suffering and who up till now have known nothing but disappointment. I am no more of a strategist than you are, but I think one must continue to have patience. It would be too serious if the operation were only half successful. You can see from here what a triumph that would be for German propaganda. If I were a German, I would defend myself to the last man in Italy, but I would hope – so long as the German morale still held good – for a hasty landing elsewhere, which would give me the chance for a violent anti-Allied propaganda.'

There was another silence . . . we had come to the dessert. General Vanier, in whose ear I had whispered a word or two, raised his voice:

'Pauline, we shall drink to the health of someone we don't yet know – a young Frenchman of tomorrow' – then turning to Claudius – 'and we shall drink to Dominique's second birthday.'

Claudius blushed and lowered his head, so moved that we all stopped talking. For a few moments each one of us thought of our own people somewhere in France. Glasses were then raised to the health of Dominique and of all the 'little ones' who tomorrow would live in freedom, holding up their heads on French soil.

All the conversation that went on until the early afternoon in the bright *salon* was directed towards the future. Beyond the immediate sufferings of each Frenchman, beyond the threats of the Gestapo, and the anguish of waiting, 'tomorrow' hovered like an immense hope. And the three men who had come here as representatives of France were for us who listened to them the witnesses of what France was hoping for.

The effect of these conversations, and others like them, on Georges Vanier was profound and lasting. No other Allied diplomat, however warm his sympathies, had a parallel insight into the epic of the French Resistance. Not all of its militants, however, shared the Vaniers' religious faith or even their liberal democratic convictions; and with the Communists there was frank and friendly argument. But they were all in such a state of nervous tension that it was difficult to make them see reason in the elaborate security measures then in force. The Allied High Command – and de Gaulle himself – had painful experience of French indiscretion; and the Vaniers sometimes wished that their visitors would understand what was at stake – thousands of British lives shortly to be sacrificed for the liberation of France. Authority had every right to its suspicions.

A few days later the three *résistants* brought another friend to luncheon, with Lieutenant de Vaisseau Savary, who had been the first Administrator of St Pierre et Miquelon, after their seizure by Admiral Musélier. Claudius Petit surprised Georges Vanier by telling him that an overwhelming majority of the Resistance favoured a political union between Great Britain and France when the war was over; and Vanier agreed that this would be a means of countering Soviet influence in Europe. He passed on these views to Duff Cooper, who was equally surprised to hear them. Savary, who was then serving with a French Division in Morocco, did not share the confidence of the others either in the French Committee or even in General de Gaulle. He reported that Communist influence in the army was very strong; the men resented the lack of consideration shown towards it by the Allied Command. But Georges Vanier, although he was in touch with men like de Lattre and le Troquer, who were building up the French Forces, and knew something of what they could achieve through his friendship with Leclerc, had few opportunities of entering into the feelings of the rank and file. The mystique of the *maquis* and the underground was more familiar to him:

'We do not know' he wrote to Robertson Fleet 'the horror of the knock on the door at midnight which may mean deportation of young men to slavery, or dishonour for women. I have seen and spoken with men who have just come out of France, having suffered horribly themselves, with tales of cruelty which sound incredible after twenty centuries of Christianity. You will not be surprised when I say that often I have not been able to listen to their stories without tears coming into my eyes.'[20]

3

The result of the Resistance was the *épuration* and this had already started in Algiers. The trial of Pierre Pucheu opened on the 6th of March. Already, in the autumn of 1935, Pucheu had launched a monthly review. *Travail et Nation*, to which Marcel Déat, one of the principal advocates of collaboration with Germany, had contributed. Later, he was a member of Jacques Doriot's 'Brains Trust', and from July 1941 to April 1942 he had

20. 26th June 1944.

been Pétain's Minister of the Interior. He was thus held responsible for the deportation of resistant Frenchmen, and notably for
the shooting of fifty hostages at Châteaubriant. Early in 1943 he
had written to Giraud from Madrid, offering his services to the
French authorities in North Africa. No reply was sent to this
letter, but in March he wrote again and was then informed that
no objection would be raised to his coming. As Giraud stated in
his evidence, 'I did not have the right to stand in the way of a
Frenchman wishing to serve in the French Army.' Unfortunately,
however, Pucheu was recognized on the convoy taking him to
Algiers, and his presence was greatly resented by his fellow-
travellers. The battle for Tunisia was then at its height, and to
avoid the risk of civil disorder Pucheu was placed in *résidence
surveillée* in south Morocco. His case came before the French
Committee in May, but it was held that a trial would be premature since the essential proofs of his guilt were not available
in North Africa. When it opened almost a year later they had been
assembled, but the witnesses who might have testified in his defence were still not available, and this prejudiced the issue from
the start.

Georges Vanier was in court throughout the trial, viewing it in
spite of his natural sympathies with a lawyer's dispassionate
objectivity. He was struck by the fundamental difference between
French and Canadian procedures. The witnesses were allowed to
make speeches as well as to answer questions. The witnesses and
the accused could interrupt each other, and the witness could
insult the accused. The prosecuting counsel, General Weiss, cut
a theatrical and emotional figure, relying on rhetoric when he
could not rely on evidence. Grénier, the Communist Deputy,
spoke with an equal passion for the martyrs of the Resistance,
although he could adduce no proof that the hostages at Châteaubriant – mostly Trades Union leaders – had been selected by the
accused. Pucheu replied that he had, in fact, saved the lives of
many hostages, and added 'I am not afraid to look Grénier in the
face.' Giraud's testimony was deeply impressive when he referred
by implication to the death of his daughter in Germany, and to
his wife and his other children who were in enemy hands. Almost
from the first day of the trial the impression was widespread in
Algiers that conclusive evidence of guilt was lacking. Vanier had
talked with most of the men who were in close touch with the
French Committee. They all wanted to see Pucheu condemned,
but most of them admitted that this was a case where politics

would have the last word. Pucheu made a moving speech in his own defence, which the future masters of liberated France would have done well to heed:

We now see clearly, gentlemen of the tribunal, what is expected of you. It is not an act of justice but a political gesture, I must pay for it with my life. To be sure, metropolitan France is of one mind in wishing at all costs to be rid of Germany, but to express the popular will over here, on any other political question, is flagrantly dishonest. If the Provisional Government, with the armies behind them, enters on the liberated soil of France with the same methods and in the same frame of mind, I do not give it a year before it leads our country into the worst internal discord.

Pucheu had a word of advice for General de Gaulle:

I hope that he will know how to raise the spirit of partisanship to the level of objective judgment, which is the test of statesmanship.

And his final declaration, heard in absolute silence, visibly impressed the court:

I have always owed my obedience, uniquely and exclusively, to what I have judged in good conscience to be the imperative needs of my country. I wish that my last word and my last thought, in this place, should be for her.

Pucheu was condemned to death and subsequently shot. The trial did no good to the reputation of the French National Committee in Allied circles, and even in Algiers the dignity and courageous bearing of the accused, with the flimsy evidence against him, the handicaps of his defence, and the emotional pressure brought on the tribunal from outside, had won for him a fair measure of sympathy. Both Duff Cooper and the American Chargé d'Affaires had expressed informally to Emmanuel d'Astier[21] their view that the evidence did not warrant the death penalty; and Georges Vanier was quick to see in Pucheu's condemnation a dark augury for the future. It was very difficult to distinguish in a court of law between 'collaborationisme' and 'attentisme'. The same tangled problems of law and politics would certainly emerge when other collaborationists were brought to justice in North Africa and later in France itself.

General Leclerc returned to Algiers at the end of March and was staying with the Vaniers at Chéragas. On Saturday, the 1st of April, Georges and Pauline were due to lunch with the Brazi-

21. Commissioner for the Interior.

lian Ambassador, and Leclerc was lunching at the Villa by himself. Just as the Vaniers were leaving Georges was handed a telegram from Ottawa informing him that a Brigade of Free French
forces under General Leclerc were to be included in the forthcoming operations in northern France. This would be a more
than token force, but it would only meet French wishes in the
matter to a limited extent. The complete text of the telegram had
not yet been decyphered, and Georges thought it best to wait until
the whole message was available before telling the news to Leclerc,
who was then at table in the dining-room – more especially since
it was apparently intended to limit the forces under his command
to a Brigade. The Vaniers returned to the Villa in the afternoon,
where the remainder of the text was awaiting them. It confirmed
that it would be difficult so to alter existing plans as to include a
larger proportion of French troops. Duff Cooper then arrived and
Georges again decided to defer telling the news to Leclerc until
he had gone. In the event, however, Duff Cooper stole his
thunder, asking Leclerc whether he were not now preparing to
move. Leclerc, obviously puzzled, shook his head; and Duff Cooper
realized that he knew nothing of the decision which had been
made in his favour. The British Ambassador had learnt of this
from Sir Henry Maitland-Wilson who was under the impression,
however, that Leclerc and his entire Division were to take part in
the operations from the north.

Georges Vanier then mentioned the telegram he had received
from Ottawa. It was a dramatic moment. The two diplomats
drank to Leclerc's health and perhaps, for once, Leclerc broke
his rule of abstinence. When Georges told them of the plan to
include only a Brigade of the Division, Duff Cooper recalled the
truth of Haig's saying that 'no news is ever as good, or ever as
bad, as when we hear it for the first time.' Leclerc naturally did
not like the idea of breaking up his Division, but Vanier reassured
him that once the principle of effective participation by the
French had been accepted, other troops could be added to the
Brigade. Leclerc suggested that the entire personnel of the Division
might be transported to England, and much of its *matériel* passed
on to other French Divisions in North Africa. This seemed a happy
solution and Vanier endorsed it. As the glasses were raised in the
cool *salon* of the Villa Simian, they were lifted not only to the
great soldier whose dearest wish was now so near fulfilment, but
to a diplomatic victory which the Canadian Ambassador had done
more than anyone to achieve.

CHAPTER 15

TOWARDS THE
LIBERATION

I

THE atmosphere of Algiers was morally enervating as well as politically tense. Even the beauty of the setting and the generous spring sunshine were felt in ironical and insolent contrast to the frayed nerves of those who were waiting to be liberated and those who were waiting to liberate them. Pauline expressed herself as disgusted with 'the Black Market, the succulent meals, and the elegant and over made-up women. What will the young men of the Resistance think of these Frenchmen who are so busy enjoying themselves?'[1] Among the callers was Père Delos, O.P., whom the Vaniers had known when he was Professor of International Law at Laval University. He had made his way to North Africa in December 1943, and occasionally celebrated Mass on Saturday mornings for the members of the Resistance then in Algiers. He also brought out to the Villa another French Dominican, Père d'Arcy, with an up-to-date account of the conditions in France. His report was extremely disquieting. The spirit of resistance was crumbling, while in Paris the wealthier classes were cheerfully paying the price of the Black Market. Reprisals were ruthless; Père d'Arcy had himself seen the Germans set fire to a house in Clermont-Ferrand and shoot anyone who attempted to escape from it. He impressed Georges Vanier as a man of intelligence and sound judgment, though leaving him with a suspicion that the majority of the French people were not really interested in whether the Allies landed or not. Of less consequence was an Abbé who wanted to go to Canada and wished on the Ambassador the MS. of an historical drama entitled *L'Ame Lorraine*. Georges Vanier was fond of reading – but there were books and books, and war-time imposed its priorities. Another friend was Andrée Chevrillon, a talented artist, who had been working for a *foyer*

---

1. Letter to Mrs Archer, 8th March 1944.

des soldats in Corsica. Now crippled with arthritis, she was living in a Benedictine convent near Algiers, and painting a mural on a theme drawn from the Apocalypse.

Visits to the Duff Coopers, whose Villa could not compare in elegance or comfort with the Villa Simian, were frequent and occasionally light-hearted. Georges willingly surrendered to Lady Diana's beauty, intelligence and charm; and she was quick to recognize his qualities of heart and mind. The talk was sometimes about politics, and sometimes about nothing at all. There was an iron bar fixed to two stone pillars at the entrance to the house, and Georges felt an irresistible desire to swing on it. Since there were obvious limits to his agility, Pauline and Lady Diana dissuaded him. The desire was contagious, and Duff Cooper could not resist it either. But he only managed to swing 'a very little, not like a monkey. He was playing safe, not as he did at the time of Munich.'[2]

Very different was a luncheon with General Catroux, the Governor General of Algeria, at the Villa Monfeld. The General had promised Pauline a *pièce de résistance* which consisted of a semolina-looking cereal. This was the prelude to a luxurious menu deplorably inappropriate in the circumstances of the time. Georges was depressed, and was glad to leave for a tour of the Casbah – the Moslem quarter of the city – under the guidance of a White Father. The houses were crowded but clean, and in thanking one of the occupants for a cup of tea Georges told her, in all sincerity, that he would rather be received by her there than in a palace by anyone else.

An invitation from Leclerc to visit him at his H.Q. at Temara, near Rabat, rescued the Vaniers from dinners that could be deadly even when they were delicious. Setting out by car, only a few days after Leclerc had left Algiers, they were received *en route* by Caid Bekkai, the Caid of Ougdo in Morocco, just over the Algerian border. He had been a Cadet student of Leclerc, and spoke freely of the mistakes the French had made in sending the wrong type of man to administer the country. 'If everyone sent to Morocco was like Leclerc, with a private life above suspicion and a deep religious faith, we should never have had the troubles we are having now.'[3] Pauline was the only woman present in a gathering of French officers, and they dined with all the ritual of a *diffa*, sitting round the table on cushions and talking till one o'clock in the morning.

2. Personal Notes, 25th March 1944.　　　3. Personal Notes, 19th March 1944.

The Vaniers reached Temara on the 4th of April and spent the next day visiting units of Leclerc's Division. Georges was deeply impressed by the discipline and grim determination of the troops and the excellent condition of armour and equipment. On advice from the French, the Vaniers kept away from the King; and also from the Gloui at Marrakesh, where they stayed at the Bahai – the Gloui's former palace – surrounded by a dozen courtyards. Fortunately it was Good Friday, and the Gloui respected Christian susceptibilities. Leclerc had no further news of his move, but when the Vaniers had returned from southern Morocco he had received orders to take his entire Division, with all its material, to England. On the night before he left, the Vaniers dined with him and Pléven in the private room of an hotel in Rabat, and then travelled with the 2nd Armoured Division to Oran. 'The dust was ghastly, but the excitement of being with the convoy made us forget the dust and the noise.'[4] In an interview with Pléven, when they got back to Algiers, Georges promised to do all he could to ensure that a second French Division was sent as well.

On the 4th of April, when Vanier was still with Leclerc, the French Committee published an Ordinance naming General de Gaulle as Chief of the Armed Forces and entrusting him with the supreme direction of the French military war effort. General Giraud had no previous intimation of this, although it had the effect of removing him from the stage, even if he remained in the wings as Inspector-General. He was reluctant to accept this purely honorific post and was surprised by an Ordinance on the 8th of April appointing him to it. For the second time a decision vitally affecting him had been taken without his knowledge. Finally, on the 15th of April, he read in a local newspaper that he had been placed on reserve and held no official appointment.

Both Churchill and Duff Cooper were anxious that Giraud should remain as Commander-in-Chief, because they believed that Washington would resent his removal, and that the morale of the French Army would be disturbed by it. In the event, how-ever, the passive attitude of the Americans seemed to indicate a conclusion that they had backed the wrong horse; and if, as some believed, de Lattre was responsible for Giraud's dismissal, the morale of the Army, which had great confidence in de Lattre, was not likely to be affected. Nothing, in fact, could equal de Lattre's confidence in himself. 'There are three Generals in the French Army' he had said 'de Gaulle, Giraud and Catroux, I am the com-

4. Pauline Vanier to the author, 8th November 1968.

mon denominator for all three, and I shall go even further.'
Georges Vanier had no very high opinion of Giraud, but he
deplored the way he had been treated. He went to the Palais d'Eté
to say Good-bye to him; congratulated him on the simple dignity
of his message to the Army; and said that history would take
account of it. To this Giraud replied – though without much bitter-
ness – that history had a way of arranging things to suit itself.
He said that good intentions were all very well, but that what
mattered was how they were carried out. Louis XI was quite
unscrupulous, yet he had done a great deal for France; Louis XVI
was an excellent family man, but he had led his country to
disaster. Giraud suggested an analogy with the present situation,
although he refrained from pointing it too precisely – perhaps for
fear of putting his own head upon the block.

The sequel to these shabby manoeuvres was a Press Conference
by General de Gaulle on the 28th of April in which he made it
clear that France would only accept a French Administration,
and that she would not accept a dictatorship either from her own
people or from anyone else. He regretted that the 'Government' –
a designation he now deliberately, and no doubt provocatively,
employed – had been unable to utilize General Giraud's experience
in an advisory capacity. He eulogized his military career and
promised that when Lorraine was liberated he should enter Metz
at the head of his army.

2

On the 25th of April Georges Vanier flew to Naples on a visit to
the French and Canadian troops engaged in the Italian campaign.
The Dakota was crowded and uncomfortable, with an American
Major-General chewing a big black cigar. On arrival Georges was
taken to his quarters at the Palazzo Prensa, and then driven round
the city and above it. Memories of his first visit to Italy in 1912
came thronging back, with stanzas from Keats and Shelley, as the
evening sun brought out the red and coral tints of the landscape.
He dined in the Canadian Mess and learnt something of the discontent of the troops because their mail was so irregular and their
compassionate leave so long delayed. On the 26th he went up to
the 1st Canadian Brigade, of which P. E. Bernatchez[5] was now
in command, and heard good reports of the Royal 22nd. The
regiment, which formed part of the 1st Canadian Division, had

5. Major-General P. E. Bernatchez.

fought its way up through Sicily and was now preparing its attack on the 'Hitler Line'. Georges had followed its exploits all through the campaign. At the beginning of the year a highly placed staff officer had written to him. 'You would be pleased if you could see the fine citations that we are preparing for several members of your old regiment.' He was as good as his word, for Major Triquet had been awarded the Victoria Cross. The regiment was in the valley of the Liri. This formed a natural corridor leading to Rome, dominated on both sides by steep mountains. The meadows of tall grass and the fields of maize gave the advantage of cover to the advancing troops. Georges Vanier described his visit in a letter to Tremblay:

The 24 hours I spent with our old regiment were for me a dream fulfilled. How I wish you had been with me, or even in my place, for the privilege was yours by right very much more than it was mine. I reached the regiment at about 5 o'clock in the evening. The wind was blowing, and a few drops of rain were falling after a day of torrential downpour. The mud reminded me of Flanders. The whole battalion gathered round me in a circle, and round the jeep from which I addressed them. I spoke of the old 22nd, and of the confidence we had in the 22nd of today which had already proved itself. I made a comparison between Triquet, Brillant and Keable. I told them (as I said so often in Quebec) that the French-Canadians at the front were not only soldiers, but the representatives of a people; that all eyes in Canada were fixed on them; that the French-Canadians were proudly counting on the 22nd to maintain our finest military traditions. No need to tell you that I was moved to tears.

I saw plenty of Bernatchez and Allard. Bernatchez, as you know, now commands the Brigade of which the 22nd forms a part. Allard is a splendid fellow and will, I am sure, prove a dynamic leader of the regiment. He is full of courage and initiative. It has really been a great chance for the 22nd to have Bernatchez and then Allard to command them. If you will allow me, I shall do them the honour of saying that they stand in the line of Tremblay.[6]

A slim volume of Georges Vanier's speeches – *Paroles de Guerre* – had recently been published. He had not seen the Preface and was annoyed by the editor's reference to himself: 'For many of my compatriots and for myself, Vanier and his companions are already legendary figures.' Georges told his former chief that the editor 'should have spoken of the 22nd and of yourself, General. Then he would have been speaking the truth.' Whenever Georges

6. May 1944.

thought of Tremblay, he saw behind him, in heraldic procession or recumbent effigy, the heroes of the past who were the exemplars of his own faith and soldiership. Tremblay had just been awarded the C.B. – 'twenty-five years too late'. He should have had the V.C. for Courcelette.

Three sons of former officers – Chassé, Dorval, and LaFlèche – were in the Mess that evening at the dinner given in honour of Georges Vanier's visit. The Menu card was illustrated with a maple leaf, and among the dishes were Potage Mediterranée and Poulet à la Triquet. The *pièce de résistance* was Tarte Vanier.

On the 2nd of May Georges flew back to Naples, and afterwards lunched with General Juin eight hundred yards from the front line and heard his views on politics and strategy. Neither the General nor anyone else had a good word to say for M. le Troquer, a judgment which conflicted sharply with Vanier's previous opinion. The following day Vanier lunched with Lieut-General Mason Macfarlane at Cescheto. An Italian General who was also there, regaled the company with amusing and somewhat scandalous stories of Turin society in 1920, with its club for men and their mistresses, and the lubricious dance at the Opera at which the ladies of the *beau monde* looked on from their boxes. In the morning of the 3rd of May Vanier called on Sir Noel Charles, British representative with the Badoglio Government. Charles was impressed with Badoglio's patriotic spirit and supported Allied Status for Italy. He warned Vanier of Churchill's hostility to Count Sforza,[7] who had returned to Italy as Minister for Foreign Affairs, and whom Vanier was to see later in the day. For Winston Churchill Sforza was 'like a red rag to a bull' – a fact of which the red rag was well aware.

Sforza received Vanier in his flat, centrally situated in Naples. With his closely clipped white beard, brown eyes, and hesitant speech, he seemed nevertheless mentally and physically alert. He had joined Badoglio's coalition Government because he believed that it represented the last chance of saving Italy from Communism. Personally he liked Togliatti,[8] the Communist leader, but if the Communists came to power he believed Togliatti would cheerfully have him shot. He thought that both King Victor Emmanuel and the Crown Prince were utterly discredited, although a Regency under the Crown Prince's son, aged six, might prove a solution for a country which had always been decen-

7. Count Carlo Sforza, 1872-1952.
8. Palmiro Togliatti, 1893-1964.

tralized in spirit and which should now be decentralized in fact. It was ridiculous to apply the same laws to the north where a girl became a woman at the age of sixteen and to the south where she matured at eleven. Sforza was emphatic in demanding Allied Status for Italy, since it was essential that he should be able to talk on equal terms with Anthony Eden. 'You will think me a conceited man for speaking in this way' he added; but Georges Vanier was by now too hardened a diplomat to agree with him.

He dined that evening on a moonlit terrace with Mason Macfarlane; and on the 5th of May he was received by Badoglio in a large room on the first floor of the City Hall at Salerno. The Marshal seemed remarkably fit for his seventy-three years. He reminded the Canadian Ambassador that he had signed an armistice with Mason Macfarlane at Brindisi, but at a subsequent meeting with Eisenhower in Malta he had been asked to agree to harsher terms. These had afterwards been modified, and he had declared war on Germany, although four fifths of the country was still under German rule. He had been urged to a greater war effort, but denied the arms and equipment that he needed for the 10,000 troops ready to go into battle. He did not mind very much whether Italy were described as an ally, or an associate, or a co-belligerent, so long as the existing situation was recognized as impossible – government without responsibility by the Allied Control Commission, responsibility without government for himself and his cabinet. Behind the Provisional Government of Italy and what was now calling itself the Provisional Government of France, the spectre of Communism loomed in warning or in welcome according to one's political sympathies. But even in this spring and summer of waiting and of crisis Georges had the power to abstract himself from politics. Young Lord Tweedsmuir remembered meeting him two months later, in the church of San Francesco at Assisi, and 'the look of beatitude on his face as he looked at the frescoes: and for a time we all forgot the war that we were fighting in the Italian hills.'[9]

On the 9th of May, just after Vanier's return to Algiers, his Air Attaché, Wing-Commander Jean-Paul Desloges, who had come through the Battle of Britain with the loss of an eye, was killed taking off from Casablanca where he had gone with Maurice Forget and the other Military Attachés on an official tour. The body was brought back to Algiers, and during the Requiem Mass General Rignot pinned the Cross of the Legion of Honour on the

9. Letter to Pauline Vanier, 9th March 1967.

Canadian ensign draped over the coffin. Desloges was buried in the British cemetery at Dely-Ibrahim, only a few kilometres from the Villa Simian where he had been living. His death was a great loss to the Vaniers and to the Legation staff.

If one link with Canada had been severed, others were strengthened when arrangements were made for the first exchange of seriously wounded prisoners of war from the two combatant sides. The Swedish ship *Gripsholm*, carrying Germans and Italians in this category, stopped briefly at Algiers, and then some weeks later returned carrying Canadian and other seriously wounded allied prisoners. Saul Rae who, with Maurice Forget, was responsible for planning which affected other Heads of Mission in Algiers, records how Georges Vanier's generally strict observance of protocol could be remarkably relaxed when it was a question of greeting his fellow-countrymen:

As the great morning approached, General Vanier's impatience to meet with the returning Canadians and other Allied prisoners of war, and to be of immediate help to them, outweighed his observance of the carefully constructed A.F.H.Q. planning. In the middle of the night, Maurice Forget and I were wakened by a fully-dressed General Vanier who said: 'Let's go now and see if we can board the *Gripsholm before* it gets to the port.' We hurriedly dressed, and drove the odd ten miles to Algiers, where Maurice, with his inimitable capacity for improvisation, managed to commandeer a small but very inadequate motor boat for our impromptu voyage. After what seemed ages, and in a fairly heavy sea, we made our way out in pitch darkness to the port towards where we thought lay the *Gripsholm*, still some distance from Algiers. After half an hour of pitching and tossing, the *Gripsholm* officers were extremely surprised to see a 'landing party' so far ahead of schedule. As we swayed in our tiny craft by the side of the huge ship, a rope ladder was tossed down from a great height above. 'Up you go', cried General Vanier, and I made my precarious way up the rope ladder. With only the Algerian boatman, our Head of Mission, and Maurice left, we wondered how the General would deal with the problem of mounting the rope ladder in a heavy sea. A Swedish voice from above said: 'Throw a rope around the old guy', and this is indeed what happened. The General half climbed and was half pulled up the rope ladder to the ship's entry, and was, therefore, the first diplomat by several hours to meet, and to welcome, the returning Allied forces prisoners of war on board.

On this occasion, Protocol was put firmly in its place. But, as an old soldier, General Vanier was not to be denied.[10]

10. Letter to the author from Saul Rae: November 1968.

The Americans on board had all received a decoration, and since no similar arrangement had been made for Commonwealth citizens Vanier regretted that the ceremony had not been postponed until the Americans landed in the United States. Among the Canadians was Lionel Massey,[11] whose fine character had evidently been tempered by adversity, 'I do not mean by this that it was not fine before, only that it is a hundredfold finer now.'[12]

There were enemies nearer at hand than the Germans in Italy and France. On the 12th of May Georges noted:

At about 11 o'clock the sound of beating on metal came to me from the fields together with many other strange noises including hand clapping and shouting. I was told that swarms of locusts had arrived and the natives were trying to keep them in flight so that they would not lay their eggs on the property.

These efforts were only partially successful, for a month later Pauline was writing to her family:

Do you remember my telling you about the locusts and their eggs? And I also told you that we had destroyed the crickets as they hatched and that we didn't fear their invasion any more! Alas! The neighbours were not able to destroy theirs so now we are having an invasion such as I could never have imagined. They arrived by the billions yesterday and these little black hopping monsters are everywhere and eating everything that they come across. They are even eating the leaves on all the shrubbery and we are told that they most probably will eat the leaves on the trees as they crawl up the trees. . . . the ground is black with them and there is nothing one can do but watch; they have dug trenches and put up zinc metal sheets up here and there to try and divert the march and then when they get some billions of them massed together they burn them. But alas! that can only be done in some places and yet there are over billions. There is a great chance that all the crops that were left and vines will be destroyed and that will mean a near famine in this part of the world.[13]

Among the numerous officials in Algiers there was even a 'Locusts Liaison Officer', whose services were desperately engaged. But the garden of the Villa Simian had other, and more welcome, guests:

The swallows are growing bigger and fatter . . . This morning I witnessed the following scene which I cannot explain. Looking up at the nest I saw five little heads waiting patiently for food, then sud-

11. 1917-1965.
12. Personal Notes, 20th May 1944.   13. 10th June 1944.

denly, all beginning to tremble with excitement, mother's voice having been heard, I imagine, in the distance, a swallow (unidentified) then flew under the portico towards the nest closely followed by another swallow (unidentified but presumably one of the parents) which fell upon the first swallow preventing it from approaching the nest. The five little swallows looking over the edge of the nest were silent and I assume terrified but they had very good ring-side seats for the fight which was of five rounds. The swallows pecked at one another and broke away five times, then flew off.

At times, quite often in fact, between meals (which appear to be almost a continuous performance), one or two swallows turn inwards and push their tail and wings over the side of the nest spreading and stretching wings and tail. After some encouragement from the parents, one of the little swallows parachutes out of the nest, flutters its wings and flies a very short way before resting. Returning to the nest is not so easy but with the help of fond but very agitated parents, little swallow is finally deposited head first in the nest where he wiggles about until he gets his tail down and his head up. The birds have been growing so rapidly that when the five of them are together it is a pretty tight squeeze and sometimes one can see more of the bodies above the nest.[14]

The little swallows are growing in size and wisdom. They now leave the nest for a short solo flight under the guidance of the more experienced parent pilots. For the first time, I saw the nest completely empty and wondered if they would come back. By sunset in fact, quite an hour before sunset, the five returned to the fold. The nest is so crowded now that I doubt very much whether mother and father can sleep in. They may have found a billet nearby. I am not sure whether the little ones sleep heads or tails inwards. I did notice however one night when it was growing quite dark that five little tails were showing over the edge of the nest instead of heads.[15]

Last night was the first night that the young swallows left the parental home. I am a little afraid that we may have frightened them on the terrace before dinner but perhaps the reason was over-crowding in the nest due to the increased size of the birds or perhaps to the spirit of adventure and independence newly born.[16]

Towards evening a high wind sprung up which sent the young swallows scurrying back to the shelter of the portico but instead of going to the now too small nest, they perched and huddled together on the top of a round metal electric light shade. I think they must have spent the night there because as the shades were falling they held together motionless like one large flat bird.[17]

14. Personal Notes, 23rd May 1944.
15. Ibid, 25th May 1944.
16. Ibid 28th May 1944.
17. Ibid, 29th May 1944.

If the first duty of a diplomat is to keep his eyes, as well as his ears, open, Georges Vanier had no reason to fear comparison with anyone.

3

On the 3rd of June, after a conversation extending far into the night, de Gaulle agreed to accompany Duff Cooper to London where important discussions were in progress. He was unwilling to leave unless he were assured that the Americans would also take part in them. Duff Cooper persuaded him that it would be very difficult for the Americans to remain aloof, and de Gaulle, although the date of 'D' Day had been kept from him, realized that it could not be long delayed. Every night the planes were flying from Algiers with arms for the *maquis*. He also would have greater facilities for speaking to French troops, and, through the services of the BBC, to people in France. Churchill sent his private plane, in which he left with Duff Cooper during the afternoon.

At 10.15 a.m. on the 6th of June Elisabeth de Miribel brought word that she had heard the voice of Eisenhower announce the news of the Normandy landings. In the evening Claudius Petit and other *résistants* came up to the Villa. They listened to de Gaulle and rose from their chairs at the sound of the 'Marseillaise'. On the following evening there was light relief at a dinner with Admiral Cunningham,[18] Naval C-in-C., who occupied one of the must beautiful villas in Algiers. The Admiral persuaded Georges to try some Spanish brandy, of which he had long been a connoisseur. When the Vaniers boasted about the value of cold baths, he said that he considered them 'an affront to the body'. No one could be in Cunningham's presence for five minutes without realizing that he stood high in the line of great fighting seamen; but another party, in those first anxious weeks after 'D' Day, struck a discordant note. Tables were set out under an enormous tree and some Yugoslav singers had been brought in to entertain the company:

Lights were turned off during singing and gave way to the sight, if not the light, of the stars. In terms of art the evening was a great success, but it was out of joint and very pre-war, certainly not war and *most* certainly not post-war, at least in France.[19]

18. Admiral of the Fleet Viscount Cunningham of Hyndhope, 1883-1963.
19. Personal Notes, 20th June 1944.

Many of the guests were about to return there by parachute, and some of them left the table because they could not stand the false gaiety of a well-intentioned but untimely *fête champêtre*. Pauline Vanier left with them.

Meanwhile the discussions in London were proceeding badly. The text of Eisenhower's 'D' Day broadcast had remained unchanged in spite of de Gaulle's objections; and de Gaulle had also forbidden his civil affairs officers to act in the wake of the Normandy campaign, because their responsibilities had not been clearly defined. There was additional conflict over the currency issued to the Allied soldiers landing in France. These *contretemps* only increased the division of opinion among the French Committee over the wisdom of de Gaulle's visit to London. Roosevelt was still adamant in refusing to recognize the Committee as the Provisional Government, and the Algiers Radio was forbidden to refer to it as such, even when quoting from its own documents. The Canadian Government favoured entrusting the Committee with the administration of French territory, but declined to authorize Vanier to communicate this opinion to the French. Such action, it believed, would only be helpful if it assisted an agreement between the Committee and the United States. Georges held his tongue, but stuck to his opinion. 'If we have a view, I believe we should express it.'[20] The Duff Coopers were dining at the Villa Simian on the 13th of June, and Lady Diana asked the company to guess whom the Prime Minister had invited to meet de Gaulle at Downing Street. Pauline guessed the answer: 'General Smuts', and Georges noted: 'What a crazy world.'[21] It was even thought that the Allies might prevent de Gaulle from visiting Normandy, but this fear had been disproved; and Georges noted again in a lapidary phrase: 'Il y a des événements qui dépassent tout, y comprises les mauvaises intentions, si vraiment elles existent.'[22]

On his return to Algiers de Gaulle received Vanier in a room with all the windows closed and heavy with cigar smoke. He was in good spirits, although he did not share Anthony Eden's optimism about an agreement with the United States over administration in France. There was now question of a visit to America and Vanier advised him to go, with or without the desired assurances. Once there, the President would find it hard to limit the

20. Personal Notes, 10th June 1944.
21. Ibid.
22. Ibid.

discussions to an exchange of courtesies. If he did not go, his refusal might be misinterpreted. This proved excellent advice. Vanier was anxious for the Canadian Government to send the General a separate invitation, but it was thought that this would be contrasted with the guarded and cautious invitation from the United States and might do more harm than good. Churchill and Roosevelt would be more likely to move on their own initiative than in response to public or diplomatic pressure. Once again, Georges Vanier disagreed:

I think that the way in which we have been approached regarding a possible visit of General de Gaulle to Canada is the greatest compliment that could be paid to this Mission. General de Gaulle and his entourage are taking for granted that the Government will be delighted to extend an invitation to him. Although very much touched by this mark of friendship and confidence, I am frankly ashamed of the situation. . . . It is all very sad. It would have been so easy to extend to General de Gaulle a contingent invitation at once instead of waiting to have the invitation wormed out of us in this way. I haven't seen any press reports from Canada but I assume that the Canadian Press as a whole will be exerting pressure on the Prime Minister to invite the General. It will look, therefore, as if the Government's hand had been forced by public opinion.[23]

On the 27th of June de Gaulle dined at the Villa Simian – 'very sympathetic under a cold exterior. It is sometimes disconcerting how jealously he conceals his sensibility.'[24] On the same day Georges had lunched with Robert Murphy, U.S. Representative on the Advisory Council for Italy, to whose Irish charm he was not insensitive. Murphy agreed that the General should go to Washington, but remarked how sad it was that out of forty million Frenchmen it should be de Gaulle with whom the Allies had to deal.

I thought he was rather guarded in conversation, perhaps he has been reading my recent broadcasts and knows that I am an out and out Gaullist. He apparently does not realize that every Frenchman, when the war is over, will be proud of the man who, at the very start, predicted and preached the rebirth of France. It is not de Gaulle as such in whom I am interested but de Gaulle (and he might be called Dupont or Smith or anything else) as a symbol of Resistance to all the weak corrupt and sinister elements in France that welcomed what they considered order (another word for protection for their vested interests) under Government domination, fearing communism

23. Personal Notes, 30th June 1944.
24. Ibid, 27th June 1944.

more than the loss of liberty. In other words, they were seeking and talking about honour in dishonour.[25]

General de Gaulle's visit to America and Canada was a remarkable success, and he returned with President Roosevelt's spontaneous recognition of the French Committee as the *de facto* Government of liberated France. Roosevelt, having obstinately opposed any such recognition, had thus stolen a march on the United Kingdom – not altogether to the satisfaction of His Majesty's Government. Duff Cooper thought the President had been clever; Georges Vanier thought he had been too clever. De Gaulle was not sorry to take note of the British discomfiture. In a long interview with Vanier after his return he contrasted Roosevelt's generous welcome with Churchill's 'deplorable' treatment of him during his recent visit to London. He was not likely to forget that he had been received in company with General Smuts, or that Smuts had accompanied Churchill on his visit to the Normandy front without his knowledge. Before leaving for Algiers he had written the Prime Minister a friendly letter to which Churchill had sent a reply that, in Churchill's own interest, had better not be published. It was inexcusable that at the 14th of July celebrations in Beirut no British officer had been present.

President Roosevelt had also stolen a march on the Canadians. Early in August Mackenzie King suggested to Churchill that to accept the title of Provisional Government which the French Committee had bestowed upon themselves would have a helpful psychological effect. On hearing of this, Vanier noted tartly:

Of course it would, but why didn't they think of it before? De Gaulle does not care now what recognition, if any, we give to his Committee or Provisional Government. Of course, some time ago when he couldn't be sure of the reception which he would receive in France, an intelligent gesture on our part would have been welcome and helpful. Ever since I came to Algiers I have been endeavouring to prove to the Department that the only reasonable course for us to follow was to acknowledge the Committee as the future and later 'de facto' administrator in France after Liberation.[26]

4

On the 1st of July Georges received an urgent message that the Royal 22nd, having fought their way up through Sicily and Calabria, and played a vital part in breaking the Hitler line, were

25. Personal Notes, 27th June 1944.
26. Ibid, 6th August 1944.

to be received in audience by Pius XII on the 3rd of July. It was greatly desired that Vanier should be present, and a priority plane was placed at his disposal. 'So another one of my dreams has come true,' he noted. 'To see Rome and the Pope, but I never could have hoped for the joy of being received by the Pope at the same time as the old 22nd.'[27] The regiment, under the command of Lieut-Colonel Allard,[28] travelled a hundred miles in convoy, arriving on the evening of the 2nd of July at Pantano, a village eight miles from Rome. Georges Vanier had reached the city on the same day. At 8.30 a.m. on the morning of the 3rd of July, the 'Van Doos', escorted by the band of the 1st Canadian Division, were driven into Rome and marched on to the Piazza of St Peter shortly before 9 o'clock. Here they were joined by twenty-five wounded officers and men who had made the journey from their hospital at Caserta, Allard handed over command of the troops to an officer of the Swiss Guard, stationed in front of the bronze doors of the Basilica, who led them to the Sala Clementina. Here Georges Vanier and Brigadier P. E. Bernatchez, who had only lately relinquished command of the Royal 22nd, were waiting to join them. At 9.30 the Pope, accompanied by his suite, came in; and after kneeling to receive his blessing, the regiment acclaimed the Pontiff with three loud cries of 'Vive le Pape!' The Pope smiled. It was the first time since 1869 that French-Canadian troops had knelt before the Supreme Pontiff; and Allard himself was the godson of a Canadian *zouave*, who had defended the Papal States against the troops of Garibaldi. More was at stake in the present conflict than the Papal States, although it was neither the time nor the place to voice such indelicate comparisons.

After the Pope had spoken with his habitual authority and charm the regiment attended Mass in the Basilica. This was celebrated in the Chapel of St Peter's Chair, and almost everyone received Holy Communion. When they had formed up again on the square Georges spotted a jeep onto which he climbed to address the men whom he could not help still regarding as his brothers-in-arms. Many of them bore names familiar from the first World War – Tremblay, DesRosiers, and Asselin. Henri Chassé was acting as his A.D.C. The regiment then marched through the streets of Rome to the Casa Madre dei Mutilati where Georges inspected them.

Among those invited to luncheon was a Nursing Sister, the

27. Personal Notes, 1st July 1944.
28. Lieut-General Jean Victor Allard.

young widow of an officer of the regiment who had recently died of wounds in Sicily. She had been asked to represent the wives of all those who had lost their lives during the campaign. When Georges heard that she had been baptized a Catholic only three months before, he said 'May we talk together after lunch?' and led her to a private sitting-room. 'There I learnt of his gift of drawing souls to himself. By his kind and courtly manner. By his simplicity, yet his profundity. By his great integrity. . . . One does not often see Christ in a general or in a statesman. But I saw Him in General Vanier.'[29]

When the troops had dispersed Georges wandered, with the gluttony of a tourist, over the city which he had not seen for nearly forty years. The view from the Pincio and the grassy slopes of the Palatine; the catacombs of St Calixtus and the abandoned tombs along the Appian Way; the Forum and the Colosseum; Santa Maria degli Angeli and the restored purity of Santa Sabina; the Janiculum where the Zouaves had fought for Pio Nono – one by one, the perspectives of history, sacred and secular, were opened out before him. It was a beautiful day, and the pavements were crowded with onlookers. In the evening the officers of the regiment gave a dinner in his honour at the Hotel Alberto Lago Maggiore on the Via Cavour.

Before returning to Algiers Vanier had a long private audience with Pius XII. The Pope was concerned about the religious situation in France. Aware, no doubt, of Georges' close relations with certain members of the Resistance as well as with the French National Committee, he asked for his opinion. Vanier suggested that a number of the Bishops had collaborated a little too openly with Vichy 'You mean with Laval?' asked the Pope; but no, Vanier meant with Pétain. He said that the conduct of the lower clergy had been admirable, but that the situation might be serious if there were no changes in the French episcopate. The Pope asked for certain details and names, but Georges did not feel competent to give them. In answering his questions he had in mind the Memorandum from a young French Jesuit, Père Ganne, who had recently come to Algiers. Père Ganne had worked with the Resistance, and his suggestions for the future of the French Hierarchy were pretty drastic. He did not believe in calling quits to collaboration, open or implicit, but in the event only five Bishops resigned from their sees. It was perhaps significant that shortly after his audience with Georges Vanier the Pope requested the

29 Letter from Helen Cannon to Pauline Vanier, 7th March 1967.

French Episcopate to give spiritual assistance to the *maquis*.

On the 13th of July the Vaniers were the guests of General and Madame de Lattre at Douera, some twenty kilometres from Algiers, where the General had organized his famous 'Cadres de l'Armée'. This was a centre of rigorous training for the officers, N.C.Os and men. The officers slept, breakfasted and lunched separately, but all ranks dined together. The purpose was to break down distinctions of rank and class, and to form soldiers who infused their spirit of hardiness and initiative into the units to which they belonged. The atmosphere and methods were similar to those one might have expected to find in a Nazi or Soviet training-camp, except that the Tricolour presided over them. De Lattre had, in fact, been greatly impressed by the Russian officers he had met in Paris before the outbreak of war, describing them as a cross between 'St Cyriens and seminarists'. This was as much as to say that they were both efficient and chaste; when it was suggested that they should amuse themselves on Montmartre, they replied that they had better things to do. De Lattre showed no consideration for his men, but was adored by them none the less. This devotion was in contrast to the criticism of many officers in those branches of the Army not under his immediate control. Whereas in other training camps the severity of the course was progressive, here the cadets were put to the most daunting tests from the day of their arrival. Once again, Vanier was struck by the contradictions in de Lattre's impulsive temperament. Hard as nails, he could yet be charming when he wished, and he had a keen sense of the beautiful. This was as evident in the decoration of the living quarters at Douera as it had been at the Centres d'Accueil in Lorraine. On the other hand he was capable of extraordinary coarseness. At the luncheon following the inspection of the school he told stories and used language more appropriate to a barrack-room than a table at which an unmarried woman was among the guests. Neither the ladies nor the gentlemen were amused, and when the meal was over de Lattre apologized to Pauline – as she, no doubt, had apologized to him on a previous occasion at Chéragas when the cook was drunk and in a fit of temper had put his fist through the window pane.

Their next meeting took place a fortnight later on the eve of de Lattre's departure for Italy. The Vaniers had invited him to dinner and found him unusually subdued. He was perhaps aware of the criticism he had incurred by having General Juin transferred from the Italian front to a Staff appointment and replaced by General Béthouard. Juin had led his troops extremely well, and some of them had wept when he was removed. But de Lattre's vendetta was implacable. Vanier wondered if his outbursts were a deliberate exercise in histrionics; otherwise disturbing conclusions might be drawn from them. When Vanier observed that as head of the Army invading France from the south his responsibility would be very great, since circumstances might arise in which the Army would have to impose its will on the people, de Lattre looked up uneasily and remarked: 'Oh! I shall stick to my rôle as a soldier.' The manner of his reaction convinced Vanier that he was not immune from political ambition; and although he regarded de Lattre as one of the two or three most interesting men he had ever met, he feared that *hubris* and vanity would be his undoing. In this case, death was indeed the leveller, and before very long de Lattre was released from his command by a higher authority than General de Gaulle. He was at the same time released from his temptations.

While the armies were fighting their way towards Paris, the world was still lagging behind events. The Canadian Radio had devoted a transmission on its overseas service to a eulogy of Anatole France, and even in Algiers the Alliance Française had devoted an entire number of its bulletin to a consideration of his work. In his conversations with educated Frenchmen, Georges learnt that Valéry and Claudel, Proust and Giraudoux, Barrès and Péguy were the authors *à la mode*. The ironical scepticism of Anatole France was regarded as 'dissolvant'. If there were a single type of man, in Vanier's opinion, upon whom the reconstruction of France should not be taken in hand, it was Anatole France. 'He does no credit to his name, and in any case it is not his own.'[30]

At the same time Godbout was defeated by Duplessis in the Provincial Elections in Quebec. The first reports announced a victory for the extreme nationalists of the Bloc Populaire, and Vanier feared that this would have compromised, and possibly ruined, the future of French Canada. Duplessis, on the other hand, though a little unstable, was not reputed for his hatred of the English. Georges liked and admired Godbout, but he foresaw no disastrous consequences from his defeat.

As the clear, blue days succeeded one another, and at night the planes flew in a continuous stream on their errand to the *maquis*, Georges Vanier contrasted the serene sunsets with the struggle for victory in France. 'One would think that all is peace

30. Personal Notes, 9th August 1944.

in the world and in the heart of man, whereas we are standing
on the threshold of the greatest social revolution which has ever
taken place in the history of the world.'[31] On the 11th of August
de Gaulle informed the Vaniers that Leclerc and his division had
been in Normandy for several days; and on the 14th a message
from Leclerc came over the radio : 'simple and direct, and all the
more moving, the clear reflection of his personality.'[32] De Gaulle
and most of his Commissioners – rightly pessimistic about the
retention of their jobs – left Algiers towards the end of the month.
On the 15th Leclerc entered Alençon, swinging his famous cane;
and on the 19th the last Mass for the Resistance was celebrated in
the chapel of St Elisabeth. On the 26th the German garrison in
Paris surrendered to Leclerc. 'Philippe enters into the history of
France. So long as France is France, children will be taught
that the German commandant in Paris surrendered to General
Leclerc.'[33] That evening Georges and Pauline were invited to
dinner at the Resistance H.Q., 18 rue Daguerre; and Georges confided the following prophecy to his diary :

The French Committee and the Consultative Assembly as at present
constituted will play a negligible, if any, part in the future government of France. The government will centre round and take its
inspiration from General de Gaulle who will endeavour to give his
country a Republican Government based on the essential principles
of democracy; namely liberty, equality and fraternity, with the addition of authority, an element sometimes lacking in democracies, particularly in time of peace. The General knows his France too well to
attempt dictatorship. He will surround himself with Ministers who
have the confidence of the people. Few of the present commissioners
will survive many months.[34]

The Vaniers, with the Duff Coopers, prepared to leave by air on
the 2nd of September, stopping off for dinner at the British
Consulate-General in Rabat. For the last time they watched the
sun go down over the unruffled waters of the bay, and felt as they
had felt six months before :

The sun retained its sharp spherical definition on the horizon as it
slipped below. . . . Two and a half minutes elapsed between the
moment when the lower edge of the sun touched the horizon and
the moment when it disappeared, leaving in its trail a brilliant red

31. Personal Notes, 11th August 1944.
32. Ibid, 14th August 1944.
33. Ibid, 26th August 1944.
34. 26th August 1944.

glow. . . . We (there were five of us) amidst the beauty and serenity looked at one another and felt uneasy. I believe we were all think-ing of the millions of people suffering on the other side of the Mediterranean.[35]

The eight months Georges Vanier had spent in Algiers would always compose a rich mosaic of memories – beautiful, dramatic, disconcerting and occasionally trivial. The temperament of de Lattre and the intransigence of de Gaulle, the driving faith of Elisabeth de Miribel, the steady support of Duff Cooper, the parties and the palavers and the protocol, were all lightened by pictures which remained in the mind's eye. Lady Diana's straw hat bought at a native bazaar; a long dissertation on the art of stalking and killing mosquitoes, which helped to keep one's mental balance on a sweltering August night; the goldfish that died in the pool at the Villa Simian; the monkey at the Hotel du Ruisseau des Singes, with the face of an old woman and a head no bigger than a tennis ball; the beetles that David Rockefeller always dis-covered at the Villa when he came to dinner, and one of which, believing it to be a sacred insect, he had mounted and sent back to the United States; and the burly black sentry, complete with rifle and steel helmet, whom Georges found lying very com-fortably on an iron post, silhouetted against the clouds, and a big black cigar between his lips.

35. Personal Notes, 19th March 1944.

CHAPTER 16

AFTER THE LIBERATION

I

THE Vaniers spent a few days at the Connaught Hotel before returning to Paris. Massigli suggested that the security situation in France was far from good, since many Germans were still in hiding, and that Georges had better return alone. Georges was not afraid of many things, but he was mortally afraid of passing on this suggestion to Pauline. 'You try to stop her,' he replied, 'I can't.' Eisenhower's British Political Advisor thought it would be wiser for her to go in uniform, if she went at all – but then the question arose, in what uniform? If she disguised herself as a C.W.A.C.,[1] she would be committing a serious military offence. The solution – which occurred to Pauline, but to no one else – was to don a Red Cross uniform, although it was difficult to find one that fitted. Pauline Vanier was a beautiful woman, but she was not exactly standard size. Eventually a uniform was shamelessly purloined from a Red Cross worker on leave, taken in, and lengthened. No doubt the explanation for its disappearance was the same explanation that Georges Vanier and Tremblay had sent to Ottawa in 1916: 'destroyed by enemy action.' It would not have been quite implausible, since the V1s and the V2s were still falling on London and proving a trial to British nerves. Pauline, aided and abetted by General Basil Price, appointed herself Canadian Red Cross representative in France and held the title until Red Cross activities ceased. It was a justified and remarkably successful usurpation.

The Vaniers arrived at Le Bourget aerodrome in a Dakota, escorted by two Canadian Spitfires, on the 8th of September. They were met by representatives of General de Gaulle and Massigli, and by Saul Rae and Forget, who had some difficulty in recovering the Citroën which they had lent to Lord Tedder – a previous arrival – in time to convey their own Ambassador into the city. The traces of battle were still evident in the streets – barricades, enemy cars overturned, abandoned tanks, the pockmarks of bullets and hand-grenades on the walls. Rooms had been reserved

1. Canadian Woman's Army Corps.

at the Ritz, depressingly pre-war in aspect and clientèle. Georges entertained the crew of the plane to champagne on their arrival, and then went down to dinner. Always a moderate drinker, he had drunk enough; and when the waiter refused service unless he ordered some wine, he walked out of the hotel, white with anger, and moved to the Westminster in the rue de la Paix. Later they settled in to the more intimate Vendôme in the rue Castiglione, where their apartment became a popular place of rendezvous for British, Canadians, and French. It was here that Père Maydieu, the irresistible Dominican, brought Edmond Michelet,[2] freshly released from his concentration camp at Dachau. Georges Vanier had secured his release through Caffery, the U.S. Ambassador, and Leclerc whose Division was then billeted near Dachau. Michelet came direct from the airport to the Vendôme, in his thin cotton garb of a deportee, to thank the General for his efforts. Peter Scarlett,[3] Head of Chancery at the British Embassy, would recall 'those weird post-liberation days in Paris when your quarters at the Vendôme were such a wonderful haven for so many young people. Night after night we came and there you both were, always welcoming, always interested in our tales (and Lord knows some of them gained in the telling) and after an hour or so we would say Good-night and return to our own quarters feeling warmed and somehow reassured.'[4]

The days were weird indeed, with their mingled tension and euphoria. There was the relief of finding old friends alive and unharmed – Charles and Elisabeth Flory, and Réquin looking very much older. Pauline had known Flory since Armistice Day 1918, when she lost her voice shouting: 'Vive la Paix' and 'Vive la France' in the streets of Montreal – the day when Georges woke up from the anaesthetic thinking he was in France because the guns were booming. During the worst stress of the occupation Elisabeth had written: 'I am sure that you will come back, and that you will come back by the Arc de Triomphe.' Now, on the morrow of the Liberation, Charles brought Bidault to dinner at the Vendôme, and described Georges as 'calm, erect, and smiling; seeming to say to us: "Here I am, and with me all the fidelity of Canada which has never questioned the greatness or the honour of France, even through the darkest days".' Elisabeth Flory was

2. Subsequently Minister for Veterans' Affairs in the Cabinet of President de Gaulle.
3. Sir Peter Scarlett.
4. Letter to Pauline Vanier, 9th March 1967.

the daughter of Maurice Blondel, the eminent philosopher of Aix-en-Provence; and when Georges was visiting Aix a little later on, a courier from the Canadian Embassy arrived with the diplomatic bag. This contained, among other things, several pounds of coffee. Georges at once handed them over to Blondel, who had been advised to drink coffee by his cardiologist, at a time when coffee was practically unprocurable. The Florys liked to refer to this as 'the first miracle of Georges Philias Vanier'.

Georges was prompt to call upon Thérèse Martin, the daughter of his old professor; and when he rang the bell of Claudius Petit's apartment a small boy opened the door. 'Bonjour Dominique' said the Canadian Ambassador, and Dominique had no idea who the strange gentleman was or how he knew his name. The Liberation meant a great deal for Dominique Petit because now his father would be at home, and his mother would not be frightened when there was a ring at the bell. And it meant something, too, for a young Canadian who had scrawled up the following inscription which caught the eye of the Ambassador when he visited the prison at Fresnes:

F/O John D. Harvie,
J 27573
R.C.A.F.
Prisoner here July 14/44 – Aug 10/44
God Save the King
Long live the Allies!
Oh to be in Canada!

But Flying Officer Harvie had been in prison for only four weeks; the French people had been in prison for four years.

On the 8th of September Thérèse arrived in beret and battle-dress from Normandy, and this time Pauline was in luck with her jewels – some friends had kept them safe all through the occupation. Yet she wrote to Mrs Archer that she would not have exchanged the emotion of those days for all the gold in the world. Outwardly, Paris had changed very little. The women and the shop windows were as elegant as ever, although the latest fashion in hats was rather hysterical. Inwardly, it was changing very fast, for there was a new social and political order in the making; and the sun shone with a gentle constant warmth, as if to moderate the drama of its birth.

But the *union sacrée* of resistance within France and beyond its shores was already showing signs of falling apart, and the *épuration* was well, and often ruthlessly, under way. By the 5th of September, 3,500 collaborators had been arrested; most of the senior officials of the police and Prefectures had been changed; and the chiefs of the French Gestapo, Borny and Lafont, had been caught. The Prefect and Chief of Police at Montpelier were condemned to death, and eight other Vichy officials were executed six hours after receiving their sentence. At Grenoble ten members of Darnand's *milice* – all of them between sixteen and twenty-six years old – were sentenced. Six were condemned to death, two to hard labour for life, and two to five years' hard labour. The death sentences were carried out immediately. Darnand himself was arrested and shot shortly afterwards. In many places women who had collaborated – often by sexual relations with the Germans – had their heads shaved; and in the remoter parts of the country, particularly in the south-west, the French Forces of the Interior, strengthened by suspiciously recent recruits, were busy paying off old scores without benefit of judge or jury, and refusing to lay down their arms.

In this situation Georges Vanier was privileged in his friendship with Pierre-Henri Teitgen, the Garde des Sceaux. Teitgen would take him, incognito, to various centres of resistance where the local militants were at odds with a Government that was trying to establish its *de facto* authority, and introduce him as his own *chef de cabinet*. Many persons under suspicion came to the Legation – which now had its offices at the Roger Gallet building on the rue du Faubourg St Honoré – wanting visas to get to Canada, or trusting to the benevolent impartiality of its Ambassador. Georges would take their names and forward them to Teitgen, who would advise according to the gravity of the charges likely to be brought against them. To some he would say: 'Go into hiding if you can'; to some: 'Give yourself up and you'll only get three months'; for others he could do nothing. There was no other envoy in Paris within miles of receiving this degree of confidence from a member of the French Government.

The problem of the higher clergy and their collaboration or connivance with Vichy was also disquieting. Among the bishops only Saliège of Toulouse and Théas of Montaubon had actively encouraged resistance. Conversations with Mgr Chevrot, the *curé* of St François Xavier – a man of balanced judgment and proved courage – confirmed that almost all the parish priests in the country, and many of those in Paris, had set an admirable example to the prelates who should have been setting an example to them. Nevertheless, the situation remained tense and troubled. Where one Archbishop – presumably Saliège – had described the last episcopal declaration as 'une manifestation éminente de la peur', the Archbishop of Aix-en-Provence forbade listening in to foreign broadcasts under pain of mortal sin. Fortunately it was not long before Aix-en-Provence had a new Archbishop. Moreover fissures were now opening between the Resistance and certain elements in the Provisional Government, Algiers was described as a 'basket of crabs', where the 'fossils' of the Third Republic had ventured to raise their heads. The impudent opportunism of the Communist leaders, and the subterranean machinations of the Masonic Lodges, were not calculated to enlighten Frenchmen of goodwill. Little by little, and almost imperceptibly, the cry went up – Joan of Arc was being burnt once more. Like Joan of Arc, the *résistants* were the madmen, the *illuminés*; like her, they were wanting in good sense; like her they were 'compromising' everything when everything was not going so badly; they were the 'rebels' and the 'anarchists'; and like the Maid they were act-ing against the 'national interest'. General de Gaulle was the last person to countenance the appropriation of a national heroine whom he regarded as his own property; but he was compelled to tread warily in this autumn of political discontent.

Massigli had been appointed Ambassador to the Court of St James and Bidault had succeeded him as Minister for Foreign Affairs. When Georges Vanier called upon Bidault on the 11th of September he seemed a very tired man, possibly on the verge of a nervous breakdown. The present writer recalls a conversation, just about that time, with a man who was to occupy, twenty years later, an important post in the cabinet of President de Gaulle. He said that it was necessary, for the health of French society, that blood should flow – as if enough blood had not flowed already. Many people felt the same way. But Bidault believed that the French wanted a revolution through process of law and not by insurrection. They would insist upon removing the abuse of property by the two hundred families, who had not been conspicuous for their resistance to the German occupation; on the abolition of corrupt political practices; and on bold measures of social reform. He did not believe that the Com-munists – despite their immediate and merited prestige – would attempt to seize power, or would be successful in doing so. He explained to Vanier the insurrection which had preceded the liberation of Paris. The order for this had only been given after the Parisians themselves had taken up arms, and the police had raised the tricolour over public buildings. It was quite untrue that the rising was ordered to forestall a Communist *coup d'état*.

Bidault had been President of the Conseil de la Résistance, and like most of the other men in de Gaulle's Government was a new face in politics. He was still sleeping in a servant's attic on the sixth floor, without any light, and he was finding it very difficult to lead a normal life. To ride in a chauffeur-driven car filled him with horror. Senator Jenneney, however, on whom Vanier called a few days later, had been President of the Senate in 1939, and had presided over the National Assembly at Vichy in 1940. He had protested firmly against the Vichy regime, and seen his country home burnt to the ground by the Gestapo in consequence. He was now well over eighty years of age, but physically and mentally well preserved. He had a high regard for de Gaulle, although he remembered riding in the same car with Clemenceau on the 14th of July 1919, and the crowd of cheering admirers as they drove across the Pont de la Concorde. Six months later Clemenceau was rejected for the Presidency of the Republic. On the 28th of September, the centenary of Clemenceau's birth was celebrated with a tricoloured scarf entwined about his statue in the Champs Elysèes. Jenneney was not in favour of a radically new constitution, and opposed to votes for women. His was the voice of the old guard – adamant, however, for the defence of ancient liberties.

The Vaniers were anxious to meet the men of the Resistance of whom they had heard so much, and shortly after their return they drove out to the Usine Gardy, a factory for electric appliances at Argenteuil. This had been a F.F.I. headquarters and the strained look on the men's faces was more noticeable here than elsewhere. Their nervous and jerky movements betrayed the tension under which they had lived for so long. They were bitter about the big industrialists who had not scrupled to manufacture small parts for secret weapons, and about the profiteers of the black market. They told of the false parachutists – Germans disguised as baled-out airmen, who then reported on those who were coming to help them. The Vaniers shook hands with them all and thanked them – to which they answered quietly that they had only done what they had to do, and that it had not been difficult.

Another visit was to the Gestapo torture chamber at Issy-les-Molineaux. Here the walls were of soft asbestos to take the imprint of human hands. The Germans had heated the floor so that the prisoners, demented with pain, had leaped against the walls in a hopeless effort to escape and left the marks of their frustration.

The French working-classes, for all their solidarity, did not have a monopoly of courage. Late one September afternoon the Vaniers drove up to the Château de Tailly, where Thérèse de Hauteclocque, alone with her children, had defied the Germans during her long vigil. One day when she was imprisoned in the *mairie*, the assembled population of two villages brought her flowers, and compelled the Germans to put a cordon of troops round the place and eventually to release her. She told their messenger: 'My husband enjoined me three years ago never to bow the head. Tell your commander that, no matter what happens, we shall carry out his instruction to the letter.' It was not far from Tailly to Belloy, where Philippe Leclerc's parents – the father over eighty and the mother not much younger – had their home. The old man was Mayor of the village, and he boasted that no one under his jurisdiction had been deported to Germany, and that not even a horse had been taken from the inhabitants. Three weeks later Leclerc, his wife and their two young children were dining with the Vaniers in Paris. 'Philippe,' Pauline noted, 'was a little sad this evening; it's hard for them to meet again and then to separate immediately.'[5]

For Georges Vanier all this country of the Beauvaisis and the Amienois held poignant memories; the towers of Amiens as he had seen them framed against the sunset as he lay on the grass before moving forward to the big attack; Notre Dame de Lorette with its 36,000 dead where he had spoken so eloquently of the 'high places of France'; and Vimy Ridge with its massive memorial to the Canadian dead, which Georges cared for 'less and less as the years go by' because he did not like 'the association of monument and studio sculptures'.[6]

If Vimy recalled the Canadian sacrifice in the first World War, Dieppe held the same hallowed and tragic associations for the second. The raid, in 1942, had been a costly rehearsal, but if miscalculations had been made lessons had also been learnt, and others would profit by them. The Vaniers went up there on the 5th of October, not a little annoyed to find an American car and American chauffeur provided for their transport. Georges – his

5. Letter to Mrs Archer, 19th October 1944.
6. Personal Notes, 23rd September 1944.

Irish blood-pressure mounting a few degrees – declared that he would not leave until he was assured that a Canadian car would be waiting in Dieppe to take him to the official ceremonies. They saw the place of the landings, and placed a wreath in the cemetery at Hautot-sur-Mer, where hundreds of Canadians lay buried. They also went along the coast to Varengeville, and had tea with M. and Mme. Pellouart with whom they had lodged during the summer of 1939. Five years ago – and although Leclerc had liberated Strasbourg, the war was not over yet.

Towards the end of November the Vaniers went up into Belgium and Holland where Harry Crerar was in command of the First Canadian Army. In Breda they were put up in a caravan, which looked like a Pullman car. It had been built for the Germans with kitchenette, living-room, and bedroom. Crerar declined to use it himself, but kept it for V.I.Ps. Georges found him in agreement with much informed military opinion that if Montgomery had been left as Eisenhower's Commander in the field, the war might already have been over. On the following day Vanier, with Maurice Forget and an A.D.C., drove on through the sparse woods to Wischen, where Lieut-General Simonds, commanding the 2nd Canadian Corps, received them. The front had been stabilized beyond Nimegen, where the parachutists dropped at Arnhem had failed to link up with the main forces, and Nimegen itself was obscured with smoke to impede visibility. The Dutch civilians were carrying on stolidly only a few miles from the enemy lines. On the return journey they watched a V2 being launched in the dusk – a long trail of smoke with a light showing for something like a minute. Georges met all the Battalion and most of the Company Commanders in the French-speaking Brigades, but with the units in the line under enemy observation, he was not able to talk to the other ranks.

Before returning to Paris the party was taken to the Vught Concentration Camp, which provided them with ghastly evidence of German cruelty and sadism. The gallows were still standing, about twenty-five yards from the crematorium. The victims had been made to stand on irregularly shaped blocks of wood with their hands tied behind their backs. They balanced themselves until they fell over and were hanged by strangulation. All the time the crematorium was before their eyes, and it was reported that some 14,000 bodies were burnt there.

In Paris the diplomatic situation was not easy owing to the Allied delay in recognizing the Provisional Government. Duff

Cooper – who on the 5th of October had not yet been received by de Gaulle – suggested to the Foreign Office that even if the British Government intended to give recognition as soon as the Consultative Assembly was reconstituted, it would be wiser not to communicate this intention to the French, since it would appear as if the British were laying down conditions. Churchill's declaration to this effect was later to infuriate them, and probably explained why the General received Vanier – on the 10th of October – before the British Ambassador. The meeting was extremely cordial. De Gaulle obviously bore Canada no grudge in respect of non-recognition, placing responsibility for this solely on Britain and the United States. There was a question of Cardinal Villeneuve coming to Paris in the course of a visit to the Canadian troops, but the General had declined to receive him – presumably because the Cardinal was proposing to stay at the Archbishop's Palace. Vanier passed on to the Cardinal a message from Bidault to the effect that it would be wiser if he confined his visit to the Army. However, General de Gaulle now agreed to receive him if he came to Paris, and no conditions were laid down as to where he should stay.

General Eisenhower, who had to deal with civil as well as military matters, was urging President Roosevelt to give immediate recognition, but Admiral Leahy[7] who had been so close to the elbow of Marshal Pétain, was now just as close to Mr Roosevelt's. The President, whose judgment in dealing with his own people rarely faltered, was losing his grip on European realities; and it was not until the 23rd of October that the Ambassadors of the principal Allies drove to the Quai d'Orsay and announced the recognition by their respective Governments of a fact that was as plain as daylight. There was only one phrase in the American and Canadian notes to which General de Gaulle took exception. He contended that from the very moment of its arrival in metropolitan France the Provisional Government had exercised full sovereignty over the liberated territory and that there could be no question of transferring responsibility. The Canadian Government disclaimed any wish to suggest that the Supreme Allied Commander had ever exercised any sovereignty in France; only that in certain parts of the liberated territory he had a temporary responsibility for administration.

Three days later Vanier dined with de Gaulle. The General was vexed by Roosevelt's statement that France would not

7. Fleet Admiral William D. Leahy, 1875-1959.

immediately participate in world security conversations, and doubted whether he really favoured recognition of the French Government in spite of his reluctant agreement to it. He was particularly annoyed because France had been excluded from the attempt to solve the *impasse* between the Soviet Union and Poland. The General spoke in high terms of Duff Cooper and was anxious to correct any impression that the delay in receiving him was due to personal dislike. This was a time when the French were quick to read between the lines of any statement. Churchill had told the House of Commons that the French could not be excluded from Allied conversations on the matter of Germany and the Rhine, and here Teitgen reacted sharply to the implication that they might be excluded from the settlement of other international problems. As for the Provisional Government, if it were not supported by the people, a thousand determined men in Paris could overthrow it.

The 1st of November was celebrated as a day of mourning for the heroes and victims of the Resistance. Immense crowds greeted de Gaulle at Mont Valérien and the Château de Vincennes. His lips were trembling as the band struck up the 'Marseillaise'; the words had suddenly acquired a tragic and sublime relevance. As he shook hands with the Corps Diplomatique, Georges Vanier observed to him that the men and women they were commemorating were 'the light which is guiding us'. Later in the day, Georges tried to explain to himself why this man, who was in some ways the antithesis of what a Frenchman is commonly imagined to be, had so evident a hold upon the people of France. He was addressing himself, as he wrote, to his Canadian compatriots:

I could give many reasons, I've given many reasons but today, I shall give you only one and a new one. After he had deposited a wreath to the memory of the 75,000 Frenchmen and women shot and murdered, he spoke to those men, women and children who have the honour of counting their dear ones among these dead. And they listened to him eagerly and bravely, stretched out hands to meet his; and I say that when the men and the women and the children of those who were shot and died for France stretch out their hands to General de Gaulle, I know that he has the confidence and the love of the people of France. The thousands of people who had friends shot, lined the streets leading to the Château de Vincennes. The people who are building France and who will continue to build it are those who have mothers, fathers, children, brothers, sisters and friends among the 75,000 shot and the 2,400,000 prisoners, forced labour people and political deportees in Germany. I know and I feel that they all accept de Gaulle. Does any one of you, my compatriots in Canada, require another reason?[8]

Both Duff Cooper and Georges Vanier were doing their best to persuade Churchill to come over to Paris and drive down the Champs Elyseés with General de Gaulle. Lady Diana was exercising her charm to the same end. The great man got so far as admitting that even if General de Gaulle was a beast, he was at least 'a big beast'. Some people might have said the same thing about Winston Churchill; big beastliness is generally the mark of high statesmanship. At last he agreed to come, although the Cabinet – prompted by Beaverbrook[9] who had no liking for the French – phoned Duff Cooper in a last minute attempt to have the visit postponed. Duff Cooper was firm, and Churchill, accompanied by his wife, his daughter Mary, and Anthony Eden, arrived on the evening of the 10th of November; were met by de Gaulle; and stayed at the Quai D'Orsay. The next morning the Vaniers were in the tribune on the Champs Elyseés for the march past. Georges' mind went back to the 11th of November 1939, when President Lebrun took the salute from an army that was thought to be invincible. For Churchill, as he stood there beside the man who had so inconveniently redeemed the honour of France, the occasion was a deeply moving one, and his lips were seen to be trembling as he laid his wreath under the Arc de Triomphe and received the acclamations of the crowd. De Gaulle gave a luncheon afterwards at the Ministry of War, and went so far in his tribute to Churchill that someone else said that he would have been furious if anyone else had dared to speak as he had done. The only discordant note was the click of M. Jenneney's knife and fork against his plate during the General's opening remarks. He was not going to be done out of his fruit, although everyone else had politely laid aside their cutlery!

Pauline Vanier had her own memories of the visit, because on the 12th of November she found herself sitting next to Churchill both for luncheon at the Quai d'Orsay and for dinner at the British Embassy. At the beginning of lunch the Prime Minister was a little grumpy, and Duff Cooper, seeing this, advised her not to worry: 'He will warm up after a glass of wine and all will be well.' Churchill assumed that the woman on his left must be the

8. Personal Notes.
9. Lord Beaverbrook, 1879-1964.

wife of a Communist Minister because she was wearing a scarlet
frock – 'the colours of her party'. Pauline replied that, on the
contrary, she was the wife of M. Teitgen, who was a good
Catholic. The Prime Minister laughed and thanked her for the
information. So the conversation turned on the realism of
Churchill's conduct of the war – 'the people of England have
never wanted anything else but the truth'; on the cabinet crisis
in Canada, the Prime Minister showing himself critical of
McNaughton and appreciative of Mackenzie King; on the punishment of war crimes – justice without brutality; on the welcome
he had received from the crowds and his insistence on standing
up in the car so that they could see him; on the Allied debt to
America and his hatred of Communism. In the evening he entered
the room with a broad grin because the *Tirpitz* had just been
sunk. After dinner he took out an enormous cigar from an individual box, which he had some difficulty in putting back in his
pocket. Pauline was quick on her cue. 'Give it to me, Mr Prime
Minister,' she said. 'I will keep it.' 'You don't want that, do you?'
he returned, making a face. 'Yes, I do,' she persisted. 'I am a
souvenir hunter.' Laughing heartily, he then handed it over.

The next day, the 13th of November, the Canadian Legation was
formally raised to an Embassy, with a reciprocal arrangement in
Ottawa; and on the 22nd Georges Vanier was formally nominated
to a rank which up to then had been only personal. With Saul
Rae as Political Counsellor and Yves Lamontagne to look after
Economics – both of whom had been with him in Algiers –
Georges had colleagues who were also friends. His secretary was
a young French girl of twenty-one. She had spent two years in the
Resistance; one of her brothers had been arrested in April; and
her parents, with her other brother, were in Germany. She knew
nothing of their fate or whereabouts. Like other secretaries, before and afterwards, she found Georges 'assez exigeant'. He was
not inconsiderate, only patiently perfectionist on paper. Indeed
Pauline was often called in to type his letters and despatches.
Saul Rae describes what it was like to work with him in a subordinate capacity:

General Vanier knew what he wanted at all times, and was a shrewd
judge of men. My own experience was that on much of the administrative, political and economic work in which we were engaged, he
shared the responsibility with the members of the staff. Once confidence was established it became a binding force, and even as a

younger officer I felt that much depended on my own judgment. But as Head of Mission he never hesitated to exercise his responsibilities, to express his own views, or to correct impressions which a draft despatch or report might have otherwise left with which he was not fully in agreement.

On matters like administration, accounts, protocol, and mess arrangements, he was a stickler for detail, and one of his favourite phrases was: 'Les bons comptes font de bons amis.' His methodical habits of mind led the General to plan matters – even of detail – far ahead, and he was seldom caught out because of lack of foresight. To younger and more impetuous men this might have seemed rather unnecessary, and even fussy; it proved itself, however, an enormous asset, whether on the occasion of a formal dinner for General de Gaulle, or when some visiting celebrity – such as Lady Diana Cooper – or others came to call. Such occasions always went off with just the touch the General was seeking. And always at such times his own private sense of humour and informality would break through and would turn a formal occasion into an event which everyone present would remember for months and even years afterwards.[10]

Not everyone, however, found him easy to work with, for the very human reason that he liked some people better than others, and when he disliked anybody he was ashamed of his dislike. This created an obstacle to easy collaboration, and it also created difficulties for External Affairs. If they asked for a confidential report on an official, they had to read between the lines of what the Ambassador wrote about him to discover what he really thought. When he learned that a report had inexcusably been shown to the person in question, he was not encouraged to be more explicit. A particularly valued colleague was Charles Ritchie,[11] and Georges was much put out by a report in Time that 'in Paris General Vanier was a barking general' because, according to Ritchie, he had exclaimed 'Press the button, Charles' in a 'barking voice' while hurrying to the lift! According to Time, Ritchie had replied 'I'm not mechanically minded'; but Georges commented, many years later, in recalling the incident to Lady Diana Cooper: 'He never said this and I don't think I barked very much, but he was sad that some people might believe he had spoken to his boss that way.'[12]

On the 20th of December the Ambassador presented his Letters of Credence at the Ministère de la Guerre where, in 1939, he had

10. To the Author, 12th November 1968.
11. Now (1968) Canadian High Commissioner in London.
12. 8th December 1959.

presented them to Daladier. There, at least, was a fossil who had
not reappeared. On the same day Jacques Maritain, Charles Flory
and Elisabeth de Miribel came to luncheon. Flory had spent some
time at the Vatican, and it was partly due to his influence that
the Papal Nuncio was returning to Rome, to be replaced by Mgr
Roncalli. Maritain had just arived from America and was suc-
ceeding Wladimir d'Ormesson as French Ambassador to the Holy
See. A week earlier Georges had seen Cardinal Tisserant, who was
opposed to a change of Nuncio and also to the displacement of
Suhard. Maritain and Flory were both agreed that some changes
in the episcopate were required, and Flory suggested that Suhard
might be transferred to another post without undue scandal.
Fortunately for the hopes of spiritual renewal in France which
Flory and Maritain – and Georges Vanier for the matter of that –
ardently cherished, Suhard was left at his post. The Cardinal became a real friend of the Vaniers and often came to the Embassy
on private visits. Georges met the retiring Nuncio, Valerio Valeri,
on the eve of his departure. He was able to bring him comforting
news from Lille where the Vaniers had been staying with Louis
Closon, the newly appointed Commissioner of the Republic and
an intrepid *résistant*, whom they had known in London and
Algiers. Here, in a Préfecture which might have belonged to a
wealthy banker out of a novel by Paul Bourget, Cardinal Liénart
had been asked to luncheon – and Liénart, formerly known as the
'Red' Cardinal, had more recently disappointed his admirers. At
a Press Conference, Georges had replied tactfully to various
questions. Were the Canadians Pétinistes? France could do with
Canadian beefsteaks; when would they be available?

During the same visit to the northern Departments the Vaniers
were welcomed at the Trappist Monastery of Mont des Cats where
Georges had spent the first days of his recovery from shell shock
in 1916. One war was very like another on territory which was
an invitation to the march and clash of armies. In a single exhaust-
ing day they had seen Calais and Boulogne and Cassel – with
official receptions everywhere – and the apocalyptic devastation
of Le Pontel, a small fishing village near Boulogne, where not one
of the 1,800 houses was still standing. Nevertheless the Préfet of
the *Nord* was presently writing to Pauline:

Perhaps, in the course of your stay in the *Nord*, you felt that you had
already seen, in some village near Quebec, that expression or smile on
the face of a child, or that window prettily decorated with geraniums,
which greeted you as you went through our countryside.

A week later they were at Lisieux and Caen. Both cities were
a heap of ruins, except for the great churches proudly intact.
They drove to the Fleury quarries where thousands of people had
lived for weeks, sheltering from the hail of Allied bombs, and
where subterranean passages led down to the banks of the Orne.

There were also visits to the Atlantic front where pockets of
the enemy were still holding out against the *maquis*, now reinforced by regular troops under General de Larminat, and presently
to be further reinforced by men of the Leclerc Division. In the
hospitals there were neither shirts nor pyjamas for the wounded,
and in one there were not even sheets. Many of the *maquisards*
had fought in cotton trousers or shorts, and some had only sandals.
Others were on guard up a tree without even a steel helmet.
Pauline brought soap, chocolate and medicaments.

The conclusion of the Franco-Soviet Treaty in December
caused the Canadian Government some disquiet. Bidault assured
Vanier that its intention was to allay Russian suspicions of the
West. When this had been done, the French would pursue agreement with their more natural allies in the search for collective
security. They preferred bilateral to tripartite pacts because they
they were easier to work. The Russians were exacting their *quid
pro quo* – which was French recognition of the Lublin Committee, to which de Gaulle had agreed to send a delegate. Bidault
had seen some members of the Committee, and had no doubt
that they were Communist agents. But if the Lublin Committee
was impossible, the London Poles were exasperating. It was time
they understood that two and two made four.

Christmas was a muted festivity with Pauline in bed with a
split rib – the result of a motor accident in Brussels – Jock in
England, and Thérèse, albeit in Paris, confined to barracks –
though not for disciplinary reasons! The Germans had para-
chuted a number of men in the Forêt de St-Germain in the hope
of kidnapping General Eisenhower – hence a state of considerable
emergency. On the 28th of December, however, the Vaniers
attended a moving occasion at the Théâtre de Paris on Montmartre, where 2,500 children between the ages of eighteen months
and thirteen years were assembled. Their parents had all been
shot by the Germans in France or deported to Germany; many
had undoubtedly died there. The Vaniers looked down from an
upper stage box on the white, peaked faces, smiling and laughing;
and on the faces of the older children, more serious, whose
thoughts were elsewhere.

A letter from two children, whom the Vaniers had invited to a party, gives the measure of the sympathy which their embassy to Paris had evoked:

Dear Ambassador:
We are Marie-Christine and Patrick, the little children that you have seen and to whom you have given many good things. I do not know if you remember us, because there were many children, but you probably remember Patrick that you had seen on the last Thursday at another Christmas tree. Marie-Christine has had a lovely little wooden train in which I shall go to Berlin to fetch my daddy. Patrick has had a little horse. But the most pleasant for us were the crackers and cakes; in France we have very seldom candies and cakes and chocolate because Boches have eaten everything. You were very kind to invite us in your beautiful house, we also invite you in our little house, but I think you are very busy to make the war against Boches and kill them. If you have time enough, come and I shall be very pleased.

Our sister helps us to write in English; we go to school and we learn to write, but we do not learn to speak English. We shall learn when we shall be older. We tell you thank you very much and we kiss you very strong.[13]

2

In the New Year Georges was away from Paris a good deal, with official receptions at Dijon, Lyon and Marseilles. He also visited de Lattre in Alsace where there had been heavy fighting around Colmar between the Vosges and the Rhine. The three Allied Governments had invited France to assume responsibility for a zone of occupation in Germany and Austria, and Vanier hoped that she would be associated with the suggested action and procedure on liberated Europe. She was, however, excluded from the Conference at Yalta in February, and was not advised of its proceedings until an account of these was handed to de Gaulle by the Allied Ambassadors – a gesture of information which was interpreted as a gesture of appeasement. A majority of Ministers, including Bidault, favoured de Gaulle's acceptance of Roosevelt's invitation to meet him in Algiers, but the General was adamant and Georges Vanier supported his refusal. More than pride and protocol was here at stake. The General had twice invited the President to France, and had he gone to Algiers he would have gone trotting in by the back door in the footsteps of the Emperor of Ethiopia, the King of Egypt, and the King of Arabia. The front

13. 1st January 1945.

door was at Yalta, and this had been closed to him. De Gaulle also declined to be an inviting Power to the San Francisco Conference, since the modification he had proposed in the form of the invitation had not been accepted by the Soviet Government. Vanier took a serious view of this abstention.

In a personal interview with the Ambassador on the 13th of March the General claimed that France should be in occupation of Germany from Cologne to the Swiss frontier – a large claim which was not subsequently allowed. If Stalin wanted his postwar defences on the Oder, de Gaulle wanted his on the Rhine. He agreed with the Canadian view that countries which could make a substantial contribution to world security should enjoy a privileged position. But since France was not a party to the decisions of Yalta, it was better that she should not be an inviting Power to San Francisco. Later in the month Vanier was in London for an audience with the King. He found Massigli much disturbed by the likely effect of de Gaulle's policy of 'greatness' on the French people. They had stood a good deal: could they stand any more? M. Luizet, the Paris Prefect of Police, had suggested that what France needed was the creation of a civic sense, and that this might take ten years. When Vanier suggested that it might take a generation, M. Luizet did not demur. Municipal elections were held in France early in May. The Communists made considerable gains in the urban centres, winning twenty-seven out of the ninety seats in Paris where they had previously held only eight. The Socialists lost slightly, and the Radical Socialists very heavily indeed. The M.R.P. made a good showing, and the results indicated that there were few Vichy sympathisers. These kept their mouths shut for the time being, but when Pétain came up for trial they would open them. Unfortunately there is no record of Vanier's view of the trial, at which he was not present. It may not have been very different from Thérèse's, who was not present at it either – 'almost nauseating in its lack of dignity and *mesquinerie*.' For there were few matters on which father and daughter did not think alike. A note of sadness creeps into a letter to Mrs Archer:

I am trying to explain to myself the disappointment we have all felt in finding this France, which we had so idealized, less perfect spiritually than we had hoped.[14]

On a visit to Chitenay Pauline was astonished to find a vital

14. 9th February 1945.

letter from Byngsie surviving amid the rubbish the Germans had left; and Jock celebrated the ending of the war in Europe with a chapter of accidents that did no particular credit to the Royal Navy. He was staying with a friend at Worcester College, Oxford; spent the afternoon in a punt and fell in the Isis up to his waist; lost his Dartmouth cap to a man in the crowd avid for a souvenir; climbed into the College over a wall; and returned to London the next morning with his friend's sports coat over his trousers, since he could not appear in uniform without a cap. In June Byngsie passed out first at Brockville Officers Training Centre and was flexing his muscles for the war against Japan; and Thérèse confessed herself not reluctant to see what the Allied bombs had done to Germany. Bernard, spending the summer at Cap à l'Aigle with Mrs Archer, for whom genealogy was a form of romanticism, sometimes wished he could discover among his Salaberry forebears a *chevalier* not quite *sans reproche* :

I have been listening to many accounts of our noble ancestors, he wrote to Byngsie. With trembling lip and eager eye, I have heard these exploits – hoping against hope to find somewhere, somewhere, some sort of a black sheep – I heard of these brave, virtuous, strong and subtle ancestors, each one better than the last, praying that we will come to a black sheep – however grey he may be – somewhere along the way. At last – success – some relative of ours was caught trying to steal a corpse from a graveyard. He fled hotly pursued, finally landing up over the border, never to be heard of again.[15]

In August the Vaniers moved into an apartment belonging to François de Menthon in the Place des Etats Unis. It had a big hall, dining-room, large sitting-room, and study for Pauline. It was here – astonishingly and no doubt metaphorically – that Georges had seen 'Thérèse kick Generals in the pants' – a gesture that did nothing to impede her rapid promotion. Two soldiers from the Royal 22nd did domestic duty, and were thought to be the cause of the cooks leaving, since they stopped them stealing. At about the same time the Chancery of the Embassy was established at 72 Avenue Foch. This was a large building, with a heavy, nineteenth century elegance; an entrance to one side; and a raised terrace with steps leading down into the narrow garden with its stone vases and conventional statuary. A laurel hedge separated the garden from the sidewalk, which was in turn separated from the main thoroughfare by a grass verge.

15. 13th August 1945.

In April, when the Allied armies were already far into Germany, Georges Vanier paid a visit to Buchenwald Concentration Camp. He wished to discover the fate of three Canadians who had been interned there; Frank Pickersgill from Winnipeg, John Mac-Alister from Guelph, and Guy Sabourin from Montreal. They had arrived at the camp on the 27th of August 1944, and been executed about three weeks later. Vanier spoke with an Austrian who knew them well; he said that their morale was excellent and their courage indomitable to the end. A fourth Canadian, Joseph Demers from St Romuald in the Province of Quebec, had died of hunger in the same camp. He was a veteran of World War I and had settled at Ramillies in Belgium, afterwards joining the Resistance of which he became a leader in his own community. He worked for eighteen months, helping Canadian and British airmen back to England. He was arrested in November 1941; placed in solitary confinement; and later transferred to Buchenwald.

Georges was moved to tears and indignation by what he had seen and heard. He broadcast an account of it to Canada, and Gladstone Murray, Director of the CBC, wrote of the speech that it was 'superbly drafted, perfectly delivered. A very deep impression was made on public opinion here.'[16] It was through these occasional broadcasts from overseas that Georges Vanier's name was kept, albeit intermittently, before the Canadian public. Even so, he must have been surprised to learn that his name was being put forward as the next Governor General to follow the Earl of Athlone. The idea was supposed to be in line with the new radical policy of Mackenzie King; the alacrity with which Canada enters a European war in the wake of Great Britain is generally followed by the determination to assert its autonomy. 'I for one am not at all sure that the rumour is not correct' wrote Robertson Fleet, 'and if it is perhaps you should brush up your Canada.'[17] He had an opportunity of doing so when de Gaulle visited Ottawa in August. It was an impressive muster of the Gaullist fidèles: Elisabeth de Miribel, Burin des Roziers, Palewski, and Juin, now Chief of Staff for National Defence – and there, immutably, at Government House was Willis O'Connor in attendance on the Athlones. In a subsequent letter de Gaulle was alert to recognize his debt to Georges Vanier:

I am not forgetting that from the very first day you were the faithful

16. 3rd May 1945.
17. 20th February 1945.

friend of the Free French and the evident defender of their cause. Every fresh proof that France gives of her vitality is a homage to your clear-sightedness.[18]

Nations relapse quickly from war into politics, and while he was 'brushing up' his Canada Georges could judge for himself the truth of Tremblay's diagnosis:

The saviours of the race are numerous and compete with their exaggerated declarations and promises. I am told that in certain quarters they no longer believe in the acts of barbarism committed by the Germans. The blindness of these people is on a level with their prejudices.[19]

On the 8th of July the French Cabinet agreed to call for the election of a Constituent Assembly, but the people would be asked to decide by referendum whether its duration should be limited to six months; whether its powers should be restricted to the study and modification of the constitution; and whether the Assembly at its first session should elect a Head of Government who, with his Ministers, would exercise legislative and executive powers for the lifetime of the Assembly. Vanier was pretty accurate in his forecast that eighty per cent of the voters would agree to these limitations. As the autumn drew on, however, the tension – always latent – between the Communist and the other members of the Government became acute. The Communists demanded that one of the three portfolios – Foreign Affairs, Interior or War – should be given to their party. De Gaulle refused and on the 16th of November had decided to resign. Vanier believed, rightly, that before the Assembly met two days later, a solution would be found; he also believed, again rightly, that this crisis was only the prelude to many others. Meanwhile de Gaulle broadcast to the nation, putting forward his candidature for re-election by the Assembly as Head of the French Government. Hitherto his election had been spontaneous; now he stepped down into the arena. He was quite prepared to be rejected, and on the 20th of November he told Vanier that he would like to go to Canada as a private citizen and rest there, very much as Churchill, after his rejection by the British electorate, was to come to France. The Canadian Government, while regretting any development which would lead de Gaulle to abandon his post, was perfectly prepared to welcome him.

18. 6th November 1945.
19. 14th May 1945.

In fact, the Assembly confirmed his mandate, the Communists being not yet sufficiently sure of their ground. He saw Vanier again on the 24th of November and explained their volte-face. The Communists were not able to count on all their followers, many of whom were not revolutionary at all; and they had failed to dislocate the Socialist party. He admitted that the Communists had not tried to foment trouble in the social and economic fields, and he reserved his contempt for the Socialists. If they had supported him in the first instance, the crisis would not have arisen. It was the problem of Soviet Russia, rather than the manoeuvres of the French Communist Party, that haunted him. Barriers must be set up beyond which Soviet Russia must not be allowed to go. He did not believe that Soviet Russia would make war, if the United States took a determined stand. General de Gaulle was not forgetting Yalta, and many other people would not forget it either.

The breathing space was short-lived. In January 1946 de Gaulle resigned, ostensibly over Army credits. Old Louis Marin, the Conservative from Lorraine, had advised him to fight it out. 'Get yourself defeated and they'll be calling you back within a fortnight.' The General replied that he had a better solution. He had told Marin that he would not enter politics at all unless he could be an arbiter above parties, and now he was disenchanted with politics – and particularly with parties. Was he already looking beyond resignation to the Rassemblement du Peuple Français? In any event, Marin told Vanier that he did not believe the General would return to power, unless there was an international or a major national crisis. In this prediction he was correct. But de Gaulle had merely retired – he had not disappeared – and for many years, from the solitude of Colombey-les-Deux-Eglises, his long shadow would continue to brood over the landscape. For many years, too, his destiny and that of Georges Vanier would be significantly intertwined; and on the 21st of January Vanier wrote him the following letter in his own hand:

At the moment when you are leaving the Presidency of the Provisional Government, I wish to make known to you the deep sadness that this separation is causing me, my admiration for the work you have accomplished, and my faith in the future.

I thank you for the benevolent sympathy you have always shown me.

I understand your decision, but I know that your mission is not at an end. France will not be able to do without you.

You can always count on my entire devotion and – if you will
allow me to say so – my loyal friendship.

I shall continue to pray for you and for France.

Saul Rae had prepared a despatch on the General's resignation,
and the events leading up to it, to which Vanier added a prophetic
postscript: '. . . and yet he will return.'

CHAPTER 17

THE FOURTH REPUBLIC

I

THE Vaniers soon acquired a residence – 5 rue Dosne – which was adequate, though no more, for the needs of diplomatic hospitality. It stood in a small street a few yards from the bustle of the Avenue Victor Hugo. Steps from the long narrow salon led to the dining-room where french windows opened on to a terrace; and the house was ready for the family as, one by one they returned from Canada. Michel, with his Nurse, and Bernard arrived in October 1945, followed by Mrs Archer early in the New Year. She stayed for a few weeks at the rue Dosne, and then moved to the Hotel Royal Monceau where she lived until her death in 1969. His parents had not seen Michel for three years and they knew that he would not recognize them; a rather spoiling grandmother was all he had known of parental care and affection. The moment came when he was alone with Georges in the car. Suddenly he turned his head, looked at his father thoughtfully, and said: 'You know, we're friends, aren't we?' It was the best way of being father and son. Very soon after entering France, Michel entered French literature. Mrs Archer – writing under her maiden name of Thérèse de Salaberry – received a medal from the Académie Française for her novel, *Michel aux yeux d'étoiles*. This was described as the story of 'a little child awaking to life under the eyes of a refined and tender grandmother.' Once again alone with his father – this time at breakfast – Michel declared that he would be either 'a soldier, an artist, or a Trappist.' Baudelaire, in establishing the hierarchy of human vocations, had said much the same thing – but it was not a thing that Michel could have been expected to know.

Byngsie joined the others in January 1946, and was writing to his grandmother from Chitenay:

We always think of you in a beautiful French garden, surrounded by lovely flowers of every colour, but above all extremely delicate. It was not without emotion – indeed it was rather like a dream – when we entered through the iron gates of the house which was our last *pied-à-terre* in France. We are now in the same rooms that we occupied in 1940. Nothing has changed – the same roses and orange-trees. It's the first Friday in May, and the same *curé* celebrated Mass . . . the church is still rather damp and you need to put on a thick coat.

Byngsie had been to Germany with Murray Ballantyne, and realized the responsibilities of victory, but his intentions were fixed elsewhere. It had been clear for some time that he had a vocation for the religious life, and it would have seemed natural for him to join the Jesuits with whose methods of education and spirituality he was already familiar. But to his parents' astonishment he expressed a wish – more exactly, perhaps, a determination – to try his vocation with the Trappists. For them, as for him, it was the hardest decision he could have made. They accepted it, not without difficulty, but without demur. When they broke the news to André Malraux, the great agnostic of the Absolute buried his head in his hands and then exclaimed: 'I understand – if one loves, one has to give everything.' They, too, understood – and for the same reason.

Mackenzie King, in response to Vanier's strong persuasions, came over for the Peace Conference which was held in Paris later in 1946. Staying, as usual, at the Crillon, he had expressed the wish to sleep in the bed where President Wilson had slept, and Georges exercised all his diplomatic finesse to evict the wealthy American lady who was in occupation of the suite. He served himself on the Canadian Delegation with Brooks Claxton[1] (Minister of National Defence), Norman Robertson, Arnold Heaney, General Pope, and Charles Ritchie. Formal treaties with Italy and the Balkan States were drawn up and signed. Among the other delegates was Jan Masaryk, whom Vanier had known and liked in London, and beside whom he found himself sitting at a luncheon given by the Czech Ambassador for the Canadian Prime Minister. 'You see that man further down the table' said Masaryk. 'He's a Communist and, mark my word, one day he's going to get me.' Shortly afterwards Masaryk was found dead in the court-yard, and the man disappeared. Diplomacy uncovered many chinks in the Iron Curtain, if one was alert to look through them. Georges Vanier also accompanied his Prime Minister to Dieppe and Caen. Mackenzie King had very little French and he therefore spoke very lengthily in English on these official occasions. Then Georges offered to translate what he had said, and the

---

1. The Hon. Brooks Claxton, 1898-1960.

audiences were surprised that the speech was so much shorter in French than in English. They did not realize that it was not the same speech. 'As the Prime Minister has told you' Georges would begin, and then continue with a felicitous speech of his own, embroidering on the well-worn themes of the historic links between Normandy and Canada, and finding some new and moving phrase for the Canadian sacrifice at Dieppe. It may be doubted whether Mackenzie King realized the extent of the Ambassador's departure from the Prime Ministerial text. In any case this did nothing to lessen his affection and admiration for Georges Vanier. The flowers which Pauline assiduously left at the Crillon to greet him on arrival, or the parcel of wine that Georges sent to the train as he was leaving, were acknowledged in handwritten letters almost effusive in their gratitude and charm. As we have seen, Georges could not forget Mackenzie King's part in the constitutional crisis of 1926, but he appreciated his services to Canada. In June 1946 King was entering upon his twentieth year as Prime Minister, and Georges wrote to him as follows:

It is no secret that Sir Wilfrid Laurier wished his mantle to fall upon your shoulders, and whenever I think of you I think of him as well. You have had to face during the war the very problems Sir Wilfrid foresaw. If he were here he would say you sought and found the solution in his message of faith and love.

Had you not succeeded, I believe that Canada might have gone through a period of disruption, the effects of which might have been lasting. This could well have happened under less understanding, less patient guidance.

As it is, the two great currents of civilization and culture with which Providence has blessed our country continue to flow side by side enriching the land and securing the harvest.[2]

Georges signed himself 'your obedient servant and debtor'; for he was always mindful of what he owed to Mackenzie King. The visit, for all its lack of bilingualism, had been a great success, and when it was over the Prime Minister was made an Honorary Citizen of Dieppe.

The honours were now flowing pretty freely. The Polish Government wished to give Pauline the Cross of Polonia Restituta, but as the wife of a foreign diplomat, she was not allowed to receive it. Perhaps it was just as well; for whatever smaller mercies Poland might have then been grateful, restitution was hardly one of them. Georges, however, was able to accept his

2. 7th June 1946.

appointment as a Commander of the United States Order of Merit. He also received Doctorates from Lyon and Laval. When the latter was bestowed upon him by M. Onésime Gagnon at the Hotel Palais d'Orsay, Etienne Gilson was present. No one, in these post-war years, had measured more exactly the scope of the Canadian opportunity – 'the union of two intellectual cultures, those of Great Britain and France, which owe everything to each other, so that to understand the one is to love the other.' These words were spoken in Toronto; they would have been just as salutary in Montreal.

On the 29th of September 1946 the Vaniers celebrated their Silver Wedding in the chapel of the Dominican house at 129 Boulevard de Latour-Maubourg. It was here that Christians, Marxists, and Existentialists had met in friendly dialogue; here that Albert Camus had stated what he expected from the Catholics of France. The anniversary Mass was said by Père Maydieu, with that face of a gentle Savonarola and a faith that was incandescent in voice and gesture. The figures of Georges Vanier and Jean Maydieu were central to the whole ferment of spiritual and social renewal which was then making Paris an arena of the world's debate. Maydieu was a frequent guest at the rue Dosne, and no one could have more appropriately presided on this occasion. Was it now, or on some previous anniversary, that the family had sent their parents the following telegram: 'Thank you for being so clever in 1921'? Neither had ever been in doubt of their own cleverness.

2

Pauline Vanier's work for the Red Cross deserves a chapter to itself. A letter from a mother on the Ile de Sein, a barren rock off the coast of Brittany, where almost every adult male among the three hundred inhabitants had joined de Gaulle, must speak for many others.

In the name of all my children I am thanking you for the clothes I received at Christmas. I don't know how to thank you for them, for since my dear son – the eldest of 8 children – left for England on June 24, 1940, we have been left without support. My husband died in 1944, after 24 years of illness. And my son disappeared aboard the submarine *Surcouf* on February 18, 1942, after fighting at St Pierre et Miquelon . . . To clothe ourselves and above all to clothe our 7 children – the oldest is only 15 and the youngest a month – is a very complicated problem on our island just now. My husband was deported after a clandestine mission in France, and miraculously came back to me.

This was only one out of nearly a hundred letters of thanks from the Ile de Sein. Elsewhere Pauline was particularly interested in the welfare of the bargees and their families – 100,000 of them – and in Normandy alone two thousand cases of clothing were distributed. All personal appeals were checked as far as possible, and now and then the appeals were extremely bizarre. One of them asked for 'a Canadian bachelor or widower, of our own social milieu, serious, a practising Catholic, very well educated, and wishing to found a Christian family *in France*? No indication was given of the person with whom the 'Canadian bachelor or widower' was expected to ally his fortunes.

A similar glimpse of the now silent and generally submerged *bourgeoisie* was caught in Notre Dame, during one of Père Riquet's Lenten sermons. There was not an inch of unoccupied space in the cathedral, and the Jesuit preacher was speaking with a sober eloquence about the Christian faced with a world in ruins. He must not be surprised; he must not try to escape; he must simply exercise the faculty of love. This was the Christian way of being 'revolutionary and absurd'. Just as Georges was mastering his emotion, a young man – obviously of the privileged classes – left his place, white with indignation, and protested to one of the clergy because a young woman near by was wearing no hat. The word 'scandal' was muttered under the venerable arches of the nave, and the priest – to avoid further disturbances – asked the young woman to put something on her head. For the Vaniers, who had reached Paris by way of Algiers, it was difficult to measure so vast a distance from reality.

Among the more interesting acquaintances that Pauline had gathered through her work for the Red Cross were Geneviève Schmidt and Abbé Depierre, a worker-priest in the industrial suburb of Montreuil. The father of Geneviève Schmidt had been converted to Christianity by the chaplain of the prison where he was awaiting execution. His daughter was hesitant to approach the rich for charity, quoting her Pascal to the purpose : 'The orders of money and of charity are so different that you cannot create charity between human beings by means of money.' Still, the Vaniers were hardly rich – and anyway they were 'different'. What the under-privileged population of Montreuil required was a cow – and a cow, five years old and due to calve in a fortnight, was duly procured from Brittany at a cost of 36,000 francs, and put out to graze at Marly.

Everyone who hungered and thirsted after social justice found a ready helper in Pauline. There was Abbé Pierre, who had turned up at Chéragas in 1944, straight from the Resistance, and slept for eighteen hours; Père Loewe, a former barrister, who worked among the dockers at Marseilles; Abbé Talvas, who rescued the prostitutes from the *trottoirs*; a young priest who was hoping to build a Boys Town among the ruins of Caen; and yet another young Frenchman was so imbued with the idea of helping pre-delinquent boys that he had sold newspapers in the more disreputable quarters of Paris to make contact with those whose feet seemed set upon the 'primrose path'. With financial help from the Canadian Red Cross and the Canadian Save-the-Children Fund, he had started a home for fifty-three of these boys in an abandoned village of the Drôme. A Massey-Harris tractor had been acquired, and the boys ran their own farm, grew their own food, were re-building the village, and had reopened two schools.

It was not only food, comforts, and layettes which were now arriving from Canada. On the 28th of February 1947, Georges inaugurated the first Canadian locomotive – 141R – at Cherbourg. A consignment of 140 similar engines, built according to French plans in the Montreal Locomotive Works and the Canadian Locomotive Works at Kingston, were shortly to follow. They were designed for passenger and goods trains to travel at a hundred miles an hour. The wheels were painted in white and the connecting rods in blue, and they were beflagged with the French and Canadian colours. They had cost half of what they would have cost to build in France. Georges Vanier went on to pay a tribute to the heroism of the railwaymen during the Resistance and their industry during the reconstruction. He recalled the marshalling yards at Trappes and Juvisy with their haunting spectacle of twisted and overturned locomotives, and the gutted skeletons of railway cars. A little further along the coast at St Malo he had recently laid the foundation stone for the reconstructed houses, reminding his listeners that, between 1688 and 1698, ships sailing from that harbour had captured 262 warships and 3,360 merchant vessels. This was not a feat to be lightly emulated; nevertheless 'down your streets, people of St Malo, runs the blood of the Corsairs.'

During April the Vaniers were in Italy, as the guests of General Lee, the U.S. Commander, and travelling in what had been

Mussolini's incredibly luxurious special train. They went down to Naples and heard Mass among the ruins of Monte Cassino; and in Rome Georges had an interesting conversation with the Apostolic Delegate to Canada, on a subject that did not officially concern him, although it interested him a great deal. The Holy See was much impressed by the firm Canadian stand against Communism; indeed anti-Communism was the first priority of Pius XII's pontificate, and it had led him to underestimate dangers just as real and rather more insidious. He was anxious, therefore, that the Holy See should be represented in Ottawa, and was willing to appoint an Inter-Nuncio, who would take precedence according to diplomatic seniority and not by virtue of his position. There were already Inter-Nuncio's in Holland, Austria, Czechoslovakia, and China. Realizing, however, that the Canadian Foreign Service was short of personnel, the Pope would be ready to accept the Canadian Ambassador to France or to Greece as Ambassador to the Holy See. He need only come to Rome three or four times a year. When Georges had an audience with the Pope a few days later, he confined himself to the expression of a hope that some satisfactory representation might be arranged. He made it quite clear that he was not speaking in the name of his Government. The Pope reciprocated the wish, but understood that there might be difficulties in the way. Georges made no comment on this although he realized the danger of stirring up anti-Catholic feeling in a country where Protestant convictions ran strongly. The President of the United States no longer had even a personal representative at the Vatican, and where the State Department watched its steps so warily, External Affairs might reasonably fear to tread.

In February 1949 Georges was officially informed that there was no immediate prospect of Canadian representation at the Vatican. This was in answer to reports that he himself would be appointed. A question had been asked in the House of Commons, and there had been strong opposition from Protestant bodies. It was thought that the opening of a mission to the Holy See would only exacerbate national tensions and be thought to contravene the principle of separation between Church and State. Rome was a valuable source of information, but there was some doubt as to how far, if it came to the point, the Catholic Church would be capable of containing Communism. The matter, however, would be kept under constant review; and it was not until 1969 that a Canadian envoy was accredited to the Holy See.

3

Important changes had now taken place in the direction of
External Affairs. Hitherto Mackenzie King had combined the
offices of Prime Minister and Secretary of State, but now he handed
over the latter functions to Louis St Laurent. At the same time
Hume Wrong, who had succeeded Norman Robertson as Under-
Secretary, was appointed to Washington and Robertson succeeded
Massey at the High Commission in London. The new Under-
Secretary, with whom Vanier had normally to work, was Lester
Pearson – a valued friend and colleague of many years' standing,
with a mind well attuned to the perils and possibilities of diplo-
macy and very alert to Canada's new position in the world.

With Byngsie at La Trappe and Jock still in the Royal Navy,
the family was a little depleted. Georges had snatched the opportunity of visiting Jock on H.M.S. *Vanguard* when she docked at
Portsmouth. Nine signals were exchanged between the British
Naval Attaché in Paris and the Captain of the ship in order that
a father should have luncheon with his son. Confusion was made
worse confounded because Georges' message was taken as coming from a French General, and French Generals do not normally
have sons on British ships. The Ambassador flew over in a plane
provided by the R.A.F. and was back in time for the President's
New Year reception at 4.30 p.m. Michel was anxious to know
what they had had to eat, and the reply – 'tomato soup and ham' –
moved him to an excitement which did less than justice to the
cuisine of the rue Dosne. In July of the same year Jock transferred to the Royal Canadian Navy.

In October Georges was himself in Canada for a medical check-
up at the Queen Mary's Veterans Hospital, and to settle a number
of personal affairs. He made two important speeches. For the
Kiwanis of Montreal his theme was the Canadian sacrifice at
Dieppe where 'the sand and the pebbles had drunk the young,
pure blood of our soldiers', and where, in the cemetery near by,
'hundreds of white crosses with the maple leaf look on to the sea.'
To the Canada Club in Toronto he spoke of the Empire that was
discarding imperialism:

I hear it said sometimes that this great political institution will never
be the same again. Of course it will never be the same. How can it
be? Life without evolution is impossible; and so the British Commonwealth must evolve and change.

I hear and read also of the decline of the British Empire. Those who dislike us point to India, Egypt, Palestine and other parts of the world. They speak of our impending collapse. They are wrong – the British Empire is perhaps the only example of an empire which has not collapsed and which will never collapse because its leaders, more particularly in the 19th and 20th centuries, understood that there could be no survival without a radical change in structure and in the relationship of its component elements. I pay tribute to the political genius of these statesmen who realized that all empires are fated to decline and fall unless we apply to them the rule of life as exemplified in the family. The father, as time goes on, passes to his children some of his goods and authority and in the end a mighty family partnership is created. And so it is with our Commonwealth with its offspring, independent, but devoted and loyal to one another through affection and also interest. Whereas yesterday they were only parts in a great organization, today they are partners. As a result there is no greater force for good in the world; one finds in the Commonwealth and Empire a political maturity born of experience. It is endowed with the qualities of courage, understanding and forbearance. It possesses a spiritual patrimony which it is our duty and privilege to share with others.[3]

Georges had already heard from more than one source that Byngsie was standing up well to the austerities of La Trappe. Père Couturier O.P. – the painter and friend of Matisse – had written:

As soon as I arrived in Montreal I lost no time in going to see your dear child. The whole countryside was deep in snow and wrapped in a great silence – like a huge and gentle Trappe without its walls. You know the place; it is very beautiful and very peaceful.

Brother Benedict is very well; he seems entirely acclimatized and perfectly happy. He has not changed in the least – only a little fatter. Already in his eyes and on his whole face you can see the wonderful peace and recollection that are the gift of the monastic life to those who are faithful to its spirit and its rules. When you see him, I am sure that his face will seem to you the face of happiness itself.[4]

Georges was naturally eager to verify these impressions. Although Byngsie had corresponded with his parents as far as the rule permitted, it was a year since they had seen him. They knew, however, exactly what he would be doing at each moment of the day. When Georges went down to Oka, his diary for those days records every detail of his visit, as if this were an opportunity that might not soon recur.

3. 6th October 1947.
4. 16th February 1947.

Sunday 19th October 1947
During the night the stump 'jumped' in such a continuous fashion (with intervals of quiet of course) that restful sleep was impossible. This is very unusual as the stump behaves very well as a rule. I can only account for this by assuming that the X-rays for the morning photographs had disturbed the nerve balance of the stump – or perhaps the devil didn't like my being at Oka. . . . 06.15 breakfast after which I lay down and slept until 09.25, when the Père Hôtelier fetched me for Community High Mass. He had placed my prie-Dieu next to St Bernard's Altar, only a matter of yards from the High Altar so that I was nearer the Sacrifice than the Community itself. Unfortunately from where I was I couldn't see 'Frère Benedict' except on his entering and leaving. A Mass beautiful, serene . . .

A little before 16.00 Brother Benedict arrived, smiling as usual. We spoke mostly of family matters. He is very serene and possesses a maturity so far beyond his years that one consults and confides in him as one would in the case of a man twice his years.

Monday 20th October 1947
07.45 Community High Mass. The Père Hôtelier placed my prie-Dieu near the Altar of St Joseph in the Choir of the brothers who did not attend the service. This was the fruit of a pre-arranged plot through which I would be enabled to see 'Frère Benedict' during the whole of Mass, but I am sure that with his eyes downcast he did not see me. It was a great privilege and a joy to hear Mass thus. . . .

From 09.00 to 11.00 I made a few notes and went for a walk in the grounds, then the midday meal (*sans* austerity) after which a siesta. Byngsie arrived at 13.15. The weather was beautiful and we decided on a walk. As the chicken farm is on high ground (opposite the Monastery) we made for it, always keen for a view. We wandered about, taking only a casual interest in the well-bred hens and proud roosters, then sat on a board spread on a chicken-wire frame. . . .

18.30. Compline, again from St Bernard's Altar. Once more the beautiful, the incomparable 'Salve Regina', followed by the filing out of all the monks before the Father Abbot who sprinkles each with Holy Water.

The Father Abbot came to see me and to bring papers reporting General de Gaulle's success at the municipal elections. I thanked him for his care of Byngsie, for standing 'in loco parentis' and when I said that Fr Benedict had perhaps a better father now, his eyes were not far from tears.

Tuesday 21st Oct.
01.45. A knock at the door tells me it is time to rise for the first Office. I wish to attend this once at least so that I may have a picture of Byngsie at prayer by night as well as by day. As I walk up to the gallery (or 'tribune') two floors above, I hear the clock strike two.

The Church is in darkness save for the small red sanctuary light. At about 02.05 the monks file in and a few moments later the signal for the Short Office of the B.V.M. is given. The office is chanted in the dark as all know the words. For twenty minutes Our Lady's praises are sung by these strong, saintly men – then lights are turned on and the half hour's meditation or 'oraison' begins. The first fifteen minutes, *with light*, enable the monks to prepare for their meditation with the help of a book, if they find this method more suited to their temperament. Some however make no use whatever of books. The second half of the meditation is completed in darkness.

After Matins, which lasted from 3 a.m. to 4 a.m., the individual Masses were celebrated and at 4.30 a.m. Georges Vanier returned to his room.

The two and a half hours passed quickly – more quickly than one would have expected. Save for the dark periods, Byngsie was in view, at times in profile, at others back but never full face. He, like the others, never raised his eyes. The memory of the scene cannot fade. Now I shall always be able to picture Bro B at early morning prayer – it will be when we are at 8 o'c Mass in Paris. Union de prière.

Later in the morning the Abbot showed Georges the Institut Agricole.

Most ingenious machine for grading apples. Bro B was in the basement busy with the lowest grade apples looking for bad ones – no compliment to his intelligence! We kept far enough away not to attract his attention – he seemed particularly interested in the disposal of one small apple, pressing it and turning it on all sides – quite a 'cas de conscience'.

After a talk with the Master of Novices, Georges saw Byngsie again for half an hour, sitting on a bench in the sun. He was proud, and perhaps a little puzzled, that his eldest son had chosen this way of life. For of all the Vanier children Byngsie had, in a quite remarkable degree, the gift of communication; and for that reason, no doubt, he had decided to communicate only with God.

4

Soon after Georges Vanier's return, Philippe Leclerc came back from Indo-China, where he had spent about nine months in a three-sided campaign with the Annamites and the Chinese. His relations with d'Argenlieu,[5] the Resident-General, had been pretty strained; d'Argenlieu, he wrote, 'combined the vanity of an

5. Contre-Amiral Thierry d'Argenlieu (Père Louis de la Trinité O. Carm.)

Admiral and the obstinacy of a Bishop.' Now, in November 1947, Leclerc was appointed to command all the armed forces in North Africa, and Georges had a long, and highly significant conversation with him as he passed through Paris. Leclerc had favoured a liberalising policy in Indo-China, although he feared the moment for it was past owing to d'Argenlieu's intransigence. What now concerned him was the threat of Communism at home. If a *coup* were successful, he would be among the first to be 'neutralized', and in fact his appointment to North Africa had not yet been signed by all the Ministers concerned. With the retirement of de Gaulle and the approval of a constitution which allowed every scope to factious party manoeuvres, the Fourth Republic seemed already headed for its downfall. It would be tedious to recount the successive ministries which fell at the whim of an Assembly that could dismiss a Prime Minister without any need to renew its own mandate. Georges Vanier's depression was shared by many impartial observers: he noted 'that after the terrible period through which France has passed, due to some extent at least to its deplorable pre-war Parliamentary system and abuses, all of those holding the highest offices are Parliamentarians of the old school.'[6]

The *malaise* had persisted all through the year, and now, with the country paralysed by strikes, Leclerc believed that it might give the Communists their chance. He was resolved, on reaching Algiers, to ensure the loyalty of the forces under his command and to use them in defence of the Republic, if need be. When Georges asked him how the army in metropolitan France would react to a *coup*, he replied that its effectives were not very strong, whereas the Communists were very well organized both in the country and the towns. What was the point of an organization if one did not use it? Leclerc believed that, on arrival in Paris, de Gaulle could have forced the Communists, by means of a plebiscite, to accept a constitution which he should have already drawn up in Algiers. Leclerc's mood was one of deep depression. He was accustomed to new departures, but he had an intuition that this one might be his last. Two days before leaving, he came to bid the Vaniers Good-bye. After saying Good-night to Michel, he remarked to Pauline as they were coming downstairs: 'If anything should happen to me, look after Thérèse and the children.' A few days later René Pléven called at the rue Dosne with the news that the

6. January 1947.

aeroplane in which Leclerc was travelling to an unspecified destination had crashed at Colomb-Bechar. Among the bodies afterwards found, one was unidentified and this gave rise to rumours, some of which were fantastic and none of which could be confirmed. If Communist sabotage had been at work, this would have been in accord with Leclerc's apprehensions. Pléven asked Pauline to go with him to Thérèse de Hauteclocque. When they had broken the news, she simply told her children to thank God for giving them such a father. Leclerc's body was brought back to France; lay for twenty-four hours at the Arc de Triomphe; and after the Requiem at Notre Dame was buried at the Invalides on the 8th of December, the Feast of the Immaculate Conception. The military annals of France do not contain a more stainless or more splendid record.

The Government was unduly worried about the public reaction on account of the general strike, but there was no disturbance and tens of thousands lined the streets in homage. Georges Vanier paid his soldierly tribute in a broadcast. 'Leclerc is not dead. I saw him today, living in the proud, sorrowful, and affectionate faces of the crowd.' Nevertheless with the death of Leclerc much of the heart had gone out of the Vaniers' mission to Paris. True, there were several years of absorbing work ahead of them, and they were not wanting for friends. But Leclerc was the closest link with a national renaissance in which they had placed their ardent hopes. Many of these were belied as cynicism and selfishness once more took possession of the political scene. The new faces were the old faces, and the new ways were the old ways. But Leclerc, ardent for reform and with face set firmly against destructive revolution, had escaped the contagion of politics. His image was as bright as on the day he knelt with the Vaniers at Farm Street in 1940. For both of them he would live beside Julian Byng in tender and admiring memory; for neither of them would the world ever be quite the same again, now that he had left it.

Moreover Leclerc's general forebodings had been correct. Robert Schuman admitted to Georges that the moment when he took power in the autumn of 1947 was the moment when France stood on the edge of the abyss. There were days when no one could tell what might happen. But the crisis passed and Schuman, with his steel and coal condominium in Luxembourg and the Saar, took the first essential steps towards European integration. The Vaniers were much encouraged by the friendship of Vincent Auriol, now President of the Republic, an honest Socialist of

humble origin and in many respects of a very different temper
to their own. They remembered him in his shirt-sleeves sweltering in the heat of Algiers; now, with his particularly charming
wife, he did the honours of the Elysée with a simple dignity.
Their friendship survived the reproduction in the press of a
private conversation with Pauline, evidently overheard and repeated by a footman. Profuse apologies were graciously accepted
and understood. Now that their old friends of the M.R.P. – Teitgen
and de Menthon – had moved from the centre of the stage, it was
with moderate Socialists like Auriol and Léon Blum that the
Vaniers were in closest sympathy. If the Socialist party in France
had reformed itself on the lines of the British Labour party, as
many wise Frenchmen had hoped, a viable solution might have
been found for the tensions which were pulling the country apart.
But the Socialists were even more sectarian than the Communists,
to whom they had forfeited their working-class support. The
nation would hardly rally to a *petite bourgeoisie* of Voltairean
school-teachers.

Each Embassy has its own style, according to its immediate
occupant. The Vaniers had not vied with the Duff Coopers in
entertaining Parisian society; apart from the diplomatic and
political figures that they were obliged to receive in the course of
duty, their guests were chosen, more often than not, from the
world of art and letters, and from their old friends of the Resistance. The test of association was whether an individual had
accepted the occupation or resisted it, actively or passively. The
Communist leader Thorez was invited, with Tillon and Billoux
who were also Cabinet Ministers, to the 1st of July reception in
1945. They were hardly *résistants de la première heure*, but they
represented the party which had made up for its hesitations by its
heroism. François Mauriac and his wife, Jacques de Lacretelle,
Georges and Blanche Duhamel, Emile Henriot, Paul Claudel, the
Prince de Broglie, Claude Bourdet, Louis Aragon and his wife
Elsa Triolet, General and Madame Catroux, Nadia Boulanger, and
Pierre Emmanuel were among those who enjoyed the Vaniers
hospitality. François Mauriac's mischievous irony could always
be trusted to set the table in a roar; there was one occasion when
the Ambassador could not help remarking: 'M. Mauriac, I like
you very much, but I would never propose you for the good
conduct prize.' Among the diplomatic visitors was Madame
Strauss, wife of the Minister from Saar, who attempted to resume
her seat on a chair which had been prematurely withdrawn. She

subsided on to the floor 'a bit wounded in pride and posture'.[7]

The Vaniers kept open house, at stated times, to Canadian students and had a sharp eye for Canadian artists performing in Paris – Raoul Jobin at the Opera, Pierrette Alarie and her husband Léopold Simoneau at the Opéra Comique, Gordon Manley, a talented pianist from Vancouver; Clermont Pepin the composer, and painters like Pierre Boudreau and Jean Bênoit. They gave a formal dinner and luncheon once a fortnight, and one cocktail party a week, which fifty or a hundred people might attend. At Christmas they enlarged the family circle to include the officials of the Embassy and their wives, with other lonely compatriots. On New Year's Day, when the rue Dosne was open to all Canadians in Paris, as many as 350 people would exchange greetings with the Ambassador and his wife.

Duff Cooper was succeeded by Sir Oliver Harvey, a cultivated career diplomat of liberal views, whom Georges had last seen during the nightmare exodus from Bordeaux. The Vaniers worked with the Harveys as easily as they had worked with the Duff Coopers, and indeed a warm friendship sprang up between them. Georges was now the senior Commonwealth Ambassador – a precedence that was given public emphasis when Princess Elizabeth and the Duke of Edinburgh visited Paris in the summer of 1948. A subsequent visitor was Field-Marshal Montgomery, who informed the French Staff College that it was their duty to be 'loyal to General de Lattre'. Georges wondered what the Staff College at Camberley would have thought of General de Lattre if he had informed them that it was their duty to be loyal to Field-Marshal Montgomery.

The Vaniers had little contact with French military circles. Although Georges inaugurated an exhibition of pictures by General Réquin, the two friends do not appear to have met very often. Too much water had flowed under too many bridges since Réquin had sent over his sketches from the Ritz to the Mayfair; and the currents had crossed. Réquin was now in honourable retirement, and Georges was not so committed to the *épuration* that he would support the French demand for the extradition of Bernonville[8] from Canada. Père Bruckberger, O.P., who knew Bernonville and vouched for his integrity, wrote to thank him for this. Bruckberger had supported de Gaulle when his cause seemed almost hopeless, and walked beside him in Notre Dame

7. Letter to Thérèse Vanier, 24th January 1952.
8. A suspected Collaborationist.

for the 'Te Deum' of thanksgiving; but he had also known Darnand and was at his side when he was shot. He sent Georges Vanier a copy of *N'irons pas au bois* – a defence of Darnand, which is in the great tradition of French polemic. Did he also know that Vanier had shaken hands with Darnand at Réquin's H.Q.? For here, in vivid illustration, were three soldiers whose personal conceptions of honour had brought France to the verge of civil war. Vanier stood for those who preferred defiance with de Gaulle; Réquin for those who preferred unity with Pétain; and Darnand for those who followed the Marshal to the last, ignoble limits of collaboration – because they had sworn an oath to him.

On the 5th of June 1948 Georges Vanier, with Oliver Harvey and the U.S. Ambassador, accompanied President Auriol to Normandy to commemorate the allied landings in 1944. Georges spoke at Airmonville where the Canadians had gone ashore, Harvey at Courseulles where de Gaulle had landed with Churchill, and the President at Arromanches. At Port-au-Bressin the fishing fleet put ceremonially to sea, with a fair wind and a general absolution from the Bishop of Bayeux. The dinner which followed gave Auriol the chance to express to Vanier his displeasure at the determination of the British and American Governments to establish a German Government at Frankfurt. He said that France had the right to ask that the enemy of yesterday should not be encouraged to arbitrate between the victors of today; a West German Government at Frankfurt was the first step towards a re-united Germany with its capital in Berlin. Auriol spoke for many Frenchmen of the old school. The necessity for Franco-German *rapprochement* had led to collaboration during the war, and when de Gaulle returned to power it would lead to collaboration during the peace. Vanier noted with surprise the absence of hatred for Germany in a country which she had invaded three times within seventy years. But if there was little hatred, there was much fear so long as Germany was not integrated in a European community. The Germans were a warlike race whereas the Russians, though politically militant, had never shown much desire to fight outside their own country.

The death of Lord Baldwin of Bewdley had left a vacancy for a foreign member to be elected to the Institut de France. The choice fell, without any prompting from Georges Vanier, upon Mackenzie King. The Canadian Prime Minister had held the chief office of state for longer than anyone else in the history of the

British Commonwealth, and he was at the same time awarded the Order of Merit. In September he came to Paris with Norman Robertson, and as usual Pauline's flowers greeted him at the Crillon. Mackenzie King was never the most popular, although he was quite the most persevering of Prime Ministers; but it says a great deal for a man when he remembers other people's wedding anniversaries. So the customary affectionate note was sent round to the rue Dosne inviting the Vaniers to dinner with Robertson and one or two other friends on the 29th of September. Oddly enough the Prime Minister's good wishes were accompanied by a quotation from Browning which Georges himself grew fond of using in the years to come:

> Grow old with me,
> The best is yet to be,
> The rest of life,
> For which the first was made.

The Prime Minister was shortly to retire, and Georges Vanier's own future came up for discussion. Mackenzie King had suggested his going as High Commissioner to London. Georges wanted this more than anything else; had often thought of it; but dismissed the idea as too good to be true. 'I think,' said the Prime Minister 'that it will be offered to you within the next few months.' At one time he had thought of bringing Georges into the Government, but suggested that things were better as they were – and Georges agreed with him.

Mackenzie King returned to Canada after a short illness in London, contemplating the carnations which Pauline had sent to the *Queen Elizabeth* at Cherbourg. His mind was still brooding on a conversation with her a few weeks earlier:

'I have had a strange feeling of an impending tragedy for our country all day' he had told her. 'As I got up this morning I felt it, and have felt it very deeply all day.'

She asked him why.

'Because at this very moment Drew is most probably being elected leader of the Conservative party, and that is the tragedy. You see, all the efforts I have made to unite our countrymen will be in vain. With the bigotry and narrow-mindedness of the Conservatives, the old hates and rivalries will start afresh and before long there will be serious trouble.'

But it was not under George Drew that the Conservatives swept the Liberals from power, and it was not from the Tory strong-holds in Toronto that the 'serious troubles' arose – whatever might be pleaded in their excuse. On the 30th of October Vanier wrote to the Prime Minister, expressing the hope that he would write his memoirs:

It is sad that no political memoirs of any importance exist in Canada. Neither Sir John Macdonald nor Sir Wilfrid Laurier left anything. Sir Robert Borden published a volume which was very scrappy with-out any claim to being more than a sheaf of personal recollections. So it remains for you to leave a record of political events which will cover not only your own premiership, but also that of Sir Wilfrid whose confidant you were.[19]

But time was running out for Mackenzie King, and all he was able to leave were his diaries. It may well be asked why Georges Vanier did not write his own memoirs when he had the leisure to do so. After all, he had once made the same suggestion to Lord Byng. But Byng had observed – pithily but not quite truly – that a man's memory seldom survived his memoirs.

Shortly after his return to Ottawa Mackenzie King retired, and Louis St Laurent became Prime Minister, with Lester Pearson at the head of External Affairs. Georges' hopes for the London appointment were doomed to disappointment for reasons that Mackenzie King explained in a subsequent letter:

Apparently Mr St Laurent had some misgivings on the score that if any differences should arise between the Government of the United Kingdom and our own, the fact that Canada was represented in London by a French-Canadian while he himself, as the Head of the Government here, was also a French-Canadian, might lead to unfavour-able comment. Personally, I should have held to a 'Canadian' and nothing else. There may have been some change in Pearson's attitude as well, though what, if so, it may have been other than the reason I have just mentioned, I cannot say. . . . I know that both you and Pauline will be greatly disappointed, and I want you both to know that I am particularly sorry for this. I, too, am disappointed; though this, of course, without any reflection upon Dana Wilgress[10] who will do, I am sure, extraordinarily well.[11]

9. 30th October 1948.
10. L. Dana Wilgress, Canadian High Commissioner in London, 1949-52.
11. 11th February 1949.

CHAPTER 18

END OF A MISSION

I

ANOTHER link, almost as close as the link with Philippe Leclerc, was soon to be partially severed. On the 2nd of February 1949, three large cars drew up before the entrance to the Carmelite Convent of Christ the King at Nogent-sur-Marne. It was 8.30 a.m. Among the eminent personalities who got out were the Canadian Ambassador and Pauline Vanier; with them were Elisabeth de Miribel and her parents. No one who had seen Elisabeth at the round of diplomatic cocktail parties, smoking a packet of cigarettes a day, and learning to dance the Samba, could have guessed the intention that was taking shape in her mind. She had never belonged to the R.P.F.,[1] regretting that former adherents of Vichy had been admitted to its ranks and that the General himself had stepped down into the arena, making of his movement a party competing with the others. Nevertheless it was over the luncheon table at Colombey-les-Deux-Eglises, one day in 1948, that she informed him of her wish to try her vocation as a Carmelite. Before doing so, she had resolved to pass the examination which would qualify her for the highest posts in the diplomatic service; and it was her friend, Père Couturier, O.P., who had himself gone to the Quai d'Orsay to discover the results, and brought them to her. 'Now' she had declared 'my real life is beginning. My admiration for the General is as pure and wholehearted as it ever was. In leaving him, I am not losing him. I shall pray for him.' But Couturier, at a small dinner given by the Vaniers for Elisabeth's friends, had spoken the truth when he said: 'Elisabeth is leaving us because we have disappointed her.' So, on this February morning, the Feast of Candlemas, Elisabeth de Miribel became Elisabeth of Jesus; and once again it was André Malraux – the unbeliever – who had understood the inexorable summons of the Absolute:

It is not necessary to believe in the community of saints to believe in the community. You wished that your decision might remain a

---

1. Rassemblement du Peuple Français.

private one. But your destiny has rubbed shoulders with history; it is symbolic, and invites curiosity. The rumour will quieten down – like the rumour of Rome, which had no idea how little it disturbed the fathomless silence of the catacombs.

The movements of history – their hopes as well as their achievements – have a way of crystallizing in certain incidents which have no influence on the march of public events. On returning to London from Algiers, Elisabeth de Miribel had obtained a visa from General Koenig to join the 2nd Armoured Division at Alençon. Leclerc had left, but she borrowed a jeep and found him in the little village of Fleuret. He looked at her, smiled, and said: 'You have won: what can I offer you?' She replied: 'To enter Paris at your side.' The wish was granted, and a little later she was munching a sandwich with Leclerc and gazing at the peak of the Eiffel Tower beckoning from the distance. A little later still, she watched the surrender of Choltitz[2] at the Gare Montparnasse. The dreams nourished in Morocco and Montreal, in London and Algiers, had dramatically come true. The Vaniers had shared them at every stage and actively assisted their fulfilment. Many of them were now buried with Leclerc in eternity, with de Gaulle in retirement, and with Elisabeth de Miribel in a silence not so far removed from the 'fathomless silence of the catacombs'. She had once said that of all the men she knew Georges Vanier and Jacques Maritain had the greatest spiritual radiation, and for the next five years she wrote constantly to Georges from Nogent-sur-Marne. But it was not a political correspondence.

2

All the family were together for Christmas 1948. Thérèse, who had been following a pre-medical course at the Sorbonne in defiance of ill health, was now studying medicine at Cambridge. Bernard was a student at the Institut des Sciences Politiques, but still suffering from a bad attack of rheumatic fever; Jock was following a gunnery course at the Royal Naval College, Greenwich; and Michel was at the Benedictine School of St Pierre-qui-Vire. This was close to Vézelay, deep in the forest of the Morvan, and the Vaniers had now rented an old house at Vézelay for their week-ends. Standing on the southern slope of the hill, it was extremely cold in winter. Empty gin bottles were therefore brought down from Paris and filled with hot water to warm the beds. The summer holidays of 1949 were spent at Guéthary, a small

2. General Dietrich von Choltitz, 1894-1966.

fishing village on the Basque Coast between Biarritz and St Jean de Luz. Pauline's Basque blood responded to the place, and the place – when it heard about the blood – responded to her. Georges interrupted his holiday to attend the annual commemorative ceremonies at Dieppe. Thirty of the original 'raiders' came from Canada to pay tribute to their dead comrades. All ranks were represented and lodged with private families in Dieppe.

Visits, complimentary or commemorative, to French cities were still the order of diplomacy, and Georges Vanier was never wanting for the *mot juste*. He congratulated the inhabitants of La Rochelle on their expertise in contraband when the company of Rouen and St Malo, which they had refused to join, had monopolized the fur trade with Canada. The famous hat that Louis XIV always wore, even at dinner, and which he raised only for women, Cardinals, and Marshals of France, had certainly come from Canada by way of La Rochelle. And there was a further link : Pauline's great-grandfather, a naval officer, had retired to La Rochelle and was buried there. At St Etienne, where the Vaniers had gone for the commercial fair, they were presented with a piece of clothing which had belonged to Lieutenant Beauregard of Montreal, arrested in Lyon on the 8th of June 1944, and afterwards shot. Receiving them at the Chambre de Commerce, Georges Bidault said : 'You are not only, for our joy, the Canadian Ambassador in France, but I will say, on condition that no one repeats it, the French Ambassador in Canada.' Claudius Petit was there, recalling memories of Algiers, and bravely standing up for St Etienne – an unattractive town distinguished for its fine workmanship in a variety of manufactures. And then there was Edouard Herriot recalling the Ursuline church in Quebec where the heart of Montcalm was buried, and where a lamp burned perpetually – the gift of a woman who was the victim of an unhappy love affair. 'For me' he said 'this little lamp is the symbol of Franco-Canadian friendship.' The veteran statesman, physically immense and immobile but mentally alert and certainly one of the best Latinists ever to sit in the Chambre des Députés, gracefully dedicated this memory of Quebec to the wife of the Canadian Ambassador.

In July 1950 Jock had quite unexpectedly resigned his commission with the Royal Canadian Navy. Vice-Admiral Grant,[3] Chief of the Naval Staff, wrote to Georges that 'the resignation of such an extremely efficient and capable young officer as your

3. Vice-Admiral Harold Taylor Wood Grant, 1889–1965.

son is a severe blow to the R.C.N., more particularly as we have all too few outstanding French-speaking Canadian officers in the Service.'[4] For a time it looked as if Jock might follow Byngsie into the Church, if not into the cloister, but he was to find his own rather tortuous way to a very special vocation. The connection between this and his training with the Royal Navy was not immediately apparent. There are more things about the Royal Navy, however, than meet the eye; and it would be interesting to know how far his later success with retarded adults was a naval secret. Naturally communicative like his brother, the 'silent service' had taught him to hold his tongue when necessary; he needed no tuition to loosen it. A fellow officer, to whom he had given his navigational books, told Georges that when he was relieved by Jock on the watch, he would sometimes stay and talk to him for an hour, just for the sake of his conversation.

On the 21st of March, 1951, the Vaniers sailed with Vincent Auriol on the *Ile de France* for the Presidential visit to Canada and the United States. David Bruce, the American Ambassador in Paris, and Robert Schuman were also on board. Scarcely had the ship berthed in New York than the news came through that Tremblay had died in Quebec. There were many still living who had heard his cry 'Allons donc, mes enfants' as the 'Van Doos' swung in a loop round the southern half of Courcelette, and closed in upon its streets; and who remembered how the victors, when the action was over, had sat down to sing the songs of old France which had become the songs of new Canada. The Tremblay, whom the Royal 22nd now buried with full military honours, had remained to the last 'the wiry man, typical of his race, modest, bright-eyed . . . such a man as Chaucer knew when Norman French was spoken in English fields' described by Philip Gibbs in 1916. Georges was present at the funeral in the Church of the Blessed Canadian Martyrs, and he now paid to his old chief the tribute, which he repeated later, when a memorial to him was erected at Chicoutimi:

Tremblay incarnated the soul of the 22nd. His place in the history of our people is assured, and I will go so far as to say that he was the greatest French-Canadian soldier since Salaberry.

The death of Tremblay left the regiment without its Honorary Colonel, and Georges Vanier was approached to fill his place. He was at first reluctant to do so, since Colonel DesRosiers – the

4. 5th July 1950.

senior of those who had formerly commanded the Royal 22nd – was still living. DesRosiers, however, was unable to accept the post owing to ill-health, and Vanier followed in the footsteps of the man he had so ardently admired. Of all the offices he filled in the course of his long career, none gave him more legitimate pride.

A very different compliment was shortly to be paid to Pauline. The nursery gardeners of Lyon decided to give a rose cultivated in their part of France the name of 'Madame Vanier'. It had been grown by Madame Orard, a rose specialist from Feyzin in the Isère. It was copper-red in colour with a particularly attractive duplication of petals. Enclosed in moss and cotton, it was handed to the station inspector at Lyon-Perrache, who gave it to the guard on the Paris express, and it reached Pauline in time to comfort her after a rather unpleasant car accident at Auteuil.

In November 1951 Georges was unanimously elected a Foreign Associate member of the Académie des Sciences Morales et Politiques to fill the place left vacant by the death of Maurice Maeterlinck. His election was proposed by Léon Noel, Ambassadeur de France, and Georges took his place among the Immortals at the opening of the regular session of the Académie on the 7th of January 1952. He had spared himself the expense of getting a uniform made for the occasion, and in his *discours de réception* he reminded his audience that three other Canadians – Senator Dandurand, Senator Lemieux, and Mackenzie King – had been similarly honoured. He spoke of certain great writers who had been members of the Institut – Louis Lavelle, who had just died, Bergson, de Tocqueville, Michelet, and Fustel de Coulanges. He said that he had read a great deal of Maeterlinck in his youth, notably *Pelléas and Mélisande*. When Norman Robertson wrote suggesting that he concentrate on *The Life of the Bee*, Georges took up the challenge.

The work of my illustrious predecessor has suggested that I raise bees in portable hives. These bees will be trained (and *are* being trained, I may add) to sting anyone who does not treat me with due respect. The main trouble we are having in training these most intelligent and industrious creatures is to make them understand the signal on which they should act ('sting' is a better word), but I hope to have everything in order before we three meet in Ottawa.

3

The political scene during the last years of the Vaniers' mission to Paris was dominated by the unsuccessful challenge of de

Gaulle's R.P.F., and by the long debate over the European Defence Community. Most observers believed that the R.P.F. would obtain about 130 seats in a house of 620. This was a very long way from a majority. Georges Vanier was convinced that de Gaulle would be hopeless as Prime Minister. Temperamentally, he was not built for co-operative work in a democratic Parliament, and the other parties would not care to work with him. The Ministers who had done so before his resignation had not relished the experience. De Gaulle did not suffer fools gladly, and he did not even suffer gladly those of his fellow politicians who were not fools. He was certainly a genius, but geniuses did not necessarily make the best Prime Ministers. He had many of the attributes of a dictator, but with his deep knowledge of history he knew that the French, whatever their need for stable government, did not want a dictator and would not stand for one. His ambition – only to be realized in the throes of a national crisis – was to create an effective democratic authority, which would not be at the mercy of partisan manoeuvrings.

In the elections of 1951 the R.P.F. won 120 seats, and within a year de Gaulle was acknowledging his failure. He admitted to Teitgen, to whom he had not spoken since 1947 and who had recently been elected President of the M.R.P., that many had joined his movement who did not share his ideas. 'On the 17th of June 1951' he said 'I needed eighty more deputies and I had eighty too many of the wrong kind.' 'In 1947' replied Teitgen 'I told you that you were going to rally round you the radicals and the old Right of the salons and the châteaux. That was why the M.R.P. could not follow you.' De Gaulle was at the limit of depression; there was nothing more that he could do; and in a moment of rare humility he admitted that he had been 'maladroit'. A comparison between Pétain and de Gaulle was now going the rounds: 'De Gaulle loves France but not the French; Pétain loves the French, but not France.' It was a succinct definition of what had divided Gaul in two parts.

A very curious incident occurred on the night following the death of Pétain in his prison on the Ile d'Yeu. A telephone call was received at the Elysée Palace at about 2 a.m. from a man claiming to be the Canadian Ambassador and asking for the President. He was informed that M. Auriol could not be disturbed, and the President's Directeur du Cabinet – M. Kosczinsko-Morizet – came to the telephone. The speaker repeated that he was the Canadian Ambassador and wished to extend to the President the sym-

pathy of the Canadian Government on the death of Marshal
Pétain. M. Kosczinsko-Morizet replied that this was obviously
untrue since he knew the Canadian Ambassador's voice very well.
The caller's identity was never known, but his nocturnal *démarche*
was an eloquent tribute to Georges Vanier's reputation as a supporter of de Gaulle. If some embittered Pétiniste had wished to
embarrass a foreign envoy, he had certainly picked on the right
man.

Of the Gaullist deputies thirty had, to all intents and purposes,
left the party and the allegiance of the others was not secure.
Jacques Soustelle, their leader in the Chamber, was compared to
a general in the midst of a dissolving army. It was in these circumstances that conversations were opened between the R.P.F. and
the M.R.P. The General agreed to accept whatever obligations
France had assumed in the field of foreign affairs, but he did so
with considerable reluctance. He was already playing with the
idea of a Franco-German confederation established behind the
Anglo-Saxon backs of the United Kingdom and the United States.
He certainly desired important constitutional amendments, but
it was impossible for the M.R.P. to accept these beforehand without knowing what they were. De Gaulle denied that he wanted
a Presidential régime on the American model. He merely wished
the President to be able to appoint his Prime Minister without
investiture by the Assembly; to be able to call for a referendum on
specific issues; and to be able to dissolve Parliament, in certain
circumstances, without consulting the Assembly and the Conseil
de la République. General de Gaulle had what W. B. Yeats
described as 'the slow, patient cunning of the born fighter', and
after six more years of Parliamentary muddle and impotence he
got his way. But when he did so, Georges Vanier was no longer a
diplomatic witness. Indeed he saw little or nothing of de Gaulle
during these years of the General's commuting between Colombey-les-Deux-Eglises, where he was writing his memoirs, and his
small apartment at the Restaurant Laperouse where the material
for future volumes was handed to him in the *va-et-vient* of political personalities, and the *va-et-vient* of political hopes and fears.
Georges stuck to his brief with the existing Governments, however fugitive; and regularly now, as the October days drew in, a
brace of pheasants would be sent down from the President's shoot
at Rambouillet. 'Qu'est-ce qu'ila, ce Georges Vanier,' Vincent
Auriol was once heard to exclaim 'qu'on aime tant?'

If de Gaulle seemed to be on the way out, Winston Churchill

was on the way in. Shortly before the return of the Conservatives to power, Georges Vanier was invited to meet him at a dinner at the British Embassy. Paul Reynaud, Georges Bidault, R. A. Butler,[5] and Mr William Hayter,[6] Minister at the Embassy, were the other guests. Georges noticed that Churchill had preserved his cherubic complexion, and that his hands were those of a man thirty years younger, with no protruding veins. He had just come from Morocco which reminded him, nostalgically, of India as he had known it as a young subaltern in the Hussars. He deplored the liquidation of the British Empire, and enquired very warmly about General de Gaulle. Both Reynaud and Bidault were amused to note that when Churchill saw pink at the mention of de Gaulle. they had admired him, and that Churchill now liked him when they admired him no longer. He thought his retirement an unmitigated disaster for France; 'who else' he exclaimed 'can maintain any semblance of leadership?' Georges asked Churchill what was the secret of his youthful appearance and good health. 'A lot of whisky and brandy' was the answer 'and sleep in the afternoon'.

He was quite definite that Great Britain would not join a European Army; she would fight with European forces, but not *in* them. He maintained that the right way to bring European armies together was to maintain their national identities and tie them together as a 'bunch of sticks', bound together by common interest in their own salvation,. rather than to mix them all up as 'wood pulp'. He did not believe in the 'wood pulp' theory of unity; and he found it difficult to understand how the French, with their strong national and military traditions, were willing to allow their army to be absorbed completely in a European force, or how their soldiers could ever loyally serve in it. He emphasized that British association with Europe would be close but not necessarily organic.

On the subject of E.D.C. Vanier had an interesting conversation with Eisenhower at S.H.A.P.E. Headquarters.[7] He observed a certain weariness underlying the General's heartiness, for he was an excellent host – although eating little himself. He had come round rather late to the notion of a European Army, having decided that it was the only way to reconcile the German point of view which insisted on equality of status and the French demand

5. Lord Butler of Saffron Walden.
6. Sir William Hayter.
7. 9th November 1951.

for a guarantee that a German national army would not be re-
created. It was more important, he thought, to appoint a responsible authority than to waste time deciding how big the army
should be. Vanier also had a qualified belief in the European Army,
provided it came under the orders of the N.A.T.O. Supreme Commander. But he also believed that once the Russian threat receded,
it would probably break up into its component parts, unless an
advanced state in European political integration had by then been
reached. No argument from political necessity ever shook Vanier's
deep distrust of German militarism. The Germans were never
more dangerous than when they were sorry for themselves, and
as he passed the scarred cities of the Rhineland on a visit to the
'Van Doos', he had noticed that they were very sorry for themselves indeed. Another guest at Eisenhower's luncheon table commented on the German capacity for hard work, and Vanier
asked whether there wasn't some way to make them work
less hard. 'And make the French work a little harder?' Eisenhower suggested. Georges agreed that this would be the ideal
solution.

Very different views were expressed by President Auriol. Was
it conceivable that the Germans would not attempt to reunite
their country and to regain the provinces lost to the Poles in the
East? General Rancke had recently spoken in this sense, and had
opposed any participation in the defence of Europe until the
honour of the German army had been restored. The President
feared that a united and rearmed Germany would make a deal
with Russia or, if that were not feasible, drag Western Europe into
a war with them to restore their eastern frontiers. Churchill's
encouragement of European integration when he was in opposition was in contrast to his isolationism now that he was back in
power. Why should integration be considered harmful to Commonwealth solidarity? Many Frenchmen hoped that despite the
decision to proceed with the rearmament of Germany, it might
never be necessary to put the decision into effect, since Russia was
apparently willing to negotiate at a meeting with the Western
powers. In the meanwhile the Government succeeded in passing
through the Assembly a considerably enlarged military budget for
1951. A Minister informed Vanier that he believed the threat
from Germany would be serious in twenty years' time if Germany
were not integrated in the Western economy.

The views of other Ministers and prominent personalities held
out little hope that E.D.C. would be ratified by the Assembly.

Herriot, Monnerville,[8] Parodi,[9] and Palewski,[10] were all unalterably opposed. Laniel, the Prime Minister, thought that if the United Kingdom had joined as a full member, there would be no difficulty, and that it was a mistake to put forward, in the first instance, proposals which involved a serious loss of sovereignty. Bidault, Minister for Foreign Affairs, though acquiescent, was far from enthusiastic. Vanier himself disliked E.D.C. for many of the reasons that the French disliked it, and he thought the 'E.D.C. or nothing' approach 'frustrating and fatal'. The alternative was the admission of Germany as a member of N.A.T.O. Failing this, he could not foresee French acceptance of any organization which did not include the United Kingdom or the United States as a long term guarantor. If the European Defence Committee had not been killed by the Assembly, it would have been summarily executed by General de Gaulle. But the Treaty of Rome was to mark the first essential steps towards economic integration, and for a time – although that time was not yet – the Franco-German honeymoon looked something more than a *mariage de convenance*.

Having lived and worked among the French for so long, and realizing that he must shortly be leaving them, Vanier took the opportunity of a visit by some members of the Canadian National Defence to set down his mature conclusions about their national character. The Frenchman was proud of his traditions, and had retained his virility; in many ways he was tougher than the Canadians. 'Go into the country and spend a night in winter in a so-called château, and you will have had enough : no heating, little hot water and no electricity. The peasant lives as no farmer or rancher would live in Canada.' The Frenchman was a magnificent fighter, and the reason for his collapse in 1940 was lack of arms to withstand a mechanized onslaught, and the terrible losses in the 1914 war from which the country had never really recovered. He was intensely individualistic and liked to argue for the sake of argument. He was also intensely human, and an appeal to his heart rarely failed unless you addressed it to a taxi-driver. Even there you might be lucky. Georges mentioned a lady, 'neither young nor beautiful', from whom the driver would accept neither fare nor tip when he learnt that she was a Canadian. The Frenchman was highly intelligent – some would say too intelligent – and he had a lethal sense of the ridiculous. He liked food and drink;

8. Gaston Monnerville, President of the Conseil de la République.
9. Alexandre Parodi, Secretary-General at the Quai d'Orsay.
10. Gaston Palewski, R.P.F. Deputy 1951-5.

but Georges omitted to mention other pleasures that he liked just as well, and he passed in discreet silence over his pathological attachment to money. He was equally attached to liberty and equality, but again Georges refrained from suggesting that fraternity came to him less easily. No country in the world was freer than France – perhaps it was a little too free. The Frenchman was an artist in everything he did; an ardent patriot; 'and, I am sorry to say, very undisciplined.' The political pot was always boiling, but as the temperature was nearing the point when the lid would blow off, something generally happened to keep it on. The French had a respect for minorities which prevented them accepting the principle of simple majority voting; and a respect for property, fearful and tenacious in the north and east where individual proprietorship was of relatively recent origin, and in the south and south east so deeply ingrained that no threat to it could be taken seriously. For the peasant in Provence or Languedoc private property was as natural and inviolable as 'the sun, the wind, and the rain'. It was a charitable summing-up, and Georges might well have quoted Father Steuart's advice to Pauline: 'Be either very good or very bad, like the French.'

4

Early in the New Year (1952) General de Lattre de Tassigny died of cancer, and Vanier was again before the microphone with a tribute that was not only generous but just. He said nothing that was not true and nothing that might have injured the memory of a great commander whose temperament he had already accurately – and apprehensively – appraised. He recalled de Lattre's motto – 'Ne pas subir' – in other words 'not to submit to the will of others, not to abdicate before the unfavourable event but to impose one's will upon people and events.' He recalled his own visit to the Rhine in 1945:

On March 24 I crossed the Lauter at his side over an improvised bridge at Scheibenhardt and entered Germany. With him I saluted the French flag – then honoured for the first time on German soil. It was at Scheibenhardt that the first sections of the 4th Regiment of Tunisian sharpshooters waded through the Lauter with the water up to their chests. It was here that the first group of Moroccan Thabers hurled themselves on towards Scheidt, infiltrating through a forest thick with mines, where the men of the 101st Goum went forward with an absolute contempt for death. Once again I realized how the Commander's will to victory had penetrated to the ranks.

On the 9th of March the Vaniers sailed for Canada to assist at Byngsie's ordination to the priesthood on the 25th. The ceremony took place in the Basilica at Montreal, with Archbishop Léger officiating, and it was here that Father Benedict said his first Mass the next morning before returning to La Trappe. These were hours of deep emotion; and equally charged, though in a different sense, was Vanier's investiture as Honorary Colonel of the Royal 22nd, in succession to Tremblay and Foch. This took place on the 17th of April. He was met by a guard of honour of fifty men, and accompanied by Brooks Claxton; Major-General Bernatchez, Commander of the Military District of Quebec; and Brigadier Allard, Assistant Quartermaster-General. After the march past, and an inspection of the troops in training at Valcartier, Georges proposed the health of the regiment at a dinner in the Officers' Mess. He spoke of Tremblay, who had stamped the regiment with the seal of his own strong personality, and brought 'sparks of glory' to its standard, and then of his own feelings. They had seldom run deeper.

This honour, this great honour and gage of your trust, crowns my lifelong attachment to the regiment. It is the culminating point of what the 22nd has meant in my life. It completes a cycle and brings me back to the first days of the regiment – I joined it in September 1914. Today, when you call upon me to become your Honorary Colonel, thirty years later, I feel that a great part of my life is gathered up, and I do not conceal from you my emotion. You know how happy I always am to come back to the Citadel, where I was in command from 1926 to 1928, and where two of my children were born; what a joy it has been to meet the regiment in Canada, in England, in Germany, in Italy, and in France. You will measure how much of my heart is on my lips when I say 'thank you' this evening. At this moment of my investiture, my first thought is for those of our number who have fallen, and I will repeat the words of Lacordaire: 'Lord, will you not look with a special favour on those who come to you with the colours for a shroud?'

A permanent residence was now bought for the Canadian Ambassador at 135 rue du Faubourg Saint Honoré, not far along the street from the British Embassy. A garden at the back extended to the rue Artois, and the courtyard had parking space for twenty cars. A feature of the house were the *boiseries* acquired by the Comte de Fels, the last occupant of the Bastille and father of the Duchesse de la Rochefoucauld. The Aubusson carpets woven à la Savonnerie and the Louis XVI painted screen, in the Grand Salon, confirmed the formal elegance of the interior. The entrance hall was austere with the stone floor and black and white mosaic left uncovered; and another narrow room, known as the *galerie*, was also left bare to display its beautiful *parqueterie*. Its high polish and length inspired Lester Pearson to christen it 'the bowling alley'. The Vaniers' private sitting-room was at the head of the stairs, with panelled walls, and yellow satin chairs catching the sunlight through the high windows, and the empty shelves waiting for the books that had not been unpacked since 1940.

Nevertheless the staffing and furnishing of the house cost months of headache to the Vaniers and Arnold Heaney, now Under-Secretary for External Affairs – for the contract had been given to two *décorateurs* one of whom had considerably more taste than the other. The bedroom tables were of uniform size and bore no relation to the proportions of the rooms in which they were placed. The lamps for the servants' quarters were far too large for the tables and had to be returned. The finish of the wood for the sofa in the Grand Salon was quite unsuitable, and the central cushion so badly made that it had to be sent back for alteration. Georges objected to the size of the Coat-of-Arms and to the placing of it inside the entrance hall. 'My views would have been the same if the sculptor had been Rodin.' He also thought that the Arms might easily be confused with those of the United Kingdom. He had no prejudice against the Union Jack, but it gave foreigners the idea that Canada was in some way dependent on Great Britain. He would have preferred the stylized armorial bearings as they appeared on the cover of the Massey Report. The house in the rue Dosne had been bought by M. Benitez-Rexach, the cultural attaché for the Dominican Republic. He was married to Môme Moineau, a celebrated variety artiste, and when the Vaniers asked her if they might remain in occupation of the house until the new Embassy was ready, she replied: 'Entre collègues on ne refuse rien.' The Vaniers moved out on the 28th of April 1953.

Pauline had returned to Canada in October 1952 to visit Byngsie who was seriously ill in hospital, and Georges went back in May of the following year. Pearson was with him on the plane and, as Georges wrote later, 'it was a bit of a shock to learn from you, exactly four days after the last move, that you were considering my transfer to another post. My wife and I had assumed that we would be left to enjoy the new house for some appreciable time.'[11] Mr St Laurent confirmed the intention of External Affairs, but suggested that a position of some importance might be offered him in Canada. This was presumably a seat in the Senate, but it would have to wait until after the forthcoming elections. There was no question of a precipitate departure, but on his return Georges wrote to the Prime Minister reminding him that now, for the first time since 1943, he and Pauline had been able to unpack and arrange their personal belongings, some of which had been in store since 1939. Moreover the installation of the new Embassy was not yet complete, and Pauline was exhausted by the move. It was surely fair that they should be allowed to inhabit the Embassy for a little time after its inauguration, which they hoped that the Prime Minister would himself perform in the autumn of 1953.

For all these reasons I am sure that you will understand our disarray if we had to envisage a fresh move before at least a year. This sort of delay would allow us to entertain suitably through the winter and the coming spring, and to say our Good-byes without undue precipitation.[12]

Alternative diplomatic appointments were discussed in Ottawa – notably Madrid, but Georges wrote later to Pearson[13] that he was not disposed to accept it. A further argument for prolonging his stay in Paris was the Presidential election in December and the consequent transfer of powers in January for which, as the Vice-Dean[14] of the Diplomatic Corps, he should properly be *en poste*. Permission was given for him to remain until the end of the year, but this did not meet the point that he had raised. Pearson then suggested that he should go to Berne and Vienna – for the two posts were served by a single representative. Georges replied, however, that such a step down in the diplomatic hierarchy would be misconstrued by French opinion as official disapproval of his mission to France, and Pearson's reassurance to the contrary did not convince him. He had consulted a number of friends on the subject – in purely hypothetical terms – and they had been unanimous that the French would never understand such a transfer. Moreover 'it would not be surprising if my friends in Canada, on hearing of my move to Berne, shared the

11. 24th June 1953.
12. 6th June 1953.
13. 26th June 1953.
14. The Papal Nuncio was *ex officio* Dean, but Georges Vanier had been *en poste* longer than any other of the envoys.

French view. A public statement to the effect that the Government was most anxious not to lose my experienced services would be taken with a grain of salt.' In the same letter he made it clear that he was not asking to be retired, and that he felt he could still 'render service at another Mission which would not be open to the same criticism.'[15] If an Embassy were to be opened to the Holy See, he would be glad of the appointment; but the post he had really wanted was the High Commission in London. In letters to Pearson and St Laurent he recalled Mackenzie King's original proposal, although he admitted that had he been in St Laurent's place, he would have shared his hesitations.

I confess that it was a great disappointment to me, all the more so as I have spent nearly 14 years in England – in hospital after the first World War, at the Staff College in 1923 and 1924, and then at the High Commission between 1931 and 1939. I was also there for quite a long time during the last war, when I was filled with a deep admiration for the English people under aerial bombardment. My wife and I have almost as many friends in England as in France. Being English-speaking on my mother's side, as my wife is on her father's, a final mission in England would have completed a cycle, and we should have found this particularly agreeable.[16]

Georges Bidault, on behalf of the French Goverment, had asked that Vanier should remain for a further spell in Paris – a very unusual *démarche*; and he regretted in a subsequent telegram that his request had not met with a warmer response. 'General Vanier will carry away with him our affection, our esteem, and something over and above. He will be difficult to replace.'[17]

Since there was now no prospect of the important position in Canada materializing in the near future, Georges cancelled his sailing in October and accepted a Directorship on the Board of the Crédit Foncier, asking that the news of his retirement should be made public as soon as possible, so that the Board might also make their announcement. He had hoped that St Laurent would come over during the autumn officially to inaugurate the new Embassy, but the Prime Minister was not able to leave Canada at the time. This was an added disappointment. And so, with only two more months of diplomatic life ahead of them, the Vaniers regretfully, and just a little resentfully, began to say their Good-byes.

15. Letter to L. B. Pearson, 12th October 1953.
16. 12th October 1953.
17. 14th October 1953.

One farewell they had said already, when General Réquin died
on the 8th of October. Weygand spoke at his funeral, and for
Georges Vanier it must have seemed as if the spectre of defeat
was once again stalking the Boulevards. Another link had been
broken when Thérèse Martin died in August 1952. Bedridden,
partially paralysed, and over eighty years old, she was living in
one room and a tiny kitchen. Georges paid all the expenses for
the funeral at Neuilly. On the 17th November the Vaniers flew
to London for a farewell audience with the Queen, and Norman
Robertson – now High Commissioner – gave a dinner for them,
at which René and Odette Massigli were among the guests. There
were luncheons at the Elysée and the Hôtel Matignon.[18] But of
all these functions the most significant and the most moving was
a dinner at the Canadian Embassy for old friends of the Resistance
and France Libre:

A Minister or former minister presided at each table. Bidault was in
his best form and his speech announcing the award of the Légion
d'Honneur to Pauline Vanier, was very moving. René Mayer,
mysterious and smiling, nonchalantly joined in the conversation
while Maurice Schumann, also at the top of his form, never stopped
reminiscing about the radio war. There were two groups of former
combatants, those of the F.F.I. and those of France Libre. Each group
was composed of people who knew each other very well and had
kept in touch since the war; but, generally speaking, the one group
had little contact with the other. It was only on an occasion like
this that they mixed – which showed, like so much else, how effectively the Canadian Embassy could act as a *liaison* when the Vaniers
were *en poste*.

General Vanier, in a very fine farewell speech, recalled his memories
of London and Algiers, emphasizing one particular example of
Franco-Canadian collaboration. Anise Postel-Vinay was the youngest
French deportee arrested by the Gestapo. She was only sixteen when
she was caught assisting some Canadian parachutists. The General
recalled that no sooner was she freed from her long Calvary at
Ravensbruck than she married another hero of the Resistance, André
Postel-Vinay, who had thrown himself out of the window of the
Gestapo headquarters to stop himself talking under torture, and had
then been recaptured by the Germans. His broken ribs were barely
mended when he escaped from the infirmary where he was under-
going treatment, after simulating madness for several weeks.[19]

Pauline was invested with the Légion d'Honneur by Bidault

---

18. Residence of the French Premier, M. Laniel.
19. Letter from Alice Gadoffre to the author, 28th September 1968.

at the Quai d'Orsay on the 31st of December, although the Canadian Government had wished her to receive it at the Gare de Lyon. 'For us,' the Foreign Minister said, 'you will always be the Canadian Ambassadress.' She was also presented with a jewelled miniature of the Cross by Henri Fresnay, a former Minister and prominent member of the Resistance. All those who had come to the Embassy dinner were invited to attend. Since Canadian diplomats were not allowed to accept foreign decorations, the French Government offered Georges the choice between a painting and a piece of Sèvres China. He chose the painting – a luminous and serene landscape by Oudot. Other gifts were a silver cigarette box engraved with the signature of the officers at the Embassy and at the Canadian mission to N.A.T.O., and a cigarette case and lighter from the Corps Diplomatique. The Vaniers would remember their last evening in the Embassy for the singing of 'Augur Maria' by Madame Héregaray. She was to sing it for them again during the desultory years in Montreal.

Georges said Good-bye to Vincent Auriol at the President's reception on New Year's Eve, and at midnight, their mission officially ended, the Vaniers embarked on the train for Montreux. Representatives of the Government, several of their diplomatic colleagues and many other friends were at the Gare de Lyon to see them off. To Oliver Harvey, Georges looked 'very livid and ill'.[20] Maurice Schumann would recall standing one day with Alexandre Parodi at the window of the Quai d'Orsay when the Vaniers were arriving. 'Would you not say' observed Parodi, 'that here were a king and queen alighting from their car?' – and Teitgen would speak of Georges Vanier's 'intelligence du coeur'. The French have tenacious memories, and the impression would not quickly fade.

The Canadian Ambassador still hoped that he might be able to serve his country in some private capacity; and the way, when it opened out before him, was not to be so private after all.

20. Letter to Pauline Vanier, 8th March 1967.

PART THREE

THE GOVERNOR
GENERAL

CHAPTER 19

RETIREMENT AND
RECALL

I

THE Vaniers were immediately bound for Gstaad, but here
Michel fractured his leg ski-ing and they had to bring him down
to Lausanne for treatment. He then caught measles and was
moved to an isolation hospital. It was not until early in March
that he was able to return to school, and the Vaniers to resume
their journey south in a new Citroen.

When Mgr Roncalli was raised to the purple in 1953, it fell
to Georges Vanier as Vice-Dean of the Diplomatic Corps to
present the congratulations of his colleagues. 'In a few weeks'
time' he had said 'you will occupy a Patriarchate which brings
with it a particular distinction in the hierarchy of the Church.'
Before Roncalli left, Georges told him that he had seen the photographs of his predecessor's sumptuous funeral, with the gondolas
draped in black moving in slow procession down the Grand Canal.
Thinking that Georges was perhaps envying him the privilege of
similar obsequies, the newly appointed Patriarch stopped him
with a gesture and said with his rather roguish smile: 'Oh, not
immediately . . . not immediately.' He was hoping that at least
there would be time for the Vaniers to visit him in Venice.

Georges was especially well placed to appreciate the finesse
with which Roncalli had handled a difficult diplomatic mission,
and he had already divined some of the pastoral qualities that
were to endear the Patriarch of Venice to his people and Pope
John XXIII to the world. Having been assured that there 'would
always be a lamp burning for them at the Patriarchate', the
Vaniers let the Cardinal know that they were in Italy. He replied
inviting them – with Jock who had joined them for a week in
Rome – to luncheon on the 7th of April. The fact that he was
suffering from a slight loss of voice would not prevent him welcoming them and offering them 'large consolations for the eyes,
the mind, and the heart'. He showed them the rooms occupied

by Pius X before his election to the Papacy; these were being
reconstituted exactly as they had been in the time of Roncalli's
saintly predecessor. He spoke to them of the poverty in Venice,
and of his own peasant origins at Sotto il Monte. Like the city
now entrusted to his spiritual care, this son of the soil had
'espoused the everlasting sea'. Neither he nor his visitors guessed
under what circumstances they would meet again.

On their return from Italy, the Vaniers spent a couple of
months at Vézelay. Georges had always found time to practise
the advice he had given to Robertson Fleet:

I have a recipe for bettering the world which is simple. Every day,
every person who has reached the age of reason should remain perfectly quiet for half an hour face to face with himself instead of
with others or events. We are suffering from too much action and not
enough reflection.[1]

The practice was easy when one stood for the hundredth time
in the narthex of the great Basilica and contemplated the tym-
panum which imperiously summed up the place and what it
stood for; a millennial witness to the power of art and faith in
victorious alliance; and a masterpiece which, through all the
metamorphoses of sculpture, would never lose its power to
subdue the eye and mind. More than any other place in France,
Vézelay was the Vaniers' spiritual home; and on the 23rd of
April 1954, Georges' sixty-sixth birthday, it was the setting for
the marriage of two very dear friends. Gilbert and Alice Gadoffre
had both been active in the Resistance, and Georges was Alice's
godfather. Most of the thirty guests had arrived in Vézelay the
previous evening, and after dinner Pauline could be seen on all
fours arranging the flowers on the High Altar, while Georges sat
in one of the choir stalls, his head bowed, practising, no doubt,
his advice to Robertson Fleet. Michel was at his side, and General
Béthouard – an old friend from Algiers and one of Gilbert's witnesses – walked up and down the nave repeating to himself:
'What an atmosphere! What an atmosphere!' Père Maydieu
blessed the marriage on the following morning, while a friend
from Paris played Couperin's Mass for the Organ. Maydieu spoke
of the Resistance, matching his memories of the Vercors *maquis*,
where Gilbert had escaped by the skin of his teeth from a burning
château,[2] with other memories of the Fighting French, of

1. 23rd February 1952.
2. See *Les Ordélies* by Gilbert Gadoffre (Editions du Seuil)

Elisabeth de Miribel, and of the Vaniers' mission to the Fourth Republic. Every marriage is an occasion for looking forward; this was also an occasion for looking back.

There was a further opportunity for retrospect before the Vaniers returned to Canada. Georges had wished to pay his respects to General de Gaulle, and a meeting had in fact been arranged for the 17th of December; but since the new President had not been elected by then, the General thought it wiser to remain at Colombey-les-Deux-Eglises, and he did not intend to return to Paris till the New Year. When, however, Georges sent him a farewell message from Vézelay, de Gaulle replied by inviting the Vaniers, with Bernard and Michel, to luncheon. Madame de Gaulle and the General's sister-in-law were the only others present. De Gaulle showed a capacity for small talk, and also an attentive charm, which he had concealed on more urgent and official occasions. He remembered that Georges did not smoke, and that Michel had been born in 1941. He was obviously in good health, although his face and figure had lost a little of their lean and chiselled strength. Above all, though, he seemed completely detached, seeing no hope – or at least no prospect – of playing a part in political affairs.

He was hard at work on his memoirs, writing them slowly in longhand and with infinite care. His daughter typed the MS., which he then revised. He had sent his pen picture of Churchill as a man to the British Prime Minister, and the sitter was not displeased with it. Although he and Churchill had often been at odds, de Gaulle admitted to Pauline that without Churchill's support he could have accomplished nothing. When Georges expressed a doubt as to whether Churchill had been wise to lead a political party after the war, de Gaulle replied that Churchill's position, with a young Queen and a well-disciplined country behind him, was different from his own. The General knew what he was writing about when he described the French as 'le peuple le plus indocile de la terre'; nevertheless his explanation of their present *malaise* always came back to the same formula – 'ils ne voulaient pas monter'. The Liberation had closed 'the last great epoque in the history of France'. The French had 'monté' behind Clemenceau, the Germans had 'monté' behind Hitler, and the Russians behind Stalin. It was only when Georges suggested it that de Gaulle admitted that the French were now too tired to 'monter' any more.

He spoke with admiration of Eisenhower and with less than

admiration of Roosevelt, but he never reacted to any mention of French personalities. Pléven, Teitgen, Parodi, Koenig and Palewski – the names seemed to pass him by, ignored for reasons of policy, or gathered up in the judicial embrace of his detachment. Before the Vaniers took their leave, the General conducted Georges into the study where he was writing his memoirs. The windows looked out on to a green and undulating landscape, and Georges commented on the distant view. 'Yes' replied the General 'one sees a long way.'

2

The Vaniers had taken an apartment on the eighth floor of the Château, a large block of flats opposite the Ritz in Montreal, and Georges' life settled down into a routine of relative inactivity very little to his liking. There were the meetings of the Crédit Foncier, and of the Bank of Montreal on whose Board of Directors he also sat. 'It is a strong proof of the Bank's ability,' he observed, 'that no unfortunate consequences have followed my appointment.' He remained, of course, closely connected with the Royal 22nd, which now comprised 115 officers and 3,850 non-commissioned officers and men. The duties of a Colonel of the Regiment – to be distinguished from the Colonel-in-Chief who was the Queen – were far from honorary. He was expected to foster an esprit-de-corps in all ranks; to advise Army Headquarters as he thought appropriate, and to act in the same capacity to Unit Commanders on such purely regimental matters as dress and customs; to advise on the administration of regimental funds, charities, organizations and memorials; to maintain a close liaison between the regular and militia units of the regiment; and to keep in touch with other regiments allied to it.

In November 1956 a new form of Royal Toast was approved: 'Mr Vice – Our Colonel-in-Chief; Messieurs – à la Reine.' In June 1958 the General visited the 4th Brigade of Canadian Infantry, of which a Battalion of the Royal 22nd formed part, then stationed near Gütersloh in Germany. He did not favour the automatic adoption by the regiment of customs and traditions common to other units, such as the Châteauguay. He thought it a mistake to have an empty table and two empty chairs at Mess dinners in commemoration of those who had been killed in action or died of wounds. A Mess dinner should be a gay affair, and it was not easy to be gay with reminders of death at one's elbow. Nor did he think it a good idea for the Officers to help themselves to cognac from a self-serving drum. He agreed to the appointment of Honorary Lieut-Colonels for each Battalion; and made himself the spokesman for those officers who were disappointed that the claim for 'Colline 227.11' had not been allowed as an addition to the general battle honour for the regiments fighting in Korea. Only 'D' Company had been heavily engaged on this operation; the others had been committed piecemeal. General Vanier had once said: 'There have been two great things in my life: my family and my regiment.' They now occupied the greater part of his time and thoughts. His portrait would soon hang in the Officers' Mess beside those of Foch and Tremblay; and some of the older veterans, whom he met at the meetings of the 'Amicale' or in hospital if they were ill or disabled, had not forgotten him.

He took all the dirty work in his stride and he was remarkable for poise, wry good humour and serenity in danger. We look forward to seeing him some day in the wards, hat cocked over one eye, cane neatly under his left arm and hear him say. 'Glad to see you again' as he used to do.

On the 26th of January 1955, Vincent Massey wished to present a goat as a mascot to the Royal 22nd, and the Queen agreed to make one available from the Royal Herd. It was to be presented during the Governor General's residence at the Citadel during September. A goat, eighteen months old and already accustomed to a halter and lead, was selected and an N.C.O. was despatched to the Zoo in order to become familiar with its habits. It was thought inappropriate that a Royal Goat should be loaded into a common truck, but this punctilio could be waived if necessary. After the harness and breastplate had been acquired from Charrington's in St James's Street the goat was handed over at a simple but dignified ceremony. It spent seventy-four days in quarantine at Glasgow before being shipped to Quebec on the 11th of July. Escorted by a corporal – with the title of goat-master – from the 2nd Battalion, it arrived on the 20th, and spent a further thirty days in quarantine at Levis. When Massey presented it on behalf of the Queen, it was led by a buckskin halter, and a buckskin strap attached the silver shield, embellished with the regimental crest, to its forehead. Georges Vanier had followed, very often with tears of laughter, each stage in the solemn comedy of its acquisition.

The Vaniers were back in Vézelay during the summer of 1955, and were just taking the road for Biarritz when Georges learnt that he was to be made an Honorary Citizen of Paris. The inaugural ceremony took place at the Hôtel de Ville in March of the following year. He owed the distinction to Champetier de Ribes, who regretted that the Canadian Government had not sanctioned his promotion to a higher grade in the Légion d'Honneur. He was received by Jacques Féron, President of the Municipal Council, and among those present – apart from Pauline, Mrs Archer and Bernard – were Thérèse de Hauteclocque, Georges Bidault, Edmond Michelet and Claudius Petit. Féron compared Vanier to Péguy's description of Descartes – 'ce cavalier Français qui partit de si bon pas' – and referred to his 'haute et fière silhouette'. In his speech of thanks Georges recalled the taste of dust and smoke in the air of Paris on the terrible night of the 10th of June 1940, and the taste of triumph in August 1944 when the city rose against the invader.

The mind naturally compares Paris to a ship, when you remember the shape of its heart – its *île de la cité* – which the waters of time lap but do not erode. Nevertheless this image is too passive, and I see it rather as an explorer, cutting loose from its moorings, navigating sometimes on the crest and at other times in the hollow of the wave, but always going forward; breaking the ice if need be; pointing the way, and bringing along in its wake all those who immediately recognize its rôle of a pathfinder and guide, armed with beauty and science, and flying the flag of hope and of discovery.

On the 3rd of June 1955 Georges received an Honorary Doctorate from the University of Montreal, and delivered the Convocation Address. The occasion has a particular significance in retrospect, because the University was to become a *foyer* of the separatism against which Georges Vanier so resolutely set his face. With no official responsibilities, he could speak his mind with perfect freedom; and it is interesting to note that he spoke very much as he had spoken to his fellow-students at Laval more than forty years before. But he now spoke with an intimate knowledge and just appreciation of the country and the civilization to which French-speaking Canada owed so much. The debt has never been more perceptively defined:

We should be very proud, we Canadians of French origin, to claim the strong and generous blood of our forebears. But this noble affiliation lays upon us a heavy responsibility – to welcome with joy and gratitude our mission to represent, to spread, and to perpetuate French civilization in America.

Our two countries, in their different latitudes, are united from within – and ever more strongly – by a long and vigorous tradition. They live under the sign of the same humanities and the same millennial patrimony. We are united in mind and heart by links forged, in the first instance, by suffering, in the struggle to win our independence and to preserve our spiritual heritage – links which could and should develop freely in peace and mutual trust.

The mission of French Canada is surely to carry the French tradition, and with it the whole Latin tradition, to peoples who are culturally remote from France. Surely it is to bring these peoples – to whom it is bound by political, economic and geographical ties – to an understanding of France – of its sufferings, its internal conflicts, its conscientious self-questionings. I have said that France and Canada are united by a tradition, and therefore from within. Canada is in communion with the mind of France; it is capable of understanding the trials and crises and events which the French have experienced in recent years, and are experiencing today. Yes, Canada ought to understand them, and to make others understand them also.

How can we discharge our mission to the full? The French survival in Canada is a fact that nothing can change. But the quality of our survival is not yet defined. It depends upon us – and especially upon you, the young men and women of Canada. Yours is the imperative duty to enrich that quality – to refine, humanize and spiritualize it. In the past we imposed our survival; let us now impose our quality. We can do it – there is nothing we cannot do – if we make the effort, if we have the will to work. Yes, we are capable of a transcendent quality, if we profit from the advantages offered us by centres of education such as this. Here you have received a doctrine – for there can be no teaching without doctrine. Here you have imbibed a philosophy, and not merely a history of philosophy where so many young people go astray before the choice in front of them. . . .

Our world is not only growing every day, it is realizing its unity on the quantitative plane. To face this frightening situation, what we need at any price is an accelerated development of qualitative values. Only the spirit can provide this element; technique alone is incapable of doing so. That is why I am speaking to you about quality and about doctrine.

But you must not think of me as a pessimist. Sometimes I hear complaints and lamentations because we are no longer living in what some people call 'the good old times'. The good time is always the present time, the time of action, and this is ours – splendid, and apocalyptic, and divinely appointed, a time of struggle between good and evil, where each must play his part and where there is no room for the cowardly or the lukewarm. . . . The motto of your University 'Fides splendet scientia' confirms this optimism. . . . If you are faithful to it, who can measure your strength? Where can you not go?

Build on the rock of truth; have faith in God, in the destiny of Canada, in your French vocation in America; and go forward without fear into the future.

This speech had an accent of authority which Georges Vanier's own future was very shortly to justify.

3

The overwhelming victory of John Diefenbaker in the elections of 1957 had brought the Conservatives to power for the first time since the premiership of R. B. Bennett. Mr St Laurent was in retirement and Lester Pearson had taken over the leadership of the Liberal Party. Mackenzie King had smoothly brought into operation his post-war policy of appointing a Canadian Governor General and of abolishing appeals to the Privy Council. Vincent Massey, though sadly handicapped by the death of his wife shortly before taking office, had proved that a Canadian could represent the Queen none the less effectively for representing Canada as well. A man of ripe experience, wide culture, and assured patriotism, he had abundantly justified his seven years' tenancy of Rideau Hall.

It was during a luncheon at the Canadian High Commissioner's, where the King and Queen were present, that Pauline Vanier had remarked, a little wistfully, to a member of the Royal *entourage*: 'Wouldn't it be fine if one day we could have a French-Canadian as Governor General?' 'Oh' came the reply 'you'll have to wait twenty-five years for that.' The prediction was curiously wide of the mark from one who knew his Canada from the inside. Already, in 1953, when St Laurent had not, after all, appointed Georges to the Senate, the idea at the back of the Prime Minister's mind, and of Lester Pearson's also, had been his eminent suitability for the post of Governor General, which an appointment to the Senate might well have compromised. But Massey's term had been extended, and the General's health was causing anxiety to his friends both within and outside the Government. He had undergone two operations for hernia, and St Laurent felt that it would be unfair to ask him to assume a burden which his sense of duty would not allow him to refuse. But now, with Massey's term approaching its end, Diefenbaker inspired a number of editorials in the Ontario press to see how digestible in those ultra-loyalist quarters the name of Georges Vanier might prove to be. Little known as he still was outside official circles, the response was encouraging. Doubts were expressed on the score of age – he was seventy-one – but if the next Governor General were to be a French-Canadian – and this was generally thought to be essential – his claims could not be disregarded.

In April 1959 Diefenbaker invited Georges to come to Ottawa. He said that he was not committed to the principle of alternating English and French speaking Canadians for the post, and he would even be ready to propose someone from outside the country if a suitable candidate suggested himself. But 1959 was the 200th anniversary of the Battle of the Heights of Abraham, and the bicentenary could appropriately be celebrated – or mitigated – by the appointment of a French-Canadian. All the veterans on either side of the language boundary would be pleased by the choice of a soldier, and official circles would be encouraged by Vanier's diplomatic record. Diefenbaker had consulted Massey, who approved of his choice; and although the Prime Minister did not know Vanier personally, he had 'heard a great deal about him'. He did not beat about the bush any further; would Georges accept the post, subject to the Queen's approval? If at the end of two or three years, he felt he could not carry on, the Prime Minister would perfectly understand; and if he found the office a financial liability, he was sure that Parliament would lend a helping hand. Georges asked when he would like an answer. The Prime Minister said that there was no dateline, except that the new Governor General must be in office to inaugurate the autumn session of Parliament.

Georges Vanier's answer was never for a moment in doubt. Pauline assumed that before accepting the offer he would of course have a medical check-up, but this suggestion was calmly brushed aside. 'If God wants me to do this job, He will give me the strength to do it.' Georges had a particular reason for this sublime confidence. Three years before, he had been laid up in the Queen Mary hospital after a heart attack. When the nurse came to take his pulse in the middle of the night, they were both astonished to find it exactly the same as before his recent attack, and he had taken this as a kind of Providential assurance that his heart would not fail him in the future. So far from wilting under the prospect of an arduous return to public life, Georges Vanier was from this moment a man rejuvenated. He wanted to be wanted; and it looked as if his Queen and his country wanted him.

The appointment was confirmed, but remained a strictly guarded secret. Georges wrote to Diefenbaker giving his movements for the coming months and expressing a wish to see 'a certain person' as soon as possible. An easy opportunity for this presented itself when the Queen came to Canada in June. One of her first engagements was to present new colours to the Royal 22nd. Georges spent four days at the Citadel, superintending the rehearsals, and went on with Pauline to Arvida, on the Saguenay, where the Queen was the guest of the Canada Aluminium Company. He presented her with the crest of the Regiment in the form of a diamond brooch which she subsequently wore at the ceremony in Quebec. On the 23rd of June the *Britannia* sailed up the St Lawrence, escorted by Canadian destroyers; and docked at Wolfe Cove, where the Queen was greeted by a guard of honour of a hundred men from the Royal 22nd. She drove up to the Citadel in the sixty-year-old, Australian built State Landau, having already warned Pauline that those who rode in it should take seasick pills before embarking. Throughout the afternoon Georges Vanier walked proudly and, as it were, paternally, by her side. Rain threatened and there was question of moving the ceremony under cover. Georges, who had not been satisfied with the last rehearsal, would not hear of this. 'If the Queen can inspect troops under rain in England, she can do so in Quebec' – and the Queen would have agreed. While the old Colours were being marched off and the band was playing 'God Save the Queen', the officers in the spectators' stand remained seated, according to their instructions. A woman journalist from Toronto criticized this as a sign of disrespect, and Georges replied with some heat to the newspaper in question. It was not for Loyalists from Toronto to teach military manners to the 'Van Doos'. After the Feu de Joie Premier Duplessis gave a state dinner to which Georges was not invited; for that devious politician could not resist so heaven-sent an opportunity to demonstrate his hatred for everything that Georges Vanier stood for. It was only out of respect for the Queen that other high-ranking officers of the Royal 22nd were persuaded to attend an occasion from which their Colonel had been excluded, and they spoke their mind very freely to the Premier of Quebec. The Queen then proceeded on her Tour, and on the 3rd of July the Vaniers sailed for Europe.

For the General there could be no better preparation for high office than a visit to his old friend Angelo Roncalli, now reigning as Pope John XXIII. The Pope received him, with Pauline, in private audience, opening out his arms as they came into the study with 'Mon cher ami!' – and then added 'Je suis toujours Roncalli, mais maintenant je suis le Vicaire du Christ.' Jock was also there, but had remained outside. After forty-five minutes Pauline wanted to fetch him in. The Pope, however, intervened – 'When one is Pope, one has to ring.' As Jock literally fell into the folds of the Johannine embrace, Pauline began to weep, and the Pope exclaimed 'I love Jock'. Georges Vanier – greatly daring – then asked if they might attend the Pope's private Mass, and at 7 a.m. the next morning they were met by Guido, the Pope's valet, and taken to his private chapel. The Mass was celebrated in dialogue, according to the new liturgical custom, and was served by Monsignor (now Cardinal) dell'Acqua. Two nuns, members of the Pope's domestic staff, were the only others present. When he came to the 'Domine non sum dignus', the Pope beckoned for a prie-Dieu to be brought for Georges so that he could kneel without difficulty to receive Communion. Afterwards he apologized for not asking them all to breakfast, and asked if they minded staying without food while he showed them his bedroom, with its family photographs – 'Bon maman' he exclaimed, pointing to the picture of his mother. They remained there talking to him for an hour. It was the first time that a layman had enjoyed the privilege of assisting at Pope John XXIII's private Mass, and the occasion roused Georges to an almost childish joy and excitement.

The Vaniers were in London, staying at the Rembrandt Hotel, when Georges' appointment was officially announced from Halifax on the 3rd of August at the end of the Royal Tour. By some miscarriage of a vital telegram all the world had public knowledge of this, except the Vaniers themselves; and when they found a substantial crowd awaiting their return to the hotel they had to pretend to know nothing – and then spent the evening watching The Nun's Story at a cinema. A few officials were, of course, in the know. Sir Alan Lascelles,[3] who knew everything there was to know about the representation of Royalty, and a good deal about Canada as well, remembered Georges 'sitting in our garden here eight years ago, and smiling his gentle deprecatory smile when I told him (with perfect sincerity and, as it turned out, with perfect prophetic accuracy) that if he accepted the offer of the Governor Generalship, he would be the best Governor General that Canada has ever had.'[4]

On the 4th of August they were the guests of George Drew, the Canadian High Commissioner in London, at a dinner for Earl

3. The Right Hon. Sir Alan Lascelles.
4. Letter to Pauline Vanier, 8th March 1967.

and Countess Mountbatten, and after ten days in Paris, where Mrs Archer had been ill, they left for Canada by sea on the 19th of August. On arrival in Montreal the General was asked whether he felt that his health and age were up to the job:

'It is not a question I would have expected,' he replied, 'but if we believe the Lord is our strength, why not act as if we thought this was true? You remember it was Shakespeare who said, "There's a divinity that shapes our ends, rough hew them how we may". Lovers of Shakespeare will pardon me if that's not quite right.'

Why had he chosen to return by sea rather than air?

'I wanted some time to rest and reflect. In fact, the time may have done my character some good.'

How should he be addressed?

'Just call me General, or if you know me well call me Georges.'

With or without an S?

'Suit your preference' – and it was observed that a man who did not care how his name was spelt was a man who did not take himself too seriously.

The General resigned his directorships and his seat on the Canada Council, where he had been very useful on the Investment Committee, and on the afternoon of the 14th of September, the Vaniers came up to Ottawa in a special Government car, 'Acadia' attached to the C.N.R. Super Continental train. They were accompanied by State Secretary Courtemanche whose Department was in charge of the arrangements for the Installation ceremony. When the train arrived at the Union Station, Ottawa, at 6.25 p.m., the Prime Minister and Mrs Diefenbaker went aboard the 'Acadia' and conducted the Vaniers to the station platform, introducing them to the Cabinet Ministers and their wives. Afterwards they drove to the Château Laurier where they were staying overnight.

The skies were lowering and the air chilly on the morning of the Installation. Georges was up at 6 a.m. putting the finishing touches to his inaugural speech. At 7.30 Abbé Leclerc celebrated Mass in the Vaniers' suite at a portable altar, since it was not customary for the Governor General Designate to be seen in public before his Inauguration. Lord Alexander[5] had worn morning dress for the same occasion, but Mr Diefenbaker thought it appropriate that a Governor General who was in fact a General

5. Field-Marshal Earl Alexander of Tunis, 1891-1969.

should dress like one on taking office. King George V had ordered a special uniform to be designed for the Governor General, and this had been worn by Lord Bessborough[6] and Vincent Massey. Bessborough and Vanier were much of a height, and Roberte Bessborough sent over her husband's uniform for Georges to wear. But he preferred to appear as Colonel of his own regiment. Madame Vanier wore a simple black silk gown, with a tiny veil over her silvery hair.

At 10 a.m. Vincent Massey left in the Viceregal train for his home at Port Hope, and at 10.50 Mr and Mrs Courtemanche met the Vaniers in a lounge of the Château Laurier adjoining the Mackenzie Avenue entrance. They drove in three cars with a motor-cycle escort to Parliament Hill, where the first Battalion of the Canadian Guards provided a band and a hundred-man Guard of Honour. The Governor General Designate and Madame Vanier were met by the Prime Minister and the Government Leader in the Senate and were then conducted to the Chambers of the Speaker of the Senate and thence to seats in front of the Dais in the Senate Chamber. The Privy Council were seated at the Council Table, with the Clerk and Under-Secretary of State at the foot and the Cabinet Ministers in order of seniority at the head on the right hand side. Over a thousand invitations for the ceremony had been sent out, but not everyone invited was expected to attend since Parliament was not in session.

The new Governor General's Acting Secretary read the Queen's Commission in English and in French, and then the Oaths of Allegiance and of Office were administered by the Chief Justice, who signed the Jurat – or attestation of the Oaths – with the Prime Minister and Clerk of the Privy Council. The Governor General ascended the Dais and took his place in front of the throne; Madame Vanier curtsied to him and stood on his left. The Secretary of State, advancing to the throne, handed the Great Seal of Canada to the Governor General, who returned it to him with the words 'I hand you the Great Seal of Canada for safe-keeping.' The Governor General then declared that he had assumed office, and sealed the Proclamation with his own Privy Seal. When the Under-Secretary had read this aloud in English and in French, the band in the Senate Rotunda played the first six bars of 'God Save the Queen'; an artillery salute was fired from Nepean Point; the Governor General's flag was raised on the Peace Tower; and Mrs Diefenbaker presented a bouquet to Pauline.

6. The Earl of Bessborough, 1880-1956.

After the Prime Minister had addressed the Governor General from his place at the Council table, Georges Vanier replied. His speech summed up with felicitous brevity many of his cherished themes. He quoted Shakespeare's *Henry VI* in paying his tribute to the Queen: 'My crown is in my heart, not on my head.' Was it surprising that such a crown should find its way into Canadian hearts as well? He paid a tribute to Vincent Massey, whose help he acknowledged and whose example he would strive to follow. He spoke of the Commonwealth whose 'potential action' conjured up 'a vision inspiring in scope and grandeur', and he spoke, with his native humility, of his trust in Divine Providence. Taking his cue from the Prime Minister, he did not forget the Plains of Abraham:

How right you are. Two hundred years ago, a certain country won a battle on the Plains of Abraham; another country lost a battle. In the annals of every nation, there is a record of victories and defeats. The present Sovereign of the victorious country, Sovereign also of Canada now, returns to the same battlefield, two centuries later, and presents Colours to a French-speaking regiment, which mounts guard over the Citadel of Quebec, a regiment of which Her Majesty is Colonel-in-Chief.

And how is the battle of 1759 commemorated? By a monument, erected in 1828, to the memory of both commanding generals, who died in action. It bears the inscription in Latin: 'Valour gave them a common death, history a common fame, posterity a common monument'. Is there a better way to heal the wounds of war, to seal the bonds of peace?

The sixty thousand French-Canadians of 1759 have become several millions. For two thousand years, more or less, the annals of history proclaim the fame and glory of Great Britain and France. The future of Canada is linked with this double fabulous heritage. Canadians of Anglo-Saxon and French descent, whose two cultures will always be a source of mutual enrichment, are an inspiring example of co-existence. They go forward hand in hand to make Canada a great nation, hand in hand also with Canadians of every origin, with their heritages, irrespective of race or creed. We are all God's children.

Here, sounded unmistakably, was the *leitmotiv* of Georges Vanier's patriotic faith. It was observed that 'the gallant old soldier was nervous, and his wife was quaking like an aspen, but the fellow who stopped a German bullet was not going to lose out in this battle of words.'[7] The speech was a characteristic over-

7. *Tribune Post*, Sackville, N.B.

ture to office, and when it had been played he stood with Pauline on the dais outside the Peace Tower steps while the Guard of Honour gave a Royal Salute, echoed by the Battery at Nepean Point. The Vaniers stepped into the State Landau, and escorted now by a detachment of the Royal Canadian Mounted Police, drove to the house that was to be their home. Here and there, among the rich foliage surrounding it, a maple leaf already transmuted to its autumn glory seemed to reflect the welcome of the nation's capital to a Governor General of whom it did not, as yet, know a very great deal.

CHAPTER 20

THE NEW ROUTINE

I

THE Vaniers had been married for thirty-eight years and they had never had a home – for an apartment in the Château was narrow quarters for two large personalities. They were not tempted, like other occupants of their high office, to hanker after an English country house left, more or less reluctantly, behind. They had made no sacrifice of business interests and severed no personal ties to arrive at their destination. If and when they retired, nothing awaited them but yet another apartment in Montreal. Where Vincent Massey had been able to escape to Batterwood for holidays or long week-ends, the Vaniers had no similar retreat. Rideau Hall became their home in a sense that it had never been a home for any previous Governor General of Canada. It was not without reason that General Vanier had remarked, on returning from his interview with Mr Diefenbaker: 'Well, Pauline, I think I've found you a house.'

As Canadians they were less diffident in asking for the improvements and amenities which their office and its functions seemed to require. Within a short time of their arrival a plate with the notice 'Résidence du Gouverneur-Général' was fixed at the main gate opposite the plate with the notice 'Government House' – a very belated concession to bilingualism. The heavy, Hanoverian dignity of the house would be all the better for a lighter and brighter touch. The old cream walls of the ballroom, darkened with age, were repainted in a pearly grey, and the vaulted ceiling, with its magnificent chandelier presented by the British Government, was trimmed with gold. A softly patterned beige rug – woven in Scotland because there were no Canadian looms big enough to hold it – almost covered the eighty-foot length and forty-foot breadth of the floor. The chairs were covered in grey-blue silk damask from Florence, and their legs were gilded. The A.D.Cs sitting-room, the small boudoir, the Royal suite, and two other bedrooms on the first floor were completely redecorated; and an elevator was installed beyond the principal staircase for the Governor General's private use. The dining-room and the long corridors were repainted, the pantry and kitchens improved, and the servants' bedrooms completely redecorated and refurnished. The secretarial offices were also completely done over, and one of the bedrooms was turned into a chapel. A sixteenth-century carved wooden chest, probably of Flemish origin, served as an altar. Elsewhere curtains, stair carpets, and chair covers were changed, and a number of attractive paintings added colour to the walls. Some of these the Vaniers had brought from the Château – Charles Camoin's 'L'Arbre de Noel', and his portrait of Thérèse when she was six years old – 'Enfant à la Poupée' – and some recent pictures by Bernard. All this embellishment naturally took time as well as money. The new red carpet which covered the whole of the entrance hall was bought for the Centennial Year, and Pauline Vanier's bedroom was redecorated only a few weeks before she left.

Many of the staff were already there when the Vaniers took over. Jean Zonda had been Assistant chef at the Hôtel du Parc in Vichy, where his recipes had nourished the senility of Marshal Pétain. He had then transferred his superlative skill to the Turkish Embassy in Paris, moving afterwards to the Spanish Embassy in London. It was here that Vincent Massey had met him and lured him to Government House, Mackinnon, the majestic *maître d'hôtel*, came from the Hebrides, and his devotion to the Vaniers was like a Highlander's devotion to his chieftain. Most important of the newcomers was Corporal (later Sergeant) Chevrier, who had served with the Royal 22nd since 1954. Georges Vanier had asked the regiment for a personal servant and had engaged him in Montreal. Within a month of the Vaniers' arrival in Ottawa, he was at a post which he never left. His loyalty to the Governor General, and afterwards to Pauline Vanier, inspired what may be described without exaggeration as an idyll of fidelity. Pauline had persuaded her cousin, Thérèse Berger, to come to Ottawa as her Lady-in-Waiting. The widow of an eminent doctor, she was a woman of unusual sensibility and charm, with a long experience of the social work in which Pauline Vanier herself was particularly interested – the Canadian Cancer Society, the Family Welfare Service, the Dominion Council of Health, and the St John's Ambulance. She had also been a Canadian delegate to the United Nations.

Much would depend on the Governor General's choice of a Secretary. He must be tactful, affable, intelligent, and discreet; acquainted with constitutional usage; and moving at ease within the limits of Viceregal protocol. Here Mr Diefenbaker had his own nominee, whose claims General Vanier resisted. Instead, he picked most happily on Esmond Butler, who had been Press Secretary to Massey, and afterwards done a spell of duty at Buckingham Palace. Sir Michael Adeane, the Queen's Private Secretary, warmly recommended him. A native of Manitoba and the son of an Anglican priest, he had graduated from the University of Toronto and since he was *persona grata* with the Queen he was not likely to be less so with her representative. He had accompanied her on the recent tour and had personally announced Georges Vanier's appointment from Halifax. He was now in London, engaged to be married to Georgiana North. They arrived in Ottawa soon after their wedding, and moved into Rideau Cottage. Georgiana was trying to bring her French up to scratch, and the General – remembering no doubt his efforts to entice Lord Byng's tongue round 'accueil' – wrote assuring her that 'it all comes in good time, with a click!' So with Commander Pemberton, R.C.N., as Comptroller of the Household, and Alain Joly de Lotbinière as Assistant Secretary, the Governor General's staff was virtually complete. He had not forgotten, however, his old friend and fellow A.D.C., William Jolliffe, now Lord Hylton, and he persuaded Raymond Jolliffe, Lord Hylton's son and heir, to join him in whatever capacities he might prove most useful. It was a happy and successful arrangement, and after a few months the General was writing to Lord Hylton:

I don't know what I would have done without him. You know as well as I how many addresses and speeches one has to make. There appears to be an idea that the Governor General can speak on any subject for any length of time. Having seen a great deal of Raymond when he was in Canada, a couple of years ago, I knew he had the qualifications necessary for research and writing. It isn't often that one can be sure that one isn't making a mistake.[1]

Butler and Jolliffe, joined later by Michael Pitfield, were, each in their different way, the ideal assistants for a man who remained indomitably young in heart. In fact it was probably the youngest staff ever assembled at Government House; only the Comptroller was over forty years old. In a house that was so much of a home the Vaniers found it easy to create the atmos-

1. 12th August 1960.

General Vanier at the Citadel, as Honorary Colonel of the Royal 22nd,
receiving the Regimental Mascot from Vincent Massey.

Madame Vanier serving the Sergeants Mess.

Arriving in Quebec after his appointment as Governor General.

The visit of President Kennedy and Mrs Kennedy
to Government House, May 1961.
Left to right: President Kennedy, General Vanier, John F. Diefenbaker,
Madame Vanier, Mrs Kennedy and Mrs Diefenbaker.

Tour of the North-West Territories, June 1961. Madame Vanier
chatting with an Indian woman.

Taking the Oath from the Chief Justice at the Inauguration Ceremony,
14th September 1959.

phere of a family. It was not long before the A.D.Cs were
referring among themselves to 'Ma Vanier', and one of them
translated 'H.E.' as 'High Explosive' – admittedly with no justification whatever, except the very occasional reminder of an Irish
heredity. This was the nearest anyone ever got to giving Georges
Vanier a nickname, and it did not get very far.

The General's daily routine, when he was in residence at
Rideau Hall, did not vary much from the day he took office. He
was woken by Chevrier at 7.45. At 8 o'clock a cooked breakfast
was brought up to him – with the Montreal *Gazette*. The Ottawa
papers, with the *Toronto Globe and Mail* and *Le Devoir*, reached
him later in the day. He was particular, though not extravagant,
about his clothes, still getting his shoes from Dangerfields, and
his pyjamas – '2-ply English fabric, Egyptian yarn, blue with
darker blue piping' – from Morgan's in Montreal; his shirts from
Austin Reed, his suits – or the material to make them – from
Welsh & Jefferies, and his hats from London also. Massey had
designed and instituted a Government House tie, but General
Vanier nearly always wore the regimental tie of the Royal 22nd.
He had several of these, and when they were worn out he cut
them in half. This was the signal for Chevrier to burn them;
merely to have thrown them away would have been an act of
inconceivable impiety. When one of them refused to fall
properly, he sent it back with a pin to mark the recalcitrant spot.

The General would come down to his study between 9.30 and
10.00 and give orders to Mackinnon for the wine to be served
that day. Pauline had already discussed the menu with Zonda,
who had passed on the information. The Governor General would
then open his mail, confer with his staff, and work till luncheon.
His desk stood in the far corner of the study, where it was easy
for him to open the window and feed the birds. A contraption
for this had been fixed just outside, for which 25 lbs. of seeds
were ordered monthly. He had two secretaries, Miss Pitney and
Mademoiselle Blais, to take dictation in English and French. It
was generally noon before he was ready for Mademoiselle Blais,
and she would sometimes come to him again later in the day. He
dictated very slowly, often asking her advice over a phrase, and
spending a long time over a single word. If the word was a wrong
word he was quick to spot it. As he was reading his first Speech
from the Throne he suddenly came upon the phrase 'unseasonal
snow', and substituted 'unseasonable' without apparent hesita-
tion. The speeches read easily because they were so carefully

prepared; one of them was revised twenty-four times. Raymond Jolliffe – and Michael Pitfield or George Cowley in later years – would do whatever research was necessary on the subject in hand, and prepare a draft which served as raw material for what was eventually delivered. As time went on, the Governor General came to treat the preliminary drafts with an even greater freedom.

After luncheon he would rest, and often sleep, for an hour or so, until Chevrier woke him with a cup of tea or glass of milk at 4 o'clock. Mass was celebrated in the Chapel adjoining his room at 5.15. The General read the Epistle of the day himself, seated before his prie-Dieu. Canon Hermas Guindon acted as Chaplain from the day the Vaniers took up residence at Rideau Hall until the day when Pauline Vanier left it. Permission had been given for the Blessed Sacrament to be reserved in the Chapel. The General always remained in front of the tabernacle for twenty minutes or so when Mass was over, and indeed he never at any time of the day passed the chapel without going inside, even if only for a few moments.

He would then work or receive visitors until seven o'clock when he took his bath and changed for dinner which was served at eight. Guests were asked to be in the drawing-room by 7.45. General Vanier would have a whisky and soda before dinner, a tomato juice before luncheon, and a glass of wine with his meals; but he was a very temperate drinker. He had, however, a passion for tomato ketchup which was not considered a suitable ornament for the Viceregal dining-table. One advantage of dining in bed – as he occasionally did towards the end of his life, and not always with the excuse of illness – was the freedom to have tomato ketchup on his tray. In the more informal surroundings of the Citadel he would hide it under the table beside his chair. After dinner he liked to watch a hockey game on the TV in the Library – a room which had been rather neglected by successive incumbents. Georges Vanier, however, was a bibliophile and whenever a book of general political or biographical interest came out, he would instruct the Comptroller to acquire it. He and Pauline had their own books in their private quarters, and Madame Vanier would take some pride in choosing appropriate reading matter for her guests, and placing it in their rooms. Sometimes a film would be shown in the evening, and at 10.30 the General liked to watch the TV news in Madame Vanier's bedroom. They retired early, though not necessarily to sleep, for this was the General's favourite time for reading – Thackeray for novels, Shelley and Keats for poetry. They were the authors of his youth and he was faithful to them. He now cared much less for French literature, although he thought that a good deal of worldly wisdom could be learnt from Montaigne, and perhaps a little unworldly wisdom from Mauriac and Claudel. He liked to quote Claudel's 'Youth is not made for pleasure, but for heroism' – although here he had his own better accredited guides; St Paul, St John of the Cross, Père de Caussade, and St Thérèse of the Child Jesus.

The protocol at Government House was correct without being fussy and, generally speaking, the Vaniers maintained the traditions they had inherited. If it were suggested that in this democratic day and age ladies should not be expected to curtsey to the Queen's representative – because, after all, they no longer curtsied to the Queen of the Netherlands – Georges Vanier replied that he represented the Queen of Canada, not the Queen of the Netherlands, and that so long as people curtsied to the Queen's representatives in her other Dominions they should continue to do so in Canada. But here, as in everything else, he had a characteristic lightness of touch; when he tried to demonstrate a curtsey to Alice Gadoffre – not easy for a man with only one leg – her laughter, and his, did not assist the experiment. Nor has the subsequent abolition of the curtsey proved so popular as its egalitarian advocates predicted. On State occasions General Vanier and his wife insisted on receiving the guests by themselves, leaving the Prime Minister, if he so wished, to receive them in another room. The Royal Toast – 'The Queen – La Reine' – was always drunk when the Governor General was at table, and when three or more persons were present. Etiquette prescribed that he should precede his wife into the dining-room, but Lord Tweeds-muir had noticed that the King always made the Queen go first, and General Vanier followed his example except on the most official occasions. He and Madame Vanier were served before any other guests; and after every formal dinner, when the men remained behind in the dining-room, the ladies curtsied to him before they left. A curious custom dictated that there should be no second helpings, and guests were encouraged to eat their fill while the going round was good.

It was noticeable that whatever their state of health or mind neither the General nor Madame Vanier ever allowed the conversation to flag, so that the rather absurd etiquette which for-

bade a guest to introduce a topic before Royalty or its representatives caused no awkward silences. Both the Vaniers were easy
and fluent talkers, and they did not talk what Lord Tweedsmuir
had called 'Governor-generalities'. It was observed, however, that
in a tête-à-tête or smaller group neither was disposed to argue.
They would listen carefully, discuss eagerly, but they were reluctant to debate. If you knew that something had happened on a
Wednesday and they were equally sure that it had happened on a
Thursday, it was useless – and indeed unwise – to produce your
evidence. In Georges Vanier the habit of command went hand in
hand with the habit of reflection. He was always liable to reverse
a decision at which he had arrived with difficulty, so that Esmond
Butler learnt to put a decision into immediate effect if he thought
it was a good one, and to procrastinate if he thought otherwise.

The General's consideration for his staff, at all levels, was
unfailing. He, or Madame Vanier, saw to it that there were hot
drinks for the Mounties on a cold night; and if an official had
not been seen around for some time, they would ensure that
enquiries were made about his health. Only on very rare occasions did the General's self-control desert him. Once, on a tour
of the North-Western territories, he exploded when Butler
warned him against over-taxing his strength. A day for rest had
been set aside, but the General could not resist the appeal of yet
another Eskimo or Indian school. Who was Butler to tell him
what he could do or not do? On another occasion a television
company had obtained permission to photograph the Governor
General at work, and a time had been chosen when the Prime
Minister was due to call – as he usually did, late on Tuesday
afternoon. The General came down to his study and finding a
barrage of cameras, and litter of cables stretching down the
corridor, raised his stick and ordered the immediate removal of
men and equipment. He had either forgotten that permission had
been given for the filming, or not realized what it entailed. Meanwhile Mr Pearson was expected to arrive at any moment, and it
required all Butler's gentle diplomacy to restore the situation.
Once it had been restored the General's apologies were as vocal
as his annoyance.

The Vaniers had very modest private means and there was
little they could do to supplement the necessary expenditure at
Government House. Vincent Massey had made no bones about
declaring, on his retirement, that the salary and allowances were
inadequate, even though the Governor General enjoyed the diplo-

matic privilege of importing goods from abroad free of duty. With a pension of only $6,600 a year Georges Vanier's private account was soon overdrawn, but he insisted on reducing it from his own resources. Nevertheless, as he reminded Pemberton, 'many of the items that appear in Account No. 6 would never have been incurred if I were not Governor General! For instance, the heavy accounts for clothes for my wife and for myself! We were living very quietly, and neither of us would have thought for a moment of buying the clothes we did.'[2] After he had been in office for some years, General Vanier made the Governor General's financial position the subject of a memorandum. There should be no question of his relinquishing such independence as he enjoyed, but he should discontinue the buying or selling of bonds or shares other than Government securities. He concluded that the only adequate solution would be the provision of a pension, as in the case of former Prime Ministers. Even if he were able to put aside $50,000 out of his salary, this would only represent an income of $3,000, on which he could not possibly live, especially if he had a family. Until Mr Pearson's Government stepped in and shouldered an extra $76,000 towards the expenses of running Government House, the position had cost General Vanier an estimated $10,000 a year from his private income.

The General found it as difficult to resist an appeal as to forget an obligation or an anniversary. If Butler reminded him that they were 'in the red', he would still spare $50 to some needy charity or Sisterhood. Had Butler remembered to send a gift to the Station Master at Vancouver, and wasn't it time that he gave something to the 'bell boy' – in fact a man of forty – who always looked after him at the Château Laurier? The Sergeant-at-Arms at the House of Commons was retiring; a letter must be sent to him. But his generosity was not spendthrift He thought it only fair that the Government should pay for local telephone calls, and he closed one London account because the firm made so many mistakes in its book-keeping. He was anxious that the French-speaking members of his staff should have French newspapers: but who paid for *Le Figaro*?

General Vanier had made it known, on assuming office, that he would attend public worship in accordance with his own religious beliefs, but that when his official duties required his attendance at the services of some other Christian denomination he would naturally be there. On Sundays the Vaniers made a practice of

2. 8th August 1960.

assisting at Mass in one or other of the churches in Ottawa or Hull, and when they were at the Citadel, in one of the parish churches of Quebec or the neighbouring countryside. In this way they became known to the ordinary people of the capital; and there were other ways as well:

One day as I returned from work, late and terribly rushed, the strap on my purse broke and it fell scattering the contents all over the street. As I frantically scrambled after the myriad objects husbands so willingly classify as junk, I became aware of someone helping me gather my possessions. After all my treasures had been retrieved I thanked my good Samaritan and went my way. Now, years later, I have never forgotten his smile of amusement or the friendly twinkle in his eye as he reached under the Viceregal car to salvage a tube of lipstick – and I cannot truthfully say I remember what he said. All I remember is the burning humiliation I felt (for I had recognized the car and must confess I was staring at the moment of my mishap) and how with a friendly smile and a friendly word my embarrassment was banished.

This letter to Pauline Vanier was signed 'a little Canadian' who mourned 'a person, not a personage; a friend, not a figure; a man not a monument.' Where another man might, or might not, have requested his chauffeur to retrieve a lady's lipstick, General Vanier insisted on retrieving it himself. Not for the first time one is reminded of Sir Walter Raleigh throwing down his cloak to prevent Queen Elizabeth I from walking in a puddle. It goes without saying that Georges Vanier would have done the same for Queen Elizabeth II. It is worth recording that he did a similar thing for the humblest of her subjects.

The figure, always distinguished – the 'haute et fière silhouette' – had now acquired a kind of majesty which might have seemed intimidating if it had not been at the same time so intimate. One is tempted to say that General Vanier knew how to unbend, but there was never any stiffness – except the stiffness of the soldier on parade – to invite flexibility. His was an integral personality, and to that extent an integral physique. His presence and demeanour combined dignity and grace, with an ease of gesture as he welcomed a friend, illustrated a point in conversation, or – and this was very habitual – twirled his greying moustaches. Yet even his attitudes were bilingual. When he was speaking in English he stood straight as a ramrod, sparing of gesture; when he was speaking in French, his body would sway with his words and his hands delicately gesticulate to emphasize his meaning.

The strength of the soldier, the suppleness of the diplomat, and the courtliness of a great gentleman complemented each other, and were each touched with a humility that uttered its unspoken rebuke to arrogance, vulgarity and pride.

During his first six months in office the General gave five official dinners, and nine official receptions. The dining-room normally used could accommodate forty-eight guests, but State banquets for anything up to a hundred people were served in the ballroom; and for the annual Garden Party in June five thousand guests would stroll across the lawns. The visits from Heads of State that followed the Vaniers' installation in office were occasions of comedy as well as of colour. The *contretemps* afforded light relief to the ceremonial. When President and Madame de Gaulle came in April 1960, French Canadian books were put out as *livres de chevet* for Madame de Gaulle, but alas! their leaves were uncut. There was a notable disparity in height between the President and his wife, and care was taken to avoid any suggestion of *lèse-majesté* in the length of the bed assigned to him. Zonda rose to the occasion of the State banquet with an Arctic fish caught by Eskimos, and with twenty-four pastel-blue sugar baskets holding French pastries and adorned with corn-flowers, marguerites and poppies – all fashioned out of sugar by his cunning hands. A Cross of Lorraine in red and white carnations and blue hyacinths decorated the centre of the table, and the guests savoured their delicacies from the dinner service of Copeland Spode.

President Kennedy admired the Canadian genius for ordered ceremonial, and the Vaniers were struck by his humility and by Jacqueline Kennedy's lack of sophistication. The Kennedys planted two trees in the grounds of Government House,[3] and in doing so the President suffered a fresh injury to his back, although at the time the fact was known only to his personal physician. He seized the opportunity to pick General Vanier's brains about de Gaulle whom he was shortly to meet – and dreaded meeting. President Bourguiba of Tunisia had come shortly before, and he too – with the Algerian crisis unsettled – was anxious to talk about de Gaulle, whose statesmanship he trusted to resolve it. There was a terrible moment when Mr Eric Williams, the Prime Minister of Trinidad and Tobago, said that he would like some rum. It was thought that he would recognize Jamaican rum, and *sotto voce* instructions were given to an

3. 16th May 1961.

A.D.C. to scour the cellars for a bottle of rum from Trinidad.

The Vaniers were careful to provide a blend of Ethiopian coffee, the gift of a Winnipeg importer, for Haile Selassie, but the Emperor did not seem to recognize, or indeed to appreciate, it. Shortly after he had left, however, Commander Pemberton phoned through to Madame Vanier with a message that 'the coffee had come'. When she asked him to send it along to the kitchen, he replied that there were *two tons* of it. The dispersal of this munificent gift to deserving recipients occupied hours of valuable time. The visit of a certain Eastern potentate was clouded by an appalling row between the guest and his A.D.C. who arrived a little late on duty. It seemed as if only the *habeas corpus* of Government House saved the unfortunate man from immediate execution. The Vaniers received the President of Iceland and Mrs Aggriessen at the Citadel,[4] but Mrs Aggriessen had brought no evening dress and asked permission to appear in national costume – which ensured the sartorial eclipse of all the Quebécoises.

No Head of State, however, gave the Vaniers more pleasure than President de Valera. Instead of returning their hospitality at the Irish Embassy, he gave a reception at the Country Club. The guests were still arriving when he embarked on a long description of his escape from Lincoln gaol, where he had been imprisoned after the Easter Rising in 1916. 'Mr President, the Prime Minister is waiting' – but Madame Vanier's curiosity was aroused and she interrupted: 'But I want to know how you got out.' Mr de Valera explained how he had collected the wax from the altar candles in the prison chapel, and used them to make an impression of the key that would unlock his cell.

Their first visitor, appropriately enough, was Princess Alice whom Georges described as 'the youngest middle-aged woman'[5] of his acquaintance. She had asked for 'nice small meals with half a dozen real pals where we can have a good talk'; and she also had her views on the thorny question as to who should precede who into the dining-room. 'We remember the advice you gave us and the solution you and I worked out (although you struggled very hard to push me forward each time) – arm-in-arm – "ensemble".'[6] This was home ground for the Princess; as it was for Vincent Massey who paid the first of many visits in the autumn of 1960. It is never quite easy to step down from the

4. 11th September 1961.
5. To Sir Bernard Fergusson, 9th January 1966.
6. 21st December 1964.

highest position in the land and Massey, though he was ripe in years and rich in honours, was a lonely man – more especially after the death of the son who had also been his Secretary. The Vaniers went all the way to make him feel at home, giving him the Royal suite and bidding him turn up with his suitcase whenever he felt inclined. He took them at their word and returned their hospitality at Batterwood. 'If you don't continue to call me Georges' the General wrote to him, 'I shall do something dramatic. I don't quite know what.'[7] Unlike his hosts, Massey had no taste for early to bed, and he would keep the A.D.Cs enthralled with his conversation until the small hours of the morning. He had the makings of a brilliant actor beneath the official or academic mask, and his anecdotes were enlivened by mimicry.

Guests did much to diversify the Vice-regal routine – Prince Philip, the Princess Royal, Lord and Lady Alexander, Lord and Lady Avon, Sir Oliver and Lady Leese, Sir Robert Menzies, U Thant, Lord and Lady Normanbrook – it would be tedious to extend the list. Harold Macmillan walked wistfully through the rooms, remembering his courting of Lady Dorothy when he was A.D.C. to the Duke of Devonshire, for the great rambling house, so stately and yet so comfortable, was part of British as well as of Canadian history. Yet the Visitors Book was very far from being a catalogue of famous names. Madame Vanier was fond of telling one, as she moved beneath those portraits – not always very good portraits – of former Governors General, that she was not 'born to the purple' – to which one was tempted to reply that if she was not, she ought to have been. But she and the General came to Government House with so rich a legacy of friendships that guests were welcomed for themselves, not for their rank or their *réclame*.

The visit of the Duke of Edinburgh in May 1962 was particularly successful. Its main purpose was to attend a Study Conference in Toronto on the human consequences of the changing industrial environment in the Commonwealth and Empire. He also found time for a fishing trip, ordering among other kit a vest of darker colour – evidently afraid lest a lighter hue might scare away the wary English or Scottish trout. When he had gone, General Vanier wrote to Sir Michael Adeane:

Last night I saw His Royal Highness Prince Philip off at Rockcliffe

7. 9th November 1959.

Airport. He was in wonderful form, leapt into his Heron and a minute later was at the controls and off to Montreal. . . . I was much impressed by the number and quality of the representatives from the 34 countries of the Commonwealth. The spirit of friendship and team-play which animated all of our guests was very comforting. There is no doubt that much good is being done by their presence in Canada. . . . I think the Prince is very pleased indeed and so are all of us. He held a Press Conference in which, in my humble opinion, he was quite brilliant, answering all questions, even some that might be considered embarrassing, in a way which won the praise of the Press itself – direct answers, pulling no punches.[8]

The General's return to Canada, and more particularly his appointment to high office, had brought a renewal of contact with old friends, lost sight of during the migrations of diplomacy. There was J. P. Cathcart, now a doctor, with whom he had stoked the fire in that icy Buxton bedroom. Whenever Mrs Cathcart saw her husband reading or watching anything about Georges Vanier, she saw his arthritic hand brushing away a tear. And for Georges 'Although our widely divergent paths have prevented me from seeing much of you since our hospital days I have always looked upon you as one of my dearest friends.'[9] There was Robertson Fleet, now a permanent invalid but 'holding his own, like the knight that he is.'[10] Georges rarely came to Montreal without seeing, or attempting to see, him. 'The next time . . . I am not going to telephone to ask whether he will see me or not, I am coming up and I am going to throw a brick through the front door to announce my arrival.'

Of his military friends Harry Crerar had also been in poor health for a long time:

If you can ever break 'protocol', he wrote to the General, we are usually in for tea, and the Medicals allow (even recommend!) a short drink before luncheon – 12.30 – or dinner, say 5.30. Have some good sherry – which you might prefer . . . I can do 'luncheon' all right?

Whether or not the General came for a drink, he came to swear in Crerar as a Member of the Queen's Privy Council[11] – a gesture that was warmly appreciated from one veteran to another.

On the 21st of September 1961, William Duncan Herridge died

8. 17th May 1962.
9. 22nd January 1961.
10. To Mrs Fleet. 1st October 1962.
11. 1964.

in Ottawa. A man of immense vitality, a keen fisherman, and lively conversationalist, he had made his reputation as a patent lawyer at the Canadian Bar. He was a close friend and supporter of Lord Byng, and very naturally became a friend of Georges Vanier. He was the second Canadian Minister to Washington (1931-1935), where his diplomatic luncheons – no cocktails, no waiting for late arrivals, excellent white wine, and all over by 2 p.m. – were carried through with unflagging verve and – according to Dean Acheson – a good deal of noise.

There was also Paul Morin who had rather come down in the world where Georges Vanier had gone up and up. In February 1960 Victor Barbeau, Director of the Académie Canadienne-Française, was writing to the Governor General:

For several years he has been leading a desolate existence, both materially and morally. In full possession of all his faculties and also of his talent, he languishes alone in a wretched little room, rue Sherbrooke 1662 East, and never comes out. The only thing that keeps him alive is the hope of publishing his book. A poet of his quality should not have to wait about in ante-rooms. Any competent and intelligent person would have immediately agreed to his request. It is surely the last joy that he will know before he dies.

Morin wrote himself a little later that he had twice received Extreme Unction – and this had given him 'furiously to think'.[12] He had also seen his library go up in flames. A telegram signed 'Gérant' was immediately mystifying, since it should have read 'Géronte' – with its reference to Morin's poem 'Géronte et son miroir'. Georges replied:

You have not altered. As ever, brilliant and sparkling, the enameller and goldsmith rising from his ashes. . . . I was reading only the other day *Le Paon d'Email* – 'de son très cher ami Paul Morin.' It revived many memories – and good ones.[13]

There followed a self-portrait, monocled, with white beard and moustache, and signed 'Facies bizarre d'un rimeur qui t'aime bien.'

I like your *facies* very much . . . it's obvious that your outlook on life has not changed; in any case your mask is no ordinary one. You still pay great attention to detail, and it was a stroke of genius to combine the hammer and the monocle.[14]

12. To Georges P. Vanier, 2nd June 1960.
13. 1st April 1961.
14. 10th May 1962.

Some of these memories went even further back than Paul Morin. When Estelle McKenna died, Georges wrote to her husband: 'Estelle and I played together as very small children, as we were about the same age, and lived next to one another on St Antoine Street. Your no was 400 and ours 398.'[15]

Certain annual events brought the Governor General into the public eye. The *leveé* in the Senate Chamber on New Year's Day – an overwhelmingly, though not strictly, masculine occasion, with most of those present, after the plentiful libations of punch, spiced with nutmeg and sharpened with lemon, dispensed in the adjoining room, trooping over to luncheon at the Rideau Club. The protests of a certain minister of the Dominion United Church that the Governor General should not connive at the consumption of the punch that contained rum and cognac among its ingredients, was firmly over-ridden by public opinion. The *leveé* tradition dated back to the days of New France when the French Governors made it known to their very much smaller population that they would receive their greetings on New Year's Day. Everybody went, from the ditch-digger to the Government official. Not quite everybody goes today; but there were enough to keep General Vanier standing for two hours, with a chair for his only support. There were also the dinners given by the Speaker of the House and the Senate. Mr Roland Mitchener was Speaker of the House when the General took office, and Mrs Mitchener had borrowed the Roman custom of having the Princes of the Blood or Princes of the Church preceded by a flunkey with a nine-branched candelabra. The Vaniers fitted neither of these categories, but they qualified. There was the opening of Parliament, and the State dinner which preceded it. Carnations from the palest of pink to the deepest maroon decorated the U-shaped table, and potted plants from the conservatory which was Pauline Vanier's pride stood in the corners of the room. Zonda's virtuosity was demonstrated by the twelve white spun sugar gondolas bringing their hint of the 'warm south' to a frosty January night; and in the morning the horses' hooves rang out crisply on the paving as the twenty-four officers of the R.C.M.P. escorted the landau to Parliament Hill, their lances gleaming in the sun – if the sun happened to be shining. Television brought to thousands of homes the figure of the Governor General pausing to speak with a member of the Guard of Honour, and then climbing the steps under the vaulted arch and the signs

15. 14th November 1959.

of the ten Provinces, whose unity in diversity he was dedicated to preserve. Within the Senate chamber and before the 'faithful Commons' summoned to the Bar by Black Rod, he sat with the Prime Minister on his right and Madame Vanier on his left to deliver his speech. Gladstone Murray thought the first of these 'really superb – easily the best of its kind I have heard in Canada or the United Kingdom during the past half century.'[16]

Then there were the reception of foreign envoys, with the protocol simplified for the representatives of nations within the Commonwealth. The High Commissioners for the monarchies handed their letters of Commission to the Prime Minister, while those from the republics handed theirs to the Governor General. They drove to Rideau Hall in the State landau, but were received in General Vanier's study instead of in the ballroom. The Vaniers gave only one ball in Ottawa, and, rather to the chagrin of local society, discontinued the parties for *débutantes*. Here they were only following Royal precedent; and the General, perfectly at home as he always seemed on ceremonial occasions, was happier at the Children's Parties with the Canada of tomorrow clambering over his knee or pulling crackers with their elders, or squatting on the floor of the ballroom and watching the comic cartoons on a screen, all the restrictions of protocol conjured away as if by a fairy's wand. 'You probably wonder what I do here all the time' he remarked to a boy from the Ottawa Boys' Club, 'I spend most of my time feeding the squirrels.'

2

Attached as the Vaniers grew to Rideau Hall, they were even fonder of the Citadel. Here Georges had exercised his first command, and it was all in keeping with a singularly rounded career that he should come back to it. Events beyond his control, as we shall see, were to cloud these happy associations; but the Vaniers spent two Christmases in those less formal but more elegant surroundings. In 1959 they attended Midnight Mass in the Salle d'Exercices Militaires at Valcartier. It was the first time in the history of the regiment that all three battalions of the Royal 22nd had been at home for Christmas; and on the 22nd of December the General and his wife donned a chef's cap and apron to serve the eight hundred non-commissioned officers and men. All the other officers did likewise in obedience to a time-honoured cus-

16. 15th January 1960.

tom, recalling the obligation of every officer to see that his men had food, clothes and lodging before making provision for himself. The Citadel was embellished, in due course, by Pauline's imaginative redecoration of the dining-room, with its black and white landscape wallpaper; and the *grand salon*, with its Louis XV armchairs, was lightened by the pearly-grey surface of the walls and the deep pink, white and bluish-grey velvet of the chair coverings. In the huge solarium, which opened on to the Queen's Bastion and overlooked the St Lawrence, the old square-paned windows were replaced to give more light and an easier view. The room itself was redecorated, and the furniture re-covered in cretonne of an audacious but successful blend of steely blue, soft green and pale yellow. This work was executed by local decorators. In the ante-room downstairs, and along the walls of the corridor leading to the Commandant's apartments which the Vaniers had once occupied, the coloured prints of Quebec and the Ile d'Orléans were an agreeable variation on official portraiture.

Recent history had left its mark on the Citadel. Bath aids had been installed for President Roosevelt when he attended the Conference of Quebec in 1943, and a commemorative painting of the President with Churchill, Mackenzie King and Lord Athlone hung over the staircase, at the top of which, at Christmas 1961, a chairlift was installed to save the General a painful climb. He owed this to the Deputy-Minister of Public Works, to whom he wrote as follows:

What a wonderful Christmas present! I can't tell you how overjoyed I was when I saw the lift! Really it will make all the difference in the world to my stay at the Citadel now and later on. Going up these twenty steps several times each day was not only a matter of fatigue, but a frustration as well, when others were taking them four at a time![17]

Lord Bessborough had planted the row of poplars along the side of the old gaol, and General Vanier planted the first of twenty-two maples bordering the central walk. In September, when the Vaniers liked to be in residence, the geraniums and petunias blazed in the flower beds and round the ornamental well-head. The heavy willows and elms still shaded the path outside the Mess and the Commandant's apartments; the Canadian flag and the Governor General's blue and gold standard flew from the King's Bastion; and the eight cannon with their gleaming black paint

17. To Major-General H. A. Young, 20th December 1961.

pointed across to Levis on the southern shore. The General was always informed at what time of day the various ships would be passing below, and the vessels of the Royal Canadian Navy were expected to blow their sirens as a mark of respect. If they forgot to do so an apology was generally forthcoming.

Quebec, no less than Ottawa, exacted its round of official duties. The General was officially welcomed by the city in the month following his installation. There was the opening of the Law Courts and procession to the Assizes; the annual dinner of the Bar Association; the Battle of Britain ceremony, with a wreath laid at the Cross of Sacrifice in the Grande Allée; the commemoration of Courcelette by the Vimy Cross, with the veterans lined up on either side, followed by Mass in the Chapel of the Citadel and a Vin d'Honneur in the Mess. Three balls were given, with supper served on the terrace walk, overlooking the docks; and the usual cocktail parties. After one of these the General observed that a good number of people had accepted the invitation, but had not turned up. He mildly suggested that they need not be invited again. Then there were visits to the women's penitentiary, to the occupational therapy and physio-therapy clinics at Ste Foy, or an initiation into the sinister mysteries of electronics and aerophysics at the Canadian Armament Research and Development Establishment. The daily routine was much the same as at Ottawa, except that the General attended Mass at noon.

In 1960 the Vaniers spent their holidays at Vézelay, taking off for Europe from Torbay in Newfoundland, where they had been on tour. They spent a few days in London, returning there to have luncheon with the Queen. On the 20th of August they lunched privately with President de Gaulle. The Governor General did not disguise his satisfaction that 'France has chosen to be governed by the man who saved its honour in 1940.'[18] But holidays did not mean relief from work. Georgette Blais, who accompanied the Vaniers to Vézelay, was writing to Esmond Butler:

H.E.'s backlog of work seems gradually to be getting down. The minute I feel it's all cleared up, he finds umpteen of them in his pockets, brief-cases etc. By the time we reach Quebec we'll start with a clean slate.

The Vaniers had always been fond of Brittany, and in 1961 they were staying at Port-Manech in Finistère; but they did not go

18. Telegram to President de Gaulle, 17th June 1959.

to Europe in 1962, since Diefenbaker's minority Government was
threatening to fall at any moment. Pauline had spent her summers
as a child at Tadoussac, a small fishing village and modest resort
at the confluence of the St Lawrence and the Saguenay. There was
some debate about the meaning of its Indian name – 'Place of
lobsters', 'turtle in fresh water', 'place where the ice is broken',
or 'mouth of river full of rocks.' It was the oldest French establishment and Christian mission station in Canada. Ships came there
for whaling, and for a long time it was the centre of the fur
trade. Jacques Cartier knew it in 1535; in 1600 Pierre Chauvin
built the first house; and three years later, at Larks Point, Champlain concluded his alliance with the Algonquins against the
Iroquois. No doubt the first Vaniers who came to Canada knew it
as well.

The little harbour was set into a rocky promontory, facing
the St Lawrence on one side, and on the other the steep, wooded
cliffs of the fjord leading upstream to Chicoutimi and Lac St Jean.
In July 1962 the Vaniers occupied a suite in the hotel, which was
then furnished throughout with antiques of considerable value.
It looked on to the wooden parade with shelters at either end,
and the earlier history of Tadoussac was writ large in the little
Indian chapel close by where two of the missionaries were buried.
The following year they rented Colonel H. E. C. Price's house
only a few yards away on the further side of a small creek. With
its wooden frame, brown shingled sides, and black shingled roof,
this was screened by pine trees at the back, and a wide verandah
ran the whole length of the exterior. It was a weather-beaten,
comfortable old place; only wild flowers grew in the garden, and
patches of the lawn were burnt brown by the sun. Here the
Vaniers could live 'a simple, family life, with no frills.' They
brought no servants from Government House; a local girl came
in to cook, and Bernard with his family were also staying there.
Sometimes he would drive the General out into the scented
countryside for a closer look at the Saguenay cliffs, so often
obscured by low-hanging clouds; and it was a pleasant conclusion
to the day when Roger Nantel[19] had caught a fat Saguenay trout.
Early in September Pauline was writing to Mrs Price:

We left Tadoussac two days ago with a heavy heart. The day was
beautiful, absolutely cloudless. It was hard to leave such beauty to
take on the harness again. I want you to know that never before

19. Lieutenant Roger C. Nantel, A.D.C.

have we enjoyed a holiday as we did in your delightful house.

For the next three years the journey by train to Murray Bay, with its wooden houses painted in pastel blues and pinks, and then by car through the lower Laurentians to the Saguenay Ferry, would be looked forward to as an overture to relaxation. The General spent much of his time in travel, but this was a journey with no official appearance at the end of it. In 1963 his personal standard was flown from the flagstaff on the lawn, and only a distant glimpse of that distinguished head bent over official papers on the Price verandah told the inquisitive that the Governor General was at work, even though he was supposed to be at play. Very often he was simply reading a book, or gazing out over the St Lawrence at an *Empress* steamer gliding upstream. Very often there were two distinguished heads close together when Pauline was sitting at his side.

In fact, there was more play in Georges Vanier's life than the casual onlooker might have imagined, who only saw his devotion to duty. A letter written to an old friend of Geneva days, after he had been in office for more than three years, reveals the secret sources of his recreation:

Thérèse will have told you something of our life here. It is alright if you don't take yourself seriously, or others as well! Bernard and his wife and Valérie (eighteen months) and Laurence (nine months) spent the month of October with us. Don't tell Thérèse this when you see her, but honestly I think Pauline and I love those two as well as (I was going to say 'better than' but I don't dare) our own children. I suppose it is because one has a good time with one's grandchildren until one gets tired of them, whilst with one's own children (there are a lot of 'ones' in this sentence, one cannot dispose of them so quickly. I remember so well that once when Pauline and I went to Paris from Geneva with one or two of the tribe and stayed at a hotel, I had to play with one or both of them from 6.00 in the morning until 8.00 in order not to earn the ire of the other 'inmates' of the hotel. I can tell you that at 8.00 sharp, I used to say 'Howl as much as you like now', feeling that at 8.00 everybody should be up and about.

While Bernard and his family were here, every morning at 8.30 they would bring me Laurence (nine months) and place her on my bed from which she would watch me shaving. She was full of something called 'pablum' (Thérèse will tell you what this is). It is a Latin drink which they have invented over here for babies. Laurence would just lie there like a female Buddha full, so full, of pablum that I didn't dare shake her otherwise she would have bubbled over. To keep her amused I gave her various things to play with: shaving stick, after-shave lotion, and any odd razor blades that might be lying about. She's wonderful, she didn't cut herself once!

Valérie (eighteen months) has a sort of 'idée fixe' about doors. They have to be shut! She would come to see me in the dressing room too because she took an interest in the various animals that came to my window, squirrels, pigeons, birds of various kinds including just common sparrows (les petits moineaux de Paris) as well as several species of 'loxia leucoptera' and 'pipilo erythrophthalmus'. Did you know that before a squirrel eats a peanut it removes very carefully the brown skin around it? – Sans blague!

To come back to the door complex of Valérie's . . . In my dressing-room here, where she came to see me a little later than Laurence, there are six doors. One through which you enter, one through which you exit, if there is a fire, three leading to cupboards, and finally the bathroom door. The man who looks after me, Sgt. Chevrier, has a sense of humour. Every time Valérie came she would close any door that might be open. It would take her some time before she got to the 6th, and following her was the Sgt. opening the doors, so that the poor thing had the time of her life satisfying this complex.

Now to be serious for a moment, you will be glad to know that Pauline and I manage to carry on somehow. Frankly when it was suggested that I take this Office, I didn't hesitate for reasons that you can guess. We simply said to the Good Lord: 'We don't know whether You willed this, but in any event You permitted it' and so we accepted and we know (especially I, parce que je n'ai plus 20 ans) that we wouldn't be able to do it without His help. We live from day to day in the shadow of His Holy Will.[20]

20. To Mrs Nora Warmington, 18th January 1963.

CHAPTER 21

THE NEW RÔLE

I

IT was inevitable at a time when Canadians were rather anxiously questioning their own identity that they should also be questioning their institutions. The Constitution itself, it was said, needed 'repatriation', and since the Crown was the corner-stone of the Constitution it could no longer be taken for granted. There were various reasons for this – the contemporary fashion for republics, even within the flexible embrace of the Commonwealth; the desire for a Head of State residing in the country and manifestly belonging to it; the 'new Canadians' having no personal or hereditary ties with the British Monarchy; the belief that a republican régime was somehow more democratic if only because it was more drab; an indifference to history; and an itch for change.

These interrogations, which were partly the result of intellectual and moral unrest, had already made themselves felt when Georges Vanier took office. Vincent Massey had replied to them with lucidity and force, and he was to reply to them again in one of the last important speeches of his long career.[1] The case for monarchy as Bagehot had stated it in the nineteenth century was equally valid today. The political system was, so to speak, personified in the Sovereign and made thereby more accessible to the people. The Crown cemented their loyalty to the State much more effectively than a flag however venerated, or a constitution however sacrosanct. It preserved certain functions from political competition and recrimination. The Sovereign with her consort and family, exposed but not over-exposed to public scrutiny, had the power to govern by example when she no longer governed by decree, and to fortify by her private virtue the essential unit of society. As for the argument that Royalty, however picturesque, was no longer relevant, Walter Lippmann, a dispassionate and acute observer from the neighbouring republic, had written:

1. To the Canada Club, Toronto, 1965.

It is significant, I think, certainly it is at least suggestive, that while nearly all the Western governments have been in deep trouble since the First World War, the Constitutional Monarchies of Scandinavia, the Low Countries, and the United Kingdom have shown greater capacity to endure, to preserve order with freedom, than the Republics of France, Germany, Spain and Italy. In some measure that may be because in a republic the governing power, being wholly secularised, loses much of its prestige; it is stripped, if one prefers, of all the illusions of intrinsic majesty.

In other words, monarchy provided a *mystique* for the mechanics of government; and it was a proved fact that no nation can survive without a mystique of one kind or another, although recent history had shown that some *mystiques* can be dangerous. A nation is ruled either by force or by tradition, and if monarchy was rooted deep in the Canadian tradition, perhaps Sir Robert Borden had been right when he described the proposal to abolish it as 'one of the most absurd suggestions ever to come to my attention.'

Sir Robert Borden would still have meant a good deal to Georges Vanier, because he had known him well. He would not have meant very much to the man on the sidewalk in Toronto watching the passage of Royalty with apparent indifference – or was it merely the canny reserve which so many Canadians have inherited from their Scottish forbears? Nevertheless, when the man on the sidewalk was asked what he thought about it all, he replied: 'It works, don't it?' The question now was – did it work any longer, and to what extent should it be made to work differently?

With the nomination of Vincent Massey the rôle of the Governor General had subtly changed, and Massey had been ideally suited to operate the transition. As an alumnus of Balliol and *persona gratissima* at Buckingham Palace, with his membership of London clubs and his links with English society, he could have represented the United Kingdom in Canada as easily as Georges Vanier could have represented France. Nevertheless, in the eyes of many Canadians, Massey's connection with the British court and society was a disadvantage which he successfully lived down. Both he and Georges Vanier had spent long periods abroad, but Massey had large business interests in Canada and his work on the Massey Commission for the Arts had given him a close insight into the problems of the country. He had travelled its length and breadth, and had come to appreciate the

French-speaking contribution to the national life more sympathetically than before. Georges Vanier had no comparable employment after his retirement from diplomacy. He may well have remembered Robertson Fleet's advice of many years earlier to 'brush up his Canada'; for like any Canadian-born Governor General he was called upon to represent both the country and the Crown. And except in the matter of French Canada, he had less experience of either than the man he followed.

Nevertheless, there was no doubt in his own mind, or in anyone else's as to where he essentially belonged. In a way he was more earthily Canadian than Massey. In his attitude to the Crown his native romanticism, now tempered and controlled, stood him in good stead. One had only to hear him speak, as he so often did, of 'our little Queen' to be reminded of some wise and gracious courtier serving his Sovereign with good counsel as well as perfect manners. His devotion to Queen Elizabeth II was personal and intense. His feelings towards her may be described as affectionate and protective admiration. He did not thrust her importunately down the throats of Canadians who may not have felt quite the same as he did, but of his fervent loyalty there was never a moment's doubt. He wrote to her, in strict confidence, about three times a year, giving a candid account of his stewardship; and he was to be at her side, as we shall see, to share the most painful ordeal of her reign.

In conversation with the present writer, only a few weeks before he died, Georges Vanier expressed his concern that the Crown had become remote for many of the Canadian people. He did not believe that Canada should become a republic; but with his eyes fixed, as they always were, on the future rather than the past he was looking forward, not very clearly as yet, to ways in which the Crown might be made more real and relevant. It was not that he was less attached to the Crown as a symbol than to the Queen as a person, but where he saw the one with personal affection, he had not quite worked out the social and political implications of the other. He clung to his belief that there was no life without movement, and that just as the Commonwealth was developing in unexpected ways, so the Crown which symbolized it would develop also.

If the Crown were not seen to be indigenous in Canada, it would wither away; and in so far as the office of Governor General was regarded as a mere agency of Buckingham Palace, it was weakened rather than strengthened by the association.

Anything that reduced the significance of the one would have a harmful effect upon the other. Georges Vanier had an abundant sense of humour, not least about himself. But he distinguished between himself and his office. When a caricature appeared in the *Ottawa Citizen*, with a report that he had been amused by it, Esmond Butler wrote to the Editor:

His Excellency wishes me to say that he was not amused by the cartoon, not because of the caricature of his own person to which he is indifferent, but because the cartoon is in bad taste considering his office as the Queen's representative in Canada.

The Governor General was very unhappy also about the statement that the cartoon 'prompted an amused and understanding smile', and that he 'understood and appreciated the nice, light touch in the topical cartoon', the quotes implying that the words were his own, which was not the case.[2]

The title of Governor General was itself a misnomer. The Queen's representative was only incidentally a general, and he did not govern. No one had ever thought of calling Buckingham Palace 'Government House', and the name was no more appropriate to Rideau Hall. Attempts were made to call the Viceregal residence by its original name, and if you ring up Government House today the telephonist will obediently answer 'Rideau Hall'. But names stick, and it will no doubt be a long time before even Governors General cease talking about 'Government House'. Murray Ballantyne, a very trusted friend in these later years, wrote to Georges Vanier soon after his appointment, reminding him that Sir John Macdonald had wished the new Confederation to be called the 'Kingdom of Canada', and that the French word 'Dominion' was substituted in order not to offend the republican sentiments of the United States at a time when the States were still casting a predatory eye to the northward. Ballantyne maintained with inexorable logic that the Governor General was the Queen's Viceroy, and that such he should be called. When he was on tour, everyone talked about the 'Viceregal train'. Why should they not describe the man who travelled in it as the Viceroy? General Vanier replied to these explosive suggestions with a cautiously non-committal – 'Who knows?'

He did believe, however, that the best way to enhance the significance of the Crown was to enhance the status of its representative, and it was his great achievement to make his office

2. 12th June 1964.

unmistakably and eloquently Canadian. This was a case where the man made the office, not the other way about. He might not govern, but he should be more than a rubber stamp. The Governor General's place in the constitution might be a modest one, its powers severely limited, but it must not be reduced to a vacuum. Sir Shuldham Redfern's[3] definition still held, and much water had flown down the St Lawrence since Sir Shuldham arrived at it.

It is often said that the Governor General is the personal representative of the King. It would be more correct to say that he is the official representative of the Crown for there is a difference between representing a person and representing the office held by a person. The King holds his position by the accident of heredity. The Crown, on the other hand, is an ancient and historic symbol of authority and it is this Crown, applied to Canada, that the Governor General represents and the traditions of which it is one of his duties to uphold.
The normal state of affairs would be for the King to live in Canada, and the absence of His Majesty from Canada should be regarded as just as much an abnormality as his absence from the United Kingdom. In the latter event a Council of State is appointed. It is a temporary expedient and if Canada and the United Kingdom are of equal constitutional status the Governor General is in the same position as the Council of State, for the King is no less King of Canada than he is King of England.[4]

This was unexceptionable as far as it went, and Father Paul Vanier – Georges' Jesuit cousin – suggested, in a most interesting private memorandum, that it might go even further. Since the Crown was divisible – and even, potentially, divisible against itself – why should not it also be pluriform, in the sense that the Queen's representatives shared in it by participation and not merely by delegated function? The argument was subtle, and might only be of interest to the metaphysicians of political theory; but it would make of the Governor General, or whatever else he was called, an actual Head of State. Moreover, it would meet Georges Vanier's strong contention that he should be able to return the visits of foreign Heads of State on equal terms; and it was prompted by a widespread regret that Canada should not have been represented by its Governor General at the funeral of President Kennedy. When, towards the close of Georges Vanier's term of office, there was question of his returning the visit of General de Gaulle, it was willingly agreed by Buckingham Palace

3. Secretary to Lord Tweedsmuir and the Earl of Athlone.
4. Memorandum, March 1945.

that he should receive exactly the same treatment as the Queen. The unwillingness of the French Government to regard the visit in the same light gave point to Paul Vanier's argument. A spokesman for External Affairs confirmed that President de Gaulle had been prepared to receive the General as an 'illustrious representative of Canada', but not as Head of State.[5]

What, then, were the Governor General's actual powers? He was authorized to make or cancel all appointments which the Queen herself could make or cancel; to summon, prorogue, or dissolve Parliament; and to do certain things 'in Council' – i.e. on the advice of the Cabinet – which the Queen 'in Council' cannot do. Certain sections of the British North America Act, limiting his powers, had in fact fallen into disuse. He could assent or refuse assent to a Bill, or reserve it for the signification of the Queen's pleasure. No such Bill had been reserved since 1886, and since the Queen would have to act on the advice of her Canadian Ministers there would be no point in its reservation. There was a provision that the Queen in Council might disallow a Bill within two years, but no Canadian Bill had been disallowed since 1873, and it was unthinkable that her Canadian Ministers would advise her to abrogate a Bill which had received the assent of the Canadian Parliament. It was also provided that the Governor General might recommend the appointment of four or eight Senators, above the normal 102, and that the Queen might direct him to appoint them. The intention was evidently that the Queen should issue her direction on the advice of the British Cabinet. On the only occasion when this provision was invoked, in December 1873–January 1874, the British Government advised the Queen not to issue the direction, and the Canadian Government's request was refused. If a Canadian Government wished to amend these sections of the British North America Act, it might be regarded as an academic exercise; but no one in Canada or the United Kingdom would lift a finger to prevent it.

In appointing a Prime Minister the Governor General had normally no freedom of choice. If a Government were defeated in the House of Commons, or in a General Election, and consequently resigned, he must call on the Leader of the Opposition to form a new Government. If the Prime Minister died, or resigned for personal reasons, he could choose whichever among the leaders of the Government party he thought most capable of

5. *Ottawa Citizen*, 20th February 1968.

commanding a majority in the House of Commons. He would naturally consult those best qualified to give him advice, including the retiring Prime Minister if he had resigned for personal reasons; but the retiring Prime Minister had no right to proffer advice unless he was asked to, and the Governor General was not obliged to take it. In Canada his choice might be temporary, until the party Convention had decided on a new leader. When the new Prime Minister presented his list of Ministers, he might criticize this or that proposed appointment, but if the Prime Minister insisted he must give way. He enjoyed, in fact, the classical Royal prerogatives: 'to encourage, advise, and warn', and he had also the right to be informed. Previous Governors General had not always been fully informed; Georges Vanier saw to it that no essential information was withheld from him.

He also enjoyed a certain discretion in the making of appointments. If a retiring Prime Minister wished to fill a vacancy for reasons too nakedly political, Georges Vanier held to the principle that if the public good were likely to suffer from that vacancy, he would agree to the appointment whether he approved of it or not. But if no harm would come from its being held over till the new Government took office, he reserved the right to refuse. He did in at least one instance very strongly object to a proposed appointment to the Judiciary. In this case he was following the example of Lord Aberdeen who had refused to fill the Senate with the nominees of a defeated Government. The Governor General might also refuse an improper request to dissolve Parliament, as Byng had refused in 1926. A Government defeated in a General Election had no right to ask for a fresh election before the new Parliament had met; and a newly elected Government defeated on a minor issue had no automatic right to a dissolution, if an alternative Government could be found. Nor had any Government the right of dissolution if a motion of censure was threatening it. Governments were made up of men, and like other men they must face the music.

Bills enacted by a Provincial Legislature might legally be reserved for the signification of the Governor General's pleasure, and they remained inoperative unless he gave his assent within a year from the date of reservation. Withholding of assent – last used in Prince Edward Island in 1945, when the Bill in question was later re-enacted and assented to – had come to be regarded as irregular. The Lieutenant-Governor of the Province had no warrant to reserve a Bill on the advice of his own Ministers; he could only do so in his capacity as an officer of the Dominion, and on instruction from the Governor General acting on the advice of his Federal Ministers. Only twenty-four Bills had been reserved since 1882, and only one during General Vanier's tenure of office. This received his assent by an Order-in-Council on the 5th of May 1961.

A more painful question was the long drawn out debate on capital punishment. The Governor General had the right to ask for the reconsideration of a death sentence, but he had no right to commute it against the advice of his Ministers. The matter had gravely preoccupied Vincent Massey, and it was only with the greatest reluctance that he had confirmed a capital sentence. He was forced to do so in fifty-five cases, whereas General Vanier, whose reluctance was no less, had only to confirm seven death sentences, and none after 1962. His personal views, as expressed to the present writer in 1966, were that only if a man committed a second murder should he pay the extreme penalty. Capital punishment was abolished by an Act of Parliament in December 1967, except for the murder of police officers and prison guards acting in the course of their duties.

There were three general elections during General Vanier's term of office. In 1962 the Conservatives lost 92 seats, dropping from 208 to 116, but they were still the largest Parliamentary group and Mr Diefenbaker continued in office. The Liberals, however, were able to assert throughout the subsequent Parliament that as a minority group in themselves the Conservatives had lost the moral, if not the legal, right to govern, and the indecisiveness of the Government, which felt its insecurity, became a matter of popular concern. In 1963 the Liberals regained their traditional hold on the province of Quebec, winning 47 of the 75 constituencies, and 41 per cent of the popular vote throughout the country. They were now the largest party with 129 seats in the House against the Conservatives' 96. The Social Creditors and New Democrats held 24 and 17 respectively. Mr Pearson took office at the head of what was still, however, a minority Government; and the psychological uncertainty in Canada, with which the General had to wrestle, was due in part to the absence of a Government that represented a decisive majority in the country. In the election of November 1963 the Liberals increased their representation in Parliament by only two seats, and the instability remained. If Quebec had returned to its old allegiance, the prairie provinces remained generally Conservative, when they were not attracted to Social Credit or New Democracy. But Provincial Conservatives had found themselves at odds with the Federal leadership, which resulted in the resignation of three Federal Ministers, and the consequent fall of Mr Diefenbaker's Government in 1962. The ostensible cause of this was the nuclear arms issue, but the 'palace revolution' had been gathering impetus for some time, and only Mr Diefenbaker's immense popularity among so many 'average' Canadians, particularly in rural areas, had prevented its earlier explosion.

It was also a period of strained relations between Canada and the United States, and here the General fully sympathized with Mr Diefenbaker's indignation over the attitude of the State Department. President Kennedy, resilient after his Cuban victory, had spoken about getting tough with America's allies as well as with her adversaries. President de Gaulle had stood up to him, where Mr Macmillan had not. 'What else could I do?' might be an excuse for the Nassau agreement, but it had not satisfied President de Gaulle, and it had probably cost the United Kingdom its entrance into the Common Market. Any suggestion that Canada would have to do as it was told by the United States was as repugnant to the Governor General as it was to his Prime Minister. When Mr Diefenbaker described a statement by Dean Rusk as 'unprecedented', the General noted : 'Unprecedented – I should think so.'

He observed these changes and chances with constitutional propriety, only intervening when he felt that his own authority was being by-passed. Mr Diefenbaker was not always predictable. He mentioned to the General – who happened at the time to be his guest at luncheon – that he would like to appoint to the Senate a certain gentleman of whom the General had never heard. This was hardly surprising since the gentleman was a conductor on the railroad. The Prime Minister thought, however, that the appointment would be agreeable to Labour. He therefore rang up the gentleman to ask him how he would like to be a Senator. He liked it very much indeed, although he was taking his Sunday afternoon nap in a caboose when this unexpected call came through from Ottawa.

Naturally the Governor General had no objection to raise – only perhaps an eyebrow – at this unusual procedure. On another question, however, he was exacting. He had been asked to sign an Order-in-Council approving a change in the Order of Precedence. This proposed to give former Prime Ministers priority over everyone except the actual Prime Minister, including previous Governor Generals. The General objected that a matter of this kind was normally discussed at some length between the Governor General, the Prime Minister, and usually the Sovereign. In one case such consultation had continued for two months, whereas in the present instance the General had merely an Order-in-Council on his desk and the Prime Minister's Deputy to discuss it with. It was quickly evident that the Cabinet had not grasped the implications of their proposal – that if, for example, Mr St Laurent came to Ottawa for an official dinner, he would have precedence over everyone, the Prime Minister alone excepted. General Vanier reserved his approval; and when the Deputy had made his report, and two letters from the General had been studied, the matter was dropped. It was not a subject of vital public concern who should sit next to whom at a dinner party, or who should precede whom in a procession. But the General's attachment to first principles included an attention to the smallest detail, just as his lack of self-esteem was matched by a punctilious respect for his office and the prerogatives that went with it. He did not consider consultation by telephone a proper procedure, and he did not hesitate to say so.

Fortunately for his peace of mind, he had no serious constitutional issues to face although with a minority Government in power they might have arisen at any moment, and this possibility weighed heavily on his mind. His anxieties were of another order; they concerned the unity of the country. Mr Diefenbaker himself spoke of launching a campaign, which the Governor General fought as a crusade. When Mr Pearson succeeded Mr Diefenbaker, General Vanier was naturally grateful to have at his side, during his last years, a man with whom he had worked for so long in diplomacy. If Mr Pearson had been in office in 1959, he might or might not have taken the risk that Mr Diefenbaker took in recommending the appointment of one who was already well advanced in years and believed to be in failing health. In the event, General Vanier was among the few points on which these two political opponents were whole-heartedly agreed. His 'royalty of nature', and that of his wife, were recognized by everybody, and by none more freely than the Carmelite Sisters of Montreal. It was their custom on the Feast of the Epiphany to choose a 'queen' from among their number. Cards were distributed bearing the names of the different 'virtues', and the Sister who drew 'charity' became the 'queen'. She then chose a 'king' and in 1961 her election fell upon Georges Vanier. Others had also chosen him 'silencieusement'. In apprising the Governor General of her choice, Sister Martha of the Presentation wrote as follows:

I take the liberty of telling Madame Vanier, by this letter, that I should have chosen her as queen with all my heart, if I had been king; but I am sure that she will understand that since I am a queen, I had to have a king. And if my choice now imposes on me the gentle obligation of praying more often and more fervently for my king, his wife will not be exempt from my prayers.

Prayers were the most grateful of gifts because, as the General wrote to another well-wisher, 'it is not easy to be humble in a post like this one.'[6]

2

The moment came – although not till seven years later – when Georges Vanier could stomach no longer the scepticism about Canadian 'identity', and he made it the subject of his New Year's message. The ideas for this had

been on my chest for some time and I finally decided that I would get rid of them. . . . It is stuff and nonsense for us to talk like some half-baked intellectuals do. . . . To show how highly regarded Canadians are abroad, I could have said: 'If I had to travel through many countries in the five continents and were given the choice of a passport, I would say: A Canadian one'.[7]

Most Canadians, however, had no chance of seeing for themselves how highly they were regarded abroad; and if they read the reports of certain foreign correspondents, they might have wondered whether the Governor General was remembering his years in Paris a shade too fondly. Immediately after the war, Canada had indeed shown all the promise of a strong second-class power. Her voice had counted for a great deal on the international scene. But she was now caught up in the general self-questioning to which all western industrial societies were subject, and in the dialogue between federalism and self-determination which the accession to independence of so many colonial territories had unloosed. It was not that any educated Canadian imagined that she was a colony, but many Canadians were nervous lest other people should think so. 'O Canada' was generally wel-

6. To Mother R. McKenna, 15th December 1959.
7. To B. C. Gardner, 6th January 1966.

comed as the official national anthem, and since it had been written originally in French, that was all to the good. If people remembered that the composer had crossed the border and become an American citizen, the fact was conveniently forgotten or tactfully not referred to.

He was not the only one. In the century since Confederation ten million people had emigrated to Canada, but eight million Canadians had emigrated elsewhere, most of them to the United States. The attraction of a gentler climate, more abundant wealth, and a higher standard of living was always a threat to patriotic attachments that did not, in many cases, reach back very far in time. The Canadian people, confined to a long and narrow strip of territory, with much of their mineral wealth difficult of access and hardly as yet exploited, needed to be sustained by the promise of a future whose possibilities no one could predict. They were not called, immediately, to an easy life; they were called to a tremendous and collective effort. Georges Vanier believed in those possibilities, and he issued the call on every occasion that presented itself. But nothing, he maintained, could be achieved without unity; and throughout his tenure of office unity was at stake. It is still very far from secure, but he designated, in season and out of season, the foundations on which it might be built.

Believing, as an article of political faith, in the bicultural character of Canadian society, he knew that the necessity for this was not everywhere admitted. It was said that English was quickly becoming the *lingua franca* of the twentieth century, and that bilingualism was a root cause of the disunity which the General deplored. To counter these arguments he relied, not only upon his own experience and common sense, but upon an interesting memorandum from his friend Gilbert Gadoffre. This pointed out that there were many parts of Europe and the Near East where French was an indispensable key for opening the door upon the outside world – not only French-speaking countries like Belgium and Switzerland, but Italy, Greece, Rumania, the Slav nations of central Europe, many parts of black Africa, the whole of North Africa, and even Portugal – in spite of its long association with England. In Latin America the French language was very quickly displacing English, which had enjoyed a temporary vogue after the war; and in Vietnam it looked as if the Americans were paying dearly for their inability to use a language common to both parts of the country. If the Canadians had found themselves in the same situation, they might well have succeeded where the Americans had failed. For a power now exerting itself on the international stage, bilingualism was an incalculable asset. If the Romans had been content merely to win their battles, they would never have built an empire and a civilization.

They were obliged to cement this empire by the bilingual and bicultural association of Latin and Greek, to assimilate altogether the Greek culture, to make their governing *élite* speak the Greek language, and use it in the administration of their African and near-Eastern territories. Without this association there would never have been a great Roman civilization nor a durable Roman peace. In the world of tomorrow biculturalism will perhaps be the Canadian opportunity, and on this ground there is no country in the world to compete with it. If the Canadians let this opportunity slip, history would never forgive them.[8]

It is a curious fact that the 'Canadian opportunity' is so often better appreciated by foreigners than by Canadians themselves. This may have been in General Vanier's mind when he stressed the value of a Canadian passport. For an historian like Donald Creighton, however, bicultural Canada was a myth – the product of a revolution not nearly so 'quiet' as it pretended to be. Of the delegates assembled at the Quebec Conference on Confederation in 1864, twenty-one came from the Maritimes and only twelve from Eastern and Western Canada, and they were more concerned to avoid the decentralizing weaknesses of the American federal system, then threatened by the War between the States, than to assert Provincial rights. If Canadians insisted, by and large, on the North American way of life – and the 'quiet revolution' in Quebec was at least a step in this direction – then they must accept the North American way of speech. Many French Canadians were in fact doing so. In Ontario one out of every three persons of French origin now spoke English, in Manitoba a little more than one in four, in Saskatchewan nearly two out of five, in Alberta one out of two, and in British Columbia two out of three. The linguistic rights in Quebec were secure; it was folly to extend them elsewhere.[9]

Creighton's arguments have been refuted by subsequent action on the part of the Federal Government, and Georges Vanier would live to see the 'sister nations' theory of Canadian nationhood consecrated as the theme of the Centennial Year. It was the

8. May 1965.
9. September 1966.

thesis which he himself had expounded on a hundred platforms, and which he reiterated throughout his term of office. But central to that thesis was the idea that the sisters belonged to the same family; that they should be made increasingly aware of the ties that bound them, and of the common destiny that beckoned to them; and that what distinguished them from each other, rightly interpreted, was a source of strength and not of weakness. It was his own strength in representing his country as well as his Queen, that if he belonged by blood as well as by adoption to one of the 'sister nations' he spoke the language of the other with an equal mastery, and understood its character just as well. He had a foot on either side of the boundary upon which he was born; or if it be objected that, anatomically speaking, he had only one to stand upon, this invites the reply that he had sacrificed the other in a common cause. With a realistic respect for frontiers, he could always look beyond them. He realized with a perfect spontaneity in himself the synthesis he was struggling to create. What he was counted for quite as much as what he said or did, in a position where there was much that he could neither say nor do. In the performance of his new rôle, age and disability imposed certain limits on his exertions; they imposed none on his example.

CHAPTER 22

COAST TO COAST

DURING his first sixteen months in office General Vanier visited every province except New Brunswick, where the Parliament was dissolved in view of elections. He took an early occasion to state his belief that Government House belonged to the whole nation, not merely to Ottawa; and that if this meant that he must be away from Ottawa more than Ottawa liked, Ottawa would have to lump it. He preferred to travel in the Viceregal train; or, more exactly, in the special cars attached to the normal railroad services. Here there had been a slight decline in grandeur since the days when Lord Willingdon entertained five hundred guests in the C.N.R. station at Vancouver, although Lady Willingdon's mauve bathroom was a reminder of that patrician pro-consulate. By 1959 the cars were, so to speak, on their last wheels. There were no electric heaters – a deficiency that was afterwards made good – and the vibration was sometimes nerve-wracking. On the other hand they were comfortably furnished, and gave the General ample time for reading, working or watching the scenery. He was normally accompanied by Butler, Chevrier, a typist secretary, an A.D.C., and a French and English dictionary. If Madame Vanier was with him, her Lady-in-Waiting came as well. On longer trips the train would often make an unscheduled halt, so that the General could step out on to the observation platform and address whoever had come to greet him from a rural area. At the larger centres a telephone was hooked on to the car so that he could attend to any necessary business. Meals were served aboard when the party were not officially engaged, and simplified to suit Canadian palates. It was twenty years since the steward was about to throw away some ducks because they were smelling high, and Lord Tweedsmuir ordered them for dinner for the same reason.

Many of the journeys were to Montreal or Toronto, where the General's attendance at the Royal Winter Fair was an annual obligation. Here he would ride round the grounds in a small motor-cart, with Madame Vanier walking beside him, and the mounted escort of his Horse Guards would execute a half figure of eight, finishing up in line facing his box. His old friend Keiller Mackay was Lieutenant-Governor of Ontario, and if the General had an evening free he would sometimes leave the train and dine with him. Seated there among the heavy mahogany and the bronze memorials of Napoleon's victories – Austerlitz, Jena, and Wagram – they would recall their first meeting in the trenches south of Ypres, and their long talks in the Buxton hospital, and the nurse with bright red fluffy hair whom they had christened the 'Bee of Buxton'. But Georges Vanier was less admiring of Bonaparte than he had once been; memories of another *petit caporal* were too recent.

It was in Toronto that the police gave warning that a bomb was set to explode during a Jewish Anniversary dinner. The General was sceptical, and merely replied: 'Bomb or not, I'm staying.' As he suspected, the scare was proved to be a hoax. The Vaniers always attended Mass at St Basil's when they were in Toronto and in the Basilica when they were in Montreal. If this was impossible, it was celebrated on the train – for the General brushed his soul every morning as other men will brush their teeth. He was the first Governor General to use a helicopter on an official tour, making thirteen hops in a R.C.N. 'eggbeater' from the deck of H.M.C.S. *Bonaventure* to drop in on coastal communities while visiting the Maritimes. Wherever possible the Vaniers wished the ceremonial aspects of their tour to be kept to a minimum – not from any distaste for ceremony as such, but because they were anxious to get through to the hearts and homes of the people. Now and again the General liked to spring a surprise. Motoring along Highway 11, with R.C.M.P. cars in front and behind, on his way to the South Saskatchewan River Dam, he noticed the little rural school of Coates, a few miles north of Dundurn. On the return journey he halted the motorcade and walked into the school, leaving teacher and pupils speechless. Sitting at the teacher's desk, he explained to the children who he was and what he did; shook hands with them all; asked for them to be excused their lessons for the rest of the day; and enjoined the teacher 'to get in touch with the school board and tell them that I, in the name of Her Majesty the Queen, request that these children be given a holiday tomorrow.' A similar request in Banff elicited the following confidence from a small boy to his teacher: 'I hope he doesn't die soon. I want to save up enough money to go to his funeral.'

In St Boniface the Vaniers would sometimes attend Mass according to the Ukrainian rite in the cathedral of St Vladimir and St Olga; and they were glad to learn from Premier Roblin that both French and English were used in the Provincial Legislature. In the Colonel Belcher Hospital at Calgary the General met an old friend – 'Frenchy' Leonard who had been his batman and runner in the first world war; and he earned the gratitude of Albertans by helping to give the Daisy Derby the status of a turf classic. In Vancouver he unveiled the statue of his predecessor in office, Lord Stanley.[1] This not very distinguished piece of sculpture had spent four years in a warehouse, while the city was rent with a municipal civil war in order to decide where it should be placed, and on what kind of pedestal. Too close a proximity to a statue of Robert Burns was thought to be injurious to Viceregal dignity. From the bridge of H.C.M.S. *Fraser* – and how evocative that name must have been! – the General watched fourteen Pacific command warships sail down the strait of Juan de Fuca, and the long distance Swiftsure Race with fifty sailing boats in competition.

Later in the year he met another acquaintance of his campaigning days. Colonel William A. Delaney, now eighty-five years old, was confined to a hospital in Quebec. In 1916 he had treated Georges Vanier for shell-shock in a hospital in London, and this unexpected encounter with an old patient moved him to tears and seemed to bring him a momentary accession of strength. From Quebec the Vaniers went up into the Royaume de Saguenay, stopping off at Arvida, Jonquière, and Kénogami, and Chicoutimi. This was country the General knew well from his travels up and down the Province in 1942, and he spoke now very much as he had spoken then, with pride in his own French ancestry but with a new emphasis on the bicultural opportunities of Canada and the need for national unity. He could exhort the Seminarians of St Charles de Bathurst: 'Soyez tous de bon Canadiens Français jusqu'à le fin de vos jours'; and then remind a Westmount audience: 'We are all the children of one French and one English parent.' How often, as he thanked municipal and academic authorities for their 'bon accueil', must his mind have gone back to his first experience of Viceregal protocol, and the quick flowering of his friendship with Julian Byng! Nowhere was the *accueil* more heart-warming than from the religious communities which received him with the faultless ritual of their

1. Lord Stanley of Preston, 1841-1908.

rule – the monks of St Bênoit-du-Lac, who brought back memories of his childhood holidays at Memphremagog; and the Carmelites of Montreal who lifted their veils in his honour.

It is the business of a Governor General to enjoy everything that is lawfully enjoyable, but he is still permitted to enjoy some things more than others. The old soldier naturally thrilled to the military occasions – the fiftieth anniversary of the 'Van Doos' in 1964, and the presentation of new Battle Honours to the Royal Canadian Dragoons, the oldest armoured regiment in Canada. As the thirty Centurion tanks, each bearing a name beginning with a letter of its respective squadron, rumbled past the Viceregal tent, they dipped their 20-pound guns in salute.

There was also an old playgoer very much alive in General Vanier, and of recent years he had been somewhat starved of entertainment. The French theatre does not seem to have much attracted him, although he attended a performance of *Tartuffe* by the Comédie Française in Ottawa,[2] and he had seen little of the English stage since his years at Canada House. Following the example of his predecessors, he became a Patron of the Dominion Drama Festival, attending its final performance whenever possible, and he did all he could to encourage the Canadian Opera and Ballet. But the Vaniers' particular joy were the Shakespeare productions at Stratford, Ontario. These they rarely missed, meeting the actors and examining the costumes and properties. Stratford, in a single imaginative stroke, had put Canada on the world theatrical map, and it was through the Vaniers' eager following of its progress that Sir Tyrone Guthrie and Jean Gascon entered the circle of their acquaintance.

The General once wrote to a friend that 'Pauline always steals the show whether I am there or not.' This was a chivalrous exaggeration; theatrically speaking, they played perfectly together, although each was capable of holding the stage by themselves. The only thing that ever stole the show was the Lieutenant-Governor's Newfoundland dog during their visit to New Brunswick. On one occasion, at least, chivalry took precedence of protocol. In 1962 they were due to see the Queen Mother off on her return to the United Kingdom and waiting in a hotel for her plane to arrive from Woodline. When it came in ahead of time, the General declared that he would not move until Pauline had had her second cup of tea. He would move, he said, in ten minutes – not before. In the event they overtook the

2. 13th February 1961.

Royal car, and Georges Vanier was there on the tarmac, bowing with a courtier's grace over Her Majesty's extended hand. He had in all the encounters of his official round what Masillon had described as 'l'affabilité si nécessaire et si méritoire dans tous les grands emplois.' But he also had what the family described as his 'custard pie' sense of humour. There was no contradiction been the two, and when he told the children's band at Fort Smith that he had always wanted to be a bandmaster, they did not doubt for a moment that a Governor General was speaking to them – and a General, *tout court*, at that.

The official tours followed a routine which it would be tedious to recapitulate. One of them, however, was of particular interest. On the 12th of June 1961, the Viceregal party of sixteen left Ottawa in a Comet for Churchill in northern Manitoba, where they were joined by Mr James W. Goodall, a member of the Legislative Council for the North-West Territories. The temperature was 35°F. Raymond Jolliffe[3] noted that on the way down to the shore 'last year's desiccated bog-cotton grew here and there, and one or two minute purple, gentian-like flowers were bravely beginning to open. Dwarf willows had catkins on them and it seemed that the beach would soon burst into flowers like the desert. We disturbed a pintail duck, some terns and a flock of small waders, probably sandpipers, as we made our way down to the now melting land-ice, beyond which stretched the chaotic mass of the sea-ice.'

Here was the northern scenery which so many Canadian artists – Lawren Harris pre-eminent among them – had tried to capture. The sun, when it came out, lit up the rocks, the pale sheets of water, and the distant spruce; and when it went down, the central column of light turned the ice to an almost sapphire blue.

General Vanier teased the children at the Garrison school – white, Eskimo and Indian happily integrated – with the expectation of a whole holiday, and did not disappoint them. (It is no small part of a Governor General's duty to provide this relief for teachers and taught, and the General had his own rather whimsical way of discharging it.) On the following day he visited Akudlik, an Eskimo village half way between the town of Churchill and the Fort. Here they were greeted by a variety of physical types, Asiatic, Indian and others more European. The

3. I am indebted to the present Lord Hylton's Diary for the details and quotations in this section.—Author's note.

majority looked distinctly Japanese and might have stepped out
of *The Mikado*. The next stop was at an Indian settlement, where
the General was greeted by a Chief called 'Duck', and where three
pipe-smoking ladies demonstrated how to clean a caribou hide.
The Indians, led by their Chief and one or two elders, sang 'God
Save the Queen' in Chipewyan to an excruciatingly slow tempo.
It seemed to the officers in attendance, standing at the salute, to
go on for fourteen verses. Later in the day the party visited the
Eskimo museum with its carvings in walrus tusk and soap-stone,
its caribou robes and fluted narwhal tusks six to eight feet long.
'What have we here?' echoed like a refrain as each new and
unaccustomed sight met the General's eye.

Visits followed to Uranium City and Fort Smith, where the
Vaniers were housed in the R.C.M.P. compound – and menaced,
incidentally, by the deer flies which had the reputation of removing a chunk of flesh with every bite. On this occasion, however,
they showed a proper sense of protocol. At Fort Smith the soil
was rich and alluvial with clumps of sizable timber-spruce, poplar
and jack pine. Here the Slave River ran through rapids which
necessitated a seventeen mile portage from Fort Fitzgerald to Bell
Rock, and in the bush sweet peas, honeysuckle and briars were
at their peak of bloom. At the Federal School 75 per cent of the
pupils were Indian, and had gathered in the gymnasium to greet
the Viceregal party:

As we entered the room recorded martial music was played and
simultaneously a band of tiny little girls (Grade 1) struck up with
cymbals, tambourines and clashing batons. They were dressed in red
tunics and pill-box hats and conducted with verve by an equally
small girl whose cap was ornamented by a feather. H.E. harangued
the children with vigour and much to the point, and gave them a
holiday.

Among those who attended the reception given by the Fort
Smith Board of Trade was an Indian woman said to be a hundred
years old.

The party next drove along the portage road to Bell Rock
where the Northern Transportation Company had its landing
point for the Lower Slave and Mackenzie rivers. General Vanier
sat down on a load of tinned chicken and was slowly driven on
board, waving Au Revoir to the great delight of the photographers
– for the Press were naturally in attendance throughout the trip.
So by river to Inuvik, and thence by air to Hay River with the

Great Slave Lake spread out below. In Hay River the Vaniers were guests of the Calgary Brewery Company, with a room looking out on to the main channel of the stream. The town was in sharp contrast to the staidness of Fort Smith – 'dynamic but also disorderly, with fishing boats, scows etc. lying about the banks of the river, broken down construction machinery, miscellaneous building materials, huge trucks and semi-trailers occupying other corners. Some of the streets have boarded sidewalks, all are unpaved though some had been oiled to keep down the dust.' When the Governor General and his wife were through with their duties – after the compliments and the presentations and 'Vive la Canadienne' and 'For he's a jolly good fellow' – they could watch from the windows of their room the sunset that Esmond Butler, and others of the party, caught as they were unsuccessfully fishing the river.

The water was dark brown with silt and probably the pickerel etc. couldn't see the lure, anyway there were no bites. The prolonged sunset from 10 to 12 was very beautiful. Occasional parties of duck flighted overhead, while a mist rose from the water as we drifted downstream between occasional tree-clad islands towards the mouth of the river which faced the afterglow across the open lake.

On Sunday the 18th of June the Catholic members of the party attended Mass in a church which Brother Bouché from Edmunston, New Brunswick, had built practically with his own hands. After luncheon they all drove south on the Hay River Highway, raising such clouds of dust even at thirty-five miles an hour that the cars had to keep two hundred yards apart. Fortunately the Mounties were at hand to halt the traffic coming in the opposite direction. The drive took them to the Alexandra Falls, where the river plunged over a limestone cliff 105 feet high, and on to the Louise Falls further down the canyon. In the evening there was talk with Brother Bouché, who was still building churches, mission-houses, and schools; and with a ninety-year-old Indian who remembered Lord Byng coming down the river in 1925. Raymond Jolliffe's father might well have been coming with him: and so might Georges Vanier himself if his training for command had not taken him elsewhere.

The next day the party flew on to Fort Simpson, where the Governor General had luncheon in a tent pitched in the Indian end of the town and overlooking the Mackenzie river. His hosts were two Indian Chiefs and their wives, who did themselves very

well on buffalo steaks that must have come from Wood Buffalo
Park. At the evening reception Indian Girl Guides served tea and
coffee with a charm so leisurely that only the tactful intervention
of the General's staff secured that many of the guests should not
go thirsty away. A subsequent entertainment was a Drum Dance
at the Community Hall:

Chief Cazon had organized three drummers equipped with shallow
drums, stretched on wooden frames and beaten with willow drum-
sticks. The performance began with a solo to a monotonous one-two
rhythm. The step is a simple hopping on alternate feet, with the
free foot sometimes extending forward and sometimes sideways. . . . Gradually more and more dancers got up and formed a
swaying conga-like line. As time went on quite a number of white
people took it up. . . . Some ladies in high heels even took part.
Eventually, after their Exs had gone, I joined in one, after two of the
photographers had taken the plunge. At times the circle would be
complete and at others broken into two or more snakelets. The
drummers sang as they drummed and the words seemed to change
from number to number. I was told that there are variations of the
footwork according to the seasons, etc.; and sometimes a circle is
formed with linked arms and the dancers facing inwards.

Bad weather compelled the cancellation of the trip down the
Bear River, and the party flew on to Yellowknife where a welcome was efficiently improvised much earlier than had been
expected. General Vanier was taken down the Giant Gold Mine,
and watched a gold brick being poured. At the end of the week
they were at Norman Wells, a strung-out riverside place on the
north bank of the Mackenzie with a baby oil refinery in the
middle of it. Here, in the mess hall of the Imperial Oil Company,
it was a mild surprise to find themselves congratulating a chef
from Parma on some of the most succulent steaks they had ever
eaten. A short flight from Norman Wells brought them to Bennett
Field, where the Vaniers climbed into a couple of arm-chairs on a
flat-topped lorry for the first stage of their journey to Bear River
Camp.

We drove across a green meadow in which a few Indians were camp-
ing in tents, to the river's edge where the tug *Radium Prince* and a
large steel barge were waiting. Both were spick and span and a fair-
sized wooden-framed tent had been put up in the middle of the barge
for H.E. It contained a bed, a table, and lots of chairs. Hundreds of
photos were taken as we went on board. Their Exs standing by the

anchor or meeting the stout Scandinavian skipper – in short the Press had a ball.

We set sail downstream with the tug pushing the barge, tightly lashed to its blunt bow. This method is always used on northern lakes and rivers, in preference to pulling, because it gives better control in shallow waters with shifting sand-banks etc. One tug will push as many as six or more barges, and manoeuvre them with precision thanks to its twin screws and four rudders in parallel.

Odd pockets of decaying snow and ice were still visible in places, and the banks had nearly been cleared by the outgoing ice for several feet above the water's edge. The river was some 200 yards wide and the icy blue-green waters wound through bush country with not much sign of wildlife. The anglers tried to fish from the barge, but we were moving far too fast for them to have any luck. There may have been no fish in any case, or if there were they certainly weren't biting.

We had a picnic on board, sandwiches and red wine. Sun-bathing followed on the open deck behind the tent, while the Press made up one of their usual bridge or poker games. After 3½ hours of this rather idyllic progress . . . we came in sight of Bear Rock. This great crag rises straight out of the water for several hundreds of feet in the angle between the right banks of the Bear and the Mackenzie. It marks the end of the Franklyn Mountains. At its foot a sharp line of division could be seen between the blue water of the Bear and the muddy flow of the Mackenzie.

At Fort Norman opposite Bear Rock the Vaniers were transported up a very steep bank, riding on a wagon drawn by a tractor. Two arm-chairs and a chesterfield had been provided for their precarious comfort. As the tractor laboured up the muddy incline, the wagon began to slide over the edge, and it was only through collective pushing on the danger side that disaster was averted. Eight diminutive scouts, formed up in two lines, greeted the Governor General, and the children of the Federal Day School presented him with a history of the Fort, written (in ink) and illustrated by themselves, and bound up between two sheets of plywood faced with birch bark. Here, as elsewhere, the scouts were multi-racial, and the schools were integrated; but at Norman Wells only two Indians were employed full time at the company's works. Others were hired in summer on a temporary basis and very uncomfortably lodged. Behind all the verbal window-dressing of an official tour, where the officials inevitably had the last word, the General's keen eye was anxious to penetrate the realities – harsh and complicated as they were – of the Canadian

North West. At Inuvik, for example, in order to provide a sufficient market for the central bakery, the hostel kitchens were
forbidden to bake their own bread. The machinery at the laundry
was so cumbersome that only when a substantial quantity of
washing had mounted up could it go into operation. There was
a danger that massive government investment at Inuvik would
so force up costs that ordinary people would not be able to
afford to live there. Socialism, which was supposed to be for the
good of the common man, was here redounding to his hurt.
Should the Indian Act be scrapped, and the Indian encouraged
to stand more independently on his own feet? Might it not be
wiser to build up an economy capable of absorbing the output
of the schools before establishing universal or semi-universal education? In Mexico economic development, road-building, and
the construction of elementary schools had been the graduated
steps towards the ending of illiteracy. In a socialist economy
on the pattern of the Canadian North rewards went to the con-
formists, but a healthy society needed its nonconformists also;
and socialist solutions had not yet commended themselves to
Canada as a whole. They rarely did commend themselves to the
pioneering spirit, and the North-West Territories were still open
to the pioneer.

In all the places they visited the Vaniers attended Mass in the
local church. At Inuvik this was built in the shape of an igloo – a
cylindrical drum, crowned with a shallow dome, a domed lantern,
and cross. The dome was covered with silvery-blue aluminium
diamonds, and the Stations of the Cross had been painted on the
inside walls by a deaf and dumb Eskimo girl. These were so
reminiscent of the Piero della Francesca frescoes at Arezzo that
Madame Vanier asked if she had been provided with 'holy pictures' to work on. The Oblate Father confirmed that this had
been the case, and that, where necessary, he had corrected the
drawing and perspective.

Inuvik was the last halt on the tour, and on the 28th of June
the Governor General and his party left for Cold Lake, Alberta,
on the first stage of their return to Ottawa. He was never to
forget 'the grandeur and beauty of the resources, human as well
as material, which are to be found in our Great North.[4]

4. 1st December 1964.

CHAPTER 23

A CRITICAL VISIT

I

DR PETER BURTON, who had accompanied the General on his visit to the North West, was a British immigrant to Canada, and so distinguished in his own person that at one point in the tour he was mistaken for the Governor General himself. An excellent general practitioner, he always knew when to call in a specialist, and since it was General Vanier's heart that needed watching he relied for expert opinion and advice on Dr Paul David from Montreal. Even as late as 1965 he was telling the General that he should do more travelling, since with proper care he always came back from a tour in a better state of health than when he had set out. In secure possession of his own 'interior castle', Georges Vanier had always thrived in contact with his fellow-men, particularly when he was trying to do them service. He was nothing of a clubman; he never sought company for company's sake; but the rediscovery of his own country, the quickened awareness of its problems, and the personal experience of its diversity, all contributed to that accession of physical and mental strength which he had felt on assuming office.

Still, it was always possible that after two or three years he would feel obliged to lay down the burden. Everything, however, went well, and in October 1962, in reply to an enquiry about his health, he could reassure Dr David that 'the Lord continues to be your collaborator'. But at 6 a.m. on the 8th of April 1963, he suffered a slight heart attack, with sudden breathlessness. He described this as 'a bit of a set-back', and indeed it was not so serious since he was able, a few days afterwards, to bid a political good-bye to Mr Diefenbaker, and to swear in his old friend, Lester Pearson, as Prime Minister from his bed where he remained for three weeks without moving. He was convalescent for a further three. The departing Ministers were deeply moved by the words he addressed to them on that occasion. Lord Alexander, who had suffered a similar but much worse attack, pointed the moral which the General had doubtless already drawn for himself.

Nature is wise, it makes a signal for us when we grow older to slow up and not try and force our bodies to do more than they can. In all seriousness I must admit that when I was laid up in hospital I not only found it a delightful rest but for the first time in a busy life I had the time to read all the books I longed to read. Tolstoi's *War and Peace* was one of them, and that magnificent story does take some reading.[1]

Georges Vanier was not a Tolstoyan, but he may well have dipped into *The Newcomes* for the twentieth time when his mind was not on higher things. By the 14th of June the doctors were well satisfied with his convalescence, and assured him that he could continue to work as usual. The holiday at Tadoussac, with Bernard, his wife, and two little girls for company, and occasionally for light relief, completed the cure.

Although the General's heart attack had not been serious, and he had quickly recovered from it, the question of his continuance in office was bound to arise in the minds of the Queen's advisers. Shortly after he had made his first public appearance – at the Requiem Mass for Pope John XXIII – Mr Pearson, the new Prime Minister, raised the matter at one of his weekly calls at Government House. A French-Canadian Governor General would be an obvious asset at a time when the tension between Quebec and the rest of Canada was threatening to become acute; and Mr Pearson hesitantly asked the General if he would be willing to carry on beyond the expiration of his five year term in September 1964. This was still some time ahead, but the General felt in duty bound to agree. The Prime Minister kept the matter to himself until the spring of 1964 when he wrote to Sir Michael Adeane as follows:

The Governor General is willing to remain in office, if requested to do so, as long as his health enables him to discharge his duties. You know how conscientious and how unselfish he is in these matters and he would not wish to stay on if he did not feel fit in every respect to do the job. At the present time he seems in really good health and I am confident that this will continue for some time. I know that, if he remains in office after September, this will be very well regarded in Canada where he and his wife have won deep respect and great affection from the whole Canadian community.[2]

Mr Pearson made the request officially to the Queen when he was in London for the Commonwealth Prime Ministers' Con-

1. 15th April 1963.
2. 6th May 1964.

ference in July, and announced Her Majesty's assent to the
Canadian House of Commons on the 21st of July. Approval was
expressed by all parties, and Mr Pearson presented the General
with a handsomely bound copy of Hansard recording it. The
Queen had already appointed him a member of her Privy Council
for the United Kingdom in February, and he was promoted to
the rank of full General in December 1964. He was the sixth
Governor General of Canada to have his term of office extended.
In this case the extension would run until September 1965, and
in the event it ran a good deal longer. The General had made only
one proviso – that he would not remain in office longer than his
health allowed him to discharge his duties effectively.

Michel Vanier was now a Lieutenant in the Royal 22nd, and
both his parents were on the ground at Valcartier to welcome
him after his first drop from a parachute. Another military
occasion which interested Pauline Vanier hardly less, was the
150th anniversary of the Battle of Châteauguay on the 20th of
October. Accompanied by the General, she unveiled the monument to her illustrious ancestor in the Parc Sauvé at Valleyfield.
If Tremblay was 'the greatest French-Canadian soldier since
Salaberry', Châteauguay was the greatest French-Canadian victory
till Courcelette. A photograph of Pauline taken at the unveiling
shows her wearing dark glasses. She was, in fact, having serious
trouble with her eyes, and her courage in carrying on as if
nothing were wrong, and the General's pretence that nothing
was wrong, although he did everything possible to spare her,
cemented the household at Rideau Hall in a quite exceptional
fraternity. In January 1964 she underwent an operation for
removal of cataract. This was completely successful and she was
back in Ottawa within a fortnight. In her absence from society,
if not from Rideau Hall, Georges dined alone with the British
High Commissioner and Lady Lintott, leaving early in order to
put the drops into her eyes. While she was still unable to read
for herself, he would read aloud to her from Vincent Massey's
Memoirs.

The family were now settled into their various careers or
avocations. Thérèse was specializing in haematology, and after a
spell at the Great Ormond Street Hospital for Children, had spent
a year in Boston. Bernard was painting, in a house which Georges
had bought for him at Marcoussis south of Paris. Jock had lived
for a time at Fatima, working on a thesis. 'Le Bonheur Principe
et Fin de la Morale Aristotélienne', which he successfully sus-

tained at the Institut Catholique. Byngsie, now fully recovered from the serious illness that followed his ordination, was thriving on the austerities of La Trappe – even more drastic then than they are today. So the wind was set fair on the home front as the Governor General and his wife, now both restored to health, rented the Tudor Hart house at Tadoussac in the summer of 1964. This stood secluded in deep woodland on the cliffs above the bay, and gave them an even greater privacy than they had enjoyed on the sea front.

2

In the five years since General Vanier had assumed office the 'quiet revolution' in the Province of Quebec had pursued a course to which no one could reasonably object. Fifty years after Ontario, and only a few years after British Columbia, the electrical power had been taken into public hands with generous compensation for its private owners. A Ministry of Education had been created, and the scholastic curriculum brought into line with the requirements of a technological society. If this reduced the influence of the Church, there were many who thought that the Church's influence had been excessive. The age of Duplessis was over, and the Québecois were no longer satisfied to have their Province regarded as a repository of folk-lore; an agrarian and priest-ridden society tolerated as a picturesque survival by their neighbours to the west and to the south. They were no longer willing to go to Ottawa as suppliants; they wished to be accepted as partners, contributing their own energies and intelligence to the future development of Canada.

For certain extremists, however, the revolution was altogether too quiet. A facetious young man had discharged his revolver in the comfortable lounge of the principal hotel in Victoria, and alarmed English-speaking sensibilities in a place where they were particularly acute. More immediately menacing were the bombs exploding in the mail-boxes of Westmount. No sane person pretended that these childish outrages were justified, but they drew attention to a situation fraught with peril for the unity of Canada. The English-speaking Canadians rarely troubled to learn the language spoken by five millions of their fellow countrymen, whereas nearly every educated French-Canadian could speak English and read it. When the editor of a French newspaper in Montreal sent free copies of his journal to 265 members of the House of Commons, two-thirds of them were sent back. When he continued to send them, he received dozens of indignant letters. 'I don't need your newspaper' wrote one Parliamentary correspondent 'because I don't read French. You can keep your filth.' Certain English Canadians were incapable of ordering a dish from a French menu; they would point to what their neighbour was eating and say they wanted 'the same thing'. The Vaniers noticed that at Tadoussac the wealthy Montrealers who came there every year for their holidays were incapable of conversing with the inhabitants in their own language. Moreover the economic influence wielded by the English-speaking minority in the Province of Quebec was still out of all proportion to their numbers. The separatist mentality was at work, psychologically if not politically, on either side of the invisible frontier which ran almost directly through Georges Vanier's birthplace, and within a few hundred yards of Government House.

The problem was not confined to the Province of Quebec. The abrogation of the Act of Manitoba, guaranteeing the use of French and the maintenance of French schools, had left sore memories in Winnipeg. Out of 647,000 French-Canadians in Ontario only 425,000 spoke their maternal tongue. In New Brunswick the Acadians formed 38 per cent of the population; yet there was not a single French school in Fredericton. In Windsor, Ontario, a group of French-speaking parishioners only obtained a French-speaking pastor by dint of suspending the Irish priest, who had been sent to look after them, over the Detroit river, and threatening to drop him in the water unless he returned where he belonged. But the issue of minority rights – and there were Ukrainian, Icelandic, German, Italian and Hungarian minorities in Canada as well as French – was quite different from the issue of separatism in Quebec. It was a social and political protest, not a constitutional challenge.

On the 16th of November 1964, shortly after the events with which this chapter is concerned, M. Jean Lesage, the Prime Minister of Quebec, speaking in Toronto, declared his hostility to either of two extreme solutions. 'On the one hand, the fusion of Quebec in a unitary Canadian state, and on the other hand the complete separation of Quebec from the rest of Canada.' The middle term between these two extremes was – and still is – under debate. How far backward could federalism bend without losing its balance? Where could one draw the line between autonomy and independence? M. René Levesque had not yet withdrawn from the Provincial Government, but his solution of 'associated status' for Quebec was already being mooted, and M. Pierre Trudeau had not yet shown his federalist teeth to the general public. On one occasion, however, General Vanier showed his. This was head-lined in the press as 'L'incident Vanier'. The General had been invited to take the salute at the torchlight procession of the St Jean Baptiste Society in Montreal on the 24th of June 1964, and had replied as follows:

After considering the memorandum submitted by the St Jean Baptiste Society to the Committee of the Constitution nominated by the Government of Quebec, I feel myself obliged to reconsider my acceptance to preside over the St Jean procession. As the representative of the Queen, it is impossible for me to support a nationalist organization which indulges in propaganda for the Republic of Quebec.

A few days later the General went back on his refusal, now foreseeing in the procession nothing more than 'a popular manifestation of all the French-Canadians'. It turned out to be rather more than that. Pierre Bourgault, the least sophisticated of the separatist leaders and spokesman for the Rassemblement pour l'Indépendence Nationale, declared in a prepared statement that the fact that General Vanier was a French-Canadian 'does not change the picture. He is still the representative of a foreign power.' M. Bourgault referred to 'this old general who speaks in the name of those who want to silence us. Let it be known that respectable old men do not impress us any more. Let Mr Vanier return as quickly as possible to Ottawa whence he came and continue to look after his dear Canadians who use him to win us over.' On the evening of the 24th of June, not only did a group of separatists shout insults at the Governor General, but they jeered at a detachment of the Royal 22nd as it was passing his stand. A snapshot taken of the General at that moment shows him bare-headed, with eyes ablaze with indignation, the jaws set above his stiff white collar, the muscles tense. The handful of dissidents stood across Sherbrooke Street, waving their placards – 'Vanier vendu', 'Vanier pour l'Angleterre'; others, headed by Marcel Chaput, forcing their way into the parade against the wishes of the organizers, pointedly refused to dip their fleur-de-lys banners as they passed the reviewing stand; and shortly before the parade was due to begin, a low-flying aircraft scattered separatist leaflets over the crowd. The booing was greeted with counter-cheers, and the incident ended in a tussle with the police and several arrests. The violence of Bourgault's attack was hotly denounced in the Ottawa press, and indeed it was only very rarely that the separatist faction showed an open hostility to the man who had done so much to win respect for the French-Canadians. The following letter was written by one who, at the time he penned it, was still being 'detained at Her Majesty's pleasure':

It is rather strange to notice that in circles like mine where people normally destroy everything, I rarely heard a critical word against this noble old man, whose attitude even the most degraded individuals could not help respecting. I remember the time when the first Separatists took up residence in this fortress. I had lively discussions with some of them about the politicians who represented English imperialism in Canada. There is no need to tell you that, whether on the federal or the provincial plane, these gentlemen had their fair share of defamation . . . but it was remarkable how even the most embittered refused to attack the Governor General.[3]

The General had minded the insult to the 'Van Doos', but otherwise he had taken the incident philosophically:

Somebody recently expressed compassion for my feelings and said he felt sorry for me and I replied 'Well, what would you like separatists to do to you – give you an ovation?' That in a way sums up the incident. I knew perfectly well I was going to be booed by a few separatists but I didn't want that to prevent me from sharing with half a million other Canadians in seeing a really imaginative spectacle. But I got my own back when, after their feeble demonstration, some thousands behind them in Lafontaine Park cheered instead and drowned their voices.[4]

It was no accident that October 1864 had brought together representatives of the three Maritime Provinces to agree on a scheme of federation – for at that moment federal democracy was being tested in the United States by the ordeal of blood and tears. Could the three British colonies to the north be more successful in reconciling the claims of central government and the claims of States rights? Their delegates met at Charlottetown on Prince Edward Island, where they were joined by representatives of Ontario and Quebec; and it was out of these conversations at Charlottetown and, later, at Quebec, and through the consummate statesmanship of Sir John A. Macdonald and Sir George

3. To Pauline Vanier 1st October 1968.
4. Letter to Thérèse Vanier, 9th July 1964.

Etienne Cartier, respectively Prime Ministers of Canada West and
Canada East, that the Dominion of Canada was born. It was not,
in every respect, an easy birth, for the notion of a larger federation was thrust upon the Maritimers, Nova Scotia and New
Brunswick being deeply divided, and Prince Edward Island – for
all its later pride in the Founding Fathers – holding out till 1873.
Although the decisions taken only assumed the force of law with
the British North America Act of 1867, they asked for public commemoration. As early as 1961 the idea had been mooted that the
Queen should visit Prince Edward Island in 1964; and it was in
the nature of the centenary that she could not visit Prince Edward
Island without also visiting Quebec. Herein lay the drama – and
the danger – of the situation.

In April 1963, immediately after taking office, Mr Pearson was
in London and broached the question of a Royal visit with Sir
Michael Adeane, leaving him in no doubt that the idea had the
support of the Canadian Government. The news of the visit was
well received when it was made known, and at a dinner given
in November 1963 for the Prime Minister and the Provincial
Premiers M. Lesage spoke of it in terms of enthusiastic appro-
bation to the Governor General. The first discordant note was
struck by the Law Students at Laval University. Wishing to
obtain publicity for a campaign against the administration over a
question of fees, they suggested that the tour be cancelled and
the money thus saved be invested in bursaries. M. Raymond
Barbeau, a Separatist from Montreal, warned the students at
Queen's University, Kingston, Ontario, that there might be
trouble, and even violence, during the Queen's stay in Quebec.
Dr Marcel Chaput, founder of the Republican Party in Quebec,
went even further. Many ardent nationalists dissociated themselves from M. Chaput; others advised cancellation of the visit
because it was ill-timed, or because the risks involved in it were
too great. Mr Pearson replied in the House of Commons that 'the
plans regarding Her Majesty's visit will not be affected in any way
by such an irresponsible statement,' and made it clear that the
Government would take 'adequate measures for the security of
the Queen'. M. Lesage, in his own Legislature, gave assurances
that 'the population of Quebec, with the exception of a few
hotheads, to whom no attention should be paid, is calm and has
a solid reputation for hospitality. Our eventual visitors can count
on the warm and enthusiastic reception which "La Belle Province"
always reserves.' And M. Auguste Choquette, a Member of

Parliament with strong Republican leanings, declared that

in no way whatever do I wish my name to be associated with Marcel Chaput, whom I consider to be one of the most harmful politicians of this decade. . . . If Her Majesty Queen Elizabeth II comes to Quebec, she must be welcomed with all the honours and consideration due to a Head of State, but this should not prevent anybody from thinking as a Canadian and wishing that all symbolic ties of colonialism be some day set aside so that Canada can be essentially Canadian.

General Vanier spoke for himself as well as for the Government when he referred to the projected visit in the Speech from the Throne on the 18th of September 1963:

The presence of the Queen of Canada will mark for our country the historic occasion of the interprovincial conference on Confederation; it will also re-emphasize the importance we attach to the Commonwealth, through which so much can be done to advance understanding and co-operation in this increasingly interdependent world.

These threats and objections were blown up by the Press – and more particularly by the British Press – out of all proportion to their importance. *Le Devoir*, responsible as always, even blamed its English-language contemporaries for making a mountain out of a molehill and thus 'playing into the hands of the Separatists and further deepening the moat which divides Canada's two communities'. Senator Cyrille Vaillancourt, a distinguished French-Canadian, inveighed against the press and radio networks for lending 'revolting and misleading publicity' to Separatist threats, and for spreading the 'absurd and divisive statements of foolish nonentities preaching hate and egoism, and acting in a destructive and irresponsible manner'. Absurd and divisive they may have been, but General Vanier and the Canadian Government were bound to take note of them. By August 1964 two schools of thought had found expression. One was in favour of cancellation. The Queen's visit was not an absolute necessity. It had been inspired by the Lieutenant-Governor and Premier of Prince Edward Island wishing to emphasize the part played by their Province in the events leading up to the British North America Act of 1867 – events with which the Crown was not concerned. 1967 was the essential centenary, and General Vanier was himself surprised by M. Lesage's enthusiasm for the Queen's visit. Some people sincerely believed that the Federal Government was using it to challenge the Separatists in Quebec by declaring, in effect, 'not only will the Queen come in 1967, but in 1964 as well.'

As a matter of fact, there was no such intention on the part of the Government. The situation reminds me of Topsy's words in *Uncle Tom's Cabin*. 'I 'spect I growed. Don't think nobody ever made me.'[5]

Cancellation was urged by *Le Devoir* and *La Presse* in Montreal and also by the St Jean Baptiste Society which 'reached the conclusion that the Queen had been badly advised and asks the Government of Canada to reconsider its decision.' The central council of the Students Association at the University of Montreal adopted a resolution to the same effect, and a leading columnist in the *Toronto Globe and Mail* shared the prevailing fears for the Queen's security.

Over the years I have covered many Royal visits to Canada and I can truthfully say that in no part of this broad Nation have I ever seen our Sovereign treated with more warmth and affection than in Quebec. But, unfortunately, there is now a small group of madmen loose in this ancient and basically loyal province. To expose The Queen to their lunacy would be a grave imposition upon a brave young woman and those who must be responsible for her safety.

The second school was opposed to cancellation, and it included many French language newspapers. *Le Soleil* from Quebec City, while admitting a more than normal risk, was convinced that a majority of the people wanted the Queen to visit them, and had 'an affectionate reception in store for her'. How, it was argued, could the Canadian Government cancel or postpone the visit without inflicting on the Queen 'an insult much worse than the one from which they wish to spare her?' Ottawa's *Le Droit* was equally categorical:

Elizabeth II remains juridically and legally The Queen of Canada until such time as Confederation disintegrates, if that ever happens, and she deserves, whether in her personal or official capacity, the most profound respect. French Canadians can, for a number of reasons, justifiably reproach their fellow citizens of British origin and of the English language; but they have no cause of complaint against The Queen, and certainly none against the noble and distinguished mother who carries that Crown today.

Some newspapers actually saw the visit as assisting the cause of French Canada. *L'Action*, again from Quebec City, pointed out that:

5. General Vanier to Sir Michael Adeane, 7th August 1964.

long before Ottawa was seized, as it is now, of the bilingual and bicultural ferment, the Crown was establishing the fact, in all its interventions in Canada, of equality of the two languages beyond the letter of the Constitution. The Queen as an ally of Quebec nationalism? And why not? In a sense she always has been.

And the Union Nationale's *Montréal Matin*, the strongly autonomist organ of the Opposition in Quebec, did not believe that 'Quebec residents who welcomed the Queen so warmly before had changed their feelings. As for young hotheads, the police could look after them.'

In the event the police did not fail to do so; it was only a pity there had to be so many policemen. Lester Pearson stood firm, assuring the House of Commons that the visit had been discussed with Premier Shaw and Premier Lesage before any formal invitation was extended; that 'when Her Majesty comes to Canada, she will receive every security protection that is possible'; and that the Government would not 'surrender to a very small minority and vicious propaganda.' General Vanier was writing to Sir Michael Adeane from Tadoussac that:

The situation appears to be settling down. On the whole, conditions are much more favourable now than many would have anticipated some time ago. There is no question now about whether the visit is opportune or not, no sinister warnings or threats. I feel sure there will be no hostile demonstration in Quebec and I doubt whether there will be any embarrassing incident. This city has a long and honourable tradition of loyalty to and affection for the Crown which the people of Quebec will not permit to be sullied.[6]

The Queen's Private Secretary replied with evident relief:

I am glad that the anti-cancellationists have won because I know how horrified the Queen would have been if they had not. She is very fond of Canada and of the Province of Quebec and it would have been a sad blow to have been prevented going there because of the activities of extremists. It is also good news that the P.M., supported by Prime Minister Lesage and Premier Shaw, is adopting an increasingly positive public position; this does not surprise me at all knowing as I have said, what his views were some time ago. I am glad, too, that he has said in the House of Commons that 'the Queen of Canada receives her constitutional advice from the Government of Canada', as this is something that though obvious, cannot be said too often.[7]

6. 7th August 1964.
7. 25th August 1964.

Many people in Canada who thought the visit untimely agreed that, once announced, it could not decently or prudently be cancelled. In a letter to the Queen General Vanier made it clear that Canada and Quebec were facing a situation in which compromise would be difficult, but where a solution satisfactory to the Province and to the rest of the country would have to be found. Meanwhile preparations for the visit, entrusted to the Canadian Government Hospitality Committee, went forward. Certain criticisms – indicative of nationalist susceptibility – were afterwards made by Marcel Faribault, who was not in principle opposed to the Crown as a symbol – although he had the intellectual's distaste for its trappings – or to Federation as a political structure for Canada:

No one seemed to realize that, to sail up the St Lawrence on a yacht called the *Britannia* was to bring back memories of the Kirk brothers, and General Wolfe – in effect, the past struggles of two peoples. Anchoring the ship at Anse au Foulon and pointing out in the Anglo-Saxon and American press (thanks to the English title of Wolfe's Cove) that the actions of the general were being followed . . . following over the Plains of Abraham the path of the conqueror of 1759 was a curious way of reminding a population of a conquest of which its ancestors were the victims.[8]

It was no wonder, said the speaker, that the citizens of Quebec were embarrassed into staying within doors; but what embarrassed them, and the Vaniers, were the elaborate precautions rightly thought necessary for the protection of the Queen's person. To drive through the streets of Quebec with every window watched and every yard of pavement closely guarded was a hideous and humiliating experience for the Governor General and his wife. An editorial in *Le Soleil* questioned whether 'the police always acted with the discernment one could have wished', and whether it was normal for journalists having no connection with the small group of demonstrators 'to suffer from a severity far too indiscriminate'. The Rassemblement de l'Indépendance Nationale had planned a large meeting of protest at which they expected 20,000 people; in fact only two hundred turned up. No doubt the R.C.M.P. might have kept order more discreetly, but this would certainly have been considered a usurpation of Provincial responsibility. Many must have wished that the Queen had been more clearly visible; a bullet-proof car with a domed bubble would have

8. Speech at the Club des Anciens du Collège Ste Marie, 26th October 1964.

enabled her to stand up and acknowledge the greetings of those who wished to protest their loyalty.

M. Faribault had also said that if good came out of the visit, it would be 'due to Providence'. He would have been nearer the mark if he had said that it would be due to the Queen. Her speech in the Quebec Parliament was universally acclaimed as a masterpiece. Using the French words which she described as 'friends of my childhood and which I have already taught to my children', the language which was a 'precious instrument of understanding', and whose 'wide diffusion could only assist the fruitful exchange of ideas' – she paid the tribute of a Colonel-in-Chief to the Royal 22nd, whose golden jubilee she had helped to celebrate at the Citadel, and then went on to speak of the future:

Compatriots should put forward and explain their point of view without passion and with respect for contrary opinions. Our problems will fall into confusion if we don't know how to illuminate them with humanity and brotherhood. So long as the dialogue remains open, it will help to unite men of good will. A true patriotism does not prevent us from understanding the patriotism of other people.

A democratic régime rests upon the conscious adherence of its citizens. The rôle of a constitutional monarchy is to personify the democratic state, to sanction legitimate authority, to assure the legality of its measures, and to guarantee the execution of the popular will. In accomplishing this task, it protects the people against disorder. But a dynamic state should not be afraid to re-think its political philosophy; and we should not be surprised if a protocol designed a hundred years ago no longer answers all the problems of today.

The Queen spoke of the forthcoming centenary of Confederation and of her desire that this should be 'a symbol of hope for the world'; and that it would demonstrate 'a free and effective understanding' between the founding races of Canada; and thus express the maturity of the nation. She concluded with an apt quotation from Lord Dufferin, a former Governor General on whose deserted mansion at Tadoussac his successor looked down from the cliffs:

Brave and noble race who first gave Europe the means of bringing civilization to the American continent. Bold and valiant race who explored the interior of the continent, and allowed the industries of Europe to settle not only on the banks of the St Lawrence, but also in the rich valleys of the Mississippi and the Ohio.

There was nothing in the Queen's speech which General Vanier would not have been glad to say himself, and he summed up his impressions of the visit in a letter to Sir Michael Adeane:

I know that uppermost in Her Majesty's mind – and I add heart – was the hope, to put it simply, that her stay with us would do some good. It has done good, a great deal of good, and more, in all the circumstances, than one might have expected.

Why? Here are some of the reasons.

The Queen's charm, her serenity, dignity, and I add, her fortitude, left a deep impression. You might ask: how can this be, since the security measures in Quebec were such that Her Majesty, except at The Citadel, had little contact with the people. But a contact was established, because everybody throughout the country saw The Queen on television, although she didn't see them. There was complete coast-to-coast coverage of all Her Majesty's activities.

Every comment, without exception, that I have heard or read speaks of Her Majesty in most glowing terms, not a single reference being made uncomplimentary to her person, or about the way she carried out her duties, or about the fact that she came to Canada – everyone knows, even the most ignorant, that the Prime Minister and M. Lesage bear this responsibility and that The Queen simply did her duty as a Constitutional Monarch.

Her Majesty's speech was an outstanding factor in her triumph. It was a complete surprise to everybody from the most loyal to the Separatists. Little thought was given to the address before or during its delivery and for a short time after. When The Queen spoke in the Quebec Parliament most people were busy thinking about possible riots and worse, stirred up by an irresponsible Press and mischievous extremists. In any event, it was generally expected that the speech would be simply a series of platitudes.

The Queen's speech drew attention to the French fact in Canada. I have said before that the majority of English-speaking Canadians do not know that there is such a thing, except in the Provinces of Ontario, New Brunswick (where the French-speaking population is roughly 35 per cent), and Quebec of course. I am not endeavouring to distribute blame of any kind, they just haven't heard about it. But the fact that The Queen has spoken about it will make them understand it exists and deserves serious thought.

Another point about the speech's efficacy is that it was made by the Sovereign for whose judgment Canadians have a high regard. The Queen's attitude may well help to mould their views.

I firmly believe that history will give credit to Her Majesty for discerning the situation and facing it. How Bagehot would have welcomed this example of the non-partisan authority of the Crown!

Quite sincerely, I believe that hope for mutual understanding, which God grant we shall attain, may result in great measure from The Queen's lead.

Another reason for saying that The Queen's presence was helpful is that Her Majesty stole the Separatists' thunder generated through threats and blackmail. Their hope was to prevent The Queen from coming. This would have been a great victory but their stock dropped sharply after her departure. I don't think, however, they ever plotted to do any bodily harm to Her Majesty. . . .

Most French-speaking Canadians are embarrassed about what went on in Quebec and by the way it was reported abroad. They see with angry surprise the mess that only a few hundred of their least distinguished compatriots and some foreigners were able to make. Demands are now being made that the Separatists step out onto the hustings at the first opportunity to show whether they have any real popular support that would give them the right to make so much noise. Many moderates, hitherto detached and silent spectators, now recognize that, whether they like it or not, they can be hurt by what is going on, with the result that they are becoming more outspoken and critical of Separatism. The English-speaking Canadians have also been embarrassed by having broadcast to the world their failure to appreciate the French position.

The Queen had to deal with such a difficult situation which required very careful treatment and at the same time positive action, that I sometimes wonder whether Providence did not play a part in Her Majesty's treatment of the whole affair. In saying this I weigh my words very carefully.

I agree with you that in the long run the decision to invite Her Majesty will prove to have been in the best interests of the Country and its Sovereign.[9]

Sir Michael Adeane had already written to the Governor General:

Last but not least, The Queen is grateful to you personally for your advice and support. It would be idle to pretend that this has been in all ways one of the easiest occasions on which The Sovereign has been in Canada, but the possible difficulties surrounding every word and action have been minimized by your forethought and your experienced advice.

It is rash for such an outsider as I am to make either comments or forecasts, but I propose to do both and say that I think that it would have been a pity if The Queen had not been able to show her real and personal interest in Canada's vital concerns by being there this year, and that in the long run the decision of Mr Pearson and Mr Lesage to invite her will prove to have been in the best interests of the country and – which is the same thing – of its Sovereign.[10]

9. 24th November 1964.
10. 14th October 1964.

CHAPTER 24

THEMES OF OFFICE

I

ONE cannot ask less of the Queen's representative – or of the Queen herself for the matter of that – than an illustration by precept and example of the great commonplaces without which a nation cannot live. To do this effectively is no commonplace achievement, and to object that there was nothing particularly original in what General Vanier said in the five hundred odd speeches he was called upon to make during his term of office is not to deny him originality of expression or, still less, of character. On every occasion he contrived to be, at some point or other, inimitably himself. An apt quotation, a personal reminiscence, or a sly twist of humour, would remind his audience of who was speaking to them. He enjoyed public speaking, as a man will naturally enjoy doing what he does well. On one occasion, when the municipal reception had been moved indoors on account of rain, he expressed the fear that he had been talking for rather a long time. 'Oh no, sir' came a voice from the back row 'please go on. It's still raining.' And on another occasion, when he was speaking without a clock, most of his audience appeared to have fallen asleep. In reply to his apologies, and to his explanation that there was no clock in the room, a voice replied: 'Thank goodness there's a calendar.' The General's humour was never livelier than when it could be turned against himself.

What he said, apart from local and circumstantial allusions, was generally related to a few important themes. In some respects his long absence abroad was an advantage to him. Having in a sense rediscovered his own country, he was able to see it in a true perspective. Other examples could be quoted of men who had come to Canada from elsewhere – a Wilder Penfield, an Etienne Gilson, or a Charles de Koninck – and discerned an unlimited opportunity of growth, where native-born Canadians were wondering whether there was any sense or significance in being a Canadian at all. General Vanier was perpetually astonished that they seemed to know and care so little about their own history, and to have so little idea of how highly their country was esteemed abroad. Boundaries had become barriers, and the General's plea for unity was based on a fact which to him was as plain as daylight. If the country did not hang together in one sense, it would certainly hang together in another.

He reminded an audience at Port Arthur that the first explorers of European stock to set foot on the shores of Lake Superior were two young French Canadians, Radisson and Groseilliers, and that these were followed by other adventurous Québecois, a full century and a half before Roderick Mackenzie built the fort which subsequently became the district headquarters of the North West Fur Company. 'My father's side of the family' he went on 'was understandably proud of these accomplishments, but you can be sure my mother was just as quick to point out the contributions made by her ancestors on her father's side, the early explorers and settlers from the British Isles.' Much of the pioneering in Canada had been a partnership, and neither the North West Fur Company nor the Hudson's Bay Company had realized the possibilities open to each of them until they had affiliated. The majestic forests and hills of Thunder Bay carried a message over and above their own magnificence; they reminded the General that 'in terms of potential resources per capita Canada may be the richest country in the world.' Just as the river Restigouche in New Brunswick was a French translation of an Indian word meaning 'a river with many tributaries', so the ethnic diversity of Canada was a constituent of its greatness.

The theme was a familiar one and the General lost no opportunity of sounding it during this western tour in the spring of 1965 – at Winnipeg and St Boniface, at Edmonton and Saskatoon, at Calgary and Kamloops – which, being translated, meant 'the meeting of the waters'.

Let us stop for just one moment to consider what would have happened to Canada had each of its founding peoples gone their separate ways. How long could we have retained an independent way of life? ... If any part of Canada were to contemplate going its separate way, could the rest of us long remain united? I am certain that if you stop for even a moment to contemplate the consequences you will agree with me that unity must be the most important single concern of all of us in this country, for on our unity depends our future, and our future is the concern of each and every one of us.[1]

1. At Edmonton, 4th June 1965.

These warnings were as pertinent in British Columbia, where certain people were looking to the United States, as in Quebec where some refused to look beyond themselves.

The General had seen in France how nearly a want of civic consciousness – or, more exactly, of civic conscience – had brought a great nation to disaster. He could not have uttered the word 'socialism' without creating a political explosion, but he was not afraid of 'socialization', and here he quoted John XXIII to his purpose:

Socialization multiplies the methods of organization, and regulates in ever greater detail the relations between human beings in every domain. In consequence it reduces the free activity of the individual. This means and the methods it employs, the atmosphere it creates, put difficulties in the way of his private initiative, the exercise of his responsibility, the affirmation and enrichment of his personality.[2]

So much might be freely admitted, but General Vanier was far from drawing a negative conclusion from this circumscription of individual effort. Everything would depend on how far men learnt to control a phenomenon which they could not escape. The precept of brotherly aid was 'among the most precious of our Judaeic-Christian heritage', and the more voluntary this aid could be, the better it would serve the purposes of a free democracy. Not everyone had the time for what was sometimes cynically described as 'good works', but everyone was called to a 'collective act of self-examination – to a serious and continuous effort, in the apostolic sense of the word, an effort of initiative, intelligence, and devotion.'[3] It was an appeal to which neither the Governor General nor his wife had ever failed to respond. An eminent psychologist in Montreal had emphasized that 'the very act of giving carries with it a reward. We are enriched as human beings by contact with another whose need may be great.' The volunteer, General Vanier went on, was:

an observer who notices the all too frequent gap between our ideals and the reality of daily life, and who then acts to bring the two closer. Volunteers in health, welfare, and education are those who see the blemishes in the social system. They live with the casualties and the victims . . . they learn to perceive real values, to spot crucial challenges, and to suggest effective remedies. They act as the eyes and ears of society and ensure by their awareness that the agencies remain

2. *Mater et Magistra.*
3. Conference des Oeuvres de Bien-Etre Social, Montreal, 15th February 1962.

in close touch with the wants, complaints and suggestions of the community.[4]

It was with all this in mind that he gave his encouragement to the 4-H Club movement, which had been founded at Roland, Manitoba, in 1913 and celebrated its 50th anniversary in January 1963. 4-H was a pledge of 'Head, Heart, Hands and Health' to the ends of a worth-while life. 72,000 young people from Canada and the United States were now bringing to farming a greater scientific and practical knowledge – and Georges Vanier reminded them that Nature was 'the living and visible garment of God', and that rural life, both in its labour and its recreation, afforded 'an education which neither city nor university could provide.'[5]

Once upon a time, in France, the General had committed himself to the opinion that if Champlain – or was it Cartier? – had been alive today, he would have been a Boy Scout. It was the sort of remark that Georges Vanier was never ashamed to make, and in Canada he did everything he could to stress his belief in scouting as a school of discipline, service and self-reliance. He was particularly pleased when the Catholic branch of the movement in Quebec joined forces with the national body. The scout's daily 'good deed' was an occasion more easily said than done. The General liked to recall the four young scouts who reported their good deed to their scoutmaster, and his astonishment that it had taken four of them to help a single old lady across the street. 'Yes' they replied 'she didn't want to go.' Equally useful was the Air Cadet League, founded by his old schoolfellow Senator 'Chubby' Power in 1940, at a time when Power was Minister of National Defence for Air; and the Commonwealth Youth Movement 'Questors' to whom the General proposed as an example the legendary figure of Sir Galahad in search of the Holy Grail, and the figure, more recent but just as legendary, of Captain Scott dying among the Antarctic snows. The heroes of mankind were 'like mountains in the moral world.'[6]

General Vanier advised the Adventure in Citizenship Students at their 14th Annual Congress[7] to ask themselves 'What is your country? How will you add to it? What will you do with it?'; and he warned the Canadian Citizenship Council that 'as soon as public service ceases to be the chief business of the citizen, and

4. Ibid.
5. 15th November, 1962.
6. Boy Scout Investiture, 25th October 1966.
7. 12th May 1964.

they would rather serve with their money than with their persons, then the State is not far from its fall.'[8] Bernard Shaw had observed that youth was a wonderful thing but that it was a crime to waste it on the young. The General welcomed the smart performance of the Ashbury Cadet Corps as an answer to such cynicism; and there was particular pleasure in a visit to the Boys' Farm and Training School at Shawbridge in the Province of Quebec. It was here that Frances' husband, Bill Shepherd, had worked for twenty-five years, and the Vaniers knew the place well. Frances had died in 1958, and now Eva was the only other member of the family still living. But these bereavements did not make Georges feel older, or turn his mind with a self-indulgent nostalgia to a past on which he might well have been proud to rest:

People do not really age by living a number of years. I am convinced that we grow old only by deserting our ideals. We are, in fact, as old as our doubts and our despairs, but we are as young as our faith and our hope, especially faith and hope in our youth, which is, after all, the same as saying our faith and our hope in our country's future.[9]

It had been said that 'the history of our society is a race between education and catastrophe', and the General was well aware that moral principles could not survive in an intellectual void. He hoped that 'dashing about the country, giving holidays right and left' was the only 'built-in difficulty of school administration' which would remain unreformed.[10] Georges Vanier was essentially a humanist, but there was Wilder Penfield at hand to remind him that there was no contradiction between science and humanism, if one allowed to humanism its ancient and honourable meaning. It was a far cry from the Montreal Medical Institution in its original garret at 20 St James Street to the new McGill Training and Research Building of the Allen Memorial Institute. McGill was justly proud of its Medical School, and in opening[11] this new centre of psychiatry the General permitted himself, nevertheless, to look beyond the confines of science. 'The power of psychiatry must be restrained within a certain morality and the keystone of that morality must be a constant attention to the

8. 14th May 1964.
9. Affiliation between the Boy Scouts of Canada and Les Scouts Catholiques de Canada, Secteur Français, 22nd February 1967.
10. Annual Convention of the Public Schools Trustees Association of Ontario, 1st October 1963.
11. 13th November 1963.

power of the spirit'; and he quoted Alexis Carrel in support of this priority. 'As a physician, I have seen men, after all other therapy had failed, lifted out of disease and melancholy by the serene effort of prayer.' The psychiatrists had the right to dissect the personality, but not to leave it in pieces. As Rabelais – to ascend no higher on the spiritual ladder – had put it – 'Science sans conscience est la ruine de l'âme.'

Only a few days later the inauguration of the programme of French studies at McGill gave the General a golden opportunity of stressing the theme which was as near as any to his heart, and to which the English minority in Montreal could rally with particular effect. Who better could interpret Quebec to the rest of Canada? Many English-speaking universities were in fact exchanging teachers with colleges in Quebec; in Victoria a 'Maison Française' had been established in co-operation with Laval. For General Vanier, France and Britain, with their ancient and complementary cultures, represented the western world at the climacteric of its middle age. Lest his audience should think him biased, he quoted his predecessors – Dufferin, Lorne and Tweedsmuir – on what France has given to Canada, and André Malraux on what Canada had given to France. 'I raise my glass' Malraux had recently declared in Montreal 'to the first French child who, on Remembrance Day, will put a flag on the tomb of a Canadian soldier.' It would have plenty to choose from in the Cimetière des Vertus at Dieppe.

Again at McGill, the General opened the Stephen Leacock Memorial Building for the Humanities and Social Sciences. In two minds as to whether he should speak about Leacock or about the Humanities, he reached for the Oxford Dictionary – never far from his elbow – and discovered its definition of the latter: 'human nature, humaneness, benevolence and polite scholarship'. This, of course, fitted Leacock like a glove. So the General remained stranded between the works of Leacock on one side of his desk and an encyclopaedia on the other. But the wit and wisdom of Leacock kept flashing across the weighty definitions of encyclopaedic learning, and won out in the end. He did not forget, however, Robertson Davies' reminder that the 'notion of Leacock simply as a funny fellow who passed his life in an atmosphere of easy laughter' left out of account 'the hints at darker things, the swift and unmistakable descents towards melancholy'. This was so often characteristic of the great comedian, and Leacock liked to tell the story of Grimaldi asking a London physician to cure his chronic depression. When the physician advised him to go and see Grimaldi, he could only reply: 'Sir, I am Grimaldi.'

General Vanier naturally received an Honorary Degree from McGill, and Madame Vanier received one also.[12] On these academic occasions there was some truth in the General's observation that she was beginning to 'steal the show'. When she was given a Degree from the University of Ottawa, the Press reminded its readers that her husband was the Governor General; and when she received one from St Mary's University in Halifax, the local paper surmised that her husband might possibly be known to some of its readers for his work in other fields. By the time the Vice-regal pair reached St John's, Newfoundland, the situation was becoming desperate. At Memorial University they were both given degrees, but the Press added as a footnote to its coverage of the ceremony, that as a token of its esteem for Madame Vanier the University had decided to confer a degree on her husband as well.

New universities were springing up fast in Canada, and the motto chosen for Brock, far south on the Niagara Peninsula, was peculiarly apt. 'Surgite' – the University did indeed rise in a single sky-scraper, and Georges Vanier was there to open it.[13] As Invigilator-General, and as a friend of its President, Dr Gibson, he watched its progress with interest, annexing Egerton Ryerson's formula for higher education of a hundred years ago.

Not the mere acquisition of certain arts, or of certain branches of knowledge, but that instruction and discipline which qualify and dispose students for their appropriate duties and appointments in life, as Christians, as persons in business, and also as members of the civil community in which they live.[14]

The transformation of Assumption College into the University of Windsor renewed pleasant associations with its Chancellor, Keiller Mackay, and its President, Dr Francis Leddy. In attending the Dedication of one of its halls, the General had been told that he might wear his academic hood – to which both he and the President had referred by the fine old French word épitoge. One of the General's secretaries, thinking that he might need an English translation, rushed into his study with the alarming information that one possible meaning of the word was chaperon! Anxious as always to avoid friction between Town and Gown, the General was glad to note that a million dollars had been subscribed to the

12. 30th May 1966.
13. 19th October 1964.
14. 14. Report on the System of Instruction for Upper Canada.

University Development by over 20,000 employees in the City of Windsor. This was a 'shining testament both to the awareness and sense of involvement of the University and to the eagerness of the community to support and nourish its cultural heart.'[15]

Later in the same year (1965) General Vanier opened the new campus at York University, Toronto. The occasion gave him an opportunity to stress the value of the tutorial system which York had adopted.[16] Universities were everywhere threatened by elephantiasis, particularly when they were situated in a large city. One solution was to found a new and separate university, with all 'umbilical vestiges' severed from the parent body – and this Toronto had been wise enough to do. In one of the larger Canadian universities the students, fearful of their growing numbers, had invented a foreign student who was unable to pay his fees in Canadian currency. The Bursar agreed that he should carry on with his studies on credit, and one of the conspirators completed an examination paper for him which was awarded a grade of high distinction. It was only when this fictitious personage ran as candidate for the Presidency of the Students' Council that his non-identity was discovered. If all student protests were as sensible as this one, academic life would be the healthier.

On the 17th of October 1964, the Governor General opened Trent University, Peterborough, Ontario. This, he hoped, would fulfil Disraeli's definition of a university as a 'place of light, of liberty, and of learning'. It certainly fulfilled Leacock's definition of it as a place 'not too near anywhere and not too far from everywhere'; and it contained more than Leacock's prerequisite of 'two dozen very old elm trees, and about fifty acres of wooded ground and lawn', since it owned 1,400 acres on the Otonobec river. Like York University, it was based on the collegiate and tutorial system.

At Lower Canada College in Montreal the General quoted the old Chinese saying: 'Great souls have wills; feeble souls have wishes';[17] and the opening of the Georges P. Vanier Library at Loyola[18] was an occasion of legitimate pride. He confessed that in his student days the Loyola Library had not been all that it should have been, and he recalled his visits to the second-hand bookshops and auction sales to make good its deficiences. 'I can

15. 28th April 1965.
16. 15th October 1965.
17. 10th June 1966.
18. 27th October 1964.

remember arriving home with great bundles of books under both arms, to be greeted by the very patient parent whom I was spending into the poorhouse. My father would often ask me if I read half of what I bought.' Was it only a verbal echo that associated the word *liber* with the word *liberty*? There could be no liberty without free access to the truth, and one way of arriving at the truth was through books. But the Vanier Library might well become a mine of something more than knowledge. The late return of borrowed books was to be punished by fines which would earn, no doubt, important accessions to the Library – but also an invective from the students which might rebound against the man after whom it had been named. The General referred to his own authorship of *Paroles de Guerre*, and his mortification at discovering that a book published at $1.50 was being remaindered at a bargain store for seventeen cents. He was not, he said, writing books any more; but it was a loss to the history of his times that he did not live to do so.

The 70th Anniversary Dinner at Loyola[19] was a celebration of constant growth and judicious foresight; and so was the laying of the Cornerstone at Lakehead University Library, Port Arthur,[20] more than a thousand miles away. Less than twenty years had passed since the University was established as the Lakehead Technical Institute in an old army hut brought out from British Columbia on a flat car and put together on a vacant lot in down town Port Arthur. It was said that in the spring, when the ice on the roof began to melt, the water leaking through the ceiling persuaded the students that they had entered an aquarium. The distance traversed in so short a space of time from a Technical Institute to a University, and from a leaking roof to a library, proved once more that where there was a will in Canada there was generally a way.

2

General Vanier was well aware that voluntary contributions to social work, however important, were no substitute for professional skill. He told the Catholic Hospital Association of Canada that:

Although I am a Fellow of the Royal College of Physicians and Surgeons, it is (I must admit) an honorary qualification. I belong to the patient class. Speaking then, as a patient, I should say that the

19. 25th March 1966.
20. 26th May 1965.

average patient looks upon medical people as a non-combatant might be expected to look upon the troops fighting on his behalf – the more trained men there are between his body and the enemy the better.[21]

Someone had apparently telephoned Government House to know whether the Governor General were really a doctor, because he heard one of his secretaries reply: 'Oh yes, he's a doctor all right, but he's not the sort of doctor that does anyone any good.' And he liked to tell the story of the patient who extracted from his physician the truth that he was extremely ill. 'Now' said the physician 'is there anyone you would like to see?' 'Yes' replied the patient in a voice almost incredibly feeble, and then, a little more strongly, 'another doctor.' The General emphasized – as he knew only too well from personal experience – that physical illness brought in its train a weakening of the spirit which it was in everyone's power to alleviate. The work of the medical technician must be completed by the 'compassionate apostle'. Both the General and Madame Vanier were particularly concerned for the care and rehabilitation of retarded children. It was not so long since 70,000 of these unfortunates had been put to death.

The thought of it alone is monstrous. Democratic countries believe that every human being, even those most handicapped mentally, have a real and profound worth; that every person has been created by God in His image and that every person passes after death into eternal life. Democratic countries believe, as well, that even in those who will never be able to lead working lives there exist those qualities of the heart in which they can and should find their fulfilment. A country such as Canada which believes in the worth of each human being could *never* consider such persons who are unable to take a full place in the work force of their country as some sort of millstone about their country's neck – a millstone to be disposed of. How much less should such a country consider hiding such unfortunates behind cold inhuman walls far from the eyes of the rest of the population, as if we should try to forget them.[22]

The Vaniers were equally concerned for the physically handicapped, and one wishes – for very particular reasons – that the General had been alive to read the following letter to Pauline. The writer had been to visit her thalidomide damaged daughter at the Rehabilitation Centre in Montreal:

21. 18th May 1964.
22. Centennial Crusade Dinner of the Canadian Rehabilitation Centre for Retarded Children, 13th September 1965.

I sat with another mother – French-Canadian – as we watched our two children play. Neither child spoke a word of the other's language, but it was no obstacle. They recognized each other as friends. I cannot explain to you how it moved me to see them, laden with their prostheses giggling hilariously, as they tried to pick up marbles with their hooks.[23]

General Vanier was Prior of the Canadian Chapter of the Order of St John of Jerusalem. The installation of Madame Vanier[24] as a Dame of Grace was an occasion of particular splendour with the cream and white ballroom filled with guests. The flag of the Order – a white cross on red, with a green and red maple leaf in the centre – was carried before the procession of the Chapter, wearing their high collars and black robes. The General admitted ninety-six Canadians to various grades of the Order, touching each kneeling candidate three times on the shoulder with his sword. The annual Investitures at Government House were picturesque occasions, and he had words of special encouragement for the 'Save a Life' programme which a branch of the Order had undertaken. This consisted of free two-hour classes in artificial respiration offered to the public across Canada. Since its inauguration in 1954 nearly 750,000 Canadians had followed the instruction, and in many cases lives had been saved as a result of it. The General was well aware that he himself had a weak heart, and in laying the foundation stone for the new Institute of Cardiology in Montreal[25] he took the occasion of paying tribute to his own specialist, Dr Paul David. Since the opening of the Institute in 1951 Dr David had been its directing spirit. His work had been recognized by his appointment as President of the Inter-American Association of Cardiology in 1964, and as a Vice-President of the International Foundation of Cardiology. In ten years 17,000 people had benefited from the professional services of the Institute, and in 10,000 cases a weakness of the heart had been diagnosed.

On the 30th of August 1965, the General welcomed the delegates to the 5th International Congress of Criminology in Montreal. Here, as always, he struck the note of intelligent and compassionate benevolence:

I think it is a natural human reaction to look on the offender with a 'holier than thou' smugness. The sight of someone who is physically

23. From Mrs Joan Niblock, 7th March 1967.
24. 14th October 1960.
25. 17th May 1965.

malformed usually calls forth our pity and our charity. Moral deformity often engenders nothing but hatred and retribution. It is the duty of the criminologist to lay bare this inconsistency and to help ensure that we never erect our prejudices into legal principles. The law must be, not only humanitarian but flexible, and responsive to the changes of our times. . . . Law is not an exact science, as Lord Halsbury reminds us. Despite the majesty and gravity with which its administration is properly invested, it is a very human affair after all. The raw material of the cases in criminal court is composed of the struggles and rivalries, the desires and emotions to which all of us fall heir. This material cannot be analysed with the cold precision of the chemist in a laboratory.

The saying went that 'every Norman is a lawyer, even when he is a soldier', and Georges Vanier had been a lawyer himself in his time, and it was to one of the greatest lawyers that he appealed in stressing that punishment was pointless without prevention. There was nothing Utopian in the counsel of Sir Thomas More, although it was quoted from *Utopia*:

For by suffering your youth wantonly and viciously to be brought up and to be infected, even from their tender age, little by little with vice, then in God's name to be punished when they commit in manhood the faults which they acquired in childhood; what are you doing but making thieves and then punishing them?

Once, as he was relaxing with Keiller Mackay in Toronto, the General had observed, a little musingly: 'I should like to leave a footprint somewhere.' It was not enough to give his name to a Library at Loyola, to a suburb of Quebec,[26] and to a number of schools up and down the country – for in the course of time names cease to evoke the persons to which they are the labels. He wanted to give something more positive to Canada – a constructive and continuing work rather than a complimentary title. Sir Thomas More had been right; if delinquency could be prevented anywhere, it was in the home. Without a strong and stable family life, the individual would go astray and the Churches – let alone the State – would have much ado to redeem him. Canada was not exempt from the moral decline of western society. Juvenile delinquency was growing out of all proportion to the increase in population, and it sometimes seemed that the better young people were fed, housed and educated the worse they behaved. As the Vaniers travelled across the country, studied the statistics, and consulted the experts, the more convinced they became that the

26. Ville Vanier.

cause of this was the disintegration of family life. It was more than a question of marital infidelity: there were

many cases of parents who, preoccupied with their problems, distracted by the television and other methods of self-indulgence, never consider their full responsibilities towards their children, and treat them with indifference, or worse – as a necessary nuisance. Their questions are ignored and their efforts to improve their knowledge are given no help, much less encouragement. They learn only that wanting to learn is an irritation to others and before they even enter school their outgoing tendencies have been sealed within a shell of self-defence and withdrawal. Strange that the children's parents are then unable to understand the failure of their offspring to make better grades in school or even to show an interest in their studies. The children's first failures are met, not with love and understanding, but with further recriminations and once again the mould is set. The rejected child becomes the drop-out; the drop-out the delinquent; the delinquent the despairing and despondent adult unable to take his place in society, much less contribute to the well-being of his fellows and his country.[27]

With this in mind the Vaniers summoned a Conference in Ottawa early in June 1964. Many distinguished people working in fields affecting the welfare of the family accepted the invitation to attend it. They represented various religions, reflected various political standpoints, and proposed various solutions, but they were united in an identical concern. The outcome of their discussions was the Vanier Institute of the Family with Dr Wilder Penfield as President, a Board of Directors, and a permanent Secretariat under Mr Stewart Sutton, a sociologist of long experience. The Ministry of Welfare in the Federal Government made a grant to an interim finance fund, to which a number of industrial organizations generously contributed. If the General were asked what exactly the Institute would do, he replied as follows:

An Institute should investigate first and act afterwards. The Vanier Institute can be compared to a Royal Commission established to investigate and learn all there is to know about the families of Canada in a world of change. But since the need for knowledge and study will continue as long as man inhabits the globe, this Royal Commission will never be discharged. Many reports will be made, reports to people, to families, and to welfare organizations and governments. And, furthermore, the Institute differs from a Royal Commission because it can take executive action. Like a medical institute, in

27. Speech at Sydney, N.S., 25th May 1966.

addition to gathering information, it is prepared to carry out treatment, although it has no authority to enforce it.[28]

The Institute received its charter in April 1965 with its secretariat in Ottawa, and a governing body of over a hundred members. Dr Penfield was known throughout the world for his extraordinary scientific knowledge and profound human insight. It was not an exaggeration to describe him as one of the greatest Canadians of modern times. As Vice-Presidents he had Mrs McCutcheon, a widely experienced social worker, Professor Garigue, Dean of the Faculty of Social Sciences at the University of Montreal, and Mr Justice Monnin, a Judge of the Manitoba Court of Appeal. Decisions were made by the Board of Directors, and General Vanier, speaking a year later, envisaged the following activities. Surveys and studies from various regions; conferences in grass-roots areas; national conferences every two or three years; publication of proceedings; the formation of a reference library on the family in Ottawa; the creation of an Information and Public Communications Service; the promotion of local teaching projects and study groups; and co-operation with relevant organizations. The Board of Directors met every month in Ottawa, and much of the programme outlined by the Governor General was quickly under way. Nothing that he did or cared for has lived more securely after him.

3

Georges Vanier had the wise humanist's respect for the scientific spirit. The scientist, he told the National Research Council, on the occasion of its 50th anniversary,[29]

contributes clarity of thought, reason before emotion, precision, caution, and integrity to the patterns of thought of his fellow citizens. The scientific spirit has done much to counter the legacies of superstition and reaction which have been the less fortunate part of our inheritance from previous ages. The scientific approach is one from which every discipline, including the arts, philosophy and the humanities, can profit. The scientific spirit has sharpened the edge of all our thinking and led to new wisdom in all our mental attitudes. . . . Science has offered man a greater potential for self-fulfilment than he has ever known before, but science by itself cannot bring happiness; no outside force can substitute for something which must come from within.

The General was in no doubt as to what that something was,

28. Ibid.   29. 21st September 1966.

and in presenting the Outstanding Achievement Award of the
Public Service of Canada to Dr Wilfrid Bennett Lewis, he referred
to the 'keen awareness of spiritual values' which had 'served to
retain for Canadian scientific endeavour a reputation for compassion and understanding which has enhanced the name of our
country throughout the world.'[30] Georges Vanier made no secret
of his religious faith, but neither in public nor in private did he
thrust it down people's throats. He would speak of 'spiritual
values' because these could mean different things to different
people, and it was his business to speak, as far as possible, to all
Canadians. But when he was replying to the welcome of the
monks at St Bênoit-du-Lac, he was able to speak in a way that
only those who shared his own faith could fully understand:

A simple Christian, reflecting in the light of his faith on the present
situation of the world, is seized with anxiety when he sees how men
develop, ever more feverishly, their scientific works and particularly
all its technical applications, and neglect at the same time with a
kind of unawareness the contemplative activity of the mind. The
more they study the means, the more they forget the ends. What is
the remedy for the evils of the present time? God had repeatedly
communicated it to us by the voice of Mary; it is prayer. At la
Salette, at Lourdes, at Pontmain, at Fatima, everywhere that Mary
has spoken she has brought us the same urgent message. PRAY.[31]

The General's piety, however, was occasionally misunderstood.
As a photographer was leaving the Cathedral in Victoria, a well-
dressed gentleman with a brief-case asked him what was going
on there. The photographer replied that the Governor General was
at Mass. 'But he went yesterday' objected the gentleman with the
brief-case. The photographer explained that the Governor General
went to Mass every day – which provoked the reply: 'He must
have been a pretty wild fella when he was young, and now he's
trying to make up for it.' No doubt, if this misconstruction had
come to his ears, the General would have welcomed it as a
salutary spur to humility.

Georges Vanier would certainly have agreed with Jacques
Maritain that it was a 'deadly error to look to art for the supra-
substantial nourishment of man.' Nevertheless he had always been
a *visuel*. He understood the abstractions of Bernard's painting
better than the abstractions of Jock's thesis, of which he confessed he grasped nothing but the title. During the years at Canada
House he had enjoyed taking the children to the National Gallery

30. 14th December 1966.   31. 8th September 1962.

on Sunday afternoons. Among the English painters he particularly admired Blake and Turner, and among the French Manet and Renoir, Bonnard and Cézanne. Later, he was attracted by the muscular romanticism of Delacroix. In January 1963 he opened the retrospective exhibition of painting and sculpture by Jean Paul Riopelle, which had filled the Canadian Pavilion at the Venice Biennale in 1962. General Vanier never made jocular, philistine remarks about modern art; nor did he judge the merit of a work by the degree to which it appeared to be Canadian. Yet although Riopelle's painting was 'the fruit of a personal adventure more than the expression of a nation', there was something in its character that proclaimed it 'the true product of a vast land of lakes and forests where dark rocks brood under the flaming leaves.' Riopelle remained Canadian 'without having intended it, and the Canadians had not attempted, in any way, to appropriate him. He is Canadian by virtue of the mimetic faculty and phenomenon. This has enabled him to preserve a prodigious memory of his native country, and to bring us in this way to a better knowledge of ourselves.' Very different was the Exhibition of Victorian Art, which the General opened – also at the National Gallery – on the 25th of March, 1965. Among the exhibits were three paintings which Queen Victoria, under persuasion from her artist daughter Princess Louise, had commissioned for the infant gallery; Millais' portrait of the Marquess of Lorne, husband of Princess Louise and Governor General of Canada; a little head of Samson by Lord Leighton; and G. F. Watts' huge 'Time, Death, and Judgment'.

'No one' observed the General 'would dare to put the Victorian painting of Landseer and Whistler on a level with the glorious flowering of French painting during the same period, from Corot to Cézanne. However, after visiting this Exhibition, I will risk the opinion that we can no longer dismiss the Pre-Raphaelites so lightly on account of their ultra-sensibility. This should never hinder us from recognizing their brilliant technique and their precise observation of nature.'

The General's comments on painting were tactful as well as true. On his first visit to Toronto after assuming office – it was tactful, in any case, to choose Toronto for his first official visit outside Ottawa – the Vaniers were presented with a painting by David Milne. In fact, it was two paintings, since the artist, who liked to give people value for their money, had painted a separate picture on each side of the canvas. In recalling his pleasure at this gift, it would have been easy and natural to say: 'When I am tired of looking at one picture, I can look at the other.' If the Governor General was tempted to fall into this trap, his second thoughts were skilful. The picture, he said, 'has been framed in such a way that one can view alternatively . . . a delightful village landscape and autumnal clouds. . . . According to my mood. I turn to one or the other. But either way I remember Toronto.'

The General was eloquent in his admiration for the revolutionary design of the new City Hall[32] – and indeed there was no finer building in the whole of Canada. He brushed aside the gloomy prognosis of the architectural students at the University that with a wind from the north-north-east of more than thirty knots the whole building would take off for Lake Ontario, merely noting that since all the windows looked inward, the people working on one side would be open to inspiration – or its opposite – from those working on the other. There was nothing more contagious than a yawn.

Georges Vanier was rather less responsive to music than to painting, perhaps because he feared its emotional effect. Yet he could still assure the Jeunesses Musicales[33] that 'life without music would be hardly bearable', quoting Beethoven's profound observation that music was 'the mediator between the spiritual and the sensual life', and Carlyle that it was 'the language of the angels'. He recalled meeting a trapper on one of his western tours who told him that, when riding through the Rockies as a young man, he had heard what sounded like a waterfall. Then he fancied it was a strong wind blowing through the trees, and then a flock of birds suddenly disturbed in their nesting place. At last, as he turned a bend in the trail, he came upon a band of Indians singing their native songs – and their songs were the music of the Nature that they knew so well.

Books, however, he loved more than either music or painting, and the annual presentation of the Governor General's Literary Awards, decided by the Canada Council, were always an occasion for showing it. These were generally divided equally between Canadians who wrote in English and in French. There was Phyllis Grosskurth whose life of John Addington Symonds had 'the colour and texture of words' and 'the restraints of the true artist in handling his medium' – qualities she had ascribed to the

32. Opened on the 13th September 1965.
33. 27th April 1964.

subject of her book. There was Père Rejean Robidoux who had written of Roger Martin du Gard – and there was no more intransigently sceptical author in contemporary France – that 'for certain minds, as philosophy is for others, literature is the instrument best adapted for the interior life.' There was Pierre Perrault's charming play, *Au Coeur de la Rose*; and Jean-Paul Pinsonneault's moving novel, *Les Terres Sèches*; and Douglas Le Pan's *The Deserter*, where the hero realized at last that only in trust and commitment were 'to be found conspicuously the final irreducible particles . . . without which nothing could be built, neither love, nor justice, nor a city, without which there could be no meaning, nor nothing but spreading tundra and despair.' For each recipient the General had the right word and the apt quotation.[34]

He was delighted to lay the foundation stone of the National Library and Public Archives in Wellington Street, Ottawa.[35] This owed much to the energy and erudition of Dr Kaye Lamb. It was during General Vanier's mission in Paris that Dr Lamb had tried to obtain permission from the French Government to copy and reproduce the documents in the French Archives concerning the relations between Canada and France, including the despatches sent to Paris by the first Governors. The General had been instrumental in securing this rare permission, and his interest in the National Library was as much historical as literary :

We in Canada have a fascinating, exciting, and often inspiring history, but do we give it the attention is deserves? . . . Is our country's heritage really a part of us, guiding our everyday decisions, maturing our philosophy, and mellowing our opinions? Or do we think and act sometimes as if we were spiritual orphans born yesterday in an historical vacuum, unaware of our forefathers' achievements and ignorant of the profound lessons of their experience?

It had become almost *de rigueur* for the Governor General to give a cup for some branch of athletic activity. There was the Stanley Cup, and the Grey Cup, and the Minto Cup for lacrosse, and the Tweedsmuir Cup for curling. The exception was the Bessborough Cup for Amateur Dramatics. So there had to be a Vanier Cup, and this was presented at the University of Toronto to the winners of the Save the Children College Bowl for Football. For the General, amateur athletics were as valuable as amateur dramatics, perhaps even more so. 'Almost every day I hear on

34. 26th April 1965.
35. 10th May 1965.

the radio about thousands, and sometimes scores of thousands of dollars mentioned in connection with baseball, hockey, boxing, football and golf. If ever young people should acquire the impression that sports are reserved for professionals, it would be very sad indeed for our country.' Sports should be played as light-heartedly as the General himself would toss the football to Esmond Butler as they were walking down the corridors of Hart House on their way to the Athletic Banquet – and none the less so for the serious and charitable purpose which lay behind this particular contest.

Lastly, there were the armed forces of the Crown to whom General Vanier could speak as one professional to another – and as a professional who had once been an amateur. Without the French, and the Scots who followed them, Canada as we know it would never have existed at all. A Mess Dinner of the Black Watch[36] was an occasion for saying some of the things about the Scots that the Scots like to hear about themselves. The Highland boatman, plying his oar on the St Lawrence and composing the 'Canadian Boat Song' in the middle of the nineteenth century, was only echoing the sentiments of the first Scots who came to Nova Scotia in 1621; of the Macdonalds, Ramsays and Frasers in Quebec of the MacNabbs and Galts in Ontario; and the men from Selkirk in the Red River Valley. If the General wished to remind himself of 'the admirable mixture of idealism and practical common sense that gave colour and form and grandeur to the Scottish character, safe as a haven in a troubled sea', he had no need to watch the Trooping the Colour by the Black Watch on television, immaculately as this ceremony was performed. He had only to look up from the table at the figure of Mackinnon, superb above the candlelight and the silver, and as sovereign in his own domain as the General was in his.

A significant naval occasion was the naming and commissioning of H.M.C.S. *Nipigon*, one of the twenty new destroyers provided for in the post-war Canadian contruction programme. It was able to operate a nine-and-a-half ton all-weather helicopter, and had the new variable depth sonar. The ceremony took place at Sorel, Quebec, on the 30th of May 1962. Madame Vanier christened the ship with a bottle of champagne, which only broke at the third try in spite of automatic control and perfect rehearsals on the eve of the big day. She took a particular interest in the ship, presenting a handsome 27-inch television set for the main cafeteria,

36. 17th November 1962.

and a gilt medal of St Christopher to be installed on the bridge. The General had his own memories of Canadian destroyers and recalled his rescue by H.M.C.S. *Fraser* twenty-four years before.

The theme of Anglo-French alliance was easier to strike when one was talking about the first World War than about the second, and General Vanier reminded the veterans of the Red Chevron Club in Ottawa that Britain and the Dominions had left 400,000 dead between Calais and Rheims – a larger army than Bonaparte had led into Russia. Out of a population which only stood at seven million, Canada had sent half a million men overseas. Moreover 'we were a citizen's army. Scarcely any of us proposed a military career.'[37] Those who wore the Red Chevron were part of the 'First Thirty Thousand', and the Governor General spoke as one who had closely followed them in a war of whose justice he had never for a moment been in doubt. More intimately bound up with his personal experience was the dinner offered by the city of Montreal to celebrate the fiftieth anniversary of the 'Van Doos'.[38] Here, among many of his old comrades, the poignant and heroic memories came back to inspire his words. The disembarkation at Boulogne with the stentorian voice suddenly rising from the ranks with 'O Canadiens rallions-nous', and the unanimous refrain

> Et près du vieux drapeau
> Symbole d'espérance

– and the proud evocation

> Jadis, la France sur nos bords
> Jeta sa semence immortelle.

– the epic of Courcelette where seventeen out of the regiment's twenty-three officers, and seven hundred out of its eight hundred non-commissioned officers were killed or wounded; the 8th of August 1918, which Ludendorff described as 'the black day of the German army', when the 22nd advanced eighteen kilometres from Marcelcave to Méharicourt; and so to Chérisy where every single officer was killed or wounded. This was Georges Vanier's last speech as Colonel of the Regiment, and he seized the occasion to pay his tribute to the ordinary French-Canadian soldier, without a star on his shoulder or a stripe on his sleeve, whom he had had the honour to command:

37. 22nd April 1964.
38. 26th September 1964

It was my privilege to know him well. For three years I lived beside him in the trenches. I saw him in the battle under fire, and I watched him die like a Christian, without fear. He has a heart.

What General Vanier expected of the officer was shown in his tribute[39] to Harry Crerar: 'If I were asked to name any of many qualities he possessed, I would say *judgment* followed by action, rapid and resolute. He was no yes-man. General Crerar believed in the human contact between officers and men.' At the 75th Anniversary Dinner of the Royal Canadian Military Institute in Toronto,[40] the General spoke of the officer's responsibility in civilian life:

Canada is the second largest country in the world and though we are barely one half of one per cent of the world's population, we have been endowed with natural resources that far exceed our present or foreseeable needs. Even a partial list of our material blessings is staggering. It is a ridiculous understatement to say that we are fortunate. We are the most fortunate people in the world. We ought to be ashamed to admit what we have – unless we do something useful with it.

In the following year (1966) the General returned to the Royal Military College at St Jean d'Yberville, and was received in the Pavilion which bore his name. What a record of growth since the raw levies of the 'Van Doos' had arrived there without uniforms in October 1914 and taken French leave to spend Christmas with their families! Now, with its faculty and cadets, it represented 'a combination of the three great hopes I hold for this country – youth, unity, and service.' They were also the principal themes of General Vanier's tenure of office. The last of them he illustrated by the story of a very rich woman visiting the outpatients ward of a general hospital, where a young nun was dressing the wounds of a very poor and badly infected patient. The work was exacting and the rich woman regarded it with distaste. 'I wouldn't do that work for a million dollars' she remarked. The nun's reply was very simple. 'Neither would I.'

39. For the C.B.C., 3rd April 1965.
40. 4th March 1965.

CHAPTER 25

THE LAST YEARS

I

THERE had been changes at Government House since the General took office. The A.D.Cs remained for two years before returning to their respective Services. Previous to their engagement they were invited to luncheon and discreetly inspected by the Governor General and his wife, who did everything possible to mitigate the embarrassment of the occasion. Colonel A. G. Cherrier had succeeded Joly de Lotbinière as Assistant Secretary. A Parisian by birth, he had joined the Queen's Own Rifles of Canada in June 1940, and later served as military attaché at the Canadian Embassy in Rome. Michael Pitfield had left to take up work with the Privy Council, and George Cowley, seconded from External Affairs, had filled his place. There were two new chauffeurs, Sutton and Hynes, now on duty with the Buick and the Cadillac. The General never entered the Cadillac without reaching forward and shaking hands with Sutton, and the glass window separating the front and the back seat was generally lowered so that he and Madame Vanier could chat with the driver.

In January 1965 Thérèse Berger left after serving her five year appointment as Lady-in-Waiting to Madame Vanier. At a farewell dinner the General presented her with a mirror to reflect the smile which had charmed so many guests. Leonard Brockington, who was born in the same year and the same month as Georges Vanier, had asked him 'to tell your Lady-in-Waiting how nobly she performs the duty of waiting and personifies the virtues of ladyship.'[1] In thanking the Governor General she recalled their journey in the latitudes of the Midnight Sun; the 1,500 sailors on the aircraft-carrier *Bonnie*, all in their white uniforms, and the 1,500 voices chanting in unison, 'Won't you come back again?'; the flowers at Government House – everywhere the flowers – and the cool elegance which Pauline had given to the furniture and the decoration, so that even the walls tempted one to cry out:

1. 13th March 1963.

'Objets inanimés, avez-vous donc une âme qui s'attache à mon âme et la force d'aimer?'; the elm-tree outside her window; and her bicycle rides through the park in spring, when a young gardener had said to her, 'You are old, Thérèse Berger, and your hair has become very white and yet you incessantly ride through the park. At your age, do you think it is right?' When she had gone, Madame Vanier was without a permanent Lady-in-Waiting for some time, but Georgiana Butler or Mrs Pemberton were at hand to discharge the auxiliary functions of hospitality.

The routine continued as before, with seven thousand people annually entertained at Rideau Hall. On the eve of his 77th birthday (23rd of April 1965) the General had travelled 64,402 miles since his inauguration, and those closest to him declared that they had never seen him in better health. After two years of disappointment five pairs of Purple Martins had nested and raised their families in the Swallow house. This was a gift from the Ottawa Boys Club, and it was placed on the south side of Government House where the General could see it from his study or his bedroom window. Esmond Butler was careful not to set it up before the swallows returned from their migration, since the starlings and house sparrows were always ready to gate-crash. There were mornings when the liquid gurgling of the Martins anticipated Chevrier's 7.45 knock on the door. On the 23rd of April another knock on the door interrupted the General while he was dictating a letter. The entire household staff, led by Esmond Butler, trooped in singing 'Happy Birthday'. Butler apologized for the appearances of a *coup d'état*.

'My wife and I are still standing' the General had written to a friend 'after which we may sit down for a few years before lying down – but I don't know, it all depends on the Lord.'[2] It was widely assumed, however, that in September 1965 he would step down from office. The names of likely successors were canvassed in the press – Wilder Penfield, Arnold Heaney, and Roland Mitchener among them. But the eyes of the Prime Minister, like those of the Governor General himself, were fixed on 1967, and General Vanier was persuaded to remain at his post for an indefinite term – which meant for as long as his age and health would allow him to perform his duties. Age was, in fact, an asset since the things he now had to say to the nation and said repeatedly – the 'themes of office' – were all the more persuasive when they had the weight of experience and personal prestige behind them.

2. To Mrs G. F. Conley, 18th January 1965.

General Vanier presenting Colours to the Royal Hamilton Light Infantry, June 1962.

General Vanier and John F. Diefenbaker;
Lester B. Pearson and Esmond Butler seen in mirror.

Three Governors General: Vincent Massey, General Vanier and Field-Marshal
Earl Alexander of Tunis.

this was a case where comparisons were dangerous – that the Trooping the Colour by the 2nd Battalion Princess Patricia's Canadian Light Infantry was the best he had ever seen. In Winnipeg he found his old friend Nurse Attrill, who had looked after him in the Buxton hospital. She was now eighty-eight and wearing almost as many medals as, on occasion, he wore himself. If only the relations between people living in Outremont and the people living in Westmount were as easy as those between the inhabitants of St Boniface and Winnipeg, Canadian problems would be less intractable. In Calgary the General was made Chief of the Stony, Sarcee and Blackfoot tribes and given the name of 'Big Eagle'. The title was appropriate, for with advancing years his features had acquired an aquiline ruggedness and strength. Here, as elsewhere, the Vaniers were greeted in French before they were greeted in English by officials who were anything but bilingual. The assembled audience sang 'Alouette' and 'Mon Merle' in their honour. In Jasper Park the Viceregal party left their railway car for a day's respite at Point Cabin. It was here that King Georges VI and Queen Elizabeth had been entertained in 1939 – the first occasion on which a reigning Monarch had visited the Dominion.

On the 2nd of July the General turned the first sod for the Battle of Châteauguay Memorial Building at Allan's Corner, Quebec. For very personal reasons, the occasion went to Georges Vanier's heart. Speaking in French, he asked his audience to:

pause for a moment and imagine what course the history of Canada would have taken if this battle had ended differently. That day might have turned the last page of Canadian history, had it not been for the dramatic morning of October 1813. Occupied by several wars in Europe, especially against Napoleon, England was obviously in no position to give more than very limited aid, although the very existence of the young Canadian nation was at stake. . . .

The Americans had a great superiority in numbers. On the 20th of August 1813 they decided on the capture of Montreal. All through the month of September they concentrated their forces and marched northward. On the 21st of October 400 infantry, with 200 dragoons and 10 cannon, invaded Canada near Athelstan; on the morrow the advance guard had pitched its camp close to the Châteauguay river. During this time, the Canadian troops had come down the St Lawrence as far as Valleyfield, and after six hours of forced marching, an uncommon test of endurance, they arrived on the field of battle.

After sundry preliminary exchanges, battle was joined on Tuesday the 26th of October. The commander of the Canadian militia, Lieut-

On the 15th of February 1965, the new Canadian flag had been
hoisted with pomp and ceremony on Parliament Hill. It had
taken thirty days of exhaustive and acrimonious discussion to
perform this comparatively simple operation. General Vanier himself sympathized with the veterans who had fought, as he had
fought, under the Red Ensign and regretted its displacement. It
was objected on the one hand that the Maple Leaf had been
adopted merely to please the French – and there were certainly
more maple leaves in the Province of Quebec than anywhere
else in Canada. Premier Lesage, who stood high in General Vanier's
esteem, described the new flag as 'something immensely simple,
like a new born baby who is full of magnificent promise', and he
hoped that it would be 'a symbol of the drawing together of all
Canadians.' General Vanier hoped no less. If the British Canadians
justified the retention of the monarchy as a symbol, it was reasonable that the French-Canadians should claim a similar justification
for the flag. But the Quebec Opposition leader, Daniel Johnson,
looked forward to the day when the fleur-de-lys would fly alongside the Maple Leaf over the Parliament Buildings in Ottawa.
Heraldically speaking, the fleur-de-lys certainly won on points. In
saluting the new flag in the Hall of Fame, General Vanier did not
forget 'the long association of the Red Ensign with the happy and
glorious, sometimes tragic, events which in peace and war have
been written into our history. As the Red Ensign is lowered, I
salute it and thank God for the blessings He bestowed upon it
and us in the past.'

Later in the month the General was in Regina for the 60th
anniversary of Saskatchewan; and in April the Shah of Persia and
Empress Farah were greeted on a State Visit to Government
House. Iranian caviare had been procured for the occasion, and
two flaming lambs were set before the Imperial guests. The new
session of Parliament was opened on the 5th of April. The Speech
from the Throne reflected the aroused sense of national consciousness, authorizing 'O Canada' as the national anthem and
proposing an address to the Queen to provide for the revision of
the Constitution by the Canadian Government. The establishment of an 'Assistance Plan' to give federal aid to needy people,
and a 'Company of Young Canadians' to promote economic and
social development at home and abroad was in tune with ideas
which the Governor General himself had done much to foster.

In May the Vaniers set out on what was to be their last tour of
the western Provinces. The General went so far as to say – and

'Big Eagle'.

The Queen's visit to Quebec, October 1964: Inside the Memorial Chapel, General Vanier explaining the windows to the Queen.

At the Rehabilitation Centre, General Vanier with a thalidomide child.

Colonel Charles de Salaberry, realized how very slim were his chances of victory, and that he would have to employ his effectives with the utmost skill if he were to have the slightest chance of carrying the day. De Salaberry knew how to rise to the height of the situation, and his principal weapon was psychology. He allowed the enemy to see his men in their grey uniforms of *voltigeurs*, and then made them disappear. He showed them again, but this time in uniforms of red – their tunics having been turned back to front – and this gave the impression of reinforcements from a large number of regiments. He cleverly deployed his men, making them appear and disappear, and seeming thus to be in command of a considerable force. He doubled the number of his buglers, ordering them to sound the advance from various points on the battlefield, and succeeded in making the Americans believe that they were faced by a formidable enemy. The despatches sent back by the American general were proof of his illusion. He thought that he was engaged with 7000 Canadians whereas, in fact, there were only 500. After fighting for four hours, the Americans, seeing the Canadians firing on them from all sides, broke their ranks and retreated in disorder. The Canadians lost five men killed and the Americans more than a hundred.

The victory of Châteauguay caused the Americans to abandon their project of capturing Montreal, and the city has never since been seriously threatened. The brilliant conduct of the Canadian militia-men would have done honour to the most hardened campaigners, but in fact the Canadian force was composed of small merchants, farmers, blacksmiths, and other colonists whose most powerful weapon was their own indomitable courage.

The summer holiday, as usual, was spent at Tadoussac, where the General kept closely in touch with public affairs. Official papers were sent down from Ottawa by plane, and copies of the *Montreal Star*, the *Ottawa Journal and Citizen*, the *Toronto Globe and Mail*, *Hansard*, *le Devoir*, *Time Magazine*, and *Maclean's* arrived regularly at the Tudor Hart House. In August the General was sending congratulations to Henri Chassé – the son of his old comrade-in-arms – on taking up the command of the 1st Battalion of the Royal 22nd; and at the same time telling Paul Hellyer, Minister of National Defence, that 'I have always thought that the Van Doos have played a part in fostering unity in our country.' The death of Madame Tremblay in November was yet a further reminder of the man whom Georges Vanier always coupled with the victor of Châteauguay. In the same month Pauline Vanier accepted the nomination as Chancellor of Ottawa University. The post had previously been held *ex officio* by the Roman Catholic Archbishop of Ottawa, but with the gradual laicisation of the

University this practice was discontinued. Another honour – though hardly an appointment – was now shared equally, or nearly equally, between the Governor General and his wife. Early in 1964 the General had received the following notification from the Minister of Mines and Technical Surveys:

It is my great pleasure to inform you that the Cabinet, on the recommendation of the permanent Canadian Committee for geographical names, has seen fit to approve the name Ile Vanier for an island not hitherto named in the North-West territories. We wish to point out that the two adjacent islands have been named in honour of the Right Honourable Vincent Massey and Field-Marshal Earl Alexander of Tunis.

The islands formed part of the Sverdrup basin, and their geological structure appeared favourable to the discovery of petroleum and gas. Ile Vanier was the most northerly of the three, with a surface of 375 square miles, and the General was gratified to learn that it was also the largest. Some time afterwards he received a second communication from another Minister of Mines and Technical Surveys suggesting that the name Ile Pauline be given to one of the remaining unbaptized islands in the Viceregal Archipelago. The General replied to this suggestion as follows:

My wife is very pleased indeed that you named the baby island next to mine after her. It is true that there is a larger one between Alexander and Massey Islands, but after 42 years of marriage she still prefers my company.

This provided the Governor General with a theme on which he embroidered in more than one public speech. Would Ile Pauline be recognized by the other three important states? Not to do so would be a denial of patent reality, but it was impossible to recognize anything without prior consultation with one's allies. There was nothing that diplomacy had not taught Georges Vanier about recognition. If only the three islands would pull together, they might become a world power – but here again there was nothing Governor Generalship had not taught Georges Vanier about the difficulties of confederation. Moreover, he liked governing his island, and Massey and Alexander liked governing theirs; and while he had no intention of taking over their islands, he was not so sure that they would not like to take over his. But what mattered at the moment was the development of Ile Vanier. A

Viceregal oil policy must be determined at once – for here, to quote Dr Johnson, was 'the potentiality of growing rich beyond the dreams of avarice.' There was also the question of a name for the inhabitants – always a difficulty for an infant nation. In 1865 it had been proposed to call the Canadian Confederation *Tupona* – based on the initials of 'The United Provinces of North America' – or even *Hochelaga*. But let the population of Ile Vanier have no fear. They would be called nothing but Canadians, if indeed there was anybody there to be called anything at all. And if the General discovered a stray Eskimo when he arrived to take possession, there would be at least no argument about the 'founding races'.

He was not perturbed by the problem of colonization. Latitude 76 and forty degrees below would be a great attraction for immigrants, and he had his list of invitations ready for Garden Party, Levée, Reception, and State Occasion. He would dispense with all but a minimum formality, remembering the answer of a lady to an invitation requesting that decorations should be worn. 'My husband has no decorations. What should he wear?' He would publish two newspapers, one to express the English half of his mind and the other the French. He would even appoint a special committee to chat with him and decide whether he was giving the right amount of time to each paper, and whether he thought more in French than in English. He would appoint as Island Manager the officer who was in charge of the arrangements when he had unveiled a memorial in honour of the Royal Canadian Signals Corps. All that the Governor General had to do was to press a button and the flag covering the plaque slid away quietly. 'I suppose' he said afterwards 'you had a man behind the memorial ready to pull a string if this electronic device didn't work?' 'I had two' replied the officer. 'Why two?' asked the Governor General. 'In case one of them fell dead' was the answer. Here, then, was a man who would leave nothing to chance. The greatest problem of all, however, remained unsolved – what should be the island's flag? At the time when *les Iles Vaniers* received their cartographical identity the matter was far too delicate for discussion. Nothing, one may suggest, would have been more inappropriate than a Maple Leaf.

2

General Vanier had always sympathized with the Poles – 'crucified' as it was said 'between two thieves'. But here was a case where his personal sympathies conflicted with his constitutional position. His patronage for the 1000th Anniversary of the establishment of Christianity in Poland was sought by those who emphasized that they had no connection whatsoever with the Polish Embassy in Ottawa, the Polish Government, or the Communist-sponsored Millenium Committee in Canada. The General had warmly advocated a welcome for Polish or Hungarian refugees, but since the Polish Ambassador was accredited to the Queen of Canada it was obviously out of the question to extend the patronage requested. What delighted him, however, in a cause even closer to his heart, was the successful exchange of students between English and French speaking Canada, organized by the Canadian Council of Christians and Jews. A student from Toronto had written to the Council's Journal:

What do you gain from the experience? Friendships are certainly created, your French is undoubtedly improved, you learn a little about the geography of the region in which you stayed. But most of all, you learn to understand and respect the differences in custom and life in general which exist in a two-language nation.[3]

The end of the year brought the news that the General's old friend Leonard Brockington had been elected for the seventh time Rector Magnificus of Queen's University. 'I always thought there was something queer – no, special – about you' the General wrote. 'Elected *seven* times by the students! Why didn't you go in for politics?' Brockington had been wise enough not to take this ironical advice; yet his political instincts were sure.

If only the newspapers would use more often their strongest weapon, which is silence, and not report to Quebec some of the stupid things said in Ontario, and not report to Ontario some of the stupid things said in Quebec, many of us would feel happier. I was born a Celtic optimist and would not be a cousin of the Bretons if I did not continue to believe that our country will survive the horrors of Hansard.[4]

General Vanier spoke to his cue in wishing him a happy New Year in Welsh, and Brockington's sentiments were surely in his mind when he broadcast his customary New Year's message to the nation. These always made a profound impression; as Senator Grattan O'Leary had written of an earlier message:

As I listened to you I remembered Morley's saying that a good speech must have three ingredients: beauty, structure and passion. You had beauty and structure (every word was made to work) and you had

3. Gavin Fraser in *Scope*, November 1965.
4. 9th April 1964.

passion – passion for what you felt to be good and true. This, indeed, was the eloquence of sincerity.[5]

In January 1966 the General defiantly affirmed his belief in Canadian 'identity', and the Queen's Printer had to be called in to ensure the circulation of 200,000 copies of his speech. It was described as a :

manifesto of fact, and appreciation, and advice. . . . It is this kind of simple, sensible analysis of our Canada and our problems and our hallucinations of dilemma that should clear the national stage of actors who would tear down our great future. Old warrior Vanier knows battle tactics. His melodramatic approach is to fight the battle. . . . Georges Vanier is not a divider : he is a builder. His tabulation of our national blessings was long and accurate. His scorn for the defeatists was well merited. There is a national count-down going on every sunrise towards Centennial Year, and the world is watching to see if the stirring giant that is Canada wants to look into the mirror of accomplishments and accept itself at face value. . . . The gauntlet was thrown down to us by a great Canadian.[6]

On the 18th of February Pauline Vanier was installed as Chancellor of Ottawa University to the ascending strains of Purcell's Trumpet Voluntary, combining 'the intent seriousness of a girl receiving her first communion and the mature serenity of a woman who fears the full meaning of her responsibility but is buoyed by the knowledge that she will do her best and be supported in that by the whole university family.'[7] For once, she 'stole the show' without a shadow of competition, the General sitting slightly to one side although certainly not in the wings. The barely perceptible pause before she began her address, and the momentary glance in his direction, indicated his presence – and her own pride in what was a compliment to him as well as to her. It was appropriate that the first Doctorate she conferred should have been given to Dr Wilder Penfield. His name now figured more frequently than anyone else's in the Visitors Book at Government House.

Thérèse was now in Uganda. She was something of an adventuress in her own way, as the General delighted to point out, and as she herself was delighted to admit. Her medical pursuits were only momentarily disturbed by an earthquake, from which she woke up thinking she was on a ship – presumably in a rather

5. 4th January 1964.
6. The *Arnprior Guide*, Ontario, 5th January 1966.
7. The *Ottawa Journal*, 19th February 1966.

heavy sea. Byngsie, the General told Mrs Archer, 'is well, physically, and as far as I know, is still a good Catholic. When we go to see him, he smiles all the time, and when he isn't smiling, he's laughing.'[8] As for the General himself, Pauline had just been declared the Woman of the Year; and he was comfortably ensconced in the shadow of her fame.

Knowing that his term of office must end soon, even if he saw it through to the end of the Centennial Year – and this remained uncertain – he was persuaded to sit for his portrait. Priscilla Tweedsmuir, who had been staying at Government House four years earlier, had suggested that this should be done by Douglas Anderson, a pupil of Annigoni; but three weeks of sittings in London would hardly have been practicable. She had made a number of sketches herself during her visit, and one of these was of the General. He had written to thank her for a photograph of it.

I like the one of me – I look so pleased with myself. You have captured a benign smile exactly like that on a cat's face after it has swallowed a canary! You have even given me nice hands which I am not sure that I have. What is important is that you have included the 'Madame Vanier' rose.

Thérèse proposed that the portrait should be done, from photographs, by James Gunn, and the General favoured the idea. But no two members of the same family ever agree about a likeness, and soon he was complaining:

You have no idea the resistance that I have met here in my own house – it is something like a révolution de palais! The attitude is akin to the one which might exist if I were thinking of committing a mortal sin.[9]

The Governor General was not a natural sitter, although the misfortunes of war had forced him to spend a good part of his life in that position. Esmond Butler agreed with a lady in New York that 'the Governor General is a wonderful man, but I am afraid that on the subject of portraits he is rather unyielding.'[10] Eventually the commission was given to Clark Cunningham, who worked afterwards from an enlarged photograph by Karsh. The General was shown, half length, in the blue uniform of the Royal 22nd; and he was more exacting about fidelity to his uniform than

8. 3rd December 1965.
9. To Thérèse Vanier.
10. To Mrs Bernard.

to his features, suggesting that 'from an artistic point of view it might be a good idea to cut out the legs – or at least part of them.'

He now rested as much as possible, dining in bed when there was no reason to come downstairs. Harold Wilson was staying at Government House in February and the Duke of Edinburgh in March. Nurse Attrill sent him a Dresden statuette of Rouget de Lisle for his seventy-eighth birthday, and Easter was spent quietly with Michel, his wife and family, and a couple of friends[11] staying in the house. News came through that Evelyn Waugh had died, and although the General did not know him he asked that Mass should be said for the repose of his soul. Shortly afterwards Sidney Shakespeare arrived to take up her duties as Lady-in-Waiting to Pauline.

In May the Vaniers set out on a tour of the Maritime provinces. The General endorsed for the students of Mount Alison University, New Brunswick, the saying that it was 'about time Canadians got off the psychiatrist's couch and enjoyed being Canadian'; and he drew an amusing analogy from the Reversing Falls at St John:

No visitor can fail to be impressed with the wonderful eagerness to please by the city planners; on the odd chance that visitors were not satisfied with the water flowing one way over the Falls, they have arranged that twice a day the whole flow should be reversed to flow the other way for the sake of the hard to please. This represents a spirit of compromise all too rare in Canada, and I suggest provides a very good example for such one-track minded institutions as Niagara Falls.[12]

New Brunswick, like Winnipeg and St Boniface, was 'a living testimony of the virtues of continuing fraternity'[13] between the two races which had founded it.

Premier Smallwood of Newfoundland was a welcome in himself, but three centuries before Mr Smallwood was born, Robert Hayman had come to the island and written to the Governor:

The air of Newfound-land is wholesome, good;
The firs as sweet as any made of wood;
The waters very rich, both salt and fresh;
The earth more rich, you know it is no less.
Where all are good, fire, water, earth and aire.
What man made of these foure would not live there?

11. Mme. Lemieux and the present writer.
12. 16th May 1966.
13. At Fredericton, 19th May 1966.

The Vaniers had a limited opportunity of testing the truth of this encomium, but they could see enough to refute the accusation that Newfoundland was 'a piece of rock entirely surrounded by fog', and to endorse the definition that it was 'a home entirely surrounded by hospitality'. They savoured its hospitality when they visited a Newfoundland family. One of the boys asked the General if he would like to see his room, in which he took some pride, and the General noticed on the wall three large photographs – one of Winston Churchill, one of Joey Smallwood, and one of himself. The boy explained, in answer to the General's questions, that the photograph on the left was of 'Britain's war time Prime Minister' and the photograph on the right of Newfoundland's 'famous Premier'. 'And who is that distinguished personage in the centre?' enquired the General. The boy frowned for a moment and then exclaimed: 'Gee, Mister, I don't know. My mother put that picture up there one day to show me what I would look like when I grew up if I didn't stop playing hooky from school.'

The General appealed, in that rugged landscape, for 'men to match our mountains', and one of those men was Olivier Asselin whose biography by his son Pierre he was then reading. He remembered Asselin on the slopes of Vimy – 'a man who combined the fine qualities of integrity and intrepidity. He loved the poor, and his wish was to die with them.'[14] The book brought back memories of the Somme. George Drew had wanted to take him back there, and now Lord Brookeborough[15] was writing: 'You wouldn't recognize anything. I had a look at the Pozière Ridge, Courcelette, etc. It is all in crop. Houses and trees look as if they had been there for a hundred years.'[16] But who was the Minister for Veterans Affairs to whom Brookeborough had given the cigarette box presented to Byng – or 'Bungo' as they called him when they were not talking to his face – by the 10th Brigade after the capture of Vimy Ridge? At Chérisy only the Quebec cemetery with its daffodils and mountain ash, and its litany of French and British names – Savarie, Duval, Moreau, Charbonneau, Pelletier, Laplante and Champlain, Duggan, Frost, Lawrence, Tucker, Hepburn, Duncan, Mortimer and Forsyth – retold the story that Georges Vanier carried in his bones, and reiterated the

14. Letter to Pierre Asselin, Canadian Consul-General in San Francisco, 10th May 1966.
15. Lord Brookeborough, formerly Prime Minister of Northern Ireland.
16. 23rd August 1966.

gospel of unity which he preached at every halting place on his last tour.

On the 1st of January the General attended the annual Parliamentary Prayer Breakfast at the Château Laurier. 'Before agreeing to read a passage of Scripture,' he told Paul Hellyer, 'I shall see if I can find something appropriate to our legislators.' He never had the least difficulty in finding something appropriate for the annual Press Gallery dinner in February. A testimonial dinner had been given to Vincent Massey, at which the Chairman had said that Mr Massey was the only Governor General who could talk to the Press in verse. This threw down a severe challenge to future incumbents, but General Vanier was not the man to refuse it. The Press had always done him justice; sometimes, perhaps, no more than justice, so that he was moved to compose a few lines of 'Meditations upon First Looking into a Press Report':

> Are these my words, retained
> So incomplete?
> Has all my thought contained
> So little meat?

He was not thinking of writing his autobiography, but duty compelled him to write his autograph, and on occasion he was asked for it in odd ways. 'I am starting a collection of different people, and would like you to be one'; and 'I would like your autograph and some from any members of your family who can write' – were among the more surprising requests. The General would recount the amusing incidents of his career, and to entertain the Press he had no need to look further than what had appeared in it. There was the Canadian who declared proudly that he himself was 'a distinct and separate Canadian identity'; and the Canadian who thought he might learn to stand up for 'O Canada' as well as for 'God Save the Queen'; and the Canadian who thought 'our politics are dull and our sports bushleague, but you can't beat the beer or the air'. The General had asked a Member of Parliament, who had attended many Press Gallery dinners, whether anyone had ever been serious at these legendary functions. 'Not intentionally' was the reply 'and anyone who tries had better sit down pretty quickly.' Legendary is here the *mot juste*, because what the Governor General said to the Press Gallery was pretty well the only thing that the Press did not report – and nothing he said was better worth reporting. There was no secret, however, about the Gallery's own victory over the Soviet Embassy staff on the Minto Skating Rink. In the heat of the engagement one of the Russian players scored against his own goal-keeper – after which the goal-keepers were exchanged to make the game more even, and the Soviet Ambassador left the ground.

The summer vacation of 1966 was spent at Tadoussac. For the last time the General was to catch his breath as the car swung round the bend in the road from Murray Bay and the junction of the St Lawrence and the Saguenay came dramatically into view. The *Nipigon* anchored off shore, and an R.C.M.P. patrol boat took the Viceregal party out to visit her. There were the customary presents to the staff at the hotel – a wallet to the chef, cigarette lighters to the stewards, compacts to the maids – and a black wallet to the Postmaster. The Vaniers were interested in the proposal to construct a chapel to Notre Dame de l'Espace on the hill upon St Catherine's Bay, and they had already contributed to the building of the new church down below. Michael Pitfield and George Cowley tried to interest the General in writing his Memoirs, but the idea never took root. He spent his days on the verandah looking out to sea through the fir trees, and reading what other men had written. The holiday seemed to have done him good.

On the 19th of September Mr Diefenbaker was thanking the General for his birthday greetings:

It brought to mind that when I recommended you to the Queen as Governor General, you were some months older than I now am. If God wills that I live until your age, I hope that the intervening years will be as worth while as yours have been. I recall that there were a number of letters received by me when your name was mooted in the Press as a possible Governor General, strongly opposing your appointment because of age. How wrong they were.

Ten days later the Household presented the Vaniers with a beautifully executed scroll for their wedding anniversary, and early in October the General was at Valcartier, to say Good-bye to his beloved regiment. The men were drawn up in deep formation on the parade ground, and the General went round the ranks in a jeep. He then took the salute from a stand, having discarded his cape. It was a day of mist and rain, but when Toby Price – the A.D.C. on duty – discreetly raised an umbrella over his head, it was impatiently brushed aside. As the General addressed the men afterwards in the gymnasium, he was observed to be coughing and it was clear that he had taken cold. He remained unwell for a week or two after his return to Government House, and on the 27th of October he went into hospital for a removal of the prostate gland. He was resigned to any consequence of the operation: 'What does it matter if I die at seventy-eight or ninety?';[17] and only a few days before leaving home he was at work on his Foreword to Robert Hubbard's illustrated history of Government House. Chevrier accompanied him to hospital, since he refused to be undressed by anyone else. Mass was said daily in his room and he stayed under observation until the 6th of November. The doctors were anxious as to whether his heart would stand the operation which was performed under a spinal anaesthetic. He rallied well, however, and the same evening was sitting up in bed, reading the newspapers.

He returned to Government House on the 15th of November. Pauline wrote to Mrs Robertson Fleet: 'He is coming home today and is really on top of the world. He will be kept quiet for another three weeks, but I am sure that there will be no holding him in after that.'[18] For three or four days he was under an oxygen tent, but he appeared to be recovering far more quickly than had been expected. Jock had come out to be with Madame Vanier during 'the very nasty days before the operation',[19] and Chevrier now slept in the room adjoining the patient's bedroom. But the General was sleeping well and never once rang for him during the night. He transacted necessary business from his room, where Mass was celebrated daily. As the days went by, however, Pauline's reports grew less optimistic. The Vaniers had planned to take a Caribbean holiday in March before the exertions of the Centennial Year, and had accepted the offer of a house at Ochos Rios in Jamaica; but on the 15th of December Esmond Butler was writing to the owner that the General's doctors felt it would be very unwise for him to undertake the journey, and to spend the month where the medical attention he required would not be available. In fact, he spent Christmas in bed, although on New Year's Day he was dressed and came downstairs to send his message to the nation. The large invisible audience noticed how thin he was, and how very much older. Thérèse had come out for Christmas, and her medical eye was alarmed by the change in his condition. Throughout his illness every foreign envoy had called to write his name in the Visitors Book, with the exception of the French Ambas-

17. To Dr Francis Leddy.
18. 15th November 1966.
19. Pauline Vanier to Lady Bigham, 8th November 1966.

sador. It was an ominous foretaste of another change of which the General was well aware, but whose climax he providentially did not live to see.

On the 26th of January Dr David give an encouraging report of his heart condition, and explained to him that if he were to carry on through the year he must now test his strength little by little. So he began to dress and to come down for an occasional meal, always in his wheel chair; but before the month was out he was able to walk to the Chapel, leaning on Chevrier's arm, and one evening at dinner he rose unaided to his feet to propose the Royal Toast. Maria Varro, the pianist, was staying at Government House and delighted an audience of invited guests with her playing, but the General did not stay up to hear her. To the present writer, who was also staying, he spoke of the Crown in Canada, and of his concern that the Governor General should be able to return the visits of those Heads of State who had been received at Government House. When a respected Ottawa journalist, Charles Lynch, misinterpreted a remark of his to mean that he thought the Canadian monarchy expendable, the General raised his cane for the last time and exacted a public apology. As to his future, he would merely remark with a smile: 'Oh, I don't know where I shall be this time next year.'

Throughout February he seemed to be regaining strength. He had always disliked being wheeled into the drawing-room before dinner, and the moment came when he dispensed with the chair and walked in, very slowly, with the help of his walnut cane. All around him were the mementos of his personal and his public life; the portrait of Thérèse as a little girl – the years dropped off him when he saw Thérèse; Bernard's abstract pictures – where his father would teasingly detect a fugitive trace of the figurative; the wooden buffalo from Winnipeg, the cowboy statue in bronze from Calgary, the caribou from Newfoundland, and the totem pole from Vancouver; the clock which had been a present from the 'Van Doos'; the signed photographs of President de Gaulle, and President Kennedy, and John XXIII; the signed photograph of the Queen. On the 8th of February he received the visit of a centenarian, Mr Weir – an old soldier like himself – and a relative of Justin Weir who had translated 'O Canada' into English. The two sat side by side on the chesterfield in the drawing-room, where the General always liked to sit after dinner. 'How old do you think I am, Mr Weir?' Mr Weir guessed that he was seventy-eight or seventy-nine. 'I am seventy-eight' the General replied, and then repeated very slowly, as if he were counting the years and wondering how many more of them there would be, 'seven ... eight'. As Mr Weir was leaving, the General warned him to beware of the little half-step in the doorway, with the lights on either side. By the middle of the month he was sending careful instructions to Welsh and Jefferies for the lightweight suits he would need for the ceremonies of the Centennial summer; and on the billiard table in the Library a huge agenda of the forth-coming State Visits was spread out for the perusal of the A.D.Cs. Towards the end of the month the film of *A Man for All Seasons* was shown; well as Paul Scofield played the principal part, some might have wondered if Georges Vanier would not have played it better.

Sometimes, in the evening, Michael Pitfield would slip up the back stairs and talk with the General in his bedroom. There, on the table beside him, was the miniature library of his spiritual life; de Caussade's *Abandonment to Divine Providence*, Saint Thérèse of Lisieux, and the Bible. The pages were worn and many passages were underlined. It was carefully noted in the margin when and where he had finished reading the book – for the second, or the third, or the fourth time. Pitfield had lent him the *Meditations of Marcus Aurelius*: 'What a very wise man'[20] was his grateful comment. He would speak of Dom Eugene Boylan, the Trappist Abbot of Roscrea, who had been killed in a motor accident:

Although I never had the pleasure of meeting him, I knew him well through his spiritual writings, all of which I have read, in some cases more than once. I feel I owe it to his memory and to myself to put on record this tribute of deep gratitude. It all began curiously enough by my reading in the French version 'Difficulties in Mental Prayer' which I picked up at a Carmel in Paris. That was the beginning of an important change in my life.[21]

And he would speak of Père Gaume, making a present to Pitfield of the Cross which Gaume had given him all those years ago. Georges Vanier's life was a life of contemplation which had over-flowed into fruitful action. Like all contemplatives, he had known periods of aridity and moments of sensible consolation. Now, in the twilight of his age, everything was reduced to a 'condition of complete simplicity costing not less than everything'.[22]

20. 3rd June 1963.
21. Letter to Dom Cami.
22. T. S. Eliot, *Little Gidding*.

At the beginning of March a decision had to be arrived at as to whether the Governor General would be able to continue in office during the arduous months ahead. To make assurance doubly certain Dr David invited the eminent heart specialist, Dr Paul Dudley White, to come from Boston for consultation. He arrived on Wednesday, the 3rd of March, and was met by an A.D.C. in civilian dress in order not to excite public curiosity. That evening the Butlers were dining at the Dutch Embassy, and Esmond was called away by telephone to Government House. On entering the drawing-room he found Madame Vanier, Dr White and the Prime Minister. Their faces told him everything. The medical verdict was decisive. If the General rested completely, he might yet enjoy several months of life, but there was no question of his remaining in office. Later he was seen coming out of the chapel in the blue woollen dressing-gown, familiar to all who had the entrance to his privacy. He was very depressed but cheered up a little when he was watching a hockey game on television with the Prime Minister. He had not been told that Dr White had arrived, although he knew that he was coming, until Dr Burton took the specialist up to his room after dinner.

Mr Pearson wished him to accept some kind of appointment at the Citadel which would keep him in the public eye during the Centennial celebrations. But the General was not interested. He spoke to a group of students from the University of Montreal for much longer than his doctors had thought advisable; and on Saturday, the 4th of March, he seemed in excellent spirits, although Dr Burton told Chevrier that 'General Vanier is very ill'. In the afternoon Butler looked into his room for a cup of tea. Arrayed on the table were six little pots of jam, a gift from Tyrone Guthrie's domestic factory in Ireland – blackberry jelly, raspberry, gooseberry, strawberry and rhubarb mixed, apple-jelly, and marmalade. It was an *embarras de choix*, and there was some cheerful discussion as to which pot they should open. Then the General said: 'We've had some good times, Esmond, haven't we?'; and Butler only remembered afterwards that instead of saying 'Good-night' he said 'Good-bye'. The General was wearing his oxygen mask, and when Toby Price, who looked in later, observed: 'You look like a man from outer space,' he replied: 'I feel like a man going to outer space.' But he was able to enjoy another hockey game on television and see the Canadiens beat Detroit. He walked to the chapel with Chevrier's assistance, and remained there for twenty minutes while Chevrier and

Pauline prepared his bed. He was reading St Paul's Epistle to the Galatians before he fell asleep.

When Chevrier called him at the usual time the next morning he was only half awake, and Madame Vanier was concerned to notice that his hands were very cold. But he ate half a grape-fruit and drank some coffee. Dr Burton called at 9 a.m. and saw immediately that he was dying. A second doctor was then summoned from the hospital. Canon Guindon arrived for Mass at 10.30 and at once gave the General Holy Communion. Pauline asked him whether they should go next door for Mass or stay with him in the room. 'No' he answered 'you go along. You will have time'; but he said to Chevrier, 'Ne me laissez pas seul', and at 10.55 he asked him, now in a very low voice, for a glass of water, murmuring 'Merci, Chevrier' – the word of thanks that had never failed to reward the least attention.

Toby Price had fetched Butler from St Bartholomew's Church, and remained in the chapel while Butler joined Pauline who had returned to the bedroom with Jock, Michel and Sidney Shakespeare, when Mass was over. It was now shortly after 11 a.m. The General lay very quietly as if he were asleep. Peter Burton held his wrist to register the failing of the pulse, and when he gently released it at 11.25 there was no visible sign to those standing around that Georges Vanier had passed from one rest to another.

CHAPTER 26

THE RECOGNITION

I

THERE was no doubt where the General had left his footprint; the entire nation was united in a community of gratitude and grief. More than 15,000 messages of sympathy poured into Government House – from those who had never even shaken him by the hand. They came from young and old, from the eminent and the obscure, from England and France, and from every part of the Dominion. To some – and indeed to most who thought about the matter – his death seemed as timely as, in a sense, it was also tragic. 'He is smiling at you from Heaven' wrote one correspondent 'and I fancy that he is doing something more – he is giving you a wink, as much as to say: "Ah! did they think I should never stand the pace during Expo and the Queen's visit? Well, I've settled the matter".'[1]

For Lord Mountbatten he was 'the greatest Canadian of his time', and Lady Diana Cooper wrote out of the fullness of her heart that he was 'the dearest man ever to be given to a generation craving for something finer and nobler than themselves.' To the officers and men of the Royal 22nd it seemed that they had lost a father, and in a way he had been a father to everyone. The civilians, also, had been strengthened by the military temper of his mind, for he had been a living example of Bossuet's 'une âme guerrière et maitresse du corps qu'elle anime'.[2] One of them recalled how the Cabinet had wished to construct a fall-out shelter in the Gatineau hills, and it was presumed that the Governor General would build one in the grounds of Rideau Hall. 'No' he replied 'I shall not be building a fall-out shelter. If there is a nuclear attack, and I am spared, I shall be out walking on Rideau Street. This will be my fall-out shelter.'

Many of those who wrote had found the apt quotation. Chaucer's 'very parfit gentle knight'; Victor Hugo's 'The tomb is

1. Mère Alice Amyot, 6th March 1967.
2. the soul of a warrior and master of the body which it animates.

not a blind alley; it is a thoroughfare. It closes on the twilight; it opens on the dawn'; and Mr Justice Holmes on the man who had seen 'beyond the gold fields the snowy heights of honour'. Others proffered their personal memories. A September night at the Citadel when he had taught – or tried to teach – a friend to play billiards, and how they had all laughed uproariously, and then walked out on to the terrace under the stars. An evening in Paris when he had read aloud a poem by Pierre Emmanuel. The first night of the London blitz in the basement at Grosvenor Square, when he and van Kleffens had told funny stories by the hour to steady the nerves of their wives. Afternoons in the oval study at Government House, when he would always insist on pouring out the tea by himself, although Joly de Lotbinière was at hand to do it for him. Rear-Admiral Landymore wrote that

Every now and then a craftsmen will produce something of exquisite beauty and perfection. When it is broken beyond repair, or when it is lost, one remembers it as it was, what it stood for, and feels a deep sense of loss because it has gone. That is how my family feels at the passing of H.E. – that a rare and gentle spirit has left us – and we are sad.

For Georges Vanier's life was a life not only lived but singularly achieved.

Nowhere had he left his footprint more clearly than in the hearts of the Canadian children. Twelve members of the same family from Calgary – aged from eighteen years to eighteen months – wrote as follows:

Our mother was American. She says Governor General Vanier was a great gentleman. Our father is Canadian. He says Governor General Vanier was a great Canadian. Please try not to worry too much. He loved Canada and we do too, and if there is anything we can do for you, we would be very glad to.

And another child wrote:

I have been sending a birthday card to the Governor General for 3 to 4 years now and I always get a nice letter from him. Our birthdays were on the 23rd April. I will be 11 this year, so I will be thinking of him too.

And on Monday, the 7th of March, a little boy from Grimsby, Ontario, came home from school and said to his mother: 'The flags are flying low today because a good man has died.' No one had said it better. The man who had illustrated all the 'virtues of the antique world' found his natural friends among those who were too young to know anything about the old world, or very much about the new.

2

For the first time in many years the family were all together. Thérèse had flown from England, and Bernard from France. Jock was already in Canada and Byngsie had permission to come up from Oka on the eve of the funeral. For two days the body of the Governor General in its walnut coffin lay in the ballroom at Government House, and on the evening of Monday, the 6th of March, it was taken down to the Senate Chamber for the lying-in-state. The coffin was draped with the Canadian flag, and the catafalque stood before the red throne and the red canopy on the expanse of red carpet. Beside it was a wreath of red and white roses from the Queen, and at each corner stood an officer from the Canadian Armed Services bowed over his sword. They came – 168 of them – at half-hourly intervals, while 30,000 members of the public filed slowly past. At Madame Vanier's wish, the coffin had been closed, so that the people imagined the General as they had seen him in life, with the medals on his chest or the carnation in his button-hole The medals and decorations now lay upon the coffin, and in front of it was the crucifix from the Chapel where he had worshipped daily. The family had placed a vigil light beside the throne.

The morning of the 8th of March broke sunny and bitter cold. The carillon from the Peace Tower tolled mournfully as the troops lining the route from Parliament Hall to the Basilica assembled in their greatcoats and the words of command rang out sharply in the crisp air. In the chamber of limestone marble, with its subdued lights and subdued voices, the cordon round the coffin was removed, as Chief Justice Taschereau, escorted by Black Rod, the Bearer Party and those who were to carry the insignia came in. The ante-chamber was filled with floral tributes. Very slowly, and followed by Madame Vanier, the members of her family, and Esmond Butler, the coffin, preceded by two officers, was carried through Confederation Hall and down the steps beneath the curved arch of the Peace Tower. The first of seventy-eight salvoes was then fired by the guns at Nepean Point.

The pall-bearers – sergeants from the Royal 22nd – donned their bearskins, and the sixty naval ratings, drawing the gun-carriage, began their slow march to the Basilica, their footsteps a little muted by the deep snow. The insignia bearers walked behind, the principal mourners and State officials following in their cars. A horse, with boots reversed in the stirrups, was led by a groom from the 8th Canadian Hussars; and the Governor General's Horse Guards from Toronto, with his Foot Guards from Ottawa, formed part of the procession. Captain Bruce Stock, an A.D.C. who had loved his chief 'this side idolatry', flew back from Germany to join it. The Band of the Royal Canadian Air Force accompanied the march, and its planes flew overhead throwing their shadows on to the street.

Hundreds of spectators braved the cold to line the pavements as the procession – 3,000 troops in all – passed the familiar landmarks – the Rideau Club, the Château Laurier – and turned into Sussex Drive. In front of the gilded statue of Notre Dame on the pointed gable of the Basilica, the cortège was halted, and the coffin – with only the General's cap and sword now resting on it – was carried down the length of the aisle to the entrance of the choir. The invited congregation were in their seats, and plenty of room had been left for the general public so that the Requiem struck a note of quiet and dignified democracy, which had marked the General's own tenure of office. Cardinal Léger had expressed the wish to officiate, and permission had been granted from Rome to celebrate the Mass in white vestments – the colour of the Resurrection. Jean Vanier read the Epistle from Corinthians in French, and the Gospel was said in English. Cardinal Léger spoke his homily in both languages. The ten concelebrants represented the ten provinces of Canada, and Father Benedict was at the altar, speaking the memento for the Dead, and stretching out his arm with the others as the long white chasubles fell in graceful folds at the moment of the Consecration. The Pater Noster, the Libera Me, and the Agnus Dei were all recited in English, and many people went to Holy Communion as if they were assisting at an ordinary Sunday Mass. Dr Reed, the Anglican Bishop of Ottawa – a very good friend of the family – and the Orthodox Archbishop from Toronto also took part in the ceremony.

The coffin was taken by motor-hearse to Ottawa station, where the family and other mourners boarded the train of ten railway cars that was to take them to Quebec. The Royal anthem was played as it slowly drew away from the platform.

The journey took six and a half hours. Many people had gathered at the stations *en route* – Coteau, Vaudreuil, Ville St Pierre – some saluting the train as it slowed down for their tributes, some standing with lowered flags. It was dark by the time it reached the Palais station in Quebec. The Lieutenant-Governor, Premier Lesage, and Mr St Laurent came on board to pay their respects; and seven hundred men from the Royal 22nd were on duty. Owing to the intense cold it had been suggested that they should wear rubber snow-shoes, but this proposal was unanimously rejected as doing scant courtesy to the occasion. The bells tolled as Colonel Richard, the Commandant from Val-cartier, led the long march of four miles through the narrow streets of old Quebec, with Bernard, Jock and Michel Vanier all walking without hat or gloves – Jock's gaunt figure contrasting with Bernard's burliness and Michel's more military address. The soft thump of feet in the darkness struck a note of weird and almost wistful melancholy, as the troops marched at full military pace to Youville Square, about half a mile from the Basilica; and only a Royal salute of twenty-one guns from the Citadel punc-tuated the deep silence of affection and respect. Tradition had been broken, for never before had the guns been fired after sunset, or the Royal colours of the 'Vingt-Deuxième' unfurled.

The body remained in a *chapelle ardente* overnight, watched over by four officers. Once again, the public filed past. On the following morning Cardinal Roy celebrated a Solemn Requiem, and the Governor General was laid provisionally to rest in the crypt, beside the Comte de Frontenac and the Governors of New France – which now claimed the right to think of itself as Old Canada. It was a claim that Georges Vanier had never contested. On the 4th of May his body was removed to its final resting place in the Memorial Chapel at the Citadel, alongside what had once been called 'the coldest sentry beat in the British Empire'. His epitaph was ready for him, inscribed around the walls:

> Ton histoire est une épopée des plus brilliants
> exploits car ton bras sait porter l'epée, il
> sait porter la croix.[3]

The windows were dedicated to the other Canadian regiments who had sent their reinforcements to the 'Van Doos'; the Fusiliers de St Laurent, the Voltigeurs de Québec, and the Fusiliers de Mont-Royal. The Governor General had died on Laetare Sunday and underneath his name on the stone, which now occupied the centre of the floor, was engraved the Introit for that day:

3. Your history is an epic of the most splendid deeds, for your arm knows how to carry the sword, and it knows how to bear the cross.

J'étais dans la joie quand on m'a dit :
'Allons dans la maison du Seigneur.'[4]

Not long after the interment President de Gaulle went ashore at Wolfe's Cove; and only a few hours before launching his 'Vive le Québec Libre!' from the Hôtel de Ville in Montreal, he drove up to the Citadel and placed a wreath on the grave of the man who had sustained him when he stood all but alone, and who had now given his life for the unity of Canada. The irony of this gesture will not escape the notice of historians, and perhaps it did not pass unnoticed by the very great Canadian in whose memory it was made.

4. I rejoiced at the things that were said to me 'We shall go into the house of the Lord.'

Index